THE CAMBRIDGE
ANCIENT HISTORY

VOLUME FIVE

THE
CAMBRIDGE
ANCIENT HISTORY

EDITED BY

J. B. BURY, M.A., F.B.A.
S. A. COOK, Litt.D.
F. E. ADCOCK, M.A.

VOLUME V

ATHENS

478—401 B.C.

Fifth Impression

CAMBRIDGE
AT THE UNIVERSITY PRESS

1958

PUBLISHED BY
THE SYNDICS OF THE CAMBRIDGE UNIVERSITY PRESS

Bentley House, 200 Euston Road, London, N.W. 1
American Branch: 32 East 57th Street, New York 22, N.Y.

First Edition   1927
Reprinted, with corrections, 1935
1940
1953
1958

First printed in Great Britain at the University Press, Cambridge
Reprinted by Spottiswoode, Ballantyne & Co., Ltd., Colchester

PREFACE

IN this volume, and in that which follows, Greece occupies the
centre of the picture, and we have distinguished the present
volume by the name of Athens because the political and intellectual activities of that city are the main subject of the history of
the fifth century, and mattered most at the time and have mattered
most to posterity.

The victory over the barbarians, which has been described in
Volume IV, was an inspiration to an Athens which believed, not
without reason, that she had saved Hellas by her example and her
exertions. With the sense of deliverance came the sense of power,
which outran the bounds that tradition had set to the ambitions
of the Greek city-states. In commerce as in thought, the Athenians were ready to take and to improve the heritage of Ionia, as
they were ready to challenge the primacy of Sparta in arms and
policy. We begin, therefore, with an account of the economic
conditions under which Athens accomplished her great achievements and made herself the acknowledged leader of Hellenic
civilization.

The main theme of the political history of this period is the
story how Athens acquired and maintained and then lost her
Empire. We have to see how, first the champion and protectress
of the Greeks of the Aegean seaboard, she then became their
mistress. With astonishing vigour and elasticity of spirit, Athens
set herself, while still at war with Persia, to turn a free alliance into
an Empire and, at the same time, to grasp at the leadership of
Greece proper. In the attempt to achieve this twofold purpose
the Athenian state was fused into a democracy which granted to
its citizens the freedom which it denied to others, and, under the
guidance of Pericles, created a splendid city which compelled
the admiration as well as the envy of its neighbours. The
story of this attempt and of the imperialistic democracy which
was at once its cause and its effect is followed by an account
of the greatest contribution made by Greece to the literature of
the world—the Attic Drama. In Chapter V will be found a study
of the development of the dramatic art, together with an interpretation of its masterpieces, which shows it as at once the product
of an age and a city and the culmination of a literary movement
which has behind it the common heritage of the Greek people.

We then turn to western Greece and may contrast the dazzling progress of an imperialistic democracy with the history of Sicily during the period in which the brilliant tyranny which had saved the island from the Carthaginians declined and was supplanted by commonplace uninspired democracies.

The Thirty Years Peace, concluded between Athens and the states of the Peloponnese, marks a moment of suspense, being an endeavour to reach a *modus vivendi*. This endeavour, made possible by the temporary exhaustion of Athenian resources, could not be permanently successful, unless Athens was prepared to abandon the tyranny which her Empire really was, and to take her place once more in the balanced circle of Greek states. The unyielding, if unaggressive, policy of Pericles now dominated his city and in the end he guided Athens into a war which might have decided the issue favourably once for all, if he had lived to see it through.

What followed was a catena of conflicts famous by the name of the Peloponnesian War. The first stage, which we have distinguished by the time-honoured name of the Archidamian War, lasted for ten years, and ended in the Peace of Nicias which was the result of the courage and tenacity with which Athens may be said to have defeated the Peloponnesian attack. It may well have seemed to an observer of the time that the future lay with Athens, had the resources of that city been guided by prudent statecraft. But the restless genius of Alcibiades, tempted by the weakness of Sparta and the hopes of brilliant conquests in the West, lured Athens into the disastrous adventure of the Sicilian Expedition, and revived the war in Greece itself. The failure in Sicily reduced the power of Athens to the level of her adversaries' resources, and the struggle entered on its final phase which all but broke down the Athenian democracy. The outcome was doubtful, even after the gold of Persia was cast into the scale, but at last the destruction of the Athenian fleet at Aegospotami left Athens at the mercy of her enemies.

The political history of the fifth century ends in tragedy and is often sordid, but it is the century which saw Periclean Athens as the intellectual centre of the Greek world, and witnessed the sophistic movement which led to an age of illumination. The Athens of Pericles was the Athens of Socrates. The outward setting of the intense life of the city was worthy of its culture, for triumphs of architecture displayed in material form the rigorous clarity that characterized Greek thinking and showed Athens great in art no less than in politics and literature. In the final chapter we read also of the pediments of the Temple of Aphaia at

Aegina, 'which, over a hundred years ago, opened modern eyes to the beauty of archaic sculpture,' the sculptures of the Temple of Zeus at Olympia, and the statues of Polyclitus. In this same chapter the painting of Polygnotus and of the Attic red-figured vases is set side by side with the masterpieces of plastic art.

Finally, this was the age made memorable to the historian by the fact that 'with Herodotus and Thucydides History as an art was born, indeed twice-born, in romantic and in classic perfection.' Above all, the political history of fifth-century Greece had the privilege of being interpreted to future generations by Thucydides. In his austere economy he ignores the achievements of Athens in art and literature, but one thing he could not hide, that this age had produced his own incomparable genius.

This volume has, then, a unity of theme and the first duty of the editors is to express their thanks to the contributors for their co-operation with them and with each other, to which is due whatever success has been achieved in the presentation of this unity. The chapter on the Economic Background of the Fifth Century is from the pen of Mr Tod. In Chapters II, III, and IV Mr E. M. Walker resumes the political history of Athens and describes the spread of the Confederacy of Delos, the struggle between Athens and the other Greek powers, and the democracy which bears the name of Pericles. In a series of notes at the end of the volume Mr Walker discusses some of the difficult chronological problems connected with this period. The chapter on Attic Drama is the work of Mr J. T. Sheppard. Mr Hackforth has written Chapter VI, which takes up the history of Sicily from the point at which the same writer left it in Volume IV. Chapters VII and VIII on the Breakdown of the Thirty Years Peace and the Archidamian War are by Professor Adcock. The history of the succeeding stages of the Peloponnesian War, including the Athenian expedition to Sicily, is related in four chapters from the pen of Professor W. S. Ferguson of Harvard. Professor Bury has described the Sophistic movement at Athens and the life of Socrates (Chapter XIII). Herodotus and Thucydides form the subject of a chapter by Dr R. W. Macan in which he sets in relation to each other and to the thought of their time the two great historians. In the concluding chapter Professor J. D. Beazley resumes the subject of Greek Art and Mr D. S. Robertson that of Greek Architecture.

The volume of plates to Volumes V and VI, which it is hoped will appear shortly together with Volume VI, is largely devoted to the illustration of this last chapter, and we would acknowledge the assistance of the writers in the selection of the illustrations. Mr C. T. Seltman is responsible for the preparation of this, as of the preceding, volume of plates. It is hoped that during the progress of the work two more volumes of plates will be published illustrating Hellenistic and Roman Republican and Roman Imperial art.

In the spelling of proper names the practice adopted in Volume IV has been followed. The purpose of the editors has been to present to readers familiar names in their familiar forms. At times their efforts may have led to uses which will appear to some readers arbitrary or unjustified, and they would make it clear that in such cases the responsibility rests upon them and not on the writers of the chapters in which the names occur. In footnotes to the various chapters will be found references to the volume of plates, which, as that to Volumes I–IV, contains letterpress as well as illustrations. The reference-numbers are to the pages of letterpress which alternate with the pages of illustrations. Throughout the volume the double form of dates, *e.g.* 452–1 B.C. is to be understood as referring to the Attic civil or archon year which ran from summer to summer.

Mr E. M. Walker has to thank Mr Tod for the opportunity of discussing with him some questions of importance chiefly connected with the quota-lists, and for putting at his disposal his store of epigraphical and bibliographical knowledge. Mr Robertson desires to express his indebtedness to Mr Gow for criticisms and suggestions; Professor Adcock would acknowledge the assistance of Mr L. Whibley and Dr A. B. West of Princeton. The editors would express their thanks to Mr Seltman for his co-operation in connection with the illustration of the Volume. Acknowledgments are due for Map 1 to Mr Tod, for Map 2 to Mr E. M. Walker, for Maps 3 and 10 to the Delegates of the Oxford University Press and for Map 10 also to Professor Ferguson, for Maps 4 and 9 to Messrs Macmillan, for Map 5 to Dr A. B. West, for Map 7 which is based on Admiralty Chart No. 211 to the Controller of H.M. Stationery Office, for Map 8 to Messrs Baedeker and to Professor Ferguson, and for Map 11 to Messrs Philip and Son. The sheet containing plans of temples at the end of Chapter XV has been arranged by Mr D. S. Robertson, and acknowledgments are due to Messrs Julius Springer, Berlin, for No. 1, to Messrs Beck, Munich, for No. 3, to the Council of the Society for the Promotion of Hellenic Studies for No. 4, and for No. 5 to Messrs Macmillan.

The general index and index of passages have been made by

Mr W. E. C. Browne, M.A., formerly scholar of Emmanuel College. Finally, the editors would express their gratitude to the Staff of the University Press for their unfailing care and resource.

The design on the cover is the bust of Pericles in the British Museum, reproduced with the permission of the Trustees.

J. B. B.

S. A. C.

F. E. A

Feb. 1927

TABLE OF CONTENTS

CHAPTER I

THE ECONOMIC BACKGROUND OF THE FIFTH CENTURY

By MARCUS N. TOD, M.A., O.B.E.

Fellow of Oriel College, Oxford, and University Lecturer in Greek Epigraphy

CHAPTER II

THE CONFEDERACY OF DELOS, 478–463 B.C.

By E. M. WALKER, M.A.

Pro-Provost of Queen's College, Oxford

CHAPTER III

ATHENS AND THE GREEK POWERS, 462–445 B.C.

By E. M. Walker

CONTENTS

CHAPTER IV

THE PERICLEAN DEMOCRACY

By E. M. Walker

CHAPTER V

ATTIC DRAMA IN THE FIFTH CENTURY

By J. T. Sheppard, M.A.
Fellow of King's College, Cambridge, and University Lecturer in Classics

CHAPTER VI

SICILY

By R. Hackforth, M.A.
Fellow of Sidney Sussex College, Cambridge, and University Lecturer in Classics

CHAPTER VII

THE BREAKDOWN OF THE THIRTY YEARS PEACE, 445–431 B.C.

By F. E. Adcock, M.A.
Fellow of King's College and Professor of Ancient History in the
University of Cambridge

CHAPTER VIII

THE ARCHIDAMIAN WAR, 431–421 B.C.

By F. E. Adcock

PAGE

CHAPTER IX

SPARTA AND THE PELOPONNESE

BY W. S. FERGUSON, Ph.D., LL.D.

Professor of Ancient History, Harvard University

CHAPTER X

THE ATHENIAN EXPEDITION TO SICILY

By W. S. FERGUSON

CHAPTER XI

THE OLIGARCHICAL MOVEMENT IN ATHENS

By W. S. FERGUSON

CHAPTER XII

THE FALL OF THE ATHENIAN EMPIRE

BY W. S. FERGUSON

CONTENTS

CHAPTER XIII

THE AGE OF ILLUMINATION

By J. B. Bury, M.A., F.B.A.

Fellow of King's College and Regius Professor of Modern History
in the University of Cambridge

CHAPTER XIV

HERODOTUS AND THUCYDIDES

By R. W. Macan, D.Litt.

Sometime University Reader in Ancient History and (past) Master of
University College, Oxford

CHAPTER XV

GREEK ART AND ARCHITECTURE

By J. D. BEAZLEY, M.A., Lincoln and Merton Professor of Classical Archaeology and Art
in the University of Oxford, and D. S. ROBERTSON, M.A., Fellow of Trinity College,
Cambridge, and University Lecturer in Classics[1]

[1] Sections I–VI (Art) are by Professor Beazley, Sections VII–XI (Architecture) are by
Mr Robertson.

CONTENTS

LIST OF MAPS, TABLES, PLANS, ETC.

CHAPTER I

THE ECONOMIC BACKGROUND OF THE FIFTH CENTURY

I. INTRODUCTION: THE NATURE OF THE EVIDENCE

WE have now traced the story of the ancient world down to the repulse of the Persian army and navy by the Greeks united under Spartan leadership. That victory inaugurated a new era, with which it is the main purpose of this volume to deal. The success of what had appeared to many at the outset a forlorn venture inspired the Greeks of Hellas with a new sense of their superiority to the great 'barbarian' powers and a new confidence in their own future. The centre of gravity of the Greek world was shifted across the Aegean from its eastern shore, the cities of which, after being subdued in turn by the Empires of Lydia and of Persia, had suffered severely as the result of the Ionian Revolt and had been reluctantly compelled to fight for their Oriental overlords against their Hellenic kinsmen. But before we deal with the political, military and cultural history of the next eighty years, we shall do well to survey in outline the economic conditions and tendencies which were not merely the background of that history but also a most potent factor in determining it.

Down to the close of the sixth century the Greeks of Asia Minor and the adjacent islands had enjoyed, if not a monopoly, at least an unquestioned predominance in literature as well as in art, industry and commerce. But the collapse of the Ionian Revolt ushered in a period of material decay from which Ionia did not wholly recover until the Hellenistic age: Athens entered into the intellectual as well as the commercial inheritance of the Eastern Greeks, and the literature of the fifth century is largely the work of men who were Athenians either by birth or by residence. But literature did not concern itself primarily and explicitly with economic history or theory. The acute economic problems of the close of the seventh century and the opening years of the sixth had been in large measure solved by the wise and moderate legislation of Solon followed by the enlightened policy of the Peisistratidae. Thus during the first seventy years of the fifth century there seems to have been little distress in Attica, where the remarkable development of trade and industry, the exploitation of the silver mines and the growth of the Athenian Empire brought a rapid accession of wealth alike to individuals and to the community. But it is sickness rather than health which, both in the human body and in the body politic, provokes comment and stimulates reflection, and throughout the greater part of the fifth century the prosperity of Athens produced a sense rather of exuberant health than of misgiving and inquiry. The century was, in the economic sphere, one of deeds rather than of words, of active achievement rather than of historical record or philosophical analysis. Only during and after the Peloponnesian War, which brought ruin upon the agricultural population and financial exhaustion upon the state, did men begin to reflect upon the economic evils of the time and to seek some remedy for them. But though the literary evidence for economic conditions in our period consists mainly of scattered allusions in the works of historians, orators and poets, we have at least this compensation that the incidental character of the references in question lessens the probability of their having been selected or manipulated in the interest of some preconceived theory.

Fortunately the literary evidence can be supplemented by that of other kinds—epigraphical, archaeological and numismatic. Though sharing some of the characteristics of literary documents, inscriptions have certain peculiarities of their own, notably their objectivity and their detail: they preserve neither traditions nor judgments but facts, and they contain not approximations but precise, and usually authoritative, statements. Few fifth-century inscriptions of economic interest have survived save at Athens. For Sparta this is not surprising, for her citizens were debarred from trade and from the possession of gold and silver, her financial system was extremely rudimentary and her conduct of public affairs was characterized by an unparalleled secrecy. Elsewhere also aristocratic principle and practice discountenanced any public record of financial administration. The Athenians, on the other hand, regarded publicity as one of the distinguishing marks of democracy and demanded that the official acts of every magistrate should be subject to the scrutiny of his fellow-citizens. Hence many financial documents were consigned to the durable keeping of marble, and of these considerable fragments survive to give us materials which are of inestimable value for our present purpose.

Hardly less important is the archaeological and numismatic evidence. The almost indestructible nature of pottery, its wide-spread diffusion and the security with which the leading fabrics can be assigned to their periods and places of origin render it especially valuable for determining the extent and intensity of the commercial enterprise of certain states, while paintings upon vases provide detailed pictures of contemporary dress, social life and industrial activities. Coins also serve to throw light not only upon the artistic development and political relations of the states which issued them, but also upon weight standards, mintage-rights, monetary alliances, commercial relations and kindred subjects.

II. POPULATION

The population of the Greek states normally fell into three main classes—the civic, the free alien and the servile. To these must be added in some states (*e.g.* Sparta, Argos and Elis) a class of subjects (*perioeci*), who, while enjoying personal freedom and certain stipulated privileges, were nevertheless debarred from the status and rights of citizens. In Sparta, for which alone we have detailed evidence, the *perioeci* were distributed over the country in settlements varying in size from considerable towns to insignificant hamlets (Isocrates xii, 179). They were liable to tribute and to military service, supplying to the Spartan army a large and increasing portion of its heavy infantry, but although subject to Spartan governors they seem to have enjoyed some measure of *de facto* freedom in communal affairs. Their land was, generally speaking, less fertile than that which the Spartans reserved for themselves; on the other hand, they had a monopoly of the industry and trade of Laconia and Messenia, due to the self-exclusion of the Spartans from these spheres, and appear in general to have been loyal and contented.

Of the political privileges of the citizens this is not the place to speak, but it must be borne in mind in considering their economic condition that, at least under democratic constitutions, they alone and directly determined the economic policy of their states and, it may be assumed, determined it primarily with a view to their own advantage.

In general, the citizen bodies of this period are marked by an exclusiveness which is the outcome partly of pride and partly of selfishness. In Sparta, where both motives operated with peculiar intensity, admission to civic status was almost unknown: Herodotus asserts that down to his time it had been granted to two men only, the Elean seer Teisamenus and his brother. The Spartan recognized no class of resident aliens (metics), and he sought to make the gulf between citizen and subject impassable by denying to the *perioeci* the right of intermarriage. The life of discomfort and apprehensiveness which he led was the price he paid. Theoretically, his position was secured by the toil of the serfs who tilled his holding (κλῆρος); practically, however, Spartan history shows a progressive decline in the number of full citizens and a growing inequality in their economic situation. In most agricultural states the citizen body must have comprised the great majority of the population. Metics were probably everywhere debarred from the ownership of land, while slavery, though by no means unknown, was restricted within narrow limits. Pericles, as reported by Thucydides (1, 141), describes the Peloponnesians as themselves engaged in cultivating the soil (αὐτουργοί) and the same might be said equally of the citizens of most of northern Greece.

In Athens the ownership of real property and the exercise of active political rights were confined to citizens, who also enjoyed a practical monopoly of one important and lucrative enterprise, silver-mining. But the development of industry and commerce led an increasing number of citizens to devote themselves to these activities, while at the same time it brought a large influx of aliens to swell the growing urban population. Even members of the aristocracy tended to migrate to Athens as the focus of political, intellectual and social life and to leave their lands to be managed by bailiffs. It would, however, be a mistake to suppose that the rural population became small or unimportant. The Attic peasantry, engaged in the cultivation of fields, vineyards or olive-groves, in the tending of cattle or the burning of charcoal, formed a numerous and sturdy stock, proud of its freedom from the monotonous and cramping work of the urban artisan. Thus Thucydides speaks of the men of Acharnae, a little country town on the slopes of Mount Aegaleos, as 'being a large part of the state' and as supplying to the Athenian army no fewer than 3000 heavy infantry. Yet it must be admitted that in the determination of public policy the urban population often exercised a preponderating influence. Every issue was decided by the citizens present in the Assembly when the vote was taken, and it was easier for those resident in Athens and the Piraeus than for those scattered over the country-side, many of them at a considerable distance from Athens, to attend meetings of the sovereign people. In the later years of the century this influence is mirrored in the increasing political prominence of representatives of the urban and industrial element—Eucrates the tow-merchant, Lysicles the sheep-dealer, Cleon the tanner, and the like.

For some time after the Persian Wars the Athenian attitude appears to have become more generous and comprehensive. But the exclusive temper of the citizens was stimulated by the material gain attendant on civic status. Not only was no regular process of naturalization opened to resident aliens, not only was citizenship granted with the utmost parsimony even to distinguished individuals (*I.G.*² 1, 110, 113, 122) but in 451 B.C. a measure was passed on the motion of Pericles rigidly restricting citizenship to those who were of civic parentage on both sides, while six years later those who wrongfully claimed a share in a generous gift of corn sent by an Egyptian prince for distribution among the citizens were sternly punished (pp. 102, 167 *sq.*). It required the shock of the defeat at Aegospotami to awaken the Athenians to a realization of the fruits of so narrow a policy, but the grant of Athenian citizenship to all the Samians in 405 B.C. (*I.G.*² 11, 1) came too late to save the tottering fabric of the Empire.

Citizens by no means dominated the industrial and mercantile life of Athens and its port. None of the important business houses of which we learn were directed by citizens, and the ranks of the shopkeepers, artisans and labourers were largely recruited from metics, freedmen and slaves. Of the 71 contractors and workmen engaged on the Erechtheum in 409–8, only 20 were citizens, while 35 were metics and 16 slaves; in other words, of the men so engaged only 28 per cent., of the free men only 36 per cent., were citizens. Nor can it be claimed that their numerical inferiority was counter-balanced by the important or lucrative nature of the tasks they undertook. In face of such evidence it is hard to accept, at least for the fifth century, the view that servile labour drove free labour from the market and the citizen fell a victim to the com-petition of slaves. These did, it is true, monopolize certain employments—*e.g.* mining and domestic service—but into those no citizen would voluntarily have entered. Elsewhere it would seem that the competition which confronted the citizen was that of the metic, rather than of the slave. But it is incredible that, if this competition had been acutely felt, the citizens, in whose hands lay the absolute determination of the conditions of employ-ment on public works, should not have safeguarded their own interests by securing for citizens priority of claim to employment, if not preferential treatment in regard to pay. Of neither privilege, however, is there any indication in our evidence. The fact is that the state was able to offer to citizens, and to them exclusively, abundant and varied means of making, or of adding to, their liveli-hood. Large numbers were drafted off to cleruchies or to colonies. The multiplication of officials, both within Attica and throughout the Empire, the large membership of the Council and the immense development of the law-courts secured the enjoyment of paid posts to a number of citizens which in normal times can hardly have fallen short of 7000. Even in time of peace considerable numbers of citizens were engaged in patrolling or garrisoning the Empire, and a period of war, while adversely affecting certain employments, automatically brought about a great increase in the demand for men to serve in the army and the navy (p. 105).

The importance of the resident aliens, the metics, varied greatly from state to state. Sparta resolutely refused to countenance them and from time to time brought into operation the alien acts ($\xi\epsilon\nu\eta\lambda\alpha\sigma\iota\alpha\iota$) which expelled them from Spartan territory. In states which were almost wholly agricultural they were probably very few, but in those which devoted themselves to industry and commerce their numbers tended to multiply. Our evidence is fullest for Athens, where they seem to have been most numerous and most highly favoured. There is, indeed, a tradition preserved in Diodorus (XI, 43) that Themistocles encouraged immigration into Attica by offering to the metics immunity from taxation, but this privilege, if granted at all, cannot have been of long duration. Nevertheless, the metics, alike Greeks and barbarians, increased rapidly, especially after the Persian Wars. They were, it is true, debarred from the exercise of active political rights and from the possession of real property, they were liable to military or naval service and to the payment of the aliens' tax in addition to the ordinary taxes, and each of them must be sponsored by a citizen patron (*prostates*). Yet they enjoyed personal freedom, the protection of the law, liberty of worship and almost unlimited opportunities of engaging in the industrial and commercial activity of their adopted home. Thus the metics remained contented and often prosperous, and the Athenians had no occasion, even in their darkest hours, to suspect them of disaffection or treachery. The great majority of them lived in or near Athens or the Piraeus and gained their livelihood as labourers, artisans, manufacturers, or traders. Of the 71 men engaged on the Erechtheum no fewer than 35 were, as we have seen, metics, and there is reason to believe that their preponderance was at least equally marked in all branches of industry, in retail trade, in shipping, in commerce and in finance. Not only so, but in the spheres of art, science and literature the metics supplied Athens with many of her outstanding men—painters, sculptors, musicians, doctors, philosophers, poets and orators.

The servile class also existed in the Greek states in different forms and in varying degrees. In some it consisted of serfs, the descendants of an aboriginal, or at least of an early, population, reduced by a victorious band of invaders and bound to the soil under the terms of a pact which secured for them certain guarantees from their masters. The best known example is that of the Spartan Helots, but the Penestae of Thessaly, the Cyllyrii of Sicily, the Clarotae of Crete and the Mariandyni of Heraclea Pontica seem to have occupied a more or less analogous position. Such a body was recruited not by purchase but by natural propagation, was engaged mainly in tillage, and was the property not of individuals but of the community. Thus the Helots, whose labour assured a livelihood to the Spartiates and so enabled them to devote themselves exclusively to military and administrative duties, could neither be liberated nor killed by the individual citizens to whose service they were assigned. Emancipation, if granted at all, was the reward of distinguished conduct in war, in which large numbers of Helots served, usually as light-armed troops and attendants on the Spartan hoplites. The enormous preponderance of Helots over Spartiates, which became more marked and more disquieting with the diminution in the number of citizens, was the determining factor in Spartan policy throughout this period. Disciplinary supervision was ruthlessly exercised by the secret citizen police under the direction of the ephors, who, to secure the right of immediate intervention without any form of trial, kept the Helot body permanently under martial law. Nevertheless, the deliberate and cold-blooded murder of 2000 Helots, whose bravery had been recognized by the state as constituting a claim to emancipation, must not be regarded as indicative of normal Spartan policy, but of the extreme lengths to which the ephors could be driven by nervous apprehensiveness at the darkest hour of the Peloponnesian War (p. 243 *sq.*).

Entirely different was the position of slaves in industrial states such as Athens. A few of them belonged to the community (δημόσιοι) and were employed in the police force or in the mint, as clerks, or as attendants on officials, or in other similar positions, sometimes of considerable importance and responsibility, as, for example, the custody of the state archives. Some at least of them received from the state their clothing and daily 'ration allowance' of three obols (half-drachma) or more, were allowed to live where they pleased, and differed little *de facto* from metics in their family and social relations.

The vast majority, however, of the slaves belonged to individual owners. They were, as a rule, bought in the market, for 'home-born' slaves (οἰκογενεῖς) were probably few in the fifth century, though the Delphian manumission records of later centuries show that then they constituted about a quarter of the total number emancipated. The slave-market was recruited from captives taken in war, the victims of slave-raids, criminals condemned for certain offences and, perhaps, a few foundlings rescued from death by exposure. They were mostly barbarians, for there was a feeling, at least in the more enlightened states, against the enslavement of Greeks, and prisoners of war, if Hellenes, were usually ransomed at the generally recognized flat rate of 200 drachmae[1] per head (Herodotus v, 77; vi, 79). Such scruples were, however, forgotten in the exasperation caused by the Peloponnesian War, as we may see from the fate of the Melians who capitulated in 416, and of the prisoners taken by the Syracusans after the Athenian débâcle of 413 (pp. 281, 310 *sq.*). With regard to barbarians, on the other hand, no compunctions were felt, or at least none were yet voiced, and the sense of superiority resulting from their victories over the mighty empire of Persia led the Greeks as a whole to accept, as a self-evident dispensation of providence, the distinction of mankind into natural masters and natural slaves. The only slave household of which we have detailed knowledge, that of Cephisodorus, a metic resident in the Piraeus, consisted of 16 persons—10 males, four females and two whose sex is uncertain. Five of these came from Thrace, three from Caria, two each from Syria and Illyria, and one each from Colchis, Scythia, Lydia and Malta (*I.G.*[2] i, 329). They were sold by auction in 414, on account of their master's actual or alleged implication in the outrage on the Hermae, and realized an average price of 168 drachmae per male and $147\frac{1}{2}$ per female: the most costly was a Syrian, for whom 301 drachmae were paid, the cheapest a Lydian woman, who fetched but 70.

Slaves were everywhere used for domestic service, assisting the mistress of the house in her tasks of baking, cooking, clothes-making, nursing, etc. The number of such household slaves in a moderate establishment varied from three to a dozen, but wealthy men occasionally had as many as fifty or even more. Greece did not, like the Italy of the late Republican period, employ masses of slaves in agriculture. In some states, such as Thessaly or Sparta, this was mainly or wholly in the hands of subjects or serfs; in others the free peasantry was almost sufficient, though some slaves were regularly employed on the larger estates and elsewhere casual slave labour may have been hired for harvesting or other special purposes. Industry, on the other hand, demanded

---

[1] It is roughly true to say that the purchasing power of the drachma varied during the century between that of 4*s.* 6*d.* and 3*s.* 6*d.* in present English currency (see below, p. 25).

the multiplication of slaves to increase production. The artist
or artisan usually had one or more working under his direction
and in close contact with him; these were regarded as apprentices
rather than as machines, for the mechanical aspect of mass-production was minimized if not eliminated, and such anticipations
as there were of the factory system were on a small scale and
appear only towards the close of our period. The slave often
engaged in the same tasks as his master and was permitted and
expected to exercise his creative faculties: on the Erechtheum,
for example, they work side by side with free men and are paid
at the same rate. Only in mining and quarrying do we find slaves,
and those usually of a low type, employed in large gangs, frequently under the supervision of slave foremen. The miner's work
was hard, the hours were long, the conditions unhealthy: as a
result the slave's life was normally short, for it was deemed
unprofitable to prolong by considerateness and care the lives of men
who could be replaced so easily and at so small a cost. Nicias is
reported to have possessed a thousand slaves whom he hired out for
this work, and to have made a profit of one obol per man per day,
i.e. an annual revenue of some ten talents (60,000 drachmae).

Yet while the law at this time regarded the slave as mere
property, protected only in the same spirit in which other
property-rights were legally safeguarded, considerations of
humanity, to which the Athenians were peculiarly susceptible,
combined with those of enlightened self-interest to secure a
marked amelioration of the lot of the domestic or industrial slave.
He was not distinguished in dress from the citizen, he was
allowed to attend certain acts of public or family worship, he was
treated frequently with kindness and sometimes even with
affection. The typical nurse or attendant of the early Attic drama
affords a picture of which Greece need not be ashamed. Indeed,
complaints were sometimes heard of the advantage taken by the
slaves of the indulgence shown to them, especially at Athens, of
the insolence of many and the luxury of some[1]. In time the
demands of public opinion and expediency led to the withdrawal
from the master of his power to kill his slave or to subject him to
prolonged cruelty; the right of sanctuary was recognized and the
slave, if habitually ill-treated, might demand to be sold to a new
master. Even the prospect of liberty was not denied to the slave.
Occasionally this was granted simply as a reward of loyalty and
good service; more often, however, the slave purchased his
emancipation by the payment of a stipulated ransom out of the

---

[1] [Xenophon], *Ath. Constitution*, I, 10–11.

savings which it was customary to allow slaves to accumulate. Regarding the amount of this ransom we have no information from the fifth century, to which very few of the extant manumission-records belong, but the Delphian and other documents supply abundant evidence for a later period. The freedman (ἀπελεύθερος, ἐξελεύθερος), whose liberty might be restricted by special conditions imposed at his emancipation, became to all intents and purposes a metic, save that he must take as his patron his former master, who also became the heir of the freedman in the event of his dying childless. Since the tendency was for the most loyal, frugal, capable and energetic members of the slave class to win their freedom, they naturally took a prominent share in the activities and enterprises of the metics which have been outlined above.

Any attempt to estimate numerically the population of the Greek world, or of any Greek state, in the fifth century B.C. is beset by almost insuperable difficulties[1]. No census was taken and, although rolls were kept of citizens, of men liable to various grades of military service, and of resident aliens, these were for official use and were not published. Few figures therefore appear in our ancient authorities and those generally approximate rather than precise. Nor can we reach satisfactory results by computing the productivity of the soil of the several states, for our knowledge of the area under cultivation in antiquity, of the average yield and of the extent to which the home-grown supplies sufficed to meet the needs of the population is wholly inadequate. Thus we are usually forced to base our calculations upon the recorded numbers of those who were liable to, or were engaged in, military service. Trustworthy records of this kind are, however, but too few, nor is it safe to assume that the number of men subject to military service bore everywhere the same ratio to the total population.

For Athens our most valuable evidence is Pericles' statement[2] that at the outset of the Peloponnesian War Athens had 13,000 hoplites apart from those stationed in garrisons and the 16,000

---

[1] The most systematic attempts made in recent times to accomplish this task are those of K. J. Beloch (*Die Bevölkerung der griechisch-römischen Welt*) and E. Cavaignac (*Histoire de l'Antiquité*, II, pp. 1 *sqq.*), but the figures at which they arrive are at best only approximations, based upon cultivable areas, tribute-payments, military strength and any other data which happen to be available, while many of them are little removed from mere conjectures. For other works dealing with the question of population see the Bibliography to this Chapter, II D.

[2] Thucydides II, 13, see below, p. 193 *sq.*

who manned the fortifications 'drawn from the oldest and the youngest and the metics who served as hoplites': she had also 1200 cavalry, including 200 mounted archers, and 1600 bowmen. Since the metic hoplites numbered 3000, Pericles seems to have assigned 13,000 citizen hoplites to the field force and an equal number to home defence. If, as has sometimes been assumed, 'the oldest and the youngest' include only the *ephebi* of 18 and 19 and adults of 50–59 years old, this equality is obviously impossible and the figure 16,000 in Thucydides' account of Pericles' estimate must be drastically reduced, perhaps to 6000. This apparently simple expedient, however, raises serious difficulties, and it is perhaps better to accept Thucydides' text as it stands and to assume that a considerable number of citizen hoplites of 20–49 years old were for physical reasons employed in home defence rather than in foreign service. If we reckon the garrison troops at 2500, this gives us 29,500 citizens of the three highest classes[1] liable to military service or about 35–36,000 in all above 18 years old. For the fourth class, the thetes, we may allow 20,000 as a probable number and 25,000 as a maximum, while the metics may have numbered 12–15,000. We thus arrive, allowing for women and children, at a total population of about 150–170,000 of citizen and 35–40,000 of metic origin. The slaves, of whom over 20,000 deserted during the Decelean War, may well have numbered 80–100,000 but are unlikely to have exceeded 120,000. At the time of the Persian Wars the civic population probably stood at about the same total, though the proportion of thetes was markedly higher, but the metic and slave classes were very much smaller. The Peloponnesian War, however, witnessed a startling decline, due in part to the havoc wrought by the plague, in part to the heavy casualties suffered in the war, while the devastation of Attica reduced to poverty large numbers of the third class, the zeugitae.

III. AGRICULTURE AND INDUSTRY

Although it is not until the time of Plato that we find the doctrine of the specialization of functions clearly enunciated, yet such specialization had made considerable strides even in the sixth century and was rapidly developed in every sphere during the fifth. Not all parts of the Greek world were equally affected. Some communities, such as those of the Ozolian Locrians, the Aetolians and the Acarnanians, were still living under primitive

---

[1] Viz. 28,500 hoplites (13,000 + 13,000 + 2500) and 1000 cavalry. The 1800 archers (mounted and on foot) belonged to the lowest class (the thetes).

conditions at the time of the Peloponnesian War, and in country districts functions were less differentiated than in the towns, notably Athens and the Piraeus. We possess no fifth-century list of trades and callings comparable to that derived from the *catalogi paterarum argentearum* of the late fourth century, but the roll of those who in 401–400 B.C. were enfranchised for their services in the recent restoration of the Athenian democracy shows a noteworthy specialization. In it we find five agricultural labourers, a gardener, a walnut-seller, an oil-vendor, a donkey-tender, a muleteer, a builder, a carpenter, a statuary, a cook, a baker, a fuller, a hired labourer and a maker or carrier of earthenware vessels (*I.G.*² 11,10). The same impression is left by the *Peace* of Aristophanes, by the Erechtheum accounts with their vivid picture of specialization in the working of wood, stone and metal, and by numerous incidental references in our sources, both literary and epigraphical.

Agriculture still held in the estimation of the Greeks a certain primacy as the most ancient and most natural of callings. Socrates, townsman though he was, is represented as uttering a fervent encomium of the physical, spiritual, social and economic results of farming, and Aristotle maintains the superiority of the agricultural over every other type of democracy. The old aristocracies were those of the *gamoroi* or landholders, and large estates survived in some districts, such as Thessaly, in the fifth century. But, even in states where a commercial oligarchy or a democracy was in power, the prestige of the farmer was maintained by the exclusion of all save citizens from the ownership of land. In Attica many large private estates had been broken up in the sixth century, though temples still retained their lands and let them to tenant farmers. But for the most part the soil was cultivated, as far as it was cultivable at all, by peasant proprietors, who appear to have been, if not prosperous, at least independent and contented until the devastation of Attica in the Peloponnesian War brought with it widespread unsettlement and ruin and inaugurated a period of hardship and struggle for the rural population. We also find gentlemen farmers, like the Ischomachus of whom Xenophon paints a detailed and attractive portrait in his *Oeconomicus*, owning and cultivating considerable farms with the aid of slaves or free labourers despite the temptation to migrate to the city and leave slave bailiffs to manage their estates. Of the price of fields inscriptions have preserved some records. In 414–13 B.C. a house and estate in Attica fetched 1200 drachmae (*I.G.*² 1, 325) and three fields 105, 205 and 10 drachmae respectively (*ib.* 1, 328). A Halicarnassian document of about the middle of the century records the prices paid for the lands, houses and persons of insolvent debtors. Of the sixteen estates which were sold separately on this occasion, eleven fetched sums under 1000 Phoenician drachmae[1], three between 1000 and 2000, one 3045 (?) and one 3600: the lowest price paid was 50 drachmae, the average 983 (Dittenberger, *S.I.G.*[3] 46). Houses ranged from 66 to 2000 Phoenician drachmae with an average of about 790.

Despite some progress in the direction of more scientific farming, agriculture remained throughout the fifth century in a backward condition. The plough, though now provided with an iron share, showed no great advance on that of Homeric times and the traditional practice of allowing the land to lie fallow in alternate years gave way but slowly to a more economical system. Ischomachus' repeated emphasis upon the extreme ease with which farming could be learned is in itself significant. Yet some farmers showed greater insight and energy than their fellows and found a profitable investment in the purchase and development of waste lands with a view to reselling them at a greatly enhanced price. In Attica especially the poverty of the soil and the shortage of water, aggravated by the progressive deforestation of the hillsides, confronted the farmer with a difficult task. Probably the cultivation of cereals never extended beyond one-fifth of the total area of the country and its productivity was reduced because in any year only half the cultivable land was actually tilled. Moreover, the greater part of Attica was unsuited for raising wheat and the ratio of wheat to barley was probably in the fifth century approximately what we know it to have been in 329–8 B.C., namely 1 : 9·8. Even in a favourable year Attica could hardly produce more than 450,000 *medimni* (*c.* 675,000 bushels) of cereals, the amount needed to feed a population of 75,000. This might possibly suffice for the needs of the rural population but was wholly inadequate to meet the requirements of the towns, and recourse was therefore had to importation from abroad. Scyros, Imbros and Lemnos may have already supplied some corn to Attica, Euboea almost certainly did so; but most of the islands required for their own consumption all the corn they produced, or even more. Many cities on the shores of the Aegean were apparently in the same position, for Methone in the early years of the Peloponnesian War asked leave to import several thousand *medimni* of Pontic wheat (*I.G.*[2] 1, 57) and about 470 B.C. Teos invoked a curse on anyone who should hinder the importation

[1] The Phoenician light drachma is a little more than $\frac{5}{6}$ of the Attic drachma.

of corn by land or sea (p. 95). Thus Athens was compelled to draw her supplies mainly from the steppes of the Ukraine, where Scythian farmers raised immense quantities of wheat for export. Athenian anxiety to keep the Pontic route open provides a master-key to the understanding of Athenian policy and strategy during this period. Sicily also supplied a certain amount of grain[1], and probably some came from Cyprus and from Egypt, which we know to have grown more corn than her own population consumed (see below, p. 167).

Athens was not the only state of Hellas which supplemented from foreign sources the internal food-supply, though she probably did so to a greater extent than any other. Thessaly, with her broad and fertile plains, was self-sufficing and perhaps exported her surplus produce; Boeotia probably met her own needs. But as early as 480 we hear of 'corn-ships from the Pontus traversing the Hellespont on their voyage to Aegina and the Peloponnese[2],' and one of the reasons for Athenian intervention in Sicily in 427 was to prevent the export of corn from there to the Peloponnese[3]. Gelon, again, is represented as undertaking, if appointed leader of the Greeks in their struggle with Xerxes, to supply corn to the whole Greek army throughout the war[4]. We must not, however, over-emphasize these references, all of which refer to periods of war, when the diversion of labour into military channels might well lessen production. The Peloponnese was probably normally self-supporting with the exception of states, such as Corinth, Aegina and Epidaurus, where trade and manufacture caused a large influx of aliens and slaves. These alone had the means of paying for imported corn; elsewhere, as in Arcadia, the problem of a growing population and a stationary food production was solved by the emigration of large numbers of men to serve abroad as mercenaries or in other capacities.

Attica with her lack of grassy plains was ill-suited to cattle-breeding; but some horses were kept for riding, mules and asses for transport and pigs for food, while sheep and goats found sufficient sustenance in the scrub and furnished the requisite supplies of wool and milk. Bee-keeping was successfully practised and provided a sugarless world with its one sweetening agent. Figs, vines and olives flourished, and Attic wine and oil were reckoned among the best in the Greek world: other fruits, vegetables and flowers were also grown near Athens, where extensive market-gardens sprang up to supply the demands of a

---

[1] Xenophon, *Oecon.* xx, 27.   [2] Herodotus VII, 147.
[3] Thucydides III, 86.   [4] Herodotus VII, 158.

great city, or were imported from Boeotia, the Megarid and the islands. Silviculture is conspicuous by its absence from Attica, where such trees as still remained were rapidly falling victims to the axe of the wood-merchant or charcoal-burner. Timber for furniture, construction and ship-building was usually imported, chiefly from Macedonia and Chalcidice but also from Southern Italy, Cyprus and Asia Minor.

While agriculture was held in honour throughout the Greek world, various judgments were passed on other forms of labour. Aristocracy tended to view them askance, notably manual work and retail trade, and many philosophers regarded the artisan and the merchant as incapable of the highest civic virtue. Socrates, however, preached the necessity of labour and its value, provided that it left the worker a sufficient margin of leisure, and in cities whose prosperity rested principally on industry and trade, such as Corinth and Athens, the disdain felt for base handicrafts (βαναυσικαὶ τέχναι) tended to become mitigated, if not to disappear altogether.

The foremost characteristic of the industrial life of the period is the absence of any save the simplest machinery. This prevented the extreme specialization and the consequent monotony which are almost inseparable from modern industrial conditions; the ancient artisan, free from the hurry, the noise and the danger attendant upon mechanical mass-production, was able to develop greater originality and artistry in his work. Further, it militated against the growth of the factory system and so gave to the worker, whether freeman or slave, an enhanced sense of his individual importance. By far the largest factory known to us was that of Cephalus, who at the close of the fifth century employed 120 slaves in making shields: this was, however, quite exceptional, and the typical workshop probably contained the master and at most two or three hands. Only in mining were labourers normally employed in large masses, and even there the number of slaves working in a single mine can rarely have exceeded a hundred. Again, the absence of machinery averted, or at least minimized, the danger that the capitalist might crush the artisan. Even when some public work was to be carried out, the separate tasks assigned to contractors were made so small that those who had little or no capital could tender successfully. Some industries, especially those of spinning, weaving and the making of clothes, were traditionally organized on a family basis, but in this sphere production far outran family requirements and the surplus became available for the local market: indeed, the specialities of certain cities—*e.g.* the silken fabrics of Cos, the linens of Tarentum and the dyed woollens of Syracuse—were in demand throughout the Greek world.

The state did not attempt to regulate the conditions of labour, the hours of work or the rate of pay, nor was there any organization which aimed at safeguarding the interests of the employed. Most workers were probably engaged from sunrise to sunset, with a break during the hottest hours of the day in the summer months; but the tension was not comparable with that of to-day, and the master often toiled alongside of, and in friendly contact with, his apprentices and slaves. Only the miner's lot was one of exacting and almost unrelieved labour, carried on in the narrow, ill-ventilated galleries of the Laurium silver-mines under the lash of a slave foreman: work went on without intermission, ten consecutive hours of employment for each gang alternating with ten of rest.

Very many producers sold direct to the consumers without the intervention of middlemen. But the needs of a large urban population brought into existence a class of retailers (κάπηλοι), who either hawked their wares about the streets or exposed them for sale on stalls and in shops erected in the Agora or elsewhere. Few of them were citizens and the non-productive nature of their work contributed to the low estimation in which they were held. Other retailers travelled from place to place, following in the wake of armies on the march, visiting the great festivals and fairs, or peddling their goods, as did the Aeginetans in especial, from village to village. Any considerable development of trade by land was, however, hampered by the mountainous nature of the country, the scarcity of good roads and of means of transport and the consequent costliness of carriage.

IV. COMMERCE[1]

Owing to the physical configuration of the Greek world, its commerce was largely sea-borne. This fact, in conjunction with the enterprise of the Greek traders themselves, gave to Greek commerce a cosmopolitan character. An Athenian citizen of the Periclean age might enjoy not only Attic olive-oil and wine but also the corn and the dried fish of the Black Sea, the dates of Phoenicia and the cheeses of Sicily; he might wear slippers from Persia and lie on a Milesian bed with his head resting on a Carthaginian pillow. During the sixth century the Ionian cities had been especially active in this sphere (see vol. IV, chap. IV), but the

[1] See map 1 above.

failure of the Ionian Revolt, the closing of the channels of trade between the Anatolian seaboard and the Persian hinterland, the political dominance and commercial enterprise of Athens, and the increasing importance of the Western Mediterranean combined to cause the transference of much of this commerce to the ports of Hellas. The power and wealth of Chalcis had been shaken by her defeat at Athenian hands in 506 (vol. IV, p. 161), while that of Eretria received a crushing blow in the destruction of the city by the Persians in 490 (vol. IV, p. 244); thus the old commercial prominence of Euboea passed away for ever. Many of the Greek states were absorbed in agriculture and the number of those which attempted to exploit the new commercial opportunities was very limited.

Among these there were three which, at the opening of the fifth century, stood in the foreground—Corinth, Aegina and Athens. Corinth reaped the fruits of her command of the Isthmus, her possession of sea-ports both on the Corinthian and on the Saronic Gulf, her direct access to the West, and her friendly relations with Syracuse, its most powerful city. On the other hand, the ill-will of Corcyra, her recalcitrant daughter, rendered her hold on the natural highroad to the West precarious, while her connections with the East were too weak to secure for her any considerable trade in the Aegean, from which, indeed, she seems to have practically withdrawn by the close of the sixth century. Aegina, peopled by an enterprising stock, which, in default of fertile lands, turned early to industry and to trade, developed a large navy and mercantile marine, carried on commercial activities over a wide sphere and amassed considerable wealth. Athens was too closely wedded to agriculture and too much distracted by internal feuds to throw herself wholeheartedly into a policy of commercial expansion in the Solonian period. Later, however, the long-continued peace and prosperity secured by the tyrants, the political reorganization effected by Cleisthenes and the development of her staple manufactures, especially oil and pottery, led her to enter the lists and compete for commercial primacy. The result was a prolonged and bitter struggle with Aegina, which was suspended in face of the common danger involved in Xerxes' invasion. At the outset Corinth seems to have favoured the new competitor, hoping that Athens would be of use to her in crushing their common rival: too late she realized that Athens had no mind to share, still less to leave in Corinthian hands, the fruits of their joint labours. In 459–8 B.C. she made desperate but unavailing efforts to avert the doom of Aegina, which after a protracted blockade became a tributary member of the Delian League: subsequently, in 431 B.C., the Aeginetans were driven from their island, which was settled by Attic cleruchs (p. 198).

Thus freed from the rivalry of Aegina, Athens was able more effectively to challenge the position of Corinth in the West, where, ever since the sixth century, Attic pottery had enjoyed a growing popularity. The possession of Naupactus, the direct access to the Corinthian Gulf secured by the accession of Megara and her hold on Achaea enabled Athens to close the Western sea-route to Corinth, and though by the terms of the Thirty Years Peace she lost Pegae and Achaea, she may well have hoped to find some compensation in the colony of Thurii which she promoted (see below p. 168 *sq.*) and in her alliance with Corcyra in 433 B.C. In the North-East there was a notable revival of Athenian trade with the Black Sea soon after 440 B.C., a revival especially important because, as we have seen, this region afforded Athens the major portion of her food-supply (see p. 173 *sq.*). Megara, which through her seaports of Nisaea and Pegae traded in eastern and in western waters, had, after some fourteen years of subjection to Athenian control, recovered her independence by the revolt of 446 and this was secured to her by the Thirty Years Peace. Athens, however, did not forget or forgive and sought, by excluding her from the Attic markets and then from those of the Athenian Empire, to compass her economic ruin. The fact that Megara survived the Archidamian War, in which her territory was ravaged twice every year, her navy and her merchant-vessels were driven from the seas, and her principal harbour was menaced from Budorum and Minoa and finally captured by the Athenians in 424, bears eloquent testimony to her resources, her vitality and her determination.

Ever since the revelation of her naval power which had come to her at the battle of Salamis and was confirmed by that of the Eurymedon, Athens had set herself resolutely to become mistress of the sea and to extend her commerce in every direction. At the instance of Themistocles, the Piraeus was superbly fortified and the Athenians began to take full advantage of its three natural harbours, which were developed not only for naval purposes but also for those of trade. A mercantile port (*Emporion*) was laid out, quays were constructed and warehouses erected, while colonnaded buildings such as the Corn Exchange (*Alphitopōlis*) of Pericles and the Deigma, where merchants displayed samples of their various wares and business contracts were concluded, served the ends both of utility and of beauty. Behind lay the city itself, with its teeming cosmopolitan population, its shrines of Greek and of foreign gods, its shops, its inns, its broad straight streets crossing at right angles according to the design of the famous architect and political theorist Hippodamus of Miletus—the earliest application on a large scale of a town-planning scheme.

A further task which Athens set herself was to police the seas effectively. At the beginning of the century piracy, fostered by the unsettled political conditions of the time, was a serious menace to trade in the Mediterranean. Herodotus' stories of some of the eminent corsairs of those days, such as Dionysius of Phocaea (VI, 17) and Histiaeus of Miletus (VI, 5, 26–28), give us vivid glimpses of their methods, and even after the defeat of Xerxes and the liberation of Ionia, Teos thought it necessary to include in her commination service (Dittenberger, *S.I.G.*[3] 37,38) a curse upon magistrates who 'should engage in piracy or wittingly harbour pirates.' The assumption of maritime hegemony by Athens brought a marked improvement. Cimon's expedition to Scyros and that of Pericles to the Thracian Chersonese were primarily directed against this scourge, and the question of safe and peaceful navigation was one of those proposed for discussion at the Panhellenic Congress projected by Pericles (pp. 93, 95). Probably this period was one of greater security for the mariner than any which had preceded since the breakdown of the Minoan thalassocracy and than any which followed until Pompey's pacification of the Mediterranean in 67 B.C. The outbreak of the Peloponnesian War, however, caused a revival of privateering, which was aimed especially at trade with the Levant[1], and the downfall of Athens, by removing the only power which could enforce the safety of the seas, led directly to a serious recrudescence of piracy.

The fifth century also witnessed remarkable progress in navigation. Larger ships were built, some of them of 10,000 talents (about 256 tons) burden, and, although the old timidity was not wholly overcome and the coastal routes were still followed by preference, sailors began to dread the open sea less and to prolong their ventures beyond the limits of the recognized sailing season. The speed of vessels also increased: in 405 Theopompus the Milesian reached Sparta with news of the victory of Aegospotami 'on the third day' after leaving Lampsacus, having covered some 290 nautical miles by sea and over 30 miles by land[2]. This speed

---

[1] Thucydides II, 69; IV, 53; VIII, 35.

[2] Xenophon, *Hellen.* II, 1. 30. We may assume that he landed somewhere on the east coast of Laconia, and did not unnecessarily prolong his journey by rounding Cape Malea and sailing to Gytheum.

was, no doubt, exceptional, but Herodotus (IV, 86) reckons about 130 nautical miles as the twenty-four hours' journey of a sailing vessel, which gives an average speed of slightly under $5\frac{1}{2}$ knots, and Xenophon (*Anab.* VI, 4. 2) states that a trireme could row in 'a long day's journey' from Byzantium to Heraclea, a distance of 120 nautical miles.

Freights and passages by sea contrasted favourably with those by land. According to Plato, the fare from Aegina to the Piraeus was only 2 obols and that from Egypt or Pontus 2 drachmae at most for a passenger with wife, children and baggage. In 329 B.C. the transport of 100 tiles overland from Laciadae to Eleusis, a distance of about 12 miles, cost 40 drachmae, *i.e.* 40 per cent. of their purchase-price, while it cost but $6\frac{2}{3}$ drachmae to bring them by sea from Corinth, three times as far. This evidence dates, it is true, from the fourth century, but it probably represents approximately the conditions which had existed in the fifth.

V. THE COST OF LIVING

The primary needs of civilized man are food, clothing and shelter. Of a housing problem we hear nothing in the fifth century save under the exceptional conditions of the Peloponnesian War, when a large proportion of the rural population of Attica was forced to take shelter, occasionally or continuously, within the fortifications of Athens and the Piraeus. Town houses were for the most part simple and unpretentious, consisting of one or two storeys and often crowded together in narrow streets, although large tenements were also found at Athens and in some other cities. On the country estates of the aristocracy, on the other hand, the buildings were frequently larger and more costly[1]. The citizen seems normally to have owned his own home, but non-citizens were legally debarred from owning real property; if, however, we may accept the evidence of Isaeus (*c.* 360 B.C.), land was leased for 8 per cent. and houses for about $8\frac{1}{2}$ per cent. of their value, a surprisingly low proportion when compared with the current rate of interest. Furniture also was in general simple and inexpensive, though there were exceptional cases like that of Alcibiades, the inventory of whose bedroom furniture has in part survived (*I.G.*² 1, 330) to give us some idea of what may well have been at the time the most luxurious palace in Athens. Yet even here the prices realized—*e.g.* 90 drachmae for eleven couches of Milesian manufacture, 16 for four tables, $1\frac{1}{6}$ for a chair, 17 for a divan—are far from extravagant.

[1] Thucydides II, 65; *Hellenica Oxyrhynchia*, XII, 4–5.

In clothing the Greeks at this period tended towards greater simplicity and uniformity. Men generally adopted the short woollen tunic (*chiton*) in place of the longer linen garment of the Ionians, while the bright hues of the previous period were discarded for a simple white or, for purposes of economy, some dark colour. At the end of the century a mantle (*himation*) cost from 16 to 20 drachmae and a workman's overall (*exomis*) about 10 drachmae[1]. Women's clothing, in which the use of linen survived to a larger extent, was less simple, and probably, as a rule, more costly, than that of men. In very many homes, however, most or all of the processes of making woollen clothes were carried out by the women of the family or by female slaves, and the cost was thus considerably reduced. Footwear was extremely varied in style and ranged from very simple and cheap shoes to elaborate and expensive boots.

In eating and drinking there were considerable differences between district and district: at one end of the scale came the Spartan, whose common table was marked by extreme simplicity, at the other the Thessalian noble or the wealthy citizen of one of the western colonies. In general, however, the Greek lived simply and frugally, and, though the professional *chef* and the cookery-book had made their appearance before the close of the century, yet even among the wealthier classes there seems to have been little tendency towards that insensate extravagance which characterized the Roman aristocracy towards the end of the Republican period. The staple food was corn, of which wheat ranked high above barley in general estimation. This was ground into flour, usually in the house, and was eaten in the form either of porridge or of flat loaves: with it were taken olives, vegetables, nuts, cheese, figs and other fruits. Meat played a small part in the ordinary diet, though pork was regarded as a delicacy; but fish was commonly eaten, either fresh or dried, in which form it was imported in large quantities from the Propontis, the Euxine and elsewhere.

Upon this basis we may seek to estimate the minimum annual outlay of the town dweller in the latter part of the fifth century. The consumption of wheat was reckoned at a *choinix* per day for each adult, *i.e.* 7½ *medimni* per year of 360 days: at 2 drachmae a *medimnus*, this would cost 15 drachmae. For other food (meat, fish, vegetables, fruit, etc.) and for drink we may allow ¾ obol a day, or 45 drachmae a year. Clothing and shoes we may estimate at about 16 drachmae, rent (in the case of one who does not own

[1] Plutarch, *Moralia*, 470 F.

his home) at 36 and incidental expenses at 8. Thus 120 drachmae a year, *i.e.* 2 obols a day, will suffice for the needs of an unmarried man. A wife will probably require less food, she will not increase the rent and her handiwork may well result in a lowering rather than an increase of the sum required for clothing: thus 3 obols a day, or 180 drachmae a year, should suffice for a married couple.

VI. MONEY, WAGES AND INTEREST

The transition from natural economy to a money economy had already occurred before the dawn of the fifth century in all the more progressive states of Greece (see vol. IV, chap. V). Sparta, however, stood aside from the general development, debarring her citizens from the possession of silver and issuing only a currency consisting of iron bars; elsewhere also, especially in the country districts, the exchange of commodities or services must frequently have been effected without the intervention of money, while rents and salaries were still occasionally paid wholly or partly in kind.

In the opening years of the century currency was seriously restricted by the scarcity of the precious metals in the Aegean area, and the withdrawal of money from circulation by hoarding, on the part both of individuals and of temples, exercised a constant influence in the same direction. Herodotus (VII, 28, 29) tells of a Lydian who possessed 2000 talents of silver and 4,000,000 staters of gold, and the story, though perhaps untrue, is nevertheless significant. The shortage of silver was remedied by the intensive exploitation after 483 B.C. of the mines at Laurium and of the mineral resources of Mount Pangaeus and the surrounding country. This led to a steady advance in the price of gold, the ratio of which to silver, fixed by Darius at $13\frac{1}{3}$: 1, had risen at Athens by 440 B.C. to 14:1 (*I.G.*[2] I, 355) and at Syracuse to 15:1 (Head, *H.N.*[2] p. 176). Towards the close of the century, however, the copious influx of Persian gold brought about a rapid fall in its relative value, which stood at 12:1 at the end of the Peloponnesian War and a hundred years later had sunk, as a result of Alexander's eastern conquests, to 10:1.

Persian gold darics circulated freely throughout the East, but gold was not minted by Greek states (with the exception of Cyrene) save as an emergency measure taken under acute pressure. Athens issued gold drachmae[1], equal in value to 12 silver drachmae, in 406, as part of her supreme effort to stave off defeat at Spartan hands (p. 355), and about the same time Syracuse, Acragas, Gela[2],

[1] See Volume of Plates ii, 4, *d*.   [2] *Ib.* 2, *a*, *b*, *c*.

and Camarina did the same, the last three presumably in face of the Carthaginian invasion which gave rise also to the earliest Carthaginian coinage[1] (see below, vol. vi, p. 110). The complex monetary conditions of the Aegean world, with its various standards of weight and degrees of purity, were further complicated by the circulation of electrum, especially the staters of Cyzicus, Mitylene, Phocaea and Lampsacus[2], which were largely used by the Greeks in their Pontic commerce. Although the proportion of gold contained in early electrum coins varies between 5 and 72 per cent. and thus the intrinsic value of coins of the same weight may differ very markedly, electrum was in the sixth century conventionally regarded as having ten times the value of silver. This convention, however, gave electrum an exaggerated value, and in the fifth century a Cyzicene stater was recognized as the equivalent not of 38 but of 24 or 25 Attic silver drachmae.

Early in the century there were many local currencies which circulated within their respective states, but few which were widely recognized and accepted. Foremost among these were the coinages of Aegina and of Corinth, but even before the Persian Wars, and increasingly after 483, the Athenian silver 'owls' gained ground at their expense, thanks to the exactness of their weight, the purity of their metal and the imperial and commercial predominance of Athens. The conquest of Aegina (p. 83) almost, if not entirely, terminated the issue of Aeginetan coins, and Athenian currency won a monopoly in the Cyclades, most of which intermitted their autonomous issues, and in many cities of Asia Minor, where only small denominations were locally struck. Even where Athens could not impose her own coinage, her influence led, *e.g.* in Rhodes[3] and Cos, to the temporary adoption of the Attic standard. Finally Athens sought by frank coercion to consummate her triumph: two decrees were passed ordering all subject cities to use exclusively Attic coinage, weights and measures on pain of a heavy fine (*I.G.* xii, 5. 480). But though Athens might threaten, her power to enforce was gone, and the rapid spread of the Chian and Abderite standards towards the close of the period clearly indicates her relaxing hold upon her empire.

Our knowledge of the normal rate of pay in this century is very restricted, but the evidence indicates a marked upward tendency during its course. Thucydides repeatedly refers to the sums paid by Greek states to citizens or to aliens who served in the

---

[1] See Volume of Plates ii, 2, *d*.   [2] *Ib.* 2, *e, f, g.*   [3] *Ib.* 2, *i.*

army or the navy, but the question is complicated by the fact that sometimes this pay was regarded as a ration-allowance while sometimes a wage was paid in addition to such allowance. According to a passage in Thucydides (III, 17), the authenticity of which some scholars have called in question, each hoplite engaged in the siege of Potidaea received two drachmae a day, one for himself and one for his servant, and naval pay was on the same scale. A drachma was also paid daily to the sailors on the Athenian armada which besieged Syracuse and to the Thracian mercenaries who arrived too late to accompany Demosthenes to Sicily in 413, while the alliance between Athens, Argos, Mantinea and Elis, concluded in 420, secured an allowance of three Aeginetan (roughly equivalent to four Attic) obols a day to heavy infantry, light troops and archers, and an Aeginetan drachma to cavalry serving in allied territory. Tissaphernes paid an Attic drachma to those serving on the Spartan fleet (*ib.* VIII, 29), but wished to reduce this to three obols and actually did so temporarily on the ground that this was at the time the normal Athenian rate (*ib.* VIII, 45). Officers appear to have received twice, and generals four times, the hoplite's pay.

We know little of the wage or subsistence-allowance granted during the second half of the century for civil service. Jurymen may have received originally one obol daily, but if so this was subsequently raised to two and again in 425, when two obols were no longer a living wage, to three. Somewhat larger sums were paid to the archons, the councillors and other magistrates. On the other hand, eminent doctors, musicians, actors and sophists frequently received considerable salaries or fees. Protagoras, Gorgias and Zeno are reputed to have charged on occasion 10,000 drachmae for the education of a single pupil; Prodicus of Ceos demanded for his courses of lectures fees ranging from 1 drachma to 50, for which latter sum he offered 'a complete education in grammar and language,' and Euenus of Paros was regarded as singularly moderate in charging only 500 drachmae for instruction in 'human and political virtue.' Poets also, such as Simonides and Pindar, and professional speech-writers, the first of whom was Antiphon, received generous honoraria.

The fullest information relative to wages is preserved in the Erechtheum-accounts for 409–8 B.C. and the two following years (*I.G.*² I, 373–4), and the payments there recorded may be taken as normal towards the end of the century, reflecting the rise in the cost of living produced by the Peloponnesian War, while at the same time reduced to the lowest practicable level in view of the financial straits into which Athens had fallen. Remuneration was reckoned either by the day or by the piece. The daily wage of the artisan, whether citizen, metic or slave, was one drachma, irrespective of the work on which he was engaged. Other rates are rare, such as the drachma and a half paid to one who erected scaffolding for encaustic work (*ib*. 374, ll. 74 *sqq*.), three obols to six men, perhaps apprentices, who took down and removed scaffolding (*ib*. ll. 151 *sqq*.) and five obols for some unidentifiable service (*ib*. l. 123 *sq*.). Even the architect received only one drachma and his assistant secretary only five obols a day, but these were regular stipends paid each prytany and not dependent upon the number of working days.

Side by side with the system of a daily wage we find that of piece-work. The sculptures of the Erechtheum frieze, for example, were paid for at the flat rate of 60 drachmae per figure; encaustic decorators received five obols per foot for their work, the makers of bronze ornaments 14 drachmae for each article, and sawyers two obols and one drachma per section for 8-foot and for 24-foot timber respectively.

The rise in wages which we have just noticed appears to have been in part the outcome and in part the cause of the rise in prices which marked the course of the century and was accentuated by the Peloponnesian War. Data are wholly lacking save for Attica and even here they are woefully meagre. A *medimnus* (*c*. 1½ bushel) of barley, which in the Solonian legislation had counted as the equivalent of a drachma, had risen to twice that price by the close of the fifth century, while early in the fourth wheat seems to have stood at 3 drachmae despite the immense quantities imported from the Euxine. Still more marked was the rise in the cost of sheep and cattle: in Solon's time a sheep cost one drachma, while at the close of the fifth century 10 or even 20 drachmae were paid for a sheep and 50 or 100 for an ox. Of the cost of clothing and furniture something has already been said. Other recorded prices from the latter half of the Peloponnesian War are of less value, for we have no means of comparing them with those paid for similar commodities earlier in the century. Thus in 408–7 the Commissioners of the Erechtheum pay a drachma for boards on which to write their accounts, 1⅓ drachmae for papyrus sheets, a drachma for leaves of gold used for gilding bronze ornaments and 5 drachmae per talent for lead (*I.G.*[2] 1, 374). Again, we know some of the prices realized by the sale of the confiscated property of those found guilty of participation in the mutilation of the Hermae or other sacrileges (*I.G.*[2] 1, 325 *sqq*.), but the general financial instability of the times and the specially fluctuating character of auction-prices must be kept in mind, nor are the descriptions of the objects sold sufficiently detailed for our purpose.

Of the normal rate of interest little evidence is available. There is reason to believe that the practice of hoarding, while it remained common throughout the period, was increasingly abandoned by the more enlightened capitalists in favour of a policy of investment—e.g. in lands or houses, in slaves, in loans or mortgages—though it is not till the age of Demosthenes that we can trace the development of the most lucrative, albeit highly speculative, type of investment, that in bottomry, which frequently brought in extraordinarily quick and high returns. Far from placing any restriction upon the rate of interest, Solon appears to have secured by definite enactment the freedom of the lender in this respect, and his law is cited as still valid by Lysias in the early fourth century. Nevertheless, the increased plentifulness of silver and the progressive stabilization of financial transactions naturally tended to lower the current rate of interest. The Delian temple under Athenian control lent money in the years immediately preceding the Peloponnesian War for terms of five years at 10 per cent. (*I.G.*[2] 1, 377), but in this case the security demanded was probably exceptionally ample, and the usual rate may well have been 12 per cent. or even higher. The Athenians paid 6 per cent. on sums borrowed from Athena and other gods between 433 and 427 B.C. and only $1\frac{1}{5}$ per cent. during the following quinquennium (*I.G.*[2] 1, 324): probably the people, in whose power it lay to prescribe the conditions of such loans, determined to pay a half, and later a tenth part, of the normal interest in order to maintain the principle that sums taken from the sacred treasures were in reality loans.

Of banking operations, apart from those of certain great temples, we find little trace till we reach the fourth century, though money-changers must have been common in the fifth, and some of them may already have laid the foundations upon which was to rise the highly developed banking system of the following period (see below, vol. VI, p. 71 *sq.*).

VII. PUBLIC FINANCE

Our knowledge of the financial organization of the Greek states at this period is practically confined to Athens. Sparta can hardly be said to have possessed any system at all and on the eve of the Peloponnesian War her king Archidamus, while admitting

that 'war is not a matter of arms but of money,' acknowledged
that Sparta had neither revenue nor reserve. The Corinthians
urged that the deficiency might be made good by contributions
from the states composing the Spartan Confederacy and by loans
from the funds at Delphi and Olympia, and we know that a sub-
scription list was in fact opened, to which miscellaneous contributions, in money and in kind, were made by Spartan sympathizers
(*I.G.* v, 1. 1). But though Sparta, thanks to her tradition of
unpaid service and the restricted area of her operations, was able
to meet the financial demands of the first eighteen years of the
war, her attempt to cope with the Athenians on their own element
after the Syracusan disaster and to carry on the struggle in
Ionian and Hellespontine waters might well have been frustrated
had it not been for the opportune intervention of Tissaphernes
and especially of Cyrus, who provided the funds necessary for the
maintenance of a large fleet and the conduct of naval warfare.

Even the Athenian ideas of public economy were in some
respects singularly rudimentary. Athens had no budget, no
public debt, no Chancellor of the Exchequer, no permanent
Treasury officials. As late as 482 it was seriously proposed to
deal with an embarrassing surplus by means of a popular distribution (see vol. IV, p. 264 *sq.*), and throughout the century
financial policy was, like every other aspect of public life, directly
subject to the decisions of the sovereign Assembly and was
supervised by the annually changing Council.

We may briefly review the principal sources of the Athenian
state revenue. The sums drawn from lands, houses, quarries and
other public property were probably moderate in amount with the
exception of those derived from the silver mines of Laurium and
from the gold and silver mines acquired in Macedonia and
Thrace. The fiscal system of the Peisistratidae, who levied a fixed
proportion of the produce of the soil (vol. IV, p. 66), was abandoned
by the democracy, which regarded such direct taxation, save as an
emergency measure, as an infringement of civic liberty. Under
the pressure of the Peloponnesian War, however, the Athenians
repeatedly imposed upon themselves the property-tax (*eisphora*),
first in 428 B.C., when they raised in this way 200 talents as a
contribution to the cost of the siege of Mitylene. On the other
hand, various indirect taxes were levied at Athens as elsewhere.
A duty of 1 per cent., later raised to 2 per cent., *ad valorem* on
imports and exports was levied at the Piraeus, and its very
moderation saved the state from the necessity of organizing
elaborate measures to deal with attempted evasion: for duties

levied on the land frontiers there is no evidence. In 413 the Athenians substituted for the tribute a 5 per cent. duty on goods passing into or out of the harbours of the Empire, hoping thus to increase their revenue; since the tribute in the preceding years had probably risen to, or above, 1000 talents, it would seem that the estimated volume of trade passing through the ports of tributary states surpassed 20,000 talents. A 10 per cent. tax (*dekate*) is mentioned in a decree of about 434 B.C. (*I.G.*² 1, 91); its nature is not there indicated, but it has been conjecturally interpreted as a toll on Pontic trade, which may have been collected by the Hellespontophylaces in the Archidamian War and was revived by Alcibiades, who in 410 instituted a toll-station at Chrysopolis on the Bosphorus. Athens further levied market-dues, a tax on sales concluded before state officials, a charge of 12 drachmae annually on metics and of half a drachma on slaves and freedmen, and a tax on those who pursued certain callings requiring special supervision, *e.g.* oracle-mongers, jugglers, and prostitutes. To the revenue so derived must be added court-fees and fines, as well as sums realized by the sale of the sequestrated property of debtors to the state.

An important part in Athenian finance was played by the sums paid by members of the Delian League, at first as a voluntary contribution to the cost of the war against Persia, later as a tribute demanded from subject states. The Treasury of the League, originally on the islet of Delos, was transferred to Athens in 454, and from that year onwards until the abolition of the tribute in 413 (see above) we can trace its fluctuations with fair accuracy thanks to the survival of considerable portions of the quota-lists, which recorded the sums paid to Athena annually on behalf of the several communities, consisting of one-sixtieth of the amount levied from each[1].

Of the total revenues of the Greek states we are ill-informed, but they must normally have been very small. Herodotus (VI, 46) estimates that of Thasos, an exceptionally wealthy community, at 200 talents on an average and 300 in years of special prosperity. At the outbreak of the Peloponnesian War Athens received, according to Thucydides' version of Pericles' speech (II, 13), 'on an average 600 talents of tribute annually from the allies exclusive of her remaining revenue,' and though the quota-lists

---

[1] The approximate totals of tribute which can be determined vary between 440 and little more than 400 talents in the period between 454 and 425 B.C., in which year the tribute was assessed so as to produce 960 talents (p. 236).

show that these words cannot be taken literally, yet they may correctly summarize the external revenue of the state. For the internal revenue we lack trustworthy data, but it can hardly have fallen short of, and may have appreciably exceeded, 400 talents.

This revenue amply sufficed to meet the ordinary expenditure of the state, all the more so because the cost of certain services involving a heavy outlay was borne by the wealthier citizens individually and not by the public exchequer. At Athens the most important of these services were the *choregia*, or maintenance, training and equipment of a lyrical, dramatic or musical chorus, the *gymnasiarchia*, which served a similar purpose for certain athletic contests, and the *hestiasis*, or provision of a banquet for the members of a tribe, to which must be added, especially in time of war, the *trierarchia*, or equipment and repair (involving also the command) of a trireme. The cost of these services varied with the public spirit and the means of the citizen concerned: the average outlay of a trierarch in the Peloponnesian War was about 5000 drachmae, while the *choregus* expended anything from 300 to 3000 drachmae, or even more, according to the occasion. One of Lysias' clients spent no less than 9 talents 2600 drachmae on 'liturgies' between 411 and 403 B.C., but this sum far exceeded his legal obligations.

In a community in which church and state were inseparably associated, the maintenance of the established cults was dependent partly on the treasuries of the divinities concerned, partly on public funds. The temples and other sacred buildings erected in Attica, especially during the Periclean period, involved a large outlay, though we cannot accept Heliodorus' statement that the Propylaea alone cost 2012 talents—a sum which probably represents the combined expenditure upon the Parthenon, including Pheidias' colossal chryselephantine statue of Athena, and upon the Propylaea. Festivals and sacrifices also were subsidized in the Greek states, above all at Athens, where such celebrations were especially frequent and magnificent; in 415, for example, 9 talents were voted towards the expenses of the Lesser Panathenaea (*I.G.* ² 1, 302), and in 410, despite the financial stringency due to the military situation, over 5 talents were borrowed for the Great Panathenaea (*I.G.* ² 1, 304). Moreover, the practice of distributing money to the citizens to enable them to view dramatic or other performances seems to have originated with Pericles, though its full development belongs to the fourth century. The state also dedicated costly offerings at Delphi and elsewhere, but the expense of these was defrayed out of the booty taken in the victories they commemorated.

Payment for public service was introduced in the fifth century and caused a serious drain upon the resources of the state. The 500 Councillors received a drachma daily; for the pay of the jurymen see p. 101 *sq.* Thus the Council and the courts cost Athens after 425 B.C. an annual sum which may be estimated at between 100 and 110 talents. We must not, however, regard these and similar payments merely as indicating the demagogic methods of Athenian politicians and the rapacity of Athenian citizens. The large membership of the Council and of the courts was fixed long before the introduction of pay and, so far from being a mere device for subsidizing a maximum number of citizens, was based upon a fundamental article of the democratic faith; but experience soon showed that, if no compensation were offered for the time devoted to public service, the deliberative, administrative and judicial work would *de facto* be monopolized by the wealthier classes and would consequently fail to embody the democratic spirit. Even non-democratic states sometimes found it necessary to adopt the same system, though within narrow limits (see below, p. 329).

The expenditure upon public works other than temples provided for the building and repair of roads, fountains, markets, gymnasia, law-courts, council-house, etc., but above all for the construction and maintenance of the massive walls which surrounded and united Athens and the Piraeus, of the arsenal and dock-yards, and for the fortification of strategic positions, especially on the frontier, such as Eleusis, Panactum, Phyle and Sunium. Even in time of peace considerable sums were spent on the military and naval establishments, for the building of ships, which in Themistocles' time had become an annual charge upon the state, the maintenance of the cavalry brigade, the provision of arms and tackle, and the payment of the forces engaged in patrolling or garrisoning important points in the Empire. Order was maintained in the city by means of a body of public slaves, originally 300 in number but subsequently raised to 1000, who were called indifferently archers or Scythians: these the state had to maintain or increase by purchase and to give them an allowance at least sufficient to provide food and clothing.

Upon education as such Athens, unlike her colony Thurii, spent nothing, though she provided gymnasia and wrestling-schools and occasionally bestowed honoraria upon distinguished literary men such as Pindar and Herodotus. She did, however, organize something of the nature of a poor-law system, granting relief to the incapacitated and maintaining till they came of age the children of those who fell in war. Towards the close of the century the ruin of the rural population, especially after the Spartan occupation of Decelea, led to a more general distribution of poor-relief and the 'two-obol payment' became one of the heaviest demands on the public exchequer (*I.G.*² 1, 304) (see below, p. 344).

The supremely disturbing factor in state finance was war, which involved the ravaging of land, the destruction of property, the impoverishment of the peasantry, the diversion of much labour into unproductive channels and the heavy cost of military, and especially of naval, warfare. Not only were mercenary troops increasingly employed, but, as war developed from a succession of short and isolated campaigns into a continuous series of operations, conducted over a wide area and often in several fields simultaneously, the payment of all the forces mobilized became necessary and costly. True, the hoplite armies engaged were rarely large: the Peloponnesian League, for example, seems to have used only some 20,000 hoplites on foreign service, the Argives had probably no more than 6000, the Boeotian Confederacy in the latter part of the century mustered but 11,000 hoplites and 1100 cavalry all told. Yet the pay of a force of 12,000 men for 150 days at the rate of four obols a day would amount to 200 talents. Naval warfare necessitated a much greater outlay. This period witnessed the universal adoption of the trireme in place of the penteconter as battle-ship. Each trireme cost about a talent to construct and its life was, at best, short. Its crew of 200 would cost the state in wages, at three obols a day, half a talent monthly. Thus the larger operations of the Peloponnesian War, especially those involving sieges or blockades, proved very expensive. Thucydides estimates at 2000, Isocrates at 2400, talents the cost of the Athenian siege of Potidaea (432–30 B.C.), and the Syracusans are said to have spent a sum far exceeding 2000 talents in the defence of their city against the Athenian Armada (415–13); the total drain on the Athenian exchequer of the Archidamian war (431–21) has been estimated at about 12,000 talents (about £3,250,000 or in terms of purchasing power £14,400,000).

It is impossible to estimate accurately the capital value of Athenian property at this period. A valuation carried out in 378 B.C. for the purpose of assessing the property-tax gave a total of 5750 talents, but this excluded the property of the state and of the lowest class of citizens. The corresponding total would doubtless have been considerably larger when Athens was at the height of her prosperity before the Peloponnesian War, though the steady rise of prices would tend to reduce the difference. Of the property of individual citizens we learn some details. Callias, the richest Athenian of the Periclean period, was popularly reputed to possess 200 talents and Nicias 100, but these sums are probably gravely exaggerated. Nicias' son Niceratus left only 14 talents at his death and Conon, one of the wealthiest men of his day, about 40. Socrates is represented as drawing a contrast between his own property, which he valued at 500 drachmae, and that of the well-to-do Critobulus, who possessed more than $8\frac{1}{3}$ talents.

The chief financial officials at Athens during this period were the *colacretae*, who received and disbursed the internal revenue, the Hellenotamiae, who administered the funds derived from the League, the Treasurers of the Sacred Moneys of Athena, usually called Treasurers of the Goddess, and the Treasurers of the other Gods, constituted probably in 435 or 434, by the decree of Callias (*I.G.*² 1, 91). The building up of a state reserve, distinct from the treasure of the goddess, seems to have been no part of Athenian policy, and it is doubtful whether there were any considerable accumulations in the League Treasury when it was transferred from Delos to Athens in 454. Normally the revenue of the state balanced or exceeded the expenditure; in emergencies any requisite sum could be borrowed from the sacred funds, to be subsequently repaid with interest. We may thus believe that the 9700 talents referred to in Thucydides II, 13, as the largest sum ever accumulated in the Acropolis, as well as the 6000 which remained there at the outbreak of the Peloponnesian War, constituted the treasure of Athena, fed largely by the balances left in the hands of the Hellenotamiae in years when military expenses had fallen short of imperial revenue.

CHAPTER II

THE CONFEDERACY OF DELOS
478–463 B.C.

I. SPARTAN LEADERSHIP

WHILE the Athenians, with those of the islanders and Ionians who had been liberated from Persia, set sail for Sestos in the autumn of 479 B.C., the Peloponnesian part of the fleet returned to Aegina, and after a few weeks spent in preparation for an expedition to Thessaly transported the troops under the command of the Spartan king Leotychidas to Pagasae[1]. It was part of the Athenian case for the justification of their Empire that after Mycale they had endured the rigours of winter in the Dardanelles, in order to reduce Sestos and open the straits once more to Greek navigation, while the Spartans and the other Peloponnesians had selfishly sailed home (see vol. IV, p. 346). This is not the only instance in which the history of Greece has suffered from being written and studied from the Athenian point of view. It was not so easy for the Greeks at the time, as it was some years later, to realize the completeness of their victory over Persia. Even after the reduction of Sestos, the other route between Asia and Europe, that by the bridge over the Bosporus, was still open to the Persians; and with the line of fortified posts which stretched from the Propontis to the frontiers of Macedonia still intact[2], it might well have appeared to the Spartans that, so long as Thessaly was in the hands of a dynasty friendly to Persia, a great and effectual door was opened into the very heart of Greece in the event of a renewed Persian offensive[3]. To secure Thessaly

Note—The main continuous sources for this and the following chapter are Thucydides I, 89–115, 128–138, and Diodorus XI, 37–XII, 7. Plutarch's *Themistocles, Aristides, Cimon,* and *Pericles* supply independent evidence; and for constitutional affairs Aristotle, *Const. of Athens.* See further the Bibliography.

[1] See note I A, 'The Thessalian Expedition of Leotychidas,' p. 466.

[2] Herodotus VII, 106.

[3] Cf. Thucydides I, 90. 'The Spartans argued that the Barbarian, if he again attacked them, would then have no strong place which he could make his headquarters.' It is clear from this passage that, at the time of the rebuilding of the walls of Athens, a renewed Persian offensive was regarded at Sparta as not improbable.

for the national cause must have seemed to them only second in importance to the opening of the Dardanelles. It is true that Sparta had private interests of her own to promote in Thessaly, for the expulsion of the Aleuadae would have meant the ascendancy of the philo-Laconian party; but it is equally true that Athens had private interests of her own in the prosecution of the siege of Sestos, where an Athenian colony had been established in the time of the elder Miltiades.

It is alleged by Herodotus[1], who is our primary authority, that the expedition failed in its object because Leotychidas accepted a bribe from the Aleuadae. It was natural that when the expedition was unsuccessful it should be assumed that its commander must have been bribed. Spartan kings were often venal, but in the present case any such hypothesis is otiose. Thessaly throughout its history was a house divided against itself, and the evacuation of Tempe in 480 B.C. was probably dictated as much by political as by military considerations. Both before and after the expedition of Xerxes, the Thessalian peasantry recognized in the rule of the Aleuadae their strongest safeguard against the oppression of the Hippēs (Knights), who formed the oligarchical and philo-Laconian party. A few initial successes were won by Leotychidas[2], but no real headway was made against the reigning house. In the following spring the expedition was recalled.

It must have been about the time that the fleet under the command of Leotychidas set sail for Pagasae that an incident occurred which revealed the latent rivalry of the two leading states in the Greek world. On the morrow of the victory at Plataea Athens was in ruins and defenceless. Only a few fragments of the city-walls remained standing. It was the policy of Themistocles both to extend the area of the former city, and to convert it into one of the strongest fortresses in Greece. It was not unnatural that Sparta should suspect that the fortification of Athens was a measure directed against herself. Owing to her geographical position Sparta had no need of walls, and nothing could have suited her interests better than the razing of the fortifications of other Greek cities. Consequently she proposed to Athens that the two states should join in imposing this policy on the rest of Greece north of the Isthmus; a policy which would have left Athens, as well as the other states, at the mercy of Sparta and the Peloponnesian League. It was not a policy that was likely to find favour at Athens, and Themistocles was resolved that Athens should be put into a state of defence before Sparta could prevent

[1] VI, 72.   [2] Plutarch, de Herodoti Malignitate, 21.

it. According to the story as told by Thucydides (1, 89–92), Themistocles persuaded the Athenians to dispatch Aristides, Habronichus, and himself, as envoys to Sparta in order to discuss the matter with the ephors. He would himself proceed at once to Sparta, but his colleagues were to stay behind at Athens until, by the efforts of the whole population, men, women, and children, the walls had been raised to a height which would permit of the defence of the city. On his arrival at Sparta he succeeded, on one pretext or another, in postponing his interview with the authorities; and when the ephors grew restive on receiving information from various sources that the walls were being rebuilt and had already reached a considerable height, he flatly denied the truth of these allegations. He urged them to send envoys to Athens who could bring back to Sparta a trustworthy report of the real position, while at the same time he sent instructions to the Athenians to detain the Spartan envoys until he and his colleagues, who had in the meantime reached Sparta, had been allowed to return home. The Spartans fell into the trap, and sent the envoys to Athens; whereupon, Themistocles laid aside the mask, and openly justified the policy of fortifying his city. The Spartans, not being prepared for a breach with Athens, accepted the inevitable, and allowed Themistocles and his colleagues to return.

There are points in this narrative which appeared improbable even to the ancient mind. Theopompus represented Themistocles as having effected his purpose by bribing the ephors[1]. Not a few modern critics are prepared to deal still more drastically with the tale as told by Thucydides. We are not, however, justified in treating the story as in the main a mere invention. It may be regarded as certain that Sparta attempted to prevent the fortification of Athens, and that her efforts were foiled by the diplomacy of Themistocles. It seems not less certain that there was at Sparta a party friendly to Athens, on whose support Themistocles could rely, and by whose aid he effected his purpose. It is inconceivable that the Spartan authorities could have been such simpletons as is presupposed by the narrative of Thucydides. The historian himself makes some significant admissions; that the Spartans were prompted to their action by the importunity of their allies, that Themistocles was popular at Sparta, and that a warm feeling of friendliness between the two cities had been created by the patriotism displayed by the Athenians in the War. An open breach with Athens was the last thing desired by any responsible statesman at Sparta.

[1] See Plutarch, *Themistocles*, 19.

If Plutarch (*Themistocles*, 20) is to be believed, Sparta made one more effort at this period to secure her ascendancy north of the Isthmus of Corinth. He attributes to Sparta the design of reorganizing the Amphictyonic League by excluding from it those states which either had joined Xerxes, or had remained neutral. The effect of the proposed change would have been felt chiefly in northern and central Greece, as Thessaly and Boeotia, as well as a number of smaller states whose votes were controlled by the Thessalians, would have lost their seats in the Council; but it would have extended to the Peloponnese where Sparta's great rival, Argos, would have been excluded. As the majority of the patriotic states were members of the Peloponnesian League, and therefore allies of Sparta, the proposal, if carried, would have given her the control of the Council. It was Themistocles, according to Plutarch, who detected the insidious designs of Sparta and induced the Pylagori, the deputies of the League, to reject the scheme. It may well be doubted if there is any historical foundation for the alleged proposal of the Spartans. It is generally assumed that Plutarch's authority in this passage is Theopompus, the historian of the reign of Philip of Macedon, and it may be surmised that we have here a typical instance of a method in favour with the writers of the fourth century B.C., that of eking out the scanty annals of an earlier period by the adaptation of well-known incidents of their own age[1]. To a contemporary of Philip of Macedon nothing was more familiar than the idea of employing the Amphictyonic League as a political instrument, but it is an idea which seems quite foreign to the mind of the fifth century.

Sparta had made two attempts to establish her supremacy north of the Isthmus; she had endeavoured to expel the Aleuadae from Thessaly, and to prevent the rebuilding of the walls of Athens. Both attempts had failed, and for the next twenty years her efforts in Greece itself are confined to the Peloponnese. It is not till 457 B.C. that another Spartan expedition is dispatched to northern Greece.

Before the beginning of spring in the year 478 B.C. Sestos had

---

[1] A good example of this is afforded by Plutarch, *Themistocles*, 25, compared with Diodorus XIV, 109. According to Theophrastus, Themistocles urged the spectators at Olympia to tear down the costly tent of Hiero, and to exclude his horses from the chariot race. That a Greek orator incited the spectators at Olympia to destroy the tent of a tyrant of Syracuse, and to exclude his envoys from the festival, is historically true, but the tyrant was Dionysius the elder, the orator Lysias, and the festival that of 388 B.C.

been reduced by the Athenians, and the Persians had been deprived of the control of the Hellespont. The liberation of the four great islands off the western coast of Asia Minor, Lesbos, Chios, Samos, and Rhodes, was a direct result of the battle of Mycale, and it may be assumed that some of the cities on the mainland of Ionia, as well as several of those on the shores of the Hellespont and Propontis, were recovered by the end of 479 B.C.[1] Much, however, still remained to be done before the task which the allies had set themselves could be regarded as accomplished. At the beginning of summer, the regent Pausanias was given the command of a fleet composed of twenty Peloponnesian vessels, thirty Athenian, and of a contingent drawn from Ionia and the islands. It might have been expected that the command would have been entrusted to Leotychidas, the victor of Mycale, but the discredit into which he had fallen owing to his mismanagement of the Thessalian campaign left the ephors no alternative but the appointment of his colleague. Pausanias had indeed incurred momentary unpopularity by a boastful inscription which he had engraved on the tripod which the Greeks had dedicated at Delphi as a thankoffering for their victory over the Persians[2]; an incident of this kind, however, could hardly have effaced the memory of the services which he had rendered to the national cause. The objective assigned to the expedition of 478 B.C. was twofold: the liberation of Cyprus, and the recovery of Byzantium. It proved an easy task to expel the Persian garrisons from the Greek cities in Cyprus, but the force at the disposal of Pausanias must have been quite inadequate for the reduction of the Phoenician cities of the island. In any case, the hold of the Greeks on the island could only have been precarious so long as the Phoenician fleet had its base so near at hand. From Cyprus the expedition sailed to the Bosporus, and Byzantium fell before the end of the summer.

This was a serious blow to Persia. Several Persians of high rank were amongst the garrison that was forced to surrender; but of even greater importance than this were the strategical results of the fall of this great stronghold. The communications between Persia and its garrisons in Thrace were cut, and the Greeks acquired complete control of the route to the Black Sea, from which region the supplies of imported corn had been largely drawn. This success of Pausanias, following on his brilliant victory at Plataea in the preceding year, appears to have turned his head. He con-

[1] Thucydides 1, 89.
[2] 'Pausanias, captain of the Hellenes, having destroyed the Persian host,
    Made this offering to Phoebus for a memorial.' See Thucydides 1, 132.

ceived the ambition of making himself master of the Greek world by the aid of Persia, and of marrying the daughter of the Great King. He adopted the Persian dress and manners, surrounded himself with a bodyguard of Persians and Egyptians drawn from the prisoners captured at Byzantium, and he showed himself insolent and oppressive towards the officers under his command. At length he entered into a treasonable correspondence with Xerxes, in which he promised to become his agent in the subjugation of Greece. So grave were the reports of his doings which reached Sparta that the ephors were compelled to insist on his immediate return. Of some of the particular charges alleged against him he was found guilty, and in consequence he was deprived of his command of the allied fleet; but the more serious charge of medism was held to be not proven, and he was allowed to return to Byzantium in an unofficial capacity. Next spring (477 B.C.) a Spartan named Dorcis was sent out by the ephors to take over the command of the fleet. On his arrival he found that the misconduct of his predecessor had had the most momentous consequences. Even before the recall of Pausanias the discontent among the Allies had given rise to a movement for the transference of the command from Sparta to Athens, but it was not until he was about to start on his return to Sparta that the transference was effected. The Peloponnesians alone of the allies refused to accept the change of leadership.

Thucydides represents this change of leadership in the operations against Persia as the outcome of two factors: the misconduct of Pausanias, and the sense of kinship which existed between the Athenians and the Greeks of Ionia and the Hellespont. He expressly says that the command was offered by the latter to the former on the ground of their common Ionian race. It has often been maintained that it was inevitable that the direction of the operations against Persia should have passed from Sparta to Athens, even if there had been no misconduct on the part of Pausanias, and no tie of blood between the Ionians and Athenians. As the war against Persia had to be carried on by sea, it was clearly impossible, so it is argued, that the command could be entrusted to any power other than Athens, which had contributed by far the largest number of vessels to the fleet which had won the battle of Salamis, and to whose navy there was now no rival in the Aegean. It may be admitted that the ultimate transference of command from Sparta to Athens was inevitable, but it is well to remember that in Greek History it is seldom indeed that the personal factor can be eliminated. Had Pausanias been a Brasidas, the change

might even so have come, but it would have come in a different
form, and it might have had very different results. As it was, the
change of leadership, coming at the time and in the manner that
it did, involved the humiliation of Sparta, and tended to the
ultimate estrangement of the two leading states. The immediate
effect, however, was to strengthen the influence of the party at
Sparta which was friendly to Athens.

In order to understand the policy of Sparta not only at this
moment, but throughout the fifth and fourth centuries down to
the rise of Macedon, it must be borne in mind that there were
two rival parties at Sparta whose influence upon her political
action can clearly be traced. One of these was a party whose view
was for the most part confined to the Peloponnese. It was opposed to a policy of adventure; above all, it was opposed to distant
enterprise across the sea. Its consistent aim was the maintenance
of a good understanding with Athens. The influence of this party
at this crisis is clearly visible in the narrative of Thucydides (1, 95).
The recall of Pausanias may have been due to a suspicion of his
intrigue with the Persian Court, and his removal from the command
may have been prompted as much by a sense of his unfitness for
the post as by the desire to avoid a rupture with Athens. It can
only have been the influence of the party friendly to Athens that
led Sparta to acquiesce in the repudiation of the claims of Dorcis
to the command, and it is Thucydides himself who asserts that
the Spartans accepted the formation of the new Confederacy under
the leadership of Athens because they were weary of the war
against Persia, because they were apprehensive of the effect of
distant service upon the character of Spartan commanders, and
because they regarded the Athenians as their friends. In the
language of Thucydides we seem to hear an echo of the arguments advanced at Sparta by the party whose influence has been
assumed. But Sparta had been humiliated, and deeply humiliated.
She had failed to expel the Aleuadae from Thessaly; she had
failed to prevent the fortification of Athens; and she had failed
to maintain that unity of command to which, as much as to any
other cause, the repulse of Xerxes had been due. Her policy had
failed, and it had failed very largely owing to the fault of those to
whom its execution was committed. Leotychidas had proved
incompetent; Pausanias had proved impossible. Such failures
and such humiliations were bound to discredit the party which
was responsible for the policy. They could not fail, however, to
leave behind bitter memories which that party would know how
to exploit to the full when the occasion should arise.

II. THE CONFEDERACY OF DELOS

As early as the autumn of 479 B.C. the Athenians had taken common action with the Greeks of Ionia and the Hellespont in the siege of Sestos, and had exercised over them a command that was independent of Sparta. Thus in the siege of Sestos, directed by an Athenian general, Xanthippus, and conducted by a fleet of which none of the Peloponnesian allies of Sparta formed part, we cannot fail to find one of the principal antecedents of the formation of the new Confederacy. The maritime league which was formed in the winter that followed the capture of Byzantium[1] is known as the Confederacy of Delos. It was here in the temple of Apollo and Artemis that the treasury of the League was established, and that the meetings of its synod were to be held. The choice of the sacred island of Delos, the ancient centre of Ionian worship, was probably dictated by considerations of sentiment as much as of convenience; and at any rate it served to throw into relief that common Ionian kinship on which the League was originally based.

In dealing with the Confederacy of Delos we are called upon to answer three questions of the first importance: what was its original constitution; what was its original extent; and what was the amount of the tribute (*phoros*) as first assessed?

It would appear that the constitution was not embodied in a document, nor expressed in any precise terms. It was more in the nature of a treaty of alliance, to which there were two parties: Athens on the one side, and the Allies on the other. It was between these two parties that the oaths were exchanged. The alliance was offensive as well as defensive, and the casting into the sea of masses of iron which accompanied the exchange of the oaths was intended to be symbolic of a determination which should last until the metal floated to the top. The object of the alliance is defined by Thucydides as retaliation for the losses inflicted by the Persians in their invasion of Greece. The task, however, of Athens and her allies must have been interpreted from the start as going far beyond a policy of mere reprisals. It must have been realized that the ultimate aim of their efforts was the liberation from the Persian yoke of the whole Greek fringe of Asia Minor. The obligations imposed upon the Allies were alternative in character. They bound themselves either to furnish

---

[1] Cf. Aristotle, *Const. of Athens*, XXIII. As the first assessment of Aristides is dated to the archonship of Timosthenes, 478–7 B.C., it must have been completed before midsummer 477, at the latest. The first steps, therefore, in the formation of the League must have been taken as early as the end of 478 B.C.

their quota of ships and crews for the prosecution of the war against Persia, or else, in lieu of this, their quota of tribute. There was to be a synod of the Allies which was to meet at Delos periodically, but what its powers and duties were it is not easy to determine. Grote attributes to it the two functions of reviewing the assessments of tribute and of sitting as a court of justice for the trial of charges, either of remissness of service or of failure to pay tribute, which might be brought against individual states. He treats it as self-evident that in the early days of the Confederacy Athens had no power to enforce any regulation not approved by the synod. 'We may be certain,' he says, 'that all which was done at first was done by general consent, and by a freely determining authority.' For these assumptions there is little evidence. It may be inferred from a passage in Thucydides (III, 11) that the synod had some control over the general policy of the League, and some say in the coercion of recalcitrant members such as Naxos or Thasos. That it acted as a court of appeal from the assessments proposed by the Athenians, or from the measures taken by Athenian commanders against defaulting states, is a view for which the authority of no ancient writer can be quoted.

In the constitution there were two defects which were to prove fatal to the success of the League as a union of free and independent allies. In the first place, Athens was unmistakably the 'predominant partner.' The contract was not between allies on a footing of equality, of whom Athens was one, but, as has been pointed out already, between two parties, of which Athens was one and the general body of the Allies was the other. To this predominant partner powers were entrusted from the first which rendered it inevitable that Athens should become the mistress of the League. It was left to her to decide which of the states included in the Confederacy should furnish ships, and which should pay tribute. To an Athenian statesman, Aristides, was committed the delicate task of determining the individual assessments of tribute. It would appear that the fleets of the League were invariably commanded by Athenian Generals, and if Thucydides is to be believed the *Hellenotamiae*, 'Stewards of the Greeks,' the officials to whom the payments of tribute were made, were Athenian magistrates from the first (see however below, p. 46). It was a singular piece of good fortune for Athens that the commander of her fleet in the Hellespontine waters at the moment when the Allies approached Athens happened to be Aristides, whose 'ostentatious probity,' to borrow Grote's phrase, inspired universal confidence.

In the second place, it was left undetermined whether each

individual state had, or had not, the right to withdraw from the League at its pleasure. It may be surmised that the right of secession was left in uncertainty, because, had it been expressly denied, the Confederacy might never have been formed. When the right to secede was claimed, first by Naxos and then by Thasos, it was easy for Athens to argue that the concession of this right could only end in the disruption of the League and the abandonment of the task which it had accepted, but when once the principle was admitted that secession was equivalent to rebellion, it was within the discretion of Athens to impose as the penalty for unsuccessful revolt such terms as were bound to make her within a few years the complete mistress of her allies. History is rich in examples of the dangers that are inseparable from such ambiguities. If the right of secession had been expressly denied by an article of the American constitution, that constitution might never have been accepted by the parties to the contract. Consequently, the right in question was neither affirmed nor denied, and the price paid for this deliberate equivocation was the Civil War of 1861.

At a later date we find the members of the Confederacy of Delos divided for the purposes of assessment into five groups: the Islands, Thrace, the Hellespont, Ionia, and Caria (see p. 168 and map 2 above). Of the insular district the nucleus was formed by the Cyclades, with the exception of the two Dorian islands of Thera and Melos. In addition to the Cyclades, there were included in this group the two important islands of Euboea and Aegina, as well as Lemnos and Imbros. The Thracian, or Thraceward district as it should more properly be called, consisted of the three peninsulas of Chalcidice, together with the cities on the northern coast of the Aegean from the Strymon to the Hebrus and the two islands of Thasos and Samothrace. The Hellespontine district comprised both the European and the Asiatic shores of the Hellespont proper, of the Propontis, and of the Bosporus, as well as the island of Tenedos. The western coast of Asia Minor from the south-western point of the Troad to the mouth of the Meander, together with the adjacent islands, formed the Ionian district. Finally, the Carian district included the whole coastline of south-western Asia Minor, from a point just south of Miletus to the city of Phaselis, in addition to a number of neighbouring islands, of which the most important were Cos, Carpathus, and Rhodes[1].

How much of what was subsequently included in these five

[1] It should be pointed out that the so-called autonomous islands (Lesbos, Chios, and Samos), and cleruchies such as the island of Scyros, did not form part of any of these assessment districts, for the simple reason that, as not paying tribute, they could not be assessed.

groups or districts formed part of the original Confederacy, when it was formed not later than midsummer 477 B.C.? From the Islands there must be excluded Aegina, Scyros, Carystus in Euboea, and possibly Andros[1]. It may be assumed that in the Thrace-ward district the two islands of Thasos and Samothrace had been recovered, and it is possible that the same may be said of the three peninsulas of Chalcidice. It may, however, be inferred with certainty from a comparison of a passage in Herodotus (VII, 105–7) with a statement in Thucydides (I, 98) that the whole coastline from the Hebrus to the Strymon, or more probably to the peninsula of Acte, was still in Persian hands. We gather from Herodotus that Persian garrisons and commandants had been established, even before the expedition of Xerxes, in all the Greek cities on the coast of Thrace and of the Hellespont, and that their reduction was not effected until the Thracian campaign of Cimon, in 476 B.C. and the following year. It is generally admitted that the Persians retained their hold on the Carian district, with the exception of Rhodes and some of the adjacent islands, until the campaign of the Eurymedon. It is more than probable that from the two remaining districts, Ionia and the Hellespont, serious deductions have to be made. It is not disputed that Ephesus and Myus in the former, and Byzantium, Lampsacus, and the greater part of the Thracian Chersonese, in the latter, were not yet in the possession of the League. Byzantium was still held by Pausanias, while more than a dozen years later it was in the power of the Great King to make a grant to Themistocles of Lampsacus and Myus[2].

It is commonly assumed that, with these exceptions, the whole of Ionia and the Hellespont had been secured by the beginning of 477 B.C.; but any such assumption seems hard to justify. It is by the merest accident that we happen to know that the places mentioned were still in Persian hands, and yet Ephesus, Lampsacus, and Myus are cities which might well have been expected to have fallen into the hands of the Greeks after Mycale. Ephesus was probably at the time the most important place on the mainland of Ionia; Myus lay next door to Miletus, while Lampsacus was a position of great strategical importance on the Dardanelles. If cities such as these were still in the possession of the Great King, what warrant can there be for the assertion that from every other place in these two districts the Persian garrisons had been expelled?

[1] For Andros, see Herodotus VIII, 111, 112.
[2] For Ephesus, see Thucydides I, 137; for the Chersonese, Plutarch, *Cimon*, 14 *ad init.*

We may conclude then that the Confederacy of Delos at the time of its first assessment (*i.e.* in the first half of 477 B.C.) comprised the whole of the insular district—with the exception of Aegina, Scyros, Carystus, and perhaps Andros—, the islands lying off the western coast of Asia Minor, and most, although by no means all, of the cities on the mainland of Ionia, and a majority of the cities in the Hellespontine district. On the other hand, the League held nothing in Caria except some of the islands, and in the Thracian district the most that it can have claimed was Chalcidice and the islands of Thasos and Samothrace[1].

The answer to the third question depends very largely on the answer to the second. If the original area of the Confederacy was at most three-fifths of what it was at the time of the Thirty Years Peace (445 B.C.), it seems reasonable to conclude that the first assessment must have produced a total sum appreciably less than those of a later period. Thucydides' answer to the question is at once precise, and unequivocal. He states that the tribute when first assessed amounted to 460 talents[2]. He is clearly referring to the first assessment of Aristides, although the 'assessment of Aristides' occurs only in a clause of the Peace of Nicias[3], and not in the passage in question. There are minds which cannot allow an appeal from the authority of Thucydides; there are others which are not content to answer the question by the aid of the simple formula, 'Thucydides cannot be mistaken.' If once this formula is ruled out, it must be admitted that there are grave difficulties in the way of accepting the figure which he gives. It is not merely that there were fewer cities included in the League in 477 B.C. than in 450 or 445 B.C.; we have also to take into account the fact that there were cities included in the League from the first which paid tribute after the middle of the century, but at the time of the first assessment supplied ships in lieu of tribute. Naxos and Thasos are the two cases known to us, but it

---

[1] It is commonly argued that the towns which are guaranteed by the terms of the Peace of Nicias the privilege of paying ὁ ἐπ' Ἀριστείδου φόρος (Argilus, Stagirus, Acanthus, Stolus, Olynthus, and Spartolus) must have been members of the Confederacy in 477 B.C. The inference is fallacious. Common sense suggests that, so long as the probity of Aristides was available, it would be employed for the assessment of new accessions to the League; but apart from common sense, this seems to be implied by the use of the plural in Aristotle, *Const. of Athens*, XXIII, 5, τοὺς φόρους οὗτος ἦν ὁ τάξας ταῖς πόλεσιν τοὺς πρώτους.

[2] Thucydides I, 96, ἦν δ' ὁ πρῶτος φόρος ταχθεὶς τετρακόσια τάλαντα καὶ ἑξήκοντα.

[3] Thucydides V, 18, 5, and below, p. 250.

is clear from the language of Thucydides that they were not the only states which were compelled to exchange service for tribute. It has been calculated from the evidence afforded by the quotalists (see above, p. 28) that the amount of tribute received by Athens between 450 B.C. and 436 B.C. never exceeded the sum of 460 talents, which is Thucydides' figure for the first assessment. The highest figure during these years is 455 talents, and the lowest 414[1]. It is generally agreed that 460 talents was the average amount of the assessment at this period, although for various reasons the amount actually received in any one year might fall below, and even considerably below, this sum. If, however, the total aimed at when the Confederacy had reached its greatest extent was no more than 460 talents, one of two conclusions must follow. Either the tribute must have been assessed on a much higher scale at the outset, when the members of the League were fewer in number, and when many of the larger states were exempt from assessment in virtue of supplying ships, or else the amount produced by the first assessment must have been little more than half the total given by Thucydides. If we take only four of the cities which in 477 B.C. either were not included in the League or were not liable to tribute, Aegina, Thasos, Byzantium, and Abdera, we shall find that between them they account for more than 90 talents in the later assessments, *i.e.* for a fifth of the total sum. The former of the two alternatives may be excluded, partly on the ground of the popularity of Aristides' assessment, partly because there is no trace of the Athenians ever having claimed credit for themselves for such a reduction in the scale of assessment, and partly because the clause in the Peace of Nicias renders it certain that the assessment of Aristides was regarded as a *minimum* rate of payment[2]. It follows, therefore, that we cannot escape from the other alternative. The tribute when first assessed by Aristides cannot have amounted to anything like so large a sum as 460 talents. It looks as if Thucydides had assumed that the total which Athens sought to secure after the transference of the treasury from Delos to Athens was also

---

[1] See Pedroli, *I tributi degli alleati d'Atene*, whose figures are here accepted for these years.

[2] For a close parallel to the provision in the Peace of Nicias compare the terms of the agreement concluded between Agesilaus and Tithraustes in 395 B.C., in which it is covenanted that the Greek cities in Asia Minor are to enjoy autonomy on condition of paying to the Persian King the ancient tribute (τὸν ἀρχαῖον δασμὸν), *i.e.* the assessment of Artaphrenes, cf. Herodotus VI, 42.

the total aimed at by Aristides. If this is so, it is probable that a similar instance of his confusing the conditions of the later period of the League with those of the earlier may be found in the same chapter (1, 96). It is there stated that the office of Hellenotamiae was then (*i.e.* at the time of the formation of the League) first instituted at Athens. The quota-lists, however, are arranged in a consecutive series[1], in relation to a certain magistracy or board (ἀρχή), and the series starts with the year 454 B.C., which can only be the date of the institution of the board. The mention of a particular Hellenotamias in the heading of certain of these inscriptions suggests that the office in question was that of the Hellenotamiae. If this inference is correct, it is clear that the office of Hellenotamiae as an *Athenian* magistracy must have been instituted at the time of the removal of the treasury to Athens in 454 B.C.; from which it follows that the Hellenotamiae of the earlier period must have been Delian and not Athenian magistrates, or else that the office was not constituted until the removal of the treasury to Athens.

III. THE RISE OF CIMON

It is not too much to claim that the Confederacy of Delos was the spiritual child of Themistocles. He was not, indeed, permitted either to have any share in its organization or to lead its fleets to victory, but it was his policy and his achievements that alone rendered possible the formation of the Confederacy and the supremacy of Athens. It was he who had created the new Athenian navy, and it was his strategy which had won the battle of Salamis. It was he, too, who was responsible for the new naval base at the Piraeus without which her maritime hegemony could not have been maintained. As far back as his archonship in 493 B.C. he had planned, and begun to construct, the new harbour which was to take the place of the open roadstead of Phalerum, which had hitherto sufficed for the needs of the Athenian fleet (vol. IV, p. 170). How much was effected, or how much of what was effected was destroyed by the Persians, we do not know. As soon, however, as the walls of Athens had been rebuilt, he set about the completion of his plan for the Piraeus. The site selected included the whole peninsula of Munychia with its three harbours; the large inner harbour known by the name of Cantharus and the two small outer harbours of Zea and Munychia. The whole of this peninsula was surrounded with a wall, which kept close to the shore and was continued along the north side of the harbour of

---

[1] *E.g. ἐπὶ τῆς τρίτης καὶ δεκάτης ἀρχῆς, I.G.*[2] 1, 203.

Cantharus as far as the promontory of Eetionea. The entrances to all three harbours were protected by fortified moles. The walls were no less than 60 stadia, or 7 miles, in circuit, and the space enclosed was almost equal in extent to the enlarged Athens. While, however, the walls of Athens had been hastily built, those of the Piraeus were a model both of design and construction. Although the walls proved amply sufficient for defence, they were carried up to only half the height that Themistocles had contemplated. It is probable that they were from fourteen to fifteen feet thick, and instead of the core being composed of rubble, according to the usual Greek practice, the whole breadth of the wall was formed of large stones, hewn square, and clamped on the outer face with iron and lead. Thus there were now two fortified cities four or five miles apart, each of which might be isolated from the other in case of invasion. So long as Athens retained her command of the sea, she could freely import her supplies of food into the Piraeus; but so long as an invading army could invest the city and cut it off from its port, there was the risk of Athens being reduced by blockade, even though it could not be taken by assault. This was the fatal flaw in the strategical position of Athens, a flaw which could only be remedied by building walls to connect the city with the Piraeus (see p. 80 and map 4 below).

It seems certain that Themistocles was never again elected General after the year of Salamis, but the story of the rebuilding of the walls, as well as the completion of his plans for the Piraeus, proved that he still exercised great influence over the policy of Athens. How long this influence lasted, and how and why it was forfeited, is obscure. He was chosen to supply a tragic chorus for his tribe in the archonship of Adeimantus (477–6 B.C.), but we have no conclusive evidence either of his presence or of his activities at Athens after this date. The ancient writers have nothing better to offer by way of explanation for his fall from popular favour than an empty phrase[1]. The decline of his influence is at least in part accounted for by the fact that he was a *novus homo*. His rapid advance to power in the interval between the two Persian Invasions had been facilitated by the rivalry of the two great clans of Philaidae and Alcmaeonidae, which culminated in the prosecution of Miltiades. The success of the *novus homo* taught the old families a lesson. If they were to retain their ascendancy, and if the democratic movement was to be checked, the Clans must present an unbroken front. In the marriage of

---

[1] Plutarch, *Cimon*, 5, ὁ δῆμος μεστὸς ὢν τοῦ Θεμιστοκλέους ('The people having had their fill of Themistocles').

Cimon with Isodice, the granddaughter of Megacles, we have an outward and visible sign of the reconciliation of the two great houses. By the marriage of his sister Elpinice with Callias, the head of the great family of Ceryces and the richest man at Athens, Cimon still further strengthened his connections. At the time of the formation of the Confederacy of Delos, Aristides was in command of the Athenian fleet, and Cimon merely a subordinate; but by the year 476 B.C. Cimon had become commander-in-chief of the Athenian forces, a position which he appears to have held without a break down to his return from Ithome in 462 B.C. (p. 71). It was the solid support of the aristocratic interest that procured for Cimon the supreme command, but it was his skill in the art of war, and the popularity accruing to him from his victories, that account for his long tenure of office. The opportunity was given him, and he knew how to make full use of it.

We owe it to Plutarch, whose *Life of Cimon* is one of the most valuable in the series of his biographies of Greek worthies, not only that we know something of his outward appearance—tall, with a great mass of thick curly hair—, but that we are in a position to appreciate the character of one who is admittedly the most prominent figure in one of the greatest periods of Athenian history, and to do justice to the greatness of the services that he rendered both to Athens and to Greece. It is seldom that we find in Plutarch a consistent picture of the subject of a biography, but what he has to tell us of Cimon is more than usually self-contradictory. In one passage[1] he quotes Stesimbrotus of Thasos, a younger contemporary of Cimon's, to the effect that the latter had never been taught music or any other of the usual accomplishments; Plutarch even goes so far as to assert that, in his earlier life, he not only was reputed to be drunken and dissolute, but was even compared by the popular voice to a grandfather who was nicknamed κοάλεμος, or booby. That a great commander should be loose in his morals, or too fond of the bottle, or even uneducated, is not incredible. Parallels from other periods of history suggest themselves. What is incredible is that the policy of the most intelligent of peoples should have been directed during one of the most eventful of its epochs by one who was illiterate in any sense of the term.

Fortunately, there is evidence of a very different tenor to be found in Plutarch's *Life*. He speaks of him as not inferior to Themistocles in sagacity, and he alleges that Aristides gave him his support because he had early perceived his good natural parts.

[1] Plutarch, *Cimon*, 4.

What is decisive is an anecdote which rests upon the authority of the poet Ion, who was himself present at the scene[1]. The whole point of the story of the supper party at the house of Laomedon is the contrast between Cimon, who could both play and sing, and Themistocles, who lacked these accomplishments. The appeal to the Assembly, in the course of the great Messenian debate, not to suffer Greece to go lame or Athens to pull without its yoke-fellow[2] (one of the few genuine specimens of the oratory of this period which have come down to us)[3] proves that, like many another soldier, he could speak with the eloquence of the heart. Cimon's mother was the daughter of a Thracian prince named Olorus; nor was he the only famous Athenian at this period who had Thracian blood in his veins, the historian Thucydides being also connected with the family of Olorus. A typical Athenian he was not; as Stesimbrotus puts it, his soul was rather of the Peloponnesian type. What contemporaries were conscious of was the contrast between him and his rival Pericles; a contrast in its way as complete as that between Gladstone and Disraeli. It was a contrast, however, not only of character and views, but between two different types of culture. Cimon had been trained in music and gymnastic as those terms were understood in the epoch before the Persian Wars. His education was that of an Athenian country gentleman of the sixth century B.C.; an education in accomplishments. He had been taught to ride, to sing, and to play the harp. It may be presumed that he was not ignorant of the poets. Of the New Learning, of the culture which had come into fashion since the days of Salamis and Plataea, the culture of which Pericles was the fine flower—of all this he had no tincture. In his public speaking he was a stranger to the conscious art of his great rival, and he would have been as little fitted to discuss the theory of music with Damonides, as to discuss the cause of an eclipse with Anaxagoras. It was left to a later generation, with its love of antithesis, to exaggerate this contrast between the two statesmen until it presents us with the Booby Cimon. Whatever verdict may be passed upon his statesmanship, there is hardly room for doubt as to his military genius. If he is to be judged either by his unbroken career of success, or by the magnitude of the results achieved, he must be ranked as one of the greatest, if not actually the greatest, of Athenian commanders.

[1] Plutarch, *Cimon*, 9.
[2] *Ibid.* 16, *ad fin.* μήτε τὴν Ἑλλάδα χωλὴν μήτε τὴν πόλιν ἑτερόζυγα περιϊδεῖν γεγενημένην. See below, p. 70.
[3] It rests on the authority of Ion.

IV. THE ACHIEVEMENTS OF THE CONFEDERACY OF DELOS

By the end of 477 B.C. the Confederacy had been organized, the tribute assessed, and the Bosporus secured by the expulsion of Pausanias from Byzantium (see note I B, p. 466 *sq.*). Thus two results had been achieved; the communications between Greece and the Pontus had been restored, and those between Persia and Europe had been cut. It must have been clear to all that the next task that awaited Athens and her allies was the expulsion of the remaining Persian garrisons from the Thracian seaboard. In the spring of 476 B.C.[1] Cimon set sail for the Strymon. We learn from Herodotus, who is our chief authority for this campaign, that little difficulty was experienced in the reduction of the Persian fortresses in this region. Only two of their commandants, he tells us, offered more than a feeble resistance. By this time the garrisons must have been thinned by desertion, and now that the communications were cut it was impossible for Persia to throw in fresh supplies either of troops or stores. The two commandants excepted by Herodotus from his general condemnation were Boges of Eïon and Mascames of Doriscus. The latter succeeded in foiling all the efforts of the Athenians to capture the town, and Doriscus never formed part of their Empire. Eïon was taken, but the resistance offered by Boges exhibits Persian courage at its highest. After Cimon had succeeded in isolating the fortress from the native tribes in the interior of the country from whom it obtained its corn, its surrender was merely a question of time. The garrison was reduced to the most desperate straits, but Boges held out till the spring, and the besiegers had to face all the terrors of a Thracian winter. At last, when endurance could go no farther, he slew his harem, his children, and slaves; threw into the river all the gold and silver in his possession; and then, having set fire to a lofty funeral pyre, himself leaped into the flames. It may be inferred from Thucydides (I, 98 *ad init.*) that the capture of Eïon was the first achievement of the allied forces in this campaign. They must, therefore, have concentrated their efforts on it, and delayed their operations against the other strongholds until the summer of 475 B.C. The strategical importance of the Strymon valley affords a sufficient explanation of their policy.

---

[1] The date of the capture of Eïon is given by the Scholiast on Aeschines, *De fals. leg.* 34, as the archonship of Phaedo (476–5 B.C.). That the siege lasted through the winter is implied in the first of the inscriptions quoted in Plutarch, *Cimon*, 7.

For the events of the next ten years no exact chronology can be attempted. The relative order of these events is not in dispute; the conquest of Scyros, the reduction of Carystus, the revolt of Naxos, and finally the battle of the Eurymedon. We have been able so far to reckon forward from Plataea and Mycale to the capture of Eïon, and the data supplied by Thucydides, supplemented here and there by the evidence of Diodorus' chronological source and of the Scholiasts, will enable us to reckon backwards from the outbreak of the Peloponnesian War to the revolt of Thasos in 465 B.C. No sufficient data, however, are available for filling in the dates between the capture of Eïon and the revolt of Thasos. It may be regarded as fairly certain that the conquest of Scyros and Carystus fall before 470 B.C., and the revolt of Naxos and the battle of the Eurymedon after that date. It is significant of the imperfect character of our knowledge of this period of Greek history that the name of Cimon is connected by no ancient writer, either with the war with Carystus, or with the siege of Naxos. It is conceivable that the conduct of the war with Carystus should have been committed to a subordinate, but it is in the highest degree improbable that the command against Naxos should have been entrusted to any lesser man than Cimon. It may be conjectured that the reason why his name is not connected with either Scyros or Naxos is to be found in the silence of Thucydides. The only events with which the historian connects the name of Cimon are the capture of Eïon, the victory of the Eurymedon, the siege of Ithome, and the last expedition to Cyprus. There were special reasons why his connection with some other events could not be forgotten. His prosecution on his return from the reduction of Thasos was sufficient proof of his command against that island; in the same way, the popularity that he acquired by bringing back the bones of Theseus established the fact that it was he that reduced Scyros. It looks as if no similar evidence in regard to Carystus and Naxos was at the disposal of later writers.

Although Scyros is a barren and rocky island, its conquest was of importance to Athens for two reasons. In the first place, its inhabitants, who were Dolopians by race, were notorious for piracy, and so long as they retained their independence there could be no effective policing of the seas. In the second place, it was a position of considerable strategical importance, lying as it did on the route to Thrace and the Hellespont. Pretexts for an attack on the island were readily found. A Delphic oracle which had been given to the Athenians in the archonship of

Phaedo (476–5 B.C.) commanded the Athenians to bring back the bones of Theseus from the island, and it was easy to allege that the Dolopians refused proper facilities for the search for his tomb. It would also appear that the islanders had been imprudent enough to refuse compliance with a sentence of the Amphictyonic Council which had condemned them to make reparation for an act of piracy against some Thessalian traders. The reduction of the island was doubtless no difficult task. The inhabitants were expelled, and Scyros re-peopled with Athenian colonists. It became a colony of the type peculiar to Athens, the cleruchy, and along with the cleruchies in Lemnos and Imbros it came to be regarded as a sort of *annexe* of Attica. It was, of course, indispensable that the tomb of Theseus should be found. It was not long before the Athenians lighted upon a grave of the Bronze Age, in which the bones of a warrior of imposing stature were discovered with his weapons by his side. The excavator is not always so fortunate. These relics were brought back to Athens by Cimon, and were solemnly interred in the city. An even greater popularity seems to have accrued to Cimon from the recovery of the bones of Theseus than from the conquest of Scyros.

The next event recorded in the annals of the League is the coercion of Carystus. The territory of this state formed the southern portion of the island of Euboea, and its inhabitants were Dryopians, and consequently of a different race from those of the rest of the island with the exception of Styra. This difference of race may account for the different policy which it pursued, and it would explain why it could not count on support from the other Euboean cities, such as Chalcis or Eretria. It was one of the states which had suffered at the hands of Themistocles after the battle of Salamis (vol. IV, p. 315), and it had refused to join the Confederacy of Delos. The motive for employing the resources of the League against a state so insignificant must have been the desire to round off the territories of the League in this part of the Aegean. Its proximity to Attica must have rendered its annexation all the more welcome in Athenian eyes. The attack on Carystus was delivered a year or two after the conquest of Scyros. There could be but one end to the conflict between sides so unequally matched. Carystus was forced to capitulate, but it received comparatively lenient treatment. Its inhabitants were neither expelled nor enslaved. The Athenians were content that the city should join the League. However unimportant the conquest may have been in its military aspect, the coercion of Carystus from another point of view is the reverse of unimportant. A free and sovereign community had been constrained to enter into the Confederacy against its will. The first step had been taken on the broad and easy way that was to lead from the voluntary union of independent allies to an autocracy exercised over reluctant subjects.

A year or two later, the second step was taken. Thirty years earlier, Naxos had been reputed the most opulent and powerful of the Cyclades, although Herodotus' statement that it could put into the field a force of 8000 hoplites may be suspected of exaggeration. The prosperity of the island must have been affected by the destruction of the town by the Persians on their way to Marathon; it is, however, surprising to find that the contingent which they supplied to the navy of Xerxes numbered only four triremes. If this was a fair measure of its maritime strength when it joined the Confederacy of Delos, it is difficult to understand how it should have ventured on secession. The mere fact of its secession suggests that discontent at the burdens imposed upon the Allies was already rife in the League, and that alarm had begun to be felt at the menacing position of Athens. Thucydides gives us no information as to the motives of Naxos, or as to the length of the siege. He does not even tell us what were the terms of capitulation. It may be taken for granted that Naxos had to surrender its fleet as well as its autonomy, and that it had to covenant to pay tribute for the future. A precedent had now been established, and the meaning of the original terms of alliance had been determined, once and for all, by the arbitrament of force. The Allies had not the right to secede.

The time had now come for Athens to complete the task which, in effect, had been imposed upon her when she accepted the headship of the Confederacy. There was one region still left in which little progress had been made in the liberation of the Greek fringe. The whole coastline of south-western Asia Minor, from a point just south of Miletus to Phaselis in Lycia, was still in Persian hands. It was probably either in 467 or in 466 B.C. that it was decided to deal the final blow to the authority of the Great King on the shores of the Aegean. At the opening of the season of navigation, Cimon collected a fleet of 200 triremes at Cnidus[1]. In the course of a few months he reduced the fortresses which were defended by Persian garrisons; the unfortified towns appear to have entered the League without compulsion. The territory

---

[1] This is the figure given by Plutarch, *Cimon*, 12. Diodorus XI, 60 gives the numbers as 200 Athenian triremes and 100 furnished by the Ionians and other Allies.

thus acquired included not only the purely Greek cities on the coast, but many, both on the coast and in the interior of the country, which were either purely Carian, or only semi-Hellenic, as well as those which were members of the Lycian League. The Dorian colony of Phaselis on the coast of Lycia, which was one of the most important centres of trade on the south coast of Asia Minor, at first held out. Terms, however, were arranged through the agency of the Chians, and it capitulated on condition of paying an indemnity of ten talents and supplying a contingent to the allied fleet. Meanwhile the Persian Court had been, at length, goaded into action. It seems to have made no effort since the battle of Mycale to check the progress of the Athenian cause, but the attack on Caria was a direct menace to their hold on the whole southern coast of Asia Minor. By the end of the summer a considerable force both on land and sea had been assembled in Pamphylia near the mouth of a small river, the Eurymedon by name. The fleet consisting of 200 vessels, mainly Phoenician, was stationed at its mouth, and the command of the whole force was given to a Persian of high rank, Ariomandes the son of Gobryas.

Of the battle of the Eurymedon we have two accounts, in addition to the brief notice in Thucydides. In the version of Ephorus[1], Cimon engaged the Persian fleet off the island of Cyprus, and defeated it with heavy loss, capturing no less than 100 vessels. On the very same day he set sail for Pamphylia, landed his troops at the mouth of the Eurymedon, and defeated the Persian army which was encamped on the banks of the river. Cimon's victory on land was achieved by means of a ruse by which the Persian commanders were misled. He picked out his best troops, dressed them up in Persian uniforms, and put them aboard the vessels which he had captured earlier in the day off Cyprus. The Persians, imagining the vessels to be a detachment from their own fleet, allowed the troops to enter their camp. In the confusion that followed, which was rendered all the greater by the approach of night, the annihilation of the Persian army was inevitable. The more this account is examined, the more incredible does it appear. A glance at the map will show that it was beyond the bounds of possibility for Cimon's fleet, after fighting and winning a naval engagement of the first order of magnitude off the coast of Cyprus, to reach the Eurymedon on

[1] Diodorus XI, 60–62. Diodorus' narrative is excerpted from that of Ephorus, some fragments of which have been discovered and edited by Grenfell and Hunt, *Oxyrhynchus Papyri*, vol. XIII, no. 1610.

the same day, in time for an army to be landed, and the Persian camp stormed, before nightfall. Difficulties almost as great are raised by the story of the ruse. The great victories of great generals are not gained by stratagems so fatuous. There can hardly be a doubt that Ephorus was led to this amazing theory of the battle by the epigram which forms the peroration, as it were, of his narrative. The epigram really related to the defeat of the Persian fleet off Cyprus in 450 B.C., but Ephorus connected it with the Eurymedon, and thus was led to make the coast of Cyprus the scene of the naval victory[1].

Very different in quality is the story of the battle which is to be found in Plutarch (*Cimon*, 12–13). His account is probable in itself, and his statements accord both with the topographical conditions and with strategical considerations. Meyer may or may not be right in his conjecture that Callisthenes is the historian whom Plutarch follows in these chapters; what is certain is that the account is ultimately derived from contemporary sources[2].

By Plutarch's aid it is not difficult to reconstruct the history of the campaign. The choice of Pamphylia by the Persians is proof that their strategy was defensive, not offensive. Had an offensive movement against Ionia been contemplated, Pamphylia would hardly have been chosen as the headquarters of the army. Both fleet and army were designed for the protection of Lycia and Pamphylia. The Persian plans were upset by the rapidity of Cimon's movements. His attack was launched while his opponents were still waiting for a reinforcement of eighty vessels from Cyprus. The Persian fleet was, therefore, unwilling to give battle, and in the confined space of the embouchure of the river there was no opportunity for manœuvring. The commanders had no alternative but to run their ships aground under cover of the force drawn up on the shore. Cimon followed up his success at sea by landing his troops and engaging the Persian army, which was completely routed. The victory was rendered even more decisive by Cimon's success in capturing the reinforcement of 80 vessels for which the Persian commanders had been looking. The victory of the Eurymedon must rank as one of the most glorious in the annals of Athens, or of Greece. To have defeated so large a Persian force both on land and on sea on the same day, and to

---

[1] This was first pointed out by E. Meyer, *Forschungen* II, pp. 7 *sqq.*

[2] There are, however, some serious objections to Meyer's hypothesis. He had been anticipated by Grote in the suggestion of Callisthenes, as in some other points connected with the Eurymedon.

have followed this up by cutting off the reinforcements, was a feat which left a profound impression on the mind of the ancients. It is a conclusive proof of the military genius of Cimon. More than that, it is the victory of which Athens had most reason to be proud after those of Marathon and Salamis. The Eurymedon was won over a foreign enemy; it is a moment in the eternal conflict of East and West. Cimon's is not the last great name on the roll of Athenian commanders, nor is the Eurymedon the last great victory that stands to the credit of Athens. But these other commanders were to win their victories over the forces of other Greek states, and the victories which they won served to exhibit the disunion of the Greek nation, if not to sap its powers of resistance. The glory of the Eurymedon is one; the glory of Oenophyta or Cyzicus is another[1].

The Eurymedon marks the climax of Cimon's career. It may be that he intended to follow up a success so decisive by a fresh expedition to Cyprus. For the moment, however, he was content that Phaselis should be the outpost of the Confederacy on the east. Little, indeed, would have been gained by the reduction of Pamphylia or Cilicia; countries which might have been conquered but could hardly have been held. The immediate task for Athens was felt to be the consolidation of the territory under its control, rather than the further extension of the League. It was to the north, rather than to the south, that the next efforts of Athens were directed. Although Sestos, and probably some other positions on the coast, had been securely held since the year after Mycale, the Athenians had been unable to dislodge the Persians from the interior of the Thracian Chersonese, just as they had failed to capture the fort of Doriscus at the mouth of the Hebrus. That the Persian troops should have had the support of the Thracian tribes of the Hinterland is only what we should have expected; that they should have been able to maintain a fleet in these waters is more difficult to explain[2]. It was probably in the spring of 465 B.C. that Cimon with only four triremes under his command attacked the enemy's squadron, and took thirteen of their vessels. He then defeated the Persian troops and their Thracian allies, and gained possession of the whole peninsula.

At this point we pass from a chronology which is approximate and conjectural to one which is, for the most part, precise and certain. A passage in the fourth book of Thucydides, supplemented by the data afforded by Diodorus' chronological source and the

---

[1] See below, pp. 82, 343.   [2] Plutarch, *Cimon*, 14.

Scholiast on Aeschines[1], enables us to date the attempted colonization of Amphipolis, and consequently the revolt of Thasos,
to the year 465 B.C.; and from this point to the conclusion of the
Thirty Years Peace the dates of all the principal events can be
ascertained, either exactly, or within a margin of a couple of
years.

In the region known as 'the Thrace-ward region' the key
position was the site on which the Athenian colony of
Amphipolis was ultimately established (see p. 172). The position
is one of great natural strength, and of great strategical importance. Its strength was due to the fact that it was almost encircled
by a horse-shoe bend of the river Strymon. It was a natural
fortress which may be compared to sites such as Shrewsbury or
Durham in our own country. Its strategical importance is illustrated both by the fact that the bridging of the river at this point
was one of the three great works preparatory to the expedition
of Xerxes that were undertaken by the Persian engineers, and by
its earlier name 'The Nine Ways.' It was here, and here only,
that the Strymon could be bridged. Below Amphipolis the river
was too wide for a bridge to be thrown across it, while above the
city the river expanded into Lake Cercinitis, the shores of which
were marshy and trackless. Hence the site commanded not only
the sole line of communication between Chalcidice and the
Thracian coast east of the Strymon, but also the only route
practicable by land between the Hellespont and Greece. From
this point, too, there radiated the roads round the rich mining
district of Mt Pangaeus. The connection of Athens with this
district can be traced back to Peisistratus (vol. IV, p. 64), and the
establishment of a cleruchy at Eïon in 475 B.C. had given Athens
control of the approach to the valley of the Strymon. If the Scholiast on Aeschines is to be believed, the Athenians followed up
the capture of Eïon by an attempt to plant a colony at 'The Nine
Ways,' although the attempt proved unsuccessful, the colonists
being massacred by the neighbouring Thracian tribes. If the
statement is correct, it is strange that this attempted colonization
should find no mention in the passage in Thucydides. It is, however, dangerous to argue from the silence of an ancient historian,
and it may be that the Scholiast is right[2]. In the summer of

---

[1] Thucydides IV, 102. Diodorus XII, 32 *ad fin.* Scholiast on Aeschines,
De fals. leg. 34.

[2] Scholiast on Aeschines, *De fals. leg.* 34. His statement seems to be
corroborated by Pausanias I, 29, 4. Cf. E. Meyer, *Gesch. d. Alt.* III, § 276
note.

465 B.C. an attempt was made to occupy the place with a body of colonists sufficiently numerous to overawe the native tribes. The settlers, only a part of whom were Athenians, were ten thousand in number; it was, in fact, to be a colony on the largest scale known to the practice of the Greeks.

Little difficulty was encountered in expelling the Edonians, a Thracian tribe who inhabited this district, and in taking possession of 'The Nine Ways.' In order to secure the plain that lay to the north of the new colony, and to obtain access to the mining region to the east of it, the whole body of settlers advanced into the interior of the country, and found themselves compelled to give battle to a strong force of confederate Thracian tribes, at a place called Drabescus[1]. The Athenian force was annihilated, and in consequence of this defeat the colony had to be abandoned. Can it be that Alexander, the king of Macedonia, had a hand in bringing about this disastrous defeat of the Athenians? When Cimon was brought to trial after the reduction of Thasos, the charge brought against him was that he had been bribed by Alexander to desist from the invasion of his country[2]. This invasion can only have been punitive in character, and, as Alexander had been hitherto in alliance with Athens, one is tempted to connect it with the disaster at Drabescus. Since the defeat of Xerxes, Alexander had succeeded in advancing his frontiers from the Axius to the Strymon, and in annexing the whole Hinterland of Chalcidice[3]. The next object of his ambition must have been the bridge-head across the Strymon. To Macedonia, therefore, the design of the Athenian colony conveyed in the plainest terms the intimation 'Thus far and no farther.' It was not the last time that Macedonian and Athenian interests were to cross at this point.

Macedonia and Thrace were not the only states that saw their interests threatened by the foundation of Amphipolis. The important island of Thasos, which was separated only by a narrow channel from the coast of Thrace, had hitherto derived a large revenue from the exploitation of the mines of Mt Pangaeus[4]. It was inevitable that the Thasians should take alarm at the revival of the Athenian designs on this region. Thucydides assigns as the pretext of their revolt a dispute which had arisen between them and the Athenians about their rights over some dependent

---

[1] Thucydides I, 100. Herodotus IX, 75. The two accounts differ in some important points. Thucydides is perhaps correcting Herodotus.

[2] Plutarch, *Cimon*, 14.

[3] Herodotus V, 17. Thucydides II, 99.　　　　[4] Herodotus VI, 46.

towns on the opposite coast and about the working of the mines of Mt Pangaeus. Here, as is so often the case, the cause was not identical with the pretext. The language of Thucydides appears to indicate that the revolt of Thasos preceded the dispatch of the colonists to Amphipolis, but the Athenian designs must have been known to the Thasians long before the ten thousand settlers landed at the mouth of the Strymon. The revolt of Thasos was far more formidable than that of Naxos. Their navy at the outbreak of the revolt must have numbered considerably more vessels than the thirty-three which had to be surrendered at the end of the siege, and its position, so near to the coast of Thrace, must have rendered an effective blockade in the winter months almost impracticable. That the siege should have lasted more than two years is sufficient evidence of the difficulty of the Athenian task. The Thasians may have hoped that their example would be followed by other members of the League, but there is no reason to suppose that it was the prospect of assistance from Sparta that emboldened them to defy Athens. It is clear from Thucydides that an appeal to Sparta was not made until some time after the outbreak of the revolt. On hearing the news of the revolt the Athenians dispatched a fleet under the command of Cimon. An engagement was fought in which the Thasians were defeated, and this success enabled the Athenians to blockade the town of Thasos both by land and sea. It was then that the Thasians made their appeal to Sparta and received an assurance from the ephors that Attica should be invaded by a Peloponnesian army. The promise could not be fulfilled owing to the earthquake at Sparta and the revolt of the Helots. In the autumn of 463 B.C., after a siege of upwards of two years, the island was forced to surrender. The terms of capitulation were terribly severe; the razing of the fortifications of the city, the loss of their fleet, an immediate indemnity, and the payment of tribute, as well as the surrender of their dependent towns and of their rights in the mining district. In future even the most powerful of the Allies would hesitate before it ventured to revolt.

V. CHANGES IN THE CHARACTER OF THE CONFEDERACY OF DELOS

Less than fifteen years had now elapsed since the formation of the Confederacy of Delos. In this comparatively short space of time the Persians had been driven out of their last strongholds in Europe, and they had lost almost the whole coastline of Asia Minor from the Bosporus to Lycia. The Aegean had become a *mare clausum.* Such is the sum of Cimon's achievements. But it was not only through the mere extension of the territories of the League that the power of Athens had grown. Her position was now, even more than before, that of the 'predominant partner.' The Confederacy of Delos had not yet become the Empire of Athens, but it was a Confederacy which was more than half way on the road to empire. It was still a Confederacy, because the Synod still met at Delos, and because the great mass of the Allies were probably still in name autonomous; but all but a few had commuted service for tribute, and some at least were no longer autonomous in name. The change from service to tribute was almost inevitable. From the point of view of the Allies, the payment of tribute was less inconvenient than the supply of ships; from the point of view of the Athenians, the more homogeneous the fleet became the greater its efficiency. The result, however, of the substitution of payment for service was not less inevitable than the change itself. At a later period, when the Confederacy had been converted into the Empire, the payment of tribute was synonymous with the loss of autonomy; those who are φόρου ὑποτελεῖς are thereby ὑπήκοοι. In the early days of the League, there was no distinction between those who were subject and those who were autonomous, and no difference between the status of those who supplied ships and of those who paid tribute. The class of subject-allies (ὑπήκοοι) must have come into existence quite gradually. The loss of autonomy must invariably have formed part of the penalty of unsuccessful revolt, and the status may have been introduced, even before the first revolt, to meet the case of Carystus. It may be inferred from Thucydides[1] that failure to supply ships, and remissness in the payment of tribute, may also have been punished by the reduction of an Ally from the more to the less privileged class. How far this change of status had gone; in other words, how many of the Allies had become subject by the end of 463 B.C., it is impossible to say. Nor does the evidence at our command enable us to answer two other questions. By the era of the Peloponnesian War, the whole body of the Allies, with the exception of Chios and Lesbos, had been brought under the jurisdiction of the Athenian law-courts. By what means was this effected, and when did the process begin? Again, at the same era, no other form of constitution than the democratic was tolerated by Athens in her Empire[2]. When did

---

[1] I, 99.

[2] With the exception, of course, of Chios and Lesbos. For Athenian influence in the constitutions of Erythrae and Colophon see *I.G.*[2] I, 10, 14–15.

Athens first adopt this policy of interference? Whatever may have been the change in the relative position of Athens and her allies in the course of the first fifteen years of the League's history, there is no reason to suppose that it was due to the policy of Cimon. He must have encouraged the substitution of tribute for ships as tending to the greater efficiency of the fleet, and the change was no doubt welcome to many at Athens for other than military reasons; but that Cimon himself deliberately aimed at the degradation of the Allies to the position of subjects is certainly not borne out by our evidence. The passage in Plutarch in which the moderation of Cimon is contrasted with the harsher methods of the other Athenian generals (*Cimon*, 11) is rhetorical, and appears to be derived from a late and untrustworthy source; it correctly represents, however, his attitude towards the Allies. The party conflict between Thucydides, son of Melesias, who succeeded him in the leadership of the Conservative Party, and Pericles turned mainly on the issue of justice to the subject-allies (p. 166).

VI. THE POSITION IN THE PELOPONNESE.
PAUSANIAS AND THEMISTOCLES

While the reputation of Athens was rising so rapidly, that of Sparta was not less steadily declining. On his expulsion from Byzantium by the Athenians in 477 B.C., Pausanias had established himself at Colonae in the Troad, a position admirably adapted for the further prosecution of his intrigues with Artabazus, the satrap at Dascylium, a town on the Propontis. How long these negotiations had been going on is uncertain, but they must have extended over a period of some years at least. The scandal became so notorious that the ephors were constrained to recall him to Sparta a second time. He hesitated to disobey the summons, which was peremptory in tone, and he was confident that, if he were brought to trial, he could procure his acquittal by a judicious use of bribery. On his return he was lodged in prison, but was soon released on the ground that the evidence against him was not conclusive. It was not long before information reached the ephors of a conspiracy more dangerous to Spartan interests than the alleged intrigue with the Persian Court. Pausanias had conceived a fresh design; that of subverting the Spartan constitution by the aid of the Helots and substituting the authority of the kings for that of the ephors. He had already approached several of the Helots with promises of freedom and the rights of citizenship. Yet the ephors still delayed to take action against him, until one of the messengers whom he had employed for the

purposes of his correspondence with Artabazus, a slave from
Argilus in the Thrace-ward region, betrayed him. Even then
they refused to act until by an ingenious stratagem they had
heard from Pausanias' own lips the confession of his guilt. As
they were on their way to arrest him, he fled for sanctuary to a
building attached to the Temple of Athena of the Brazen House
at Sparta. The ephors had the doors of the building walled up
in order to starve him to death. Just before he expired, he was
brought out still breathing, and died outside the sacred precinct.
The only explanation that Thucydides assigns for the hesitation
of the ephors, which is so remarkable a feature in the story, is
that their reluctance to act was in accordance with an invariable
principle of their government. They were always slow, he asserts,
to take irrevocable action without incontestable proof, even
against a private citizen. In view of the facts admitted in his
narrative, this is an explanation which it is difficult to accept.
He himself admits that when Pausanias was on the point of being
arrested he was warned by one of the ephors. It is fairly evident
that there were many at Sparta who could not forget the services
which he had rendered to the national cause, and who were
unwilling to believe that he was either a traitor to Greece or a
conspirator against their own state. And there must have been
still more who at the time of his deposition from the command
of the fleet were indignant that the victor of Plataea should be
sacrificed in the interests of an *entente* with Athens.

The fate of Pausanias involved that of Themistocles. It was
alleged by the Spartan government that conclusive proof of the
complicity of Themistocles had been found among the papers
of Pausanias. The growing unpopularity of Themistocles had
culminated in his ostracism. As to its date, opinions are divided.
There are some grounds for connecting the year 471 B.C. either
with it, or with his flight from Argos; but the evidence is not
conclusive[1], and the date may be connected equally well with
either event[2]. It was certainly not later than the spring of 470 B.C.,
and it may well have been a year or two earlier, that he left Athens
and took up his residence at Argos. The choice of Argos was
dictated by its position on the flank of the Peloponnesian Con-

---

[1] Cicero, *De Amicit.* XII, 42, *Themistocles fecit idem quod viginti annis
ante apud nos fecerat Coriolanus.* (The date for Coriolanus is 491 B.C.)
That Diodorus (XI, 54–8) should record under the archonship of Praxiergus
(471–70 B.C.) the whole career of Themistocles from his first trial to his death
affords no presumption whatever that this was the date of his ostracism.

[2] E. Meyer connects it with his ostracism; Wilamowitz with his flight.

federacy, as well as by its perennial hostility to Sparta. Making Argos his headquarters, he visited from thence a number of the other Peloponnesian states in order to carry on an anti-Laconian propaganda which was to bear fruit in the near future. It is evident that he responded to the advances of Pausanias, and that, whatever his motive may have been, he allowed himself to be deeply compromised. It is scarcely probable that he should have wished for the subjugation of Greece by Persia, or that he should have imagined that Pausanias was a fit instrument for carrying out any such design, although he may well have welcomed his conspiracy against the Spartan constitution as promising the overthrow of the Lacedaemonian hegemony. There must, however, have been *prima facie* evidence of his complicity in the schemes of Pausanias, not only so far as they were directed against the authority of the ephors, but also in their relation to Persia. Envoys were dispatched to Athens by the Spartan government to prefer the charge of medism, and to demand his punishment. The leaders of the Conservative Party, the influence of which was now predominant at Athens, welcomed this opportunity of getting rid, once and for all, of so dangerous an opponent. The coalition of the great houses was still intact, and it was an Alcmaeonid, Leobotes son of Alcmeon, who acted as prosecutor. The charge was one of high treason, and the proceedings were to be before the Assembly, probably in the form of an *Eisangelia*, or impeachment[1]. Themistocles did not venture to return and stand his trial. He fled from Argos, and disappeared from view. Rumour carried him to Syracuse, to the court of Hiero[2]. In reality he had sought an asylum in Corcyra, where he had some reason to anticipate protection. The Corcyraeans, being indisposed to incur the enmity of the two leading states in the Greek world, conveyed him to the coast of the mainland. Here, in order to escape from the emissaries of Sparta and Athens who had been sent to effect his arrest, he was driven to appeal to the magnanimity of Admetus, the king of the Molossians, to whom he had formerly done some disservice. By the aid of Admetus he succeeded in making his way over the mountains to the coast of

---

[1] Plutarch, *Themistocles*, 23. E. Meyer is certainly right in his view that the court which was to try the charge was the Assembly. Wilamowitz, *Aristoteles und Athen*, I, 140, maintains that it was the Areopagus.

[2] Stesimbrotus (*ap*. Plutarch, *Themistocles*, 24) is probably good evidence that the story of his visit to Hiero was current at the time of his flight. It certainly does not prove that Syracuse was the original objective of Themistocles, as E. Meyer contends.

Macedonia. He took ship at Pydna, and reached Ephesus, which was still in Persian hands, after narrowly escaping capture by the Athenian fleet which was blockading Naxos at the time. From Ephesus he wrote to Artaxerxes, who had just succeeded to the throne of Persia, offering his services to the King for a fresh invasion of Greece. At the end of a year he went up to Susa, where he acquired a greater influence than any Greek refugee at the Persian Court had ever exercised before. Honours and rewards were showered upon him. He even received a grant of three cities: Magnesia on the Meander, Myus near the mouth of this river, and Lampsacus on the Hellespont. We may form some idea of what this meant from the fact that the revenue of Magnesia alone amounted to fifty talents a year[1]. His promises, however, remained unfulfilled, as he died at Magnesia (probably about the year 450 B.C.) before any fresh invasion of Greece had been attempted. There were rival stories both as to the manner of his death and the place of his burial. It was a widespread belief at the time that he poisoned himself with bull's blood in order to escape the fulfilment of his promises[2], but Thucydides prefers the more prosaic version of a death from natural causes. His place of burial appears to have been Magnesia, but it was asserted by his family that his remains had been carried back to Athens at his own request, and secretly buried there.

In this account of the flight of Themistocles the narrative of Thucydides has been followed, but it differs in some important points from the statements of other ancient authorities. According to Ephorus and Aristotle[3], there had been a previous prosecution of Themistocles for medism at the instance of the Spartans, and an acquittal before his ostracism; and according to Aristotle this first trial was before Ephialtes' reform of the Areopagus in the year 462–1 B.C. According to Ephorus and a number of later writers it was not Artaxerxes, but Xerxes, to whom Themistocles addressed his letter, and according to the authorities followed by Plutarch (*Themistocles*, 26)[4] Cyme, not Ephesus, was the port at which he landed on the coast of Asia Minor. There can hardly be a doubt that on all these points the verdict must be in favour of Thucydides. On the all-important question of which king it was to whom Themistocles appealed, Xerxes or Artaxerxes,

---

[1] For coins of Themistocles issued in Magnesia see Volume of Plates ii, 2, *h*.
[2] Thucydides I, 138. Cf. Aristophanes, *Knights*, 83.
[3] Diodorus XI, 54. Aristotle, *Const. of Athens*, xxv.
[4] Wilamowitz's suggestion that some of Thucydides' information was derived from Lampsacus is attractive.

Thucydides is supported by Charon of Lampsacus, the earliest of our authorities[1]. The presence of Themistocles at Athens at the time of Ephialtes' reform is chronologically impossible. Thucydides' own version, however, is not altogether free from difficulty. The siege of Naxos cannot be put later than 467 B.C., and the previous year is not an unlikely date for it. Artaxerxes, however, did not come to the throne till the beginning of 464 B.C. There was, therefore, an interval of upwards of two years at least between Themistocles' arrival at Ephesus and his appeal to Artaxerxes. The interval may be filled up in various ways, but the important point is that Thucydides is unaware of its existence.

'Such was the end of Pausanias the Lacedaemonian, and Themistocles the Athenian, the two most famous Hellenes of their day[2].' The fate of Pausanias makes little appeal to the modern mind. He was a capable commander, and at a great crisis in the nation's history he had rendered it a great service, but his understanding of things did not extend beyond the art of war. Of statesmanship he was wholly destitute. The most that can be pleaded in his excuse is that his narrow Spartan training had unfitted him to deal with any but Spartans, or to play a part on the stage of international politics. With Themistocles it is different. It is to the modern mind, even more than to the ancient, that his career appeals as among the most tragic in Greek history. No man ever rendered his country, either in the narrow sense of Athens, or in the wider sense of Greece, a service more splendid; and yet he died an outlaw from Athens, and a pensioner of the Persian Court. Thucydides devotes a panegyric to his memory, and from the verdict of the historian there can be no appeal. It is a panegyric prompted by the calumnies that were current at the time; almost certainly it is a protest against Herodotus' caricature of the great statesman. But Thucydides in his appreciation of Themistocles is concerned solely with his intellectual qualities. Here more than anywhere else it is true that the standpoint of the historian is non-moral. A non-moral standpoint cannot reasonably be expected of contemporaries. Themistocles' ethics were neither better nor worse than those of many Athenian statesmen; but they were not better. He was unscrupulous in his choice of means, and his ends were not always disinterested. It is not surprising that he should have suffered by contrast, not only with the 'ostentatious probity' of Aristides, but even with the more commonplace qualities of Cimon.

About the time of the recall of Pausanias and the flight of

---

[1] Plutarch, *Themistocles*, 27.　　　　[2] Thucydides I, 138 *ad fin.*

Themistocles, Sparta found her headship of the Peloponnese seriously menaced, and she had to fight two battles, and to win two victories, before she could restore her authority. It is characteristic of the fragmentary nature of our knowledge of this period of Greek history that we should owe the little information that we have about this crisis to an incidental allusion in Herodotus (IX, 35). His interest in soothsayers, and in the oracles given from Delphi, leads him to mention two Spartan victories which he ranks with Plataea and Tanagra. The first of these was at Tegea in a battle against the Tegeates and Argives, and the second at Dipaea in Arcadia against all the Arcadians except the Mantineans. To Dipaea there is a reference in Isocrates (*Archidamus* 99),—it would be an enigma apart from the notice in Herodotus—and that is all but all. From Herodotus it may be inferred that the two battles come in between the Persian invasion and the third Messenian War; *i.e.* between 479 B.C. and 464 B.C. It may also be inferred that Sparta was confronted by an alliance between Argos and Tegea, and that the victory at Tegea was not sufficiently decisive to restore her authority; for it was not long before she had to deal with a more formidable movement, the revolt of all Arcadia with the exception of Mantinea. But we cannot infer from Herodotus either the precise dates of the two battles, or the reasons for the absence of the Argive army at Dipaea and for the part played by Mantinea. The battles are usually assigned to the years 473–1 B.C., but the arguments in favour of these dates are inconclusive. If the Archidamus to whom Polyaenus (I, 41, 1) makes reference is the king in the fifth century, and not his namesake in the fourth[1], it would follow that Dipaea, if not Tegea, must be put as late as 469 B.C.; and in that case it would be possible to find an explanation of the absence of the Argives from Dipaea in their desire to crush Mycenae while Sparta was unable to protect her ally[2]. From Thucydides it may further be inferred that Themistocles had a hand in bringing about the alliance of Argos with Tegea and, not improbably, with the other Arcadian towns.

Dipaea was a decisive victory won against great odds. It proved, once more, the immeasurable superiority of the Spartan hoplite. It

[1] Busolt and E. Meyer connect the incident in Polyaenus with the Archidamus of the fourth century and refer it to 369 B.C.

[2] Diodorus XI, 65. Diodorus assigns the war between Argos and Mycenae to the year 468–7 B.C., which is almost certainly the correct date. The reference to the earthquake and the Helot revolt is a touch added by Diodorus in characteristic fashion.

put an end to the anti-Laconian movement, and it enabled Sparta
to strengthen the bonds that held the Peloponnesian League
together[1]. The success of Sparta, however, was not entirely due
to the discipline and courage of her soldiers. Political causes
contributed to the failure of the movement. The democratic
revolution which had resulted in the foundation of the city of
Elis in the year 471–70 B.C. had failed to impair the ties that
bound the Eleans to Sparta. Both states had still a common
interest in the Messenian question, for it was as much in the
interests of Elis that Pisatis and Triphylia should find no support
in Messenia as it was in the interest of Sparta that the Messenians
should receive no aid from the subjects of Elis. It may be conjectured, too, that the revolution which seems to have taken place
at Mantinea after the battle of Plataea had put into power a party
friendly to Sparta[2], and that it was the influence of this party that
prevented the secession of their state. Of even more importance
to Sparta than her relations with Elis and Mantinea were the
policy of Argos and the attitude of Athens. Had Argos thrown
her whole weight into the anti-Laconian movement, the result
of Dipaea might have been different, and the defeat of the Spartans
in the field would have meant for Argos the annexation of Mycenae and Tiryns, and much more besides. As it was, she preferred the lesser but more immediate gain to the greater and more
remote. Fortunately, too, for Sparta, the foreign policy of Athens
was still directed by a statesman the steady aim of whose efforts
was the maintenance of the alliance between the two leading
states of Greece. Had the democratic party been in power at
Athens at the time, Dipaea might have proved an anticipation
of Leuctra.

[1] The institution of *Xenagoi* is usually attributed to this period. For the
Xenagoi, cf. Thucydides II, 75.
[2] Cf. Herodotus IX, 77. It was the prompt intervention of Mantinea
that saved Sparta at the time of the earthquake. Cf. Xenophon, *Hellenica*
V, 2, 3.

CHAPTER III

ATHENS AND THE GREEK POWERS
462–445 B.C.

I. END OF THE COALITION

IN the winter following the fall of Thasos (463 B.C.) Cimon
was brought to trial in connection with the audit of his official
accounts as general during the siege. He was charged, as has
been explained in the previous chapter, with having accepted a
bribe from Alexander of Macedon. Such charges of corruption
were part of the stock in trade of the Greek demagogues. They
serve to illustrate the low level of probity in the public life of the
ancient democracies, but they are not to be taken too seriously
in any particular case. In view of Cimon's wealth the charge
brought against him seems peculiarly improbable, and it can
hardly have been expected that the prosecution would succeed.
It was intended as a test of the relative strength of the Conservative Party and the Opposition, and herein lies the interest and
importance of the trial. So far as we know, it was the first occasion
on which the democratic party had ventured to try conclusions
with Cimon and his followers. It was also the first occasion on
which Pericles played a part in Athenian politics. His share in
the prosecution was inconsiderable, and the manner in which his
task was performed almost perfunctory. Yet the trial, though it
ended in Cimon's acquittal, was a turning-point in the history of
Athens at this epoch. The appearance of Pericles on the side of
the prosecution proclaimed to the whole world that the coalition
of the great aristocratic houses was at an end. Aristides was dead[1],
and his death must have been a serious blow to the party to which
he had lent the great authority of his name. Xanthippus, too, was
dead, and the leadership of his group of nobles had passed to his
son Pericles. That Pericles should have thrown in his lot with
the Opposition need not surprise us, for in so doing he was but
reverting to the policy of Cleisthenes, his mother's uncle. As yet,
however, he was merely the leader of the Alcmaeonid faction, not
the leader of the democratic party. To a later generation, indeed,

[1] His death was four years after either the ostracism or the outlawry of
Themistocles, *i.e.* not later than 464 B.C., and probably a few years earlier.
Cf. Nepos, *Aristides* 3, 3: *Decessit autem fere post annum quartum quam Themi-
stocles Athenis erat expulsus.*

it seemed a thing incredible that he could ever have been anything but the leader of the party to which he belonged. Theopompus goes so far as to claim for him forty years of political supremacy[1], but these flights of rhetoric must not mislead us. If anything is certain, it is that Ephialtes was the leader of the party down to his assassination, and that Pericles was his subordinate. It was Ephialtes, not Pericles, who led the Opposition in the great debate on the Messenian question; it was he that conducted the series of prosecutions of the members of the Areopagus, which led up to the attack on the Areopagus itself; and he, not Pericles, was the author of the laws which deprived it of its prerogatives[2]. Few things are to be more regretted in the history of this period than that we should know so little about him. His fame was so completely overshadowed by that of Pericles that he became to later writers little more than a dim and unsubstantial form. The most that we can gather is that his father's name was Sophonides; that, in spite of his poverty, he was reputed honest; and that he showed himself relentless in the prosecution of his political opponents. It is not uncharitable to surmise that he was bitter and fanatical. We have no information as to when his political career began. He once held the office of General, and was given the command of a fleet of thirty vessels which ventured eastward of the Chelidonian Islands; but when this was we cannot guess[3].

II. THE REVOLT OF THE HELOTS AND THE FALL OF CIMON

It was not long before Ephialtes and his followers had a further opportunity of testing once more the strength of their opponents. In the year 464 B.C., towards the end of spring or the beginning of summer, Sparta had been visited by an earthquake of unusual severity. It was said that only five houses remained standing in the villages of which the city of Sparta was composed, and that 20,000 of the inhabitants lost their lives[4]. Figures such as these have little value. Recent experience reminds us that in times of panic the imagination, even of eyewitnesses, is prone to run riot. It is certain, however, that the town was all but destroyed, and that the loss of life was heavy. By the Spartans themselves the

---

[1] Plutarch, *Pericles*, 16. Forty years reckoned from the date of his death, 429 B.C., would give 469 B.C. as the beginning of his supremacy. This is probably Theopompus' date for the death of Aristides.

[2] Plutarch, *Cimon*, 16 *ad fin.*, Aristotle, *Const. of Athens*, xxv.

[3] Plutarch, *Cimon*, 13.

[4] Plutarch, *Cimon*, 16. Diodorus XI, 63, 1.

earthquake was viewed as a visitation of the god Poseidon, the 'earthshaker,' for a recent violation of his sanctuary at Taenarus, from which some suppliant Helots had been dragged away for execution. However serious the losses occasioned by the earthquake may have been, its indirect effects were even graver. The Helots in Laconia itself, who must have viewed the disaster as an encouragement of their cause given by the god himself, rose in revolt, and advanced against the ruined city. Some even of the Perioeci joined them, and the insurrection became general in Messenia. Thanks to the courage and presence of mind of the young king Archidamus, and to the timely aid of the Mantineans[1], the attack on Sparta was repulsed. As might have been expected, isolated bodies of Spartan troops were massacred, especially in Messenia; but a decisive success seems to have been won by the Spartans at a place called Isthmus, somewhere in Messenia[2], and in the course of the next year, 463 B.C., the insurgents were compelled to take refuge on Mt Ithome, a lofty hill which rises out of the Messenian Plain. It is a natural fortress, and it had been the stronghold of the Messenians in their long conflict with Sparta in days gone by. The Spartans were notoriously unskilful in siege operations, but in view of the area of Mt Ithome and of the steep, or almost precipitous, nature of much of the ground, it may well be that the forces at their disposal were insufficient for an effective blockade.

By the beginning of the next year, 462 B.C., it had become evident to them that the Helot stronghold was not likely to be reduced by their present methods. It was resolved to appeal for help to the general body of their allies, and in particular to the Athenians, from whose skill in siege work much was hoped. It must have been in the spring or early summer of 462 B.C. that the appeal of the Spartan government came before the Athenian Assembly. It was only to be expected that the appeal would meet with the fiercest opposition from Ephialtes and his friends, who saw in the embarrassment of Sparta a long-wished-for opportunity for her humiliation. The Spartan cause found its champion in Cimon, who pleaded, with all the force of a double metaphor, that Greece should not be allowed to go lame, and that Athens should not consent to lose her yoke-fellow. The result of this memorable debate furnished fresh evidence that the ascendancy of Cimon was still unshaken. The Assembly voted a force of 4000 hoplites, under the command of Cimon. The Athenian

---

[1] For the Mantineans, see above, p. 67, n. 2.
[2] Herodotus IX, 35, 64.

contingent arrived in Messenia and took part in the siege of Ithome, alongside of the other allies of Sparta who had come to her aid[1]. Whatever the reason may have been, the Athenians failed to accomplish what had been expected of them, and the Spartan authorities, becoming suspicious of their intentions, abruptly dismissed Cimon and his troops. It may well seem surprising that the Spartan government should have taken a step which they must have known to be fatal to the political influence of one who had done so much to maintain intact the alliance between the two states. We must remember, however, that we have only the Athenian account of this incident. The suspicions of the Spartans may not have been without some foundation, for it is more than probable that in the Athenian ranks there was a good deal of latent sympathy with the insurgents. In any case, Spartan notions of discipline were different from Athenian, and this fact of itself was bound to give rise to friction. Our own experience in the South African War may remind us how easily misunderstandings may arise between the Regular soldier and those who have been trained in a different school.

The effect of Cimon's dismissal from Ithome was instantaneous, and the triumph of the democratic party complete. Athens withdrew from the anti-Persian Confederacy which she had joined in 481 B.C., and at once concluded alliances with Thessaly in the north, and with Argos, Sparta's rival claimant for the hegemony of the Peloponnese. Next spring Cimon was ostracized, and his party, demoralized by the loss of their leader and discredited by his fiasco in the field of foreign policy, found itself powerless to prevent the crowning triumph of the democratic party, the overthrow of the Areopagus itself.

It has been the general tendency of writers on Greek history since the days of Grote to brand Cimon's policy towards Sparta in the crisis of the Helot Revolt as a piece of quixotic generosity. Nothing could be more unfair. It must be remembered that Athens was still a member of the alliance which had been formed against Persia under the presidency of Sparta, and that it was on the ground of this alliance that the ephors appealed to Athens[2]. It follows, therefore, that a refusal to send a force to the assistance of Sparta would have amounted to a repudiation of the alliance. It should, further, be remembered that the whole foreign policy of Cimon was based on the maintenance of this tie between the

[1] The Plataeans and Aeginetans happen to be mentioned. Thucydides III, 54; IV, 56.

[2] Thucydides I, 102.

two Great Powers in the Greek world. It is true that it is alleged, and that by no less an authority than Thucydides himself, that the Spartans played the Athenians false at the time of the revolt of Thasos. He asserts, not merely that the Spartans gave a promise to the Thasians that they would invade Attica, but that they would have fulfilled their pledge had it not been for the earthquake. The statement is precise, but it presents great difficulties. It would be natural to suppose that the moment when the fact of the Spartan promise would be disclosed would be the morrow of the surrender of the island. What is quite certain, however, is that not a rumour of the promised invasion can have reached Athens at the time of the Messenian debate. Had Ephialtes been able to point to any evidence of such bad faith on the part of Sparta, Cimon's eloquence would have fallen on deaf ears. It may be conjectured that the story was derived from the Thasian Stesimbrotus; but how much, or how little, of truth there is in it cannot perhaps be determined. It is clear that the ephors who were in office at the time belonged to the anti-Athenian party, and it may be that they gave some such pledge. Can we be certain, however, even if we grant that the pledge was given, that it would have been fulfilled but for the Helot Revolt? An invasion of the Athenian territory must have been preceded by the convening of a congress of the members of the Peloponnesian League, and a declaration of war against Athens by a vote of the congress.

III. PERICLES' ACCESSION TO POWER

Within a few months of the ostracism of Cimon[1] Ephialtes was assassinated after carrying through his reform of the Areopagus (p. 69)[2]. It may be taken for granted that the assassin, Aristodicus of Tanagra, was the agent of one of those secret societies whose activities in the interests of the oligarchic cause can be detected from time to time in the course of the fifth century B.C. It was the death of Ephialtes that gave Pericles his opportunity. In him the democratic party found a leader whose fame was destined to eclipse that of Ephialtes; and the eclipse was to prove all but total.

There have been few statesmen, either in ancient or modern times, who have combined in so high a degree the qualities of birth, character, and intellect. On his mother's side he belonged to the Alcmaeonidae, whose influence in this and the preceding century appears to have been greater than that of any other of

[1] For the date of Cimon's ostracism see chronological note I D.
[2] Before midsummer 461 B.C. Aristotle, *Const. of Athens* XXV, 4; XXVI, 2.

the Athenian Clans. His father was Xanthippus, the commander of the Athenian fleet at Mycale, while his mother Agariste was the niece of Cleisthenes the reformer, and the granddaughter of that other Agariste, the daughter of Cleisthenes the tyrant of Sicyon, whose wooing by a goodly company of suitors forms the subject of one of the most famous passages in ancient literature. In the combination of these three qualities he presents a striking contrast to the other two most notable names in the political history of Athens in the fifth century B.C. In respect of pure genius Themistocles may well have been his superior; but Themistocles was a *novus homo*, and his character was more than suspect. In birth Alcibiades was not inferior to Pericles, and his intellect, though undisciplined, was brilliant; but his lack of principle and his levity of conduct were to prove ruinous to his career. The two teachers to whose influence Pericles seems to have owed most were the musician Damonides, of the deme Oea, and the philosopher Anaxagoras of Clazomenae. The former of these, who was interested in political speculation as well as in the theory of music, is said to have suggested to him the introduction of that system of payment for public service which forms one of the most striking features of the Athenian constitution. The story may well be apocryphal[1], but it is not unlikely that it was from Damonides that he derived his bias in favour of democracy. It has, indeed, been maintained that Pericles attached himself to the popular cause from no higher motive than the furtherance of his personal ambition, but for this there is little evidence and less probability. The hypothesis that explains most simply the whole of his political career is that of the sincerity of his democratic creed.

From Anaxagoras he derived his interest in philosophy. He had as little belief in the popular religion and in the superstitions of the multitude as the historian Thucydides himself. The fact that he was a free-thinker does not seem to have affected his influence with the masses during the greater part of his career, although the masses were far from friendly to free-thinkers; but a time came when his opponents succeeded only too well in making political capital out of his association with so notorious a sceptic as Anaxagoras (pp. 175, 382). In temperament there was much of the aristocrat about him. He was distant and reserved in his intercourse with his fellows, and even his opponents could not impute to him the arts of the demagogue. At least in the latter

[1] Aristotle, *Const. of Athens*, XXVII, 4. He is said to have advised Pericles, διδόναι τοῖς πολλοῖς τὰ αὑτῶν ('to bribe the people out of their own pockets').

part of his career, when his authority was unassailable, he did not hesitate to tell the people truths, however unpalatable they might be. There was something almost of ostentation, alike in his avoidance of society, and in his devotion to public duty. It is reported that the only occasion on which he was seen at a social gathering was at the wedding of a near relative, and that even then he left before the ceremonies were half over; and it was a common saying that the only streets in Athens that he habitually traversed were those that led to the market-place and the Council Chamber. The modest estate which he had inherited was entrusted to the management of a steward, and his household was administered with so rigid an economy that he was freed from all fear of pecuniary embarrassment.

As a speaker he was ranked by his contemporaries as unrivalled in his power of swaying the multitude by his words. From this verdict of his contemporaries there can be no appeal, for there have never been better judges of oratory than the Athenians of the Periclean Age. In his eloquence there is to be found one of the chief secrets of his influence with the Assembly. It was eloquence of the kind in which clear expression is but the outcome of clear thought. It was an eloquence, too, that was reserved for great occasions; he spoke only when it was necessary for Pericles to speak. There is as little reason to doubt his love of art as to question the sincerity of his democratic professions. We may believe the ancients when they assert that Pheidias the sculptor was as intimate a friend as Anaxagoras the philosopher. It must be admitted, however, that in the discharge of his military duties he proved himself little more than a competent commander. He has no claim to rank with Cimon, Myronides, or Alcibiades. His foreign policy, too, down to the conclusion of the Thirty Years Peace, was based on a complete miscalculation, both of the resources of Athens, and of the attractive power of the democratic ideal; in spite of its initial successes, it brought Athens to the brink of the abyss. It was in his domestic, rather than in his foreign, policy that his genius stood revealed. In his constitutional reforms we see the democratic principle carried out to its legitimate conclusions with an inexorable logic. If by democracy we mean government by the people, as well as for the people, we can but recognize in the constitution which was the creation of his intellect a democracy the most complete that the world has ever known. Yet it was that constitution which in the long run proved the undoing of Athens. On what, then, rests the claim of Pericles to greatness? His fame is inseparable from that of the Athens which he ruled. The epoch of Athenian history to which he belongs is known, and must always be known, as the Periclean Age. It is an age in which we see the whole energies of a society, and that the most gifted known to history, consciously directed by a single will to a given end. There is no need to dwell on what we owe to the art and letters of this Periclean Age. If anything is certain, it is that our debt would have been appreciably less had there been no Pericles.

IV. OUTBREAK OF THE FIRST PELOPONNESIAN WAR. THE GREAT EGYPTIAN EXPEDITION

The alliances which Athens had concluded towards the end of 462 B.C. with Argos and Thessaly were a direct challenge to Sparta. The step which had been taken could only mean that Athens was prepared for war with the Peloponnesian League. But if Athens were going to be involved in hostilities with Sparta and her allies, an effort must be made to secure peace with Persia. Since the battle of the Eurymedon both sides appear to have remained quiescent. Athens had had her hands full with the suppression of the revolt of Thasos, and Persia was, doubtless, only too glad to be left undisturbed. There was every prospect, however, that she would attempt to recover the seaboard of Caria and Ionia, when once the efforts of Athens were concentrated on the Peloponnesian War. A peace with Persia on any tolerable terms must have been the immediate object of the foreign policy of the democratic party. The alliance just concluded with Argos seemed to offer to the Athenian government a favourable opportunity of opening up diplomatic relations with Susa. There had been a secret understanding, if not a formal alliance, between Argos and the Persian Court at the time of Xerxes' invasion, and the friendly relations between the two states seem to have continued down to the death of the Persian monarch. Now that Argos had entered into the Athenian alliance there was reason to anticipate that, in the event of a Peloponnesian War, she would have to bear the brunt of a Spartan offensive. It is intelligible that, under these circumstances, she should endeavour to secure the help of Persia, possibly in the form of subsidies. Even the moral support of the Great King might be of value. It was, perhaps, in the spring of 461 B.C. that the two embassies arrived simultaneously at Susa; the Argives to secure from Artaxerxes, who had succeeded Xerxes on the throne, the renewal of the former relations; the Athenians, whose spokesman was Callias, the son of Hipponicus, to conclude the treaty of peace. Nothing could have been more friendly than the response of Artaxerxes to the Argive envoys; it is evident, however, that the only terms that Persia was prepared to grant to Athens were such as no Athenian statesman could venture to commend to the Assembly. The least that Persia is likely to have asked was the recognition of her claim to the tribute of the Greek cities in Asia Minor; but the glories of the Eurymedon were too fresh in the memory of the citizens for any responsible statesman to advise the concession of this claim. The democratic leaders, therefore, saw themselves confronted with the prospect of a conflict on both sides of the Aegean at once[1].

The outbreak of hostilities was not long delayed. The alliances with Argos and Thessaly were followed a year or so later by one with Megara. This state had reason to complain of encroachment on its territory by its neighbour Corinth, and failing to obtain redress, it placed itself under the protection of Athens. No alliance could have been more welcome at the moment. The control of the Megarian territory secured to Athens two advantages of the utmost importance. In the first place, it enabled her to hold the difficult passes over Mt Geranea by a strong force of troops, and thus to render an invasion of Attica through the Megarid all but impracticable; in the second place, the Megarian port of Pegae gave her a naval base on the Corinthian Gulf. The price paid for the Megarian alliance was the ineradicable enmity of Corinth.

The first use that the Athenians made of this alliance was to connect Megara, which was built on a hill at a distance of about a mile from the coast, with Nisaea, its harbour on the Saronic Gulf, by building 'Long Walls' between the city and the port. Megara and Nisaea now formed parts of a single fortress, which the Athenians proceeded to occupy with a garrison of their own troops. So far as we know, this was the first instance of the building of 'Long Walls'; a process afterwards repeated in other places, and on a larger scale. It was, as Grote puts it, 'an ingenious invention for the purpose of extending the maritime arm of Athens to an inland city.' Either in 460 B.C. or the year following (we cannot be quite certain which of the two it was), Athens struck the first blow by landing a force at Halieis, on the southern coast of the Argolic peninsula. In an engagement which followed with some Corinthian and Epidaurian troops the Athenians were defeated; but shortly afterwards in a sea-fight with a Pelopon-

---

[1] For the two embassies see Herodotus VII, 151. For the date here suggested for the embassy of Callias see note 3 at the end of the volume (p. 470).

nesian fleet off the island of Cecryphaleia, midway between Aegina and the coast of the Argolid, they were victorious. Neither engagement was probably of much importance in itself[1]. It was now apparent to Aegina that she must throw in her lot with the other allies of Sparta who were vitally interested in the control of the Saronic Gulf. Aegina had even more to fear than Corinth from the ambitious designs of the democratic party at Athens. The trade of Corinth had always been mainly with the West; that of Aegina was almost wholly with the East. Athens had not as yet stretched out her arms to the West, but in the East the growth of the Athenian Empire must have involved the decay of the commerce of any rival power. With the aid of the Aeginetans a large Peloponnesian fleet was assembled in the Saronic Gulf, and gave battle to the Athenians off Aegina. The defeat of the Peloponnesians was decisive, seventy of their vessels being sunk or captured. The Athenians were thus enabled to land a large body of troops upon the island, under the command of Leocrates, and to blockade the city both by land and sea.

Meanwhile the energies of Athens were diverted to another direction. Shortly before this time an insurrection had broken out in Egypt[2]. The leader of the insurgents was Inaros, who was king of the Libyan territory, to the west of the Egyptian. He captured Marea near the site of the later Alexandria, and after this initial success had little difficulty in bringing the greater part of the country under his control. The revolt was clearly doomed to failure unless he could secure the support of an ally, and above all of an ally who held the command of the sea. It was inevitable that he should appeal to Athens. It may well have seemed to Pericles and the other leaders of the democratic party that here was a golden opportunity for teaching Persia the lesson that she needed. If Persia would not have peace with Athens, she should learn once more what war with Athens meant. At the moment (in 460 or 459 B.C.) a fleet of 200 sail, supplied partly by Athens and partly by her allies, lay off Cyprus. This fleet was at once dispatched to Egypt. It sailed up the Nile, and, with the help of his new allies, Inaros succeeded in capturing two-thirds of Memphis, the capital of the country, and in investing the citadel, known by the name of the 'White Castle,' in which the Persian

[1] The battle of Oenoe (Pausanias I, 15, 1; X, 10, 4), if historical, probably belongs to the next century. The silence of Thucydides and Diodorus is, to the present writer, decisive. For a discussion of the problem see the works cited in the Bibliography, and Beloch, *Griech. Gesch.* II², 2, pp. 206 *sqq.*

[2] See further, for these events from the Egyptian side, vol. VI, pp. 138 *sqq.*

troops had taken refuge. For the moment the Persian Court was content to rely on the methods of diplomacy. An envoy, Megabazus by name, was sent to Sparta to see what could be effected by a liberal use of Persian gold. It was hoped at Susa that Sparta might be induced to invade Attica at the head of a Peloponnesian army, and that an invasion of Attica would compel the recall of the fleet from the Nile. The embassy ended in failure. The bribes were freely accepted, but no invasion followed. The fact, however, remained that, while Athens was engaged in a conflict with the allies of Sparta which must ultimately involve the intervention of Sparta herself, a fleet of 200 vessels and a force of 50,000 men were engaged in an enterprise in Egypt which must ultimately involve a collision with the forces which the Persian Empire had at its command[1].

The victory of Athens in the sea-fight off Aegina was followed, at no long interval, by an invasion of the Megarid by the Corinthians. They calculated, not unnaturally, now that so large a part of the Athenian forces were either engaged in Egypt or occupied with the siege of Aegina, that Athens would have no troops available for the defence of Megara, and that consequently she would have to adopt one of two alternatives; either she must abandon Megara to her fate, or she must raise the siege of Aegina. In spite of the fact that practically the whole force which was usually employed for service in the field was absent, at the moment, either in Egypt or Aegina, Myronides, the Athenian general, did not hesitate to advance to the relief of Megara with such troops as he could raise. These consisted of 'the youngest and the oldest'; that is, of the youths who were undergoing training, and of those who were past the age of active service. Two battles were fought outside Megara, the first of which was indecisive; but in the second Myronides compelled the Corinthians to evacuate the Megarid. That the mere rump of the Athenian army should have inflicted a defeat upon the best troops that Corinth could put into the field was a feat of arms of which Athens had good reason to be proud. There is conclusive evidence that the whole series of events, from the Athenian alliance with Inaros and the battle of Halieis down to the victories of Myronides, took place within the space of twelve months; perhaps between midsummer 459 and midsummer 458 B.C. On a marble slab on the walls of the Louvre in Paris there may still be read

---

[1] For a smaller estimate of the Athenian forces engaged see M. Caspari in *C.Q.* VII, 1913, pp. 198 *sqq.*, and F. E. Adcock in *Proc. of the Camb. Phil. Soc.* (1926).

the names of those 'who fell in the same year in Cyprus, Egypt, and Phoenicia, at Halieis, in Aegina, and in Megara.' The marble is a signal tribute to the spirit of a free people at a great epoch; it is not less signal evidence of the extent to which the states of antiquity overtaxed their resources in men and money.

V. THE BATTLES OF TANAGRA AND OENOPHYTA

The moment had come for Sparta to take action. Hitherto her energies had been absorbed in the suppression of the Helot revolt, and she had been compelled to remain a passive spectator of the success of Athens, and of the humiliation of her own allies. By the beginning of the year 457 B.C. the resistance of Ithome was breaking down[1], and Sparta might venture to dispatch an army outside the Peloponnese. It had become by this time evident to the ephors that, if the progress of Athens were to be checked, an ally must be discovered north of the Isthmus who could serve as a counterpoise to her influence. As Thessaly was on the Athenian side, it could only be to Boeotia that Sparta must turn. A generation earlier the Boeotian League under the presidency of Thebes had been one of the chief military powers in Greece; but the edifice of the federation now lay in ruins. The discredit into which Thebes had fallen, in consequence of the active support which she had lent to the Persian cause, had led to the virtual dissolution of the League. The other Boeotian cities repudiated her supremacy, and, by way of asserting their independence, proceeded to issue coins of their own[2]. In order to restore the League, and the influence of Thebes in its councils, it was resolved to send into Boeotia so large a force as would crush all opposition.

A pretext for sending an army into northern Greece lay ready to hand in the appeal addressed to Sparta by the little state of Doris, which had recently had reason to complain of the aggression of her more powerful neighbour Phocis. According to the legend of the return of the Heraclids Doris had been the starting-point of the movement which led to the conquest of so much of the Peloponnese by the Dorians, and, as far back as the time of the poet Tyrtaeus, it was regarded by the Spartans as their metropolis, or mother-city. That the Phocian attack on Doris was a mere pretext, and that the real objective was Boeotia, is proved by the

[1] There is no sufficient reason for altering the reading in Thucydides I, 103, from 'in the tenth year' to 'in the fourth year.' It is clear from Diodorus (XI, 64, 4) that the siege of Ithome was commonly reckoned as having lasted ten years.

[2] See Volume of Plates ii, 2, *j*, *k*, and Head, *H.N.*[2] pp. 343 *sqq.*

numbers of the expedition. The army, which was placed under the command of Nicomedes, who was regent for King Pleistoanax who was a minor, consisted of 1500 Lacedemonian hoplites and 10,000 Peloponnesian allies (a third of this force would have sufficed for the coercion of Phocis), and found its way, it would appear, by sea, across the Corinthian Gulf into Northern Greece. Having effected its object in Phocis, the army entered Boeotia. The League was restored under the supremacy of Thebes, the fortifications of which were extended and strengthened.

It was inevitable that the Athenians should take alarm at these proceedings. They occupied the passes of Mt Geranea with a strong force to prevent the return of the expedition by way of the Isthmus, and they were on the watch to intercept its return by sea across the Corinthian Gulf. Nicomedes could not fail to realize that, in order to effect his retreat through the Megarid, he must give battle to the Athenian army. With this end in view, he advanced on Tanagra, which was not far from the frontiers of Attica. His object, however, in taking up this position was not merely strategical. The Athenians were at the moment engaged in building 'Long Walls' of their own. The new invention, which had been employed a year or two before at Megara, was now to be applied to Athens, but on a far more stupendous scale. Two walls were being built to connect the city with the sea; one to the harbour of Piraeus, a distance of four and a half miles, and the other, somewhat shorter, to the open roadstead of Phalerum. The design was a legitimate development of the plan of Themistocles in fortifying the Piraeus, and, if carried into effect, it would render it impossible for a Peloponnesian army to reduce Athens to surrender by a blockade on land, so long as she retained the command of the sea. The scheme formed an integral part of the policy of the democratic party, and was for this very reason obnoxious to the opposition. The secret societies saw their opportunity in the presence of the Peloponnesian army in Boeotia. They managed to get into touch with Nicomedes, by whose aid they hoped, not only to arrest the building of the 'Long Walls,' but also to effect the overthrow of the democratic constitution.

Rumours of these plots reached the ears of Pericles and the other leaders of his party, and impelled them to anticipate the projected invasion by launching an offensive against the Peloponnesian army in Boeotia. The force employed amounted to 14,000 men, and consisted partly of the Athenians and partly of their allies, amongst whom were 1000 Argives and some Thessalian cavalry. These are the figures attested by Thucydides, and it is

evident that no Athenian general would have risked an engagement with upwards of 11,000 of the best troops in Greece, unless
he had at his disposal a force superior in numbers and not much
inferior in quality. Yet they are figures that present a grave
difficulty. A year or so before, in the battles in the Megarid,
Myronides had been unable to oppose to the Corinthians any
troops but 'the youngest and the oldest,' and we are expressly
told that the reason for this was that the rest of the Athenian
army (*i.e.* those of the usual age for service in the field) were
serving at the time in Egypt or Aegina. It is possible that by
the summer of 457 B.C. it was deemed safe to withdraw from
Aegina some of the hoplites engaged in the blockade; none, however, can have been withdrawn from Egypt. If we allow one
thousand for the Argives and another thousand for the Plataeans,
we have still to account for 12,000 'Athenians and Allies.' If
these consisted mainly of 'the oldest and the youngest,' and of
contingents from Ionia and the islands, we should have expected
that the Spartans would have made short work of such indifferent
stuff.

The two armies came into conflict in the neighbourhood of
Tanagra in May or June 457 B.C. The engagement was protracted, and the loss on both sides heavy. In the end the Athenians
suffered a defeat, chiefly owing to the defection of the Thessalian
cavalry. The victory, however, was not sufficiently decisive to
encourage the Spartans to march on Athens itself, or to attempt
to interfere with the building of the Long Walls. They were
content with effecting their return to the Peloponnese by the
Isthmus, and with ravaging the Megarian territory on the way.
The Athenians seem to have thought it prudent to allow them
to retire unmolested[1]. We may well be surprised that the victory
of the Spartans was not decisive, and that the Thebans took no
part in the battle, but no light is thrown by our ancient authorities
on either of these points. On the eve of the engagement, as soon
as the Athenian army had crossed the frontier, Cimon, who had
now been in exile for more than four years since his ostracism,
appeared on the scene, and begged to be allowed to take his place
in the ranks. When the Council instructed the Generals to refuse
his request, he conjured his friends to disprove any suspicion
that might rest on his loyalty and theirs by their conduct on the
field of battle. They took his suit of armour, and set it up on
the spot where he would himself have stood, and fell fighting

[1] For the four months truce alleged by Diodorus (XI, 80, *ad fin.*) see
note I D at the end of the volume (p. 468).

desperately to the number of a hundred. The story was current in antiquity that in consequence of their heroism Cimon was recalled from exile, and it was even said that the decree which permitted his return was proposed by Pericles himself[1]. It seems more probable, however, that he was not recalled, and that he did not return to Athens until the spring of 451 B.C., when his ten years of ostracism had run out[2].

The evacuation of Central Greece by the Peloponnesians left the Athenians a free hand in Boeotia. The political conditions of this state present a striking contrast to those which prevailed in the rest of Greece. The factor which elsewhere was of primary importance, the opposition of 'the Many' and 'the Few,' is here but secondary. In Boeotia the fundamental question was that of federalism or autonomy. The federal party, with Thebes at its head, was in alliance with Sparta, and for this reason it was oligarchical in sympathy; the anti-federal party looked to Athens for support, and was therefore democratic. Sixty-one days after the battle of Tanagra the Boeotians were decisively defeated by the Athenians under Myronides at Oenophyta, which was probably in the neighbourhood of Tanagra and not far from the Athenian border. This reverse was fatal to the power of Thebes, and to the ascendancy of the oligarchical party in Boeotia. The other cities seceded from the League, which had been so recently reconstituted under pressure from Sparta, and the whole of Boeotia, with the exception of Thebes, passed under the control of Athens[3]. Democracies were everywhere set up, even at Thebes itself. From Boeotia Myronides advanced into Phocis, which at once joined the Athenian alliance. The resentment felt at the intervention of Sparta must have secured him a welcome from the Phocians. Finally he invaded the territory of the Eastern or Opuntian Locrians, which lay to the north of Phocis, and commanded the communications with Thessaly, which was still regarded as an ally of Athens in spite of the desertion of the cavalry

[1] Plutarch, *Cimon*, 17; *Pericles*, 10. It is possible that the story of the loyalty of Cimon's friends may have been invented to explain his supposed recall after Tanagra.

[2] See note I D at the end of the volume, p. 468 *sq.*

[3] That Thebes was not captured by Myronides is expressly asserted by Diodorus (XI, 83, 1), whose statement finds confirmation in the speech of the Thebans in Thucydides III, 62: Ἀθηναίων κατὰ στάσιν ἤδη ἐχόντων αὐτῆς τὰ πολλά ('when the Athenians owing to our divisions had actually conquered the greater part of Boeotia'). Thucydides' narrative of these events (I, 108) is misleading owing to its compression. Diodorus furnishes a most valuable complement.

at Tanagra. The government of Locris was in the hands of a landed aristocracy, and was vested in a body numbering one thousand selected from this class. The oligarchical character of the constitution rendered an alliance with Athens distasteful to the population; coercion therefore had to be employed, one in ten of the governing body being carried captive to Athens as hostages for the good behaviour of the rest. It was probably before the end of the year that the Long Walls were finished, and Aegina compelled to surrender. The terms were harsh. The island had to enter the Confederacy of Delos as a subject-ally, and to pay a tribute of thirty talents, the same as that imposed on Thasos, but much in excess of that paid by any other of the members of the League.

The power of Athens had now reached highwater mark. On land, the whole territory from the Isthmus of Corinth to the Malian Gulf was under her control, and even to the north of the Gulf Thessaly was her ally, at least in name. The possession of Aegina, Megara, and Troezen on the coast of Argolis, gave her complete command of the Saronic Gulf. The foreign policy of the democratic party had not as yet met with failure in any direction. It remained to bring the Corinthian Gulf as completely under the control of Athens as the Saronic now was. It was probably in 455 B.C. that the Athenian general Tolmides was sent on an expedition round the Peloponnese. He burnt the Spartan arsenal of Gytheum, and ravaged the territory of Sicyon. The expedition served not only to display the naval power of Athens, but also to achieve results of substantial value. Achaea, on the southern shore of the Gulf, was brought into alliance, and a garrison of Messenian Helots established on the opposite coast at Naupactus, which had recently been captured from the Ozolian Locrians. It was a position of great strategical importance, commanding as it did the entrance to the Corinthian Gulf. Ithome had surrendered earlier in the year, and by the terms of capitulation its defenders had been permitted to go free where they would outside the Peloponnese. It was a piece of singular good fortune for Athens that some of the best fighting material in Greece should thus at this juncture have become available for its purpose.

VI. THE FATE OF THE EGYPTIAN EXPEDITION

Meanwhile the tide had turned. After the failure of Megabazus' mission to Sparta, the Persian Court roused itself to a great effort for the reduction of Egypt. Early in the year 456 B.C. a large army was raised, and placed under the command of

Megabyxus, the son of Zopyrus. It marched through Syria, and succeeded in penetrating into Egypt. It looks as if Charitimides (or possibly Charmantides), the Athenian general, must have been singularly incompetent, for the invasion of Egypt by the land route is proverbially difficult for a power which has not the control of the sea. We hear indeed at a later stage of the Phoenician fleet, and it may have lent its support to Megabyxus during his march; but the narrative of Thucydides suggests that Charitimides had allowed his ships to be locked up in the Nile. Whatever the explanation may be, the success of Megabyxus was complete. The Persian garrison in the White Castle was relieved, Memphis recovered, and the Athenian troops driven into the island of Prosopitis, which was formed by a canal that intersected two branches of the Nile. Here they were blockaded for eighteen months, until at length Megabyxus drained the canal, which separated the island from the mainland, by diverting the water. The Athenian ships were left high and dry, and the capture of the island and the capitulation of the Athenians followed as a matter of course. Only a small body of troops succeeded in making their way across the desert to Cyrene. Shortly after this, a fresh force of fifty vessels which had been sent in order to relieve the original expedition, in part at least, and had sailed into the Mendesian mouth of the Nile in ignorance of the disaster, was captured by the Phoenician fleet, only a few ships escaping. The insurrection was suppressed, and the whole country was reduced, with the exception of a district in the delta known as 'the Fens,' where an Egyptian prince named Amyrtaeus still held out. Inaros surrendered to the Persians, and was later, by a breach of faith, crucified or impaled. Thucydides has devoted two whole books to the great Sicilian Expedition, while he disposes of the Egyptian in a couple of pages. It is not easy to view things in their true proportions when the scale of the narrative differs so much. For all that, the expedition had lasted six years, and it meant the loss of something like 250 vessels and 50,000 men, Athenians and Allies together. Beyond all doubt, the Egyptian disaster is the greatest in Athenian history until we come to the battle in the Great Harbour of Syracuse and the surrender on the banks of the Assinarus (p. 310).

Although the precise dates cannot be determined, it is probable that the news of the disaster reached Athens early in the summer of 454 B.C. Even before the news of the final catastrophe had been received, it had been thought prudent to remove the treasury of the Confederacy from Delos to Athens, in view of a possible

descent of the Phoenician fleet upon the island[1]. At the beginning
of the campaigning season, the Athenians had sent an army,
reinforced on its way northwards by contingents from Boeotia
and Phocis, into Thessaly, where things were going badly for
their cause. The politics of Thessaly are never easy to follow,
but it would appear that at this period the country was divided
between two interests; the oligarchical, the party of the Knights
or landed aristocracy, and the monarchical, which had the support
of Athens. The leader of the latter party had been Echecratides,
but he was now dead, and his son Orestes had been driven into
exile. The Athenian expedition was undertaken in the hope of
restoring him to power, and its immediate objective was the
capture of Pharsalus. The Thessalian cavalry proved too strong
for the Athenian force, which must have consisted mainly of
hoplites. Orestes was not restored, and Pharsalus was not taken.
The expedition was compelled to make its way back to Athens,
having accomplished nothing. On its return, it was met with
the news from Egypt. A few weeks later, in the latter half of the
summer, a fresh expedition, although on a small scale, was undertaken, and this time Pericles himself took the command. A
thousand hoplites were embarked at Pegae, and landed on the
coast of Sicyon. After a skirmish with the Sicyonians, in which
the Athenians had the advantage, Pericles re-embarked his force,
and sailed along the coast to Achaea, from which he obtained
some troops by way of reinforcement. His ultimate aim was the
capture of Oeniadae, a place of some importance near the mouth
of the river Achelous, in Acarnania. He failed, however, to take
the town and he returned home at the end of the summer. This
expedition was as abortive as that to Thessaly; but it is probable
that it was intended merely as a demonstration. Athens would
prove to the rest of Greece that her spirit was not yet crushed, in
spite of the calamity which had befallen her in Egypt.

VII. THE FIVE YEARS TRUCE AND THE DEATH OF CIMON

For the next three years there was a lull in the operations on
both sides. Early in 451 B.C. the term of Cimon's ostracism ran
out, and he returned to Athens. Reference has already been made
to the story which was current in antiquity of Cimon's recall
from exile after the battle of Tanagra by a decree proposed by

[1] The quota-lists start with the Attic year 454–3 B.C., the removal of
the treasury must therefore have been effected sometime before midsummer
454 B.C.

Pericles himself. It was part of this story that, before Pericles consented to propose the decree, a compact had been arranged, through the skilful diplomacy of Cimon's sister Elpinice, to the effect that Cimon should have a free hand against Persia, while Pericles' control of domestic policy was to go unchallenged. Such facts as we know point in an opposite direction. The return of Cimon to Athens seems to have been the signal for the renewal of the old struggle for supremacy between him and Pericles. There are reasons for assigning to the year 451 B.C. two measures, both of them proposed by Pericles, which are most naturally interpreted as a bid for popular support. The first of these measures is the introduction of payment for the jurors, and the second the limitation of the franchise to those who could prove Athenian parentage on both sides[1]. The latter is expressly assigned to the archonship of Antidotus (451–50 B.C.), and it is implied in Aristotle's *Constitution of Athens* (xx, 3; xxvii, 4) that the former was introduced at a moment when Pericles and Cimon were the leaders of the two opposing factions. Thanks to these measures Pericles was enabled to maintain his position so far as domestic policy was concerned.

In foreign politics, however, the victory remained with Cimon. Within six months of his return he had procured the Five Years Truce from Sparta, and the renunciation on the part of Athens of the alliance with Argos. By the beginning of the next year (450 B.C.) the Assembly had voted him a fleet of 200 vessels for the resumption of the war with Persia, and had appointed him to its command. The meaning of all this can hardly be mistaken. The alliance with Argos had been the keystone of the anti-Laconian policy of the democrats; its conclusion had been the outward and visible sign of Cimon's fall. This policy was now reversed. In the latter part of 451 B.C., probably at the same time as the signing of the Five Years Truce, a treaty of peace for thirty years between Sparta and Argos was concluded, on the understanding that the alliance between the latter state and Athens should be dissolved[2]. The assumptions on which Cimon's policy had been based before his ostracism, that if Athens were to prosecute the war with Persia, she must be secure against attack

[1] For a discussion of these measures see the next chapter, pp. 101 *sqq.*
[2] The date of the Thirty Years Truce between Sparta and Argos follows from a comparison of Thucydides v, 14, 4, with v, 28, 2. For the dissolution of the alliance between Argos and Athens see Pausanias v, 23, 4, from which it appears that Argos was not one of the allies of Athens at the time of the signature of the Thirty Years Peace (see p. 91).

at home, and that the prosecution of the war with Persia was her primary duty, were those which underlay the policy to which the Assembly was now committed. That at so critical a moment a respite of five years should have been granted to Athens suggests that the reappearance of Cimon in the political arena had gone far to restore the influence of the moderate party at Sparta.

At the beginning of the summer of 450 B.C. Cimon set sail for Cyprus with a fleet of 200 triremes, furnished partly by Athens and partly by the Allies. After detaching sixty of these vessels for the support of Amyrtaeus, who still held out in 'the Fens,' he employed the rest of his fleet in the siege of Citium, on the south-eastern coast of the island. He died, either of disease or wounds, before the place had fallen, and shortly after his death the siege was raised. At the end of the summer, or early in the next year, the Athenians won a decisive victory, both by sea and land, at Salamis in Cyprus. The fleet which was defeated in this engagement consisted of Phoenician and Cilician vessels. No further effort was made to complete the conquest of the island, and the Athenian forces returned home. Cyprus remained in undisturbed possession of the Persians, but the expedition had achieved its primary object. Athens had proved that, in spite of the overwhelming disaster which she had sustained in Egypt, she could still hold her own against Persia on the sea. The prestige of the Eurymedon was revived, and it was owing to the prestige thus restored that the authority of Athens in the Greek fringe of Asia Minor was to remain unchallenged for another generation.

Cimon was dead, and his policy died with him. Even his followers must have recognized that no further successes against Persia could be looked for, now that the great commander to whose genius so much of the past successes had been due had passed away. To Pericles, who still clung to the hope of maintaining the Empire on land, a cessation of the hostilities with Persia would be welcome. He, too, at length had learnt the lesson that the conduct of war on two fronts at once was far beyond the resources of the state. It is not disputed that warfare between Athens and Persia ceased soon after the death of Cimon, and that for the future Athens abstained from any intervention in Cyprus or Egypt, or any aggressive action against Phoenicia and Cilicia, and that Persia on her side sent no fleets into the Aegean. What is in dispute is the conclusion of a formal treaty. In the fourth century B.C. the belief was current, although it did not go unquestioned, that a treaty was concluded (which was sometimes called the Peace of Cimon, and sometimes the Peace of Callias), by which Persia bound herself not to send a fleet into the Aegean or troops within three days' march of the coast of Ionia, while Athens bound herself to refrain from attacking the territories of the Great King. This treaty is a commonplace with the Orators, and it was accepted by Ephorus. The authority, however, of Theopompus and Callisthenes, two of the greatest names among the historians who were his contemporaries, can be set on the other side, and even those moderns who believe in a Peace of Callias are compelled to admit that there is no agreement, either as to its terms or its author, among the ancients on whom they rely (see note 3 at the end of the volume).

VIII. COLLAPSE OF THE LAND EMPIRE. INVASION OF ATTICA BY THE PELOPONNESIANS

Meanwhile in Greece an incident occurred, which although dignified by the name of a Sacred War, was of little importance in itself, and did not constitute a violation of the Truce. It was ominous, however, of what might happen on its expiration, now that the moderating influence of Cimon was removed. It was probably in 448 B.C. that the Spartans sent an army across the Corinthian Gulf to expel the Phocians from the temple at Delphi of which they had taken possession. The status of Delphi was at all times a burning question in the politics of Greece. The Phocian claim was that Delphi was an integral part of Phocis, and that the right to control the temple was consequently theirs; the Delphian, that the administration of the shrine was solely their concern. As soon as the Spartans had effected their object, and withdrawn, Pericles himself marched out at the head of an Athenian force, and reinstated the Phocians, who were still in alliance with Athens.

The first blow, however, was struck not by Sparta but by Thebes, and that a year before the Truce had run its course. The democracy which had been established at Thebes after the battle of Oenophyta was short-lived. Its misgovernment was such that it provoked a counter-revolution[1]. Thebes now became the asylum of the oligarchs who had been expelled wholesale from the other Boeotian cities in which democracies had been set up by the aid of Athens. We may be quite sure that it also became an active centre of anti-Athenian propaganda throughout the country[2]. The insurrection, which had been doubtless planned

[1] Aristotle, *Politics*, VIII (v), 3, 1302 b 25.
[2] The concise narrative of Thucydides I, 113 must be read in the light of the Theban speech at Plataea (*ib.* III, 62), in which Coronea is claimed as a Theban victory.

at Thebes, broke out in the extreme north-west of Boeotia, close
to the borders of Phocis, where the important city of Orchomenus,
together with Chaeronea and some other places, was seized by
a body of oligarchic exiles[1]. The Athenian Assembly failed to
appreciate the significance of the movement, and, in spite of the
warnings of Pericles, was content to dispatch the general Tolmides
with a body of 1000 volunteers, mostly youths belonging to the
best families, reinforced by a small number of Allies. Tolmides
captured Chaeronea, into which he threw a garrison, but he did
not attempt to recover Orchomenus. He then began his retreat,
but at Coronea, which commands the communications between
western and eastern Boeotia, he was met by a force consisting
partly of the oligarchs who now held Orchomenus and partly of
exiles from Locris and Euboea. The Athenians were defeated
with heavy loss. Tolmides fell, and a large part of his army was
captured. To recover the prisoners, Athens consented to evacuate
the whole of Boeotia. But the loss of Boeotia was not the full
measure of the disaster, as Phocis and Locris at once renounced
their alliance. Thus the whole fabric of the empire of Athens
north of Cithaeron collapsed at a single touch, like a house built
of cards.

At the end of the next summer (446 B.C.) the Five Years Truce
was due to expire, and the plans of the Peloponnesians were carefully laid in view of this date. As soon as the Truce had run out,
Euboea rose in revolt. Pericles crossed over into the island with
the bulk of the Athenian army to suppress the insurrection; but
before he had time to effect anything he received the news that
Megara had also risen and that the Athenian garrison had been
massacred. Only the two fortified ports of Pegae and Nisaea
were still held. The three regiments which alone remained at
Athens were dispatched against Megara under the command of
Andocides, the grandfather of the orator of the same name; but
so small a force could not venture on an engagement with the
Megarians, who had received reinforcements from Corinth, Sicyon,
and Epidaurus, and Andocides, who found his retreat cut off by
the enemy's army, was compelled to make his way back by the
difficult road that ran from Pegae through Aegosthena, Creusis,
and the Boeotian border[2]. The evacuation of Euboea was now
inevitable. Pericles crossed back into Attica, only to receive news

[1] Late in the summer of 447 B.C., or perhaps in the spring of the next
year.

[2] For Andocides, *I.G.*[2] 1, 1085 (Hicks and Hill 38); Köhler, *Hermes*,
XXIV, pp. 92 *sqq.*

even worse than that of the revolt of Megara. The Peloponnesian army under the Spartan king Pleistoanax had already crossed the frontier, and had reached Eleusis. It looked as if a Spartan invasion of Attica might well prove fatal to the power of Athens. Pericles could not risk a battle against forces far superior to his own, and, although Athens was invulnerable now that the Long Walls had been completed, her Empire was not. Discontent was rife amongst her allies, and the example of Euboea might prove infectious. The Peloponnesian army, however, withdrew from Eleusis without striking a blow. It was alleged at Sparta that the young King Pleistoanax and Cleandridas, who had been appointed by the ephors as his adviser, had been bribed by Pericles; and the War Party procured the deposition of the king and the exile of his counsellor[1]. The allegation may have been true or it may have been false, but it is evident that it does not explain the facts. That which needs explanation is, not merely the evacuation of Attica, but the readiness of Sparta to grant to Athens terms so generous as those of the Thirty Years Peace. If she had been bent upon the ruin of Athens, she could not have signed a treaty which was based upon the recognition of the Athenian Empire. The terms embodied in the Treaty must have been substantially the same as those arranged between Pericles and Cleandridas.

The retirement of the Peloponnesian army left Euboea at the mercy of Athens. Pericles crossed once more into the island with an army of 5000 hoplites, supported by a fleet of 50 triremes. With a force such as this he made short work of the insurrection. The whole island was compelled to surrender, terms of exceptional severity being reserved for two of the leading cities, Chalcis and Histiaea. From the former the *Hippobotae*, a landed aristocracy, were banished; at Histiaea the territory was confiscated, the inhabitants expelled, and an Athenian cleruchy established under the name of Oreus.

IX. THE THIRTY YEARS PEACE. FAILURE OF THE FOREIGN POLICY OF PERICLES

In the winter the Peace Conference assembled at Sparta. The basis of the negotiations agreed to by both sides was the surrender by Athens of what remained to her of the Empire on land (the two Megarian ports of Pegae and Nisaea, together with Achaea and Troezen in the Peloponnese), and the recognition by Sparta of the Athenian Empire in the Aegean. Controversy must have centred on Naupactus and Aegina. Corinth must have resisted

[1] See Thucydides I, 114, and v, 16. Plutarch, *Pericles*, 22, 23.

the Athenian claim to a fortress which commanded the entrance
to the Corinthian Gulf; Sparta was bound by every consideration
of honour to secure the independence of Aegina. In the end,
Athens gained her point on both these issues. Corinth was induced
to concede the Athenian claim to Naupactus; Sparta saved her
face by the proviso that Aegina was to enjoy autonomy, although
she was to pay tribute to Athens and to be included in her Empire.
This proviso was a safeguard of a kind that is not unfamiliar to
the diplomacy of our own days. Athens had no intention of
carrying out this article of the Treaty, and Sparta had no desire
to find a *casus belli* in its non-fulfilment. The further provisions
of the Treaty were that neither of the contracting parties should
give help to the allies of the other in case of revolt, but that states
at present neutral should be free to join either confederacy; and
that, if any occasion of conflict should arise between the two
parties to the Treaty, recourse should be had to arbitration.
Although Argos, as being no longer an ally of Athens, was not a
party to the Treaty, it was specifically provided that Athens and
Argos might conclude a separate alliance with each other, if they
wished it[1]. As Argos was bound by the terms of the thirty years
truce which had been made between her and Sparta in 451 B.C.,
it was necessary to assert explicitly that she was free to enter into
alliance with Athens. Such an alliance could not, of course, be
directed against Sparta till the truce of 451 B.C. had expired.
If the Treaty was a humiliation for Athens, it was a triumph for
Pericles. He had appreciated with the utmost nicety the strength
of the motives which would determine the action, not only of
Sparta, but of Corinth. However unwilling the latter might be
to leave Naupactus in the hands of Athens, she could not fail to
see that the Treaty restored to her the freedom of the Corinthian
Gulf. The grip of Athens on that Gulf during the past few years
must have almost throttled the trade of Corinth with the West.
For the humiliation which was involved in the terms of the Treaty
the Athenian public can hardly have failed to find some degree
of compensation in the fate of Euboea. In spite of the services
which the island had rendered to the Peloponnesians by its revolt
at so critical a moment, it was abandoned to the mercy of the
Athenian Assembly, and left to feel the full measure of its resentment.

Naupactus and Aegina were all that Athens retained as the
result of her efforts since the breach with Sparta. And at what a
price had these gains been purchased! It had now been demon-

---

[1] Pausanias v, 23–4.

strated by the relentless logic of events that it was far beyond the capacity of Athens to fight both Sparta and Persia at once. The number of Athenian citizens available for service in the field at this epoch can hardly have been greater than at the outbreak of the Peloponnesian War, when it is computed by Thucydides as 13,000 hoplites (p. 10). Aristotle (*Const. of Athens* XXVI, 1) puts the loss in hoplites during this period of Athenian history as high as two or three thousand a year. This is, doubtless, an exaggeration, but there must have been years in which the losses fell not far short of the higher figure. The inscription in the Louvre, to which reference has been made above, shows that in a single tribe close upon 170 fell in a single year; and if it is permissible to argue from one tribe to the rest, this would give a total of 1700 for the whole army. The year in question was a heavy one, but there were others in which the total must have been even greater.

The policy pursued by Pericles, however, stands condemned not merely on account of the inadequacy of his resources. An Athenian empire on the mainland of Greece was a vain dream. It is to be remembered that at the time of the breach with Sparta democracy was, so to speak, a new thing in the experience of the Greeks. It was, at least, enough of a novelty to excuse the belief in those who were themselves convinced democrats that the population of every state in Greece would choose the 'government of the many,' if once they got their chance. The leader of a popular party in all ages is apt to indulge in the illusion that 'the flowing tide is with him.' It was as natural for Pericles to imagine that the states in which oligarchies were established in power would declare for democracy as soon as Athens intervened, as it was for the Jacobins in France to persuade themselves that all Europe would embrace the principles of the Revolution when once the malign influence of priests and princes was removed. The policy pursued by Pericles broke down for two reasons. In the first place, in some of the states at any rate (*e.g.* in Boeotia and Locris), both the economic conditions of the country and the traditional sentiment of the people were favourable to the rule of 'the Few,' rather than to that of 'the Many.' In the second place, it was beyond the strength of Athens to maintain her ascendancy by force. Coronea showed that it was beyond her strength even to coerce Boeotia. Athens had been driven to hold Megara and Troezen with a garrison of her own troops, and to exact hostages from Locris. The result could only be that she would have to reckon with one of the strongest of all forces in Greek life, the sentiment of autonomy. When a state was confronted with the alternative of democracy or autonomy, there could be little doubt as to what its choice would be.

It is commonly argued that the policy of Cimon was bound to fail because a breach between Athens and Sparta was inevitable. It may be that a breach was inevitable in the long run; but, after all, Ithome was an accident. Had there been no Ithome, there would still have been an Inaros, and then how differently the history of Athens might have read. It is true that the great Egyptian expedition ended in disaster; but is it unscientific to conclude that, if all the conditions had been reversed—if Athens had been at the time of one heart and of one mind; if her energies had been concentrated on a single task; above all, if Cimon had been in command instead of the incompetent Charitimides—, the least that would have been accomplished would have been the permanent detachment of Egypt, and perhaps of Cyprus, from the Persian Empire? If this had been achieved, a day would have come when it would have been recognized even by Sparta that Athens was now supreme in Hellas.

It is probably to the interval between the death of Cimon and the beginning of the building of the Parthenon, in 447 B.C., that we are to assign the proposal of Pericles for a Congress of delegates from the Greek cities, to discuss the rebuilding of the temples which had been burnt by the enemy in the course of the Persian Wars[1]. Although Plutarch (*Pericles*, 17) is our sole authority for this proposed Congress, there is no reason to doubt the accuracy of his statements, which may possibly have been ultimately derived from Craterus' *Collection of Decrees*. The delegates were to be sent to all Greek cities, great and small, whether in Europe or in Asia, although the Greeks of Southern Italy and Sicily were naturally not included, as they lay outside the sphere of the Persian invasions. The Congress was to meet at Athens, and it was to discuss the payment of the vows made in the crisis of the Persian Wars and the policing of the seas, as well as the rebuilding of the temples. Twenty commissioners were dispatched to convey the invitation; five to the Dorians and Ionians in Asia Minor

---

[1] The proposal for a Congress implies that Sparta and Athens were at peace and that the hostilities with Persia had come to an end; *i.e.* it must be later than 449 B.C. It is usually assumed (*e.g.* by Busolt, Beloch, and E. Meyer) that the invitation must have been issued before Athens had herself begun the building of the Parthenon. The argument is not conclusive, but in default of any more positive evidence, it may be allowed to weigh in favour of a date within the Five Years Truce, as against a date after the signing of the Thirty Years Peace.

and to the islands in the Aegean, five to the Hellespont and the coast of Thrace as far as Byzantium, five to Boeotia, Phocis, and the Peloponnese, and thence to Locris, Acarnania, and Ambracia, and the remaining five through Euboea, to the Malian Gulf and Thessaly. The scheme failed at the very start, as the commissioners sent to the Peloponnese met with a blank refusal. It is difficult to believe that any other result could have been expected by Pericles himself. A statesman of his sagacity could hardly have imagined that Sparta would accept the proposal for a Panhellenic congress to be held at Athens on the invitation of the Athenian State. Had Sparta accepted the invitation, her action could only have been interpreted as a tacit admission of the Athenian claim to the hegemony of Greece. It was a proposal which must have been received in the Assembly with rapturous applause, and it must have contributed in no small degree to the popularity of Pericles; but that he himself anticipated any further result may well be doubted.

X. THE ATHENIAN EMPIRE AT THIS EPOCH

In the last chapter it was pointed out that by the time of Cimon's ostracism the Confederacy of Delos was well on its way to becoming the Empire of Athens. There can be little doubt that by the time of the Thirty Years Peace the process of transformation was complete, and that this transformation of Confederacy into Empire was the deliberate aim of Pericles and his party. The evidence at our command does not enable us to determine with precision how far the conditions which we find prevailing in the Peloponnesian War can be assumed for this earlier period; but it will be convenient to describe the status of the subject-allies, and to discuss their grievances, at this point rather than in a later chapter. What is true of the Empire in 425 B.C. holds good of it, in all essentials, twenty years earlier.

The synod had ceased to meet; the treasury of the League had been transferred from Delos to Athens, and the board of Hellenotamiae had been converted into an Athenian magistracy; the jurisdiction of the Athenian courts had been extended to the whole body of the Allies, and it probably included all the more important criminal cases as well as commercial suits[1]; all the

---

[1] Antiphon, *de Caede Herodis*, 47 proves that the death penalty was reserved for the Athenian courts. At Chalcis cases involving exile and disfranchisement were also reserved. *I.G.*² 1, 39 (Hicks and Hill 40). [Xenophon], *Ath. Const.* 1, 16 seems to imply a general jurisdiction of the courts: τοὺς συμμάχους ἀναγκάζουσι πλεῖν ἐπὶ δίκας Ἀθήναζε.

Allies, with the exception of Chios, Lesbos, and Samos, had lost their autonomy, had ceased to supply ships, and had become tributary. It can also be proved, although it has frequently been denied, that Athens tolerated no form of constitution other than the democratic in the cities that were subject to her[1]. Where she did not find democracy already existing, she imposed it[2]. It must be admitted that Athens rendered two great services to her subjects: she kept the Persians at arm's length, and she suppressed the evil of piracy. Persia never abandoned her claim to the Greek fringe of Asia Minor and to the great islands off the coast. Had the Athenian Empire disappeared, she would certainly have been able to make good her claims. Piracy was rife in the Aegean except during the existence of the Empire. We have evidence of its prevalence on both sides of the sea in the early days of the Confederacy of Delos. On the western side the island of Scyros was a pirates' nest from time immemorial, and on the eastern side the pirate was viewed as a public nuisance. In an inscription relating to Teos in Ionia, which may be put about 470 B.C., foremost amongst those against whom imprecations are decreed are those who practise piracy or harbour the pirates[3]. The evil survived in the Thracian Chersonese as late as the middle of the century[4], but there is no trace of it elsewhere during the ascendancy of Athens. The moment the Empire of Athens was overthrown, the evil revived[5].

In spite of the services which Athens thus rendered, her authority was resented. Both Herodotus (VII, 139) and Thucydides (II, 35) have to admit that the Empire was unpopular. It cannot be denied that the subjects of Athens had more special grievances to complain of than the mere loss of autonomy. No doubt the jurisdiction of the Athenian courts was favourable to the commercial interests of the Allies, in so far as it rendered it possible to enforce a claim against the citizen of another state. Yet there is nothing that men cling to so tenaciously as their own legal system and their own courts of law; the independent jurisdiction of their own courts was to the Greek mind an integral part of the conception

[1] With the exception of Chios, Lesbos, and Samos. These being autonomous had the right to choose their own constitution, and all three chose oligarchy.

[2] See note 4 at the end of the volume.

[3] For Scyros cf. Plutarch, *Cimon*, 8. For Teos cf. *C.I.G.* 3044 (Hicks and Hill 23).

[4] Plutarch, *Pericles*, 19.

[5] For the revival of piracy in the fourth century see Isocrates, *Panegyricus*, 115, Demosthenes, *in Aristocratem*, 166.

of autonomy. There is evidence, too, that the courts were made an engine of political oppression. It seems to have been no uncommon thing for the aristocrats in the subject-states to be brought to trial at Athens, and convicted on some trumped-up charge, at the instance of the local party leaders[1]. It must, again, have been deeply resented that Athens should claim the right to spend the tribute on any object that she pleased. The principle was expressly asserted by Pericles that, so long as Athens kept Persia at bay, she was under no obligation to render to her subjects any account of the monies contributed by them. He even claimed the right to spend these funds on the adornment of Athens, and the protest of the Conservatives, to which their leader Thucydides, son of Melesias, gave expression, was all in vain (p. 166)[2]. If it be argued that the amount of the tribute before the great re-assessment of 425 B.C. (p. 236) was not excessive, it may be answered that, although this is true, there was a substantial grievance in the fact that it was assessed by Athens, and that this power of assessment might be used inequitably[3]. It was indeed only to be expected that Athens would use this power of discrimination to the advantage of states like Miletus that were friendly, and to the detriment of those which, like Thasos and Aegina, were hostile.

Finally, there was the grievance of the cleruchies. The cleruchy was not the invention of Pericles. The earliest example of this peculiar species of colony goes back to the time of Cleisthenes, when no less than 4000 cleruchs were settled in the territory of Chalcis in Euboea. To the period between the Persian Invasion and the fall of Cimon there can be assigned the cleruchies at Eïon and Scyros, and perhaps those at Lemnos and Imbros, if these latter are not of much earlier date. It was Pericles, however, who made the cleruchy an important part of the imperial system. It served two purposes, an economic and a military. On the one hand, it provided relief for the Athenian 'unemployed'; on the other, it helped to secure some of the more important strategical positions in the Empire. To the Periclean period down to 445 B.C.

---

[1] [Xenophon], *Ath. Const.* I, 16 and 18; the latter a most impressive passage.

[2] Plutarch, *Pericles*, 12: χρημάτων μὲν οὐκ ὀφείλουσι τοῖς συμμάχοις λόγον προπολεμοῦντες αὐτῶν καὶ τοὺς βαρβάρους ἀνείργοντες.

[3] That the assessment was in the hands of the Council is attested by [Xenophon], *Ath. Const.* III, 5. It would appear from the quota-lists (*e.g.* *I.G.*[2] I, 212, Hicks and Hill, 48) that in a few exceptional cases the right of self-assessment was conceded.

belong the cleruchies in Naxos, Andros, the Thracian Chersonese, Brea, Oreus, and perhaps others in Euboea. By the time of the Sicilian Expedition the list is much enlarged. The cleruchy was not infrequently the penalty for revolt, as at Histiaea, Potidaea, and Lesbos; and sometimes it involved the expulsion of the whole population, as in the case of Scyros, Potidaea, Aegina, and Melos. In other instances the cleruchs were settled side by side with the native population, and there is some evidence to show that, where this happened, the cession of land required for the settlement was compensated for by a reduction of tribute[1]. There is no need to dwell on the bitter feeling engendered by the expulsion of the rightful possessors of the soil; but where the native population was allowed to remain, and even where it received some compensation, there was still a grievance. The cleruchs were not, in the proper sense of the term, the subjects or the dependents of Athens. They were themselves Athenians, and the cleruchy constituted, so to speak, a detached portion of the Athenian State[2]. They paid no tribute; they even remained members of their tribe and deme. They were thus a privileged order, and as such not exempt from the odium which privilege excites.

[1] The quota-lists show that in 447 B.C. the Chersonese pays 18 talents, whereas after that the tribute of the Chersonese as a whole disappears and in its place we have the contributions of separate communities, which together amount to about 2 talents, and that Andros, which paid 12 talents in 450 B.C., pays only 6 in 449 B.C. As Naxos, a wealthier island than Andros, pays only 6⅔ talents in 448 B.C. (see West-Meritt, *A.J.A.* xxx, 1926, p. 137), it looks as if here too there had been a reduction of tribute.

[2] It would appear from an inscription relating to Histiaea (*I.G.* i, 25, *I.G.*² i, 42) that the cleruchs were liable to the payment of *Eisphora*, or property-tax levied on the three higher classes of Athenian citizens. See M. Cary, *Athens and Histiaea*, J.H.S. xlv, 1926, pp. 243 *sqq.*

CHAPTER IV

THE PERICLEAN DEMOCRACY

I. EPHIALTES' REFORM OF THE AREOPAGUS

IT would appear that no measures of constitutional reform are to be attributed to the period between the invasion of Xerxes and the ostracism of Cimon. There are indeed two changes of great importance which are assigned to this epoch, the one by Aristotle and the other by Plutarch. It is asserted by Aristotle that the patriotism of the Areopagus in the crisis of the evacuation of Athens in 480 B.C. secured for it the revival of its old ascendancy in the state, and that the supremacy thus restored continued for some seventeen years until the fall of Cimon from power. On the other hand, it is asserted by Plutarch that Aristides, in recognition of the services rendered by Athenians of every rank and grade in the repulse of the Persians, threw open the archonship, apparently in 479 or 478 B.C., to all four of the Solonian Classes. There are good grounds for regarding both these statements as mere inventions[1]. It is not until we come to the fall and ostracism of Cimon that we enter on a further stage in the development of the democracy.

The measure which comes first in point of date, if not of importance, is Ephialtes' Reform of the Areopagus. That, under the provisions of his law, the Areopagus was deprived of all its powers except its jurisdiction in cases of homicide, and that the powers of which it was deprived were divided between the Council, the Assembly, and the popular courts of law, may be regarded as certain. But what these powers were, other than the guardianship of the laws, is quite uncertain. It is probable that by the 'guardianship of the laws' we are to understand, not the right of vetoing any proposed alteration of the law, but merely the right of compelling the magistrates to conform to the laws in the administration of their office[2]. It is more than likely that the importance of the measure lay, not so much in its practical results, as in the assertion of a principle. The principle involved was none

---

[1] See notes 5 and 6 at the end of the volume, pp. 472 *sqq*.

[2] Cf. Aristotle, *Const. of Athens*, IV, 4 with the Decree of Tisamenus, Andocides, *De Mysteriis*, 84. These two passages appear to indicate that the 'guardianship of the laws' was interpreted in this sense at the end of the fifth century B.C. See, however, vol. IV, p. 52.

other than that of the Sovereignty of the People. If sovereignty were vested in the people, it seemed to follow that the will of the people, as expressed either in the Assembly or in the law-courts, must be final. The right of either directly overruling the decisions of the people, or indirectly interfering with their execution, could be conceded to no other body in the state. If the guardianship of the laws is to be interpreted as the right of veto, it meant that the Areopagus could directly overrule the decisions of the Assembly and the law-courts; but even if it meant nothing more than the right of compelling the magistrates to conform to the laws, it gave the opportunity for indirect interference with the popular will. The constitution too of the Areopagus can have been hardly less offensive to democratic sentiment; for the members of the Areopagus were appointed indirectly, and they held office for life. The archons, it is true, were appointed by sortition in conformity with democratic principles, but they entered automatically into the Council of the Areopagus at the end of their term of office, and hence over their appointment as Areopagites the people had no direct control. In the democracy of the fifth century no other office could be held for more than a year; even a *strategos autocrator*, such as Pericles, had to be annually re-elected. The Areopagite alone held office for life.

Whatever may have been the importance of the Reform in its practical results, there can be no question of its importance as the assertion of a principle. By the Athenians themselves it was always regarded as the turning-point in the history of their constitution. It was the first of a series of reforms which changed the moderate constitution of the epoch of the Persian Wars into the extreme democracy of the Peloponnesian War. The virtual disestablishment of this venerable Council must have come at the time as a severe shock to a great body of religious sentiment at Athens, and it is not unlikely that in this religious sentiment we are to find the explanation of the hold which the Areopagus seems to have retained on the Athenian mind for more than a century after the reform of Ephialtes. Not only was Ephialtes' measure repealed by the Thirty (p. 367)[1], but it was to the Areopagus that Athens turned in its hour of need, alike after Aegospotami and Chaeronea[2].

It is probable that a substitute for the guardianship of the laws

---

[1] Aristotle, *Const. of Athens*, xxxv, 2.
[2] Lysias, *In Eratosthenem*, 69. Lycurgus, *In Leocritem*, 13, 52. Aeschines, *In Ctesiphontem*, 252. Lycurgus goes so far as to claim that the Areopagus played the chief part in saving Athens after Chaeronea.

hitherto exercised by the Council of the Areopagus was provided by the institution of the *Graphē Paranomōn*, one of the most characteristic features of the Athenian State in the latter part of the fifth century. It is remarkable that no hint is given in the *Constitution of Athens* as to the date of its enactment, although it is referred to in the account of the Revolution of the Four Hundred, by which time it had come to be regarded as the chief constitutional safeguard of the democracy (see below, p. 328). It was an indictment for bringing before the Assembly measures which were unconstitutional; *i.e.* in conflict with the laws of the state. Although any Athenian citizen was at liberty to bring forward a motion for a new law, or for the amendment of an old one, the proposer was liable to be prosecuted on the ground that the proposed enactment was inconsistent with the law, or contrary to the public interest. Even if the proposal had become law, its author was still liable to prosecution under the *Graphē Paranomōn* until the expiration of a year from the passing of the measure.

II. ADMISSION OF THE ZEUGITAE TO THE ARCHONSHIP

Ephialtes' Reform of the Areopagus was effected in the archonship of Conon (462–1 B.C.), probably after the ostracism of Cimon early in the year 461 B.C. The next measure of reform recorded by Aristotle belongs to the year of Mnesitheides, 457–6 B.C. The archonship, in common with the more important magistracies, had hitherto been confined to the two highest classes in the Solonian system, the Pentacosiomedimni and Knights (vol. IV, p. 51). It was now thrown open to the third class, the Zeugitae. From a passage in the *Constitution of Athens* it would appear that the disability of the lowest class, the Thetes, was never formally removed, although in practice the disqualification was evaded by a legal fiction[1]. It may well be, however, that the legal fiction belongs to the restored democracy of the fourth century B.C., and that the Thetes were ineligible for this office, in practice as well as in theory, throughout the fifth century. Once more it is probable that the reform was more important as the assertion of a principle than in its practical effect. The introduction of sortition in 487 B.C. had reduced the archonship to a magistracy with purely routine duties (vol. IV, p. 156). So far as the conduct of the business of the state was concerned, it mattered little who held this office; but in virtue of the old

---

[1] *Const. of Athens*, VII *ad fin.* The passage seems to imply that according to the letter of the law the Thetes were not eligible for any office whatever.

associations which gathered round its name, the archonship must still have made some appeal to the imagination, and it had thus become a position of dignity such as was admirably calculated to reward the modest ambition of the humbler class of citizens. The principle, however, which was asserted by the reform, that of the equal eligibility of all, was fundamental in the ancient conception of democracy.

III. PAYMENT FOR THE JURORS AND THE RESTRICTION OF THE FRANCHISE

The next change in the constitution to which we come is of a very different character. It is possibly the most far-reaching of all the reforms of this period in its effect on the working of the constitution. In the fully developed democracy there is no feature more characteristic than the system of payment for service. It meant the assertion of the principle of equal opportunity for all, and in its practical effect it enabled even the poorest members of the citizen body to take part in the work of administration, in a degree, and to an extent, that is well-nigh inconceivable to those who are familiar with democracy only in its modern forms. The first step in the introduction of this system was taken by Pericles himself, when he introduced payment for the *dicasts*, or jurors. The precise date of this measure, and the original amount of the payment, are both uncertain. The only indication of date is afforded by the statement of Aristotle that the measure was brought forward by Pericles as a bid for popular favour, and in order to counterbalance the wealth of Cimon[1]. This would point to a period when Pericles had succeeded to the leadership of the popular party, and Cimon was still the leader on the other side. The date, therefore, cannot be before the ostracism of Cimon, for Ephialtes, not Pericles, was then the leader of the popular party (p. 69); and it cannot be during the exile of Cimon, for Aristotle's statement implies his presence at Athens. It must, therefore, fall between his return from exile, which happened probably in 451 B.C., and his sailing for Cyprus in 450 B.C. It will be seen that the question of date is of some importance in its bearing on the connection between this reform and another measure attributed to Pericles, that of the restriction of the franchise. In the period of the Archidamian War (431–21 B.C.) the jurors were paid at the rate of three obols, or half a drachma, a day, but there is some

---

[1] *Const. of Athens*, XXVII, 3: ἀντιδημαγωγῶν πρὸς τὴν Κίμωνος εὐπορίαν.

evidence that the fee was originally fixed at two obols, and that it was raised to three obols by Cleon in 425 B.C.[1]

The last of the reforms enumerated by Aristotle is the law of Pericles, passed in the archonship of Antidotus (451–50 B.C.) which confined the franchise to those of citizen birth on both sides[2]. From two other references to this measure[3] it may be inferred that, although the law was passed in 451–50 B.C., it was not carried into effect until half-a-dozen years later. In the year 445 B.C. an Egyptian pretender named Psammetichus sent a present of 30,000 medimni (c. 45,000 bushels) of corn, in order to secure the support of Athens. As a preliminary to the distribution of the corn, the list of citizens was revised, and nearly 5000 names were struck off the register (p. 168).

To those who are unacquainted with the Greek conception of democracy it may seem a paradox that the name of the most famous champion of the popular cause in the ancient world should be associated with a measure which seems to the modern mind so essentially undemocratic. It may at once be admitted that few measures of constitutional reform at Athens have a better right to be called reactionary. Cleisthenes had broken down the old barriers which excluded, not only the resident alien, but the off-spring of mixed marriages, from the franchise, and the presence within the citizen body of a numerous class who were partly of non-Athenian origin must have constituted a strong link of senti-ment between the sovereign people and its subject-allies. The repeal of the liberal legislation of Cleisthenes, and the restriction of the franchise to those who could prove Athenian parentage on both sides, meant the assertion of the principle of privilege in its most offensive form. It proclaimed that the Empire existed for the benefit of Athens. But, although the measure was re-actionary, it was not undemocratic in the ancient sense of the term. Democracy in the modern world has had monarchy and the feudal system as its antecedents, and it has meant the overthrow of privilege. Democracy in the ancient world had oligarchy, not monarchy, as its predecessor, and it was a form of oligarchy which had little in common with the feudalism of the Middle Ages. To

---

[1] See Scholiast on Aristophanes, *Wasps*, 88. The addition of one obol to the fee of the jurors would give point to a passage in the *Knights*, l. 798, in which it is predicted that the jurors will exercise their office in Arcadia, and be paid at the rate of five obols a day. The *Knights* was produced early in 424 B.C.

[2] Aristotle, *Const. of Athens*, XXVI *ad fin.*: ἐξ ἀμφοῖν ἀστοῖν γεγονώς.

[3] Philochorus, frag. 90; Plutarch, *Pericles*, 37.

the Greeks democracy meant, not the overthrow of privilege, but merely the extension of its area. To them it seemed that democracy was as much rooted in privilege as oligarchy itself. It was the grounds on which privilege was based and the number of the privileged that constituted the difference between the two forms of government. Cleisthenes was a reformer born out of due time. The pretext for the law of Pericles is stated to have been the excessive number of the citizens; in other words, it was alleged that the citizen body had become unmanageably large. It may be surmised, however, that the real motive of the measure was to enhance the value of the lucrative privileges attaching to the franchise, by limiting the number of those entitled to share in them. Hence it is not difficult to trace an organic connection between the two measures of reform of which Pericles was the author; the introduction of pay, and the restriction of the franchise. It is a connection which becomes all the more evident, if we are at liberty to assume that both these laws were passed within the same twelve months, and that both were bids for popular favour in the strife of parties which had broken out afresh on Cimon's return from exile.

IV. THE DEVELOPMENT OF THE DEMOCRACY

There are two questions that are suggested by Aristotle's enumeration of the successive changes in the constitution between the Persian and Peloponnesian Wars[1]. It may be asked whether Aristotle's list of reforms is complete; it may also be asked how far the development of the democracy was due to causes other than mere legislative enactment.

To the first question there can be but one answer; the list of changes is clearly incomplete. As has been pointed out (p. 99 *sq.*), there is no mention of the *Graphē Paranomōn*, although its institution almost certainly belongs to this period. The payment, again, of the jurors is the only form of payment for public service which is mentioned by Aristotle in this passage; yet in a preceding chapter (XXIV) he has himself enumerated the various other forms of payment, both civil and military, which were in force at this epoch. We may safely ascribe to the period of Pericles' ascendancy the introduction of payment for the members of the Council, who received a drachma a day, and for all the magistrates, with the exception of the generals and the other military officers. The number of these magistrates is put by Aristotle as high as 700. To Pericles, too, there are probably to be ascribed two other forms

[1] *Constitution of Athens*, XXV–XXVII.

of payment; a payment of three obols a day for the soldiers and sailors on active service, over and above the allowance for rations which they had previously enjoyed, and a payment of two obols a day from the Theoric Fund to the poorer classes for each of the three days of the performance of the plays in the theatre[1]. In regard to this latter measure it may be assumed that at this period the system was confined to giving the poor citizen the price of his theatre ticket. In the next century, however, the principle was established of making large distributions of money from this source on the occasion of the more important religious festivals, the whole surplus revenue of the year being ultimately credited to this Fund, which thus became a most serious drain on the financial resources of the State. It may be presumed that no such extended application of the principle could have been anticipated by Pericles and his contemporaries.

On the other hand, it seems certain that payment for attendance at the meetings of the Assembly, which is one of the most familiar features of the extreme democracy of the fourth century B.C., found no place in the constitution of the Periclean Age. A comparison between the *Acharnians* of Aristophanes (produced in 425 B.C.), in which it is implied that there was at times a difficulty in securing a quorum, with two other of his plays, the *Plutus* and the *Ecclesiazusae*, (both later than the restoration of the democracy in 403 B.C.), in which there are frequent references to this form of payment, is sufficient to establish the fact. If further proof is needed, it may be found in Aristotle's statement[2] that it was Agyrrhius, a leading statesman in the early days of the restored democracy, who was responsible for this further extension of the system of payment. The rate was fixed in the first instance at one obol a day, and subsequently raised to three.

Critics of the Athenian democracy, both in ancient and in modern times, have not been slow to direct their attacks against this system of payment for service. Plato, in a well-known passage (*Gorgias*, 515 E), brings against Pericles the charge of having corrupted the Athenian character by the introduction of pay. He had made the citizens, it is alleged, indolent, cowardly, greedy of filthy lucre, and loquacious. To the ancients who had watched the effects of the system when carried to its logical conclusion in the course of the century after Pericles even so sweeping a condemnation might seem not unwarranted, and the authority of Aristotle can be adduced in support of Plato's view. He asserts

---

[1] Plutarch, *Pericles*, 9, and above, p. 29.
[2] *Constitution of Athens*, XLI *ad fin.*

that the number of those maintained by the state in the fifth century B.C. was not less than 20,000[1]; *i.e.* one-third of the citizen body, if we accept Eduard Meyer's estimate of 60,000 for the total number of citizens, or one-half of the whole, if we accept the alternative estimate of 40,000[2]. He regards the system of payment for service as a means of maintaining the poorer classes in idleness; 'a nation of salaried paupers' seems to be implied in the passage. It would be, however, in the highest degree uncritical to accept either Aristotle's figures or Plato's verdict, as applying to the fifth century B.C. Any such number as 20,000 can only be arrived at by including the sailors and soldiers when engaged on active service. The jurors constituted the larger part of those who received payment for other forms of service, and they appeared to have been, as a rule, elderly or old. The conditions of life in ancient Athens were so extraordinarily simple that for those who were past middle life, and whose working days were at an end, the modest rate of pay that was offered might serve as a sort of Old Age Pension. It is difficult to believe that it could have appealed to the vigorous and young.

It would also be uncritical to confuse the conditions of the Demosthenic age with those of the Periclean. In the fifth century B.C. the source from which payment was provided was the tribute of the subject-allies; in the fourth century B.C. Athens had no empire, and consequently no tribute. In the age of Pericles, payment for the jurors, the members of the Council, and the magistrates, imposed on the state a burden that could be borne, although it was inevitable that, in the course of a war so protracted as the Peloponnesian, it should become a burden that was felt. In the Athens of the fourth century B.C., with its payment for attendance at the Assembly and its abuse of the Theoric Fund, and with no source save the internal revenue from which the expenditure could be defrayed, the effects of the system may well have been as demoralizing for the character of the citizens as they were, beyond all question, for the finances of the state. It may be assumed that when the system was introduced by Pericles it was intended, not as a means of maintaining in idleness any class of the citizens, but as the means, and the sole means, of enabling all classes of the citizens alike to take their full share in

[1] *Const. of Athens*, XXIV, 3. Aristotle, it is true, attributes the introduction of the system to Aristides instead of Pericles, but this does not affect his view of the results of the system in the Periclean Age.

[2] So Beloch, *Griech. Gesch.* III[2], 2, p. 393, for the years immediately preceding the Plague (430 B.C.); see, however, above, p. 11.

the work of government. If government by the people, in the strictest sense of the term, is an ideal that was attained more completely in Periclean Athens than in any other society of which we have any record, this was in some degree at least the result of the introduction of payment for public service.

But even if Aristotle had given us a complete enumeration of all the measures of reform which were placed on the Statute Book in the second and third quarters of the fifth century B.C., the sum total of these measures would have failed to explain the change from the constitution as it stood in the time of Themistocles to the full blown democracy of the days of Cleon. The explanation is to be sought, not merely in any list of legislative enactments, but also in the change in the conditions, social, economic, and political, of the Athenian State. It may be permissible to look for an analogy in the history of that constitution which is as typical of modern, as the Athenian constitution was of ancient, democracy. No changes of any importance, with the exception of the Articles relating to the Abolition of Slavery, were effected in the constitution of the United States during the first hundred years or more of its existence; yet the whole character of the constitution was profoundly modified in the course of the nineteenth century. When we reflect on the extension of the area of the United States, and on the increase in its population during this period; on the industrial revolution which had transformed a society mainly agricultural into one in which the predominant interests were commercial, manufacturing, and financial; on the influx of a vast foreign population, and on the introduction of railways, steamships, and telegraphs, we need not be surprised to find that, while the letter of the constitution remained unaltered, the spirit in which it was worked was no longer the same. Things have doubtless moved far more rapidly in the modern world than they ever moved in the ancient, but movement there was at Athens in the fifth century B.C., and the character of Athenian society, and of the Athenian State, underwent modification in more respects than one in the period that followed the Persian Wars.

V. THE RISE OF THE DEMAGOGUES

By far the most important of the changes in the character of the Athenian constitution during this period is to be found in the rise of the Demagogues. Hitherto it had been the rule that the political leader should have held office as General, and this meant that he must belong to one of the old families who had a tradition of military skill and command. Shortly before the outbreak of the Peloponnesian War a leader of a new type appears on the scene. He is of humble origin (a tradesman or a skilled mechanic), and he has never held office as General. As yet the popular party had been content to find its leaders among the members of the old families, just as in England after the first Reform Bill the Liberal Party was content to find its leaders among the Whig peers. It was only to be expected that a time would come when 'the People' would claim to be led by those who were themselves men of the people. The first demagogue of any importance in the constitutional history of Athens is Cleon, but it is commonly inferred from a passage in Aristophanes[1] that he had two predecessors, at least; Eucrates and Lysicles. From Cleon to the Battle of Chaeronea the succession is unbroken. The contrast between the new type of political leader and the old is thus twofold. In the first place, there is the social contrast. Miltiades and Cimon, Xanthippus and Pericles, Thucydides, son of Melesias, and Nicias, even Aristides and Ephialtes, all belonged to what may be called the 'county families.' Themistocles is the one exception to this rule. The demagogues were town-bred men, whose manners and mode of speech were alike offensive to the aesthetic sense of well-bred Athenians. It is a common charge against them that they were violent and unrestrained in gesture; and the fact that in the Old Comedy they are twitted with foreign birth and a foreign accent may possibly find an explanation in the vulgarity of their language and pronunciation[2].

The second contrast lies in the unofficial character of the demagogue. To Grote the demagogue is 'essentially a leader of opposition.' He illustrates, for example, the respective positions of Cleon and Nicias by the relations of the Leader of the Opposition to the Prime Minister in the British Parliament. He even goes so far as to excuse the part played by Cleophon in securing the rejection of the terms of peace proposed by Sparta after the battle of Cyzicus[3] on the ground that 'a mere opposition speaker like Cleophon...did not look so far forward into the future as Pericles would have done.' In short, the demagogue is, first and

---

[1] *Knights*, 128–140.

[2] It may be that the charge of foreign birth is meant to suggest that they belonged to the class which ought to have been disfranchised under the provisions of the Periclean law. A passage in the *Athenian Constitution* of the Pseudo-Xenophon (II, 8), in which it is asserted that the Athenian dialect is a blend of tongues both Greek and Barbarian, suggests that there was a marked difference between the pure Attic of the upper classes and the country population and the colloquial speech of the industrial and mercantile classes in the city and its port.　　　　[3] See below, p. 344.

foremost, a critic of measures, not a formulator of policy. Grote, who was much better acquainted with our Parliamentary system than most of those scholars in other countries who have either accepted his premises or attacked his conclusions, intended the comparison of the demagogue with the Leader of the Opposition as a mere illustration; as an analogy that was not to be pressed. What is fundamentally true in Grote's view is that the demagogue need not, and commonly did not, hold any office whatever. His legal position differed in no respect from that of any other member of the Assembly.

That it was possible for one who held no official position to 'exercise,' for all that, 'by far the greatest influence over the people,' as Cleon did at the time of the debate on the fate of the Mytilenean prisoners[1], finds its explanation in one of the most characteristic principles of the Athenian constitution, the initiative of the individual. To critics of the constitution it appeared one of its gravest defects that any individual citizen had the right to put forward any proposal, however insane it might be[2]. It is true that no decree could be submitted to the people unless it had been sanctioned by the Council, but the liberty of amendment allowed to the Assembly was so large as to render this constitutional safeguard far less effective in practice than had doubtless been intended. In no respect does the Athenian constitution differ more profoundly, both from the Roman Republic, and from the modern systems of Representative Government, than in this. At Rome the initiative lay with the magistrate, while in a parliamentary system even the Private Member, to say nothing of the individual citizen, has surrendered almost all his right of initiative to the Cabinet. Hence no change in the letter of the constitution was required to enable the new type of political leader to emerge. His influence, however, extended far beyond that of the mere critic. Measures of the first importance could be carried in the Assembly in direct opposition to the advice of the Board of Generals, and if this happened no political crisis was involved. Neither the Board as a whole, nor any individual General, was called upon to resign. Consequently, the policy of Athens might be that of 'the Leader of the Opposition,' rather than that of 'the Cabinet.'

It was the rise of the demagogues that first revealed one of the most fatal defects in the Athenian system. There are few constitutions in history that have made more ample provision for

---

[1] Thucydides III, 36 *ad fin.*, see below, p. 217 *sq.*
[2] [Xenophon], *Athenian Constitution*, I, 6.

official responsibility. By the system of *Euthynae* every magistrate, civil or military, was called upon to render an account at the end of his year of office, and prosecutions for peculation, or other offences, on the part of the official were not infrequent. For political responsibility, however, there was no such provision; indeed, the very theory of political responsibility, *i.e.* of the responsibility of the statesman for the policy which he advocates, was imperfectly apprehended by the ancient mind. Thucydides, in one passage (VIII, 1), seems to imply that in his view the responsibility for the Sicilian Expedition lay with the Assembly which had voted it, rather than with the speakers who had advised it. This defective theory of responsibility mattered little as long as the political leader held an office; for, so long as this was the case, the political responsibility was merged in the official, and could be brought home to the statesman because he was also a magistrate. Miltiades could be convicted for his failure in the Parian Expedition (vol. IV, p. 253), Cimon ostracized in consequence of his dismissal from Ithome (p. 71), and Pericles himself brought to trial for the disappointing results of his plan of campaign in the Peloponnesian War (p. 202), because each one of these was accountable for the execution of the policy which he had himself proposed. But how could responsibility for a policy be brought home to the orator who had proposed it, when its execution had necessarily to be entrusted to others? It was inevitable that the statesman should contend that his policy had failed, not because it was faulty in itself, but because the soldiers, or the envoys, who were commissioned to carry it out had proved incompetent or corrupt. To take a single example from the history of the Peloponnesian War, the first Sicilian Expedition failed because it was bound to fail under the existing conditions, but the penalty for failure was visited, not on Hyperbolus and the other demagogues whose scheme it was, but on the unfortunate generals, Pythodorus, Sophocles, and Eurymedon, who were fined and exiled, after the Congress of Gela in 424 B.C., because they had failed where failure was inevitable (see p. 225).

The rise of the demagogues was itself a symptom of a change in the economic conditions of Attica, which affected the working of the constitution in more ways than one. Down to the Persian Wars the landed interest was still predominant in the state, but in the course of the next half century industry and commerce became serious rivals to agriculture. The centre of gravity was shifting steadily from the country to the town. If we include in our estimate the slave as well as the free and the alien as well as

the citizen, we may assume that at the outbreak of the Peloponnesian War the larger part of the population was resident in
Athens and the Piraeus, although it is clear from a passage in
Thucydides (II, 14) that, if the citizens proper are alone taken
into account, the reverse of this would be true. He expressly
says that the majority of the Athenians down to the year 431 B.C.
still lived in the countryside. The plays of Aristophanes afford
ample evidence, if evidence were needed, that the country population was conservative in instinct. It was natural that the small
farmer should look up to the wealthier landowners who were his
neighbours, and that he should be disposed to follow their lead.
No such ties of sentiment could exist between the old families
and the population of the town. It was in the urban proletariat
that the demagogues found their chief support. Whatever may
have been the relative proportion of the rural and urban populations so far as they consisted of citizens, it is quite certain that it
would be the urban population, rather than the rural, that would
furnish a majority of the voters in the Assembly. The inhabitant
of Athens or the Piraeus was on the spot; it would cost him little
time or trouble to attend. The dweller in the more distant demes
of Attica would hesitate before he sacrificed a day's work on his
farm (and it must often have meant two days rather than one), in
order to exercise his political rights. When payment was once
introduced, the attractions of office, as magistrate, or on the
Council, or in the law-courts, would make a stronger appeal to
the town than to the country. Even a drachma a day would
hardly be a sufficient compensation to the farmer or the fisherman;
to the poorer sort of citizens in the City and the Port half this
amount proved an alluring bait. It was from this class that the
jurors, at any rate, must have been chiefly recruited. It followed
that the policy of Athens came to be determined more and more
by the votes of the urban population, and that the interests of
the country were subordinated to those of the town. Nor can we
take the tone and temper of the Assembly in the Periclean Age
as a fair criterion of the sentiment of the citizen body as a whole.
It hardly admits of doubt that the Assembly was more radical in
its views than the people.

VI. THE DEMOS AND THE EMPIRE

Two other changes remain to be noticed, each of which contributed to render the constitution still more democratic in spirit. Both were the outcome of the rise and development of the Athenian Empire.

Down to the beginning of the fifth century B.C., Athens was a land, rather than a sea power. Its navy was insignificant, and the military strength of the state resided in the quality of its hoplites or heavy infantry. This force, being mainly recruited from the small farmers of the countryside, was conservative in sentiment. The Persian Wars and the policy of Themistocles converted Athens into a naval power of the first rank, and with the growth of her Empire her superiority at sea to all other states in the Greek world became more and more marked. After the Thirty Years Peace it was evident that it was to her fleet, and solely to her fleet, that Athens must look for the maintenance of that Empire. Those of the seamen who were citizens were drawn from the class of Thetes, who for the most part were resident in Athens and the Piraeus, and formed the radical element in the community. In one of the most striking passages in the *Athenian Constitution*, wrongly ascribed to Xenophon[1], the writer is at pains to point out the connection between the Athenian Empire and the Athenian Democracy. The Empire, he argues, depends on the navy, and the navy on the seafaring population, and it is precisely because it is the navy that maintains the power and prestige of Athens that the class from which the crews are drawn is paramount in the Assembly. The first article in the programme of the Reactionaries after the failure of the Sicilian Expedition was the disfranchisement of this class (p. 327); but if the disfranchisement were to be permanent, the price which would have to be paid for this reform was the surrender of the Empire. To the conservative thinkers of the next century, to Isocrates and Aristotle, it seemed that the policy of Themistocles and Pericles had been the undoing of Athens. It is Isocrates who, amid the humiliations of the Social War in the middle of the fourth century B.C., preaches the doctrine that the one chance for Athens lies in the renunciation of her last claims to empire or supremacy in the Aegean.

The second of these changes is to be found in the gradual process by which the Athenian courts acquired jurisdiction over the whole body of the subject-allies. It would be difficult to exaggerate the effect of this jurisdiction as an instrument of

[1] I, 2.

political education. It rendered a large proportion of the citizen body familiar with the circumstances and conditions of any number of states within the Empire; and it was the experience thus gained by the jurors in the courts of law that qualified them to deal with questions of imperial policy, when they came before them in the Council or the Assembly. It would also be difficult to exaggerate the influence of this imperial jurisdiction on the character of the constitution, and on the spirit in which it was worked. It was the citizen of the poorest class who was attracted by the pay, and it was he who sat enthroned in the courts. It is a remark of Aristotle's[1] that it is by means of the popular courts of law that the masses have gained their strength, since, when the democracy is master of the voting power in the courts, it is master of the constitution. The courts were in almost perpetual session; their jurisdiction extended to every aspect and department of public life; and from their decision there was no appeal. In the age of Cleon the sovereignty of the people finds expression in the law-courts even more effectively than in the Council and Assembly.

[1] *Constitution of Athens*, IX, I.

CHAPTER V

ATTIC DRAMA IN THE FIFTH CENTURY

I. THE ORIGIN OF TRAGEDY

At first mere improvisation, beginning with the leaders of the Dithyramb....

> Zeus, Zeus Accomplisher, fulfil my prayer.
> What Thou intendest to accomplish be Thy care.

So Clytaemnestra prays, intending death to Agamemnon, vengeance for her child. Her creator, long before he 'dignified the tragic trumpery,' had heard and watched the Rhapsode, staff in hand, his hair dressed high in old Ionic fashion, vested in crimson for the passion of the *Iliad*, in sea-purple for the adventure of the *Odyssey*, impersonating Homer's gods and heroes, 'singing Odysseus as he leapt upon the threshold, or Achilles rushing against Hector, or some pitiful thing about Andromache or Hecuba or Priam,' till 'his soul, enthusiastic, could not but think herself in Ithaca or Troy.' He had pondered on the oath of Homer's Zeus to Thetis that her son should be avenged—

> Go thou apart, lest Hera note our conference. I swear,
> By my own Head I promise it, these things shall be my care—

and on the sequel, when Achilles cried 'My mother, all these things hath Zeus accomplished, but my friend is dead.' Homer gave him the conception of a tragic hero, and from the *Iliad* he learnt his art of composition—Oikonomia. The Wrath, which sprang from the rejection of an old man's prayer by Agamemnon and the insult to Achilles, developed slowly to a moment of suspense when Agamemnon would have made amends, had not Achilles, now himself the victim of Illusion, stubbornly rejected 'Prayers, the daughters of high Zeus.' After the growing tension of a second movement, Achilles in his turn was stricken by Patroclus' death. In the culminating fury of a third, he took the field and all the gods trooped down to battle, though the fight between two mortals made the tumult of the gods seem child's play. At the end, when Achilles granted Priam's prayer and gave the body of his enemy for burial, the discord was resolved as if by music. From the contemplation of this sequence—three movements with a quiet close crowning the third—the pattern of the Aeschylean trilogy evolved. Clytaemnestra's Wrath, engendered when her husband killed her child, waits, in the *Agamemnon*, 'terrible, abiding, unforgetful,' till she kills him in his triumph. In the second movement, she herself is killed by her own son. In the third, the Furies claim Orestes, and the conflict grows into a cosmic struggle, gods striving on both sides, until at last Athena's intervention brings deliverance and peace. Homer's technique, the shape and structure of his paragraphs, his balancing of themes and episodes, like figures on a vase or pediment, even the distribution of his images—similes of fire and flood, for instance, sparsely used at first, but afterwards reiterated, reinforced, combined, accumulated, till the images become reality, the Trojan rivers are in spate and fire devours the plain—all this was studied and adapted to dramatic purposes by Aeschylus. Whether he said it or not, his plays were slices from the Master's feast.

They were more, of course. Since Homer's Muses answered Apollo's harping and Demodocus sang while the Phaeacians danced, poet-musicians, leaders of choruses, had re-woven old heroic stories into innumerable lyric patterns. Some drew inspiration from the *Odyssey*. Alcman, for instance, with his choir of Spartan girls, re-told the Phaeacian story—how the maidens 'cowered helplessly like birds when a hawk hovers,' how Nausicaa whispered 'Father Zeus, I wish he were my husband', how Odysseus was invited to the royal table. At moments Alcman and his dancers must have mimed their tale, but the moments passed. Alcman-Odysseus was a music-master again, teaching his choir 'the songs of all the birds.' Yet his half-dramatic lyrics held the promise of the 'antique honeyed songs' of Phrynichus, the master in this kind of Aeschylus. Sometimes the music of the *Supplices*, our earliest surviving play, echoes this lyrical apprenticeship—

> Birds are calling in the land.
> Is there one can understand?
> He will tell you. He will know,
> 'Tis the hawk-chased bride of woe,
> Tereus' luckless bride, who wrought
> Sorrow from a bitter thought,
> The sweet nightingale, bereft,
> Longing for the home she left,
> Grieving in some leafy grove
> And weaving a strange tale of love,
> How love by hate to death was done
> When a mother slew her son. (58–69.)[1]

So Homer's Penelope had mourned her husband, 'like the nightingale in the thick leafage of the wood, lamenting Itylus, whom her own folly slew.'

---

[1] References are given according to the texts cited in the Bibliography.

More important perhaps for Aeschylus was the sterner lyrical tradition which drew inspiration from the *Iliad* and Hesiod and Delphi. Stesichorus had re-told and moralized tales of the Argonauts, Medea, Alcestis, Helen and the Sack of Troy. Above all he had made a lyric *Oresteia*, in which Clytaemnestra took her right place as a tragic wife and mother (vol. IV, p. 503). In particular, the Dithyramb, associated by tradition with the cult of Dionysus, was by this time a grave narrative-lyric form. Since Archilochus boasted, 'he knew how to lead the Dithyramb in honour of King Dionysus when his wits were thunderstruck by wine,' successive masters had elaborated the convention, and evolved a stately type of dance and song, performed by fifty persons at an altar, and relating any tale of gods or heroes that the poet-leader chose. When Peisistratus inaugurated his new festival for Dionysus of Eleutherae, he could hardly fail to make provision, besides obvious delights of sacrifices and processions, for this kind of entertainment (vol. IV, p. 67).

What was more important, he encouraged local talent with a prize for 'Tragedy,' 'goat-singing,' which was won by Thespis of Icaria. Why the village-mummers of Attica were called *Tragōidoi*, whether they dressed in goatskins, or were goatlike in behaviour, worshipped or sacrificed a goat, or danced for a goat-prize, no one knows. The use of masks, the prevalence of lively dancing, and the fact that only men took part, points to some ritual origin. But what? Icaria was a Dionysiac cult centre. Had Thespis once impersonated the god? Was his waggon, which survived as a stock property, originally the god's chariot? Had Eleutherae a ritual drama, representing nature's annual death and resurrection? Was there a birth-and-passion play in the Lenaea? Or a drama of the dead in the Anthesteria, when ghosts walked abroad? What was the Eleusinian mystery-play? Out of such *drōmena* secular drama might have sprung. That it did, there is no proof. The various villages which sent competing teams may well have had their various traditional mummeries, based on different and now irrecoverable 'origins.' At Sicyon in the Peloponnese, we know, a man, Adrastus, not a vegetation-spirit, had been honoured 'with tragic choruses in reference to his sufferings' till the despot Cleisthenes 'duly gave them' to Dionysus (vol. III, p. 555). For Attica in Solon's time such celebrations at a hero's tomb are not improbable, but not yet proven. Thespis may have secularized a service for the dead. We do not know, nor does it greatly matter. Savage analogies, modern 'survivals,' traces of 'ritual sequences' in extant plays, prove nothing. Suffering and struggle, death and mourning, with some hint of victory, some 'theophany,' often a little 'faded' are a common lot, and Greek Tragedy was not false to nature's 'ritual sequences.' At any rate, when Peisistratus first countenanced the mummers, their shows, which the cautious Solon deprecated in his time, must have been crude and racy of the soil, primitive, rustic affairs, in some ways like the unpremeditated Dithyrambs of an Archilochus, or like the rudimentary attempts at drama, known as 'Satyr-plays,' performed by goatish followers of Dionysus in the Peloponnese.

Public recognition was a challenge. Let Athenian wits devise a way of story-telling as impressive as Ionic epic recitations, and more vivid than the Dorian choral lyric, yet as beautiful as either. Thanks to Peisistratus, both models were before Athenian eyes. Neither poets nor spectators were content to leave the native art a thing of shreds and patches.

In one generation 'Tragedy' shed its grosser elements. The jog-trot of the dancing, trochaic, measure and the clumsy rustic diction yielded, in the songs, to the subtler rhythms and the mixed poetic dialect, Aeolic with a Dorian tinge, already recognized as suitable for lyric; in the spoken interludes, to such Atticized Ionic as was used for spoken verse by Solon and to the six-footed iambic ancestor of our blank verse. The mummers' costumes were exchanged for robes of majesty, the ritual masks ennobled, not abandoned. How far the tendency had gone when Aeschylus (524–456 B.C.) began his work, we do not know. He is said to have first competed against Pratinas (of Phlius in the Peloponnese) in 499, and Pratinas is said to have first introduced the Satyr-play about that time, as a distinct form, and a frankly comic relaxation after 'Tragedy.' If so, grotesqueness and buffoonery, though still popular, were beginning to seem inappropriate to the main business. On the most important point Aristotle's testimony is decisive. If the evidence of extant plays were wanting, we should still know that the 'origin' of Tragedy in our sense of the word was to be sought, neither in savage ritual nor rustic mumming, but in the transformation of these beggarly elements into a new art by a man of genius, who studied, reinterpreted, and then exploited for dramatic purposes in the theatre the high thought and the subtle music first of Homer, then of the sophisticated lyric.

II. AESCHYLUS: THE GROWTH OF HIS ART

Tragedy was late in acquiring dignity, because it evolved from a satyric type. Aeschylus raised the number of Interpreters from one to two, diminished the choral element, and gave the chief part to the spoken word.

Aeschylus created Attic Tragedy. In the *Supplices* we happily possess an early work which shows him as a master in dramatic lyric, but a novice still in the manipulation of the tools which he himself invented, the second actor and dramatic dialogue.

Into the circular orchestra, which is to represent for the imagination, as the first scene tells us, a meadow with an altar-shrine near Argos, throng the Chorus, fifty men disguised as wild and swarthy women. They are the Danaids, who have fled from Egypt to escape the persecution of their cousins who desire to force them into marriage. Danaus, their father, 'captain of their counsel, leader of their cause,' is with them, an impressive figure, though his part in the performance, we shall find, is strangely insignificant. He is, in fact, a primitive chorus-leader, only half transformed into an actor. From the first he stands silent, while they appeal to Zeus for help—

> May the city, the soil and the bright rivers welcome us,
> The gods in the height, and the heroes, dread possessors of the tomb,
> And third, the Keeper of all good men's homes, the Saviour Zeus,
> Welcome this company of women and of suppliants with a breeze of pity
>   from the land,
> Driving the men, the insolent, swarming brood of Egypt,
> Back to the sea, in storm-lashed hurricane to perish! (23–36.)

In form their invocation is a triple litany of Zeus, as god of suppliants, as lover of Io, their ancestress, an Argive maiden, third, and last, as Saviour. In effect it is dramatic, a charm to raise a storm.

A choral Ode repeats the triple formula. May Epaphus, son of Zeus and Io help them, as their sorrows are like hers. May Zeus, the Saviour, save. If not, they will appeal from Zeus above to Zeus below, pollute the shrine with blood and shame the gods by suicide—

> Beware! This dark sun-smitten band
> Will seek that other Zeus in Dead Man's land,
> The god who never turn'd his guest away.
> And these strange garlands, we shall say,
> So fast about our throats are tied
> Because the gods to whom we pray
> Refused us, and we died. (160–167.)

The formula which underlies the structure—'Zeus, Lord of Io, hear! Zeus, Saviour, save! Beware, or we shall turn to Zeus, the Saviour of the dead!'—is, in its origin, Homeric—'Sing, goddess of the Wrath of Achilles son of Peleus...and the woes it wrought in the fulfilment of the will of Zeus...beginning when the son of Atreus quarrelled with divine Achilles.' The keystone and the centre of the composition is a meditation on the mystery of Zeus the Saviour, in which Homer's phrases are transformed and blended with the thought and language of Pythagorean mysticism—

First Voice.   The doom by Zeus decreed,
          Once by His Nod confirm'd, falleth aright,
          Thrown by no wrestler—
Second Voice.   Blind
          The secrets of His Mind,
          As tangled o'er with weed,
          Pathways in thickets, lost to human sight.
All.   From Hope's ambitious height
          He hurleth men away,
          Needing no weapon for the fight
          Nor armour for the fray,
          No force, but in His Mind the Thought
          Whereby the Harmony is wrought,
          No stirring. On the Holy Throne
          He labours not, yet all is done. (88–109.)[1]

Tragedy was born when these old stories were re-told by Aeschylus in the full consciousness that this demand for justice in an ordered universe was hard to reconcile not merely with old tales but with the facts of life.

This animated choral introduction leads to an anti-climax. Our actor has been waiting, silent, dramatically useless. When he speaks, it is to give the cue for a re-grouping of the Chorus. He relapses into silence when the Argive King appears, and leaves his children to conduct negotiations. Strangest of all, when he sights the ship of the pursuers, he makes no attempt to protect his terrified charges, but retires, on the pretext that he has to fetch assistance. The truth is, he has to change for a new part. He re-appears, dressed as a Herald, at the head of a wild company, the negro servants of the Egyptian suitors, shouting in broken Greek, 'Quick to the boat! There shall be branding, plucking of hair, bloody, murderous cutting away of heads!' The Argive King arrives in the nick of time to save the women and dismiss

---

[1] The version and interpretation of this passage are based on those of Walter Headlam, *Book of Greek Verse*, pp. 68–75, 277–280.

the savages. Our actor can return, as Danaus, with a bodyguard and in the highest spirits, to give the cue for the last Ode.

Lively and charming all this is, but dramatically rudimentary. Two transitional plays, the *Persae* (472 B.C.) and *Septem* (467), show us how Aeschylus, without abandoning his formal patterns and his silent actor, learnt to use them for dramatic purposes and concentrate the interest on a central tragic figure. The brooding lyrics of the Elders in the *Persae* wake expectancy, create the atmosphere required by the first actor. The Myriads of Asia have gone out with Xerxes. We are anxious, for the King is young. They have gone in their strength and splendour and the motherland that nursed them grieves for them with fierce desire. Their parents and their wives tremble because the time is long. The multitude with which the King has crossed the straits seemed irresistible. Yet when a god deceives, no man escapes. The riders and the footmen with the captains of the army have gone over. The Persian women make their beds in tears with longing for their men. Each, in a luxury of grief, because she has sent out her soldier husband, lies alone. Enter Atossa, the King's mother, the embodiment of Persian pride, a woman haunted by bad dreams and omens. They try to comfort her, but when she hears of the Athenians, 'called no man's slaves,' who proved a match for a great army of Darius, 'Terrible words' she says 'for those whose sons went forth.'

The colloquy is broken by a Runner with news of the destruction of the fleet. Amid his clamour and the wailing of the Elders, she stands silent, but the Prelude has enabled us to read her thought. When she speaks, she is too proud, perhaps too anxious, even to frame her question plainly, but the Messenger understands.

Atossa. I have been silent long. Your evil news
   Appals me. Here is a calamity
   Too great for speech, too sad for questioning...
   Who has not fallen? Whom shall we lament?
   What Captain, or what Prince, has left his post
   Unmann'd because he died there?
Messenger.   Xerxes lives. (293–5, 299–302.)

It is a light to her, she says, like dayspring. She has yet to hear the catalogue of nobles who fell fighting, till her son, who watched the battle from a throne in safety, rose and tore his robe and gave the signal for retreat.

Here was the promise of a Niobe, dumb in her anguish, an Achilles, sullen while the Myrmidons clamour for battle, a Prometheus, silent till his persecutors leave him, then crying to the Earth and Sea and Sky, a Clytaemnestra, kindling incense, pouring oils, while old men mutter that no sacrifices can appease the wrath of God. Again, the fantastic ritual by which Atossa and the Magi bring Darius from the shades, is a link in the development from the grotesqueness of the black Egyptians to the vindictive energy of Trojan captives summoning the spirit of the murdered Agamemnon to revenge, and to the hunting of Orestes by the Furies. If we smiled when the good Argive King marched in to save the Danaids, we shall not smile when Pallas comes to save her suppliant.

So Aeschylus learnt to link the Chorus with the action, and to use the silent actor. In the *Septem* he has concentrated interest on one central tragic figure. The valiant young prince, for whom we tremble, though his perfect bearing almost makes us hope, is changed and driven to his crime and death by hatred of his brother and a false conception of a soldier's honour. This climax is a great achievement. The dialogue is still clumsy, not yet fully dramatized.

In the *Prometheus*, where the hero is a Titan, the old stiff convention is deliberately used to make his torments seem to last an age. This is mature work, though the form is archaistic. The music of the Ocean-Nymphs, embodiments of mists that rise from waters to hover on the mountain-side as sun-flecked clouds, shows that the poet could still sing a honeyed song, like Phrynichus. But it is now a foil to a high tragedy of gods. Zeus, the author of the law, 'By Suffering, Wisdom,' had to learn, when he was young in power, that force without intelligence cannot prevail for ever. Prometheus, humanist and rebel, had to learn that bounds are set by nature even to intelligence, certainly to its power, perhaps to its rights. That was a lesson in high policy for Athens.

III. AESCHYLUS: THE *ORESTEIA*

After many changes it achieved its natural form.

Sophocles (496–406) first competed against Aeschylus in 468. Soon afterwards the number of actors was increased to three, and the *Skene*, or dressing-booth, beyond the orchestra, hitherto dramatically negligible, was decorated as a stately building, a low range consisting of a central block with a flat practicable roof and two projecting wings, each with its door of entry. The scheme was symmetrical, and the great door exactly in the centre of the main façade was now to prove not less significant in the dramatic picture than was the central phrase in the archaic lyrical-dramatic paragraph. Henceforth the action took place partly in the orchestra, as heretofore, but partly on a stylobate or terrace which connected the two wings of the stage-building, and to which the central door behind, and probably shallow steps from the orchestra in front, gave access to the actor (see below, pp. 459 *sqq.*).

In the *Oresteia* (458) the stage-building represents for the imagination, first the Fury-haunted house of the Atreidae, then Apollo's shrine at Delphi, then Athena's temple on the Acropolis at Athens.

On the roof of the Atreidae's palace stands a Watchman, praying in the night—

> Deliverance, O ye gods, the same prayer still
> This year of nights, high on the Atreidae's roof
> Set watching, doglike, till I know by heart
> The stars in their nocturnal sessions met
> With those pre-eminent bright potentates
> That bring men signs of storm and summer weather,
> Waning and waxing—well I know the times—
> Yet still must wait and watch for one bright sign,
> One gleam of news from Troy, the beacon-flare
> Of capture—Why? Because a woman's will,
> Strong as a man's, controls me, sanguine still.
> Pacing my beat, this dew-dank roof my bed,
> Unvisited by dreams—no dreams for me,
> But fear for company instead of sleep—
> Fear of a sleep indeed too deep for waking—
> Well, when I think to sing or hum a tune,
> My dose of cheerful song, sleep's antidote,
> Turns to a sorrowful wailing for this House
> That is not what it was, a home well govern'd.
> Come, it is time, glad messenger of light,
> Shine out with good Deliverance on the night! (1–21.)

Theme after theme from this Prologue, the night, the stars, the sleeplessness and fear, the songs that turn to wailing, the light that seems to bring relief, but is the herald of worse gloom, will be woven in the fabric of the sequel, like strands of colour in a tapestry, like the images of fire and flood in Homer's *Iliad*.

The prayer for good Deliverance, the first note of the drama, is an aspiration, baffled yet persistent, which will find fulfilment only in the last words of the trilogy. Its repetition here drives home the thought that worse things in this house require a remedy than the monotony of a night watch. Within, as at the centre of the paragraph, there lurks a woman with a man's will and a woman's sanguine heart.

He sees and hails the beacon. 'Many a dance shall Argos celebrate for this event.' He shouts, 'Ho there, within!'

> That makes all plain for Agamemnon's wife
> To rise with instant pious Hallelujah
> And greet the light.... (25-9.)

He dances. The side-doors open, and messengers run out, as to the city. Suddenly he stops—

> As for the rest, I'm silent. A great ox,
> They say, on the tongue. This house would tell a tale
> If it could find a voice.... (36-8.)

A woman cries a sinister 'Hallelujah' within.

Old men gather in the imagined morning twilight. 'Ten years of war' they mutter, 'since the Kings went out for vengeance, with a war-cry like the scream of vultures, robbed of their young. God hears the cry and sends upon the malefactor an avenging Fury.' Enter, by the central door, which now flies open, Clytaemnestra. Unnoticed by the Elders for the moment, she burns incense, pours libations, while they mutter, 'So Zeus sent the sons of Atreus against Paris, In vain the sinner pours libations, kindles sacrifice. The Wrath of God is not appeased.' They see her at last, and question her, 'What is the meaning of your sacrifices?' but she gives no answer, and departs in a religious silence, as if to pray at other altars in the city.

While they wait for her return, they sing, recalling the first days of war, and the strange sign which came to the two Kings, two royal eagles, feasting on a pregnant hare. The prophet read it as a promise and a threat. No Greek sportsman should allow his hounds to kill a mother-hare with the young in the womb. Troy would fall, but Artemis be angry. What if the huntress-goddess claimed a forfeit? A sacrifice in kind? The young of the eagle? They shudder, 'Say *Ailinon*! Woe for Linos! Yet may good prevail!' Long ago, on Achilles' shield, the vintagers responded with shrill cries to a boy's harping and his tale of Linos, a sweet singer whom Apollo slew. Calchas was hinting that he meant to claim, for Artemis forsooth, a sweet young singer, Clytaemnestra's child.

Amid such memories their only comfort is the thought of Zeus, men's chastener, who schools unwilling souls by suffering to wisdom, in the watches of the night, when old wounds ache and conscience broods on sin.

The sign was fulfilled. When the prophet clamoured for his victim, Agamemnon yielded to 'the Wretch Temptation.' 'Blowing the war the wind blew, criticizing no prophet,' he gave his daughter to the butchers. They gagged her for fear of an ill-omened cry, and she stood, waiting for the knife, 'as in a picture, her robe of saffron falling about her, wishing to speak to them, as often in her father's hall, after the men's banquet, lovingly, a pure maid, with clear voice she graced the hymn for her dear father's happiness at the outpouring of the third libation. What ensued, I did not see, nor do I tell. Only the prophet's scheme was not without fulfilment....May the end be good, as is the wish of this, the nearest....' Clytaemnestra has returned. When she speaks, thanks to the Prelude, every word betrays her outraged motherhood.

Clyt. Just as the proverb has it, with good-news
    May the Dawn issue from her Mother, Night.
    The message you shall hear is fraught with Joy
    Greater than Hope, The Greeks have taken Troy.
Chor. Is it possible? *Clyt.* It is true. The Greeks in Troy.
Chor. I weep for joy of it. *Clyt.* So the eye betrays
    The heart. *Chor.* Have you some proof? *Clyt.* Yes, I have proof,
    Unless the god deceive. *Chor.* Some happy dream?
Clyt. I am not one to prate of dreams. *Chor.* A breath
    Of rumour? *Clyt.* Nor am I a witless girl
    To be chidden thus. *Chor.* But when...? *Clyt.* This Night, I say,
    This very Night, the Mother of to-day. (276–91.)

That is the consummation of the long apprenticeship. Each paragraph of Prologue, Anapaests and Ode, and even dialogue, preserves the old symmetrical design, now fully dramatized. Thanks to the form, though Clytaemnestra cannot hint her purpose to the crowd, we know she is set on vengeance.

One detail in the picture of the child whom Agamemnon sacrificed requires a word of explanation. To Athenians the scene 'at the outpouring of the third libation' was familiar. At their dinner-parties, when the meal was finished, the host would pour libations from a bowl of unmixed wine, first to the gods, then to the spirits of departed heroes, third and last to Zeus the Saviour. At the third was sung the Paean, a hymn to the 'Good Spirit of the House' for health and happiness. So Iphigeneia sang, and wished her father all good luck. He sacrificed her, and he has won the prize of his ambition. 'Troy has fallen in the Night, the Mother of this day' cries Clytaemnestra. 'What messenger could come so fast?' 'The god of fire!' The beacon lit at Troy, has sped from peak to peak until it found the mainland—

    Swoop'd on the Spider's Crag near home, and thence
    Reach'd Agamemnon's palace-roof, a light
    Whose first progenitor was the fire at Troy. (321–3.)

The streets of the captured city will be ringing with the ill-accordant cries of friends and foes—

> Your oil and vinegar, pour'd in the same flask,
> A sorry mixture...   (334–5.)

The vanquish'd 'wail for husbands, brothers, children...'—

> What of the victors? A night's foraging
> Sets them down hungry to a morning meal
> Of what the city offers, discipline
> Forgotten, every man as Luck provides
> Snatching at Fortune. In the captured homes
> Of Troy they lodge, deliver'd from the dews
> And frosts of the cold sky. What happiness,
> To sleep the whole night through, secure at last,
> No guard kept.   (342–9.)

Security, she knows, is mortal's chiefest enemy. Luck has smiled on Agamemnon. Will he be careless? She intends to tempt him, and to catch him in a net of sin and ruin. 'Bid the King come' she cries, 'and find me faithful, as he left me'—

> I know no touch of joy, no breath of shame
> From any other man, more than I know
> The way to temper sword-blades.   (616–7.)

He comes, secure as she expected, applauding his own justice. She waits. He does not speak to her. What will she say?

> Good citizens, my reverend Argive Elders,
> I shall not blush to publish openly
> My love for this my husband. Modesty
> Fades out in time.   (846–9.)

And so, through the long speech, to the superb conclusion—

> As for myself, the fountains of my tears
> Have run themselves quite dry, not one drop left.
>   (878–9.)

But words enough left for flattery. She is Deceit personified, incarnate Temptation, a second Helen. When she bids her women 'strew his way with purple, that Justice lead him to a home scarce hoped for,' he resists. But when she urges him again, he thinks she loves him, and he yields.

> There is the Sea, and who shall drain it dry?
> Breeding fresh purple, every drop worth silver,
> Oozing abundantly, for dipping robes
> In colour.   (949–52.)

As the King goes in, the women cry 'Hallelujah,' and the Queen prays 'Zeus Accomplisher, fulfil my prayer.'

After that, Cassandra sees, not as mere shadows of the fancy,

but as visible realities, the evil shapes which haunt the house.
The Good Spirit has become a grim Avenger, gorged, yet craving
blood. The revel-song is now a chant of Furies, dancing on the
roof, ingeminating sin. Cassandra's innocence is touchingly contrasted with her vision. At the end, though she knows her fate,
she is quiet, full of pity—

> Alas for mortal life, its happiness
> A shadow merely, and adversity
> A sketch by a wet sponge at a touch dash'd out. (1326–7.)

New images are developed, but the old persist. When Clytaemnestra boasts her triumph—

> I have said much before to serve the time
> Which now I shall not blush to contradict....
> I stand here where I struck, the work well done.
> I wrapp'd the rich robe round him, caught my fish
> Fast in the blind inextricable Net,
> Then struck two blows, and with a groan for each
> He slack'd his limbs there. On the fallen body
> I struck a third blow, grace of prayer to Zeus
> The Saviour, who keeps dead men safe below.
> So down he fell, gasping his life away,
> And the sharp jet of blood which suddenly
> Gush'd, and besprinkled me with a dark shower
> Was welcome as the god's bright gift of rain
> To cornland in the travail of the ear...
> If we could pour it, what drink-offering
> Were fit for this dead man, just, more than just? (1371–95.)

She shows the blood on her hands and robe—

> This—for the bowl of curses and of wrong
> He fill'd high in his house, now drinks it, and is gone. (1396–7.)

That is the sequel to the hymn for Agamemnon's happiness, sung
long ago, 'at the outpouring of the third libation' to the Saviour.
'Deliverance!' the Watchman prayed, but Clytaemnestra,
pouring oils and kindling incense, prayed for vengeance. It is
granted. It will bring no light of joy.

'Save me and fight with me,' Orestes prays in the *Choephoroe*
to Hermes and the dead. Clytaemnestra's cry of fear is heard,
and lights are kindled. At last she sends her husband his drink-
offerings. They are useless. The offended spirit still craves vengeance, and Cassandra's countrywomen cry their 'Hallelujah,
for the light has come!' over a grim libation, the drink-offering
of Clytaemnestra's blood. Orestes sees the Furies.

In the *Eumenides*, a gentle priestess prays to Earth the Mother,

Apollo, Pallas, and last, highest Zeus. Apollo gives Orestes all the cleansing that religious ceremony can afford. But Clytaemnestra's spirit wakes the Furies—

> Sleep, would you? Fie! What use are you asleep?...
> Behold my wounds. . . . (94, 103.)

From the Furies, clamouring for blood in the name of Justice, Pallas, the child of Zeus, and representative of the divine Persuasion, saves the victim. The Trilogy is a symbol of the birth, through reason, of a moral order out of chaos. Its three movements are conceived as three libations, to the gods, to the heroes and the nether powers, then to Zeus the Saviour. The Paean at the third drink-offering is the poet's *nunc dimittis*—'For the citizens of Pallas, Zeus and Righteousness are reconciled. Crown the song with Hallelujah.'

IV. SOPHOCLES

The presentation of an action, serious, complete and having magnitude, in language sweetened for delight.

When Aeschylus died, in 456, an exile, at Gela in Sicily, Athens decreed his works should not die with him, but compete at festivals with plays by Sophocles or any other on whose shoulders the mantle fell. In the next year Euripides (*c.* 480–406 B.C.) competed for the first time, and for half a century, with Sophocles, he continued the tradition. Both were children of the Periclean age, and Sophocles, though born some fifteen years before his rival, died a few months later. The extant plays of the 'artist,' and the 'thinker,' belong to the same decades. Both were primarily men of the theatre, concerned, by music, dance and gesture, poetry and rhetoric, to represent for the imagination and intelligence, not theories, but life.

Sophocles, it is true, had something of the Periclean reserve. His art, like that of Pheidias, was austere. With dextrous subtlety he modified the old convention, sharpened his tools of character and plot and diction, banished superfluous ornament, and concentrated interest on one single tragic issue in each play. Modern critics, faintly praising his dexterity, are wont to hint that it implies some lack of feeling or defect of vision. Could a man draw life so steadily who saw it whole? The truth is, the detachment of this artist's contemplative mood was an achievement won from life 'by many journeys on the roads of thought.' No golden mediocrity created Oedipus, Antigone and Ajax.

His gods, Homeric in their clarity of outline, were, for good and evil, pagan, the embodiment of circumstance, the representatives of stern realities against which human energies are spent in vain. Ajax refused Athena's help in battle. He trusted his own strength to win success without the gods. When the Greeks adjudged the armour of Achilles to Odysseus, he brooded on what seemed to him a slight, and formed the mad design of murdering the chieftains in their tents. Athena foiled him. At the moment of the execution of his plan, she turned his moral blindness into physical delusion, his folly into frenzy, so that he attacked the innocent flocks and herds and slaughtered them, believing them to be his enemies. In a sense, her intervention is a symbol merely of the facts of his psychology. Morbid egoism is akin to madness: there are obvious conveniences for drama in presenting, as the agent of disaster, a personal and visible divinity. So Euripides in the *Hippolytus* and *Bacchae* represented Aphrodite, Artemis and Dionysus as embodiments of human instincts.

But Sophocles, we are told, attributes to Athena a resentment which is human, or sub-human, rather than divine. Gods are gods, no doubt, and will not abide our question. But this goddess who delights in the humiliation of our hero does more credit to the poet's orthodoxy than his heart.

It is at best a half-truth—hardly even that. Left to himself, Athena's victim would have killed the chieftains and have died a traitor and a murderer. If she foiled him and humiliated him, at least she saved him from a 'joy' that would have been 'irreparable.' Nor is it mere vindictiveness that makes her force upon her favourite, Odysseus, the spectacle of Ajax in the frenzy which will lead to his despair and suicide. Odysseus is to learn the lesson of *Sophrosyne*—

> He was my enemy, but I pity him....
> For all of us, I see, are merely shadows. (121–2..., 125–6.)

At the end, when the two Kings, as normal men, forget their comrade's services, it is Athena's pupil who declares, 'This was the best man of us all, except Achilles'—

> If you dishonour him, your injury
> Is done to heaven's own laws. (1342–4.)

Aeschylean in the rhythm of events—pride, madness, outrage and disaster—the play is Sophoclean in the subtlety which makes Athena's servant vindicate the honour of her victim, whom Athenians also loved.

Sophrosyne, safemindedness based on self-knowledge, that is, on recognition of the limitations of mortality, afforded many minds a standard and a refuge in this perilous age. But for the deeper human tragedies *Sophrosyne* suggests no remedy. 'Honour the gods, your parents and the law' said old morality; 'above all,' Pericles insisted, 'those unwritten laws of which the violation is admittedly disgraceful.' Sophocles, accepting all these loyalties, knew that they might conflict. When Creon, in the name of Zeus and Law, denies his nephew burial, Antigone defies him—

> Because Zeus made me no such proclamation.
> Because the Justice of the gods below
> Gives no such ordinance validity.
> Because you are a man, and your decrees
> I thought of no effect to override
> The sure, unwritten Laws of God, which live
> Not for to-day alone, or yesterday,
> But always.... (*Antig.* 450–7.)

At that moment she is certain of her faith. But when Creon tells her that, by honouring the traitor, she offends the brother who was loyal, she can only falter 'Who knows if the dead approve? My nature is to join in love, not hate.'

As the play goes on, she realizes that she stands alone. Ismene, with a touching and impulsive gesture, tries to share her sister's danger. It is too late. At the moment of decision Ismene failed. Antigone repudiates her firmly, even harshly. She must make Creon understand, this is her business, not Ismene's. She alone must suffer. But she loves Ismene, and the separation hurts.

She was betrothed to Creon's son, and Creon tells her she has lost him—

> Dearest Haemon, how your father wrongs you! (572.)

The cry is an act of faith, but no help comes. She does not hear her lover pleading with his father, and when she goes 'to that one bridal-chamber where all rest at last,' she thinks that, like Creon, he renounces her. That is why she harps so bitterly on marriage. 'Alas for the disaster of my mother's bridal. Brother, in thy marriage thou wert most unfortunate, and by thy death hast slain me.' Her sense of betrayal makes her even wonder why she made her sacrifice—

> Had I been mother of a child, I would not,
> Or had it been a husband who lay dead. (905–6.)

Her friends, her lover, even the gods, she thinks, have failed her.

> Why should I look to heaven? What god have I
> To help? For faithful service my reward
> Is this, that all the world esteems me wicked. (922–4.)

Yet, at this last, when she is least assured of faith, she is still generous—

> If what they do to me seem good to heaven,
> When I have suffered I shall know my fault.
> But if the fault be theirs, may nothing worse
> Befall them than the wrong they do to me. (925–8.)

Retribution strikes at Creon, blow after blow. His *Hubris* culminates in a magnificent blasphemy—

> Not if God's eagles tear the dead man's flesh
> And take the carrion to the throne of Zeus,
> Not that pollution shall dismay my soul. (1040–3.)

Then, under stress of the prophet's fulminations, he repents. It is too late. Antigone, impulsive to the end, has killed herself, before her lover finds her. Haemon dies over her body, cursing his father, spitting in his face. Eurydice, his mother, follows him, and Creon stands alone, his life in ruins.

This swift and violent conclusion leaves us breathless, but perhaps uneasy, half-aware that interest has been somehow shifted from the heroine to Creon. Is there a flaw here in the tragic structure? Has the dramatist imperfectly combined his own discovery, the pure tragedy of heroism, with the Aeschylean formula of *Hubris* and its chastisement? If so, he made amends in the *Oedipus Tyrannus*, his masterpiece, for which the character of Creon, his encounter with the prophet and the silent exit of Eurydice appear to be rough sketches. Jocasta has her guilty secret, since she sacrificed her child to Laius: but her tragedy is subordinated to the main design. The hero himself, like Creon in the earlier play, is suspicious, hasty, obstinate, over-confident, but, unlike him, he is brave, intelligent and generous. His intellectual and moral courage, not his defects of temper or of judgment, lead him to disaster. Acclaimed at the beginning almost as a god for wisdom and beneficence, he loses the fight with circumstance, but keeps his honour and humanity.

A sound tradition had saved Tragedy from journalism. The exceptions prove the rule. Phrynichus was fined for his *Capture of Miletus* (vol. IV, p. 171). Salamis was celebrated twice—by Phrynichus and Aeschylus: Themistocles and Pericles respectively were their Choregi—but, for the rest, the tragic criticism of events was indirect and incidental. None the less it was significant. The Periclean claim that Athens was the school of Hellas, an embodiment of the due measure, and a mistress of whom subjects could be proud, was implicit in the *Oresteia*. It was challenged by the Samian revolt, when Sophocles, the friend of

Pericles, was a General. His own *Antigone* might have warned the statesman of incalculable forces and unwritten laws, not lightly to be disregarded. If the sequel, as recorded by Thucydides reflects the movement of an Attic Tragedy, it is not because his memories of poetry confused his judgment, but because the facts were tragic. Whether or not the dramatist so designed it, the analogy between the Alcmaeonid statesman and the hero who saved Thebes, yet proved her ruin, is instructive.

> O Wealth, O Kingship, and thou, gift of wit
> Surpassing in life's rivalry of skill,
> What hate, what envy come with you! (*Oed. Tyr.* 380–2.)

So might Pericles have said in those last days, when he declared to the Athenians, 'I am the same man still. It is you who change.' The path he had chosen as by every calculation of material resources safe and profitable, led to miseries of war and plague and civil discord.

Sophocles was neither blind nor heartless, nor is it true, though it is often said, that he lived through the agony of war—he died a few months only before Aegospotami—serene, and unaffected by the tragedy of Athens. Electra's cry, 'Set in the midst of evil, we must needs do evil too,' refutes the notion that the play which bears her name is optimistic, a light-hearted vindication of the legend that Apollo sanctioned matricide. She is a normal woman, changed by circumstances and a bad creed to the wretch who bids her brother 'Strike again, if you have strength,' although the victim is her mother. War, in fact, is 'a violent schoolmaster, who makes men's tempers like their circumstances.' The creator of a Neoptolemus, discovering the clash between ambition, cunningly presented as the call of patriotic duty, and his impulses of honour and humanity and friendship, understood the war-psychology of generous youth. He advocated neither a retreat from facts nor supine acquiescence in old superstition. Witness the cry of Hyllus in the *Trachiniae*:—'These things are pitiful for us, and shameful to the gods, but hardest of all to bear for him who suffers.' No hint of his father's destined apotheosis is vouchsafed him for his comfort.

If, in spite of all, the poet kept his faith in Athens as a benefactor of humanity; if, in spite of all, he hinted to the last at the existence of high secret laws, which somehow chime with human aspirations, are we certain he was wrong? In the *Oedipus at Colonus*, Theseus and Athens are the representatives of old *Sophrosyne*, Creon and Polyneices, and in some degree even Oedipus, of *Hubris*. Oedipus claims that 'suffering and long com-

panionship of time and his own honour' have taught him moderation. Yet, when he meets his son, his passion is ungovernable. He
is deaf to Antigone's appeal. The splendour of his passing, a
majestic symbol of the mystery of life, is not allowed to veil the
deeper mystery of her unfailing, unrewarded love. 'I knew' said
Anaxagoras, when he was told his son was dead, 'I knew my
child was mortal.' 'You know' said Pericles to parents, mourning
for their sons, 'the various conditions of our lives, and that to
have an honourable end, like theirs, an honourable grief, like
yours, is fortunate.' 'I knew' Antigone once said to Creon, 'I
knew that I should die, even if you had made no proclamation.'
And now perhaps the last words written by the poet of Colonus
were 'Lament no more. These things are fixed and certain.' He
had kept his faith. He had served the Muses well. He had tried,
at any rate in poetry, to realize the harmony which Aeschylus
discerned as an ideal inherent in the world, in part attainable by
man, in part beyond his reach.

V. EURIPIDES

We should not try to keep at all costs to traditions.

Sophocles re-created the heroic world and peopled it with heroes.
Euripides fixed his eyes on Athens. His imaginative world was
peopled by Athenians. When he ascribed to them the notions,
even the cant phrases, of contemporaries, he was not in general
allowing a delight in controversy or in novelty to turn him from
his purpose, though sometimes, no doubt, he strained the form
or sacrificed his art to propaganda or sensational effect. His
purpose was to represent, so far as that was possible in the convention, the normal play of character and passion as he watched
it in contemporary life. This meant that much which had remained suppressed or only half expressed in the crude jumble of
the myths and in the Sophoclean presentation, had to be dragged
to light and stated plainly. His puppets must expound, as fully,
lucidly, and almost as ingeniously as pupils of the sophists, all
the arguments which bore on their own situations. They must
conduct in public and in measured speech the obscure debate
which half-unconsciously precedes and follows action in real life.
There is hardly a topic mooted in this time from which antholo-
gists cannot collect conflicting verdicts from these characters. The
time was pregnant. Systems were decaying and a new world being
born. Its midwives and its educators were Euripides and Socrates.

Besides the main tradition of high Aeschylean drama, the
lighter, more romantic inspiration of the *Odyssey* was now to

claim its part in the creation of a new and charming type of play. The heritage was never quite forgotten. Phrynichus made an *Alcestis*, and Sophocles, as a young man, a *Nausicaa*, in which he charmed spectators by his graceful dancing in the ball-game. But when Euripides in 438—only three years later than the *Antigone*—produced his own *Alcestis*, he secured a place for Attic Tragedy in the ancestry both of New Comedy and of the romantic novel. This is a domestic play, with a happy ending, a delicate blend of humour and of pathos, and a gentle malice of portraiture. It was presented, as a substitute, we are told, for the traditional Satyric drama, in a group of 'Tragedies' which included a romantic melodrama, lost, but very famous, the *Telephus*, which shocked the orthodox by introducing a high tragic hero in a beggar's rags, and the Achaean warriors at dice round the camp-fire, like any group of bored Athenian campaigners. The success of the new methods is attested by the long-continued onslaughts of comedians.

Admetus, a pattern of all virtues, was rewarded with an extra span of life, if he could find a substitute to die for him. None volunteered, except his faithful wife. She died, and, in his grief, a friend claimed hospitality. He gave it readily, concealing his bereavement, and again his generous virtue was rewarded. The friend was Heracles, who, when he learnt the truth, went to the grave, fought Death, and brought Alcestis home alive.

Such was the folk-tale, but Euripides created an Alcestis who, although she loved her husband well enough to die for him, was not a fool—

> You see, Admetus, how it is with me,
> And I will tell you, ere I die, my thought...
> I am dying for you, though I need not die.
> I might have lived with any prince I pleased
> Of Thessaly, in ease and luxury.
> I would not live, parted from you, to see
> Our children fatherless. I did not grudge
> My gift of youth, though I had pleasure in it,
> And though your parents failed you. (280–90.)

They were old. The gift for them would have been easy. She is perplexed, but unresentful—

> It must have been
> Some god's will that these things are what we see.
> Ah me! Then by your grateful memory
> Repay—no, not repay, there is no gift
> So dear as life—but what I ask of you
> Is just, as you yourself will say. (297–301.)

With this quiet survey of the truth, she begs him not to take another wife, a stepmother for her children. He promises that, and more. He will never marry: no beauty or wealth shall tempt him. He will mourn, and his people too: there shall be no mirth or music in the streets. He will make an image of her, and cherish it. It would have pleased her better had he said 'I love the children for your sake as well as for their own.' But Admetus lives by formulas, not love. She urges him again, and again he promises. Then she entrusts her children to him, and with one word, 'Rejoice,' she dies.

Normal life resumes its claims. The moral pedant is to be tested and found wanting. The concealment of his wife's death from his friend is not, as he conceives, a sacrifice to friendship, but an outrage, as his friend, a boisterous, crude, warm-hearted creature, presently will tell him. No code provides for everything, and in fact Admetus does not really know what friendship is. Still, he suffers. There is hope for him.

Worse follows. The selfish father comes to take part in the funeral, and this model son, because forsooth he would not die for him, denounces and disowns him. Admetus hears a plain analysis of egoism from a man as egoistic as himself. By his code, he stands condemned. Then, alone, by his own action friendless, he goes his way with the body.

When he returns, he is changed. The spirit of Alcestis has prevailed. Stripped of pretensions, and alone with memory, he has discovered what was meant by her choice of love and death. He has begun to know himself and love his wife.

In the *Medea* (431 B.C.), for the first time in our extant plays, this ruthless intellectual analysis is applied to a high tragic theme. The story of a woman's passion, changed by a lover's perfidy to monstrous hatred, is re-told, not as an echo from a far-off world, but as an incident which might have happened in contemporary Greece—in a Corinth of intrigue, ambition, jealousy and vengeance, not, it is true, in Athens, where 'the Loves are throned with Wisdom.' The Athenian interlude, which opens a window to a saner world, is essential to the poet's scheme.

No glamour of the golden fleece redeems this Captain of the Argo who would settle down and rid himself of old entanglements. The enigmatic woman who proved useful in his dangers and has borne him children is no wife for a Greek gentleman. And respectability is more to Jason than romance—

> You thought, as you grew old your foreign wife
> Would cost you something of the world's regard.   (591–2.)

It is Medea's penetrating comment, a warning to male egoists not in one generation only. The study of Medea, with her irony, her ingenuity, her scorn of the Greek commonplaces about foreigners and women, and of Jason's talk about the golden chance she had of winning a good name for her undoubted talents from the only judges in the world that count, is a masterpiece. She is now a broken-hearted woman, weeping helplessly for her lost home and children, now a wild beast, caught and caged and tamed, it seemed, for a time by a keeper's fascination, but with savage instincts waiting, till the keeper took another animal for his favourite.

But Euripides is happier in the portrayal of two creatures naturally lovable, the victims of their generous impulses, misunderstood and misdirected—

> Chaste hath she proved, although from grace she fell.
> Virtue I loved, but have not served her well. (*Hippolytus*, 1034–5.)

So Hippolytus thinks, when he hears that Phaedra is dead, hunted to death by his impetuous denunciation. He misunderstood the Nurse's garbled tale. He failed in sympathy. Nature takes vengeance for resistance to her instincts, though it be a noble instinct which resists. Theseus, with his warm heart, his hasty temper and his fatal lack of subtlety, is a good foil to the son whom he regards as crank and hypocrite. The Nurse, a mixture of rough sense and meanness and affection, has her own sordid reading of *Sophrosyne*. Nothing too much, is her motto, in love and virtue. She is a foil to Phaedra, whose resistance to dishonour is not wholly free from sophistry. When Phaedra tries to save her children's reputation by betrayal of the youth whom, much against her will, she loved, she yields to that false *Aidōs*— excessive pride in a good name—of which she spoke in the first scene as one of women's 'pleasant' dangers. In this exquisite work the two traditions, the romantic and the heroic, meet in a harmony which marks the consummation of the Euripidean art.

Throughout the war, with a penetrating, if not quite impartial analysis—he was the champion of the under-dog—he dramatized the clash and interaction of male and female, Greek and barbarian, parents and children, rich and poor, master and slave, in the partnership and conflict of contemporary life. He has a gallery of portraits, the intriguing Spartan Menelaus in the *Andromache*, the plausible Odysseus and the temporizing Agamemnon of the *Hecuba*, to tell us what he thought of politicians—to say nothing of adventurers like Polyneices, homicidal maniacs like Pylades,

Orestes and Electra. Loathing as he did the cruelty and cynicism bred by war, his inspiration sometimes flags. The patriotic commonplaces which contrast the city of ideals with knavish enemies, become mechanical, as in the *Supplices*, when the Athenian declaims his homily on the folly of aggressive war, or in the *Heracleidae*, when Alcmena, clamouring for her oppressor's blood, stands rebuked by the respect of her Athenian champions for law and decency. In the *Hecuba* he rises to a higher plane. Polyxena, the victim of a superstitious statecraft, keeps the freedom of her spirit—

> You men of Argos who have sacked my city,
> I die of my own will. Let no one touch
> My body. See, I give my throat to the knife
> Bravely. I pray you, let me die unbound.
> Leave me free. I am royal. (547–52.)

Her selfless heroism turns her tragedy to beauty and enables Hecuba to keep her sanity—

> I cannot so forget as not to weep.
> Yet you have robbed grief of its sting, because
> They say that you died noble. (589–92.)

In the sequel this Queen, who has kept honour in adversity, hates sophistry, and can appeal sincerely to that sense of law which seems to justify the thought that there are gods, becomes a fiend of cruelty, exploiting her intelligence for an ignoble and outrageous vengeance. We are reminded of the Thucydidean analysis of *Stasis* and its consequences.

The scepticism of Euripides, it has been said, 'blurred those Hellenic ideals which were the common man's best,' without replacing them. It is not true. When Heracles, in his agony of shame and grief, intends to kill himself, Theseus, his friend, inspires him to the harder, more heroic choice of life. He thinks himself an outcast from humanity, polluted, and a pollution to his neighbour. Theseus tells him, in a phrase which implies a new gospel, 'No friend can bring pollution on a friend.'

To the brief respite of the Peace of Nicias we owe the *Ion*, the study of a charming youth, reared in a faith too simple to survive experience. The freshness and the ingenuity with which Euripides re-fashions an old patriotic myth, are admirable. Yet a certain, wholly honourable inconsistency demands indulgence. The tale implies that, by descent through Ion from Apollo, the Athenians are natural leaders of the Greeks not only in Ionia but in the Peloponnese. As a patriot and a lover of romance Euripides has told his story well. But as an honest man, for whom 'gods who do evil are not gods at all,' he probes his theme until his play becomes, if not by his intention, in effect, a damaging attack on Delphi, an exposure of the patriotic legend as immoral and improbable.

Politicians and oracle-mongers certainly were not idealists. The *Troades*, composed soon after the Melian outrage, is evidence both of the poet's disillusionment and of his faith. It is inspired, as Professor Murray has well said, by 'pity for mankind exalted into a moving principle.' When the Hecuba of this play appeals for vengeance to a half-discerned mysterious energy, world-sustaining, world-sustained, which works in silence, but for righteousness, it is idle to contend that, since no vengeance follows, the appeal can tell us nothing of the poet's mind. A dramatist who makes his heroine identify divinity with one or other of these unexplained creative powers, Constraint of Nature or the Mind of Man, and neither choose nor dogmatize, but leave a question-mark, has made a contribution to religion.

In 412 B.C., when the city, mourning for the expedition lost in Sicily, was not grasping at supremacy, but fighting for her life, Euripides, as if to comfort, not to chasten, by the power of poetry, turned again to romance. The *Andromeda*, a love-story, and the *Palamedes*, a tale of adventure, are lost, but the *Helen* remains, a tragi-comedy of errors, playing lightly on the folly, not the wickedness, of those who put their trust in war-mongers and prophets. When he made his Helen sing how Joy—

> Died beside the streams of Troy
> For the phantom of a face
> And the shadow of a name, (249–51.)

Euripides was thinking of young men who died in Sicily for Athens; of whom some might say 'They died for Helen's sake,' others 'They live, as gods in starry shape'—

> Silent lies the Spartan plain,
> They shall never ride again.
> Silent is the meadow-close
> Where the reedy river flows.
> They shall never more contend,
> Youth with youth and friend with friend. (208–11.)

In the same play, with the sailor's sensible advice still in our minds—

> Take my advice, 'twill save you much expense,
> The best of prophets is your own good sense— (756–7.)

we hear Theonoe declare—

> Living and dead
> Are subject to God's Justice, and the soul,
> Merged in immortal Aether, deathless still,
> Lives not, yet keeps Intelligence.... (1013–6.)

We begin to understand why in the *Frogs* Euripides appeals to 'Aether, Intelligence, Tongue-Trickery and the Critical Nostril' as his gods, and why the poets of a younger generation would have hanged themselves to meet him, had they been sure of immortality.

In 408 B.C. he left Athens, for Macedon, where he was joined at the hellenizing court of Archelaus by Agathon, the youth whose victory (*c.* 416) was immortalized by Plato in the *Symposium*, and whom Dionysus in the *Frogs* calls 'a good poet, and much missed by his friends.' A disciple of Euripides, Agathon had pushed experiment far: he was the first to make his choral odes mere interludes between the acts, and he produced the *Anthos*, the one ancient Tragedy of which we are told the plot was freely invented, based on no myth. In the new environment Euripides found fresh inspiration, and composed a masterpiece of authentic Tragedy, the *Bacchae*, an unrivalled study of religious ecstasy, its heights and depths, its perils and allurement, the splendour of its promise and the cruelty of its effects. The news of his death reached Athens in the spring of 406, in time for Sophocles to put his Chorus into mourning at the Dionysia.

VI. COMEDY: ARISTOPHANES

'*I woke,*' *he said,* '*at daybreak, when the cocks were already crowing, and found the rest had gone or were asleep. Only Socrates and Agathon and Aristophanes remained awake, drinking from a great bowl, while Socrates discoursed. He was trying to compel them to admit, it is the same man's business to have knowledge how to make both Comedy and Tragedy.*'

Aristophanes (*c.* 446–388) began his work precisely at the moment when both Sophoclean and Euripidean Tragedy had 'found their natural form' in the *Oedipus Tyrannus* and *Hippolytus*. His predecessors, men of the great age which had created Tragedy, invented for him his convention and the attitude, as licensed critic of all eccentricity, in politics and poetry and thought, which so exactly fitted his own instincts, prejudices and convictions.

The development of Comedy from mere buffoonery to art came later and was less complete than that of Tragedy, though the *Kōmos*, out of which the art evolved, had from the first formed part of the Dionysiac festivals. A procession of masqueraders, fantastically dressed, often as birds or beasts or monsters, wearing and carrying the emblems of fertility, danced and gesticulated in the orchestra, and improvised both song and speech with an extravagance not only tolerated, but demanded as essential for the efficacy of the rite. At a certain moment they would throw off their disguise and their leader would harangue the people about things in general. That episode developed into the *Parabasis* of the convention. Sometimes they broke into disputing factions, each with its champion and spokesman. That was the germ of the comic *Agōn*. As time went on, short farcical scenes were added, analogous to those of the contemporary Dorian farce, including characters from Attic life, as well as the stock Dorian types, cook, doctor and old woman, for example. At first, says Aristotle, the performers were volunteers. It was not till late that the Archon granted a Chorus. The conventions were already fixed when first the names of poets began to be recorded, and the framing of invented plots originally came from Sicily—that is, from Epicharmus, who was fifteen years the junior of Aeschylus. The first regular competition may have been held in 487, when Chionides is said to have been victor, or even somewhat later.

Aristophanes, though he claims much credit as a reformer, an artist, not a mere buffoon, acknowledges by implication his debt to many predecessors—to Magnes, with his choruses of 'Lute-players and Lydians, Frogs and Flies and Birds,' to Crates of the 'happy thought and polished phrase,' but above all to Cratinus, whose vigorous invention and tumultuous invective, in his prime, was like a flood which swept away obstructions, 'oaks and planes and rival poets,' with an irresistible impetuosity. With characteristic impertinence he adds that the old man's music has now left him, and he wanders drearily through Athens, with a withered garland, caring for nothing but drink. So said Aristophanes in 424, flushed with the consciousness of his audacity in bearding Cleon. Nemesis followed with the failure of the *Clouds* in 423, and the triumph of Cratinus with his *Wine-Flask*, a fantasy in which he posed as victim of a jealous wife, Dame Comedy, who prosecuted him for flirtation with the disreputable lady Winebottle.

From the first, scurrility in these performances was thought to be a safeguard against fortune's malice, and indecency a help to nature in her fertilizing work. That was true in the time of Aristophanes, and was in part the explanation of the licence on the whole triumphantly retained by Comedy throughout the war. Everywhere and always war has been the enemy of freedom, but in Athens the tradition of free speech died hard. Pericles tried to clip the wings of Comedy at the time of the Samian revolt, and failed. Cleon prosecuted Aristophanes for daring in his *Babylonians* to criticize Athenian administration at a festival at which the Allies, whom he championed, were present. The Council rejected the bill of indictment, and two years later Aristophanes produced the *Knights*. No doubt, as a member of a cultivated aristocratic circle—the *Symposium* attests it—he had influential backing. No doubt he could rely on the support, by no means negligible, of the Knights themselves—although his claim that they consented to appear in person in his play is not intended to be taken seriously. But it needed courage to assail the demagogue who had so lately been invested with a crown of honour for his services at Pylos. There is no sign that the poet ever forfeited his independence or became a party hack. He criticized the Demos as its friend, and gave no countenance to oligarchic faction or intrigue. He denounced the war as a patriot, and he was right. The impunity which he enjoyed attests the candour of his countrymen, who loved to hear both sides, and liked ideas for their own sakes.

As portraiture his caricature of Cleon is fantastic, not to be used as evidence. But his Demos is a person recognizable in all free countries—

> A little old man fed on voting-beans,
> Quick-tempered, rustic-minded, hard of hearing, (*Knights* 41–3.)

easily cajoled by promises and doles, opening and shutting his ears 'like a parasol' to the flatteries of politicians, ready to fight when they prime him with their garlic or dope him with oracles, absent-minded when the soldiers look for pay—a disreputable creature, but with such a mixture in his composition of good-humour, gaiety, and shrewdness that we like him and applaud, though we are not convinced, when, from the Sausage-Seller's magic cauldron he emerges as a worthy representative of 'shining, enviable, violet-crowned Athens,' a young Prince, 'fragrant with peace and myrrh.'

To make distinction in the work of this exuberant and reckless artist between foolery and serious opinion is a thankless task. It was not his business to provide material for a just estimate of Cleon, Socrates or the Tragedians. Nevertheless, besides his famous victims, he drew many Attic types in normal focus, as foils to heighten and make plausible his high fantastic comedy.

Such are Peithetairos and Euelpides in the *Birds*, two solid human beings, whose talk, when we first meet them, is so homely as to make their enterprise seem almost credible—

> Gentlemen, we are the victims
> Of a strange fancy. We don't share the taste
> Of those eccentric aliens who flock
> To Athens. We're respectable, blue-blooded
> And undeportable Athenian voters
> Who've run away from Athens. Yes, no doubt,
> A great and happy land, where everyone
> Is free to pay his taxes.... (30–8.)

The admission of absurdity disarms us. Had not Sophocles made a play about the Thracian Tereus who became a Hoopoe? What more natural than for these gentlemen, who want to lead a simple life, to visit him and ask him to suggest a suitable retreat? So gradually Aristophanes transports us from reality. We reach the Hoopoe's nest, and are received first by a servant, plausible and human, though his beak is certainly astonishing, then by the crested Hoopoe, somewhat shabby, and still sensitive about his transformation. The serenade which wakes the Nightingale and the summons to the birds take us a further step into poetry, till at length, when a company of many-coloured birds assembles, as large as human beings, obviously human beings dressed as birds, and last of all, Athena's bird the Owl, we are ready to believe that birds can be taught Greek, and men grow wings and Peithetairos rise to godhead.

Once at home among the birds, Peithetairos, as a plausible Athenian, cannot resist the impulse to create and organize. His scheme for Cloudcuckooland involves him in a hundred problems, all of which he tackles with Athenian resourcefulness and humour. His city is invaded by the pests of war-time Athens, the prophet, mouthing oracles to the effect that he is worthy of his hire, Meton, the calendar-reformer and town-planner—type of the expert who would clear away the small anomalies which make life pleasant—poets, of course, a youth deluded by the sophists, last and worst a sycophant, whose business is to trump up accusations against citizens and Allies, spying, threatening, blackmailing. His well-merited castigation is the climax of these farcical interludes.

At the outset Peithetairos was a commonplace, intelligent Athenian. As he conceives, expounds and executes his plan, he becomes a Themistocles or Alcibiades, contriving victory. When a Messenger reports that the bird-citadel is finished, he listens, like a poet wrapt in wonder at the beauty of his work, silent, amazed, still gaining dignity. In the end, when he has conquered gods and men we are delighted to acclaim him, more than human, as he wafts his goddess-bride in triumph to a home in the cloud-palaces of *Nephelokokkugia*.

The play was produced at the time of the Sicilian expedition. Was it a warning? Or, since Peithetairos is successful, a defence of Alcibiades? We shall be wise if we leave such hypotheses, and visit the Assembly in the company of Dicaeopolis, and listen to his chatter about poetry and music and the price of oil and vinegar in war-time, or go to the Council with the Sausage-Seller, and hear the patriotic cry 'Peace at this time? Let the war go on' —since sprats are cheap. Lantern in hand we may pick our way, with Philocleon's friends, through muddy lanes in the cold darkness before dawn—'More rain in the next few days'—hurrying because we must not miss our place in the jury-courts, beguiling the way with a song from Phrynichus or gossip about our youth, a little anxious where we shall find the price of supper, if by any chance the courts are not in session, but certain, if they are, both of a feast of argument and of the happy consciousness that on our verdict will depend the fortune, and perhaps the life, of a fellow-citizen. Or, soaring with Trygaeus on the dung-beetle to Zeus, we may learn that on one theme at any rate there is no doubt about the poet's serious conviction. Trygaeus cannot bear to hear the children—

> Asking for bread and calling me papa,
> With not a penny in the house.... (*Peace*, 119–21.)

And so, like an Euripidean hero, he mounts his unsavoury Pegasus and rides to heaven to lodge a protest and demand an explanation.

Aristophanes was probably a youth of about fifteen when war began. For him it meant the exchange of a happy country life, never forgotten, for the narrow quarters, jostling crowds and bitter politics, as well as the alleviating humours of the town. He rebelled against the conflict between Greek and Greek, the atmosphere of mutual suspicion, and the exploitation of the Allies. For his generous Hellenism it would be hard to find a parallel in his time. It is true that in the *Peace* his celebration of the coming days of plenty dwells on the material side, not without grossness. That is in the traditional comic vein. The holy Mysteries themselves suggest to Xanthias the pleasant savour of roast sacrificial pork. But eating, drinking and promiscuous embracing are not the only joys of peace. At the sight of burnished pitchforks and of mattocks gleaming in the sun, Trygaeus breaks into song about his vines and figs and olives and his 'bank of violets beside the well.' He is a statesman and a poet when he prays—

> Put an end to our fights and our feuds and division,
> Till all men shall hail thee, our Lady of Peace,
> Put an end to the whispers of cunning suspicion,
>   And mingle all Greece
> In a cup of good fellowship. Teach us at last
> To forgive one another forgetting the past. (991–8.)

That was written in hope, before the Peace of Nicias. In darker times, when revolution and defeat impended, after the Sicilian disaster, the same spirit inspired Lysistrata's fantastic and audaciously improper but effective bid for peace. She is a living refutation of the doctrine that Athenian women were reduced by their secluded lives to blank stupidity. Weary of being told to stick to her spinning, 'War is the business of men,' tired of the sight of swaggering hoplites, haggling for shrimps in the market-place, cavalry-captains, stowing their purchases in their helmets, Thracians, shaking their javelins and targets at the frightened market-girls, then sitting down to eat their fruit, she is determined that the women shall take charge, and end the war by their own patient method, washing the filthy fleece, picking out burs, unravelling knots, then carding, combing, spinning the good wool, till they can weave a robe of peace for the whole people. Such ideas do not convince a venerable member of the Committee for Public Safety. 'Impertinent' he repeats 'for you to talk—you women, who have nothing to do with war'—

Lys.   Nothing to do with it, wretch! When it is we
            Who bear you sons and send them to the war.
Magistrate. Hush, hush! No bitterness!   (*Lysistr.* 588–90.)

The attacks on Socrates and on Euripides were, in intention, much less serious, though for Socrates the consequences were disastrous. The tone of the *Symposium* suggests that Plato did not think the poet, in whose soul the Graces sought and found a shrine, had meant to do such harm. It was traditional for a comedian to launch his shafts against whatever in the age appeared eccentric, popular, disruptive and potentially ridiculous. Aristophanes disliked the sophists. He connected, not without some sort of justice—he mistook the symptoms for the cause of the disease— the sordid scramble of the politicians and their dupes with the new education, logic-chopping, hair-splitting, phrase-hunting, the fine art of 'making the worse argument prevail.' He idealized the past when healthy minds in healthy bodies were in fashion—

Happy runner, still contend
With your modest-hearted friend
'Neath the olives in the shade
Of the Academic glade,
Garlanded with rushes pale,
Fragrant with sweet galingale,
Fresh with nature's choicest scent,
Innocence and heart's content,
Drenched with blossom which the lime
Sheds to greet the happy time
When the planes are whispering
To the elms the news of spring. (*Clouds*, 1005-8.)

It is a charming picture, and, no doubt, sincere, but it was drawn by a sophisticated artist, as the epilogue shows—

If you do what I tell you, you quite understand,
Your shoulders will swell and your chest will expand,
　Your complexion be glowing,
　Till soon you are growing
A bottom superb, a diminutive tongue,
And a what-you-may-call-it just right and not wrong. (*Ib.* 1009–14.)

The version is less frank than the original. The excellence of the Aristophanic art in fact depends on its amazing combination of good spirits, 'mindless laughter'—of the kind which finds an inexhaustible supply of entertainment in the gross indignities inflicted on our pride by nature's queer contrivances, digestive, reproductive—with the purest poetry, with subtlety of thought, with shrewd and vivid observation. Aristophanes was himself a creature of the new age, and Cratinus made a palpable hit when he described his impudent young rival as a picker up of trifles from the Euripidean store—

'Who are you, sir, pray who?'
Some supersophistical, would-be logistical,
Hypereuripidaristophanistical
　　Spark will remark.　　(*Frag.* 307, Kock.)

For twenty years, from the *Acharnians* to the *Frogs*, he assailed Euripides with joyful and not always over-scrupulous impertinence. But it is a gross mistake to treat such pleasantries too tragically. The flexibility, lucidity and grace of his own style, the quality of his lyrical inspiration, as well as innumerable happy reminiscences, and even many of his sober judgments, reveal him as a pupil, and not merely a student of the tragic poet. From the moment in the *Acharnians*, when Dicaeopolis, in search of tragic gear to make a plea for peace more touching, calls on Euripides

to ask a loan from his theatrical equipment, and is met at the door
by the Euripidean Porter, the poet's friend Cephisophon—

> *Ceph.* Who's there? *Dic.* Euripides at home? *Ceph.* Yes! No!
> *Dic.*   At home and not at home? *Ceph.* Exactly so.
>   His Mind goes out collecting things to say
>   While he lies down upstairs and writes a play— (396–400.)

to the last scene of the *Frogs*, when Dionysus, after the great
critical encounter, can still hesitate between Euripides and
Aeschylus—

> The one I think so clever, and I find
> The other so delightful— (*Frogs*, 1413.)

Aristophanes never for a moment suggested that among the
myriads of tragic scribblers, 'Choirs of chattering swallows, pests
of art,' there was one except Euripides worth pitting against
Aeschylus or Sophocles.

CHAPTER VI

SICILY

I. THE TYRANTS OF SYRACUSE AND ACRAGAS

WE have now to resume the story of Sicily from the death of Gelon which occurred in 478 B.C., two years after the victory of Himera (vol. IV, ch. XI). At that date the island seemed destined to enjoy a period of tranquil prosperity: in his own city the steps by which the ruler of Syracuse had risen to power had been forgotten, the usurping tyrant had been an acknowledged king: outside it his hegemony, resting in part upon a cordial alliance with Theron of Acragas, was, if not welcomed, at least unquestioningly accepted; and the common victory over the Carthaginian invader might seem to have drawn together the Greeks of Sicily into a strong and abiding union. But this was not to be. Such union could only be maintained by the sacrifice of independence, by the subjection of Syracuse to a single ruler, and of the other cities to Syracusan domination. As in Old Greece, so in Sicily, centrifugal tendencies proved too strong. Less than twenty years after Himera, tyrants and 'kings' had disappeared, and the several cities regained their full autonomy.

If we accept the account of the division of power determined upon by Gelon before his death, we may believe that it was intended to secure his dynasty and to prevent friction between its members; but in this his judgment was mistaken. The arrangement for the succession met with no opposition from the citizens of Syracuse; but from the first the real power seems to have been in the hands of Hiero; in fact our principal authority, Diodorus, speaks of Hiero as the successor of Gelon without qualification: a fact which supports the suggestion that Polyzelus was not a partner in the rule of Syracuse, but a vice-gerent at Gela (vol. IV, p. 382). Whatever the position of Polyzelus may have been, it was such that Hiero determined to get rid of him. An opportunity soon presented itself. The people of Sybaris, who since the

Note. The sole continuous ancient authority of importance for this period is Diodorus (XI, 38–92, XII, 8–36), probably following the Sicilian historian Timaeus. The Sicilian odes of Pindar and Bacchylides are valuable as reflecting contemporary opinion before the tradition had been fixed by Timaeus.

overthrow of their city had maintained themselves in their colonies of Laus and Scidrus, were once more hard pressed by Croton, and appealed to Syracuse for help. In response, Hiero enrolled a force, largely consisting of mercenaries, and ordered Polyzelus to proceed to the assistance of the Sybarites. He thought that there would be little chance of a successful resistance to Croton, and that his brother would fall in battle; failing that, the mercenaries might be trusted to see to it that he did not return victorious to Syracuse. Polyzelus, however, suspecting the plot refused the commission, and an open breach ensued between the brothers. According to another less probable account, he accepted it and waged a successful campaign in Italy. In any case he found it necessary to leave Syracuse, and threw himself upon the protection of his father-in-law, Theron of Acragas. The result was that Hiero declared war upon Theron. This bare fact is all that we are told. It seems astonishing that Hiero should have been so ready to attack a state which had so recently been his predecessor's ally; we can only suppose that, with the removal of the barbarian danger, the friendship between Syracuse and Acragas had cooled, and the relation of suspicion and jealousy, normal between Greek states whether in east or west, had re-appeared at the death of Gelon, or before it.

Theron marched into Syracusan territory and the two armies faced one another on the banks of the Gela river. An actual conflict, however, was averted at the last moment through the mediation, it is said, of the poet Simonides, who held an honoured position at the court of Hiero. The nature of his pacifying counsels we do not know, but it is clear that Theron at least had reasons for suspending hostilities. It was probably at this time that he was embarrassed by the rebellion of his cousins, Capys and Hippocrates, while further trouble was threatened from Himera. That city was now under the rule of Theron's son, Thrasydaeus[1], and to escape from his oppression her citizens had turned to the tyrant of Syracuse, promising to surrender to him their city and to join in the attack upon Theron. In the upshot Hiero, whose motives are unknown to us, betrayed the Himeraean plot to Theron, who massacred the ringleaders and made peace with Hiero on the condition of Polyzelus' restoration to favour. It does not appear, however, that Polyzelus hereafter exercised any power at Syracuse; he passes out of the story and certainly died before 466 B.C.

Hiero's intervention in favour of Sybaris may perhaps have

---

[1] For a coin of Himera issued under the rule of Acragas, see Volume of Plates ii, 2, *l*.

had another motive besides the wish to get rid of his brother. From the outset of his reign he showed a desire of making his influence felt amongst the Italiotes. In this sphere he had a competitor in the person of Anaxilas, tyrant of Rhegium and Zancle. The rivalry between Anaxilas and Gelon has been described in an earlier chapter (vol. IV, p. 376); it seems that after the rebuff encountered by the pro-Carthaginian tyrant in the battle of Himera Anaxilas had made some sort of submission to Gelon. For the moment his ambitions had been crushed, but it was not for long. In 477 we hear of him threatening war against Locri, whose maidens, as Pindar sings, owed their deliverance to the generous intervention of the lord of Syracuse. We may conjecture that a stronger motive than the befriending of a weak state was Hiero's determination to cut short the ambitions of a reviving opponent or rebellious vassal. The mere threat of intervention in arms was sufficient. What Hiero especially desired to prevent was the growth of a strong power in southern Italy, especially in the hands of the tyrant of Zancle. The support accorded to the Sybarites may be explained as another instance of the same opposition to the growth of a strong Italiote power.

To the year 475 we may ascribe an act which Hiero reckoned as perhaps his greatest title to fame, the foundation of the city of Aetna[1]. If we knew more of the story, and could more fully understand the motives of the act, we might perhaps appreciate better the praises heaped by the lyric poets upon the founder of Aetna and upon the son, Deinomenes, whom he charged to rule it. The account as we have it from Diodorus is a mere record of wanton cruelty and vaingloriousness. The inhabitants of Naxos and Catana, cities which formed part of the inheritance of Hiero, were driven out and transplanted to Leontini, while the site of an enlarged Catana was assigned to ten thousand new settlers, half drawn from the Peloponnese, half from Syracuse. Thus Aetna was but Catana enlarged and re-peopled. The motives assigned by our historian are, first, the desire to have a city of refuge in emergency—by which presumably is meant a revolt at Syracuse—and, secondly, the hope of posthumous honour. We need not reject these motives, though possibly they were deduced from subsequent events: Hiero was, in fact, honoured as a 'hero' by his new city after his death, and his son and successor did receive timely support therefrom in his hour of need. But what chiefly needs explanation is the treatment of Naxos and Catana. If, as

[1] This foundation is attested and illustrated by a famous coin, now in Brussels; see Volume of Plates ii, 2, n.

seems probable, Hiero's foreign policy was largely dictated by fear or jealousy of Rhegium, it is tempting to conjecture that the two Chalcidian colonies had been, or seemed likely to be, attracted within the sphere of influence of Anaxilas. By removing their inhabitants to Leontini Hiero would have them close under his eye, and at the same time the new settlers would be well placed to keep vigilant and faithful watch upon their founder's rival, the ruler of Zancle and Rhegium.

A year after the foundation of Aetna there occurred an event of far greater significance. The Chalcidian colony of Cumae, the oldest of Greek colonies in the west, was hard pressed by the Etruscans. In the sixth century the power of Etruria had been at its height, but by now it was on the decline (see vol. IV, p. 390). Latium had thrown off her yoke, and the result was that the Etruscans in Campania were now separated from their fellows in the north. By sea, however, they were still powerful and threatened to subdue the Greek settlements on the Bay of Naples. The people of Cumae appealed to Hiero and a squadron was sent to their defence. In a great battle the Etruscans were humbled and Cumae relieved of her fears. The prince of Syracuse had rescued Greece from the burden of slavery to the barbarian, as Pindar proudly claims in lines which set the deed of Hiero side by side with that of Gelon six years earlier[1]. A memorial of the victory is still preserved in the bronze helmet dedicated by Hiero at Olympia, now in the British Museum, on which the inscription tells of 'the spoil won by Hiero, son of Deinomenes, and the Syracusans from the Etruscans before Cumae.' But while defending Greek civilization from barbarian aggression, Hiero was also extending the power of his own city and of his own dynasty. Syracusan influence in this distant region was to be maintained by a colony or garrison on the island of Pithecusa (Ischia) just outside the Bay of Naples. This had previously been the site of an Eretrian settlement, which had been abandoned in consequence of earthquakes and volcanic eruptions. The same cause very shortly terminated its occupation by the Hieronian settlers.

The several attempts made by Syracuse to extend her influence in the Italian peninsula came indeed to nothing, but that they did not escape the notice of rival powers is shown by the events of the following years, 473–471. The Greeks of Tarentum who had for long been extending their territory at the expense of

---

[1] Syracusan coins, presumably struck after his victory, are in type analogous with the *Demareteia* issued after Himera. See Volume of Plates ii, 2, *m*.

their native neighbours, the Iapygians and Messapians, were suddenly faced with strong resistance. A boundary dispute led to plundering raids, and these to regular warfare. The battle that decided the issue in favour of the native peoples is described by Herodotus as involving greater carnage than any battle hitherto fought by Greeks. But from the point of view of Sicilian history the interesting circumstance is that Tarentum was supported, and her defeat shared, by the troops of Rhegium. Anaxilas had died in 476 and Rhegium was now ruled by one Micythus as the guardian of his two young sons. The action of Micythus in thus allying himself with a distant city, though he had nothing to fear from barbarian attacks, calls for explanation, particularly as we learn that the alliance was forced upon the citizens of Rhegium against their will. The probable explanation is that the successor of Anaxilas sought to continue his policy of opposition to the ever-growing power and prestige of Syracuse. Hiero's championship of Locri, his oppression of the Chalcidian cities of Naxos and Catana, and, above all, his recent establishment in the neighbourhood of the Chalcidian colonies on the Bay of Naples, must have strengthened the apprehensions of the Chalcidian city on the Straits of Messina. An alliance with Tarentum seemed to offer the needed support.

In addition to a military pact there was probably a commercial agreement. Since the early sixth century trade-rivalry had played an important part in the history of the Italiote cities, and the progress of Hiero was now menacing the trade interests of Tarentum and Rhegium alike. With the passage through the Straits of Messina liable to be blocked by the vessels of the Syracusan fleet, it was to their joint interest to develop an alternative route for the extensive trade passing between Greece and the shores of Campania, Latium and Etruria, or farther west. The key to the situation lay in the re-settlement, now undertaken by Micythus, of Pyxus on the Tyrrhenian Sea. It cannot be doubted that this is to be brought into connection with the Rhegine-Tarentine Alliance. Tarentum, at whose excellent harbour all ships coming from the east put in, was to give Rhegium a commercial preference by developing or rather re-developing the old trade-route up the Siris valley and across to Pyxus (vol. III, p. 675). This was the return for Rhegine military assistance: the military and commercial pact between Rhegium and Tarentum was thus an answer to the political and commercial hegemony which Syracuse was endeavouring to secure in southern Italy. We have seen already how the plan of Hiero miscarried: equally unsuccessful was the attempt at opposition; for in addition to the severe defeat of the allies by the Iapygians, the new life of Pyxus came soon to an end.

This fact is perhaps to be attributed to the intrigues of Hiero. It is at least certain that the last recorded action of that prince, whose death occurred probably early in 466, was a direct attempt to weaken the power of Rhegium. Sending for the sons of Anaxilas, who were by now of full age, he reminded them of the clemency shown to their father by his own predecessor Gelon after the battle of Himera, and urged them to call upon Micythus for an account of his stewardship and to assume the reins of government for themselves. Micythus, thus challenged, defended his acts as regent with such complete success that the young princes and their friends were fully satisfied and begged him to retain the government. Their request however was refused by the regent, who left Rhegium and ended his days at Tegea in Arcadia[1]. The sons of Anaxilas ruled Rhegium and Zancle until 461–460, when they were expelled by a democratic revolt. The story plainly reveals an effort on the part of Hiero, at least partially successful, to weaken the position of Rhegium by getting rid of the able and experienced Micythus and substituting the young princes, whom he counted upon over-reaching or bending to his own designs. But, as has been said, his own death ensued after a few months.

Except for this intrigue our record of Hiero's actions between the battle of Cumae and his death is practically a blank. Of the general character of his reign we have two sharply contrasted though not necessarily contradictory pictures: the one from the court poets, Pindar and Bacchylides, the other preserved by Diodorus. Hiero in fact appears now as an Augustus, now as a Tiberius. On the one side is the prince 'kind of heart to his citizens, envying not the good, wondrous to strangers,' 'plucking the topmost fruits from every tree of excellence,' 'holding the scales of Justice in even poise,' 'the favourite of the gods, the lover of horses, the warrior who bears the sceptre of Justice-guarding Zeus, and has fellowship with the Muses of violet locks.' On the other side is the crafty and suspicious despot with his swarms of spies, propping up his throne by the aid of mercenary hirelings, feared and hated. Two generations later, it is Hiero that is taken

---

[1] This is the account given by Diodorus (XI, 66), possibly after Timaeus; it seems open to suspicion, and Herodotus (VII, 170) says that Micythus was banished.

by Xenophon to sit for his portrait of the typical evil tyrant. It may be that the account repeated in Diodorus blackens him unduly, but it has been justly observed that even amongst the praises heaped by Pindar upon the munificent patron of the Muses and the Stadium there runs an undercurrent of warning, such as the hint that Croesus is a better model for tyrants than Phalaris. But undoubtedly Hiero did good service to Greece and to the world in fostering the new literature of lyric; nor should it pass unmentioned that the founder of Greek Comedy won kindly welcome at his court, and the greatest master of Greek Tragedy not only saw acted at Syracuse his drama portraying Greece triumphant over Persia, but also composed a play whose title is plainly a tribute of honour to the founder of Aetna. In partial defence of Hiero's tyranny must be set the fact that for the last seven years of his life he suffered from a painful disease.

Meanwhile at Acragas Theron had reigned until his death in 472 B.C. In these eight years after Himera, Acragas had flourished and prospered exceedingly. The large number of Carthaginian prisoners that fell to her share had given an impulse to the adorning of the city with magnificent temples, amongst which that of Zeus is said to have been the largest in European Hellas. We hear also of the construction of water-courses, of a huge artificial fishpond, and an extensive drainage system. Moreover it is very probable that it was in these years that the circuit of the walls was widened, as part of the scheme of temple-building. Of Theron, unlike Hiero, the voices of history and of poetry unite in a common strain of praise. Diodorus tells us in general terms that he was a good ruler, thoroughly popular with his citizens, who followed the examples of the Syracusans at the death of Gelon by according him the worship of a hero. The honour was well deserved, for it has been justly said that if Gelon was the second founder of Syracuse, Theron was equally the second founder of Acragas. Hiero too was accorded the same honour, not however at Syracuse, but at Aetna, the city of his foundation and the place of his death.

II. THE FALL OF THE TYRANTS

The successors of Theron and of Hiero alike failed to maintain their power for more than a few months. Of Thrasydaeus, son of Theron, we have seen something as tyrant of Himera: as ruler of Acragas he displays all the regular characteristics of the 'bad' tyrant; lawless, cruel and arbitrary, hated and distrusted, he relies for support on large mercenary forces. We are told that these, with a leavening of citizen troops from Acragas and Himera, amounted to 20,000 horse and foot. It was perhaps for no better reason than a belief that his position would be strengthened by successful military adventure that Thrasydaeus entered upon a war with Syracuse; if there was any better reason, we are not told it. Hiero, however, was more than ready for him, and a battle ensued which, according to Diodorus, established a record for carnage as between Greek and fellow Greek: but the Syracusan loss was only half that of their enemies. For Thrasydaeus it meant the end of his career not merely at Acragas and Himera, but in the whole island. He fled to Megara in old Greece, where he was condemned to death and executed: so much our brief record tells us and no more. Such was the end of tyranny at Acragas, which now established a democratic government, and made peace with Hiero, receiving, we may suppose, the status of a quasi-independent ally; for it is hardly probable that the ruler of Syracuse would demand no sort of requital for an unprovoked attack. Himera, too, which was bound to Acragas only through subjection to a common master, regained its freedom.

At Syracuse the citizens found the recovery of liberty a harder task. On Hiero's death, early in 466 B.C., the power passed into the hands of the youngest and only surviving brother, Thrasybulus. The character of his rule is described in precisely the same terms as that of Thrasydaeus. It appears, however, to have been challenged from the outset. The son of Gelon was now growing, or grown, to manhood, and a movement in his favour was initiated by certain members of the ruling house who are unnamed, but may probably be identified as Chromius and Aristonoüs, brothers-in-law of Gelon appointed by him as guardians of the young prince. But their revolt was soon merged in a wider movement, a general rising against tyranny itself. The bid for freedom was bold and by no means certain of success. The tyrant could depend not only on his mercenaries but also upon the citizens of Aetna, who doubtless felt their fortunes bound up with the prosperity of their founder's dynasty. He displayed promptness by occupying the fortified parts of Syracuse, the 'island' of Ortygia and Achradina to the north. The citizens had no choice but to establish a position in the quarter called Tycha, to the west of Achradina, of which we now hear for the first time. Help was sought in all possible directions, and it was not refused. From Gela, Acragas, Himera and Selinus came contingents of horse and foot, so that the forces of the liberators outnumbered the 15,000 troops disposed of by the tyrant. Warships too were provided by some of the allies, for Thrasybulus must be defeated on sea as well as on land. It was in fact on sea that the first conflict took place, and Thrasybulus was defeated with heavy loss. A sally from Achradina led to an equally decisive defeat on land. We hear that, before the actual fighting began, the tyrant had been abandoned by his allies and had to trust to his mercenaries alone. The reference to allies would seem to mean that the men of Aetna proved faithless in the end. After his second defeat Thrasybulus capitulated, and was permitted to withdraw to Locri, where he ended his days.

Thus in 466 fell the house of the Deinomenidae. Its fall is attributed by Diodorus to the evil character of its last representative, but in truth the progressive deterioration of Syracusan tyranny, as shown in the succession of the three Deinomenid brothers, is a regular feature in Greek history. The rule of the first tyrant is tolerated and even welcomed because it frees the mass of citizens from oligarchical oppression, or from foreign menace. But with his successor the normal Greek hatred of autocracy revives and the tyrant has to base his rule on fear and force: it is probable that Thrasybulus could not, even with the best intentions, have won the goodwill accorded to Gelon. In the *Politics* of Aristotle (vɪɪɪ (v) 12, 1315 b) the tyranny at Syracuse, which is reckoned as having lasted eighteen years, is mentioned as an example of duration beyond the ordinary.

The fall of Thrasybulus is noted by Diodorus as marking the beginning of a period of freedom and renewed prosperity for Sicily in general: and though for some years longer tyranny or kingship continued both at Zancle and at Aetna, all the cities which had been subject to Syracuse now became free and independent. At Syracuse itself the new constitution was inaugurated with great enthusiasm: annual games and sacrifices were instituted on the day that marked the tyrant's fall. Nevertheless within a very few years further troubles arose. Amongst the citizen body there were left some seven thousand of the ten thousand foreign mercenaries settled there by Gelon, and not unnaturally their presence excited the distrust and suspicion of the older citizens; if Syracuse were to be made safe for democracy, these quasi-aliens must be at least debarred from holding magistracies. A resolution to this effect was therefore passed. Whether this measure was adopted simultaneously with the democratic revolution in 466, or not till three years later, is not clear; in any case it was in 463 that the excluded mercenaries decided on an appeal to force. The situation of a few years earlier was now repeated. The mercenaries seized Ortygia and Achradina as Thrasybulus had done; the citizens occupied Tycha and the high ground in the direction of what was afterwards known as Epipolae: a wall was built opposite the wall of Achradina which cut off the mercenaries from the interior. A sea-fight was fought in which the citizens gained the day, but by land the attempts to drive the mercenaries from their positions failed owing to their superior military skill. In the end hunger compelled them to risk a battle outside their fortifications: it was a desperate struggle, but at last the citizens proved victorious. Of the subsequent political settlement we are told nothing, but it may be assumed that Syracuse was troubled by the presence of these aliens no longer: the aftermath of tyranny was swept away and democracy was left with a clear field.

In the other cities of Sicily a similar re-settlement occurred at or about the same time. At Zancle the rule of the sons of Anaxilas came to an end in 461–60 B.C., and with it her political union with Rhegium. At Acragas, Gela and Himera the foreign elements, whether mercenaries from abroad or Siceliotes transplanted by the tyrants from other cities, were removed. At Acragas and Gela at least, force was required for their removal; on this point we are fortunately able to supplement the account of Diodorus from a recently discovered papyrus (*Ox. Pap.* iv, 665). The mercenaries of Gela took refuge at two places in the vicinity, Omphace and Cacyrum, those of Acragas at Heraclea Minoa. In the struggles which ensued both cities obtained the aid of Syracusan troops. Finally by common agreement the several cities took back the exiles into their citizen bodies, and settled the mercenaries all together in the territory of Zancle, which from this time comes to be regularly called by the name of Messana given to it by Anaxilas. The choice of Messana for this settlement was a happy one, for the mixed population which had existed there since 486 would have less distaste for this new admixture than any other city in the island. It is interesting to find that on occasion the Siceliotes could thus act together for the common interest: and it may be supposed that Syracuse took the lead in a measure which is explicitly attributed to the general desire to avoid further conflicts.

Among the cities now re-settled was Catana, the Aetna of Hiero's foundation, where Hiero's son Deinomenes probably still ruled. The story of its re-settlement is interesting, more particularly because a part was played therein by the Sicels. It was of course at the expense of the natives of the island that Hiero had enlarged the territory of Catana before handing it over to its new inhabitants. No resistance was offered at that time, but now in 461 there was a favourable opportunity at hand and a man of enterprise to seize it. The overthrow of Deinomenid rule at Aetna was desired alike by Ducetius the Sicel leader and by the Syracusans, and the work was done jointly. The Hieronian settlers were driven out, and established themselves in the Sicel town of Inessa, ten miles distant and close under the mountain; and with them they took the name of their city, so that Inessa becomes Aetna and Aetna becomes Catana once again, its old inhabitants returning from their exile at Leontini[1]. The story however is in some points obscure or incomplete. We hear of a partition of lands between the Syracusans and their Sicel allies: if correct, this can only refer to the additional territory by which Catana had been enlarged for Hiero's foundation, for it must be presumed that the original site of Catana was restored intact to the returned exiles: it is quite possible that the sacrifice of some Sicel territory was the price which Ducetius had to pay for Syracusan help. A similar difficulty arises in regard to the occupation of Sicel Inessa by the men whom Sicels had helped to expel from Aetna: we can hardly believe that Ducetius welcomed this arrangement, and it seems clear that of the fruits of the joint victory the greater part went to Greeks and not to Sicels—a circumstance which may help to account for the subsequent career of Ducetius.

Before we come to the story of that career there is one further act of re-settlement to be recorded, namely the restoration of Camarina. It will be remembered that since its original foundation in 599 B.C. Camarina had been destroyed by its Syracusan founders as punishment for its revolt, had then been re-established by Hippocrates, and again wiped out by Gelon, who transported its inhabitants to swell the population of his enlarged Syracuse (vol. IV, pp. 364, 369, 373). The present restoration was the work of the citizens of Gela, but in this its third lease of life neither Gela nor Syracuse attempted to violate its political independence. Within a few years of its restoration an Olympic victory won by the son of a citizen of Camarina gave Pindar, or more probably an imitator of Pindar, the opportunity of celebrating in lyric song the reviving aspirations of the new-built city.

III. THE SICEL REACTION

For the next twenty years our interest is centred in an enterprise of a different nature from any that we have hitherto had to record. It is a determined effort made by the Sicel communities of the

---

[1] The coins of Aetna are now replaced by a new issue bearing the legend KATANAION, see Volume of Plates ii, 2, o.

island to establish political domination over the Greeks, an effort which seems to have come very near success. That this was the aim of Ducetius, there can be no reasonable doubt; but if it was not less than this, it was also not more. There was no question of exterminating Greek civilization, as there had been, and as there was to be again, half a century later, in the Carthaginian invasion. If the Sicels had realized their aspirations, the Greeks would have lost political freedom but Greek culture would have continued to develop under Sicel protection. For by this time the native communities must have gone far in the direction of Hellenization, which in another hundred years was complete. The whole career of Ducetius proves that a strong national sense animated the Sicel tribes against the Greek enemy: yet at the same time the Greeks were, as has been justly said, not merely their enemies, they were also their masters and their models: and on the other side the dealings of the Greeks with Ducetius prove that they were far from thinking of the Sicels as barbarians. Hence the attitude and aim of Ducetius have not unfairly been compared to those of Philip of Macedon.

It was in 459 B.C. that Ducetius began his work of welding together the separate Sicel communities into a political federation, and it was not until 453 that that work was finished. Of the way in which it was done we know hardly anything. Force was sometimes necessary, as in the case of the powerful town of Morgantina, and one place, Hybla, the so-called Galeatic Hybla south of Mount Aetna, stood aloof to the end. The centre of Ducetius' power was at first at Menaenum or Menae, a stronghold situated high on a peak at the northern end of the Heraean range of mountains, some thirty miles west of Leontini. Later he abandoned this site in favour of one in the plain below, where he founded Palice, so called from its proximity to the sanctuary of the divine Palici, the ancient protectors of the Sicel folk. This act shows that Ducetius was not insensible to the importance of attaching religious sentiment to his political schemes. As to the position of Ducetius himself it is impossible to speak with certainty, for our sole authority, Diodorus, has not cared to explain it: it may be that he ruled as king at Menaenum and Palice, while acting as President of the Sicel confederation. But we have no information as to Sicel political institutions at any period. In any case the essential point is clear, that for some years Ducetius was the acknowledged leader of practically the whole Sicel population.

That he attained this position unmolested by the Greek states is to be attributed to the internal troubles in which they became

involved during these years. It is of Syracuse alone that we have
any details. The compressed narrative of Diodorus (xi, 86–7)
sets all the events that follow under a single year, 454–3, but it is
impossible that this can be correct, and we shall be fairly safe in
supposing them to cover about the same six years as those in which
Ducetius was consolidating his position. In part, the troubles
of these years were the after effects of tyranny. Syracuse had
expelled her tyrants, she had expelled the mercenaries that supported the tyrants, but not all traces of the tyranny were thereby
effaced. Disputes arose in particular about the tenure of land,
much of which had no doubt been confiscated or changed hands
under the tyranny: its redistribution could hardly be effected
without raising grievances. Another source of difficulty lay in
the register of citizens: for the rule restricting citizenship to the
pre-Gelonian inhabitants must have been found difficult or impossible to apply in all strictness, and doubtful cases must have
been numerous. Party distinctions began to emerge, and we seem
dimly to descry the lines of cleavage familiar to the Greek
commonwealths, the 'respectable' as Diodorus sympathetically
calls them, that is to say the wealthy and conservative classes,
ranged against the 'revolutionary' poor. It is hardly surprising
that in these circumstances a candidate for tyranny appeared in
the person of one Tyndarion or Tyndarides. He is described in
conventional terms as a bold demagogue surrounding himself
with the inevitable bodyguard. After his trial and condemnation
to death an attempt was made by his followers to rescue him, and
a riot occurred which led to the execution, or perhaps the lynching,
of the revolutionaries.

After Tyndarion other would-be tyrants arose, either in
reality or in the imagination of the conservatives, and to safeguard
the constitution a measure was introduced directly copied from
Athenian ostracism (vol. iv, p. 151). By the law of *petalism*,
so-called because the olive-leaf took the place of the potsherd, it
was enacted that the citizen assembly could pronounce a decree of
banishment for five years against any one whose power they
deemed excessive. So far as we know, petalism could be applied
without restriction whenever the majority of the assembly desired
it, and nothing beyond a bare majority was required either in the
vote for its application or in the selection of the individual to be
exiled. Fortunately this amazingly crude and ill-considered
imitation of ostracism, which, even with the restrictions limiting
it at Athens, was oppressive enough, lasted only for a short time:
it is peculiarly vexatious that the negligence of Diodorus in

matters of chronology prevents us from knowing its duration more exactly, but from his account it would seem to have been a question of years rather than months. Its consequences were what might be expected; men of ability and character were deterred from public life, and political influence became the monopoly of unprincipled adventurers and glib demagogues. The cure in fact had but aggravated the disease: the old disorders and dissensions continued and increased, until the law was repealed.

It is to be supposed that other cities as well as Syracuse experienced similar troubles. At Acragas the democracy established after the expulsion of Thrasydaeus had found an ardent supporter in one of that city's most famous sons, Empedocles. Embedded amongst the mass of legend which became attached to his name we find a few words of serious historical import. It appears that during the first years of the city's freedom oligarchical tendencies had made themselves felt: the Council of the Thousand, which is evidently the administrative body, had become a preserve of the wealthy and acted in the interests of a class. This Council Empedocles, by means unknown to us, reconstituted in the interests of the democrats. For some years the reformer exercised great influence on the politics of Acragas and we are even told that he refused an offer of kingship. But he had made enemies, and ultimately was forced to leave the city, perhaps by a formal decree of banishment. It is most likely that this happened in 461 when the old citizens came back to Acragas as to other places: for their numbers would strengthen the opposition to the advanced democracy and its champion. What is certain is that Empedocles spent a considerable part of his life in exile, that the party opposed to him were able to prevent his return, and that he died in the Peloponnese about 436.

In addition to her internal troubles, the attention of Syracuse was diverted from the doings of Ducetius by an external menace. The Etruscans who had had twenty years to recover from their defeat at Cumae, were in 453 infesting Sicilian waters with their pirate galleys. A squadron was sent to the Etruscan coast under Phayllus, who however did nothing beyond carrying out a raid on the island of Aethalia (Elba): on his return he was condemned to exile on the ground of accepting a bribe from the enemy. A second expedition under Apelles raided Corsica, then an Etruscan possession, and occupied Elba, bringing back a large amount of spoil and a number of prisoners. The Etruscans were quieted, but no permanent occupation of Elba was maintained. In this same year 453 a war broke out in the west of Sicily, quite unconnected with events in the east of the island, except in so far as any troubles in which Greek states were involved may be deemed to have favoured Ducetius. The record of this war is so confused that we cannot be absolutely certain who the combatants were, but it was probably fought between Selinus and Elymian Segesta, cities which we shall find again at variance in 416 B.C., and it arose out of a boundary dispute. It seems that Segesta was supported by a neighbouring Elymian town, Halicyae, but that the victory went to Selinus: for an inscription of about this date is extant which records a victory of Selinus over some unnamed enemy. But the interesting point is that Sicilian cities are now for the first time brought into political connection with Athens. In 453 the Athenian Assembly received an embassy from Segesta which resulted in a treaty between Athens, Segesta and Halicyae (*I.G.*[2] 1, 19–20). Its terms are unknown. If, as seems probable, military aid against Selinus was asked for, it was certainly refused: Athens was in no position to accede to such a request, weakened as she was by the recent disaster in Egypt (p. 84). We may however see in this treaty both a continuation by Pericles of that policy of developing Athenian connections, political and commercial, with the West which had been foreshadowed by Themistocles, and also the first step on the road that was to lead to Athens' great disaster forty years later (chap. x).

The work of union completed, Ducetius began his greater task in 451 B.C. by a successful attack on Aetna, the formerly Sicel Inessa. He captured the town and slew by craft its ruler, whom we may suppose to have been Deinomenes, son of Hiero. He next invaded Acragantine territory, and besieged and captured a fort called Motyum. These successes alarmed Syracuse, which sent troops to the support of Acragas. The allies however were defeated in a pitched battle. During the winter of 451 operations were suspended and the Syracusan commander Bolcon was executed on a charge of treachery during the campaign. Early in the summer of 450 a new and strong force was sent from Syracuse, and a second battle ensued at an unidentified spot called Noae in which the Syracusans, this time unsupported, utterly defeated the Sicels. At about the same time the Acragantines recovered Motyum by an assault. A group set up by Acragas at Olympia described by the traveller Pausanias (v, 25. 5), representing boys stretching out their hands in prayer, probably commemorates the recovery of this fort. Thus in less than a year the success of Ducetius had been completely reversed. Those of his troops who survived the battle took refuge for the most part in various Sicel strongholds: a few remained to share the fortunes of their leader, but even these he had reason to suspect of plotting against his life. In his extremity Ducetius took the bold step of throwing himself on the mercy of the Syracusans. Riding across country by night, he entered Syracuse before day-break and threw himself down a solitary suppliant at the city's altars.

The scene which followed in the assembly has seized the imagination of Diodorus, and recalls to us a more famous debate to be held a quarter of a century later in the Assembly of Athens (p. 217 *sq.*). But when Cleon and Diodotus come to plead for and against the extremity of punishment for conquered Mytilene it is a question of justice against expediency: here at Syracuse the city's honour is involved, for her defeated enemy is a suppliant at the altar of her gods. The appeal to generosity and religious scruples prevailed, and the cry of 'Save the Suppliant' rang out on all sides. It was decided that Ducetius should be sent to Corinth, and a grant for his maintenance there was allotted from the Syracusan treasury. Four years later he returned to Sicily, and the circumstances of his return demand some discussion, for the narrative of our single authority again presents difficulties. One point however at least is clear: in returning to Sicily about 445 Ducetius violated a pledge given to Syracuse on his departure, and this fact is irreconcilable with the supposition that it was with the permission or connivance of Syracuse that he came back. In the next place the return of Ducetius was in some way connected with a dispute between Syracuse and Acragas which led to a declaration of war by the latter city in this same year. The grievance felt by Acragas is said to be, not that the Syracusans had suffered the common enemy to return, but that they had let him escape without consulting her. This in itself need not imply that the quarrel between the two cities broke out before the return of Ducetius: it might mean that Acragas complained that his return had been made possible by the fact that Syracuse had previously let him go. Nevertheless it is likely that Ducetius would choose for his return a time when the minimum of opposition would confront him; in other words, a time when the two cities whom he had chiefly to fear were in conflict with each other. For these reasons it seems probable that the declaration of war by Acragas upon Syracuse occurred shortly before Ducetius set foot again in Sicily, and that he saw in that war a favourable opportunity for renewing his designs. It has indeed been argued that he would not have been permitted to leave Corinth with a large company of followers unless the authorities there were assured that Syracuse approved his doing so. But we do not know that it was from Corinth that he sailed: the narrative is quite compatible with the supposition that he remained at Corinth not for four years but for as many months.

The ostensible project of the Sicel prince was to found in obedience to an oracle a settlement in the district on the north coast known as Cale Acte, the district to which Scythes of Zancle had lured the unfortunate Samian emigrants in 494 (vol. IV, p. 367 *sq*.). The colonists consisted partly of Greeks brought by the founder from the mother-country, partly of Sicels from the domain of a neighbouring chief, Archonides of Herbita. There can be little doubt that the foundation of this new colony was regarded by Ducetius simply as a step towards the recovery of his hegemony over the Sicels, and that he intended in due time once again to try conclusions with the dominant Greek powers in the island. Nevertheless it may well be that his sense of racial antagonism had been somewhat weakened during his four years' sojourn in Greece: he may have aimed now rather at personal leadership of Sicels and Greeks alike rather than at the establishment of a supremacy of Sicel over Greek: such at least is a natural inference from the mixed population of his colony, and perhaps also from the Greek name of his chief ally, Archonides. Whatever may be the precise nature of his plans they were cut short by death in 440 or 439 B.C.

Meanwhile Cale Acte had flourished, and that seemingly without opposition: a remarkable fact, for the explanation of which we are driven to conjecture. That Acragas should have offered no opposition is natural enough, for she had been decisively defeated by Syracuse and was consequently weakened: other cities—in particular Himera and Messana—may not have felt their interests threatened: but the inaction of Syracuse is difficult to explain, especially as she entered upon a fresh Sicel war immediately after Ducetius' death. It looks as if there were some agreement between Ducetius and Syracuse, entered into after the defeat of Acragas—perhaps an undertaking to enlist Sicel aid in keeping Acragas quiet. Moreover the action of Ducetius' ally, Archonides of Herbita, has to be taken into account. In the war between Syracuse and Acragas we are told that the Sicel cities were engaged, some on one side, some on the other. If we may assume that Archonides supported Syracuse, it would help to explain why Syracuse tolerated the existence of the colony which Archonides helped to establish. The death of Ducetius in some way changed the situation, for in 439 we hear that Syracuse, which had already brought all the other Sicel cities under her subjection, proceeded to reduce the most important of them all. This city appears in the text of Diodorus (XII, 29) as Trinacia, but no such place is elsewhere heard of, and from the description given it is highly probable that Palice is meant. Syracuse had suspicions that Palice, the former capital of Ducetius, had inherited his plans for hegemony of the Sicels: and after a desperate resistance offered by the men of Palice, unsupported by allies, she was conquered and destroyed. This was the end of Sicel resistance to the Greeks: but the statement of Diodorus that the whole body of Sicels had now become subject to Syracuse is certainly untrue; the evidence of Thucydides[1] shows that Syracusan dominion was confined to the more low-lying districts of the middle and lower Symaethus valley, whereas the Sicels of the northern districts, the upper Symaethus valley and the Nebrodian mountains, never lost their independence.

IV. SYRACUSAN HEGEMONY

The defeat of Acragas in 445 B.C. is taken by Diodorus as marking the definite establishment of Syracusan hegemony in Sicily, a hegemony acknowledged by all the other cities. And it is probable that Diodorus is right in saying that Syracuse aimed now, as she had perhaps before aimed under Hippocrates and Gelon, at something more than hegemony. The measures adopted in 439 included the building of 100 new triremes, the doubling of the cavalry, and the reorganization of the infantry: and they were measures which aroused the apprehensions of other Sicilian cities, especially the Chalcidian, and which led indirectly to the more active intervention of Athens in Sicilian affairs. We have seen that in 453 Athens made a treaty with Segesta and Halicyae; there is no reason to suppose that her motive in doing so was fear of Syracuse, but, once involved in political connections with Sicilian cities, she could not remain indifferent to the advance of the most powerful amongst them. The policy adopted by Pericles was to support the Chalcidian cities, Rhegium and Leontini, which were most hostile to Syracuse and which alone were in a position to check Syracusan aggression. We do not know the precise date of the treaties made by Athens with these two cities; but two inscriptions of the year 433 record their renewal[2], and we may suppose that they were then not less than

[1] VI, 88.

[2] W. Bauer, *Epigraphisches aus dem Athener National Museum* (Klio xv, pp. 188 *sqq.*) has shown that the upper halves of the extant inscriptions

ten years old. It is thus at least probable that Athens and the Chalcidian cities took steps to protect their joint interests in the island very shortly after Syracuse had attained her dominant position by the defeat of Acragas in 445. For Athens the alliances were destined to have momentous consequences in years to come; but a policy of aggression in Sicily was not contemplated by Pericles and was only adopted by Athens after his death. The story of the active intervention of Athens in Sicily, which begins in 427, is bound up with that of the Peloponnesian War, and will be reserved for a later chapter (see below, pp. 222 *sqq.*).

If the date above suggested for the Athenian alliances with Rhegium and Leontini is correct, they may be brought into connection with another act of Athenian policy in the West, the foundation of Thurii on the site of Sybaris in 443. The history of southern Italy is always bound up more or less closely with that of Sicily; and although the settlement of Thurii was not, so far as we know, in any sense a move against Syracuse, yet in so far as it turned the attention of Athens towards western waters it was a step towards the expedition of 415; and we shall find Thurii supporting Athens at the siege of Syracuse, though not in the operations of 427–4 B.C. The details of the settlement will be given elsewhere (p. 169): what needs to be mentioned here is that Syracuse must have felt a potential menace in the establishment of a city, Panhellenic indeed in population, but under Athenian auspices. The intention of Pericles was plainly not aggressive: we need attribute to him no more than the desire to improve Athenian trade facilities in the West and to increase Athenian prestige. But this could hardly be appreciated at Syracuse, where the event would naturally be viewed in relation to the support given by Athens to the Chalcidian cities.

Although the record of Sicilian history from 466 to 439 is mainly one of wars and civil disturbances, yet the period is one of continued prosperity, and indeed this holds good of the years which follow down to the second Carthaginian invasion in 406. The cities which the tyrants had enriched and adorned with splendid buildings continued, as free republics, in the paths marked out for them by the tyrants. At Acragas, the line of temples along the southern wall, begun under Theron, was still in course of completion when the Carthaginian invader returned. It is of this

(*I.G.*[2] 1, 51, 52), which fix their date at 433 B.C., were superimposed by erasure of an earlier incision, *i.e.* that the treaties were not first made, but only renewed, in 433.

city's wealth and splendour that we hear most in this period, owing to the fact that she was destined to be sacked hereafter by the barbarians, but the general picture may be taken as applying to the other cities also, in varying degrees. It is a picture of wealth and luxury, but not of vice or moral decadence: the bounty and liberality of some of the citizens of Acragas became proverbial, and her culture is attested by the numerous pictures and statues in the possession of private individuals which were carried off later as spoil by the invaders. The main source of her prosperity was her trade with Carthage, to which she exported the fruits of the vine and the olive. At Selinus the famous sculptures of her temples show to how high a point Greek art was developed even in one of the less important of the Sicilian cities (vol. iv, p. 593). It was in Sicily too that the art of rhetoric, of such vast importance both in the literary and political history of the Greek peoples, had its first beginnings. Initiated by Corax and Tisias of Syracuse in the early days of Syracusan democracy, when the ability to argue a case with force and persuasion was coming to be a practical necessity in the assembly and the law-court, it was carried on by one of the most famous of Greek teachers, Gorgias of Leontini, whom we shall meet later pleading his city's cause at Athens (see below, p. 223). It is perhaps enough to say of Gorgias here that he, more than any other, inspired the prose of Thucydides. Another famous Sophist,—Gorgias is generally classed amongst the Sophists, though he himself disclaimed the title—Hippias of Elis, is said to have visited Sicily, and to have won fame and profit in a place where we might hardly have looked to find such appreciation of the new learning, the Sicel town of Inycum[1]. The statement, which there is no reason to doubt, shows as much as any single fact could show, how highly developed was the intellectual life of Sicily in the middle of the fifth century, and how rapidly the Sicels were becoming assimilated to the Greeks.

[1] Plato, *Hippias Major*, 282 D–E.

CHAPTER VII

THE BREAKDOWN OF THE THIRTY YEARS PEACE B.C. 445–431

I. THE FIRST YEARS OF PEACE

THE Thirty Years Peace was for Athens a sign of exhaustion. Pericles, who had come to control Athenian foreign policy, recognized that it was no longer possible to maintain both her Empire overseas and her more recent acquisitions in Greece proper. The population of Attica was not large enough to provide a force which could face the Peloponnesian League and Boeotia in the field, and, before the days of mercenary armies, the treasures on the Acropolis could not make good this deficiency. The contingents of the Empire could not be at once so strong as to be useful and so weak as not to be dangerous. By sea Athens was invincible, but her fleets could not defend Megara or Troezen or Achaea. Pericles decided to hold no more for Athens than could be held with safety. Her one vital interest in Greece proper lay in Euboea, and the Euboeans, who had dared to bell the cat, were abandoned by Sparta to Athenian vengeance. The lands of Hestiaea were confiscated to provide farms for a garrison of Athenian cleruchs, and Chalcis was bound to Athens in naked subjection. The Thirty Years Peace recognized the Athenian Empire and bound the Peloponnesians not to interfere on behalf of the states scheduled as the allies of Athens. Greece, in fact, returned to the old dualism: Athens and her Empire predominant by sea, Sparta and her allies predominant by land. With Sparta unambitious by nature and Athens half-cured of ambition by adversity, there was a chance that the Thirty Years Peace would prove to deserve its name.

Sparta might well be content, for politically she had gained all that it was worth her while to gain. What she had missed was the chance to demonstrate the power of her military machine in a great battle which would have won for her no more than she

Note. The continuous ancient sources of the narrative of this chapter are Thucydides I, 115–17, 23–88, 118–46; II, 1–6, and the portions of Diodorus XII, 9–42 which refer to Greek affairs. These latter are mainly derived from Ephorus. Plutarch, *Pericles*, supplies some independent information. For further details, especially of inscriptions, see the Bibliography.

gained without it, and would have weakened her army, already none too large to maintain the Spartan régime at home. For indeed the Spartan army was becoming something which her enemies dared not face and Sparta dared not use. It is true that the military party overwhelmed with reproaches the politic king Pleistoanax and drove him into exile, but his policy was not reversed. Equally at Athens Pericles had to face disappointment and disillusionment, but, after all, a great defeat on land had been averted, and Athens seemed secured in an empire which was as splendid as it was profitable.

The revenues of the Empire supplied far more than was enough to maintain a fleet to police the Aegean and conserve Athenian naval skill, and the Peace left Athens free to exact the full payment of the tribute by the pressure of her naval strength. To this temptation the Athenians fell. They had saved and protected the Greeks of Asia Minor and of the Aegean and now they claimed their reward. Pericles believed that the spiritual greatness of Athens was rooted in her political power, and the tough imperial conscience of a profit-sharing democracy was untroubled by the thought that it was sacrificing the virtue of honesty to teach the Allies the virtue of gratitude. The full tribute was extorted and spent, in part, on great buildings which made Athens splendid and brought work and wages to many Athenians.

It is true that this policy did not go unchallenged. In 447 B.C. the Athenians had begun to build the Parthenon, the visible symbol of their greatness, and before the end of 444 their own treasures were giving out. It was therefore proposed to divert to this purpose the balance accumulated or accruing from the tribute of the Allies[1]. The aristocratic or oligarchical opponents of Pericles could not let this pass without a struggle. To do so was to betray their own principles and, still more, their fellow-aristocrats throughout the Athenian Empire, who were ill-content to bear the burden of tribute to a state which everywhere upheld their democratic enemies. So their leader Thucydides son of Melesias, who was, at the least, an adroit party-manager, attacked the proposal on high grounds of principle. The tribute was paid to defend the cities from Persia; Athens had no moral right to take it 'to deck herself like a courtezan with thousand-talent temples.' Pericles was well able to supply whatever answer was needed, and was content to stake his career against that of his

---

[1] See p. 177. For the view that only the quota $(\frac{1}{60})$ of the tribute was spent on the Parthenon, as on the Propylaea, see Dinsmoor, *A.J.A.* XVII, 1913, p. 53, XXV, 1921, p. 233.

rival on such an issue. In February 443 the Athenians voted which of the two leaders they could spare. Thucydides was ostracized and Pericles remained the autocratic leader of the Athenian democracy[1].

The building of the Parthenon went on apace, until after nine years it was ready to receive the gold and ivory statue of the goddess, the masterpiece of Pheidias; and, before the temple sculptures were finished, the Athenians began to build the Propylaea, which were not completed when the Peloponnesian War broke upon Athens. The sanctuary for the mysteries at Eleusis, which the Persians had destroyed, was rebuilt on a grander scale by the skill of Ictinus, the architect of the Parthenon. Athens became daily more splendid and also more nearly what Pericles called it, 'the School of Hellas.' A new building, the Odeum, served the needs of musical festivals (pp. 448 *sqq.*). Not less imposing in their way were the works which added to the military strength of the city. A third Long Wall was built parallel with the northernmost of the two which had existed since 457 (p. 80). This inner wall made the whole system more defensible and the southern wall to Phalerum was abandoned. At the Piraeus the war-harbours were organized and equipped, and the triremes, the truest servants of Athena, were housed in fine new sheds where they lay against the day of battle. Aristophanes has described the bustle of life which filled the dockyards when the word went out to launch the squadrons. At the same time the mercantile harbour was improved to receive the increasing volume of Athenian trade, and the Piraeus itself was laid out with the ordered symmetry of a colony, by the town-planning expert Hippodamus of Miletus (p. 18 *sq.*, p. 463). All this involved vast outlay but most of it had been completed within ten years of the Peace. From that time onwards, as will be seen later, Pericles turned his energies to the building up of a great war reserve fund.

The vigour of Athens may well have aroused the admiration and possibly the envy of her neighbours. Her favour was well worth purchasing. As early as 445–4 B.C. the Libyan prince Psammetichus, perhaps at the request of the Athenian government, sent a gift of some 45,000 bushels of corn to be distributed among the citizens. His object may have been not only political, to conciliate Athenian favour against a possible attack by Persia, but also commercial, to secure a larger market at Athens for Egyptian corn. So striking an example of the value of Athenian citizenship led to the retrospective enforcement of the law passed in 451 B.C.

---

[1] On the date of the ostracism of Thucydides see chron. note 7, p. 474.

which limited civic rights to those born of citizen parents on both sides (p. 102). A scrutiny was held, and, according to an ancient calculation which we cannot control, nearly 5000 persons were struck off the list of citizens, doubtless from among the poorer classes who would claim a share in this corn[1]. No doubt the vast majority of them remained at Athens with the status of resident aliens. But even so this narrow policy was a grievous error. The limit of Athenian greatness was the limit of her devoted citizens, and this action is a great reproach on the state-craft of Pericles, a denial of Athens' past, and a menace to Athens' future.

The more the democracy was organized to share the spoils of empire, the more natural it was to organize the Empire to produce them. The struggle between Thucydides and Pericles raised acutely the whole question, and Pericles followed up his victory by dividing the cities for the purposes of tribute into five groups or districts, Ionia, the Hellespont, the 'Thrace-ward regions,' Caria, and the Islands (see above, p. 42 and map 2). This division facilitated the control of payments, and the quota-lists which have survived show that for two or three years the payments were regular. At the same time it was a further visible sign of the subordination of the cities to Athens, and it must have suggested the satrapies of Persia imposed on what had been a free Greek alliance. But Pericles remained unmoved. His policy was 'to keep the allies in hand,' and to exploit to the full what the Thirty Years Peace granted him, while abiding loyally by its restrictions. He was under no illusions about the envy which Athens inspired and he had not forgotten old and new grudges, but for the time being what Athens needed was peace.

The one sphere in which Athens might pursue a policy of adventure without infringing the terms of the Peace was in the West. In 445 Athenian colonists had gone out, together with other settlers from Greece, to help to refound a new Sybaris[2] in South Italy. But the remnant of the Sybarites claimed privilege over the newcomers and were driven out, leaving the new settlers with more territory than they could occupy. They appealed to Athens, and now was the opportunity to plant in southern Italy

---

[1] Philochorus Frag. 90 F.H.G. i, p. 398. Plutarch, *Pericles*, 37. The latter repeats an assertion that all these were sold as slaves, but that can be no more than a deduction from the penalty inflicted in the fourth century on those who appealed unsuccessfully against ejectment at the time of such a scrutiny.

[2] The rare coins of new Sybaris bear the devices of both states, the head of Athena and the bull of Sybaris. The first coins of Thurii, which follow, have the same types but the different ethnic. See Volume of Plates ii, 4, *b*, *c*.

an outpost of Athenian power, perhaps a stepping-stone to Athenian empire. But Pericles, without entirely rejecting the appeal, refused to adopt a provocative forward policy. He declared the undertaking open to all the Greeks and, when a new band of colonists set out, only two-fifths of them came from Athens and the Empire. They planted in 443 the city of Thurii, which was laid out by the skill of Hippodamus. It is possible that the work provided by the new buildings and the growing trade of Athens left no great surplus population willing to emigrate; it is possible, too, that it was an honest piece of broadminded statesmanship. At the least, it was a gesture that while Athens claimed the Aegean for herself, she claimed no predominance in the West. Nor did Pericles make any attempt to secure permanent Athenian influence in Thurii itself, but allowed the colony to be managed by the non-Athenian settlers and to be driven, after a war, to a disadvantageous peace with Dorian Tarentum. An Athenian who visited Olympia might see a dedication of the Tarentines commemorating their war with Thurii, but Athens made no attempt to protect the new city[1]. In Sicily Syracuse had been increasingly dominant since 445, and her close relations with Corinth might make her a potential enemy of Athens; but Pericles was content with a promise of possible support to Rhegium and Leontini, the two Chalcidian cities who might be trusted to watch with jealous care the growing strength of their Dorian neighbour (p. 223). Not even the news that Syracuse was building a great navy moved Pericles from his course of watchful and defensive quietism.

II. THE SAMIAN REVOLT

For the last decade Athens' imperial policy had been successful. Timely relaxations of tribute had eased the difficult moments of 446 and then after the Peace her hold upon the cities had tightened again. But 'in the sixth year of the Peace' (the winter of 441 B.C.) Samos, which with Lesbos and Chios still possessed both independence and a fleet, was driven into open secession. It began with a dispute between Samos and her neighbour Miletus over the possession of Priene which lies between them on the mainland of Asia Minor: Athens, not wishing to see her independent ally strengthened, favoured Miletus, and when the latter, hard pressed in the war which followed, appealed to the Athenian democracy

---

[1] Unless it was at this time that Athens made an alliance with the Messapian chief Artas (Thucydides VII, 33; Demetrius *ap*. Athen. III, p. 108 *sq*.) which might be intended to embarrass Tarentum, an old enemy of the Messapians.

against her oligarchic enemy, Pericles himself set out with a fleet
and took occasion to establish in Samos a pro-Athenian democracy.
But Samian oligarchs, who had thought it prudent to retire before
the Athenian triremes arrived, turned for help to Pissuthnes the
restless Persian satrap of Sardes and he allowed them to hire
mercenaries in his satrapy. Hardly had Pericles sailed for home
than they landed in Samos, attacked the democrats, and gained
control of the city. The hostages whom Pericles had taken and
placed in the island of Lemnos were recovered, and the Athenian
garrison in Samos surrendered and were handed over to Pissuthnes.
The Samians may have hoped to engage the whole-hearted
support of Persia; they may, too, have realized that to massacre
the prisoners would mean that there was no hope of mercy,
should Athens prevail. And then, as if Athens would be slow to
strike, they turned to renew the war with the Milesians.

But Pericles was quick to take up the challenge, and was soon
at sea again with a fleet of sixty triremes. Sixteen of these were
dispatched to summon the squadrons of Chios and Lesbos and
to watch for a possible naval attack by the Phoenician fleet. For
the actions of Pissuthnes, the Great King's nephew, might be the
prologue to a new war with Persia. With the remainder Pericles
intercepted the Samian fleet as it was returning from Miletus.
The Samians had seventy ships, twenty of them transports
crowded with troops. There was an engagement off the island of
Tragia some fourteen miles south of Samos. The forces with
Pericles failed to win the decisive victory that might have ended
the revolt. The Samians broke through and part at least reached
home and were blockaded by the Athenian fleet which was soon
reinforced from Athens and from Chios and Lesbos. The reinforcements brought enough troops to drive the Samians from the
field and lay close siege to the city. The one immediate hope was
now from Persia and it was known that the Samians had sent
begging for help. To meet this danger Pericles took the risk of
dividing his forces and with sixty triremes sailed off to Caunus
which lay on the regular route of fleets from Phoenicia to the
Aegean. The fleet of the Great King did not appear, but meanwhile the Samians under the philosopher Melissus plucked up
courage and surprised and defeated the blockading squadrons.
For a fortnight they held the seas and used the time to provision
their city. Then Pericles returned and the blockade was restored.

New squadrons arrived from Athens under Hagnon, Phormio
and others, and thirty ships from the Allies. Before such a concentration of triremes and notable commanders Samos was

helpless. The siegecraft of Artemon, an engineer from Clazomenae, was baffled, but after eight months the city was starved into
surrender (spring, 439 B.C.). The walls were dismantled, the
Samian fleet surrendered, and the cost of the siege was repaid,
partly by the surrender of land, partly by annual instalments in
money. The island of Amorgos was taken from Samos and appears
in the quota-lists as a tributary of Athens. The oligarchic leaders
were exiled and settled at Anaea on the coast opposite, perhaps
under Persian protection. Thence they were to give trouble during
the Peloponnesian War both to the Athenians and to the democracy which was set up in their place.

The course of the campaign, if not creditable to Pericles or
to the Athenian higher command, showed how overwhelming
was the power of Athens at sea. Persia had not dared to strike.
The Samians had appealed to Sparta and the Peloponnesians had
discussed intervention, how seriously we do not know. Corinth
some seven years later took credit for declaring on the side of
peace. Anyhow nothing was done. Apart from some disorders
in the Thracian Chersonese, the cities of the Empire remained
quiescent except Byzantium, and on the surrender of Samos
Byzantium came meekly to heel. Athens had weathered a severe
crisis and stood unshaken. Her finances had stood the strain and
her treasury had provided no less than 1400 talents for the
expenses of the siege. Pericles himself delivered the funeral oration
over the Athenian fallen, and generations remembered his fine
phrase of the young men who had died for Athens, that it was
as if the spring had been taken from the year. Many of the allies
were secretly disappointed, and the scandalmonger Ion of Chios
retails the story of Pericles' boast, that while Agamemnon had
taken ten years to reduce a barbarian city, he in nine months had
subdued the proudest and strongest state of Ionia.

III. PROBLEMS OF EMPIRE

During the revolt of Samos there had been some fighting in the
Thracian Chersonese[1] which may have been due to the presence
of the Athenian cleruchs whom Pericles had established there
some ten years before. This trouble was quickly suppressed and
Madytus and Sestos were visited with an increase of tribute, as
was Parium on the opposite coast. The Athenian hold in the
Hellespont proved too firm to be shaken. Far otherwise was the
action of Athens on the south-eastern borders of her Empire,
in the tribute-province of Caria. The little Carian communities

[1] *I.G.*[2] 1, 943 (Hicks and Hill, 46).

had taken the side of Athens in the conflicts fought off their coasts during the last thirty years, but they were not by nature willing tributaries and they were open to Persian intrigue and Persian pressure. In 440 B.C. forty-three Carian towns or communities paid tribute; of these some twelve do not appear again in the quota-lists. An attempt to coerce the recalcitrants might well have cost more than it was worth—for the annual loss involved was about ten talents—and it might besides have led to a war with Persia, the destruction of the *modus vivendi* with which Athens was well content. Wisely enough, the Athenians decided to cut their losses, and when the tribute was re-assessed in 438 B.C.[1] the remnant of the Carian province was merged in the Ionian.

In the Thrace-ward district the Athenians were faced by a more complicated problem which, to the end, baffled their statecraft. The little towns of Chalcidice[2] found themselves between the reviving power of Macedon on the north-west, a new and vaguely formidable Thracian empire on the north-east, and the exigent navalism of Athens on the south. Their natural instinct was to coalesce into some kind of league and then to lean on the least dangerous of these three powers. Events were to show that the right policy for Athens was to encourage such unification and support it, in return for the economic advantages to be gained from trade with the Thracian hinterland. But the expansive power of Macedon was underrated in the person of its shifty king Perdiccas, and the timid state-craft of ancient Imperialism forbade the Athenians to trust to goodwill instead of to the maxim *divide et impera*. And so the incipient movement towards coalescence among these towns was checked by the device of *apotaxis*, that is, the breaking up of the little groups into yet smaller units for the purposes of tribute. As a further fortification of Athenian power, a colony was sent out in 437 B.C. to resume the old plan of occupying 'The Nine Ways,' the crossing of the river Strymon (see above, p. 57 *sq.*). There was founded a city, Amphipolis, to be a centre of Attic political influence, to block the road to Thracian expansion westwards and to monopolize for Athens the exploitation of the mines and the forests which lay behind it. Communications with the sea were secured by the port of Eïon which lay at the mouth of the river. The quota-lists of the years 438–4 B.C. show more increases of tribute than reductions in this area, and at the assessment of 434, the city of

---

[1] B. D. Meritt, *The Reassessment of Tribute in* 438–7, A.J.A. xxix, 1925, pp. 292 *sqq.*

[2] See on Chalcidice, E. Harrison in *C.Q.* vi, 1912, pp. 93 *sqq.*, 165 *sqq.*

Potidaea was compelled to pay fifteen talents instead of six, an increase which was to cost Athens dear. We may assume that Athenian power in the North-East seemed to be secured[1], and Amphipolis rapidly became a flourishing and peculiarly prized possession.

East of the Strymon there were the cities which now bordered the new Thracian empire of the Odrysian king Teres, which stretched from the Aegean to the Danube and the shores of the Black Sea and Propontis. With this power Athens had good reason to be friendly, for the plain between the Hebrus and the Ergines was rich in corn which might be shipped to Athens from the port of Aenus. We may attribute to this time the beginnings of friendship with the king of the Odrysians (whom some Athenians affected to connect with the Tereus of Attic legend) and a shrewd concession which lowered the tribute of Aenus from ten talents to four. An even more striking reduction from five talents to 900 drachmae was granted to Selymbria, which might be a useful neighbour to the Odrysians and a watchful neighbour of Byzantium.

But Athenian policy ranged farther afield. On the coasts of the Black Sea lay Olbia and the state which the Greeks called the realm of the Cimmerian Bosporus, the modern Crimea. Here were inexhaustible supplies of the staple foods of the Greeks, bread and fish. The steppes of southern Russia grew wheat which travelled and kept peculiarly well, and from the Black Sea ports came jars of fish-pickle, a delicacy like caviare, and piles of stock-fish for less sophisticated palates. A century before, Athens had had trade-dealings with these regions, as is attested by the black-figured and early red-figured Attic vases which have been found in southern Russia[2]. Then with the Persian Wars came a break; the exploitation of these regions which had begun to pass definitely from Miletus to Athens was in the main enjoyed by Heraclea Pontica. Now Athens, at peace with all the world, might revive and increase her old commercial interests.

The prime motive was the need for security and privilege in the purchase of food. For a hundred years Attica had grown more and more olive-trees and less and less wheat and barley, and the population of Athens itself had grown with increasing speed as the city became more prosperous and attractive. The cleruchies

---

[1] There is no good evidence for defections from Athens before the revolt of 432 B.C. See A. B. West in *Class. Phil.* XXI, 1926, p. 253.

[2] See E. v. Stern, *Die Griechische Kolonisation am Nordgestade des Schwarzen Meeres.* Klio, IX, 1909, pp. 139 *sqq.*

had done something to relieve the pressure of population, and Athenian settlers in the Chersonese and in Lemnos, Imbros and Euboea might not only feed themselves but send foodstuffs to their parent-city. But there was a limit to the exportation of citizens, and more and more cargoes of wheat were needed to fill the new grain-warehouses at the Piraeus. There was corn in Egypt, but high policy forbade Athens to interfere between the Egyptian and Libyan chiefs and Persia. Sicily produced corn as well as cheese, but Syracuse, the Dorian colony of Corinth, was a potential enemy and her rapidly growing power might set an embargo on export to Athens or give priority to other customers. The Thracian wheat was within the borders of the king of the Odrysians, too powerful to be coerced, too barbarous to be trusted. While, for the present, Athens might buy in all these markets, she could not be sure of controlling any of them. And so, not without reason, Pericles turned his attention to the North-East.

The moment was opportune. In 437 B.C. sovereign power in the realm of the Cimmerian Bosporus had passed to a successful soldier Spartocus[1], and the new dynast proved willing to give to Athens commercial advantages in return for recognition. So began a friendship which was to benefit both parties for a century. The corn-barons of the Crimea soon became amateurs of Attic pottery and terracottas, and from this time onwards Athenian wares are found in their houses and Attic writing in their inscriptions. To achieve this friendship was a task worthy of Pericles' diplomatic skill and he himself (c. 437 B.C.) led a splendid squadron into the Propontis and Black Sea to reinforce his persuasions. An Athenian post was established at Nymphaeum, which became so prosperous that at some later date, perhaps in 425 B.C., its tribute was assessed at one talent. Athenian citizens were planted at Sinope after room had been made for them by the expulsion of the local tyrant Timesilaus. Amisus received Athenian colonists and a significant new name, Piraeus. In 435–4 Astacus in the Propontis, which had been harried by its Bithynian neighbours, was saved for Hellenism and secured for Athens by a garrison of Athenian settlers. From the cornlands of South Russia to the wharves of the Piraeus the food of Athens could pass in safety sheltered by Athenian power, and when the Peloponnesian War broke out, it was easy for her to ration those of her Aegean subjects who had come to depend on the importation of Pontic corn.

[1] Diodorus XII, 31, 36; XIV, 93. The most probable date for the accession of Spartocus is that given in Diodorus XII, 31. See E. H. Minns, *Scythians and Greeks*, pp. 570 sqq.

So much had been done to strengthen and consolidate Athenian power within the Empire and to secure the food and promote the trade of Athens. In the city itself the Parthenon was nearing completion and in 438 the Athena of Pheidias took her place in her new temple. The temple was the embodiment in marble of Athenian pride and love of beauty; its creation was the achievement of Pericles the aesthete and the realist. To the Allies a more comfortable symbol was the statue of Athena Promachos which stood to protect as well as to rule. This moment marks the summit of the splendour if not of the power of Athens. The great days of the Erechtheid inscription when Athens faced Persia and half Greece in arms had passed: the spring had gone out of the year, but this was the high summer of Athenian greatness. In the words which Thucydides puts into the mouth of his hero Pericles, all mortal power is doomed to decline, but the memory of greatness stands for ever.

But there was in Athens, besides the resolute Olympian will-to-power, the lively, critical, ungenerous spirit of the everyday Athenian. The dedication was followed by a *cause célèbre*. Pheidias was promptly accused of embezzling the gold and ivory bought for the making of Athena's statue, and, like so many great servants of the Athenian people, he was driven into exile. The brilliant circle which surrounded Pericles was assailed by scandal, envy, and prejudice. The tradition that good women should be neither seen nor heard had resulted in the presence at Athens of a group of polished Ionian courtezans like the Thargelia who, in the interest of the Persian secret service, was the mistress of a generation of Athenian notables. The most brilliant of this group, Aspasia the Milesian, became Pericles' concubine, for Attic law forbade her to be his wife. That she was clever and sympathetic is beyond doubt, but we need not follow Attic gossip either about the lowness of her morals or the highness of her mind. Pericles had no need of an Aspasia to teach him eloquence, and there is no reason to suppose that her attractions deflected the compass by which he steered the ship of state. Of more influence with Pericles on the intellectual side was the physical philosopher Anaxagoras, on the political side an early friend, the musician Damon (or Damonides) of Oea (p. 73). Both of these were driven from Athens, probably before this time[1]. To be the friend of Pericles was little protection from the Athenian courts which were no respecters of persons and slight respecters of justice.

[1] On the dates of these attacks on Pericles' friends see chronological note 8, p. 477.

Again and again he had to see his friends baited before jealous dicasts, perhaps a fair retribution for the cynicism with which he had used the beliefs of others for the ends of art and empire. During the crisis of the Samian revolt a decree had forbidden the mockery of living persons in comedy; but within three years this was repealed, and jests which the serious in antiquity and modern times have sought to translate into history were showered upon the 'Olympian' 'squill-headed' autocrat. For the Athenians might offer to their leaders obedience, admiration, even affection, but hardly ever respect.

But in matters of state Pericles was supreme. Fifteen times in succession he was elected General-in-chief. He had outlasted all possible rivals—Cimon, Tolmides, Thucydides the son of Melesias. He stood alone and indispensable with one lieutenant, a brilliant admiral, Phormio the son of Asopius. Nowhere else in Athens was there a sign of political genius, though in the house of Pericles there was a boy Alcibiades, whose abilities and weaknesses were to conspire for the destruction of the power which his guardian was so laboriously building up.

The policy of Athens was that of Pericles, a policy steady and farsighted. The age of adventures was over; now came a quiet determined increase of influence, prestige and financial strength against an evil day. The Athenian fleet was kept efficient by constant practice, and every summer a squadron took the sea and displayed the invincible power of Athens. About 437 B.C. Phormio was sent to north-western Greece, which had long been the preserve of Corinthian influence and trade[1]. The city of Amphilochian Argos had been in dispute between the Acarnanians and Ambracia, the chief Corinthian colony in those parts. The Ambraciotes had brought to this more barbarous Argos the blessings of Greek civilization and had ended by ousting the Argives from their own city. The refugees had appealed to the Acarnanians and they in turn asked for help from Athens: the intervention of Phormio's squadron turned the scale and the northern Acarnanian communities who had been concerned in the war became the allies of Athens. The incident was in itself unimportant, for such treaties of alliance might mean little more than the registration of an Athenian claim to gratitude. There is no evidence that Corinth protested or that this intervention was made a grievance. At the cost of slight exertions Athens had made friends who might be useful one day, but the mere fact that

---

[1] Thucydides II, 68. See chronological note 7, p. 474 *sq.*

states in north-western Greece had seen another power active besides Corinth was soon to have serious consequences.

Far more significant was a reform to secure financial preparedness. We may assume that the Athenians, in particular for the building of the Parthenon, had begun by drawing upon the accumulated treasures of Athena and the lesser funds of the other gods. When these were exhausted the funds of the Empire were used, after the great controversy of 444–3 B.C. The Assembly, as a set-off to this use of the tribute, decreed that any surplus in each year should accumulate on the Acropolis until the sum of three thousand talents was reached, and that then the other gods should receive repayment. By the year 435–4 the Parthenon and most of the other buildings in the Periclean programme had been practically finished and paid for, and, despite the heavy cost of the Samian War, the three thousand talents were deposited on the Acropolis. Now came the turn of the other gods. A decree was passed on the proposal of Callias to collect evidence of the amounts due to these gods and make repayment from the funds set aside for the purpose[1]. Any balance left over from these funds was to be spent on the dockyards and the walls, and the treasures of the other gods were to be placed in the care of a special board (the Treasurers of the other Gods) like the existing Treasurers of Athena. The whole financial reserves of the Athenian State were now under the care of these two boards of Treasurers and any surplus of tribute passed automatically into their keeping. Thus was created a consolidated reserve which was rapidly increasing. After the completion of the Parthenon there was little building apart from the Propylaea, and when in 431 Athens found herself at war, Pericles could point to an accumulation of six thousand talents which the state might borrow for her military expenditure. There was no question of a separate treasure of the Confederacy of Delos available only for the purposes of the Confederacy (see above, p. 32). What Athena guarded, Athens might use.

IV. CORINTH AND CORCYRA

We may therefore attribute to Pericles as early as 435 B.C. and possibly as early as the action of Phormio in c. 437 B.C. the consciousness that a general war might come. To this moment

---

[1] *I.G.*[2] 1, 91. A date not later than 434 B.C. is here accepted for this inscription. The other inscription on the same slab (*ibid.* 92) which may be later, is not here adduced as evidence, see below, p. 280, n. 2. The earlier decree referred to in *I.G.*[2] 1, 91, ll. 3–6, is here assumed to have been passed in 444–3. This date appears to the present writer the most probable

may belong one of his few recorded sayings, that he saw a cloud of war advancing from the Peloponnese. But the day of conflict can hardly have seemed either inevitable or very near at hand. The Peloponnesians had resisted the temptation to strike at Athens, while she was embarrassed by the Samian revolt. Athens herself had done nothing to challenge the position of Sparta, had not revived her claim to dominate Greece proper, and by the partial diversion of her trade-interests to the far north-east must have reduced rather than increased her competition with other Greek states in other markets. Such Peloponnesian cities as may have needed to import corn or other necessities had less reason to be alarmed than at any time in the last thirty years. On the other hand, the growing strength and prosperity of Athens was as apparent as the sanguine spirit of the Athenians, who seemed born 'neither to be at peace themselves nor to leave mankind at peace.' The Athenian Empire was the negation of Greek ideas of right and, when the moment came, envy, anger, timidity, and militarism might reinforce themselves with righteous indignation. For the present, however, the Peloponnesian League was passive, almost dormant. Its most influential member, after Sparta, was Corinth and so long as Corinth did not make for war, it was most improbable that the League would move.

Corinth was a commercial state, and, as such, inclined to peace. She might, however, see in Athens a successful trade-rival (though that was now an old story), and if she found her trade decaying, she might be tempted to prefer war to a slow decline. Yet if the remedy was war, it might well seem worse than the disease. Next to Megara, Corinth of all Greek states stood to suffer most from a war with Athens, for her overseas trade must pass either through the entrance to the Corinthian Gulf where lay the Athenian Gibraltar, Naupactus, or within easy reach of the war-harbours of the Piraeus. There is no good reason to suppose that the trade of Corinth was at the moment especially threatened by Athens. The Corinthians might hope to gain from the increasing power and prosperity of Syracuse, however complete became the Athenian monopoly of trade with Asia Minor and the Black Sea. Their true embarrassment was elsewhere, in the unfilial conduct of their colony Corcyra, which by the use of its geographical position both hampered Corinthian commerce with Sicily and South Italy and challenged the Corinthian monopoly of trade with the hinterland of north-west Greece.

Out of a petty quarrel with Corcyra was to spring the first of the two 'grievances' which were to lead to a war which in the end was to be ruinous alike to Corcyra, Corinth and Athens. Epidamnus, a colony which Corcyra had planted to the northward on the coast of Illyria, had become a considerable city by exploiting the trade which came down from the hinterland along what was later the *Via Egnatia*. Many years of internal strife had ended in a war with the neighbouring barbarians helped by the aristocracy who had been expelled from the city. The democrats, harried by land and sea, appealed to Corcyra to intervene and make peace between them and their enemies. The Corcyraeans refused, and in their despair the Epidamnians bethought themselves of Corinth. According to Greek practice, that city, as the mother-city of Corcyra their immediate founder, had supplied the oecist or leader of the settlement. Fortified by a ruling from Delphi, the source of law on these matters, envoys were sent to Corinth. The merchant princes of Corinth, though no democrats, seized the opportunity of injuring Corcyra and making Epidamnus in fact a colony and dependency of their own. Possibly, too, they realized that it might serve as an alternative half-way house to Italy such as Dyrrhachium, which took the place of Epidamnus, became three centuries later. Accordingly, in the full consciousness of profitable benevolence, they sent out colonists and troops of their own as well as from their dependencies of Ambracia and Leucas. These were dispatched overland and arrived at Epidamnus unchallenged. The news of their coming, brought by fugitives from the exiled oligarchs, roused Corcyra to a counter-intervention and a squadron was sent to demand the dismissal of the new settlers. The Epidamnians naturally refused and the Corcyraeans besieged their city, whereupon the Corinthian government began to collect a fleet, requesting help of their maritime neighbours and inviting further colonists, thus proclaiming their persistence in their policy.

Corcyra, sobered by the news of these preparations, sought to settle matters peaceably. In the spring of 435 B.C. their envoys, with the moral support of Sparta and Sicyon, appeared at Corinth. They offered to submit the whole question to the arbitration of agreed Peloponnesian states, but refused to abandon their case beforehand by admitting the right of Corinth to send settlers to what they claimed to be a Corcyraean colony. If Corinth forced them into war, they would be driven to seek new allies not where they wished but where they could. The intention of the hint is plain. As the Acarnanians had called in Athenian help against the Ambraciotes some two years before, so now the Corcyraeans might invite help from the same quarter. It is significant that at

12-2

this time Spartan policy had showed itself pacific and sought to avoid complications which might endanger a settlement that suited Spartan interests sufficiently well.

But Corinth cared for none of these things, and in the summer (435 B.C.) a fleet of seventy-five triremes, thirty of them Corinthian, the others drawn from her allies, set sail. Such a force was small indeed in the face of the Corcyraean navy which was reported to be a hundred and twenty ships strong, though many of these were in bad repair. Brusquely as negotiations had been broken off, the Corcyraeans had time to put their fleet in some sort of trim, and eighty ships faced the Corinthians while forty maintained the blockade of Epidamnus. The Corinthians forced on a battle near the promontory of Leucimne, were defeated, and drew off with the loss of fifteen ships. Of such prisoners as they took the Corcyraeans kept the Corinthians in bonds while they put to death the allies of Corinth who had joined in a quarrel which was not theirs. On the very day of the victory Epidamnus capitulated. Here, too, the Corinthian settlers were handed over to be kept prisoners, the other new colonists were sold into slavery. Thus, while Corcyra had staved off the attack, her harshness made certain a renewal of the war, for Corinth could find allies whose desire for revenge would serve her own desire to make good her humiliating failure. For the rest of that campaigning season Corcyraean squadrons held the sea, harried the nearer allies of Corinth, especially Leucas, and burnt Cyllene, the dockyard of the Eleans, who had supplied the Corinthians with ships. Corinth presently replied by establishing troops and a squadron at Actium and near Cheimerium in Thesprotis to cover their chief allies in the West. Throughout the next year, the two powers watched each other, but all the time Corinth was busy preparing a yet stronger fleet and spending her wealth in hiring rowers throughout the Greek world. The Athenians, who so far had made no sign, did not forbid to them the Athenian recruiting-ground, the maritime states of the Eastern Aegean.

V. ATHENIAN INTERVENTION

By the spring of the year 433 the Corinthian preparations were so far advanced that the Corcyraeans were forced to act upon the hint which they had given, and seek help where they could. The splendid isolation which had been their pride was now their danger, and they sent envoys to Athens to sue for help. Corinthian envoys followed them and the Athenian Assembly met to listen to the rival suitors. Thucydides has given us two speeches which appear to present the substance of the contending arguments, though their form is an essay in sophistic sententiousness. We shall not err in supposing that this whole group of events was recorded by the historian soon after they occurred and that to Thucydides at the time this debate seemed of crucial importance. The arguments are set out under the two topics of Justice and of Expediency. On the narrower ground of legal correctness Athens was justified in accepting Corcyra as an ally, for the Thirty Years Peace allowed her to make an alliance with any state not scheduled as belonging to the Peloponnesian group. On this point the arguments of Corinth fail. On the broader issue of Justice Corinth pleaded past services, but against these might be set the activity with which Corinth had made war against Athens some twenty-seven years before. The issue of Expediency was not so clear. The Corinthians made in effect a diplomatic offer. Let Athens and Corinth agree that the common interest of imperial states is to be obeyed, and Corinth will facilitate the pursuit of that Athenian interest in the Aegean, if Athens will do the like for Corinth in the Corinthian sphere of influence, western Greece. Such a bargain is in the spirit of the Peace; to refuse it, to use the power of Athens to cross the purposes of Corinth, is the road to war. Such an argument might well give the Athenians pause, but the Corcyraeans urged a point which in the end proved more convincing. Their navy was the second in Greece. If Corinth mastered them, that fleet might be used against Athens in the general war which, they represented, was near at hand. But if Athens made Corcyra her ally, she transferred to her own scale the weight of the Corcyraean navy, and gained the strategic advantage to be derived from the position of the island on the route from and to Italy and Sicily[1].

The Corcyraeans who had taken the initiative spoke first and the Corinthians followed. In the debate which lasted throughout the remainder of the meeting the balance of the opinion went with the Corinthians but the Assembly was adjourned and next day we may suppose that the governmental policy was declared. The Corcyraean arguments had prevailed, but the alliance that was made was to be only defensive, as offensive action against Corinth would constitute a breach of the Thirty Years Peace. Whether the Athenians, or Pericles who probably swayed the Assembly, did wisely, it is hard to say. There is no evidence which justifies

[1] Thucydides 1, 36. The strategic rather than the commercial advantages of Corcyra appear to the present writer to have been the important factor.

us in supposing that a general war was in reality inevitable. Thucydides does not commit himself to that opinion as his own. The bargain which Corinth suggested would suit the interests of Athens but only if the bargain were kept. If, despite it, war did come, Corinthian control of Corcyra and of the Corcyraean fleet would cripple any Athenian offensive in western Greece, and would make it easier for Syracuse, the colony of Corinth in Sicily, to send naval help on which the Peloponnesians did in fact count when the war began. Pericles had in all probability already pigeon-holed his plan for a war if war should come, and an integral part of that plan was precisely the naval offensive in the West. His policy was unaggressive but unyielding, and once Greek states were at war, it was hard to foresee the future. The choice lay between a great risk of war and a small risk of defeat in a possible war, and that choice is easy for patriotic imperial statesmen. Pericles chose a great risk of war and in so far is responsible for what followed.

The alliance was made in the early summer[1]. The Corinthians, none the less, pressed on with their preparations, and, on the news that their ships had started, the *casus foederis* arose. At the beginning of August the Athenians dispatched ten triremes, and, some three weeks later, a second squadron of twenty[2]. The smallness of these forces was canvassed even in antiquity. Had the Athenians sent a hundred ships to Corcyra earlier, the Corinthian armada might well have turned back. But Athens must wait until the Corinthian offensive was under way, and, besides, the Athenians had no interest in preventing a collision between the opposing forces. They would, after all, gain more by the sinking of each Corinthian trireme than they would lose by the sinking of each Corcyraean trireme. It was better to allow the two sides to fight, provided only that Corinth did not win an inexpensive and decisive victory. The two squadrons, which, it was expected, would arrive in time, were, as it appeared, a sufficient force to save the Corcyraeans from complete disaster. Its very smallness was a claim to naval superiority; a touch of that *panache* so dear to the Athenians which Pericles sedulously fostered.

By the first half of September 433 B.C. the Corinthian fleet of a hundred and fifty ships anchored off Cheimerium on the mainland south of Corcyra, and thence, cleared for action, they advanced. At dawn next day they came upon the Corcyraeans who were at sea with a hundred and ten ships of their own, many of them old and not so well manned as those of their enemies

---

[1] On the renewal of the alliances with Leontini and Rhegium see above, p. 162 n. 2 and below, p. 223.   [2] *I.G.*[2] 1, 295 (Hicks and Hill, 53).

and, besides, the first Athenian squadron of ten triremes; the second had not yet arrived. The result was a fleet-action off the islands of Sybota. The Athenian commanders, in accordance with their orders, at first only threatened attack, but when the Corcyraeans were defeated, they were forced to act to cover them from pursuit. Late in the day, as it was growing dusk, the Corinthians formed line to deal the *coup de grâce*. The remnant of the Corcyraean fleet and the ten Athenian ships prepared to fight to the last, when suddenly the Corinthians stayed their attack and backed water. They had caught sight of the second Attic squadron advancing through the gathering darkness. It was, for all they knew, the advance guard of the main battle-fleet of Athens. On the next day the united Attic squadron with such Corcyraean ships as were still capable of manœuvre offered battle. The Corinthians refused the engagement, and sailed home, erecting a trophy on the way for the victory which they had won, while the Corcyraeans raised a like memorial of the victory which they would have won. This, Thucydides says, was the first grievance from which the Peloponnesian War arose, because Athenians as allies of Corcyra had fought with Corinthians though still at peace with Corinth (1, 55).

The Attic squadrons returned. They had resisted the Corcyraeans' wish to force on a second engagement which might have led to the destruction of the Corinthian fleet, but equally might have resulted in a reverse damaging to Athenian prestige. Instead they had allowed the Corinthian armada to return baffled by thirty Athenian triremes. This was a lasting injury to the morale of the Peloponnesian sailors, and at Athens the returned sailors talked of the clumsy, antiquated tactics of their friends and enemies alike (Thucydides 1, 49).

The Athenian government might now assume as beyond question the tactical superiority of their squadrons which for more than twenty years had not been tested against a Peloponnesian fleet. This was a gain, but the price was the active resentment of Corinth. Some twenty-seven years before, Athens had crossed the path of the Corinthians by admitting Megara to her alliance (p. 76). The result had been the first Peloponnesian War. Now a second time Attic intervention had snatched victory from their grasp. Twenty-seven years before they had conceived against Athens what Thucydides calls 'their extreme hatred' (1, 103). The Thirty Years Peace had lulled it to sleep: now it awoke. A second time their shrewd quietism was interrupted by un-reasoning passion, and they forgot what it would mean to be at war with the Athenian fleet. The merchants of Corinth set their wits at work to find a means of striking at their enemy. As yet it was vain to appeal to Sparta. No doubt the Spartans had already intimated that they did not regard the Athenian alliance with Corcyra as an open violation of the Thirty Years Peace. Two years before, Sparta had urged upon Corinth a peaceful settlement with Corcyra. All the Corinthians would have got from Sparta would have been good advice two years old from the shrewd king Archidamus. If then the Corinthians wished to involve the Peloponnesian League in a war with Athens, they must find a second, more definite, grievance to reinforce their plea.

VI. POTIDAEA

The second grievance was soon found, in Chalcidice. The establishment of Amphipolis had strengthened Athenian power but had alienated both the Chalcidian cities and the king of Macedon. The Chalcidians saw in the new colony a favoured rival in trade which made them less able to pay a tribute which had ceased to be justifiable now that Persia was a hypothetical as well as a distant danger. The movement towards union was too strong to be checked and it was shrewdly encouraged by King Perdiccas who offered land for settlements near the lake of Bolbe. Many of the small cities on the coast were deserted by the bulk of their inhabitants who migrated to the city of Olynthus and so escaped from the immediate reach of Athenian naval power. Perdiccas was the ally of Athens, but the Athenians, often too fond of being too clever in such matters, had allied themselves with his brother Philip who, with a chief named Derdas, was at enmity with the king, for the domesticities of the Macedonian royal house did not make for fraternal affection. The near approach of Athenian power must have been unwelcome and Amphipolis offered a permanent obstacle to Macedonian expansion eastwards. Accordingly Perdiccas began to intrigue with the Chalcidian cities to bring about a revolt. The Athenian alliance with Corcyra opened a new door to his activities for now he could hope to find in Greece itself enemies of Athens. On the news of Sybota, Macedonian envoys began their travels inciting the animosity of Corinth and undermining the placidity of Sparta. The Chalcidians were ready to support any state bold enough to declare against their common enemy, and Corinth seized her opportunity.

An old Corinthian colony, Potidaea, situated on the Isthmus of Pallene within reach of Macedonian help, had no cause to love Athens, which had more than doubled its tribute. It had the right to receive each year magistrates from its mother-city and these now became the agents of Corinthian hatred of Athens. Before the winter of 433 B.C. was over the Athenians had good reason to suspect that Potidaea was planning a revolt. They thereupon demanded the surrender of hostages and the dismantling of the walls on the side of Pallene, hoping to check the revolt before it could spread. The Potidaeates replied by sending envoys with dutiful protestations, for they were not ready and wished to wait until Corinth would implement her promises of gaining them support from the Peloponnesians. The farce went on until at last the Athenians prepared to dispatch a fleet, and the Potidaeate envoys took the road to Sparta. There they found the ephors inclining to war and lavish with promises; and when at last the Athenians sent the general Archestratus with 30 ships and 1000 hoplites to impose their will on Potidaea, the city with the support of its Chalcidian and Bottiaean neighbours openly revolted. The rebellion spread rapidly except in the three promontories of Pallene, Sithonia and Acte and among the Andrian colonies of the east coast. In Chalcidice proper the very union which the Athenians sought to prevent became a fact[1].

The expedition of Archestratus set out at the end of June or the beginning of July 432 B.C., just before the change of magistrates at Athens, a fact which suggests that the Athenians, as later at Mitylene, aimed at a surprise. It is possible that, until the last moment, Pericles had hoped either to detach Perdiccas by fair words or to hold him in check by supporting his brother or that Potidaea would find Sparta discouraging. But, apart from such hopes, the moment was well-chosen. It left Athens time enough to begin a siege before the winter and left the Peloponnesians little time to prepare an invasion of Attica. For, as Pericles well realized, the Peloponnesian League was ill-organized for swift action. But the Corinthians were ready to move and, the moment news of the revolt arrived, one of their leading citizens, Aristeus, set out by land with a force of 2000 Peloponnesian volunteers. Within forty days of the revolt this semi-official filibustering expedition had arrived at Potidaea. Meanwhile Archestratus'

[1] Thucydides 1, 58. For the evidence for this from tribute-lists see especially A. B. West, *The History of the Chalcidic League*, pp. 14 *sqq.*, and articles by West and Meritt cited in the Bibliography. For the union of the Chalcidians during the Archidamian War see Busolt-Swoboda, *Griechische Staatskunde*, 11, 1926, p. 1502. The earliest coins of a formal Chalcidian League are to be set about the time of the Peace of Nicias. See H. Gäbler, *Zeit. f. Num.*, xxxv, 1925, pp. 193 *sqq.*

army, which was too weak to act effectively against the Chalcidians, had taken Therma in order to isolate Potidaea on the north-west and had then turned against Pydna, for a demonstration in force might well daunt the unstable Perdiccas. By the end of August or the beginning of September a new general, Callias, was sent out with 40 ships and 2000 hoplites. Too late to intercept Aristeus, he joined the force at Pydna and patched up an arrangement with Perdiccas. By the end of September the combined armies were before Potidaea and won a victory outside the town which was then besieged with Aristeus leading the defence.

Thus in the autumn of 432 Athenian hoplites were attacking a city defended by Peloponnesian volunteers led by a Corinthian general. This, according to Thucydides, was the second grievance which preceded the war (1, 66). The moment that Aristeus started from Corinth, one of two things was certain: either Sparta must lead the Peloponnesian League against Athens, or she must face the defection of Corinth, her most powerful ally, who was now deeply committed to save Potidaea. There was a third possibility: that Athens would abandon the attempt to subdue Potidaea rather than face a war with the Peloponnesian League, but to do so risked the break-up of her Empire, and there was no party at Athens prepared to choose that alternative.

VII. THE DECISION OF PEACE OR WAR

Pericles was ready for war but also for peace, if peace could be kept without sacrifice. But what was needed was first a reply to Corinth which might daunt her friends. On the news that Aristeus had started, the Athenian Assembly passed the famous decree which excluded the Megarians from the markets of Attica and the harbours of the Athenian Empire. Pericles declared that this decree was not a violation of the Thirty Years Peace, and we may accept his testimony against that of the aggrieved Megarians. The Athenians had recent causes of complaint against Megara, and, besides, they had yet to revenge themselves for the massacre of their garrison fourteen years before (p. 89). But, though anger may have chosen the victim, it was policy that directed the blow. The war which now seemed inevitable was to be a test of morale and Pericles chose this way of demonstrating from the very outset how formidable a power the enemies of Athens were daring to challenge. The decree was not what vulgar tradition came to see in it, a cause of war, it was an operation of war, the first blow at the courage and will of Athens' adversaries. The state which could, by a single decree, close a hundred harbours despite all the hoplites of the Peloponnese, was not an enemy to be lightly challenged, least of all by Corinth.

This shrewd stroke displays, alike in its force and adroitness, the intellectual clarity of Pericles, who believed that the issue whether Sparta would move must be made plain and that at once. Pericles forced the issue, not because his personal position was shaken, but because, if war came, it must come before he was too old to guide Athens to victory. He was now sixty and it was no easy task to control for ever the sanguine fickle adventurous Athenian demos, and he foresaw how lightly they might squander the strength which he had built up.

The Athenians were thus ready to bring matters to a head but their zeal was cold beside that of the Corinthians. Even before the news came of the Athenian victory before Potidaea they had stirred up all the allies of Sparta who had grievances against Athens, and before the month of September ended they gathered at Sparta to persuade the Lacedaemonians that the Thirty Years Peace was at an end. The Megarians had their new grievance which they declared meant the breaking of the Peace, and envoys came secretly from Aegina complaining that Athens did not leave them autonomous as the Thirty Years Peace had provided. Their precise grievance is not revealed to us, but Aegina had once been a member of the Peloponnesian League and in the Thirty Years Peace there may well have been a clause providing that the Aeginetans should be autonomous so long as they paid their tribute to Athens. It was at least a strange interpretation of autonomy that the Athenian Assembly should, by its bare fiat, deny to Aeginetans the right to import desirable woollens from their Megarian neighbours.

These grievances were real enough, but more powerful was the Corinthian veiled threat which followed, that if Sparta would not fight for her allies, they must look elsewhere for a leader. Thucydides takes occasion to put into the mouth of the Corinthians a brilliant contrast between Lacedaemon and Athens, which illuminates not only the crisis itself but the ten years of war which followed it. The Corinthians did not go unanswered, for there is no reason to doubt the historian's statement that Athenian envoys, on some pretext or other, were at Sparta at the time. These now gave the Periclean answer that Athens stood by her rights and her Empire, but was ready, as the Peace provided, to submit disputes to arbitration[1].

[1] Thucydides I, 67 *sqq.* For the view here taken of dates of composition of these parts of Thucydides Book I, see below, note 9, pp. 480 *sqq.*

Opinion at Sparta was divided. As in every state with a proud military tradition, there was a party unwilling to see its bright sword rust, anxious to cut a straight road through the maze of statesmen's calculations. But the Spartans were cautious legalists, especially while they viewed the grievances of others. On juridical grounds the offer to accept an arbitration placed Athens in the right. The offer might prove illusory, for there was no impartial state considerable enough to be judge in such a cause. But that did not justify its summary refusal. Athens and Corinth were not formally at war before Potidaea, or, if they were, Corinth was the aggressor. Sparta had condoned the Athenian intervention to protect Corcyra by a year of inactivity. And far more cogent were the arguments of the wise king Archidamus that Athens was no ordinary Greek power to be lightly attacked and quickly defeated. The Spartans should think long before they began a war which their children might inherit. Let Sparta test the truth of the Athenian protestations and meanwhile prepare for war if war must come. The answer to these politic considerations was given by the ephor Sthenelaidas who led the war-party. 'Athens was plainly the offender; the Thirty Years Peace was at an end; Sparta must stand by her friends.' This thesis, so manly and so intelligible, prevailed, and the Lacedaemonian Assembly voted that the Truce was at an end and that war was justified.

But the victory of the war-party was not yet complete, not yet even certain. For, according to Greek practice, Sparta was still far from a declaration of war, and the Peloponnesian League as a whole could only make war if a majority of its members voted for it. So a meeting of the League was summoned and meanwhile the Spartans sent to consult Apollo at Delphi 'whether it would be better for them if they made war.' 'And the god replied, it is said, that "if they made war with all their might they would win, and that he himself would help when summoned or even uninvoked."' It was to take nearly thirty years to prove the god right and meanwhile the news from Potidaea was none too good. Corinthian envoys feverishly frightened or cajoled the Peloponnesian states, and when the conference met they ended the debate with a speech of resolute and resourceful optimism. Thucydides has put together, in their name, a masterly analysis of their advantages as against the Athenian position, the possibilities of attack, the glorious uncertainty of war, the claim to be fighting for Greek freedom against a city that had become a tyrant.

The decision was taken, a majority voted for war and, as it

was now October or November, the Lacedaemonians settled down to a winter of diplomatic manœuvring for position.

At this game they found their master. First came an antiquated gambit, the demand that the Athenians should expel the tainted house of the Alcmaeonidae, the family of Pericles. It was a test of Pericles' personal position, which proved too strong to be shaken. The Athenians invited Sparta to clear herself of newer guilt, the killing of Helot suppliants and the death of Pausanias (p. 62). Thucydides (1, 139) then describes more serious demands, first, the raising of the siege of Potidaea, second, the restoration of autonomy to Aegina, third, the repeal of the Megarian decree. 'There would be no war if they repealed the decree.' This can hardly be the whole truth, for Sparta was bound at least to satisfy Corinth, and the simple repeal of the Megarian decree would hardly do that.

The Athenian answer was to bring justificatory charges against the Megarians and to refuse the other demands. Whereupon Sparta sent three new envoys with the message: 'The Lacedaemonians desire the peace to continue and it would continue, if you leave the Greeks autonomous.' It is often said that this was an ultimatum which struck at the very existence of the Athenian Empire. But legalists might have debated for ever how far the Athenian Empire infringed the autonomy of each of its members. The studied vagueness of the proposal, perhaps due to a change of feeling in the Spartan ephorate, seems devised not so much to close the negotiations as to keep them open, and, to judge from the account of the debate which followed, that was the view of the Athenian Assembly.

This was the crucial debate and at this point Thucydides brings in a speech by Pericles. It is quite possible that he has put together what Pericles said on two occasions, the first at which the Megarian decree was more specifically the point at issue, the second the debate on this vaguer demand.

The attitude of Pericles is that Athens cannot yield to a threat of force, that the Athenians cannot hold their own in fear. They will accept an arbitration but until their case is tried they will neither cease to besiege Potidaea nor to exclude the Megarians from their markets and the harbours they control. This last may be the answer to a hint attributed to a Spartan envoy by Plutarch (*Pericles*, 30) that if the Athenians will not repeal the decree, they may at least disregard it. This unyielding attitude was justified by pertinent criticism of the Corinthian plans for the conduct of the war. Behind the question of formal right or wrong stands the shadow of a military calculation. And one factor in the calculation was the moral effect of confident unwavering acceptance of every challenge. Pericles prevailed; the Lacedaemonian envoys received their answer and returned, and after that no further embassies were sent.

The issue was only too plain. In the barren field of diplomatic dialectics Pericles had scored a notable success. It was logically impossible for Sparta to accept an arbitration under the Thirty Years Peace which it had already declared to be at an end. It was practically impossible, now that so many questions had been brought in and the Greek world was ranged in two camps. Above all, Sparta could not now recede a step without admitting a diplomatic defeat which would have meant the loss of her leadership of the Peloponnesian League. The break-up of that League would enable the subtle and patient state-craft of Pericles to achieve for Athens all that a war could give to her. The 'violent hatred' conceived by the Corinthians, the fumbling policy of Sparta, following in order to lead, the resolution of Pericles to make no sacrifice of security or prestige for the sake of peace and to face the issue while he could control the event, had combined to make inevitable a war for which an unbiassed study of the ancient evidence can find no single cause which appears sufficient to the modern mind. Neither rivalry in trade, nor prejudice of race, nor the opposition of political ideas, nor a chivalrous sympathy on the part of the Peloponnesians with the subjects of Athens, can be promoted to be more than elements which went to make war possible but not inevitable. The ancient fiction that Pericles 'set Greece in a blaze' from vulgar personal motives rests on a naïve evaluation of the jests of comedy and on a chronological confusion which concentrated in the year 432 the attacks on Pericles' friends which belonged to the past and the attacks on Pericles himself which belonged to the future[1].

'The truest explanation (ἡ ἀληθεστάτη πρόφασις),' writes Thucydides (I, 23), 'though it appeared least in what was said, I consider to be the growing power of the Athenians which alarmed the Lacedaemonians and forced them into war.' It has often been pointed out that neither the history of the ten years which preceded nor of the ten years which followed the outbreak of the war justifies this statement. It seems to explain more truly why the war began again in 413 and ended as it did than why it began at all in 431. In the opinion of the present writer, the

[1] Diodorus (Ephorus) XII, 38–9, Plutarch, *Pericles*, 31–2. See below, chronological note 8, pp. 477 *sqq.*

words were written by Thucydides after the fall of Athens as he looked back to the Archidamian War and saw it darkened by the tragic shadows of the Sicilian Expedition and the Decelean War, after Alcibiades had made Athens more aggressive and Lysander had made Sparta more determined. But the historian's conception of the whole period as a unity made one by the logic of events is not binding upon us, and we have the right to appeal from the Thucydides of the day after to the Thucydides of the day before. In the earlier stratum of the Thucydidian history on which the preceding narrative is based we have an account of the antecedents of the Archidamian War which is true to fact and true to the Greeks and Greek wars of that time. Angry men at Corinth had not feared fire, clever men at Athens had played with it, a generation of ill-will had lowered the flashpoint and a conflagration was only too easy.

VIII. THE FRONTIER INCIDENT

Negotiations between Athens and Sparta were broken off and both sides were pressing on their preparations for the next summer, but as yet there was no declaration of war. Some of the more ardent partizans of Corinth may still have had a suspicion that the peace party or the temporizing party at Sparta might at the eleventh hour postpone the war, possibly for ever. What was needed was an act of open hostilities, and this came from Thebes. The ambition of the Thebans to make a solid united Boeotia impervious to Athenian intrigue and with frontiers rectified in their favour was best served by war. And in Plataea, the renegade Boeotian city which was an ally of Athens, they found a most suitable objective. If it could be seized at this moment, Thebes would at once make the war actual and would have achieved part of her purpose. There was in Plataea, as in almost every Greek city, a party that would betray the city in order to gain power. A plot was laid with the chief of the Theban government to open the gates to a small force which would be supported by the whole force of Thebes. The other Boeotian cities took no part in the enterprise, no doubt for fear of news of it spreading abroad.

On an evening early in March 431 B.C. the advance party, three hundred strong, left Thebes and before midnight they had been admitted within the gates of Plataea, and the Plataeans were awakened by the voice of a herald summoning them to declare for Boeotia. For the Thebans, anxious to have a good title to the possession of Plataea, began with a proclamation instead of with the massacre that seemed wisdom to the Plataean traitors. The citizens remained in their houses until, plucking up courage, they realized how small a force had entered the town. Then they quietly prepared an attack and just before dawn they rushed the market-place where the Theban hoplites were collected. In a storm of rain, amid the shrieks of the Plataean women, pelted by tiles from the houses and attacked by superior numbers, the Thebans at last broke and were hunted through the streets, trapped within the walls of the city. A part of the invaders had held together and sought to cut their way out, but the gates which they forced led, not into the country, but into a building that was part of the city-wall. The Plataeans after debating if they should burn the building with the men within it, finally allowed these and other Thebans to surrender at discretion. They thus held hostages against the attack of the Theban reinforcements.

The news of the disastrous failure of the surprise reached the Theban main body as it pressed on delayed by the rain-swollen Asopus which it had to cross. They debated what to do and decided to seize as hostages for the safety of the prisoners within the city such Plataeans as were in outlying farms. Before they had done so, the Plataeans sent out a herald to denounce the Theban action and to threaten to kill their prisoners if the Thebans advanced. The Thebans retired on some kind of understanding about their comrades in the city and on their retirement the Plataeans hastily brought in their goods from the country-side and then put the prisoners to death. That the Thebans were tricked in some way is certain, though the Plataeans declared that all they promised was to negotiate about the fate of the prisoners and they denied that they had bound themselves by a solemn oath. Whether they added perjury to deceit may be left undecided. This affair, which crowded into twenty-four hours all the vices of war and of civil strife, was a fitting prelude to the struggle that went far to undermine the spiritual greatness of the Greek people.

The Athenians, who had received news first of the entry of the Thebans into Plataea and then of their defeat in the town, at once seized all Boeotians in Attica, rightly regarding this attack as an act of war against themselves. They sent a herald to instruct the Plataeans to take no action about their prisoners until they, the Athenians, were able to advise them. But hatred had outrun prudence and the herald found the prisoners already put to death. A second attack from Thebes might now be expected, and the Athenians sent troops to help to garrison Plataea and removed all but combatants to the safe shelter of Athens. The Thirty Years Peace was plainly at an end.

CHAPTER VIII

THE ARCHIDAMIAN WAR

B.C. 431–421

I. PERICLEAN STRATEGY

THE news of the events at Plataea was the signal for the mobilization of the enemies of Athens. Argos, the old rival of Sparta, remained neutral, as did the Achaeans except the canton of Pellene. But the remainder of the Peloponnese belonged to the League and obeyed the call of Sparta. Two-thirds of the troops from all these states marched to the Isthmus where, with the Megarians, they formed an army of some 24,000 hoplites attended by swarms of light-armed troops. In Central Greece the Boeotians were in arms and, with the support of the Locrians and the Phocians, they could place in the field some 10,000 hoplites and at least 1000 cavalry. In the north-west of Greece Ambracia Leucas and Anactorium prepared ships and men to fight in the quarrel of Corinth. The naval strength of the Peloponnesians may be assessed at rather more than 100 triremes, but this force was not as formidable as it might appear, for we may assume that the rowers hired throughout the Athenian Empire two years before (p. 180) had returned to their homes or to the quays of the Piraeus.

In the meantime Athens had mustered her forces. Her own troops, citizen-hoplites and metics, provided an active field-army of 13,000 men, and men enough to garrison the city and the Long Walls and to hold the frontier fortresses Eleusis, Oenoe, Panactum, Phyle, Decelea, Aphidna, and Rhamnus[1]. Of the

Note. The main ancient source for the narrative of this chapter is Thucydides (II, 7–v, 23). To this primary source Diodorus (XII, 37–74) and Plutarch (*Pericles*, 33–8; *Nicias*, 1–10) add little of value. For politics and popular feeling at Athens, Attic Comedy, in particular Aristophanes, *Acharnians*, *Knights*, *Wasps* and *Peace*, affords valuable evidence. Of equal importance are the inscriptions (see Bibliography) which supplement Thucydides on finance and, here and there, confirm and supplement his chronology (see the synchronistic table facing p. 252, in which references are given).

[1] The evidence for these fortresses, several of which were strengthened and enlarged in the fourth century, is collected by Miss Chandler in *J.H.S.* XLVI, 1926, pp. 1–21. Eleutherae (Gyphtokastro) appears at this time to be outside Attica or at least outside the Attic defences. The forces needed for their defence may be set at 2000–3000 men. Their strategic value is hard to estimate, but they must have hindered raids and supplies from Boeotia to an invading army in Attica.

field-army 3000 hoplites were in the lines round Potidaea and the admiral Phormio had taken a further force of 1600 to operate in Chalcidice. The cavalry comprised 1000 horsemen and 200 mounted archers and the Thessalians sent a body of horse. In light-armed troops Athens was definitely inferior to her enemies, for the first duty of Athenian thetes was to row in the fleet. The Empire supplied a revenue which Pericles assessed at 600 talents a year, all of which was available for the needs of the war, and the reserves laid by against this emergency reached 6000 talents. It was possible to raise a considerable force of troops from the subject cities, but it was dangerous. Indeed, as regards troops, the Empire of Athens was rather a liability than an asset. The real contribution of the cities was their tribute and the rowers for the Athenian fleet, which was put on a war footing and reinforced by the squadrons of Lesbos and Chios. Besides the Empire, Athens had allies in the north-west of Greece, Corcyra, Zacynthus and part of Acarnania. Naupactus near the mouth of the Corinthian Gulf was firmly held for Athens by Messenians, and Plataea, faithful by tradition and necessity, lay on the main road from Boeotia to Attica.

The strength of the Peloponnesians lay in an army of hoplites so superior in numbers and quality that in a single battle they could count on victory. Their strategy was dictated by this fact and suggested by their knowledge of the history of the last thirty years. At Tanagra a smaller Peloponnesian army had been victorious, at Coronea the Boeotian levies had shown their mettle, while, fifteen years before, Athenians had made a bad peace rather than risk all in a great pitched battle. Thus the first move was to invade Attica in full strength. Pride might compel the Athenians to fight; the alternative, to watch the Peloponnesians devastate the cornfields and olive-yards of Attica might be more than either pride or self-interest could endure. Beyond that immediate direct action lay the plans attributed to the Corinthians (p. 188): to occupy a permanent position in Attica and to raise fleets which could match the Athenians by sea. The first was not immediately practicable, for the Peloponnesians and their allies had not as yet the margin of military strength necessary to hold a position near Athens permanently and effectively in face of the Athenian army. The second demanded the possession of large funds, together with such a diminution of Athenian naval prestige as would encourage the rowers of the Aegean states to throw in their lot with the Peloponnesians. Nearly twenty years were to pass before these two conditions were fulfilled. It is true that the

Corinthians pointed to the treasures of Delphi and Olympia, but, for whatever reason, the Peloponnesians did not mobilize for war the resources of these two sanctuaries. Embassies were sent to the Great King, but he preferred to keep his gold and wait upon events. There were exaggerated hopes of naval help from the Sicilian states, above all from Syracuse, but these hopes were quickly disappointed.

The Athenian strategy was that of Pericles. He, too, had reflected on the history of the past thirty years, and had realized that he must refuse a decisive battle and rely on the great linked fortress of Athens and the Piraeus for defence, or on the action of the Athenian navy and landing-forces of Athenian hoplites for attack. He must first prove that the existence of Athens and of the Athenian Empire could not be destroyed and then that Athens, too, could harm her enemies. The most vehement of these was also the most vulnerable. The possessions and allies of Corinth in north-west Greece lay within the reach of a naval power that was allied with Corcyra, and the sea-borne trade of Corinth must pass either through the entrance of the Corinthian Gulf or within reach of Athens herself. The coasts of other Peloponnesian states such as Elis and Lacedaemon could not be effectively blockaded. Squadrons of triremes were expensive to maintain, almost helpless at night, and dependent on secure bases near at hand. The development of tactics had made them nimble to defeat their own kind but unsuited in build or complement to roam the seas attacking sturdy merchantmen manned by crews fighting for their lives. Nor was the strategical position entirely in favour of Athens, for the possibility of dragging ships across the Isthmus of Corinth gave to the Peloponnesians an advantage not unlike that which the Kiel Canal afforded to the Germans in 1914–18. Nerveless as was the naval strategy of her enemies, Athens was forced to keep a reserve of triremes to meet a raid in her own waters. On the other hand, the Aegean could be policed and the important routes of Attic trade and food effectively guarded, though enemy privateers might make captures and find refuge on the coasts of Caria and Lycia, the traditional home of piracy. Thucydides (II, 67) attributes to the Peloponnesians the terrorism characteristic of the weaker naval power, which did not spare neutrals or the very subjects of Athens whom they declared they wished to liberate. But the defence was on the whole successful, and neither the historian nor the comedians reflect any anxiety about Athenian food during the whole of the Archidamian War. Finally, the fleets of Athens were a menace to the security of the Peloponnese in that any day in the summer months might see an Attic landing-force attacking villages, burning crops or driving cattle.

Such were the weapons in Athens' armoury, and their effect was not to be despised. It was a reasonable calculation that the nerve and will-power of her opponents might well be exhausted before the treasures on the Acropolis, and that they might admit that the power and determination of Athens were invincible. If that result was achieved, Pericles' task was done and the greatness of his city vindicated. Geography and man-power forced upon him the strategy of a Frederick; it is idle for critics to demand from him the strategy of a Napoleon. Once it is granted that a decisive battle offered no prospects of victory, the defence of the Attic country-side became impossible, with the road through the Megarid open to the enemy and the Boeotians, with levies almost a match for the Athenian field-army, pressing on the northern line of fortresses. The Periclean calculation stood the test of ten years war and was not entirely refuted by two factors which were unforeseeable, the Plague and the unspartan enterprise of the Spartan Brasidas. The struggle was a contest of morale, and with all their faults, the Athenians were a people of singular resolution and elasticity of spirit, quick to learn and slow to forget the pride of empire. Their pride was a match for the Corinthian anger, their ambition more than a match for the self-protective instinct of the Lacedaemonians. Their opponents enjoyed wide-spread sympathy, 'especially because they declared that they were giving freedom to the Greeks.' But the beginning, the course, and the end of the Ten Years War show that this claim was a battle-cry and not an ideal, and we need not attribute to Peloponnesian statesmen or to good honest Peloponnesian hoplites sympathies which they never felt or quickly learned to forget. It is no wonder that the Archidamian War was singularly devoid of heroism and of self-sacrifice, or that the perverted idealism of Athens outlasted the determination of her enemies.

The imposing array of the Peloponnesian hoplites concentrated at the Isthmus, and even now, Archidamus, who had not ceased to be a statesman on becoming a general, sent an envoy, the Spartan diplomatist Melesippus, to give Athens a last chance of making concessions to avoid invasion. But Pericles had passed a decree to admit no negotiation under the pressure of an armed threat, and all that the envoy gained was the opportunity to make the prophetic announcement: 'This day will be the beginning of great evils to the Greeks.' The Peloponnesians, reinforced by contingents from Boeotia, moved on to the Attic frontier and sat down before the border-fortress of Oenoe, a place worth taking for it guarded the direct routes between Athens and her ally Plataea and between Thebes and an army in north-west Attica. But while Archidamus vainly practised the arts of siege-warfare, his army grumbled, for what offered most chances was a swift invasion of the Attic country-side. The king, it was said, still hoped against hope that the Athenians would not at the last make the sacrifice of their farms, but agree with their adversary. But no herald came from Athens. Reluctantly enough, the Athenians had brought their families and movables into the city and transferred their sheep and cattle to the safe shelter of Euboea and the neighbouring islands. The vacant spaces in Athens, at the Piraeus and between the Long Walls, were soon crowded with improvised dwellings, and the people comforted themselves by watching the preparation of a great fleet to harry their enemies.

By the end of May the siege of Oenoe was abandoned and Archidamus moved into the country of Eleusis and the Thriasian plain. The standing corn was ripe to burn and the Peloponnesians burnt it, and then moved off to the left on Acharnae, the largest of the Attic demes, where Archidamus made a standing camp, ravaged the country-side, and waited for the Athenian army. Acharnae was the home of prosperous growers of vines and olives and of sturdy irascible charcoal-burners, and these, from within the walls of Athens, could see the smoke that meant their ruin. They led the clamour to go out and fight, and the whole city was in an uproar, moved by pride and anger and a multitude of oracles which prophesied to suit all tastes. But Pericles remained unshaken. By the exercise of his powers as General-in-chief and of his unrivalled personal ascendancy, he prevented any meeting of the citizens which might cross his plans, and the crisis passed. The Athenian and Thessalian cavalry did what it could to protect the fields near the city, but the hoplites of Athens were kept within the walls. The Peloponnesian army was too large to live on the country for long, and presently moved north-east to regain touch with supplies from Boeotia and, after gratifying their allies by the devastation of the territory of Oropus, the debatable land between Attica and Boeotia, they marched off home and dispersed to their several cities. The invasion had lasted a month and in that time, despite the losses it had inflicted on the Attic country-side, it had done little to undermine either the will or the power of Athens.

Then came the counter-strokes. Even before the Peloponnesians had left Attica, a hundred triremes, carrying 1000 hoplites and 400 bowmen, had sailed from the Piraeus to repay them in their own coin. The fleet coasted along the Peloponnese, landing troops to ravage the country, and contingents from the western allies, above all 50 ships from Corcyra, joined in the good work. The Athenians suffered one check, at Methone in Laconia, due to the resourceful daring of Brasidas son of Tellis, a Spartiate, who 'chanced to be in the neighbourhood.' It was not the last time that chance and Brasidas were to conspire to discomfit the Athenians, and the reputation which he acquired by his exploit brought into the Spartan counsels the one man of initiative whom the Peloponnesians produced during the whole Archidamian War. With the Athenians were Messenians who had age-long grudges against Sparta; and these, when a storm left them marooned in the territory of Elis, led a bold and successful raid on the town of Pheia, and then succeeded in escaping to the ships under the eyes of the whole Elean army.

But more vulnerable than the Peloponnese were the western dependencies of Corinth, and before the fleet returned to Athens, it captured Sollium and gave it to the Acarnanians, ejected a pro-Corinthian tyrant from Astacus, and won over the island of Ce-phallenia, the outer-guard of the Corinthian Gulf. In the following winter the Corinthians sent a fleet and army which restored their friend Evarchus at Astacus, but elsewhere they achieved little. The Athenians had given as good as they had got, and their defensive measures were equally energetic. The squadron which guarded Euboea raided the coasts opposite the island, and a fortified post was established on the barren island of Atalante to check privateers from the Malian Gulf. A like danger to Athenian trade in the Saronic Gulf might be anticipated from the people of Aegina, whose intrigues at Sparta had come to light, and the whole population was ejected and replaced by Athenian settlers. The Aeginetans were allowed to find a home, granted to them by the Spartans, in the Thyreatis. Judged by Greek standards, their treatment was clement; some seven years later they were to learn how the long-drawn course of war made the Athenians cruel.

The one other state within reach of Athens was Megara, and in the autumn, when the Peloponnesians were busy with their crops and vintage, Pericles himself led the full available field-army of Athens into the Megarid. There he joined hands with the fleet and, after ravaging the country, fleet and army returned in vindictive triumph to Athens. This was the first of a series of invasions of the Megarid which reduced the Megarians to the straits which made them a good jest to Aristophanes. It was a classical example of the principle *odisse quem laeseris*.

All this time the blockade of Potidaea continued. The inhabitants were to be taught how little they gained when the promised invasion of Attica became a reality. The lines drawn round the city were firmly held. Perdiccas was now active on the Athenian side against the Chalcidians, and Phormio could spare men to help in ravaging the country. A timely alliance with Sitalces, the king of the Odrysian Thracians, brought to Athens present security and future hopes. The fall of Potidaea seemed only a question of time, and that time the nearer because the inhabitants had refused to listen to the Corinthian Aristeus when he advised them to abandon the city, leaving him and 500 men to hold it to the last. Aristeus himself escaped and did what he could to keep alive the anti-Athenian movement in Chalcidice and Bottice. Apart from the drain on the Athenian treasury—for the pay and maintenance of the besieging army alone cost about a talent a day—the position in the north-east gave, at the least, no cause for disquietude.

So ended the operations of the first year of the war, and Pericles might well be content. According to the custom there was the formal eulogy on the citizens who had fallen, and though these were few and not the heroes of any great feat of arms, Pericles himself, as was natural, was spokesman for the city. And Thucydides is spokesman for Pericles. With consummate art the historian has taken this occasion to draw a picture of Athens which is, first of all, a justification of her before the Greeks who, when the words were written[1], had ended by destroying her political greatness. The ritual is described as if to strangers; then follow the words, in the simple style of a Simonidean epitaph: 'And when they have laid them in the earth, a man chosen by the city who is reputed to possess insight and understanding and is highly thought of, speaks over them such praise as befits them. And after this they go away.' And then, in phrases unmarred by the bitterness of defeat or the memory of crimes and follies, there is described the Athens for which men had lived and died, to which the exiled historian avowed his devotion in a world which had proved hostile, faithless, or fainthearted. For the faults of Athens we have only to look elsewhere in the Thucydidean history: if Athens was the school of Greece, she was a hard school and taught much that was evil. It is not easy to forget the cost to Greece of all this greatness, or the justice of the nemesis that

[1] See note 9, p. 480.

struck Athens down, but it remains true that nothing greater
than Periclean Athens had ever yet been achieved by the mind
and will of man.

II. THE PLAGUE AND THE FALL OF PERICLES

The winter ended and, as soon as the campaigning season
opened, Archidamus led the Peloponnesian army into the central
plain of Attica. That was foreseen, but within a few days of their
coming came the Plague. Athens and the Piraeus were crowded
with the refugees from the country-side, and an epidemic, which
had already ravaged the East, reached the Piraeus and spread to
the city. The disease was beyond the skill of the Athenian phy-
sicians, who themselves fell victims as they sought to save others.
'Nor did any other human skill avail. And men's prayers at temples and their recourse to oracles and the like were all in vain.'
Penned up within the walls, many of them in stifling booths under
the summer heat, the Athenians perished, and as the Plague raged,
demoralization spread. Meanwhile the enemy marched on to
ravage the coasts of Attica, until after forty days they evacuated
the country for fear of infection.

When the Peloponnesians were far enough engaged in Attica
and before the Plague had reached its height, an expedition sailed
against Epidaurus (towards the end of June 430 B.C.). The forces
used showed the importance attached to the expedition, 150 fighting triremes (50 of these from Chios and Lesbos), 4000 hoplites
and 300 cavalry in old triremes converted into transports. Pericles
himself was in command. This was to be no mere raid but a serious
attempt to take Epidaurus, thus securing a foothold in the Peloponnese and possibly inducing the Argives to strike in against
their old enemies the Spartans. Epidaurus was strongly walled
and a set siege would soon be interrupted by the return of the
main Peloponnesian army. We must therefore suppose that the
Athenians were relying on that common phenomenon, a party
within the city ready to betray it. But, if such were their hopes, they
were disappointed; an attack just failed, and the great expedition
had to be content with ravaging the lands of Troezen, Halieis,
and Hermione and with sacking the Spartan coast-fort of Prasiae.
The Plague had infected the troops and crews engaged in the
expedition but not so badly as to ruin its effectiveness: it was,
accordingly, dispatched under the tried commanders Hagnon
and Cleopompus to operate against the Chalcidians and press the
siege of Potidaea. The blockade was turned into an active attack
but without success. What was worse, the infection in Hagnon's

army spread to the force already before Potidaea, which had so
far escaped. The result was that in some forty days Hagnon returned home with the loss by plague of 1050 of his 4000 hoplites.
Phormio's detached force had been recalled before Hagnon's
arrival; the remainder of the army in that sector were enough to
maintain the blockade, but that was all.

The Plague at Athens continued during the year 430 and 429
and then, after a partial cessation, broke out again in the year 427.
In the course of that period, it swept away about one-third of
the population. Three hundred of the 1000 Athenian cavalry
perished and 4400 hoplites of the field-army, which, including
garrisons, may be set at 15,500 men (Thucydides III, 87). Of
these losses, we may fairly assume that the greater part fall within
the summer of 430 B.C. The effect was permanent, for the classes
of new recruits during the next twenty years were thinned out.
The land forces of Athens were so far weakened as to fall to about
the level of the Boeotian army. While at sea their superiority was
maintained, it became impossible during the next few years to
man such large fleets as before, because it was not to be expected
that the rowers from the Aegean states should venture themselves
in the plague-stricken city or risk infection from the Athenian
oarsmen. Thus the intensity of the Athenian counter-attacks was
diminished, while their enemies could pursue plans which before
had been at the least hazardous. Attica itself was protected from
invasion so long as it was plague-stricken.

The morale of the Athenians was shaken, and their depression
turned into anger against Pericles as the author of the war. His
calculation, which was to have been triumphant over accident,
had been, in part, refuted. It was undeniable that the concentration of the Attic population within the linked fortress of Athens-
Piraeus had turned the Plague from a small to a great disaster,
and the very reduction of the defended area due to the abandonment of the Phalerum wall (p. 167) had increased this result. If
Athens must lose 4000 hoplites, would it not have been better to
lose them in the forlorn hope of a great battle, than vainly and
ingloriously in the agonies of the Plague? To many at Athens,
the Plague was more than Fortune's criticism of a calculated plan
—it was a sign that the wrath of heaven rested on their city. They
remembered that Apollo had promised to the Spartans his help,
and now he was helping them with the farshooting shafts with
which he had avenged the wrongs of his priest on the Greeks
before Troy. They saw the Peloponnese almost free of the Plague,
and may well have forgotten that the Athenian hold on the Aegean

was a kind of quarantine which prevented evils as well as goods from reaching the Peloponnese from the East. On the house of Pericles himself rested the taint of blood-guiltiness and the gods who had turned Pericles' wisdom into folly may have judged more truly than they about Pericles' innocence or guilt. Epidaurus had proved a failure; the sending of the army to Potidaea was, to all appearance, a blunder, though to keep it at Athens during the heat of the summer might well have been greater folly.

The first sign of the Athenian change of mood was the dispatch of envoys to open negotiations for peace. What offers they made we do not know; very possibly the Lacedaemonians believed that they had nothing to lose by leaving the Plague to do its worst. At all events, the envoys returned unsuccessful. The war must continue, and Pericles, who still held the office of General-in-chief, summoned the Assembly and faced his fellow-citizens. We cannot deny to him the unbending spirit which inspires every line of the speech which Thucydides puts into his mouth, little as that speech is calculated to conciliate, or to arouse the sanguine optimism which was half the courage of the Athenians. The historian has given us less what Pericles must have said than the authentic accents of Pericles himself as possessing 'the quality which marks the greatest men and the greatest cities—to be least depressed in thought and most resolute in deed, when misfortunes come.'

His speech, and still more his example, had their effect; the Athenians rallied to their own greatness and made the sacrifices demanded by the war. But their private griefs bit deep. Many poor farmers had lost all that they had: the rich had lost much and the burdens of war bore heavily upon them. Pericles was deposed and accused of malversation, a charge which, however untrue, he had not the means of disproving. Fifteen years of uninterrupted power had involved expenditure of which he could not now give an account. The verdict under a procedure amended by his colleague Hagnon declared him guilty, but the penalty was not death but a fine of 50 talents. The explicit testimony of Thucydides to his probity, and his reinstatement as soon as the anger of the Athenians had passed, clear his character: his fault, if it was a fault, was to worship too well an Athens made in his own image.

III. THE NORTH-EAST AND THE NORTH-WEST
(430–429 B.C.)

With the fall of Pericles the war enters upon its second phase. It is true that when the elections came round in March or April of 429 Pericles was elected General again. But he was a broken man. His two legitimate sons had been carried off by the Plague and he himself had been stricken by it, and within three months of entering on his last term of office he was dead. The unrivalled authority which he had wielded from the ostracism of Thucydides, son of Melesias, to his own deposition, an authority austere, arrogant, and self-reliant, had prevented Athens from being a school of statesmen. The state had become a veiled autocracy: now the autocrat was dead, and the city was plagued by the rivalries of leaders none of whom possessed Pericles' greatness of mind, or united in themselves his military, financial and diplomatic capacity. The impulse which he had given to Athenian policy kept it on its course. Among the leaders who came forward at this time were none who thought of surrender, none willing to buy peace by abandoning the Empire. It is true that there was a small set of aristocrats who hated the democracy and Empire and would destroy both in order to reduce Athens to an aristocratic well-ordered country town, but they played no part in Athenian public life, where democratic principles were orthodoxy and other principles were blasphemy. For years to come they had to work in secret, protecting each other by the subtle use of private influence, comforting themselves by the sense of their superiority. They had at least the intellectual comfort of adhering to a lost cause, of despising the busy vulgar world around them, in which it was hard to tell who was slave and who was free man. About this time one of their number, armed with an incisive candour which must have surprised old oligarchs, wrote a pamphlet which, by some irony of chance, has been preserved along with the writings of Xenophon. Superficially this pamphlet is an unwilling tribute of admiration to the logical self-protective instinct of the imperial democracy, but between the lines may be read the message, 'do not seek to mend the democracy, but wait—until one day you may convert loyalty to the good cause into triumphant treason.' The lesson was well learned, and for the next decade at least there is no sign at Athens of a declared aristocratic party.

But within democratic Athens there was a divergence of opinion due to an economic difference. It is roughly true to say that the rich who bore the financial burdens of the war and the farmers, whose lands were exposed to the enemy, looked forward to peace with a greater longing than the sailors and craftsmen and traders to whom the war brought pay and profit and little danger so long as the naval power of Athens stood above serious challenge. These last found leaders of their own class, Eucrates, Lysicles and Cleon, who sought to convert what was in essence a defensive war into a war of definite triumphant aggression. On the other hand the generals, elected at a time when the farmers were in Athens, were as a rule men who, by position, temperament or training, followed the tradition of Periclean strategy. Chief among these was Nicias son of Niceratus, whose cautious skill and good fortune made him, on the whole, the most trusted commander in the Ten Years War. Devoid as he was of any touch of genius, the very negative quality of his mind fitted him to guide a people which had more to fear from their own errors than from the enterprise of their enemy. But the existence of more adventurous politicians and more adventurous soldiers, together with his own lack of moral courage, left Athenian policy and strategy without continuous direction, the sport of programmes, promises and personal ambitions.

Even had there been at Athens continuity of policy and the possibility of directing widely separated operations to a single end, the material resources of Athens were so diminished by the Plague that for the next four years the initiative lay with her enemies, who showed themselves singularly unfitted to use it to advantage. Before the summer of 430 was over an expedition of 100 triremes under the Spartan admiral Cnemus sought to seduce Zacynthus from the Athenian alliance by the potent argument of ravaging her fields. That they could do this without interference from Corcyra or from other Athenian allies in the west suggests that the news of the Plague had weakened Athenian prestige. Athens herself could do little to help her friends especially as long as her main fleet was off Potidaea. The efforts of Cnemus did not succeed, but it was important to show that Athenian naval power was still to be reckoned with, and in the early winter Phormio, who had returned from Chalcidice, was dispatched with 20 triremes to operate from Naupactus against Corinthian trade and to maintain Athenian influence in the North-West. His naval skill, his earlier dealings with the Acarnanians and the liking which he inspired, all justified his appointment.

Meanwhile the diplomatists on either side had not been idle. The hopes of naval reinforcements from Sicily which the Peloponnesians had entertained had proved false. It is possible, though it is nowhere expressly stated, that the populous Sicilian cities had not been unvisited by the Plague. Persia was a doubtful neutral and Spartan envoys together with Aristeus the Corinthian sought to approach the Great King, taking with them an Argive Pollis who, though not commissioned by his government, might play upon the ancient friendship of Persia for Argos. The mission was hazardous, for Athens controlled most of the approaches to Persian territory, but there was the chance of travelling across Thrace to the Propontis and so evading the watch kept on the Hellespont. The envoys presented themselves at the court of Sitalces and asked for a safe passage and sought to detach the Odrysian from his new alliance with Athens. But they found at his court Athenian ambassadors to whom Sitalces handed them over as an earnest of his good will. They were taken to Athens and promptly executed, a violation of Greek diplomatic usage which was justified as a reprisal for the Peloponnesian treatment of neutrals at sea.

The failure to win over Sitalces to act against Athens sealed the fate of Potidaea. Before the winter was over, the citizens were driven by hunger to approach the generals of the besieging army, Xenophon, Hestiodorus and Phanomachus. These, anxious to end an expensive war which kept Athenians in a land where winter was an infliction, granted good terms. The inhabitants were allowed to go free, the men with one garment and the women with two, and to carry with them an agreed sum of money to support them by the way. The refugees found homes where they could in the towns of Chalcidice. The Athenians who had not felt the rigours of a Thracian winter censured their generals and presently sent out settlers to occupy the deserted city. The siege had cost 2000 talents: it may be doubted if even this striking example of Athenian tenacity was worth that price.

But more than the capture of Potidaea was needed to secure Athenian power in the Thrace-ward districts. The three generals had still with them a force of 2000 hoplites and 200 cavalry, and towards the end of May 429 B.C. they advanced against the Chalcidians and Bottiaeans. They hoped to win over Spartolus where there was a party friendly to Athens, but the Chalcidians sent help, and their cavalry and light-armed troops had the better of the Athenians until at last the Athenian hoplites, who had hitherto more than held their own, broke and were driven back on Potidaea with the loss of all three of their generals and 430 men. The Athenians, discouraged, withdrew the remainder of their army. To continue so distant a war which demanded considerable land forces was perhaps beyond their means, the more so as Perdiccas was the least trustworthy of allies. Indeed in the summer of this year he sent help to the Peloponnesians who were operating in Acarnania.

The other ally of Athens was Sitalces, whom the Athenians hoped to use for their own ends. The Athenians had sent envoys headed by Hagnon to arrange with him a march west against the Chalcidians and Perdiccas. He was to be joined by an Athenian fleet and army and the two powers were to settle affairs to their liking. Amyntas the son of Philip was to be set on the throne of Macedonia, and, we may assume, the Athenians were to retain the coast towns while the Chalcidians and Bottiaeans were to be subject to Thrace. It was possible, as the Greeks feared, that the Athenians might recruit a barbarous army to give them a chance of victory at least in Central Greece.

But this far-reaching combination failed. In the early winter Sitalces appeared with an army which rumour declared to be 150,000 men. He overran most of Macedonia and then turned against Chalcidice, where he found, not an Athenian fleet and army, but only envoys with presents. Thucydides (ii, 101) states without comment that the reason for the non-appearance of a fleet was that the Athenians did not believe that Sitalces would come. The reason rings false and may well be no more than the official explanation, while we may suspect that the true cause was that Sitalces seemed too formidable and that the plan of joint action with him had been abandoned. Perdiccas had contrived to win over Sitalces' nephew Seuthes who urged retreat, and the provisioning of so great an army was difficult, so that after 30 days the Thracians withdrew again to their northern home. Stratonice, Perdiccas' daughter, married Seuthes and the two kingdoms remained on amicable terms. The Athenians continued to hold most of the coast towns of this area, but Perdiccas and the Bottiaeans and Chalcidians remained as possible allies for anyone bold enough to move against Athens. Such an enemy was to appear five years later, when the Athenians must have repented of their half-hearted action.

Thus in the North-East the Athenians had forfeited the initiative which they had spent so much to gain. Affairs in the North-West were equally urgent. The alliances of Athens with Corcyra, Cephallenia, Zacynthus, and part of the Acarnanians, while they made it possible to injure Corinthian commerce by sea and Corinthian trading interests by land, had imposed upon Athens the obligation to defend her friends.

As has been said, the Athenians had replied to the abortive

but menacing enterprise of Cnemus by the dispatch to Naupactus of their best admiral Phormio with twenty ships 'to prevent anyone sailing from Corinth in or out of the Crisaean Gulf.' Such a force might go far to achieve its immediate purpose, but it was insufficient to carry out what was plainly the ideal strategy, namely to destroy the last remains of Corinthian influence and leave to Corinth and her allies no foothold from the Gulf of Corinth to Corcyra. This strategy was consistently urged by the Acarnanians, who knew the politics of the North-West; and the need to adopt it was the greater because Corcyra had ceased to co-operate actively in the war and might be seduced by Corinthian intrigue or deflected by the violence of her own internal party warfare. 'May Poseidon destroy the Corcyraeans in their hollow ships' wrote the comedian Hermippus about this time 'for they are double-minded[1].' For the present, however, Phormio, though a good diplomatist and personally acceptable to the western allies of Athens, could do no more than hold Naupactus and watch the entrance to the Gulf of Corinth.

His weakness was due to the effects of the Plague and the fact that Athens was already feeling the need to husband her financial resources. Early in 429 B.C. the Ambraciotes, who realized their opportunity, appealed to Sparta to send a force which might help them to destroy the Athenian hold on Zacynthus and Cephallenia and to reduce the Acarnanian communities which held to Athens. Possibly they might even succeed in taking Naupactus. Thus the Athenian fleets would find no friendly harbour to receive them when they sailed round the Peloponnese. Corcyra would soon become neutral and Corinthian influence would be restored. The Corinthians naturally supported these suggestions and the Spartans were wise enough to appreciate the importance of the project. In the summer of 429 they dispatched their admiral Cnemus with 1000 hoplites and a few ships to Leucas. Thence, with the Ambraciotes, Leucadians and Anactorians, and their barbarian allies from the interior of Epirus and the islands, he was to effect a landing and march through Acarnania from north to south. Meanwhile a Peloponnesian fleet was to follow and join the squadrons of Leucas, Anactorium and Ambracia. This combined force would demonstrate off the coast of Acarnania and thus, it was hoped, the country would quickly be overrun or submit.

Cnemus succeeded (August 429) in evading the attentions of Phormio, and his part of the scheme was put into operation. He landed with his troops within the Ambracian Gulf perhaps at

---

[1] In the *Phormophoroi*, Frag. 63 Kock.

Olpae or Metropolis, marched through the territory of Amphilochian Argos leaving the city on his left, sacked Limnaea which was unfortified and thence marched on Stratus. His forces moved in three columns, the centre column consisting of barbarians especially Chaonians, who pushed on rashly and met with a check outside Stratus. On this the other two columns joined forces only to be harassed by the skilful slingers of the Acarnanians. Under cover of night Cnemus retreated to the river Anapus 10 miles away and there, after admitting the Stratians' victory by recovering the dead under a truce, effected a junction with the forces of Oeniadae and retired to that town, where they did not find the reinforcements which they expected. Apparently the plan had been for the fleet from Corinth to land some troops at Oeniadae on its way to join the ships of Leucas and the rest. But the fleet from Corinth did not appear and, as the campaign had clearly broken down, the troops dispersed to their several homes.

The reverse on land was made worse by a reverse by sea. About the same time as the success of the Stratians the fleet from Corinth fell in with Phormio's squadron just outside the Gulf of Corinth. The Peloponnesians had 47 ships but these were laden with men and stores for a land campaign rather than cleared for a naval action. They trusted that their numbers would be enough to discourage Phormio's squadron from attacking them if they fell in with him. In the evening they sighted his twenty triremes coasting along parallel with them and they tried to slip past in the night. But Phormio caught them in the open sea as they were crossing from Patrae in Achaea in the direction of Oeniadae. They formed in a circle, hoping thus to offer no opening for the Athenian skill in naval attack. With great daring Phormio sailed round and round them, until the circle contracted more and more, and then, as Phormio had anticipated, the east wind from the Gulf arose towards morning and threw them into confusion. The signal was given to charge and the Athenians scattered them with a loss of 12 ships. Some of the Peloponnesians fled to Dyme and others back to Patrae while Phormio sailed back in triumph to Molycrium and thence to Naupactus. The fleet from Corinth felt its way round to the safety of Cyllene where they were joined by Cnemus and the other ships from Leucas. Here the defeated general and the defeated admirals compared defeats, assisted by the reproaches of three commissioners from Sparta, Timocrates, Brasidas and Lycophron, sent with the message to fight another better-managed battle and not be shut off the seas by a few ships.

With the advent of Brasidas came courage and skill, and the fleet prepared to renew the battle, while their allies were instructed to send reinforcements of ships. Phormio got wind of these preparations and sent word to Athens of his victory with an urgent request for reinforcements; for he expected every day to have to fight another engagement.

The Athenians decided to dispatch 20 ships, but, overestimating the slowness of Peloponnesian preparations, sent them first to Crete in the hope of winning over the city of Cydonia. They were persuaded to this by their *proxenos* at Gortyn, a Cretan named Nicias. But Cretans were deceivers ever, and the Athenian squadron ravaged the territory of Cydonia with no result except the waste of time, and after that they were hindered by bad weather. Phormio looked in vain for their coming, and was left, with no more than his 20 triremes, to face the new Peloponnesian offensive.

With reinforcements chiefly from the western ports of the Peloponnese, for the Athenians barred the way from Corinth and Sicyon, the enemy fleet had been raised to 77 ships, all prepared for sea fighting, and at last they moved to a point on the coast just west of the narrow entrance to the Gulf of Corinth and anchored under cover of a land force. Phormio had brought his squadron just outside the entrance of the Gulf though not so far as to be beyond the support of covering troops from Naupactus. This position would enable him to manœuvre towards the open sea if the Peloponnesians forced an engagement and would give him the chance of getting into touch with the reinforcements expected from the south-west. This last reason prevented him taking up a safer position just within the Gulf itself. For six or seven days the two fleets moved to and fro along the opposite coasts. Every day was a gain to the Athenians, and the Peloponnesians at last had to force on a battle. They moved in four lines ahead towards the Gulf while Phormio, afraid that they might capture Naupactus, now that its garrison had been brought west to support his fleet, followed in single line ahead along the coast. Thus he covered Naupactus and might hope for a chance of attack as the Gulf widened.

The Athenians needed all their courage based on superior skill to move so near a fleet of nearly four times their number. And in the enemy's fleet was as enterprising and ingenious a commander as Phormio himself. As Phormio's squadron was rounding the promontory of Antirrhium the Peloponnesian fleet, instead of pursuing its course, wheeled and charged. The Athenian squadron

was cut into two. The eleven leading ships by hard rowing
escaped into the entrance of the Gulf; of the other nine one was
captured and the remainder driven on shore. The twenty fastest
Peloponnesian triremes which had been put at the head of their
formation chased the eleven Athenian ships into Naupactus.
Ten of them reached the harbour and turned to face the attack,
the eleventh, chased by a Leucadian ship in advance of its fellows,
rounded an anchored merchantman and rammed its pursuer. This
touch of daring turned defeat into victory. The Peloponnesians
were taken aback and stopped rowing; their triremes lost way, and
then 'daring fell on the Athenians and at one command they
shouted and charged.' After a short confused resistance the
Peloponnesians were driven back to their anchorage with
the loss of six ships, while the Athenians recovered some of
their triremes which the Peloponnesians were preparing to tow
away.

The moral effect of this reverse was decisive. The Peloponnesian fleet retired to Corinth and, on the advent of the 20 ships
from Crete, the Athenians were able to keep them cooped up in
the Gulf. Cnemus and his colleagues took the one chance that
was left to them, and transferred their crews by land to Megara,
where they found 40 triremes not in the best of condition. Manning these, they attempted to surprise the Piraeus. But during
that night beacons flashed the news to Athens and at dawn the
Piraeus was strongly held and an Athenian fleet was at sea.
Whereupon the Peloponnesians hastily retired, having achieved
nothing except the destruction of a station in the north of Salamis.
The Athenians' reply was the protection of the Piraeus' main
harbours with a boom and the re-doubling of their vigilance.
Perdiccas, miscalculating the chances of the Peloponnesian offensive had sent 1000 men to join Cnemus, but they arrived too
late and, no doubt, returned to Macedonia without revealing
their true intentions. At least Athens took no official cognizance
of this move, and Perdiccas was well able to explain anything
away. But in the *Phormophoroi* of Hermippus, the comedian did
not scruple to include among the imports of Athens 'cargoes of
lies from Perdiccas.' Judged by that Macedonian barometer of
success, the fortunes of Athens from now onwards began to improve. Phormio, once winter had set in, made a triumphal progress along the coast of Acarnania and, landing a force at Astacus,
restored the influence of the friends of Athens by the expulsion
of their political enemies. There remained Oeniadae in the south,
which sided with the enemy, but in the winter the lagoons formed

by the river Achelous protected the town from assault, and an attack was reserved for the next summer.

By the early spring of 428 Phormio had returned to Athens with his prizes and prisoners, but only to meet vigilant auditors instead of grateful and admiring fellow-citizens. He was accused of peculation and disgraced. No more is heard of him, but his son Asopius was elected General and, at the express request of the Acarnanians, was dispatched in August 428 to resume his father's good work. He was only able to keep 12 ships of his squadron, for the remainder were needed against Mitylene (p. 215) and with these he joined the Acarnanians in an unsuccessful attack on Oeniadae. He then turned against a more important objective, Leucas, the last considerable ally of Corinth in western waters. The island, as will be seen later (p. 221), was of great strategical importance and its capture would have added enormously to the risk and difficulty of any Peloponnesian naval movement in that region. Attempting what may have been no more than a reconnaissance in force, Asopius was defeated and killed. His squadron sailed off to its base, and with his death, what may be called the Phormio phase of Athenian operations in the North-Western theatre of war was ended.

The results achieved were not to be despised. The interests of Corinth had been gravely injured, serious efforts by the Peloponnesians had been frustrated by comparatively slight exertions on the part of the Athenians themselves, and the naval skill of their fleet had been triumphantly vindicated. But, as in the North-East, Athens had not been able or willing to complete her successes and in the enemy's hold on Leucas and the wavering policy of Corcyra there remained the possibilities of grave embarrassments in the future. The achievement of incomplete successes with small forces was in the end to prove false strategy as well as false economy.

During the campaigning season of 429 B.C., the main Peloponnesian army had not invaded Attica, chiefly, no doubt, because the country-side was protected by the presence of the Plague. Otherwise it is possible that they might have taken advantage of the serious weakening of the Athenian field-army to establish a strong point such as Decelea was to prove some sixteen years later. Another objective, however, was within their reach. Plataea guarded the road between Thebes and Attica and was to the Thebans Boeotia irredenta. To control the road the neutrality of Plataea would suffice, and Archidamus after moving the Peloponnesian army into Plataean territory replied to the citizens' protestation that their country had been promised independence after the crowning mercy vouchsafed to Greece beneath its walls, by offering them the choice of strict neutrality or the safe-keeping of their possessions by Sparta until the war was over. The offer was fair enough and in such matters the Spartan conscience might be trusted, but with pathetic loyalty the Plataeans consulted their ancient ally, Athens. The Athenians encouraged them to resist and made what may have been sincere promises of support which decided the Plataeans to reject Archidamus' offers. The king called the gods of Plataea to witness the correctness of his procedure and then laid siege to the town, actively supported by the Boeotians, who had far other intentions than their scrupulous allies. Plataea was well prepared for a siege, and as hunger was the most dangerous enemy, the garrison was reduced to 400 Plataeans and 80 Athenians, with 110 women to keep house for them. The city was strong and the circumference of its walls no greater than could easily be defended by this force. Indeed it remained defensible when, some eighteen months later, nearly half the garrison escaped to Athens. In the hope of avoiding the tedium of a blockade, the Peloponnesians pressed the siege by every manner of device but the variety of the attack was defeated by the ingenuity of the defence. The last expedient was an attempt to fire the town. No such conflagration caused by the hand of man had been seen by anyone then alive, but in the nick of time, a thunderstorm quenched the flames. There remained the slow pressure of a blockade, and while part of the Peloponnesian army was sent home, the remainder completed a double wall to shut in the city and ward off any attempt at relief from Athens. By the middle of September the walls were built and a force was left to hold one half, while the Boeotians made themselves responsible for the rest. Thebes was near enough to reinforce the garrison of the circumvallation in case of need, but the Athenians did not raise a hand to implement their promises, and Plataea waited for the day of its inevitable surrender.

IV. THE REVOLT OF MITYLENE (428–7 B.C.)

With the early summer of the year 428 came the Peloponnesian army which set itself to destroy the crops that had been sown by Attic farmers who hoped to harvest them. But more serious was the news that Mitylene the chief city of Lesbos was preparing to secede from the Athenian alliance. Lesbos, like Chios, had remained so far independent that it paid no tribute, maintained its own fleet, and managed its own domestic affairs. But there was no certainty that it would remain an island of freedom in the Empire, or that Athens might not prefer a faithful and subservient democracy to the moderate oligarchy which ruled in Mitylene. Even before the war there had been intrigues with Sparta, but Sparta was not then ready to give active support. But now the Plague and the inactivity of Athens emboldened the Mitylenean oligarchs to try their fortune before it was too late. Both Sparta and the Boeotians were willing enough to encourage a movement which might be the signal for a widespread revolt, or, at the least, distract the Athenians from ravaging the Peloponnese or attempting to relieve Plataea. During the winter of 429–8 the Mityleneans had quietly prepared their plans, and begun to improve the fortifications of their town and harbour and to import corn and archers from the Pontus. News was brought to Athens by her friends in Mitylene and by the governments of Methymna, the second city in Lesbos, and of Tenedos. For the Mityleneans aimed at nothing less than the domination of all Lesbos. The news was too unwelcome to be readily believed, but it soon became clear that Athens could not evade the challenge to her authority.

Envoys were sent demanding that these suspicious activities should cease, but the demand was refused, and the Athenian government decided to follow up their threats by a sudden stroke. The general Cleïppides, with a fleet of 40 triremes which was under orders to sail against the Peloponnese, was dispatched to attempt a surprise of Mitylene while the citizens were outside the city at the feast of Apollo Maloeis. The news of its coming outstripped the Athenian squadron, and, when Cleïppides appeared off Mitylene, it was to find the city and harbours in a state of defence. He accordingly presented an ultimatum and, on its refusal, opened hostilities. The Lesbian fleet, weakened by the absence of 10 triremes which lay at the Piraeus as a proof of loyalty, was driven in, but the Athenian force, though sufficient for a surprise, was not strong enough to undertake a siege and an armistice was agreed upon, during which the Mityleneans might satisfy Athens of their virtuous intentions. At the same time a trireme slipped out carrying envoys to procure help from Sparta. In offering the armistice the Mityleneans were over-clever, for what the moment demanded was not words either at Athens or at Sparta but deeds in Lesbos which might set the Athenian Empire aflame with revolt. While the Athenians turned a polite though incredulous ear to the protestations of the Mity-lenean envoys, Cleïppides called up reinforcements from the cle-ruchies of Imbros and Lemnos and from such allies as were near and loyal. Methymna sent help, and when the armistice ended with the return of the Mitylenean ambassadors, the Athenians were able to maintain themselves in their camp to the north of the city. A second post was soon occupied south of the main har-bour and the Attic triremes held the approaches by sea and waited for an army from Athens.

In the meantime, the shipload of Mitylenean envoys who had reached Sparta were asking to be formally enrolled as members of the Spartan alliance so as to engage the honour of the Pelopon-nesians in securing their safety. The answer was an invitation to plead their cause before the Greeks assembled at the Olympian festival. Accordingly, about the middle of August, they addressed the Peloponnesians, justified their revolt, and called for a vigorous offensive against Athens by land and sea. A second invasion of Attica might prevent the dispatch of a besieging army to Lesbos, a naval attack on the Saronic Gulf would force Athens to recall either the 40 triremes which lay off Mitylene or the 30 triremes under Asopius which the Athenians had sent out to sail round the Peloponnese. The Spartans were convinced, and prepared to drag across the Isthmus the fleet which Phormio had driven back into the Corinthian Gulf, while, at the same time, they called up the contingents of the Peloponnesians.

This well-conceived operation failed. The Peloponnesian hop-lites, who had already spent a month ravaging the Attic fields instead of harvesting their own, were now busy with the vintage and the gathering of their figs and olives, and mustered 'slowly and grudgingly.' The naval threat was vigorously countered, for the Athenians' spirit rose with the danger. It was easier to find ships than crews. Year by year since the war began, 100 triremes had been set aside to meet precisely this emergency, but the Plague had thinned the ranks of the Athenian thetes who served in the fleet, and the treasury could ill afford to maintain a reserve of hired rowers from the rest of the Aegean world. At this crisis the hoplites of the zeugite class and the metics were called out to act as rowers and the 100 triremes put to sea. Part of Asopius' squadron was recalled but not a ship was moved from before Mitylene. The Athenian armada demonstrated before the Isthmus, and then moved off along the coast of the Peloponnese, and as the levies of their enemies marched into the great camp at the Isthmus, it was to hear that Athenian raiding parties were destroying the vintage which they had left ungathered. The troops were sent back to their homes and, though the military value of the Athenian reserve fleet with its admixture of untrained rowers was more than doubtful, the Peloponnesians abandoned their naval offensive. Phormio's victories had not been forgotten. At no moment in the war was displayed so clearly how well Athens faced a danger and how ill her enemies used an opportunity.

The immediate danger was overpast but there remained the heavy task of besieging Mitylene. The first few years of war, above all the siege of Potidaea, had been very costly, and a second operation of that kind might well exhaust the reserves of the state. The Plague must have affected Attic trade, there had been loss of tribute in the Thrace-ward region, and cities in Caria and Lycia had refused to pay their contributions and killed the Athenian general Melesander who tried to exact the tribute as well as to protect the trade-route from Athens to Phoenicia. In this very year a like fate befel the demagogue Lysicles who was defeated and slain by the Carians while engaged on the same errand. And yet the money for a siege must be found at all costs. For the first time as a free democracy the Athenians imposed upon themselves an *Eisphora* or property-tax, which brought in 200 talents. Such a measure pressed hardly on the richer Athenians, who already bore the burden of equipping triremes and had seen much of their property destroyed by invasion. When, in the second half of September, a force of 1000 hoplites were sent out under Paches who took over the command in Lesbos, the hoplites themselves acted as rowers in order to spare the Athenian treasury.

If Athens was to carry on the war two things were needed: resolution in raising money and economy in spending it. And the man who did most in both directions was Cleon son of Cleaenetus. Both in the *Knights* and the *Wasps* of Aristophanes he is represented as extorting money from the Allies and the rich for the demos. But the small peasantry of Attica and the poorer town citizens could supply little and money must be found where money was. What Cleon did at this time is what Pericles himself would have done. Cleon was charged with personal corruption, but as he was bound to make very many enemies, it is hard to believe that, if he had been corrupt, no one could be found to prove it in a court of law. And, once such a charge was proved, his career was ended. But, if not personally corrupt, he was without shame or mercy, and, no doubt, his patriotism and his self-seeking were two facets of the same jewel. Insensitive, unscrupulous, plausible, vain, resolute, and violent, he was one of the necessary evils of an aggressive democracy. But he was led captive by his own policy. To impose on half the Athenians the sacrifices needed to avoid losing the war, he was forced to make the other half believe that the war could be gloriously won. It was his fate at once to make a good peace possible and then to refuse it for the mirage of a better. The immediate danger of his policy was the exhaustion and discontent of the rich Athenians and the resentment of the Allies. But the leader of the rich Athenians, Nicias, while prepared to accept a reasonable peace, was not for surrender, nor willing to see the Athenian Empire broken. To the discontent among the Allies Cleon opposed frank terrorism. The Empire was a tyranny...*oderint dum metuant*.

Athens found the money and the determination to hold on. With the arrival of Paches' force, the rebels were driven from the open field and by the beginning of the winter Mitylene was blockaded both by sea and land. Its fall was only a question of time unless the Peloponnesians could send help by sea. Towards the end of the winter the Mitylenean position was becoming desperate, but they were encouraged to hold on by Salaethus a Lacedaemonian, who made his way into the city with the news that a Peloponnesian fleet would be sent to their relief. The campaigning season of 427 B.C. opened with the invasion of Attica— probably about the end of May. Towards the end of June a Peloponnesian fleet of 40 ships under the Spartan Admiral Alcidas had evaded the vigilance of the Athenians and reached Delos before the Athenians knew that it had started. But it came too late. Mitylene had fallen. Salaethus had despaired of relief and found the food of the city exhausted. Accordingly, as a last resort he armed the mass of the people to make an attempt on the Athenian lines. But no sooner were the people armed than they declared that the rich had supplies of corn which must be divided or they would hand over the city to the besieging army. The oligarchic government, anxious not to be the last to make peace, surrendered to Paches on such terms as they could get. The Athenians were to decide their fate. Salaethus was sent to Athens and put to death at once.

The Peloponnesian fleet reached Embatum near Erythrae seven days after the city had fallen, but before Paches had received warning of its coming. Had Alcidas possessed the resolution to attack at once, all might yet have been retrieved. And that course was urged upon him by one Teutiaplus an Elean who has the honour of pronouncing Thucydides' verdict upon war, that the good general is he who guards against surprises and watches his opportunity of inflicting them upon the enemy. Three years later the historian was to write or re-read those words with his own bitter experience to prove them true. Alcidas, who appears to have regarded the art of war as a method of avoiding conflict, was not convinced, nor would he adopt an alternative plan of seizing a city in Ionia or Cyme in Aeolis and making it a centre of disaffection against Athens. Optimists declared that perhaps the Satrap of Sardes, Pissuthnes, might strike in on the Peloponnesian side. But Alcidas was no optimist, and did not desire the glory of a forlorn hope. He began to feel his way homewards, slaughtering the unfortunate subjects of Athens whom he caught at sea, until the nimbler-witted exiles from Samos convinced him that his conduct was neither honourable nor politic. By this time the presence of a Peloponnesian fleet in what had become an Athenian lake, had caused widespread alarm, and messages had poured in to Paches culminating in the arrival of the state-triremes, the Paralus and Salaminia, which had themselves sighted Alcidas' squadron on their way from Athens. Paches gave chase at once; but Alcidas, who could at least understand the mission of the state-triremes, 'sailed swiftly and fled' and escaped, having suffered as little injury as he had inflicted.

The whole affair from the false hopes with which the Mityleneans had been lured to their ruin to the enterprise of Alcidas, which atoned for the rashness of its conception by the timidity of its execution, was a fine commentary on the Spartan programme of freeing the Greeks, and a welcome strengthening of the prestige of Athens.

What remained to be settled was the fate of the people of Mitylene. Alcidas had done them the disservice of inflicting on the Athenians a moment of alarm which reinforced their natural anger. Cleon, a connoisseur of the baser emotions, persuaded the Assembly to decree the indiscriminate slaughter of all Mityleneans of military age, whether democrats or oligarchs, and the enslavement of the women and children. This ferocious folly, the *reductio ad absurdum* of Periclean imperialism, was not consummated, for the Athenians, though swift to anger, were not without pity and intelligence. The very next day the decree was re-considered in a debate which Thucydides has made the setting for a contrast between passion and reason. An Athenian Diodotus appears for a moment in history as the mouthpiece of reasoned state-craft[1]. The Athenian Empire was possible because democrats in the allied cities preferred the rule of the Athenian demos to the domination of their political rivals. To slaughter the democrats at Mitylene who had, after all, turned against the oligarchs, was to alienate the democrats in every city of the Empire. Such arguments prevailed over the angry rhetoric of Cleon, though it was by the narrowest of majorities that the decree was reversed. The trireme which had set out for Lesbos with its heavy freight of doom was almost overtaken by the ship which carried the reprieve, and news of the second decree reached Paches between the reading and the execution of the first. 'So near was Mitylene to destruction.'

Cleon had his way with the ring-leaders of the revolt, the walls of the city were dismantled, and its fleet was surrendered. Apart from the faithful Methymna, the lands of the Lesbians were divided into 3000 lots, and these, after the gods had received their tithe, were assigned to Athenians who garrisoned the island, living on the rent paid to them by the former owners, who continued to farm them[2]. The possessions of Lesbos on the mainland became tributary subjects of Athens. Farther south Paches had taken occasion, as he returned from the chase of Alcidas, to re-establish the Athenian hold on Notium where an anti-Athenian faction held the city with the help of mercenaries hired from Pissuthnes. This success, gained by an adroit treachery, was permanent. The general himself came to a bad end, for he was attacked at the expiry of his year of office, perhaps for malversation in Lesbos, and stabbed himself in open court[3].

[1] On the reflection of current philosophical thought in the speech of Diodotus see below, p. 384.

[2] A fragmentary inscription (*I.G.*[2] 1, 60 = Hicks and Hill, 61) implies that the Athenian settlers did in fact migrate to Lesbos and not remain absentee landlords in Athens. This was first pointed out by Swoboda, *Serta Harteliana*, p. 28.

[3] The story that his crime was the violation of Mitylenean women is a conjecture of Niebuhr, based on an epigram (*Anth. Pal.* vii, 614) composed by Agathias nearly a thousand years after the Fall of Mitylene.

V. CORCYRA, SICILY, AND THE NORTH-WEST

The reduction of Mitylene marks a revival of Athenian vigour. When the Peloponnesian army retired, Nicias led a force which established a fortified post Minoa at the very entrance to the southern harbour of Megara. From this advanced point the Athenians could observe more promptly the naval movements of the enemy and hinder the coming and going of Megarian commerce and privateers. The mere presence of an Athenian force so near to the city of Megara was a standing invitation to any party within the city to intrigue with the enemy for personal or party ends. We may see in this operation the foreshadowing of a policy which, two years later, was to dominate Athenian strategy.

But the pre-occupation of Athens with Mitylene had proved fatal to Plataea and had seriously endangered Athenian influence in the North-West. The Plataeans had received assurances from Athens that she would not desert them, but these assurances flattered only to deceive. To fight a great pitched battle to force the raising of the siege, would have led to certain defeat and would not have saved the city, but it is at least possible that a surprise attack on the besieging lines might have enabled the whole garrison to escape in safety. No such attack was made. As the second winter of the siege wore on, the defenders were driven to decide between the danger of remaining and the danger of attempting escape. About half the garrison chose the nearer risk, and on a night of sleet and rain, in the dark of the moon and under cover of an easterly gale, they crossed the enemy's lines and reached Athens. Their departure enabled the remainder of the garrison to hold out longer on their store of provisions but by the middle of August 427 B.C. they were so weakened by famine that they could no longer defend the walls and there was nothing left to them but to surrender. They had no hope but in the memory of their city's past services to Greece and in the mercy of the Spartans. This hope was destroyed by the triumphant malice of the Thebans, who pointed out the undeniable fact that the Spartans were judging not the Plataeans of the Persian wars, but the Plataeans who had stood by Athens and had slaughtered their Theban prisoners four years before. The Spartans, who wished to please Thebes and were no doubt exasperated by the long siege, put to each prisoner the question, 'Whether he had done any service to the Lacedaemonians or their allies during the present war?' The only possible answer meant death, and 200 Plataeans and 25 Athenians were killed, while the women were sold as slaves. After a year of occupation by refugees from the former Theban party in Plataea and from Megara, the city was razed to the ground, and the land became the property of the Theban state. Plataea had ceased to exist, and the Athenians conferred the solatium of Athenian citizenship[1] on the Plataeans who survived.

In North-West Greece since the death of Asopius (p. 211), the interests of Athens had been neglected. The general Nicostratus had 12 triremes at Naupactus and the Messenian garrison could provide a force of 500 hoplites. But these forces were small and sufficiently occupied with the duty of guarding the entrance to the Gulf of Corinth. Meanwhile at Corcyra the oligarchical faction which did not wish to serve the interests of a democratic Athens was reinforced by the return of 250 aristocrats whom the Corinthians had taken prisoner at Sybota (p. 183) and now sent home under a show of ransom. The oligarchs hoped to bring back Corcyra to her traditional detachment from Greek politics, while the democrats wished to give more active support to their Athenian allies. At the moment Corcyra was in effect neutral, and Athens and Corinth had each a ship with envoys lying in the harbour. In July 427 B.C. the struggle of parties proceeded from impeachment and counter-impeachment to assassination. Peithias the leader of the pro-Athenian faction successfully defended himself against a charge of treason, and retorted by accusing five of the richest aristocrats of having cut vine-props in the precinct of Zeus and Alcinous. They were convicted and condemned to the enormous fine of a stater for each stake, a fine which Peithias proposed to exact with the full rigour of the law. Whereupon the oligarchs broke into the Council-hall and killed him with sixty of his followers. Having thus gained control of the executive, they forced through a decree declaring neutrality in set terms.

Had Athens accepted the *fait accompli* the oligarchs might have been contented, and they dispatched envoys to test the feeling of the Athenians. They arrived to find that the news had outstripped them, and that orders had been sent to Nicostratus instructing him to intervene. The envoys and any other Corcyraeans of their party whom the Athenians could lay hands upon were interned in Aegina. In the meantime, Lacedaemonian envoys arrived at Corcyra with promises of help, and the oligarchs decided to force the issue by attacking their democratic fellow-citizens. A force of 800 mercenaries was brought over from the mainland

---

[1] [Demosthenes] LIX, 104–6; Isocrates, *Panathenaicus*, 94. The grant of citizenship is to be placed after the Fall of Plataea, despite Thucydides III, 55, 3 and 63, 2. See Busolt, *Griech. Gesch.* III, 2, p. 1038 n. 2.

but their help was more than counterbalanced by the fact that the greater part of the large slave population of the island took the side of the democrats. After three days of street-fighting the oligarchs had the worst of it, but before the democrats could complete their victory, Nicostratus with his twelve ships and 500 Messenian hoplites appeared in the harbour. The Athenian commander sought to make a peaceable settlement, provided that Corcyra adhered to her alliance with Athens, but this settlement was too gentle for the passions of Greek party warfare. The democrats, who rightly distrusted their power to live in peace and safety with the oligarchs, requested him to leave five of his triremes while they would man five others to take their place. The five others were to be a floating prison for aristocrats, but these latter, with the rest of their party, preferred the shelter of a temple until they were induced to leave their asylum for a small island off the city.

In the meantime, the fleet of Alcidas, which had returned from its inglorious adventure in the Aegean, was reinforced by 13 ships from Leucas and Ambracia and dispatched to assist the oligarchic *coup d'état*. Within a few days of Nicostratus' arrival, the news reached Corcyra that this fleet was approaching the city. Sixty ships were manned which, with the Athenian squadron, should have been enough to defeat Alcidas, but with a nice appreciation of the relative merits of their enemies, the Peloponnesians detached 33 ships to face Nicostratus, while the remaining 20 defeated the Corcyraeans as they straggled up to the battle. The Athenians, who were on the point of repeating Phormio's manœuvre in his first naval victory of 429, were forced to be content with covering the retreat of their incompetent allies, and the day ended with the Corcyraeans making hasty preparations to repel an attack on the city. But Alcidas saved them further anxiety. He had with him Brasidas, sent no doubt to lend him a little resolution, but the leaven failed to leaven the whole lump, and Alcidas exercised his right as Admiral to order a useless landing at Leucimne. At nightfall beacons from Leucas warned him of the approach of a second Athenian fleet, and he hastened home, evading the enemy by hauling his ships across the narrow spit of sand which joined Leucas to the mainland, while the Athenians were sailing west of the island. Thus, twice within twenty-four hours, Leucas proved useful to the enemies of Athens.

The retreat, if timid, was wise, for the Athenian fleet consisted of 60 triremes under Eurymedon, dispatched as soon as the news of the oligarchic *coup* reached Athens. The fears of the

Corcyraean democrats turned to savage triumph and they massacred their opponents, public and private, with every circumstance of sacrilege, treachery and judicial murder. For seven days this went on under the eyes of the Athenian generals and moved Thucydides to analyse, with a psychological insight which surpassed his powers of expression, the effect of war on the intensely political minds of the Greeks. We are presented with a picture of the Greek city-states, as they were to be for the remainder of the Archidamian War, and from this point onwards, intrigue with parties within other states becomes an increasingly common operation of war.

A remnant of the oligarchs escaped to the mainland and harried their enemies with raids until they were emboldened to cross over and seize Mt Istone some four miles south of the city[1]. Thence they continued their depredations until in 425 B.C. an Athenian squadron on its way to Sicily helped the democrats to storm the fort on the mountain and the remnant of the oligarchs surrendered on the promise of a trial at Athens. They were tricked into attempting escape, and Sophocles and Eurymedon, two generals in a hurry, handed them over to the Corcyraean democrats. Sixty of them were killed as they were driven along between two files of hoplites, each of whom struck and stabbed such prisoners, in passing, as chanced to be his personal enemy. The remainder tried to bar the way into their prison and called on the Athenians to be their executioners. All one night they endured a rain of arrows and tiles from the roof or sought to end their own lives. At dawn the tragedy was over; the Corcyraeans heaped the corpses on waggons and carried them out of the city; and all the women taken in the fort were enslaved. 'Such was the way in which the Corcyraeans of the mountain were cut off by the democrats: and thus the sedition after being so violent ended, so far at least as concerns this war. For there were none of the aristocratic party left worth mentioning. The Athenian fleet then proceeded to Sicily' (Thucydides IV, 47–8).

We may now return to the year 427 in which the Athenians were persuaded to intervene actively in Sicilian affairs. As has been said, the power of Syracuse had grown rapidly since the defeat which she inflicted on her rival Acragas in 445 B.C. (p. 162). In the decade which preceded the outbreak of the Archidamian War her navy had increased, and in 431 B.C. the Peloponnesians entertained high hopes of help by sea from their friends in Sicily. No help was sent, and we may assume that this was due to the

---

[1] See P.-W. s.v. Korkyra.

facts that Syracuse was still pre-occupied with her own ambitions, and that the states in Sicily which had reason to fear her were encouraged by Athenian diplomacy as well as by their own interests to produce embarrassing complications. In 433–2 B.C. the Athenians had renewed in identical terms existing treaties with Leontini and Rhegium (p. 162 n. 2), and these cities were or became allied with the other Chalcidian cities of Sicily and with Camarina. In this way during the early years of the war there was formed a group of cities, predominantly Ionian, which had some claim on Athenian support if only because its continued existence was in the interests of Athens. In natural opposition to this group was Syracuse, the head of the Siceliote Dorian cities whose sympathies were on the side of the Peloponnesians, with whom indeed they were nominally in alliance. The adhesion of Italian Rhegium to the Ionian group was balanced by that of Locri to the Dorian combination.

By the summer of the year 427 the opposition between these two groups had ended in open war, in which the Ionians had the worst of it. Leontini, thereupon, sent envoys, among them the famous sophist Gorgias, appealing to Athens to fulfil her treaty obligations and send help to her Ionian kinsfolk. Greek states, although scrupulous in avoiding what treaties forbade, exercised great freedom in deciding whether to do what treaties prescribed. But the danger that the Ionian group would collapse and that Syracuse would be free to bring powerful help to her mother-city Corinth was decisive. The Athenians voted to dispatch 20 ships to the west and these sailed under the command of Laches and Charoeades about the end of September 427 B.C. The smallness of the squadron, the fact that no considerable body of troops was sent, and the character of the operations on which the Athenians embarked, all show that both the generals at Athens and the generals in command of the fleet were pursuing a strictly limited objective, the maintenance of a political equilibrium, however unstable, in Sicily.

A by-product of hostilities in Sicily would be the cessation of the export of corn thence to the Peloponnese. The natural effect of the war with its destruction of peaceable activities had been to make it more convenient, if not necessary, to import corn, and the readiest market open to the Peloponnesians was Sicily, where they may have enjoyed favourable terms because of the sympathy of the Dorian states. No blockade which the Athenians could institute would suffice to prevent merchant-ships reaching the western Peloponnese, but if the Sicilians fought instead of working in the fields, the Peloponnesians might have to work in the fields instead of fighting. So far the purpose of the Athenians may be described as in essence defensive. But, besides the plans of the generals, there were the hopes and promises of demagogues like Cleon and a new parody of Cleon, the lampseller Hyperbolus, who spoke of a possible conquest of the whole island of Sicily. To them this expedition was the first step on a long and glorious road and they taught the Athenians to expect far more than lay within their power to achieve.

Laches set out with the forces and for the purposes of a defensive policy, and for a year he discharged his mission with success. As Leontini was too near Syracuse to be a secure base, the Athenians established themselves at Rhegium and engaged in minor operations against the north coast of Sicily[1], gained a victory at Mylae, and won over Messana. Thus they secured command of the Straits of Messina and so isolated Locri from her Sicilian allies. But they and the Rhegines failed to do more than win some small successes in southern Italy. Locri itself proved too strong for them and an attempt to raise the Sicels against Syracuse ended in a defeat at Inessa. Charoeades had fallen in battle and Laches must have displayed great tact and resource in making the most of his fleet and the best of his allies. By the close of the campaigning season of 426, the tide of war was beginning to set in favour of the friends of Syracuse. It became plain that the Athenians must send reinforcements to avert the defeat of their allies or, in the phrase of optimistic demagogues, to end the war more quickly. The Syracusans were rapidly gaining the command of the sea and what was needed was a stronger Athenian fleet. Athens had ships and crews to spare, now that the Peloponnesians, since the end of 427 B.C., had not ventured to send out a fleet. As Athenian naval supremacy was secured by constant practice, the use of a fleet in Sicilian waters could be represented, not entirely without reason, as a good thing in itself. It was decided to send out 40 triremes, and meanwhile the general Pythodorus was dispatched with a few ships to supersede Laches and announce the coming of the remainder of the fleet in the following spring. Laches, who had been engaged in campaigning with the Sicels against Himera retired to Rhegium to find himself superseded and after his return to Athens he was prosecuted for peculation, but acquitted. Pythodorus proved incompetent or unfortunate, and allowed the Syracusans to win back Messana, and so re-open communications with Locri. Rhegium was in her turn isolated

---

[1] Renewing an old alliance (p. 159) with Segesta, Thuc. vi, 6, 2, where read [Λεοντίνων]

and, although the Athenians and Rhegines had rather the better of it in a series of naval engagements, they were unable to regain Messana. The alliance with part of the Sicels assisted the Ionian cities in Sicily to hold their own with fair success, but Dorian Camarina showed signs of deserting their cause and, what was more important, the main body of the second Athenian fleet was detained in Greek waters until the summer of 425 B.C. was over.

It had by now become apparent even to the Ionian allies of Athens that the Athenian policy was purely egotistical. Those Athenians who thought only of defence desired the continuance of evenly balanced wars in Sicily, those who had wider ambitions and thought of conquest were as prepared to conquer Ionians as Dorians. For the other cities of Sicily the alternative to becoming either the catspaws or the subject-allies of Athens was to make a reasonable peace with Syracuse and there was a Syracusan states-man, Hermocrates, who realized that the interests of his own city would be better served by a peace which excluded Athenian in-fluence than by a war which had proved so hard to win. In the summer of 424 B.C. a Conference met at Gela, and the Siceliote cities agreed upon a general peace, which removed any justifica-tion for the presence of an Athenian fleet. Eurymedon and Sophocles, the commanders of the new Athenian fleet, and Pytho-dorus, although he had spent 100 minae on a sophistic training, could hardly defend either the actions or the speeches of the Athenians and acquiesced in the inevitable and returned home, leaving the Siceliote cities to live at peace with each other. But, if we may judge by a hint in a speech which Thucydides puts into the mouth of Nicias (VI, 13), they did succeed in making some kind of a bargain whereby the Sicilian cities renounced any intention of interfering in the politics of Greece proper. That very modest though real achievement did not prevent them from becoming the victims of the Athenian demos, which had been en-couraged by Cleon to expect the impossible and fined Eurymedon and banished his colleagues. Two years later (422 B.C.) during a revival of Cleon's influence, an Athenian envoy, Phaeax, was sent to Italy and Sicily to fish in the troubled waters of interstate politics, but his mission came to nothing. The Syracusans had not proved very formidable enemies and Sicily had become a de-sirable prize, so that nine years after the Conference at Gela the half-formed plans of optimistic demagogues became the considered policy of the Athenian state.

Having traced the course of the first operations of the Athe-nians in Sicily to their close, we may now return to the main theatre of war. If intervention against Syracuse is regarded, in its inception, as defensive, the general result of the year 427 B.C. was that Athens had overcome or neutralized the attacks upon her interests. There are signs that the old vigour and initiative were returning. But with the winter of 427–6 came a second visitation of the Plague which lasted a year and reduced the fighting strength of the Athenians. Equally serious was the depletion of the Athenian treasury. The average cost of the last five years of war may be set at about 1400–1500 talents of which more than half had to be met by borrowing from the state reserve. We possess accounts which show that between 433–2 B.C. and 427–6 B.C. the Athenians had borrowed not far short of 4800 talents, so that even if we allow for some revenue from sacred property accruing to the reserve fund, the 6000 talents with which Athens began the war must have been reduced to little more than 2000[1]. It is to this fact as much as to the difficulty of obtaining crews that we must attribute the smallness of the fleets which from now onwards are sent to sea. None the less the spirit of the people remained high and at the elections for the office of General in 426 B.C. Nicias, the opponent of adventure, was not reappointed, nor Hipponicus, a general who shared his strategic views. Eurymedon, who appears to have combined high democratic orthodoxy with a purely professional attitude towards the war, was re-elected and Laches, though of the party of Nicias, was continued in his Sicilian command. Otherwise, a troop of nonentities was chosen to lead the forces of Athens, with one exception, Hippocrates the nephew of Pericles, who begins a short and unfortunate military career. It may be suspected that the influence of the demagogues, above all of Cleon, was in the ascendant and that the Athenians wished for a more violent prosecution of the war. In the *Babylonians* produced at the Great Dionysia of 426 B.C. the young poet Aristophanes dared to attack Cleon and his drastic policy towards the Empire with such vigour that he was haled before the Council and narrowly escaped severe punishment.

With the spring of 426 there came the possibility of peace. Archidamus had died and his son Agis had succeeded him, a young man as yet with little influence. At the same time Pleistoanax had been recalled from exile and his influence was thrown on the side of peace. Sparta had little cause to be satisfied with the events of the last two years and Athens appeared to be invincible. Accordingly, in the Spartan manner, the ephors took advantage of an earthquake which hindered the invasion of Attica

[1] *I.G.*[2] 1, 324, with the literature there cited.

to open negotiations for peace. We are not informed what offers were made, but it is possible that they proposed to return to the position as defined in the Thirty Years Peace. Such proposals involved the restoration of Aegina to its old inhabitants and the dispossession of the Athenian cleruchs (p. 198)[1]. The sanguine and violent popular leaders found it easy to arouse the spirit of the demos, and the Lacedaemonians were dismissed with contumely. It is significant that Thucydides does not think it worth while even to mention these proposals which were rejected as soon as they were made.

The earliest operations of the year 426 were directed by the generals still in office, but more in the spirit of their successors. Towards the end of May Demosthenes of Aphidna and Procles were sent with a fleet round the Peloponnese to continue the war in North-Western Greece. Soon afterwards, Nicias, as the closing exploit of his year of office, set out with 60 ships and 2000 hoplites to the Dorian island of Melos which refused to take its due place in the Athenian Empire and did not surrender, despite the ravaging of its fields. The returning fleet took part in an interesting operation. The 2000 hoplites were landed at Oropus and advanced on Tanagra while the remainder of the Athenian field-army under Hipponicus and Eurymedon marched to join them. We may suspect that the movement was intended to entrap the Boeotian army but, if so, it failed, for only the contingents of Tanagra and a small Theban force was brought to battle and defeated. Nicias ravaged the coast of Eastern Locris while the Athenian field-army returned home. The Boeotians made one effective retort in the autumn of this year by razing Plataea to the ground, so that nothing of the city might remain to be bargained away by their half-hearted allies, the Lacedaemonians.

This campaigning season was marked by two offensives in the North-West, the first by Demosthenes, the second by the Peloponnesians, both of which ended in failure. The Athenian strategy in that area was complicated by the conflicting interests of the Acarnanians and of the Messenian settlement at Naupactus. Demosthenes was at first guided by the advice of the Acarnanians. The strategic importance of Leucas had become more apparent than ever during the operations of the previous year, and the Athenian fleet, supported by the full strength of the Acarnanians, Corcyraeans and other allies of Athens, attacked the island. The Leucadians were driven into their city and the Acarnanians urged Demosthenes to beleaguer the city and thus finally secure Athenian

[1] Aristophanes, *Acharnians*, 653.

interests in the North-West. But the tedious operation of a siege did not appeal to the enterprising nature of the Athenian admiral, and a more ambitious and seductive plan was proposed to him by the Messenians of Naupactus. They suggested that the moment had come to subdue Aetolia and thus strengthen Naupactus and Athenian influence on the western mainland. To this attraction his own imagination added a yet more alluring prospect, the opening up of a new avenue for an attack upon Boeotia. Beyond Aetolia eastwards lay the Ozolian Locrians, who had promised help, and beyond them the Phocians, who might be brought to remember their old friendship with Athens (p. 88). Phocis marched with Boeotia, and Demosthenes might hope to force the Boeotians to face an attack on their western border, while the Athenian field-army stood ready to strike in at the right moment, and complete the work of their allies from Western and Central Greece. Such a far-reaching combination reveals in Demosthenes strategic imagination and the spirit of the offensive, but his brilliant conception was not based on an accurate calculation of the forces in the field, and his faith in his own star could not remove the mountains of Aetolia. It is possible that personal considerations weighed with him, for he had not been re-elected in the previous spring and this was perhaps the last opportunity which he would have of distinguishing himself. To the annoyance of the Acarnanians, who retired to their homes, he yielded to these temptations, and broke off the attack on Leucas, and began the new campaign with insufficient preparations, not waiting for contingents of light-armed troops promised him by the Ozolian Locrians. He landed at Oeneon and advanced into Aetolia. There he found his hoplites almost helpless against the Aetolian javelin-men and must have missed the Acarnanians who were masters in the art of skirmishing. After losing 120 out of the 300 Athenian hoplites whom he had with him, he was forced to retire. The Athenian fleet escorted the remainder of the expedition to Naupactus, and thence sailed home. But Demosthenes did not return, for he knew well that the Athenians did not forgive failure.

There was soon a better reason for his presence at Naupactus. The Aetolians had appealed to the Corinthians and Lacedaemonians for help, and these now proposed to send a strong force to take advantage of Demosthenes' failure. About September 426 3000 Peloponnesian hoplites concentrated at Delphi and the second offensive began. The Ozolian Locrians did not dare to offer resistance and Eurylochus, the Spartan commander of the Peloponnesians, pushed on and appeared before Naupactus about the middle of October. Demosthenes showed in adversity the boldness which had tripped him up in prosperity. He succeeded in persuading the Acarnanians to raise 1000 hoplites and with these he made good the defence of Naupactus. Eurylochus moved on into Western Aetolia where his presence emboldened the Ambraciotes to revive the old plan of the conquest of Amphilochia and Acarnania (see p. 207). They were to advance south, while Eurylochus marched north to join them. The Ambraciotes began by investing Olpae (November 426) and this threat to Amphilochian Argos roused the Acarnanians to put their full forces in the field and to invite Demosthenes to lead them. Calling up a squadron of 20 Athenian triremes that had appeared off the north-west of the Peloponnese with two generals, who were no doubt sent to supersede him, he brought his Messenians and 60 Athenian archers and took command. Meanwhile Eurylochus had joined forces with the Ambraciotes. A battle followed, in which Demosthenes showed great qualities and won a decisive victory with inferior numbers. Eurylochus was killed; his successor, Menedaeus, negotiated to secure the safe withdrawal of the Peloponnesians, leaving the Ambraciotes and the barbarian mercenaries to the tender mercy of the Acarnanians. Demosthenes hastened to agree, for such a desertion of their allies by the Peloponnesians was worth more to Athens than another victory. The Peloponnesians withdrew and their allies were chased with heavy loss into the shelter of the neighbouring Agraeans. At dawn of the next day a second Ambraciote force was trapped and destroyed at Idomene, north of Olpae.

Demosthenes could now sail off to Athens in triumph. He was elected General for the year 425 and his voice carried weight in the military councils of the Athenians. The Acarnanians, who had refused to complete the destruction of Ambracia, concluded a peace marked by distrust of Athens. The Ambraciotes on the one side and the Acarnanians and Amphilochians on the other made a treaty pledging themselves to take no offensive action on either side in the war. The Ambraciotes bound themselves not to help their neighbour, the Corinthian colony of Anactorium, which was taken by the Acarnanians in the next year, with the help of Athenian forces from Naupactus.

The result of what may be called the Demosthenes phase in the north-western area of war was to establish his personal reputation, justly enough, for his indomitable energy had more than atoned for his sanguine over-haste. But Athens had gained less than she might have hoped, for it would have been better to capture Leucas and retain the whole-hearted support of the Acarnanians. It was, none the less, true that the power of Corinth was weakened and the military prestige of Sparta was damaged by the discreditable fiasco of Eurylochus' expedition. Most important of all was the encouragement which these dramatic events gave to the optimists at Athens. In Demosthenes they had a general from whom they might hope the impossible, who had the ingenuity to invent new and promising schemes as well as the capacity to direct their execution. It was all in vain that Aristophanes in the *Acharnians* attacked the party of adventure, with their wild schemes for bringing in help from the ends of the earth, of finding war profitable and exciting, at the expense of honest Athenians who hated the Lacedaemonians but realized the blessings of peace. The Plague had ceased, Apollo's island of Delos had been purified, and Nicias displayed his piety and wealth in reinstituting the Delian festival. The anger of heaven was appeased and over, and the Athenians began the campaigning season of 425 B.C. in a spirit of resolute hopefulness.

VI. PYLOS AND SPHACTERIA

The Peloponnesians opened the campaigning season of 425 B.C. with an invasion of Attica and planned to send a fleet of 60 triremes to assist the exiles who were harrying the democrats in Corcyra (p. 222). In answer to this threat, the Athenian reinforcements for Sicily (p. 224) were ordered to sail first to Corcyra and, when the position there was secured, to continue their voyage to the West. Such were the instructions with which the two generals, Eurymedon and Sophocles, left Athens before the end of May. But with them went Demosthenes, general-elect for the civil year 425–4, who had obtained from the Assembly leave to employ the fleet off the coast of the Peloponnese if he thought fit. As the Athenians coasted round Laconia, they received the news that the enemy fleet had reached Corcyra and that their help was urgently needed. The two generals who would have to answer for it, if any delay of theirs caused disaster to the friends of Athens, were naturally disposed to abandon or postpone any scheme of Demosthenes. At this juncture, so says Thucydides, Fortune intervened in the shape of a storm which drove the Athenians to take shelter in the harbour of Pylos on the west coast of the Peloponnese, the very point at which Demosthenes had intended to employ the fleet. Here, well informed by Messenians, who knew the country, he had designed to establish a force to be a centre for depredation and a rallying point for disaffection in the territory of the Spartans.

The position was well chosen. The peninsula of Pylos was defensible and a garrison could keep in touch with the fleets of Athens. There would be no need to subject Athenians to the tedium and danger of holding the position once it was occupied, for there were Messenians only too ready to raid the fields of their old masters the Spartans. The country round was bare of troops, and the Athenians could occupy and fortify Pylos before the enemy could hinder them. While the storm raged outside, the Athenian commanders disputed within the harbour, until the sailors beguiled their enforced leisure by strengthening the position with rough walls. The storm abated, and Eurymedon and Sophocles hastened on their way, leaving behind them Demosthenes with five triremes to meet disaster or achieve success. The immediate effect went far to justify his boldness, for the Lacedaemonian government recalled their army from Attica, though it is true that bad weather and the unripeness of the Attic crops made them not unwilling to find a good reason for retirement. At the same time their fleet was ordered back from Corcyra and, evading the Athenian main squadron, it reached Pylos and the Spartans prepared for an attack by land and sea. This was the test of Demosthenes' scheme. He had worked hard to strengthen his defences, and the long arm of coincidence, if indeed it was that, had brought along two Messenian privateers with some hoplites and arms, but, even so, his force was small indeed to face a determined attack by the armies and ships of the Peloponnese. With the Spartan forces was Brasidas, his equal in courage, enterprise, and resource.

The peninsula of Pylos, or Coryphasium as the Spartans called it, was joined to the mainland on the north by a neck of sand[1]. At some point, either across the neck or where the high ground of the peninsula sloped down towards the open sea, the Athenians had built a wall which they might hope to hold against any assault not supported by siege-engines. A greater danger was from a simultaneous and resolute attack made from the sea. The east side of the peninsula and the greater part of the west face was sufficiently protected by a high line of cliffs, but at the south-west corner a landing was possible, although difficult because the sea-front was broken by rocks. Here a second wall had been built, but it was weak, and might be taken if the Spartans could land

---

[1] See map 7. On the topographical problem see the works cited in the Bibliography, especially G. B. Grundy and J. Kromayer in *Text zu Schlachten-Atlas, Griech. Abt.* 1, Bl. 3.

troops on the beach in front of it. At this, the point of danger, Demosthenes himself with a picked force of 60 hoplites and a few archers faced the enemy at the very water's edge, while his main body, perhaps 600 strong, held the land wall to the north. The Spartans attacked at both points. Brasidas was with the sea attack and pressed it with characteristic vehemence, but the defence held. Brasidas was wounded; the Athenians won his shield and the Spartans lost his counsel. The attack on the north also was repulsed, and the enemy had to expect the appearance of the Athenian fleet which was now no longer needed at Corcyra. On the naval side the position was that Pylos and the island of Sphacteria to the south guarded what is now the Bay of Navarino. From the mainland to Pylos there now stretches a sandbank, but we must assume, what is in itself probable, that in the fifth century B.C. this sandbank did not make a barrier as far west as Pylos but left open a channel from the bay into an inner harbour which is now the lagoon of Osmyn Aga. A second channel, some 130 yards wide, separated the north of Sphacteria from the peninsula. Thucydides attributes to the Spartans the design of blocking up the entrances to the bay by arranging their ships across them. We must interpret these words as referring to the two channels already mentioned, for the only other entrance, that south of Sphacteria, is 1200 yards across and the water is too deep for anchoring. While the main bay was thus open, it was at least possible to hold the inner harbour and, to assist this operation, the Spartans landed a force on the northern end of the island of Sphacteria. Having done so, they failed to do what gave the landing its meaning, and, after all, left the two channels unblocked.

The attack by land, though renewed, ended in failure, and after two days the Spartans sent away for timber to make siege-engines. But on that day the main Athenian fleet arrived. With tired rowers, Eurymedon and his colleague did not seek to force an engagement at once, but spent the night off the island of Prote, eight miles to the northward. Next morning they attacked, took the Peloponnesian fleet by surprise, and won a decisive victory which gave them the command of the sea and cut off the force on Sphacteria, which consisted of 420 Lacedaemonian hoplites with their attendant Helots.

In a moment the position was reversed and the Athenians became more besiegers than besieged. Their grip on Pylos was secure, for their troops could hold the land wall with the help of the fleet. The Peloponnesians were too shaken to face another battle by sea, and the hoplites on Sphacteria were out of reach of rescue. The heads of the Spartan government came down to see if things were as bad as they were reported to be, and arranged an armistice on the spot, while envoys carried to Athens proposals for peace. The terms of the armistice reflect the anxiety and depression of the Spartans. The Peloponnesian fleet, including all warships in Laconian waters, was to be placed in the hands of the Athenians for the duration of the armistice. A fixed, though ample, ration was to be supplied to the Spartans on the island, while each attendant Helot received half as much as his master. The Athenians retained the right to patrol the waters round the island but not to land upon it, and neither side was to make any attack. Any breach of these conditions ended the armistice, which was to last until the return of the Spartan ambassadors.

The Spartan envoys proposed not only peace but alliance between Athens and Sparta. The terms of the settlement would naturally be a matter for private negotiations, and, if the two powers agreed together, no other Greek state would be strong enough to cross them. It was clear that Sparta would make great sacrifices, if only at the expense of her allies, in order to redeem her citizens imprisoned at Sphacteria. But the negotiations broke down before the opposition of the more optimistic or grasping Athenians, adroitly led by Cleon. He demanded that the Spartans should begin by surrendering the hoplites on the island to be held as pledges for the fulfilment of further demands—the surrender to Athens of what she had given up twenty years before, Nisaea and Pegae, Troezen and Achaea. Moreover, he insisted that the negotiations should be conducted openly. Whatever sacrifices Sparta was prepared to make, it was impossible for her to bargain away in public the possessions of her allies, and if the negotiations after all broke down, she would be left without peace and without friends. After a severe struggle in the Assembly, Cleon had his way, and there was nothing left for the Spartans but to return home. With their return the armistice ended. The Athenians refused to hand back the enemy fleet, adducing petty infringements of the armistice.

It now remained to achieve by war what Cleon had failed to attain by negotiation, if that is the word for his conduct, namely, the surrender of the Spartan hoplites. Thucydides does not pronounce judgment on the wisdom of the Athenians at this moment, but the speech which he puts into the mouth of the Spartan envoys contains in itself his criticism. He gives no reply; to him, the Spartans' arguments were unanswerable. The situation in which the Spartans were placed did not reflect the permanent relative strengths of the two contending powers. The momentary advantage given by fortune, if exploited to the full, leaves the exploiter himself at the mercy of fortune. The right course is to make peace and friendship without undue regard to the advantage which one side holds at the moment; only such a peace can be enduring. To Thucydides, these Spartan envoys grace the triumph of Pericles, not of Demosthenes. It is the policy of Pericles which has brought down the Spartan spirit so low that at a single reverse they come to ask for peace. The logical conclusion of the Periclean strategy would be to make peace now, without insisting on the possession of those places which Pericles had surrendered because Athens was not strong enough to hold them. The policy of Pericles was based on the permanent resources of Athens, and these were not enough to secure all that Cleon hoped.

Thucydides believed that the wise general is bold in making war, temperate in making peace. Cleon was to justify his policy for the moment by a striking success, but Thucydides was right in thinking that Cleon's success was only less fatal to Athens than its failure would have been. For the time it looked as though Cleon's policy would soon be refuted by events. The Athenians did not venture to attack the island, occupied as it was by Lacedaemonians screened from observation by the woods which covered it. The blockade was difficult to maintain and not wholly effective, since provisions were brought to the island both by swimmers from the mainland and by daring small craft which ran in from the open sea when westerly winds drove the Athenian triremes into shelter. Weeks passed and the end of August approached without any sign of surrender. Once the autumn gales set in, the blockade would be impossible, and the Spartans on the island might escape to the mainland in the small craft that had brought them food.

From this situation Nicias, the General-in-Chief at Athens, drew one deduction, that it was unfortunate that Cleon had hindered the conclusion of a favourable peace. Cleon, whose political existence was at stake, refused to believe that nothing could be done, and his view was shared, if not prompted, by Demosthenes, who was ever sanguine and resourceful. He had learnt in Aetolia the value of light-armed troops against hoplites and was convinced that with reinforcements, especially of peltasts and archers, a successful attack was possible. His plans were aided by an accidental fire which laid bare the island, denied to the Spartans the advantages of their knowledge of the terrain, and disclosed the fact that their attendant Helots had deserted them[1]. Cleon clamoured in

[1] Thucydides' account of what follows implies the absence of the Helots.

the Assembly for the sending of reinforcements and Nicias retorted that if Cleon was so confident of success, he might take whatever troops he needed and make good his words. He was prepared to waive his powers as general, and have them transferred to his critic for the purposes of this adventure. Cleon, between fear of political ruin and confidence in Demosthenes, accepted the commission and promised to capture or kill the Spartans within twenty days. Thucydides, who knew Greek war and autumn weather, judged the promise madness, but Demosthenes supplied a method to make it come true. On Cleon's arrival at Pylos with troops from Imbros and Lemnos, peltasts, and a force of 400 archers, he found Demosthenes with his plan prepared. An ultimatum was sent offering to admit to surrender the Spartans on the island. The offer was refused, and after a day's interval, a landing was effected just before dawn with 800 hoplites who surprised the Spartan pickets and covered the disembarkation of the light troops and of some 8000 men from the crews of the Athenian fleet.

In that broken country the Lacedaemonian hoplites were almost helpless before a well-handled attack. But their defence was worthy of the Spartan reputation. After hours of struggle against overwhelming numbers, they sullenly withdrew to make a last stand behind an ancient line of walls on the high ground at the north of the island. Shielded from any but frontal attack, they held their own until the leader of Demosthenes' Messenians led a force which by climbing round the cliffs appeared suddenly on the sky-line behind the Spartan position. Then at long last the defence broke down. Demosthenes and Cleon, who realized how much more valuable to Athens the Spartans were alive than dead, held up the final attack and offered quarter. Epitadas the Spartan commander had fallen, his lieutenant lay wounded and unconscious, the third in command asked leave to communicate with the Lacedaemonians on the mainland. At last he received orders. The force was to consult its own safety so long as it avoided dishonour. Under cover of this phrase the Spartans surrendered, after having done all that brave men could do. Worn out, tortured by thirst, and with no hope of relief, their surrender seems beyond reach of all censure, yet the Greeks wondered that, in any circumstances, Spartans should surrender while they had arms in their hands. Of the 420 Lacedaemonian hoplites 128 had fallen, the rest surrendered, including about 120 full Spartiates. The Lacedaemonian land army retired, and Cleon returned to Athens in triumph with the prisoners of Demosthenes' bow and spear.

VII. CLEON: THE OFFENSIVE

Cleon was the man of the hour, and from the moment of his return to Athens he dominated Athenian policy for more than a year. He was strong enough to carry through something like a doubling of the tribute and the prestige of Athens stood so high that no revolt followed, though we must not take it that all the states that were assessed actually made payments[1]. The increase was not without some justification. The states of the Empire might expect to make greater contributions of men and money during a war, even if the war was not of their making or in their interest, and Athens had not called on most of them for contingents of troops and had paid their sailors. It might further be argued that the purchasing power of money had declined and that it was not unreasonable to raise the nominal amount of the tribute. As far as we can check it, the increase was greatest where the Athenian hold was most secure, that is, in the islands, which had been taught by the failure of the Mitylenean revolt that they were at the mercy of the Athenian fleet. This increase of revenue rendered possible a more vigorous prosecution of the war and the raising of the dicasts' allowance from two obols to three (p. 101 *sq.*). The Athenian courts were kept busy with prosecutions of all kinds, which gratified the censoriousness and sense of power of elderly jurymen who saw in Cleon the watchdog of the people.

The triumph at Sphacteria enabled the Athenians to use the Spartan prisoners as hostages to secure the immunity of Attica from invasion, and that fact alone brought a spirit of renewed confidence into their military policy. The Messenians at Pylos raided the country-side and made a refuge for Helots who deserted their masters' estates. The very security which Lacedaemon had enjoyed for so long made the Spartans peculiarly apprehensive of a widespread Helot revolt and repeated embassies visited Athens in the hope of regaining by concessions both Pylos and their prisoners. But the Athenians were in no mood for peace, and the envoys returned empty-handed. The policy of establishing fortified posts in the enemy's country (ἐπιτειχισμός) had proved so successful that it now dominates Athenian strategy.

[1] This important financial step is not mentioned by Thucydides. The sole definite evidence is the inscription, *I.G.*[2] 1, 63, which gives not the quota but the total assessment of the cities so far as the stone is preserved. A finally accepted arrangement of these fragments has not yet been reached. To the text in *I.G.*[2] should be added the restorations of Meritt in *A.J.A.* 1926, p. 26. The total of the assessment slightly exceeded 960 talents.

Nicias himself was glad enough to take an occasion to repair his damaged reputation and very possibly to be spared the spectacle of Cleon's insolent triumph. He was still General-in-chief and he set out with 80 ships, 2000 Athenian hoplites and 200 cavalry and some forces from Miletus, Andros and Carystus and sought to establish a second Pylos in the territory of the Corinthians. The general purpose of his expedition became known to the Argives, who let pass none of the advantages of neutrality, and these sent early news to Corinth. But the exact point of attack was unknown and the Corinthians accordingly concentrated a striking force at the Isthmus and guarded the whole line of their coast along the Saronic Gulf. The Athenians first made a landing at Solygeia to the south-west. But before they could establish themselves and fortify the place, a part of the Corinthian reserves came up and after a stubborn engagement in which the Athenians gained a dubious and barren victory, Nicias withdrew his men and sailed off to Crommyon at the other end of Corinthian territory. It may be that, as later in Sicily (pp. 291, 293), he had meant to feint at one point and make his true landing at another, using to the full the mobility afforded by sea power. But if that was his purpose, he failed to carry it through, and after ravaging the country round Crommyon he set off the next morning and contented himself with establishing a fortified post on the isthmus which joined the peninsula of Methana to the territory of Epidaurus and Troezen. This post proved sufficiently injurious to those states but its establishment was of second-rate importance as compared with the occupation of a point in Corinthian territory.

But the new policy and yet larger hopes of decisive action prevailed at Athens. The comparative failure of Solygeia might be attributed to over-caution; what was needed was *l'audace* and of that Cleon was the embodiment. In February 424, before the elections for the next Attic year, Aristophanes attacked Cleon in the *Knights* and pointed out that at Pylos Demosthenes was the true architect of victory. The Athenians admired boldness whether in comedians or in politicians and gave the first prize to the one, and elected the other. Demosthenes was also appointed general together with Demodocus, Autocles and Aristides, officers of established reputation. Two new names appear, those of Eucles and Thucydides the historian, neither of whom was to enjoy a successful term of office. The skill of Nicias in amphibious operations could not be spared, but, though he was re-elected, the post of General-in-chief seems to have passed to Hippocrates, the nephew of Pericles who as a strategist proposed to improve upon his uncle. The campaigning season of 424 B.C. was to test the capacity of Athens to force a speedy victory.

The first major operation, undertaken before the new generals entered office in July, was directed against Laconia. Nicias with colleagues of his own mind, Nicostratus and Autocles, led an expedition against the island of Cythera off the south-east corner of the Peloponnese. The island was carefully guarded by the Spartans, as it was a favourite landfall for the trading ships that came from Egypt and Libya and apparently a guard station against pirates or privateers. Besides, as appeared from the sequel, the moral effect of its occupation on the already shaken Spartan régime was certain to be considerable. Nicias had with him 60 triremes and 2000 hoplites, some cavalry and allied contingents, and quickly mastered the island. Thence, leaving a garrison, he ravaged the coasts of southern Laconia. The Spartans were much alarmed and found themselves obliged to keep standing forces to protect their coasts. The attrition of their morale was proceeding rapidly, and the weapon of ἐπιτειχισμός was proving its worth. The Spartans were being reduced to act like the barbarian boxers in the orator Demosthenes' analogue, who do not ward off the blows but clap their hands on the afflicted spot. The Athenian fleet ravaged the coasts of Epidaurus Limera and then descended on the Aeginetans who had been settled at Thyrea. The Spartan garrison of the upper town of Thyrea left them to their fate and the Aeginetans were killed, or carried off to Athens and executed in cold blood.

The exultation of the Athenians was dashed by the news from Sicily (p. 225), though, as has been said, the settlement of Gela removed a temptation rather than added a danger. But, with the entry of the new generals into office, Athenian strategy took a wider range. With the Lacedaemonians immobilized by fear both for their captured citizens and for their coasts, the moment had come to seize the Megarid and then to master Boeotia. The Megarians, worn down by constant invasions, with their northern harbour, Pegae, in the hands of exiles and their southern harbour, Nisaea, blocked by the Athenian occupation of Minoa, had found the war intolerable, and the leaders of the ruling democracy, to save their own skins, made overtures to Hippocrates and Demosthenes. A plot was laid to isolate the Peloponnesian garrison which held Nisaea, by seizing the Long Walls which joined the port to the city of Megara, and to open the gates of the city itself. At first the plan succeeded brilliantly: the Long Walls were occupied and the garrison at Nisaea surrendered. Though the conspirators within Megara itself had failed in their part of the scheme, the surrender of the city seemed a question of days.

At this point Fortune intervened through her chosen instrument, Brasidas, who happened to be in the neighbourhood of Sicyon and Corinth, preparing an expedition against Thrace. He realized the danger of Megara and he sent word to the Boeotians, who had already divined the ulterior significance of the Athenian *coup*, to concentrate on Tripodiscus, seven miles north-west of Megara, while he raised what troops he could from Corinth, Phlius and Sicyon. By a night march he reached Tripodiscus and, without waiting for the Boeotians, pushed on to Megara. The Megarians, in a lively state of dissension, refused him admittance and waited to see which side would prove victorious. The Boeotians reached the rendezvous at dawn with 2200 hoplites and 600 cavalry, while the remainder of their levies returned home, willing to leave Brasidas to fight their battles. He had now 6000 hoplites in all and after an indecisive cavalry skirmish he took up a position covering the city and awaited the Athenian attack. But Hippocrates and Demosthenes, whose force was slightly inferior in numbers, did not risk the loss of what they had already gained and, leaving a garrison in Nisaea, retired to Athens. Brasidas was free to resume his preparations to deal the Athenians a more serious blow. Those Megarians who had been openly implicated in the plot left the city, the rest of their party came to terms with the oligarchic exiles who returned from Pegae and, after securing the death of a hundred of their opponents, established a strong and long-lived oligarchy.

The first part of the Athenian strategic scheme had failed, though the occupation of Nisaea and part of the Megarian Long Walls[1] could be counted as a success. None the less, the second part of the scheme, the attack on Boeotia, was put into effect. Here as in the Megarid the Athenians might hope for support from within. In Phocis there was a band of exiles who had hired troops in the Peloponnese, and in Orchomenus, the old rival of Thebes, there was a party which promised to open the road into Boeotia by helping to seize the border-city of Chaeronea. Siphae on the Crisaean Gulf was to be betrayed to Demosthenes who was to come by sea from Naupactus with 40 ships and contingents of the western allies of Athens. On the day that he reached Siphae, Hippocrates was to cross the border in the east near Oropus and

---

[1] In the winter of 424–3 B.C. this part of the Long Walls was retaken by the Megarians and destroyed (Thuc. IV, 109). Nisaea remained in the hands of Athens (p 252).

seize the sanctuary of the Delian Apollo. The Boeotians would have too much to think about, with a democratic rising in the north and a hostile landing in the west, to prevent the fortification of Delium. If the anti-Theban movement spread, Demosthenes and Hippocrates might strike in with decisive effect, while, even if the Thebans held their own at first, the presence of the Athenians at Delium, raiding the country and supporting movements of revolt, would end in breaking down the Theban hegemony in Boeotia and the position as it was before Coronea might be regained. The plan, worked out in secret conclaves at which no doubt the historian Thucydides himself assisted, was well conceived. For its complete success three things were needed, continued secrecy, accurate co-ordination, and commonplace leadership on the side of the enemy.

Delay was the enemy of secrecy, and delay was unavoidable. After the partial failure at Megara, Demosthenes set out with 40 ships and raised the contingents of the western coalition. But before the full forces of the west would engage in the enterprise, they must be secured at home, and Demosthenes had to spend time in bringing into the alliance Oeniadae and Salynthius the king of the Agraei whose hostility might threaten either the Acarnanians or the Aetolians. The second cause of delay was the presence of that disturbing element, Brasidas, who presently completed his preparations and marched through Boeotia into Thessaly. As news came of his progress, the Athenians discerned his objective, Thrace; and Thucydides and Eucles were dispatched to guard Athenian interests with a small fleet instead of a large army. The full hoplite strength of Athens was needed for the great *coup*. At last, just before the close of the campaigning season, all was ready, but the secret was out. The Boeotian exiles in Phocis had not been silent, and a Phocian, Nicomachus, had taken the news to Sparta. The ephors warned the Boeotian federal executive—the Boeotarchs—and at the critical moment strong forces occupied Chaeronea and Siphae. The full federal army took the field and pro-Athenian intriguers in the various cities did not dare to move.

The enterprise of Demosthenes, once known to the enemy, had small chance of success, but its failure was made doubly certain by a mistake as to the day on which he and Hippocrates were to invade Boeotia. Demosthenes arrived too soon, realized that his project had been foiled and sailed off to suffer a reverse in an attempted landing on the coast of Sicyon.

Thus both secrecy and co-ordination had broken down, and with them two-thirds of the great scheme. There remained the occupation of Delium by Hippocrates, who, according to plan, marched out with the Athenian field-army, 7000 hoplites and something less than 1000 cavalry, together with a rabble of unorganized, ill-armed levies, labourers rather than soldiers. He seized Delium without resistance and it was busily fortified under cover of his regular troops. By noon of the third day the fortifications were complete. Hippocrates had heard nothing or only news of failure, and realized that, as at Megara, he must be content with the occupation of this strong point in the enemy's country. The light-armed troops resumed the rôle of soldiers and streamed back along the road to Athens, followed by the hoplites who stood fast on the frontier about a mile from Delium while Hippocrates left final instructions before overtaking them with the cavalry. At this moment news came that the Boeotian army was upon him. By the morning of that day the levies from all the eleven districts of Boeotia had concentrated under their various federal commanders at Tanagra five miles to the westward. A majority of the Boeotarchs was for allowing the main body of the Athenians to retreat unchallenged, now that they were no longer in Boeotian territory. But the chief representative of Thebes, Pagondas, was for fighting and his resolution and energy prevailed. At this critical moment the Boeotians had found a leader. Hippocrates sent word to the hoplites to stand to their arms, left 300 cavalry to hold Delium and to watch their opportunity to strike in during the battle that was imminent, and rejoined the army.

The battle that followed, the most considerable in the Archidamian War, was most probably fought rather more than a mile south of Delium which lay just to the east of the modern village of Dilesi[1]. The Boeotians, after leaving a force to mask Delium, were equal in hoplites, slightly superior in cavalry. They had with them 500 peltasts and 10,000 light-armed troops while the Athenians had practically none, and those few of little military value. The Athenian position was well chosen, for its flanks were protected by ravines on either side of a plateau less than a mile across. It was already late in a November afternoon and Hippocrates might hope for an indecisive battle. But Pagondas was as skilful as he was energetic. The Thebans on the right wing of his army were ranged in a column 25 men deep which pushed back the Athenian left and then proceeded to roll up their line. A like advantage gained by the Athenians on the other flank, where

---

[1] See Kromayer-Veith, *Schlachten-Atlas, Griech. Abt.* 1, Bl. 3 and *Antike Schlachtfelder* IV, pp. 177 *sqq*.

stood the men of Thespiae and, no doubt, contingents of light-armed troops to prolong the shortened hoplite line, was countered by an adroit movement. The Theban cavalry on the right which could not come to grips with the enemy because of the ravines was moved round under cover of a hill and suddenly appeared behind the victorious Athenian right wing. They were taken for the vanguard of a new army and the enemy were seized with panic and broke in flight. The fugitives were cut up by the Boeotian cavalry and some 'Locrian horse, who came up as the battle was decided, until darkness came on.' Hippocrates fell and nearly 1000 hoplites. Part of the fugitives who had made for Delium or the sea were taken off by a supporting Attic squadron, the remainder made their way across Mt Parnes and took the news to Athens.

Reinforced by troops from Corinth and Megara, the Boeotians then set themselves to take the fortified precinct at Delium. Part of the hastily constructed wall was of palisades and they succeeded in setting fire to this by means of a gigantic kind of blow-pipe. Most of the garrison escaped on shipboard, the remainder were killed or taken. The siege had lasted 16 days, but its success had proved, what had become doubtful, that a fortification could be taken without recourse to blockade. The theory of the new offensive made three postulates: the practicability of synchronized surprises, effective support from sections of the enemy states, the impregnability of fortified points in touch with the sea. All these three were denied by the events of this disastrous campaign. Besides that, the small and precious hoplite force of Athens had suffered a severe defeat, Hippocrates was dead, Demosthenes had failed and news came that the ablest of Athens' enemies was winning rapid successes at the weakest point of Athenian power.

VIII. BRASIDAS: THE COUNTER-OFFENSIVE

During the five years which followed the fiasco of Sitalces' invasion (p. 206), Athens had given little attention to her possessions in the North-East. The Bottiaeans and Chalcidians were not coerced, Perdiccas continued in name to be the friend of Athens, but, justly enough, was both suspected and suspicious. The town of Olynthus grew in power as the centre of some kind of Chalcidian federation which was so far organized as to possess a common foreign policy. The cities eastwards round the coast from Potidaea remained members of the Athenian Empire, and we have no record of any secessions at the time of the revolt of Mitylene. The Athenians had nothing but small garrisons in some of the towns and their triremes were content to apply pressure here and there where the tribute fell into arrears or was refused[1]. Once only, in the early summer of 425, the Athenian general Simonides sought to distinguish himself by scraping together a force of Athenians and Allies to capture the western of the two Eïons which lies in the country of the Chalcidians or Bottiaeans. The place was betrayed to him, but his success was short-lived for he was speedily ejected.

In the course of the next year, the feeling against Athens spread among the coast towns which had hitherto been faithful. The increase of the tribute and the domineering policy of Cleon aroused resentment, while the pre-occupation of Athens with her schemes nearer home facilitated anti-Athenian intrigues on the part of the aristocrats in the several cities. The very successes of the Athenians roused both Perdiccas and the Chalcidians to action, the Chalcidians had reason to fear a day of reckoning for Spartolus, while the King of Macedon had a bad conscience and the recollection of old quarrels. Besides this, Perdiccas had a troublesome neighbour, Arrhabaeus the prince of Lyncestis, whom a new ally might help him to coerce. Accordingly, in the summer of 424 B.C., these two powers approached the Spartans and suggested the sending to Thrace of an expedition by land. The idea was not entirely new at Lacedaemon; when the Spartans founded Heraclea in Trachis two years before, one reason according to Thucydides was its position on the road to Thrace. It is at least possible that the project was then in the mind of Brasidas, a mind which the historian seems to have known, perhaps from conversations after the one had caused the exile of the other. But no action followed the founding of Heraclea. In 424, however, the very alarm of the Spartans and their sense of the danger of a Helot rising made them willing to engage in an adventure which might distract from themselves the pressing attentions of the Athenians, and enable them to employ Helots where they would not be dangerous. In Brasidas they had the man for such an undertaking and possibly it appeared more comfortable to employ his restless talents for Sparta but not at Sparta. They provided him with funds to hire 1000 hoplites from the Peloponnesian states and placed under his command 700 Helots armed and drilled in the Spartan fashion. These Helots were more fortunate than 2000 of their like whom the Spartans had chosen out as of especial bravery. 'For these were crowned with garlands and attended the temples as having

---

[1] Such were the petty operations of the generals Demodocus, Aristides and Lamachus in the Hellespont and Euxine; see Thucydides IV, 75.

been enfranchised, and not long afterwards the Lacedaemonians caused them to disappear and no man knew how each perished.'

After organizing this small force, Brasidas made his way through Thessaly, where the mass of the people favoured Athens, partly by the help of various aristocratic dynasts and the agents of Perdiccas and the Chalcidians, partly by his own adroitness and energy. Realizing that Perdiccas was deeply compromised, he refused to be his tool and, at the cost of forfeiting some Macedonian support, he made a truce with Arrhabaeus and marched on; so that he reached the territory of Acanthus before the citizens had gathered in their vintage. The presence of his army among the ungathered grapes was a powerful argument which Brasidas reinforced by his own words, 'being no bad speaker for a Lacedaemonian.' He pledged the faith of Sparta that they should have real freedom if they abandoned Athens, and the anti-Athenian oligarchs carried the day. And soon afterwards Stagirus followed the example of her neighbour.

On the news that Brasidas had reached the districts towards Thrace, the Athenians declared war upon Perdiccas. To the two generals, Eucles and Thucydides, was assigned the duty of guarding, as best they could, the interests of Athens in the North-East. Of these generals the qualifications of Eucles are unknown and are not disclosed in the operations which follow. Thucydides had family and financial connections with Thrace and, if we may believe the apologia which underlies this part of his narrative, he might well hope to secure Thracian help to defend his charge (iv, 105). This task, however, was not made easier by the death of Sitalces, who at this very moment fell in fighting against the Triballians, and the succession, not of his phil-Athenian son Sadocus, but of his nephew Seuthes, Perdiccas' son-in-law. While Thucydides stationed himself with a small squadron at Thasos and plied his diplomatic arts, Eucles took charge of Amphipolis. Both generals, perhaps, trusted overmuch to the rigours of the Thracian winter which had by now begun.

But Brasidas, like Philip of Macedon, was no respecter of seasons and on a wintry day he marched eastwards from Arnae. He had secured partisans both in Amphipolis itself and in Argilus the city to the south-west of it. By a night march he reached Argilus where his friends were awaiting him and at dawn the bridge across the Strymon was in his hands. The Athenians in Amphipolis and those of their party closed the gates and sent word to Thucydides who, with seven triremes, raced into the river in the evening of that day. But it was already too late.

Brasidas had offered easy terms, allowing any who wished to leave the city with their goods within five days, and offering to the remainder the peaceful possession of their rights and property. Eucles had little to say or said little, and the city capitulated. Thucydides beat off an attack on Eïon at the mouth of the river, thus denying to Brasidas access from Amphipolis to the sea. But he was without the means to attempt the recapture of the city.

This disaster caused consternation and rage at Athens, for the country behind Amphipolis had supplied them with money and, what was of equal importance, timber for shipbuilding. The road farther eastward was now open, though we need not credit Brasidas with any wild schemes of marching to the Hellespont. At least we hear nothing of any such attempt or of an alliance with the Odrysians which would be its necessary preliminary. But Myrcinus, Oesyme and Galepsus came over to him and the Athenians feared further defections. The diplomacy of Brasidas was as dangerous as his army, and the recent reverses in Boeotia had damaged Athenian prestige. But it was winter, and the Athenians contented themselves with sending some troops and banishing Thucydides. Of Eucles we hear no more. There is no good reason to suppose the historian to have been either corrupt or incompetent, but he had failed. He had failed to be wiser than his colleagues or his countrymen, who might have crushed Brasidas with half the force that was defeated at Delium.

Fortunately for Athens, the government of Sparta was more ready for peace than for victory. The influence of the king Pleistoanax was steadily pacific, and the ephors had achieved their object of distracting the attention of Athens and, after Delium, might hope for a peace which would restore to them their imprisoned hoplites. They refused to send to Brasidas the reinforcements he requested and were more concerned to exploit his successes than to assist them. Despite this disappointment Brasidas was active, building triremes on the Strymon against the day when he might capture Eïon and intriguing with the disaffected oligarchs in the coast cities. During the winter, he won over the towns on the peninsula of Acte except Dium and Sane, and then marched into Sithonia. The chief city in that peninsula was Torone which was held by a small Athenian garrison. But the walls had fallen into disrepair or had even been dismantled to place the city at the mercy of Athens, and the garrison kept bad watch. Torone had been forced to pay twelve talents instead of six as tribute for at least the last two years and there was a party in favour of Brasidas[1].

[1] *I.G.*[2] 1, 218. This increase preceded the general doubling of tribute.

With their help the city was surprised and taken, as was soon afterwards the fort of Lecythus to which the Athenian garrison had retired. The Athenian possessions west of the Strymon had shrunk to little more than the peninsula of Pallene, which was guarded by Potidaea, now an Athenian stronghold.

The cumulative effect of the series of disasters which began with Delium and ended with Torone was the temporary eclipse of Cleon's influence. Nicostratus who shared the views of Nicias seems to have been elected in place of Hippocrates after Delium, and during the winter there were negotiations for an armistice. About April 20th the Athenian Assembly accepted proposals for an armistice which, to judge from the text which is preserved in Thucydides (IV, 118–9), was drafted at Sparta[1]. It was to last for a year and it was made with the definite object of preserving the status quo while a definitive peace was arranged. The Athenians retained their strong points in enemy territory but were bound not to receive deserters or fugitive slaves. On the other hand, the Lacedaemonians and their allies were not to send out any ships of war, though their trading ships might pass freely on their lawful occasions. There is little doubt that the Spartans hoped to negotiate the Athenians out of Pylos and Cythera and their prisoners out of Athens, while the Athenians hoped to negotiate Brasidas out of the region towards Thrace.

These hopes were soon shattered. Two days after the armistice was ratified, Scione, the second largest city in Pallene, declared for Brasidas, who did not hesitate to throw a garrison into the town. He had now a footing in the peninsula and planned to attack Mende and Potidaea. At this point arrived commissioners from Sparta and Athens with news of the armistice. Agreement was reached about all the cities except Scione. The Athenian commissioner declared that Brasidas must withdraw; Brasidas refused and asserted, with more vigour than truth, that the revolt happened before the armistice was ratified; the Lacedaemonian government proposed arbitration; the Athenian Assembly declared its intention to take the city and put the inhabitants to death. This motion was proposed by Cleon.

The Greeks had a notable capacity for simultaneous peace and war. The armistice continued in force in Greece proper, while the most active and bitter hostilities were pursued in the peninsula of

---

[1] Formulated at Sparta, reported verbally by Spartan envoys at Athens and reduced to writing by the Secretary of the Athenian Council for the approval of the Assembly; see A. Kirchhoff, *Thukydides und sein Urkundenmaterial*, pp. 4–27.

Pallene. An oligarchical minority in Mende contrived to bring about the secession of that city and the two towns were put in a position of defence. The women and children were removed to Olynthus and 500 hoplites and 500 peltasts were sent to assist the citizens to face the impending attack from Athens. A larger force would have been in place, but Brasidas had to reckon with the fact that, while the Athenians in Potidaea controlled the isthmus, the peninsula was, in effect, an island, in which his whole army might be interned by the Athenian fleet until it starved or out-stayed its welcome. He had to choose between besieging Potidaea and using the main body of his army elsewhere. He chose to march with Perdiccas against Arrhabaeus, though possibly the choice was dictated by the fact that the king had been contributing to the support of his troops and claimed his reward. The expedition ended in the flight of Perdiccas and the retreat of Brasidas, who was left unsupported to face the Lyncestians and their Illyrian allies. His troops in anger plundered the baggage of the Macedonian army, and Perdiccas retorted by making peace once again with the Athenians[1].

Meanwhile Nicias and Nicostratus with a fleet of 50 triremes and an army which contained 1000 Athenian hoplites had landed in Pallene and had taken Mende all but its citadel. With wise clemency the lives of the citizens were spared, the oligarchic conspirators being handed over to their democratic townsfolk for judgment. Brasidas was helpless so long as the Athenians held Potidaea and the sea, and sat at Torone while blockading lines were drawn round Scione. Perdiccas had used his influence to prevent Lacedaemonian reinforcements from traversing Thessaly. In their place came a Spartan commissioner Ischagoras, who brought with him Spartiate governors for the new allies of Lacedaemon. It is unlikely that these shone by comparison with the Athenians who had preceded them. Nicias and Nicostratus returned to Athens leaving Scione closely besieged. The Athenians could afford to wait for their revenge.

The armistice continued in force until April 422 B.C., but in an atmosphere of recriminations and distrust no progress had been made towards a definitive peace. At the elections in March of that year Cleon was chosen General, and he intended to repeat in the North-East his military triumph of 425. He planned the punishment of Scione, the restoration of Athenian power throughout Sithonia and Acte, and, most resounding success of all, the recovery

[1] Thucydides IV, 132; *I.G.*[2] I, 71 and J. J Hondius, *Novae Att. Inscr.*, pp. 22 *sqq.*

of Amphipolis. In April the armistice was not renewed, but military operations were postponed until after Cleon entered office in July. Even then there was delay, for the Etesian winds in the Aegean hinder an expedition to the north during the month of August. But meanwhile Athenian diplomacy was active. The Bottiaeans and Chalcidians were too near neighbours to be lasting friends and an alliance was made with the larger part of the Bottiaean communities[1]. Perdiccas was pledged to give help, and the expedition which sailed at the beginning of September had good hopes of success. The troops blockading Scione might be drawn upon, and Cleon took from Athens 1200 Athenian hoplites, 300 cavalry and contingents from the Allies. His success was greater than Thucydides describes. Besides taking Torone, he succeeded in winning back to Athens a string of towns, Singus, Mecyberna, Gale, Cleonae and Acrothoï. At least all these re-appear in the assessment of the year 421 B.C.[2] Part of his task was done, and Scione might be left to starve. There remained Amphipolis, where Brasidas, after failing to relieve Torone, had concentrated his forces. Cleon moved to Eïon where he waited for reinforcements from Perdiccas and from Polles, king of the Odomantes, and meanwhile won back Galepsus, but failed in an attempt upon Stagirus. Brasidas had forces equal to his own, but the impatience of the Athenian hoplites, who disliked their general as much as the prospect of a Thracian winter, forced him to make a demonstration. With the hardihood of his ineptitude, he trailed his army along within striking distance of Amphipolis and was defeated. As better soldiers have done, he ran away, and was killed, along with 600 Athenians. Sparta suffered a greater loss, for Brasidas fell in the moment of victory. As the Spartan prisoner said after Cleon's triumph at Sphacteria: 'The arrow would be a valuable weapon if it could single out the brave.'

---

[1] *I.G.*[2] i, 90. See B. D. Meritt, *Peace between Athens and Bottice*, *A.J.A.* xxix (1925), p. 29.

[2] See A. B. West and B. D. Meritt, *Cleon's Amphipolitan campaign and the assessment list of* 421, *A.J.A.* xxix (1925), pp. 59 *sqq.* The terms of the Peace of Nicias appear to imply that at the time when the Peace was made, only six towns, apart from Scione, were successfully resisting Athens (p. 250). It is possible that, despite the return to Athens of the main army, there were desultory operations during the winter 422–1 (to which may perhaps be assigned the recovery of the three Thracian towns, Zone, Sale and Drys, see *I.G.*[2] 64), but, even so, the Athenians must have achieved considerable successes during the campaigning season of 422 B.C.

IX. THE PEACE OF NICIAS

The death of Brasidas removed the last obstacle from the path of the peace party at Sparta. The king Pleistoanax was anxious to end a war in which the blame for all misfortunes was laid at his door by those who alleged that he had impiously bribed the priestess at Delphi to procure his return. Delphi itself had, doubtless, become more anxious to see Hellas at peace than to witness the victory which Apollo had promised to the Spartans. The kinsmen and friends of the Spartiate prisoners at Athens were prepared to purchase their freedom by any sacrifice. The Thirty Years Truce made with Argos in 451 (p. 86) had almost reached its term, and Argos would soon be free to head an anti-Spartan movement in the Peloponnese or to strike in openly on the side of Athens. Finally, the defeat of Cleon had made the Athenians inclined to peace, while his death had removed the most serious obstacle to a settlement by understanding and compromise. Nicias, who resumed the direction of Athenian policy, cared more to avoid disaster than to achieve victory, provided only that the power of Athens was left unimpaired and free to restore her hold on the Thrace-ward district. If the limited objective of Pericles—the demonstration of Athenian invincibility—could be attained, the moment for peace had arrived.

During the winter of 422–1 B.C. envoys went to and fro between Athens and Sparta and the two powers reduced to a minimum the grounds of dispute between them. At Athens Aristophanes wrote his comedy, the *Peace*, to be performed at the Great Dionysia in March 421 B.C. (p. 141 *sq.*). The play reflects the growing desire for peace, the realization that fratricidal strife was grinding Greece to powder, and that now there was hope because the two 'pestles of war,' Cleon and Brasidas, had vanished. Equally clearly are revealed in the play the cross-currents of self-interest which made it hard, even now, to reach a settlement. Sparta was prepared to sacrifice the interests of her allies, but it was imperative that the extent of these sacrifices should be concealed until the last moment; at the same time, the Lacedaemonians could not allow the negotiations to be protracted until the termination of their peace with Argos. They forced the issue by announcing a mobilization of the Peloponnesian armies with the object of establishing a fortified post in Attica, thus turning against Athens her own weapon. Within a few days of the performance of the *Peace* in the theatre at Athens, the two powers agreed together, and the Spartans summoned a meeting of their allies and laid before them the bargain that had been made.

Thucydides (v, 18) has preserved for us the very phrases of the document which was the product of six months of cautious bargaining after nearly ten years of ruinous, demoralizing war. The Delphians, those honest brokers, received their reward in the formal recognition of their independence as against the Phocians (p. 88), and of their control of the oracular wisdom of Apollo. Then come clauses in the regular form establishing peace between the Lacedaemonians and Athenians and their respective allies for fifty years. As in the Thirty Years Peace it is provided that any disputes shall be settled by arbitration. The governing principle of the settlement which follows is the restoration of what each belligerent had taken in the course of the war. But the application of this principle was beset with difficulties, above all in the region towards Thrace, for a number of cities in that area were still in revolt from Athens with the declared support of Sparta, and of these at least two, Olynthus and Spartolus, had seceded from the Athenian alliance before the war began. In return for the handing over to her of her cherished colony, Amphipolis, and for a free hand with the remaining cities of that area, Athens acquiesced in a compromise as regards Argilus, Stagirus, Acanthus, Stolus, Olynthus, and Spartolus. These towns were not to be allies either of Athens or of Sparta, except that they might of their own free choice join the Athenian alliance at any time. The inhabitants might, if they wished, remove themselves and their property whithersoever they would, and Athens pledged herself to take no hostile action against these cities so long as they paid 'the tribute assessed by Aristides' (see above, p. 45). They are therefore in a special position with no obligation to render to Athens and no right to ask from Sparta the military assistance of an ally. The tribute which they have to pay is not affected by the re-assessment of 425 and they are secured against further increases in the future. With the exception of these six towns, the Athenian control of the Thrace-ward area is admitted. Express provision is made for the independent existence as cities of Mecyberna, Sane, and Singus, a provision which is best interpreted as a continuation of the Athenian policy of preventing the absorption or coalescence of the small towns in this region (p. 172)[1]. As regards cities held by Athens, among

---

[1] Steup, *Thukydideische Studien* I, pp. 40 *sqq*. That the Chalcidian League is not mentioned or assumed in the Peace does not prove that it did not exist, but only that Athens was unwilling to acknowledge its existence. See p. 185, n. 1.

which is included Scione then blockaded beyond hope of relief, the Athenians receive a free hand to deal with the inhabitants at their discretion, and the same clause is extended to cover any of the present members of the Athenian Empire. The implications of the Peace are clear. All the states which accept it accept this settlement and are pledged to abide by its conditions. Against any states which do not accept it, Athens is entitled to make war without hindrance from the other signatories of the Peace. If the other allies of Sparta accept the Peace, the Chalcidians and neighbouring cities are given the choice between abandoning their hopes of complete freedom and facing, unaided, the full power of Athens. Throughout the remainder of the Empire Athens may work her will.

If the war was an attack on the Empire of Athens, the Peace acknowledged its failure. A decade of peace would replenish the treasures on the Acropolis. The two remaining pillars of Athenian power, the linked fortress of the city and the Piraeus and the Athenian fleet, were unchallenged. During the war Athens had lost only two places which could be called integral parts of her own territory, the colony of Amphipolis and the border-town of Panactum betrayed to the Boeotians in the summer of 422 B.C. It was expressly stipulated that these should be restored to her.

The apparent price to be paid for all this was the surrender of what would only be of use while the war continued. The Peloponnesian prisoners, above all the Spartiates whom the Athenians had taken on Sphacteria, were to be handed back. Included among these were the allies of Sparta who formed part of the garrison of Scione. In return Athenian and allied prisoners were to be restored to their several cities. Further, Athens was to place in the hands of Sparta the strong points occupied for the purpose of war in the Peloponnese and Central Greece, Coryphasium (i.e. Pylos), Cythera, Methana, Pteleum and Atalante[1].

---

[1] Coryphasium p. 231; Cythera p. 238; Methana p. 237; Atalante p. 198. The identification of Pteleum is doubtful. Thucydides gives us no help and has omitted to mention its occupation. The other names in the list are in geographical order and Busolt argues that Pteleum must lie between Methana and Atalante. This suits Pteleum in Boeotia S.E. of Thebes attested by Pliny, N.H. iv, 7. 26. But the reading in Pliny is suspected (see Mayhoff, ad loc.) and it is improbable that the Athenians should have taken and held Pteleum while they lost Panactum. The Pteleum in Messenia or Triphylia mentioned by Strabo VIII, 349 may not have existed in historic times, except as an uninhabited tract of woodland called Ptelasium (ib. 350). Unless it lay on the coast a permanent Athenian occupation is improbable, and we would expect it to be mentioned along with Coryphasium. There remains Pteleum

With the satisfaction of Athenian and Lacedaemonian interests, the force of principle was exhausted. There follows a significant silence, eloquent of Sparta's betrayal of Corinthian interests. During the war Corinth had lost practically all her allies and dependencies in North-West Greece. There is no word of their restoration. The formal reason for this may have been that what had been taken in war had not passed into the possession of Athens or even of states which, at the moment, were allies of Athens. The very fact that the Acarnanians and Amphilochians had already withdrawn from the war (p. 229) placed their acquisitions at the expense of Corinth outside the purview of a peace which concerned only the allies of Sparta and Athens. Corinth might embark on a private war to regain what she had lost, but she had no claim on Lacedaemonian support, and was too broken in power to contemplate such an adventure unaided. Nor was there anything in the Peace which would preclude Athens from renewing her alliances in North-West Greece at a moment convenient to her and inconvenient to Corinth. The treaty is equally silent about Nisaea, the port of Megara which remained in the hands of Athens as an asset for bargaining. The especial interests of Boeotia were entirely disregarded. Such was the settlement to which the allies of Sparta were invited to assent and pledge themselves by solemn oaths to be renewed each year. The record of this piece of cynical state-craft was to adorn the three centres of Panhellenic religion, Delphi, the Isthmus, and Olympia, as well as the Acropolis of Athens and the Amyclaeum at Sparta. Finally the right of future amendment of the Peace was reserved to the two High Contracting Powers, Athens and Sparta.

It was easy for Athenian and Lacedaemonian envoys to exchange oaths ratifying this arrangement. The problem was to impose the settlement on the allies of Sparta, and the failure to solve that problem and the consequences of the failure form the subject of the succeeding chapter. The breakdown of the Peace marks the beginning of a new epoch; the achievement of it is the legacy of Periclean state-craft. Athens had secured by the war what Pericles set out to attain, the vindication of Athenian power. But this result might have been reached four years before, after the occupation of Pylos, had Athens been guided then by wiser counsels than those of Cleon. In 425 the Thrace-ward cities had

on the coast of Phthiotic Achaea, which may have been occupied for the same reason as Atalante, viz. to limit the activities of privateers. This identification seems to the present writer most probable, though if the order is strictly geographical, Pteleum should follow, not precede, Atalante.

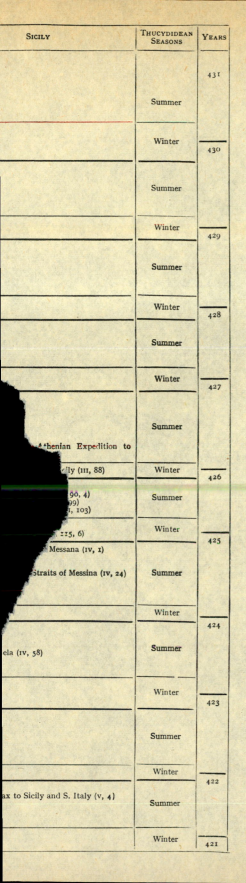

SICILY	THUCYDIDEAN SEASONS	YEARS
		431
	Summer	
	Winter	430
	Summer	
	Winter	429
	Summer	
	Winter	428
	Summer	
	Winter	427
	Summer	
Athenian Expedition to Sicily (III, 88)	Winter	426
90, 4) 99) , 103)	Summer	
115, 6)	Winter	425
Messana (IV, 1)		
Straits of Messina (IV, 24)	Summer	
	Winter	424
ela (IV, 58)	Summer	
	Winter	423
	Summer	
	Winter	422
ax to Sicily and S. Italy (v, 4)	Summer	
	Winter	421

SYNCHRONISTIC TABLE OF THE ARCHIDAMIAN WAR[1]

[1] The references throughout, where no author or collection of inscriptions is mentioned (*I.G.*[2] 1 = *Inscript. Graec.* ed. minor, 1; H.-H. Hicks and Hill) are to the chapter or, where closer definition is needed, the section of Thucydides from which dates may be deduced. For the chronology see *Fasti Attici* in I.G.[2] 1, pp. 286 *sqq.* and Beloch, *Griech. Gesch.* II[2], 2, pp. 228 *sqq.* and Busolt, III, 2 *passim*. The present writer is inclined to accept, though with some hesitation, Keil's theory of a separate Council Year and not to attach independent value to the archon-dates in Diodorus for the closer chronology of these years 431–21 B.C. Thucydides' synchronisms cannot well be quite exact, but may be used allowing a small margin for error. Hicks and Hill 58 is no longer evidence for the Athenian expedition to Lesbos under Paches. The first decree on Methone (Hicks and Hill, 60), should be set in 430–29 (see A. B. West, *A.J.A.* XXIX, 1925, p. 440). The Thucydidean summer is regarded as lasting from about the end of March to the end of October.

[2] Generals. The Roman numerals denote their tribes according to their official order. Where two generals are elected from the same tribe, one of them is General-in-chief. † means that a general met his death during his year of office. Names in brackets are of generals who, in default of direct evidence, may fairly be assumed to have held office. See Beloch, *op. cit.* II[2], 2, pp. 260 *sqq.*, where the evidence is collected. The work of Beloch is the starting-point for all inquiry on this topic. Of value also is A. B. West, in *A.J.Ph.* XLV, 1924, pp. 141 *sqq.* A. Krause, *Attische Strategenlisten*, Jena Diss. 1914, adds little for these years. Paches disappears from the list for 429–8 B.C. now that *I.G.*[2] 1, 105 (H.-H. 58) is more correctly dated 411–10. The tribe of Eurymedon is not known, since Busolt's restoration of *C.I.A.* IV, 1, 179 c. fr. B 4, which assigned him to tribe IV or V, must be abandoned since Bannier's article *B.P.W.* 1913, col. 1613; see *I.G.*[2] 1, 297 and *ibid.* p. 288. This makes feasible the reconstruction given here. Pythodorus may be assigned to tribe VIII (West) which makes possible Laches as general in 426–5. The tribe of Nicostratus is not attested, but it is possible that he belonged to the same tribe as Hippocrates and was chosen to fill his place after Delium. The generalships of Lamachus are doubtful. The generalships of Demodocus, Lamachus, and Aristides in 424–3 appear probable, that of Pythodorus more doubtful. If he did not hold office, there is no need to suppose (with West) any by-elections in 424 B.C. except one to fill the place of Hippocrates.

[3] Assuming that ἐβδομήκοντα in II, 75. 3 is corrupt: see Beloch, *loc. cit.*

F. E. A.

To face p. 252.

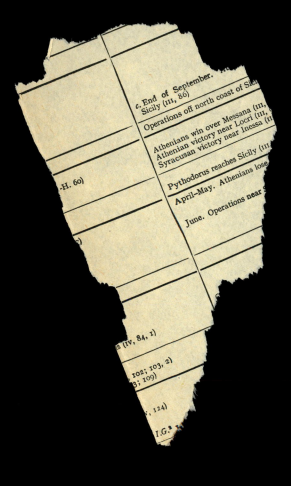

c. End of September.
Sicily (III, 86)

Operations off north coast of Sic

Athenians win over Messana (III,
Athenian victory near Locri (III,
Syracusan victory near Inessa (II

Pythodorus reaches Sicily (III

April–May. Athenians lose

June. Operations near s

-H. 60)

)

s (IV, 84, 1)

102; 103, 2)
3; 109)

, 124)

I.G.

...WEST GREECE	THE AEGEAN, ASIA MINOR	THE THRACE-WARD RE...
e (II, 30)		Siege of Potidaea continues. Athenians allied (II, 29) ? Phormio returns to Athens (II, 58, 2)
, 33)		
		August. Hagnon before Potidaea (II, 58)
	Melesander fails in Lycia (II, 69)	Surrender of Potidaea (II, 70) First decree passed about Methone (I.G....
rth-West (II, 80) (II, 86; 92, 7)		End of May. Athenians defeated in Cha... Athenian army withdrawn (ibid.)
		c. November. Sitalces' invasion of Macedonia...
(III, 7)	June. Lesbos revolts (III, 2) Armistice at Mitylene (III, 4)	
	September–October. Paches reaches Lesbos (III, 18, 3)	
	Lysicles killed in Caria (III, 19) February–March. Salaethus reaches Mitylene (III, 25)	
76, 1) a (III, 76 sqq.)	End of June. Alcidas reaches Delos (III, 29, 1) Fall of Mitylene (III, 27) Mid-July. Alcidas reaches Embatum (III, 29) Paches at Notium (III, 34)	
, 91) (III, 95) nania (III, 102)	Athenian expedition to Melos (III, 91)	Second decree about Methone (I.G.² 1, 57=
lpae (III, 105)	Purification of Delos (III, 104)	
		Simonides defeated at the western Eïon (IV,
1; 29, 1; 39, 1) Capture of Anactorium (IV, 49)		
(I.G.² 1, 324, l. 19)	Athenian envoys to Persia (IV 50)	
, 76)	Athenian minor operations in Hellespont and Euxine (IV, 75)	
e (IV, 89)		September. Brasidas arrives before Acanthu...
		c. December. Brasidas takes Amphipolis (IV Spread of revolt in the North-East (IV, 107,
		c. April 22. Revolt of Scione (IV, 120) May. Revolt of Mende (IV, 123) Brasidas and Perdiccas attack Arrhabaeus (I Nicias retakes Mende (IV, 129) Nicias besieges Scione (IV, 131; 133, 3) Perdiccas makes peace with Athens (IV, 132,
		Brasidas fails to take Potidaea (IV, 135)
		Athenian alliance with Bottiaeans (I.G.² 1, 90 September. Cleon takes Torone (V, 3, 2) October. Further operations of Cleon (V, 6) Battle of Amphipolis (V, 7, 1; 12, 1; Andr... Pacem 48)

not yet been inspired by the courage of Brasidas and Argos was not about to enter on the stage of Greek politics as a menace to Sparta and a temptation to Athens. And, further, both then and now, the true price of Sparta's surrender of her allies was that Athens should help to secure her against their resentment. For, as will be described below, the Peace of Nicias was followed by the formal conclusion and publication of an alliance between Sparta and Athens. It is possible that Nicias looked back beyond the policy of Pericles to the policy of Cimon, and was willing to make some sacrifice of Athenian interests in order to revive an ancient dualism. But, whether Athens was inclined or not to entangle herself by this alliance, we should be doing Spartan diplomacy less than justice if we did not suppose that Pleistoanax and the ephors insisted upon receiving in advance the promise of this insurance against the danger from Argos and the emotions which the publication of the Peace was certain to evoke in the hearts of their deluded allies. Sparta was not yet so reduced that she could be forced to face the risks of the Peace without the security of the alliance. Had Greece been a chessboard, this combination would deserve high applause. But its immediate result was to destroy far more good will than it created and to involve Athens as well as Sparta in numberless complications. Athens had won the war; to win the peace called for the steady patient guidance of a statesman powerful enough to impose upon the Athenian democracy a cool and consistent, above all a pacific, foreign policy. This task was too high for Nicias, too long-drawn for Alcibiades. To complete the victory of Periclean state-craft, the one thing was needed which Athens could not produce—a second Pericles.

CHAPTER IX

SPARTA AND THE PELOPONNESE

I. THE SPARTAN-ATHENIAN ALLIANCE

THE treaty which ended the Archidamian War was never executed in its entirety. In their eagerness to recover Pylos and the citizens lost at Sphacteria, the Spartans had assumed obligations which they could not fulfil, and since it was upon Sparta that the lot fell to make restitution first, Athens was automatically absolved from doing its part. What the Spartans could do without regard to others, they did at once: they released their Athenian prisoners. Then two impossible tasks confronted them, to induce their recalcitrant allies to accept the treaty, and to restore Amphipolis to the Athenians.

At the moment, the officer who had succeeded Brasidas was inside the walls of Amphipolis; and, since he had a Lacedaemonian garrison with him, the home authorities ordered him to put the city into the hands of the Athenians. But Clearidas, for such was his name, disapproved both of the treaty and of the mission entrusted to him and professed to be unable to surrender the place against the wishes of the inhabitants. His hesitation was probably fatal. Some precious weeks were spent in backing and filling, and then Sparta virtually accepted his opinion (which he had returned home to present personally) by giving him permission to withdraw his troops from Amphipolis altogether. The evacuation of this key position, and the subsequent recall of all the Lacedaemonian forces in Thrace (summer 421 B.C.) formally disassociated Sparta from direct resistance to the treaty, but thereafter the Spartans lacked physical means of redeeming their pledges in that district.

Note. Thucydides (v, 20 to end of book) is the chief source for this chapter. His narrative is less straightforward than usual partly because of the intricacy of events and partly because of literary troubles incident to his change of general plan (p. 480 *sq.*). Diodorus (XII, 75–82), who has used Ephorus, adds little or nothing to Thucydides and confuses what he gives. Plutarch's *Lives* of Nicias and Alcibiades are valuable, particularly for the circumstances in which Hyperbolus was ostracized and for personal detail derived not, as is the thread of each biography, from the ancient historians, but from comic poets and writers of memoirs, speeches, chronicles (*Atthides*), and dialogues, of which the great part has perished. The inscriptions serve to check Thucydides and to acquaint us with some important happenings, chiefly in Athens. See the Bibliography.

The restoration of the Athenian Empire in the Thrace-ward parts—one of the primary objects of Athens in ending the war—would perhaps have lain within the moral power of Sparta had it succeeded in holding its alliance together. But the nature of the peace precluded this. The terms of the treaty had indeed been ratified by a majority of the Peloponnesians and their allies; but the opposition comprised Elis, Corinth, Megara, and Boeotia, the most important members of the coalition after Sparta itself, and these states refused point blank to abide by the decision reached.

The real basis of Elean dissent was private—a bitter quarrel with Sparta over Lepreum—and when Mantinea also joined the opposition, it, too, acted for reasons unconnected with the peace; but in the cases of Corinth, Megara, and Boeotia it was the treaty alone that determined their attitude.

After a ten years war, during which its maritime traders had enjoyed only the privileges of pirates, Corinth was asked to accept without compensation a peace which confirmed Athens in the possession of all the objects in dispute. For not only was Corcyra definitely lost to its mother country, but Sollium and Anactorium, Corinthian colonies in Acarnania, were also left with the enemy; so that Athens was better able than before the war to control the passage of merchant ships and naval expeditions to and from the Adriatic and the West. To the Corinthians this seemed a betrayal of Peloponnesian interests—a demonstration that the Peloponnese needed a new leader. With Athens, therefore, they suspended hostilities, but did not even make a truce.

The outcome was even more intolerable for Megara. For its chief harbour, Nisaea, remained in the hands of Athens, which refused to give it up unless Thebes surrendered Plataea. This, however, Thebes would do only under compulsion. The votes of Plataea sealed its preponderance in the Boeotian League. It saw no reason why it should make a concession thus doubly important to secure peace. The Boeotians were not war-weary. To them alone the war had been really profitable. For ten years they had been engaged (under cover of the Peloponnesian armies) in transferring to their own towns the movable property of neighbouring Attica. Unaided they were not strong enough to carry on war with any hope of conquering Athens, but after Delium they believed they could repel an Athenian invasion of Boeotia without the assistance of the Peloponnesians; so they simply made a truce for ten-day periods. In the meanwhile they retained their Athenian prisoners and the frontier post of Panactum which they had captured in the course of the war.

The insubordination of these five states gathered significance from the fact that at the very time at which Sparta had failed to live up to its military reputation and their expectations, the treaty lapsed by which thirty years earlier (451 B.C.) Argos had withdrawn from the struggle for the headship of the Peloponnese. The sympathies of Argos were preponderantly with the enemies of the Lacedaemonians; for the Spartan hegemony was an affront to ancient Argive traditions. And in form of government the Argives stood close to Athens. But thus far they had remained neutral in the war because, isolated as they were in the midst of the Spartan confederacy, they were too weak to defend themselves; and, because of the Athenian strategy of non-resistance on land, they saw no possibility of being helped from outside. And had Sparta succeeded in getting rid of Athens in April 421 B.C. without alienating its most powerful confederates, it would not have had to beg a peace from Argos. In the circumstances, however, the prospects that opened out to Argos were so alluring that it declined to bind itself again to neutrality.

What was Sparta to do? It could not break with Athens if for no other reason than because the Athenians still held captive five per cent. of its citizens. The alternative was to bind Athens yet further—a contingency contemplated doubtless on the conclusion of peace (see above, p. 253). Hence in May 421 B.C. the two states concluded a fifty-years alliance, which pledged each to bring military assistance to the other in the event of an attack by third parties, and forbade either in such a case to make peace without the other. Athens, moreover, undertook to aid Sparta should a Helot uprising occur.

This was a sudden reversal of policy for both, and it put a severe strain on public opinion in each. But a re-orientation was justified as *Machtpolitik* by the failure of a ten years war to upset the equilibrium between them. The alliance, too, evoked memories of Cimon and of glorious days when they mauled the Persians instead of mauling one another. But what commended it chiefly was the exigency of the moment. By it the Spartans hoped to keep Argos quiet, since they believed that if Athens were on their side, neither would Argos attack them nor the Peloponnese secede to Argos. The immediate gain of the Athenians was security from invasion for Attica should they proceed, as was natural, to restore by force of arms their Empire in Thrace.

The arrangement thus contained a double threat, but only in case Argos and the dissidents proceeded to gain their objects by war. The original treaty, however, had provided for alterations in the covenant at the discretion of Athens and Sparta alone,

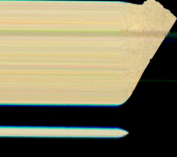

and in the light of the alliance, this clause, which concealed in an unaccented formula a claim on Sparta's part to act for its allies as Athens acted for its subjects, was construed to forecast positive measures, jointly taken by the two Hellenic great powers. In Sparta, as well as in Athens, a party existed which favoured a policy of co-operative aggression, and to strengthen its hands as well as to create an atmosphere more favourable to peace, the Athenians now released their Spartan prisoners.

The result was not a lessening of the tension. On the contrary, the Spartans assumed a firmer tone in their dealings with Athens, and pressed for the evacuation of Pylos. Since Athens could not continue instigating a Helot revolt while pledged to aid in its suppression, the demand was not unreasonable; but seeing that Sparta now avowed its inability to restore Amphipolis, and would not set a time limit to the undertaking it gave[1] to treat as its enemies allies who by refusing to accept the peace had remained enemies of Athens, the Athenians yielded only partially in the matter of Pylos: they withdrew to Cephallenia the Messenians and deserting Helots by whom it was garrisoned, but put in their place a detachment of their own troops.

If Sparta did not go far enough to convince the Athenians of its good faith, its gestures were sufficiently menacing to produce an effect on its late associates; but the effect was directly the opposite of that intended. Instead of submitting they simply made haste to secure the only protection visible to them, as well as furtherance of their quarrel with Athens, by the creation of a new coalition based on Argos.

II. THE ARGIVE COALITION

The capabilities of Argos for Hellenic leadership were now to be tested. The Argives had not shared in the wastage of strength and energy which the long struggle had brought on most of the belligerents; and thus, as Thucydides says, they had reaped harvests from their neutrality. But they possessed weaknesses which more than balanced their prosperity. Their citizen body was divided against itself on the fundamental issue of ulterior relations with Athens and Sparta; and the opposition to war with Sparta was at the same time opposition to the democratic form of government. Moreover, the democratic institutions of Argos, while attracting

---

[1] Thucydides v, 35, 3. Part of this transaction, entered into by ten pleni-potentiaries on each side (Diod. xii, 75, 4), was probably the undertaking 'not to make peace or war except together' (Thucydides v, 42, 2; 39, 3; 46, 2). See below, p. 261.

the Mantineans, repelled the Megarians and the Boeotians. Thus the tendency for democratic states to take their place on one side and aristocratic states on the other ran counter to the project of Argos to form a new coalition on foreign issues wholly, and confused the political situation in Argos itself. It was, therefore, doubtful whether the constitution of Argos would stand the strain of a prolonged struggle or defeat.

The Argives had thought it incompatible with the liberal character of their domestic institutions to keep their entire citizen population trained and fit for war like the Spartans. Yet they could not close their eyes to the superiority of their neighbour's army. They had, therefore, adopted the plan used in Great Britain and America to-day of selecting a fraction of the men available for military service and maintaining them at professional standards of manœuvring and marching, leaving the rest comparatively undisciplined and untrained—a dangerous experiment when in the corps of 1000 *élite* thus constituted were enrolled, for the most part, young men of aristocratic families.

Lest Argos should awaken slumbering animosities by seeming to seek power for itself, Corinth undertook the task of organizing the coalition. Its first step was to have the Argives designate twelve of their citizens as a commission with full power to conclude an alliance 'for mutual defence of territories' with any state that wished, except Sparta and Athens. With both or either of these an alliance was not precluded, but it was to be negotiated only after authorization had been given by the Argive people. This adroit bid for members for a third coalition, to be independent of the other two, was so presented as to enable states to make overtures privately when they did not wish to compromise themselves needlessly. The amplitude of the movement could be kept hid till the moment for disclosure had arrived.

The second move of the Corinthians was to convene in their own city a general conference of states that were ready to come out in the open. Their hope was to secure unanimity on the part of all the communities that had rejected the peace. In this they were foiled; not so much by Sparta's denunciation of their conduct as sacrilegious, in that, having sworn to abide by the decisions of the Peloponnesian Congress 'unless there was some hindrance from gods or heroes,' they had none the less repudiated the treaty; for to this the answer was ready that the real sacrilege was the desertion of the Chalcidians, whom they had all sworn to defend. What mainly foiled them was the unreadiness of the Megarians and the Boeotians.

In consequence, the secession from Sparta took place piece-meal. First Mantinea and Elis, then Corinth and the Chalcidians, joined themselves with Argos, the former being actuated, as we have seen, by hostility to Sparta, the latter by hostility to Athens. There was thus something inherently self-contradictory about the Argive coalition from the very beginning, and ardour on its behalf was at once damped when Tegea refused to have anything to do with it, and Megara and Boeotia, acting in accord now as throughout, continued to temporize. The decision of so important a place as Tegea caused the rest of the Peloponnese to pause, and by preventing the secession from Sparta from becoming a land-slide, it daunted even the Corinthians. Elis, Mantinea, and Argos went on to convert their agreement for mutual defence into an alliance for common action in waging war and concluding peace; but Corinth refused to commit itself thus far. Yet the movement for a reorganization of the Peloponnese could not be said to have failed so long as the attitude of Boeotia remained undefined. Hence Boeotia became the next battleground.

The spirit of government in Boeotia was aristocratic, and those in authority there looked askance at states which were ordered on democratic principles. Hence the Boeotians had no predisposition to throw in their lot with Argos, and would only do so when they were certain that Sparta would join Athens in compelling them to disgorge the spoils of the Archidamian War. Hence when the Corinthians approached them directly in the summer of 421 B.C., urging them to enter the Argive confederation, they simply bade them wait. Nor did they annul their truce with Athens, as the Corinthians requested, when it proved that Athens was unwilling to extend it to include Corinth also. Obviously their course was to make no move till the plans of Athens and Sparta were farther disclosed.

Do what it might, Sparta could not evade the initiative. What was it to do? The course set by the Peace of Nicias and the alliance with Athens was clear enough: Sparta must join Athens in co-ercing its former allies. But supposing this course were followed and Sparta and Athens were to crush an Argive-Corinthian-Boeotian confederacy, what then? The gain would be mainly on the side of Athens, since the reduction of Argos would be a small compensation for the re-establishment on a firm basis of Athenian dominion in Central Greece. Clearly the course must be modified; but the Spartans did not know what new direction they should take. The anti-Athenian party, led by Cleobulus and Xenares, wanted to annul the peace altogether; but to violate treaties, even though they had served their purpose, did not come easy to the Spartans. Yet they swerved thus far in this direction that, when the elections occurred, they rejected the ephors who had conducted the negotiations with Athens, and among the five who took their places were Cleobulus and Xenares (autumn 421 B.C.).

But they continued none the less to try for a settlement by understanding. In the course of the winter a meeting of the Peloponnesian League, attended by envoys from Athens, Corinth, and Boeotia, was held in Sparta, and even when nothing came of the discussion, it was not the government of Sparta, but Cleobulus and Xenares who set on foot a plot, with the connivance of Corinth, to bring Boeotia into the Argive alliance and then swing the whole block into the Spartan camp. To this scheme two of the highest Argive magistrates lent themselves, and they prevailed upon the Argives to undertake that, in case Boeotia should throw in its lot with them, Argos would leave it to a general conference to decide with whom the coalition should make war and peace—Sparta or another. The Boeotarchs, on being apprised of what lay behind the proposal, decided to open negotiations with Argos. But before going thus far, they thought it wise to insure that the Corinthians, Megarians, Chalcidians and themselves would act in concert in whatever contingency should arise—a step all the more necessary in that the anti-Spartan members of the proposed coalition (Elis, Mantinea, Argos) were thus confederated. A treaty to this effect was accordingly concluded, which the Boeotarchs submitted, as required by law, to the Council of the Boeotians. There, however, they came to grief. What was open and above board was the anti-Spartan policy of Corinth and the Chalcidians: to join them seemed, therefore, to take sides against Sparta, and this the Boeotians were resolved not to do so long as Sparta left them alone. The *point d'appui* which the project had in the war-party in Sparta and the design that underlay it of winning Argos for the war and repudiating the peace with Athens, the Boeotarchs (for obvious reasons) were unable to disclose to the Council. Hence the Council rejected the treaty; whereupon the Boeotarchs let the whole matter drop.

Officially Sparta had no part in all this. It continued *pourparlers* with the Athenians, which simply revealed that Boeotia was the key to the whole diplomatic problem. It saw no way forward except to get from the Boeotians their Athenian captives and Panactum for surrender to Athens in exchange for Pylos. That they would agree to this without a price was hardly to be expected, even after the illumination the Boeotarchs had recently received on currents of opinion in Sparta. What the Boeotians demanded in return was that Sparta should make with them, as with Athens, a separate alliance. And this condition, for which, in view of its inevitable effect on Spartan-Athenian relations, the pro-war ephors fought, the Spartans accepted (March 420 B.C.). As Sparta had given the Athenians a definite undertaking to conclude no alliances except in conjunction with them, it knew that it was breaking faith. Its only possible defence was that, by surrendering Panactum and the captives, and thus complying with the substance of the treaty of Nicias even if not putting their signature to its text, the Boeotians had in fact made peace with Athens. This defence crumpled up when the Boeotians razed Panactum before abandoning it. As was natural, therefore, the Spartan envoys who came to Athens to deliver the prisoners and Panactum got in exchange, not Pylos, but a harsh dismissal.

III. THE QUADRUPLE ALLIANCE

The fate of the Argive coalition was sealed by the return of Boeotia to the Spartan camp. There was no room in Hellas for a second land power when the first possessed the two strongest armies. Greece was accordingly denied the experience of a tripartite division. And it was Argos itself that took the lead in restoring the dual system. Its first move, made in panic on the false news that the Spartan-Boeotian alliance had been concluded with the knowledge and consent of Athens, was to leave the Mantineans and Eleans in the lurch, and seek a renewal of its treaty of neutrality with the Lacedaemonians, who of course were ready to accommodate them even to the extent of agreeing to settle their long-standing quarrel over Cynuria by a preposterous trial by arms. But when the strained nature of Spartan-Athenian relations became known in Argos, less ignominious counsels prevailed. The Argives yielded to the suggestions of Alcibiades; and, acting in concert with Mantinea and Elis, sent envoys to Athens to negotiate a quadruple alliance. If thus supported, Argos was ready to try conclusions with Sparta.

Sparta had scored heavily by regaining Boeotia. But it had incurred the risk of having the Athenians make a separate alliance also—with its Peloponnesian enemies. Of two evils it had chosen the lesser, certainly the less imminent; for there was still a chance that if Athens were approached in a friendly spirit, when its anger at the demolition of Panactum was less fresh, it might yet leave Sparta's antagonists unsupported and evacuate Pylos. Hence close at the heels of the Argive ambassadors three Spartans, known for their Athenian sympathies, Philocharidas, Leon, and Endius, arrived in Athens, vested (so they informed the Athenian Council) with plenipotentiary powers to settle all outstanding questions, and authorized to state that the alliance with Boeotia had not been concluded to the detriment of Athens.

Seldom had the Athenians a more momentous decision to make, and never perhaps did they have to make it with so much misdirection. Their accredited leader was still Nicias, and, as it was by his persuasion that the peace and alliance with Sparta had been made, so it behoved him to put the best construction on Sparta's failure to live up to its engagements. To the man in the street it seemed clear that Sparta should have put its army into action and compelled Corinth, Megara, Boeotia, and the Chalcidians to accept the peace. Nicias had a much juster sense of what was possible for Sparta in the circumstances; and thus far he had convinced a majority of the Athenians that, except under intolerable provocation, it was not for them to reopen a war which had ended so ingloriously for Sparta, so advantageously for themselves. His second line of defence, moreover, was unassailable—that the disruption of the Spartan coalition was of quite as much value to Athens as the strict fulfilment of the terms of the treaty. But now that Sparta had found a way of regaining its allies by ceasing to press them for the satisfaction they owed to Athens, his position became difficult. Clearly, Sparta should not be allowed to discontinue the pressure; on this point Nicias was in agreement with his political opponents.

Among these was Hyperbolus, whose political début has been noted already (see above, p. 224)—now as then a reincarnation of the tenets and methods of Cleon. But Nicias had long since taken the measure of men of his stamp. It was a recent recruit to the ranks of the war-party that now made it formidable. This was Alcibiades, whose coming of age politically was signalized by success in winning a generalship at the spring elections. His father was Cleinias, who had died for his country at Coronea (447 B.C.), and on his mother's side he was, like Pericles, an Alcmaeonid. Brought up as a ward in the house of this great master, he drew thence, as well as from his own ardent nature, an impetuous desire to dominate which led him inevitably on to the political stage. He grew to manhood with a generation upon which (for reasons set forth elsewhere) neither the authority of elders nor the conventions of society nor the rational justifications of morality imposed their usual restraints. In the case of his contemporaries the feeling with which their society was suffused, that 'each individual should live as he pleased,' was controlled by the practical necessity to respect the rights of others of which the popular tribunals were the constituted guardian. But Alcibiades was permitted to be a law unto himself. Arrestingly handsome, he received from men in Athens the recognition and privileges ordinarily given in other societies to extraordinary beauty in women; and his insolence he draped in such charm of manner that, when he showed respect for neither gods nor man, age nor authority, guardian nor wife, the outrageousness of the act was often forgotten and only the air of the actor remembered. In these circumstances his very infirmities became fashionable; and his engaging lisp, his rakish method of trailing his robe, his preciosity of speech and insistence on attention till the right phrase came, no less than his wild pranks, were imitated by the gilded youth of the city.

His personality was thus as intriguing in his own day as it has remained ever since, and he cultivated it with a vanity which, thus indulged, became unfortunately a rival of his intelligence for the determination of his conduct. It was not through dullness of vision that he came to grief so often. For his mind was as quick and penetrating as it was free and ranging. The attraction which Socrates had for him—their fate had been curiously linked on the battlefields of Potidaea and Delium—arose not simply from the unequalled practice in discussion to be got in the great teacher's company, but from the apparent freedom from pre-conceptions with which Socrates approached his problems. As an intellectual game the new dialectic fascinated Alcibiades greatly.

Thus endowed with imagination, insight, eloquence, and personal distinction, he was versatile enough to master at the same time the art of war and the art of the demagogue, so that he was qualified by training as well as by inheritance to become a great force in the public life of Athens; but that it should be an incalculable force was certain. For his petulance, self-will, recklessness, and contempt for dullness and goodness—the joint product of a wilful nature and his youthful career as a people's pet—could not fail in the long run to speed him on courses of which his better judgment would disapprove and to intensify unnecessarily the passions of political controversy. He had almost all the qualities needed for greatness in a democracy except the supreme one—character; a lack that was not mitigated, as in the case of Themistocles, by devotion to a great cause. Loyalty in others he could inspire, though he did not display it himself;

and, while he could on occasion win the support of the populace
for a project on which his heart was set, he proved unable to
maintain the people's confidence, as Pericles had done. Nor did
he deserve it; for the projects he championed, provided they were
in the interests of his own ambition, need not be for the public
good.

His first opportunity to prove himself came after the death of
Cleon. Old ties of family, which he had taken pains to renew,
bound him to Sparta (his grandfather had been Spartan *proxenos*
in Athens); and had the Spartans used his good offices, instead
of those of Nicias, in 421 B.C., the incentive of piqued vanity
would have been lacking to the vehemence with which thereafter
he strove to annul the peace. Convinced by this one attempt
that he could not hope to oust Nicias from the leadership of the
conservatives, he threw in his lot with the radicals. He was,
moreover, too clear-sighted not to see that the drift of events
opposed collaboration with Sparta and favoured an Argive-
Athenian alliance. And now that Athens had arrived at the cross-
roads he determined to use every means in his power to thwart
the hope of Sparta of completely isolating Argos and its associates.

The general point of view he presented was that Sparta meant
first to crush Argos and then to attack Athens. This was, of
course, to give the lie to Spartan professions; which probably
were sincere enough, since it seems clear that Sparta was ready
to give Argos peace on the old terms and had had enough of war
with Athens. Hence, to win ground for his main contention and
at the same time to nullify the good impression certain to be produced if the Athenians found that at last they had to deal with
envoys possessed of full powers to make a settlement, Alcibiades
staged a convincing demonstration that the Spartans were not to
be trusted. By promising the ambassadors his support, for which
he pledged his word of honour, he got them to disclaim before
the Athenian people the plenipotentiary authority they had
claimed while dealing with the Council. The first to denounce
the duplicity of it was Alcibiades himself. And so incensed did
the Athenians become that they did not stop to consider whether
Boeotia had not accepted the peace sufficiently to qualify as their
ally also. They imagined that Sparta was simply trying to get
Pylos vacated so as to be able to begin another war; and had not
an earthquake occurred to postpone a decision to the following
day they would at once have concluded with Argos a treaty with
an avowedly anti-Spartan intent. As it was, all that Nicias could

do at the later meeting (for, though taken aback like the rest by the unintelligible *volte-face* of the ambassadors, he had kept his head) was to re-state his general position and have himself dispatched at the head of an embassy to deliver to the Spartans what was virtually an ultimatum; that, besides rebuilding Panactum and restoring Amphipolis, they should renounce their alliance with the Boeotians; otherwise, Athens would make a separate alliance too—with the Argives.

And with this *démarche* we have virtually come to the end of this involved passage in the diplomatic history of Greece. For in the circumstances Nicias could accomplish nothing in Sparta. The party of Cleobulus and Xenares scored a complete victory. Sparta reaffirmed its signature to the treaties—that was all. Accordingly, in July 420 B.C. Athens concluded with Argos, Elis, and Mantinea an alliance for one hundred years that was defensive in form but offensive by implication. For two of the new allies whom Athens undertook to defend were already at war with Sparta; the Mantineans because Sparta in the summer of 421 B.C. had driven them out of Parrhasia by an overwhelming display of force, and Elis because of Lepreum, in which Sparta planted at this very time—during the holy month (August) of the Olympian games—a military colony of 300 Neodamodes and 700 Helots. This was a distinct provocation, and the retort of Elis—the exclusion of Sparta from the great games—was another. In the grouping and re-grouping of the states that had been unloosed from their political moorings by the Peace of Nicias forces too strong for Greek diplomacy thus brought about in fifteen months, as in Europe in 1914, a formidable coincidence of antagonisms. The contacts of adjacent peoples (centred perversely, as happens so frequently, on controversies over frontier-areas) tended to lead neighbours into hostile combinations: witness Argos-Sparta, Elis-Sparta, Mantinea-Tegea, Athens-Thebes, Argos-Epidaurus. The atmosphere surrounding city-nations was not easily penetrated by the spirit of neighbourliness. But the spirit of party was more pervasive. As in the United States during the critical period of Western expansion, allegiance to party was a unifying force that ignored ordinary frontiers; and its potency in this epoch of readjustment is revealed in the outcome—the consolidation of Athens, Argos, Mantinea, and Elis into a democratic block and the gravitation back to Sparta of aristocratic states like Boeotia, Megara, and Corinth.

But the propensity of like in government to seek like was controlled by a yet superior force: the need to obtain security.

This it was that impelled strong states to keep their coalitions well in hand, weaker states to seek a considerate protector. Thus driven, the group of peoples that seceded from the Athenian Empire and the two groups that renounced the leadership of Sparta tested the fitness of Argos to be their common head. But the fact that the first problem contemplated for the new coalition was whether it should side with Athens or Sparta needed only the panic of Argos once the scheme had broken down to prove that there were but two states in Greece strong enough to offer the menace and the protection requisite for a coalition. The ultimate facts of Greek international relations were therewith disclosed in all their nakedness—the army and discipline of Sparta and the fleet and enterprise of Athens. But the Greece of this revelation did not include the West where Syracuse was soon to show that it had sufficient power to stand on its own feet.

IV. THE WAR OF ALCIBIADES IN THE PELOPONNESE

After the peace Athens continued the blockade of Scione (p. 251), and, when it finally surrendered, treated it with exemplary rigour, the adult males being put to death, the women and children sold into slavery, and the land given to the Plataeans. Further operations could only concern places for the restoration of which Sparta was responsible. Hence 'war-worn as they were in every particular,' the Athenians even endured fresh losses in Thrace without stirring. They had enough to do at home in repairing the damages caused by the long struggle. Attica had indeed been free from invasion for three summers, and as early as 422 B.C. the state had begun putting things to rights. The temple service at Eleusis, for example, was made a charge on the agriculture of Attica and the Empire[1]. But more was needed than to propitiate Demeter. There were vineyards to reset, olive trees to replant, houses and outhouses in the devastated regions to rebuild and the neglect of a decade to be redressed, both in town and country.

Thus engaged, and relaxed for the enjoyment of peace, the Athenians were in no mood to resume war with Sparta. The Spartans, too, wanted peace. It was awkward to be encircled by Athens' new allies, and it did not seem impossible to sweep this barrier aside; but the prospects of reaching results in a war with Athens were more remote than ever. Some embarrassment was caused by the arrival home in the summer of 421 B.C. of the 120 Spartiatae who had failed to die at Sphacteria, and the 700 Helots

[1] *I.G.*[2] 1, 76.

who had served the state so well under Brasidas. The former seemed more dangerous to the existing régime as citizens fearing punishment than as outcasts on whom the punishment had fallen. Hence the time-honoured penalty for cowardice—loss of civic rights —was imposed upon them—and removed not long afterwards. The reward given to the Helots was emancipation and permission to reside where they pleased. They chose Sparta, thus increasing dangerously a class which had its next of kin among the serfs; but the opportunity soon came to settle them and 300 other Neodamodes as a military colony at Lepreum, and it was seized upon as a godsend. The menace from the serfs was ineradicable. Like Napoleon the Spartans were prisoners of their conquests; but they experienced a valued relief when Pylos ceased to be the terminal of 'underground railways' for the escape of Helots and the point of departure of expeditions that plundered their estates and seduced their serfs. Thus the peace meant an alleviation of their domestic situation.

Accordingly, for the greater part of a year after the formation of the quadruple alliance, neither Sparta nor Athens did anything further to endanger the peace. But during the interval the Spartans were given a rude reminder that their prestige abroad was not what it had been. Their ally, Boeotia, took off their hands, unsolicited, their colony Heraclea in Trachis, on the ground that, weakened by a defeat it had sustained at the hands of the neighbouring tribes, it was in danger of falling into the possession of the Athenians. Alcibiades, too, was industriously employed all this while fomenting the war spirit in Athens. What he wanted was for the Athenians to put their army and navy unreservedly at the disposal of their Peloponnesian allies, and for himself to be given general conduct of operations, that should have as their object to crush Sparta completely. That was a clear-cut policy, and it appealed strongly to the restless spirit of action that was strong among the Athenian youth and to the hatred of the Lacedaemonians and dreams of dominion over all Hellas to which masses of the people were instinctively responsive.

Nicias' idea, on the contrary, was to insist on the purely defensive character of the new alliance, and avoid a rupture with Sparta by leaving unsatisfied both the territorial claims of Mantinea and Elis and the aspirations of Argos for leadership in the Peloponnese. That, too, was a clear-cut policy; and with it Sparta would no doubt have been content. But for its execution, no less than for the execution of Alcibiades' alternative, singleness of purpose and tenacity of judgment were required of the Athenian people; for, once the quadruple alliance had been concluded, Argos, Mantinea and Elis would defer to nothing but a certainty that Athens would stand aside if they assumed the offensive. But these were precisely the qualities that the Athenian people lacked at this time. And their indecision came out clearly at the elections of the spring of 419 B.C. when Nicias and Alcibiades were both re-elected to the generalship.

Alcibiades chose to regard this half-success as a confirmation of his policy. And thus far he was justified, in that the Athenians let him act as if their intentions were his. He went to the Peloponnese, and with an armed force made up of local troops and a few Athenian hoplites and archers, proceeded from place to place consolidating and extending the alliance. Patrae in Achaea was won, and he persuaded its inhabitants to bind themselves firmly with Athens by carrying their walls down to the sea. He would have built a fort at Rhium to guard the exit from the Corinthian Gulf had not the Corinthians and Sicyonians come up in force and prevented it. This was to singe the Spartans' beard and implicate Athens more deeply; but it was his next move, in which the Argives were his voluntary agents, that brought on the crisis.

They picked a quarrel with Epidaurus, a loyal member of the Peloponnesian League, meaning to win it for their alliance, by force if necessary, and thus join hands directly with Athens across Aegina. This stirred the Spartans to action. They moved their whole army to the frontier, but did not cross it. The Carnean month was approaching during which Dorians were required to refrain from military operations. It was at its expiry, therefore, that their allies were ordered to be ready for war. Undeterred by this threat, the Argives, after juggling with their calendar so as to defer the sacred month artificially, overran the open country of the Epidaurians. An eleventh-hour effort to preserve the general peace was made by Athens, undoubtedly at the instigation of Nicias. A conference of envoys 'from the cities' was convened at Mantinea. It suspended its deliberations when the Corinthians insisted that it was absurd to be discussing peace while the Argives and Epidaurians were fighting; resumed them when Argos, deferring to the wishes of Athens, recalled its army, but broke up without reaching an agreement. Again the Lacedaemonians mobilized their entire army and marched to Caryae. This time Alcibiades crossed the Saronic Gulf with 1000 hoplites, but the Spartans came no farther, and the Athenians returned home. The Argive-Epidaurian struggle remained localized; and eventually the defenders must have given in, had it not been for the landing,

unmolested, at Epidaurus during the winter (419–8 B.C.) of a
Lacedaemonian garrison. The chagrin was great at Argos, where
the Athenians were held to have been remiss in allowing the troops
to pass through their territory, *i.e.*, the sea; and the Athenians,
too, were so angered that, at the request of their ally, they restored
the deserters to Pylos, and on the motion of Alcibiades, affixed
to their copy of the treaties with Sparta the declaration that 'the
Lacedaemonians had not kept their oaths.'

But when Athens had come thus to the verge of war the people
drew back. The rural population saw their homesteads in Attica
again burning. Men recalled the lessons of Pericles and Delium
—not to risk all by incurring certain losses and possible disaster
in a great battle on land. Nicias charged his antagonist with
having been wilfully and needlessly provocative. The reaction
went so far that Alcibiades failed of election to the generalship
for 418 B.C.; so that the conduct of military operations in what
proved to be the critical year came into the hands of Nicias and
his associates, Laches and Nicostratus. This was to play straight
into the hands of the Spartans. After June 418 B.C. Athens could
be counted on to limit its participation in a Peloponnesian war to
a force proportionate only to the needs of defence, and to refrain
from operations elsewhere.

Sparta, accordingly, waited till midsummer notwithstanding
that Epidaurus was now in sore straits, and then proceeded to
concentrate at Phlius for attacking Argos 'the finest Hellenic
force assembled up to that time.' The Boeotians, relieved of
anxiety for their Attic front, sent 5000 hoplites, 500 horsemen,
and 5000 light-armed troops; the Corinthians 2000 hoplites,
and Megara, Sicyon, Phlius, and Pellene the pick of their field-
armies. King Agis with the Spartans, Tegeates, and the rest of
the Arcadians that were on their side won the first, and in many
ways the decisive, round of the struggle by superior strategy.
Finding the combined armies of Argos, Elis, and Mantinea in
position at Methydrium in Arcadia determined on bringing him
to battle before he reached the point of concentration, he eluded
them by a night march and arrived at Phlius the same day. There
he took command of the whole group of armies, now comprising
20,000 hoplites and many light-armed troops, besides cavalry and
their auxiliaries. Meanwhile, the Argives and their allies, hurrying
to Argos, took up a defensive position on the main road coming
from Phlius. Their forces numbered perhaps 10,000 hoplites
and they had no cavalry. The strategy of Agis aimed not merely
at their defeat but at their annihilation. He divided his army into

three corps. One, including the Boeotians, waited until daybreak and then advanced by the direct road through Nemea. A second, half as strong, started during the night and keeping well to the left, descended into the Argive plain by a steep road: while a third, which Agis led himself, like the first about 8000 hoplites strong, to which belonged the Lacedaemonians, made a night march round the right flank and descending into the plain, likewise by a steep road, ravaged Saminthus and proceeded to interpose itself between the Argive army and the city.

Had the movements of these three armies been timed precisely the Argives and their associates must have been overwhelmed. As it was, the Argive generals fell back before the central army came up. They seem to have brushed off the smaller of the two encircling armies. Then they confronted Agis in the plain, and both sides prepared for battle. Did the Argives and their allies possess an opportunity to try conclusions with Agis before the Boeotians arrived? If so, he might have been assailed in the rear by troops issuing from the city at the same time that he was engaged in front with an army numerically his superior. In these circumstances a defeat would have been disastrous. Should, however, his other two armies come up while the battle was still in progress, the Argives were doomed, especially since the Boeotians had cavalry and they had none, the Athenians upon whom they relied for this arm having not as yet put in an appearance. As it happened, the case was not put to the test of actuality. Two prominent Argives, Thrasyllus and Alciphron, the former one of the five generals, the latter Lacedaemonian *proxenos*, both undoubtedly members of the aristocratic faction in Argos that wished to overthrow the democracy and substitute a Spartan for the Athenian alliance, came to Agis on their own initiative as the battle was on the point of beginning, and urged him not to engage since the Argives were ready to give satisfaction and make peace.

Without consulting anybody except one of the ephors, Agis took the suggestion and offered the Argives an armistice of four months in which to conclude a treaty. Without getting the assent of the soldiers, or, what was even more important, of their associates, the Argive commanders accepted the proposal; and Agis at once led his great army off and disbanded it. The feeling was general among both Spartans and their allies that he had thrown away a precious opportunity, and this feeling was shared by their military experts as well as by the rank and file. With the Argives the situation was different in that the leaders, by accept-

ing the offer of an armistice, registered seemingly a judgment that
their tactical position was bad. But since the soldiers believed
that it was extraordinarily good, they ascribed to their generals
treasonable motives and would have stoned Thrasyllus to death
had he not taken sanctuary. Nor can we be sure, in the light of
subsequent happenings, that they were altogether wrong in
thinking that their generals were swayed mainly by political considerations. Certainly many Argives who were not traitors were
canvassing the wisdom of withdrawing from the alliance with
Athens. For Athens had proved a broken reed in the crisis. Even
the limited assistance, on which alone they had had reason to
count, had started too late. Hence when the Athenians arrived
with 1000 hoplites and 300 cavalry, under the command of
Laches and Nicostratus, the Argive magistrates bade them begone;
nor did they give them an audience with the people, notwithstanding that it was for Alcibiades (present as a special diplomatic
agent) for whom the privilege was requested, until they were
forced to do so by the insistence of the Eleans and Mantineans.
And it was as spokesman for all three that Alcibiades drove home
the point that the Argives had no right to conclude a separate
peace with the Spartans. It may be doubted whether he would
have carried the day for all his charm and eloquence, had the
Argive people not been convinced that they had been cheated out
of a victory by their generals, and that they, too, like the Mantineans, Eleans, and Athenians, had been victimized by the truce.

The political morale of the coalition had been seriously impaired by the incidents just described; but it had still sufficient
coherence for the fatal decision to be reached to assume the offensive in turn. They made Orchomenus the first object of attack,
the design being to get possession of the Arcadian hostages whom
the Spartans had deposited there. But when Orchomenus capitulated harmony ended. The Eleans urged an utter foolishness—
the recovery of Lepreum—and when the Argives and Athenians
sided with the Mantineans, who were bent on settling private
scores with the Tegeates, the Eleans refused to concur in the
decision and weakened the coalition by withdrawing 3000 hoplites. The confederates can hardly have hoped to capture Tegea
by assault. Nor did they need to. They had friends within the
city—democrats no doubt—who were prepared to admit them,
and it was the news that Tegea was all but lost through treachery
that forced the Spartans to abandon recriminations and bestir
themselves for its rescue.

For a fortnight they had indulged themselves in the unwonted pleasure of king-baiting. Agis' military judgment had been censured from the day of the armistice, and the political foundation on which his defence rested had given way completely when Argos went back on its generals. The loss of Orchomenus drove the Spartans to fury. But even so their respect for Agis' gallantry prevailed. They let him off, but required him thenceforward to take with him on military campaigns a board of ten advisers selected by the people. Though he was erratic as a tactician Agis had undoubted ability in planning strategical movements and executing them with celerity. Never had so complete a muster been dispatched from Sparta at so short notice as the one with which he started for Arcadia. On reaching Orestheum, where he learned perhaps that the confederates were divided, he sent home the older and younger classes, in all one-sixth of his forces. At Tegea, according to instructions previously given, he was joined by reinforcements from Lepreum, Heraea, and Maenalia; and without waiting for the Corinthians, Boeotians, Locrians, and Phocians, whom he had ordered to join him at Mantinea with such speed as they could, he sought out the enemy, meaning to give battle at once.

Finding the narrows between Mytika and Kapnistra[1] undefended he advanced to the Heracleum, where he pitched a camp and proceeded to ravage the country. The confederates had resolved to decline an engagement in the open with the Eleans absent and reinforcements which were coming from Athens not yet present. Hence Agis ordered his army to attack them in their chosen position, a height (Alesion) with steep and difficult approaches overlooking Mantinea from the east. But when his men came within a stone's throw of the enemy he countermanded the order and withdrew his troops rapidly. Whether it was a jibe on the part of an old soldier—that he was planning to mend one error by another—or the presence in his mind of a different strategical conception that prompted him to draw off in this abrupt fashion, we may, like Thucydides, refuse to decide. His unmolested retirement caused a clamour in the Argive army that their generals had let him escape a second time; and it was with feelings of contempt for an enemy who seemed now, as at Sphacteria, to possess none of the ancient Spartan virtues that the confederates came down into the plain later on in the day, and on the following morning drew up in battle-order eager to engage the enemy wherever they should happen to find him.

[1] See map 9 facing p. 274.

In any event Agis *had* had a different strategical conception—
to entice the confederates to do what they had thus done without
further provocation—abandon the heights and furnish an opportunity for battle on level ground. He had set his army to work
diverting into the territory of the Mantineans, to their great
harm and, presumably, indignation, a stream (Sarandapotamos)
about the canalization of which the twin Arcadian cities were
always fighting. Then he, too, set out on the morning after,
intending to resume his position at the Heracleum, ignorant
apparently that the enemy had moved, or had moved so far.

Thus it was that with his army still in column of route he came
suddenly upon the confederates already deployed for battle. For
a moment the consternation in his ranks was as great as it was
unusual; but the discipline of the Spartans soon asserted itself.
The movement of the Lacedaemonians from column into line
was completed in time despite the initial confusion; and when
the other contingents had taken the posts assigned to them and
the 400 horsemen had gained the flanks, Agis was ready for battle.
The highland brigade, the so-called Sciritae (600 strong), occupied the extreme left as usual. Next came the detachment from
Lepreum, 1000 men at the most. The main Lacedaemonian army
occupied the centre, with the Tegeates (stiffened by two Lacedaemonian battalions, commanded by Aristocles and Hipponoidas) on the extreme right, and the rest of the Arcadians in
between. Thucydides estimates the Lacedaemonians (Spartans
and Perioeci together) exclusive of the Sciritae—but whether
exclusive or inclusive of the ex-Helots from Lepreum is uncertain
—at 3584 men, distributed in seven battalions (*lochoi*) of 512
combatants. As near as we can judge there were from eight to
ten thousand men in the whole army.

Singing their war-songs and keeping step and evenness of front
with the aid of music furnished by flute-players stationed at
short intervals along the entire line, the Lacedaemonians came
on deliberately, each man with his shield on his left arm and
seeking the protection of his neighbour's shield for his exposed
side. Since their adversaries likewise and for the same reason
edged off towards their right, Agis sought to prevent the Sciritae
and ex-Helots from being taken in flank, by having them move
out to the left and thus make room next themselves in the line
for the two Lacedaemonian battalions, whose services the Tegeates
did not require to complete the envelopment of the enemy on their
front. Had Aristocles and Hipponoidas moved across promptly,
instead of refusing to budge, or had the enemy advanced less

impetuously, Agis would thus have used his greater length of line to advantage. But, as it happened, owing to the gap in the line, the Sciritae and the ex-Helots were assailed simultaneously in front and on both sides and driven back to their camp. But their opponents—the Mantineans and their Arcadian allies and the 1000 Argive regulars—had gained a fruitless victory. For in the meanwhile the Lacedaemonians in the centre, with whom were Agis and his bodyguard of 300 picked men, had fallen upon the Argive territorials ('the older men of the Argives, the so-called five companies, and the Cleonaeans and the Orneates'), who gave way with little or no resistance and carried along with them in precipitate flight the adjoining files of the Athenians. The rest of the Athenians being thus exposed from two directions—for the Tegeates and the Lacedaemonians were enveloping them from the left—were saved from disaster only by the superiority of their cavalry, and by the promptitude with which Agis, letting the Athenians and the Argive territorials go, wheeled about his centre and right, and advanced to the rescue of his left. Outnumbered three to one the Argive regulars and the Mantineans sought safety in flight.

Since the Lacedaemonians made no use of their cavalry and did not think it wise to submit their hoplites to the fatigue and disorder of a long pursuit, the casualties of the vanquished (1100, including the two Athenian generals, Laches and Nicostratus) consisted of the dead alone, and the fugitives quickly reassembled in Mantinea, where they were joined shortly after by the Eleans and 1000 fresh troops from Athens. But they were in no mood to try their luck again. The strength of the Lacedaemonians and the weakness of the Argives were only too apparent already. By a single battle, with a loss of only 300 men, the Spartans reestablished completely their military prestige, and twenty-four years were to elapse before any Greeks ventured again to face them in the open field.

V. THE DISRUPTION OF THE QUADRUPLE ALLIANCE

The campaign in Arcadia came accordingly to an abrupt termination. The Lacedaemonians dismissed their allies, both those on hand and those coming from Corinth and beyond, and returned home to celebrate the Carnea (August), perhaps already overdue. Their opponents could not take time even for recriminations. For on the day before the battle the Epidaurians had attacked Argos in full force, and had killed many of the guards that had been left behind for its protection. The confederates resolved on an united effort to save the Argives from such unpleasantness in the future and to open the direct road to Athens. They accordingly marched on Epidaurus, and, dividing up the work among themselves, proceeded to surround the city by fortifications which would make rescue impossible and surrender inevitable. But the Athenians alone had the skill and the patience to complete the portion assigned to them. The others soon gave up, and, leaving a mixed garrison in the Athenian section, they all withdrew.

The disintegration of the confederacy revealed in this paltry result of so formidable an enterprise was soon shown to have its centre in Argos itself. The friends of Sparta there had once already all but succeeded in withdrawing their state from the quadruple alliance. Now they were to be completely successful. For in the autumn (October 418 B.C.) Agis led the Lacedaemonian levy to Tegea, and from this point dispatched Lichas, Argive *proxenos*, to Argos, giving the Argives the choice of war or peace. Alcibiades went to Argos and fought hard to keep the Argives in the fighting—but unsuccessfully. The aristocrats, who had already reached a private understanding with Sparta, came out in the open and carried the day against him.

Their programme called next for a reversal of foreign policy. This, too, they effected. Argos repudiated its treaty with Elis, Mantinea, and Athens, and entered into a fifty-years alliance with Sparta. In this the rest of the Peloponnesian states were to share on the basis of freedom and autonomy, and the allies of Argos and the extra-Peloponnesian allies of Sparta on the same terms as Argos and Sparta themselves. Its fundamental condition was a notable concession to Argive pride and ambition—that in case a general expedition of the Peloponnesians and their allies were necessary, not Sparta alone, but Sparta and Argos, deliberating together, should decide what forces each member should contribute.

A corollary to this pact was an agreement on the part of the two principals to declare war on the Athenians if they did not evacuate the Peloponnese, and an undertaking 'not to conclude peace or wage war with anyone except together'; and a consequence of it was that Athens came to terms with Epidaurus and withdrew its garrison, Mantinea released its dependencies and made a thirty years alliance with Sparta, and Perdiccas of Macedon joined the Sparto-Argives as a first step to deserting Athens—an event of considerable importance to his neighbours, the Chalcidians, whom the Sparto-Argives likewise admitted to their coalition. By the end of the year 418 B.C. the Lacedaemonian victory at Mantinea had yielded this rich crop of political fruits, and at this moment the position of Sparta in Greece seemed stronger than it had been at any time since the formation of the Delian Confederacy.

The opportunity for its triumph had been afforded by the aggressive acts of Alcibiades and Argos. The triumph itself had been assured by the refusal of the Athenians to risk their main army in the Peloponnese. The irreconcilability of this refusal, for which Nicias was primarily responsible, with the provocative conduct of Alcibiades, is traceable to the weakness of government in Athens occasioned by the violence and equality of parties. Clearly the leader of one of the two great parties was a menace to the republic: the question was, which? A majority voted to find the answer by ostracism. But when the votes were counted (spring 417 B.C.) it appeared that the individual designated for exile was neither Nicias nor Alcibiades. On the initiative of the latter the two protagonists had united to ward off the common danger, and each had got his own supporters to vote, not against the other, but against Hyperbolus. The result caused guffaws at the moment, for Hyperbolus had been the foremost in inviting the trial of strength, little dreaming of the issue, and the feeling was widespread that 'it was not for such as he that the sherd-test had been invented.' But the occasion was not one for levity. Once the way had been found to circumvent ostracism its usefulness was gone, and with it something archaically wholesome disappeared from the public life of Athens. It had succeeded when political controversy was more sincere and parties less amenable to personal control (see, however, vol. IV, pp. 151 *sqq.*). So the division of public opinion continued and for the time being Athens was without resource against it. In the ensuing elections both Nicias and Alcibiades received generalships.

The alliance of Athens with Argos, Elis, and Mantinea was not inevitably an error. The mistake was the use to which the Athenians had let it be put. Nor was the game wholly lost; for a chance was soon given them to regain Argos under circumstances which weakened again the loyalty of the Peloponnesians to Sparta. The parties mainly responsible for this were the Argive friends of Sparta, the ultimate goal of whose programme had always been an oligarchic revolution in their own state. And indeed the admission of Argos to partnership with the Spartans in the headship of the Peloponnesians was tolerable to the latter only when partisans subservient to themselves controlled the Argive government. Hence a force of 2000 men, half of them

Lacedaemonians and half Argive regulars, whose aristocratic sympathies were notorious, was called out, the Lacedaemonians to set up an oligarchy in Sicyon, the two together to overthrow the democracy in Argos (early spring 417 B.C.).

VI. SPARTA AGAINST ARGOS

This done, and matters put to rights in Achaea, the Spartans felt secure. But they had overreached themselves. Their activity in setting up oligarchies through whom they could have their own way, created uneasiness in other parts of the Peloponnese. The best check to Spartan arrogance was, after all, the freedom of Argos; so the Corinthians, for example, seem to have thought, all the more so, since it was quiet and autonomy alone to which the Argive populace now aspired. In the movement of revolt which grew in Argos from the day of the *coup d'état* the Argive democrats did not lack outside sympathy, nor inside provocation. Their political degradation was brought home to them so forcibly by individual acts of outrage that they coalesced in ever greater numbers round a central revolutionary body till, choosing a time when Sparta was preoccupied with religious celebrations (the *Gymnopaidiai* of July 417 B.C.), they rose up against their masters. The street fighting that ensued was prolonged; and the oligarchs could have been saved had the Spartans started promptly. But they broke away so reluctantly from their festival that when they reached Tegea they were met by fugitives from Argos with word that the struggle was over—that some of the oligarchs were slain, others expelled, the rest cowed, and the demos master of the government. The movement had thus gone so far that it required action by the entire coalition, if any—a point debated at length at a Peloponnesian Congress to which the question was referred. There were advocates of Home Rule for Argos present besides the Argive democrats, and when the decision went against them the Corinthians refused to take part in the joint expedition which was authorized.

The Argives chose autonomy in preference to quiet since they could not have both, and, with Alcibiades as broker, they renewed their alliance with Athens, this time for fifty years only. Their thought was no longer of challenging Sparta's headship in the peninsula, but simply of preserving their independence. What they had to fear principally was betrayal, but a blockade was not impossible. This could be eliminated by connecting Argos with the sea by long walls—a project which doubtless originated with Alcibiades and certainly received the approval of the Athenians, since by it their task would be lessened and their influence increased. They accordingly sent over carpenters and stone-masons to help the Argives, who turned to, men and women, free and slave, and pushed on with the gigantic work; but before it was finished the Lacedaemonians, after 'postponements and hesitations' at length arrived (winter 417–6 B.C.). They were foiled of their hope that the oligarchs who had stayed in Argos would rise in their support. So they dismantled the uncompleted walls, massacred the inhabitants of Hysiae, which they had captured, and departed. The Argives retaliated by a raid into the territory of Phlius, which had given hospitality to most of the oligarchic refugees; and the following spring Alcibiades took off from Argos on Athenian ships 300 men who were thought to be disloyal to the democracy and friendly to Sparta.

During the next two years (summer 416 to summer 414 B.C.) the efforts of Sparta were directed towards restoring the oligarchy in Argos, and the efforts of Athens, though no longer centred exclusively on the Peloponnese, were exerted for the preservation of the democracy. Four times the Lacedaemonians mobilized their forces for an invasion of Argos, and on two of these occasions they and their allies actually entered and ravaged the Argive country (winter 416–5, summer 414 B.C.). Twice the Athenians came by sea and found the Peloponnesians already gone. Thus, as it happened, the Spartans and the Athenians did not cross swords in the Argolid. But not content with seeking out twice more the refugees in their rendezvous at Phlius and with expelling (with Athenian aid) an oligarchic colony which the Lacedaemonians had planted at Orneae in Argive territory (spring 415 B.C.), the Argives retaliated for the second Peloponnesian devastation of their country by invading and plundering the Lacedaemonian land of Thyrea (summer 414 B.C.). And on this occasion the Athenians themselves, prematurely elated because of their successes in Sicily (in the 'mood of adventurous speculation and sanguine expectancy, dreaming of some great and wonderful change for the better' exhibited 'with good natured banter in the fanciful comedy entitled the *Birds*' brought out by Aristophanes at the Great Dionysia of the preceding March), sailed with a fleet along the coast of the Peloponnese and put landing parties ashore in Laconia, at Epidaurus Limera and Prasiae—thus giving the Spartans the pretext for which they were waiting for reopening the general war with a clean conscience.

VII. ATHENS AND ITS EMPIRE

By the summer of 417 B.C. it was abundantly clear that if Athens was to retrieve its position in Thrace it would have to be by its own exertions. Probably the secession of Dium, which first absorbed Thyssus (421 B.C.) and then went over to the Chalcidians, established Nicias' contention that here, and not in the Peloponnese, was the area in which Athens should conduct military operations. So he launched an expedition at this time which counted on being able, with the help of Perdiccas, the shifty king of Macedon, to master the rebels; but Perdiccas, already secretly in league with Sparta, deserted the Athenians, and the whole enterprise came to grief. Patching up an armistice with the Chalcidians, the Athenians turned on their disloyal ally, blockaded his coast (winter 417–6 B.C.), where too they organized at Methone a sort of second Pylos (winter 416–5 B.C.); and, since the Spartans and the Chalcidians left him in the lurch, they finally constrained him to change sides again. The object to which they next directed their attention was the recovery of Amphipolis; but, though they were assisted both by Perdiccas and by numerous Thracians, they failed in their attack on the city and a blockade had not yet yielded results when bad news from Sicily forced them to suspend operations.

The truth is that neither in the Peloponnese nor in Thrace did the Athenians care to commit themselves seriously. The ideas that became dominant after 421 B.C. were those of the Periclean peace—to make Athens the most splendid and enjoyable place in Hellas for men to live in and to restrict activity abroad to exploiting the gains and opportunities of naval power. There was, accordingly, a revival on a small scale of pre-war building projects. It seems that new temples of Athena were erected or begun[1], yet further to embellish the Acropolis, and the Periclean programme for accumulating reserves of money now yielded good results. A new festival with musical and gymnastic features was established in honour of Hephaestus, and a new cult—that of Asclepius —was introduced with the help of the poet Sophocles. The spirit of the epoch, like that of Nicias himself, was conservative. Protagoras was indicted for impiety, Diagoras outlawed for atheism, and Alcibiades caricatured on the stage as the celebrant of lewd, outlandish orgies. In piety Alcibiades could not compete with Nicias, for he was as much in advance of the sober

[1] *I.G.*[2] i, 88/9. We should probably date at this time the construction of the temple of Athena Nike and the greater part of the Erechtheum.

thinking of his time as Nicias was behind it. But none knew better than he the uniqueness of the opportunity afforded by the great religious festivals to transform a national into a Panhellenic reputation. Nicias had selected Delos as the scene of his most spectacular act of devotion (p. 230). Alcibiades chose Olympia to be the herald of his magnificence. He entered no less than seven four-horse teams in the chariot race of 416 B.C., and surpassed all records by gaining first, second, and third, or possibly fourth, places. Nor did he miss the occasion to impress upon the world the eminence he enjoyed at home. While attending the fête he acted like the lord of Athens, using its silverware for his private banquet and taking gifts from its subjects almost as if he were entitled to tribute; and on his return home he had Euripides compose for him an ode of victory. By his very ambition and energy he magnified for Athens the triumphs of peace. Simultaneously he and his city sowed the seeds of *hybris*.

The gains of naval power were the Empire, which the treaty of peace (while safeguarding the Chalcidians) left to Athens to dispose of as it saw fit. The tribute, though reassessed in 421 B.C. in a downward direction[1], was kept high enough to permit the raising of the reserve to something like 3000 talents in six years[2]. The officials of the Athenian courts came and went, bearing condemnations here summons there, organs of a sovereign tribunal with an unlimited range of commercial and criminal jurisdiction and alone competent to dispose of serious political offences. Transmarine traffic continued to be regulated in the interest of the Athenian market, and finally, by a single decree of the people, Athenian weights and measures were prescribed for all the Empire's business, the minting of silver by the 'cities' was forbidden and the silver currency of the metropolis made obligatory even in local transactions[3]. Deeper and deeper the idea penetrated into the sub-consciousness of the Athenians that the sea and all that used it were theirs—subject as well to their authority as to their protection. Had not the Spartans recognized this in 431 B.C. by treating even neutral seafarers as enemies, the Argives in 419 B.C. by claiming that a hostile expedition that went by water had passed through Athenian territory? The most palpable offender

---

[1] A. B. West, *A.J.A.* xxix, 1925, pp. 135–51.

[2] Approximately, this sum is obtained by calculation (Beloch, ii², 2, p. 352). The precise figure comes from *I.G.²* i, 99, l. 28.

[3] *I.G.* xii, 5, 480. For portions of a third copy of this decree see Wilhelm, *Wien. Anz.*, 1924, pp. 157 *sqq.*, Hiller and Klaffenbach, *Zeit. f. Num.*, 1925, pp. 217 *sqq.*, and Hiller, Ἐφ. Ἀρχ., 1923, p. 116 *sq.*

against this fantastic extension of the conception of sea-power was Melos—a sturdy little Doric community. It had disregarded the assessment of tribute made against it in 425 B.C., and both before and afterwards had defied Athens, trusting to its inoffensiveness and the assistance of the Peloponnesians. Now (summer 416 B.C.) it paid the penalty for its temerity and the world was informed in unforgettable language that islanders had a master. Athens, Lesbos, and Chios furnished the ships, 38 in all, Athens and its allies the troops, 2700 hoplites, 320 archers, by which the Melians were driven into their city and there surrounded by walls which enabled a garrison to starve them into submission. Again, this time on the motion of Alcibiades, the Athenians decided to make an example of the 'rebels.' So they slew all the adult males, sold the women and children into slavery, and re-peopled the island with 500 Athenian colonists. And one of their own citizens pilloried them in words, penned seemingly without passion, which yet, by their pitiless exposure of the soul of a despot nation, have power even to-day to rouse the conscience of mankind against states that act as if the weak have no rights which the strong need to respect.

Another island remained to tempt Athens to its nemesis.

CHAPTER X

THE ATHENIAN EXPEDITION TO SICILY

I. THE DESIGNS OF ATHENS IN THE WEST

IN 416 B.C. the situation in Sicily again demanded the attention of Athens. For a second time since the peace of Gela (424 B.C., p. 225) an Athenian ally felt the heavy hand of Syracuse. Earlier it had been Leontini. Now it was Segesta. A war had arisen between Segesta, a hellenized Elymian city with its outlet to the sea on the north, and Selinus, the most westerly Greek city on the south coast. Though the two places were fully thirty miles apart, their territories were contiguous, and trouble as to frontier lands and mixed marriages brought on the struggle. It became unequal when Syracuse, summoned as an ally, joined Selinus. Hence the Segestans, hard pressed by land and sea, were forced to look outside for assistance. Acragas and Carthage rejected their appeal. With Athens they had not only a treaty of long standing but a recent alliance (p. 224 n. 1). They knew, too, how reluctant the Athenians had been to withdraw from the island in 424 B.C. Accordingly they sent an embassy thither in the winter of 416 B.C. and called on Athens in its own interest to intervene in the West to checkmate the dangerous projects of the Syracusans.

Note. For this chapter Thucydides (VI and VII) is all important. We can do little but paraphrase his famous narrative. The account he gives of Syracuse and its environs betrays autopsy; and for precision and completeness the work leaves little to be desired Diodorus (XII, 82, 3–XIII, 33) gives at second hand a digest of Thucydides bristling with inaccuracies and expanded at certain points (the last battle in the Great Harbour and the trial of the Athenian captives) by rhetorical embellishments due probably to the intermediary or intermediaries between him and Thucydides (Ephorus, Timaeus). Plutarch (*Life of Nicias*) adds a detail or two drawn perhaps from Philistus. We have two speeches of Andocides dealing with the mutilation of the Hermae, one (*On the Return*) delivered in 407 B.C. before, and the other (*On the Mysteries*) delivered in 399 B.C. after his restoration to Athens in 405 B.C. They contradict one another in some points but add much to our knowledge of the incident. Besides the *Life* by Plutarch there are three speeches extant in which the career of Alcibiades, both before and after his exile, is overhauled—one by Lysias (XIV) one by Isocrates (XVI) and one falsely attributed to Andocides (IV). Their statements need to be used with caution. The inscriptions are few. They corroborate Thucydides and add a point or two. See the Bibliography.

The argument of which they made most use was that, if Syracuse were permitted to become mistress of Sicily, it would some day lead thence vast armaments to aid the Peloponnesians in a renewed effort to destroy the Empire of Athens. The embassy affirmed the ability of Segesta to meet the expenses of the war. On this point Athens desired confirmation, and accordingly voted to send envoys who should see for themselves the treasures alleged to be stored in the temples of Segesta. They were also to ascertain the exact state of the war between Segesta and Selinus. Thus far the Athenians acted circumspectly; but privately they were debating in a spirit of adventure, aggrandizement and greed the chances of a war of aggression in the West.

Generally they had little knowledge of the magnitude of Sicily and the number of its inhabitants. They were quite unaware that it was larger in extent than the Peloponnese, and that it possessed a Greek population not much less than that of the League headed by Sparta. And even when well-informed Athenians knew that Syracuse was comparable in size with Athens and the world in which it moved with the Athenian Empire, they were not always deterred thereby. Was it not by greatly daring that their fathers had acquired and maintained their dominions? At this particular moment the youth of Athens were fretting at the ineffectiveness to which the state seemed condemned by the cautious healing policy of Nicias. Diverted from enterprises near at hand, in the Peloponnese or Thrace for example, by the quarrels of evenly-matched parties, they saw in Sicily a chance to do something spectacular.

The possible scope of operations in Sicily was conceived differently by different groups of the Athenians. Of the aims of the expansionists we need not speak; but there were those who favoured the dispatch of a strong fleet, yet had no thought either of conquering the whole island or of besieging Syracuse. To them the real object of Athenian interference was to keep alive local opposition to the imperial projects of Syracuse, and, by showing that Athens was still a factor in the West, to create more favourable conditions for the trade of the Piraeus and the Empire. None imagined that even if they engaged in a blockade of Syracuse they could not withdraw from the island, as in 424 B.C., when it should seem wise to do so. Many thought of the enterprise simply in terms of wages to be earned, spoils to be brought back or sold on the spot, and possible increase of tribute to be enjoyed in the future.

The masses in Athens were thus favourably predisposed to a

policy of western expansion, to which, too, their triumph over Corinth in the Archidamian War logically looked, so that its powerful advocacy by Alcibiades (desirous primarily of securing an occasion for the display of his own conspicuous ability) served but to make its acceptance more unanimous. Hence when the envoys returned from Segesta with sixty talents in hand (a month's pay for sixty ships) and the report, which proved to be inaccurate, that the money to defray the cost of the entire expedition was actually in the possession of the Segestans, the Athenians voted to send to Sicily a fleet of sixty ships and to put in charge of it, not, as was proposed, one commander with full powers, *i.e.* Alcibiades, but three generals, to wit, Nicias, Alcibiades, and Lamachus. The instructions given them were: specifically, to aid Segesta against Selinus and restore Leontini; generally, in case of success, to use their own judgment in settling matters on the island to the best interest of the Athenians.

Neither in the constitution of the command nor in the formulation of the instructions did the Athenians make their mind clear. Nicias it was who brought out the fact that at any rate they were thinking of something big. His real desire was to get the whole enterprise abandoned, and at a meeting called five days later to consider details he pleaded for the reversal of what he termed a hasty decision taken on the prompting of the young to satisfy the desire for vainglory of a youth who also sought, at the peril of the state, to rehabilitate a fortune wasted on horses and extravagant living. Nor did he confine himself to an attack on Alcibiades. He restated succinctly the arguments that condemned the project: the unwisdom of engaging in a great war in Sicily while powerful enemies at home, restrained merely by a temporary or discredited treaty, and chafing under defeat, were planning to fall upon Athens, if not at the moment its forces became divided, certainly in case of a reverse; the folly of seeking new subjects far afield while old subjects near at hand were still in revolt, especially since the latter, when subdued, could be held, whereas even if the Siceliotes were conquered, they could be kept in subjection only with great difficulty, or not at all; the unsoundness of the assumption that forces from Sicily would be more likely to join in an effort to tear down the Athenian Empire if they were controlled by Syracuse than if they were free to move individually, whereas precisely the opposite was to be inferred from the considerations that it would not be to the interest of one empire to attack another, and that nature itself had laid down boundaries between the two worlds in the Ionian and Sicilian Seas upon the observance of which the Athenians should insist, and which they should recognize themselves.

The reasoning was cogent. There was indeed no answer to the contention that even if Athens conquered Sicily, it lacked the forces to keep it conquered. But to see that this was so implied a calculation of their strength on the part of the Athenians which they were in no mood to make. The rebuttal of Alcibiades was characteristic. In a strain of mingled insolence and candour he justified his right to lead by his exceptional abilities, and his princely outlays at home and abroad by the glory and prestige they brought both to him and to Athens. Deprecating the effort of Nicias to set the young against the old, he pleaded for union in action, and declared that a people with an empire could not rest on its oars as other peoples could, but must always forge ahead, preserving its superiorities by practising them, striking down enemies before they declared themselves, making every call for help an opportunity for expansion. In Sicily, he averred, the citizen populations, made up of new and old elements as yet unfused, lacked national spirit, and were thus both amenable to corrosive propaganda and destitute of the preparation requisite for war. Beyond the immediate undertaking, which the navy rendered safe (for without imperilling its maritime superiority at home Athens could send out ships enough to defeat the combined fleets of Sicily), Alcibiades opened out prospects of vastly increased armaments, of an assault on the Peloponnesians with irresistible strength, and of dominion over all Greece.

Nicias was worsted. But he did not give up. He made a move by which, like an unwitting figure in a tragedy, he implicated himself and Athens more deeply in the calamity he sought to avert. He tried to deter the Athenians from the enterprise by magnifying the equipment of soldiers and ships, transports and stores, required for its successful prosecution. And the Athenians forthwith accepted his estimates of at least 100 triremes and 5000 hoplites, and voted to give him and his colleagues full power as to the size and despatch of the armament. Three thousand talents—the balance in the treasury in 421 B.C. plus the savings of six years—were set aside for the expedition to be appropriated as needed.

II THE FIRST EXPEDITION

There was now no turning back. With an enthusiasm and energy commensurate with the exaltation of spirit under which they were acting the Athenians went ahead with their preparations, putting their triremes into sea trim, mobilizing the naval and land forces required of their allies, selecting the quotas of heavy-armed troops from their own citizen-regiments, assembling ample supplies of grain and the personnel of an extensive commissariat as well as the merchant ships needed for their transport. For the following three or four months the city was full of the bustle of preparation.

Shortly before the time fixed for departure nearly all the busts of Hermes which, carved on square pillars of stone, stood in large numbers in shrines and at the entrances to private houses were mutilated during a single night. The occurrence was a sign of the times—a manifestation of the irreverence for sacred things which had made its appearance as a by-product of the contemporary enlightenment, and it evoked an outburst of exasperation and fanaticism that was even uglier than the outrage itself. Who the perpetrators were would perhaps have been a matter for the police and not for the historian, had not the enemies of Alcibiades, by widening the scope of the investigation instituted so as to include in it other similar acts of impiety, implicated him in charges of having burlesqued in a private house the sacred Mysteries of Eleusis. Nor did they hesitate to interpret in a political sense the number, prominence, and affiliations of the persons denounced by mercenary informers, so as to plant in the heated minds of the populace the conviction that they had to do with a conspiracy widely ramified in fashionable society to overthrow the demos.

Alcibiades demanded an immediate trial, fearing the campaign of calumny certain to be conducted against him during his absence. But his enemies, the most active of whom were the demagogues Peisander and Androcles, prevented it. When the army, which was friendly to him, was gone, and there was no longer any danger of losing the Argive and Mantinean contingents, which he had procured, the chances of having him condemned were infinitely better. Merely to be able to have him recalled at the right moment was to make them, not him, the master of his military career. To have set sail under such conditions was a hard blow to Alcibiades; but he could neither win consent for a hasty trial nor detain the expedition for a searching one. Besides, there was always the hope that the frenzy would die down.

The battle-fleet for Sicily was ready in the Piraeus in June 415 B.C. The ships were appointed regardless of expense, manned with the best crews attainable, and perfected for speed and manœuvring. The soldiers were picked men, young and often well-born. There had been rivalry among trierarchs as to vessels, and among hoplites as to arms, each individual striving to make his the best; and neither publicly nor privately had money or effort been stinted to make the expedition equal in all respects to its mission. An impressive ceremony marked the starting. When the ships were in the water, the rowers at their oars, and the soldiers at their posts, a trumpeter gave the signal, and amid a solemn silence, as the officers and marines poured libations from gold and silver cups, all together, led by a herald, repeated the prayer that was customary before putting out to sea, which in turn was taken up by the immense throng that had gathered on the shore from all Attica (anxious at once and exultant) to see their friends and relatives off. This done, the battle-cry was sounded and the ships, filing one after another out of the harbour, raced at full speed as far as Aegina, there to settle down to the long haul that was to take them to Corcyra.

At Corcyra they picked up the sailing vessels that had gone ahead with supplies, and then the whole armament put off for Italy. It comprised 134 triremes, and 130 supply boats. Of the triremes 100 were Athenian, 40 of them being used to convey troops. The other triremes were furnished by the allies. The army consisted of 5100 hoplites, of whom 2200 were Athenians, of 30 Athenian cavalry, and 1300 light-armed troops (400 being Athenians). The crews of the triremes may be reckoned at 20,000, and the total of all forces at 27,000. It was a huge and formidable armada—so huge that it seemed wise to divide it into three squadrons so as not to overburden the facilities of the ports *en route*; so formidable that on its arrival in Italy the cities of Magna Graecia were afraid to admit it, and until it reached Rhegium, except for water and anchorage, it received no hospitality, and even these were refused by Tarentum and Locri. At Rhegium the Athenians were permitted to land and stretch their weary legs, and a market was set up for them outside the walls; but this was the only concession made by the people to their comradeship with Athens in the former war and their kinship with the Leontinians, for they kept their gates closed and affirmed their intention of remaining neutral in the war. Coming on top of the coolness or hostility of the other Italiotes, with whom the Rhegines said that they meant to act in concert, this rebuff was extremely disappointing to the Athenian generals, and it augured badly for their success in winning allies in Sicily. Nor did it help matters that at this point a squadron of three triremes, sent forward from Corcyra, returned from Segesta with the news that except for thirty talents there was no money there, the envoys despatched from Athens having been made the victims of an elaborate hoax. So a council of war was held to decide what to do next.

And it was not before time. For there were as many opinions as there were generals. Nicias was for dismissing all larger projects and moving at once on Selinus; Lamachus favoured a brusque assault on Syracuse; and Alcibiades pleaded for securing by negotiations all the support they could in Sicily before attacking either place. Too unimportant politically to win his powerful colleagues for his own plan, Lamachus rejected the programme of Nicias, which seemed faint-hearted, and inclined the balance in favour of opening the campaign with a struggle for allies. So the Athenians approached Messana, which would have nothing to do with them; Naxos, which admitted them; Catana, into which their soldiers broke by a postern gate while the citizens were gathered in assembly intent on hearing what Alcibiades had to say; and Camarina, which drew back after making friendly overtures. Messana Alcibiades had tried to win by argument alone: to the other cities he and his colleagues went accompanied by a battle-fleet of sixty triremes; and from Camarina all returned to Catana, which they had made their base of operations in Sicily. As yet they had few results to show for the loss of so much time and credit. And now they were to lose the driving force, not only of their diplomacy, but of the entire enterprise; for at Catana they found waiting for them a despatch-boat from Athens summoning Alcibiades home to stand trial for sacrilege.

By this time the mutilation of the Hermae had been traced (to the satisfaction at least of the Athenian courts) to an oligarchic club, of which Euphiletus was the head and Andocides a member. The information on which this conclusion rested had been given by a resident alien named Teucer; but, though the accused were condemned, credence was none the less given to the later tale of a certain Diocleides implicating a party of about 300, whom he professed to have seen at the work, and 42 persons named by him, among them a brother of Nicias, were indicted. At this moment a small Lacedaemonian force advanced to the Isthmus and simultaneously a movement of soldiers occurred in Boeotia; whereupon the whole city was called to arms in the belief that a *coup d'état* was imminent. Nothing came of it, but the air remained charged with suspicion, and many innocent persons would certainly have perished, had not Andocides confirmed by confession, at least in a general way, the information of Teucer, adding the quieting explanation that the outrage was conceived in drink. The case was therewith settled; but the facts were as obscure as ever. Meanwhile charges of burlesquing the Mysteries had been laid yet twice against groups of which Alcibiades was the centre. Why should he alone escape punishment? All the accusations of conspiracy, too, which were flying loose without a destination were seized upon to corroborate the belief, founded on his general behaviour, that the goal of his ambition was tyranny. There was hardly a politician in Athens who did not dread for himself or the city the predominance that awaited Alcibiades should he return victorious from Sicily. Cimon's son, Thessalus, was found to bring the indictment against him; and lest he should make a disturbance in the army, the emissaries who went to Sicily for him were instructed not to arrest him but to let him accompany them home in his own ship. Alcibiades seemed to have acquiesced, but at Thurii he gave his guards the slip and reached Elis shortly after. From there he went on a safe conduct to Sparta. In Athens he was condemned to death *in absentia*.

The recall of Alcibiades enabled Nicias to conduct the campaign more on his own lines. So he embarked on an expedition to the west of Sicily in the course of which he visited Segesta. The armada made a display of force on the north coast, and the army caused unrest among the Sicels by marching back through the centre of the island; but otherwise they had nothing to show to offset a rebuff at Himera and the loss of much precious time, except the spoils of the petty Sicanian town of Hyccara and the thirty talents of the Segestans. Then they tried to take Hybla by storm, but without success; so that the Syracusans now viewed the expedition not with consternation but with contempt.

III. THE SIEGE OF SYRACUSE

Like Athens, Syracuse was ruled by the people. Hence it too lacked a 'government' in the modern sense of the term, by which reports from abroad could be appraised authoritatively. Neither there nor elsewhere in Greece did state organs exist for collecting and forwarding trustworthy information from other political centres. It was a poor substitute for official reports that leaders of parties had private correspondents and contacts abroad by which they were rendered in a measure independent of the news which, transmitted by traders and travellers from one to the other arrived ordinarily in the form of unauthentic rumours. For information reaching the people through political channels was suspect, oftentimes (especially in Syracuse) deservedly so. Thus

it happened that even whilst the Athenians were already in
Corcyra the Syracusans were unconvinced that their city was the
object of the expedition. To the leader of the popular party,
Athenagoras, it seemed incredible that Athens should commit
an act of such great folly as to attack Syracuse; and from
the facility with which (as he thought) an Athenian force could
be repelled he inferred that the report of its coming was
spread abroad by the oligarchs with the sinister design of stam-
peding the people into entrusting extraordinary power to military
authorities hostile to democracy. His opponent Hermocrates,
on the other hand, was much better informed. He appreciated
justly the scope of Athenian ambition and the need for immediate action to thwart it; but he rather welcomed the coming
of the Athenians on the consideration that it could not but promote the union of all Sicily under the patronage of Syracuse—his
favourite political conception. His proposal was to arouse the
Greeks on the island and in Magna Graecia to a sense of their
common danger; and, by concentrating all available warships
at Tarentum, to force the Athenians to fight, while still suffering
from the effects of their long voyage, at the very threshold of the
West. Whatever may be said for its military wisdom, the scheme
was politically impracticable. Hermocrates was unable to convince the Syracusans of the imminence of danger, much less the
others. The generals, of whom they had no less than fifteen,
professed to have the situation well in hand.

And so matters rested till the Athenians arrived at Rhegium.
Then there were hurried dealings with the Sicels, dispatch of
garrisons to frontier-posts, and inspection of the arms and horses
to be used in operations based on the city. The likely and dreaded
thing was that the Athenians would arrive at the heels of the news
of their approach. Such, however, proved not to be the case. The
great fleet finally hove in sight off the city, but when the Syracusans
prudently kept their ships in port, it simply sent a squadron into
the Great Harbour to reconnoitre and issue a negligible proclamation. They then began to feel that they had been needlessly
scared. A little later their cavalry drew first blood while ejecting
an Athenian landing-party from Syracusan territory. And when
week after week passed and they remained unmolested, passing
from panic to temerity, they made up their minds themselves
to attack the Athenians at their base in Catana, and thus gave
Nicias a chance to show that he could strike as well as threaten.

Apprised of the fact that the Syracusans had fallen into a trap
he had set for them, and were on the march to Catana with their

entire army, he sailed during the night to Syracuse, and, without meeting any opposition, put his whole force on shore at daybreak within the Great Harbour opposite the Olympieum[1]. The enemy did not return till evening, and by then he had increased the natural strength of the position (it had cliffs on one side and on the other walls, houses, woods, and a marsh) by throwing up a wall at Dascon where it was most accessible, destroying the bridge over the Anapus river, and planting a wooden stockade on the beach by the ships. Nicias had no intention of suffering a disaster in case he proved the weaker in the field. Nor could he take any chances with the enemy's cavalry, which outnumbered his little detachment forty to one. A secure base was thus essential; but so was a prompt trial of strength with the Syracusan army. Hence the very next morning he advanced into the plain, where the enemy had bivouacked behind the Helorine road, and forced on a general engagement before they had got their minds set for it or their ranks consolidated. But they did not flinch. With their cavalry on their right and their phalanx sixteen men deep they sustained with courage the onset of their more experienced adversaries. A thunderstorm occurring in the midst of the fighting terrified particularly the less seasoned troops. The Syracusan left gave way and the rout spread along the entire line. Only the presence of the cavalry prevented a disaster. As it was, the army regained its initial position with a loss of only 260 men, and, after garrisoning the Olympieum, withdrew within the fortifications.

Nicias seemingly was now free to occupy the entire plain. Instead, he at once put his army on board ship and sailed back to Catana. The reasons for this disconcerting move have been given fully by Thucydides, whose account of the Sicilian expedition, here as throughout, we can do little but paraphrase: it was now, he tells us, winter; to carry on the war across the plain required strength in cavalry; the victory afforded prospects of gaining new allies, the delay, opportunity to prepare additional material, with which to push the attack with greater vigour in the spring. Since all these reasons for withdrawing were visible before landing, it is probable that Nicias was acting in the hope of creating, without the waste and risk of besieging Syracuse, a situation in Sicily with which the Athenians at home would be satisfied. Nor was such a hope groundless now that the moving spirit for war *à l'outrance* was out of the way. But seeing that Nicias himself was rendered politically ineffective by absence, and the men now most prominent at Athens, Androcles and

[1] See map 10 facing p. 289.

Peisander, belonged to the war-party, the Athenians, far from being content with defeating the Syracusans, voted the money (300 talents) and cavalry (250 horsemen and 30 mounted archers) requested for continuing the siege.

The Syracusans, too, had as yet no thought but to prepare themselves to make resistance successful. After being beaten in the open field they had to envisage the certainty that the Athenians would try to enclose their city by a wall of circumvallation. If they could not prevent this they must surrender, since their population of 100,000 could not subsist on the supplies which might elude the vigilance of the Athenian fleet. A wall of circumvallation, however, must cross Epipolae, a triangular plateau with precipitous edges, which, sloping gradually down from the west, was accessible from the plain below at two points only, its apex, Euryalus, and where it fell off less abruptly to form a broad bridge-head for the neck of land connecting Ortygia with the mainland. The land-wall of Syracuse ran from sea to sea across the base of this plateau, including in the section known as Achradina the portion of the bridge-head on which Ortygia abutted directly. The rest, designated Temenites, extended for some distance outside the fortifications to the west. By building an advance wall so as to cover this area the Syracusans secured for themselves all the easy passages between the heights above and the plain of the Anapus and at the same time lengthened appreciably the distance from sea to sea which would have to be covered by the Athenians with a wall of circumvallation.

With this they occupied themselves during the winter (415–4 B.C.), but they did not neglect other matters. Attributing their defeat to lack of discipline and of unity of command, they decided to substitute for their fifteen generals a board made up of Hermocrates and two others with more strictly military authority; and, besides working with diplomacy and arms to counter the moves made by the Athenians to win allies among the Greeks (notably at Camarina, and at Messana, where the treachery of Alcibiades proved fatal to his friends) and to stir up insurrection among the Sicels, they dispatched envoys to Corinth and Sparta to get aid if possible and to persuade the Lacedaemonians to renew the war with Athens. These found the Corinthians eager to help— they were already at war with Athens—the Spartans, on the other hand, hesitant. They did not want to recommence hostilities until Athens, not they, incurred the anger of the gods by breaking the treaty, and until they saw some reasonable prospect of success. Waging war so far afield as Sicily had no attractions for them.

But they could not escape the conclusion that they must do something to help Syracuse. As to its peril there was agreement between its envoys and Alcibiades, whose bitterness against his native land lent weight to the authority with which he disclosed the expectations, plans, and fears of the Athenians: once Syracuse had been starved into submission, all Sicily and Italy would be mobilized for a grand attack by sea and land on the Peloponnese. This should be forestalled by sending to Syracuse, if not Spartan soldiers, at least a Spartan general; and it would especially help to keep the Athenians from dispatching further troops to Sicily and to bring them into a frame of mind to accept terms, should Sparta do what Athens above all else dreaded—seize Decelea in Attica. To the one of these suggestions which committed them least the Spartans at once acceded and nominated Gylippus, son of Cleandridas, to take command both of the Syracusans themselves and of an expedition to be set on foot from Corinth for their relief. A better choice could not have been made.

During the winter of 415–4 B.C. neither Syracuse nor Athens had much success in stirring up the Siceliote Greeks to take a hand in the war. The record of both for unfair dealing with allies was against them. The idea uppermost on the island was to be on good terms with the victor. Hence the Athenians profited little in this particular by the winter's delay. And an effort to capitalize the ancient enmities toward Syracuse existing in the West outside Sicily yielded them only three shiploads of troops from 'Etruria.' Carthage refused to aid them. When, too, spring came the Athenians were still unready. The cavalry from Athens was not yet there. The interval of waiting they filled in with unimportant expeditions. Then, when the Athenian horsemen finally reached Catana and mounts had been secured for them and they were about to be augmented by 300 cavalry from Segesta and 100 from Naxos and elsewhere, Nicias and Lamachus concluded that they were in a position to strike (May, 414 B.C.).

The Syracusans had long since put a garrison at the Olympieum and lined the shore of the Great Harbour with a stockade on the chance that the Athenians would try again to land where they had landed before. The importance attached by their adversaries to cavalry suggested, however, an alternative—an advance on Epipolae from the north. For this Hermocrates and his colleagues set about arranging a defence—the constitution of a picked force of 600 men to guard the approaches to the heights. But they had waited too long and were caught napping. For on the very morning on which they assembled the troops on the meadow by the Anapus for the purpose, in connection with a general review, of selecting the men and organizing them in a special detachment, Nicias and Lamachus, having come, not by land, but by sea during the night, disembarked their entire force at Leon, and rushed it forward so rapidly that it had mastered the ascent at Euryalus and debouched on the highest point of the plateau before even the 600 guards, who had a slightly greater distance to traverse, had come up to dispute their passage. In the battle which ensued the Syracusans, attacking in the disorder of their approach, were defeated, and retired within their walls leaving the Athenians in possession of the key position to the defence of the city.

With a celerity in action that contrasted strangely with the hesitancy of their decisions Nicias and Lamachus next fortified a base at Labdalum 'on the verge of the bluffs looking towards Megara,' and bringing up all their cavalry advanced to Syke, where they built with staggering speed the first section of the 'circle,' which with one wall facing out and another facing in and a passage between was planned to run for a distance of more than three miles across the heights and down on each side to Trogilus on the north and the Great Harbour on the south. The progress of this work the Syracusans sought first to impede by bringing their mounted troops into action, but these too the Athenians worsted by using in conjunction with their cavalry a regiment of foot. Then they sought to stop it by constructing a counter-wall out from the city below the southern cliffs across its projected line, the course selected being so situated that they could protect the approaches to it from the heights by palisades and force the Athenians to divide their army dangerously should they intervene.

But the Athenians went on with their own job extending the circle toward the north and laying down wood and stone in the direction of Trogilus. They waited till the Syracusans had finished and had resumed their various stations. Then choosing the time of the midday siesta when their adversaries were off their guard, a picked Athenian corps rushed the counter-wall at its end, driving the Syracusan garrison before it, while one Athenian army advanced to contain the enemy's troops in Achradina and another to assail his works at a point near the postern gate leading into Temenites. The latter was unable to intercept the garrison, but it entered Temenites simultaneously, and, though it was immediately thrown out again with losses, the main purpose of the attack was achieved. The cross-wall was destroyed and its materials appropriated by the Athenians to their own uses.

With this incident is doubtless to be connected the fact that on resuming operations on the circle next day it was no longer with its extension toward the north that they busied themselves but with the carrying of it to and over the southern bluffs to the low-lying land that ran thence for over half a mile to the Great Harbour. While they were thus employed the Syracusans set to work to head them off a second time, and this they did by constructing a stockade and digging a ditch through the middle of the marsh across their path. And a second time the Athenians bided their time and then intervened. Having ordered the fleet to sail forward from Thapsus into the Great Harbour, they advanced, Lamachus leading, across the marsh at daybreak by the aid of doors and planks which they carried with them, and mastered the enemy's works and defeated his army. But the enterprise was not completed without incidents. The Syracusan right was thrown back on the city, but the left, repulsed on the Anapus, made for the bridge to escape toward the Olympieum. An Athenian regiment, which tried to head them off, was itself cut to pieces by the Syracusan cavalry, and while stemming the panic that ensued Lamachus exposed himself rashly and was slain. Simultaneously the Athenians narrowly escaped losing their other general. For, taking advantage of the crisis below, the Syracusans who had fled to the city launched an attack on the heights above, which were now denuded of defenders, and Nicias, who had not participated in that day's offensive because of illness, kept them at bay till help arrived only by setting fire to the engines and timber that lay in front of the circle. At this moment the Athenian fleet appeared in the Great Harbour; whereupon the Syracusans, extricating their left wing somehow, retired everywhere within the city, gave up the struggle, and let the Athenians—sailors reinforcing soldiers—go ahead with the envelopment. The circle was soon carried to within a short distance of the shore, and, since in the case of the two-mile stretch between Syke and Trogilus, the materials were for the most part in place and some sections were already finished, the complete circumvallation of Syracuse was now only a question of time.

Of the two methods by which at that epoch walled cities were wont to fall—blockade and betrayal—it was not clear, however, that the Syracusans would chose the sterner; for a party within the city was conducting private negotiations with Nicias; and the citizens collectively were debating, both among themselves and with him, the possibilities of peace. A symptom of profound dissatisfaction and distrust appeared in the dismissal of

Hermocrates and his colleagues and the appointment of other generals in their place.

IV. GYLIPPUS AND THE SIEGE OF NICIAS

The essence of the matter was time, and this the Athenians had squandered. But even yet, at the height of their fortunes, when at the eleventh hour help was about to reach Syracuse, they might have remained master of the situation if they had been reasonably vigilant. Lamachus was sorely missed. It was a curious accident that a man who disbelieved in the ultimate utility of capturing Syracuse should have been left alone to prosecute its siege. Yet how much depended upon personality in warfare was shown no less in Gylippus' case than in his. For without waiting for the thirteen ships of which his relief expedition mainly consisted, this able and enterprising man put off from Leucas for Italy with four vessels only, notwithstanding that he was in receipt of false news from which he judged that his mission was hopeless. The Italian Greeks refused to back an enterprise so weakly equipped. Nor did Nicias treat it seriously till it had arrived at Locri, when he sent against it four triremes, which, however, arrived too late to prevent it from passing through the straits. Gylippus thus arrived at Himera, where he scored a remarkable success. The Himeraeans embraced his cause wholeheartedly, furnished arms, by which he transformed 700 of his sailors into soldiers, and put 1000 of their own infantry and 100 of their cavalry at his disposal. The masterful way in which he lived up to his reputation as a Spartan won the interest of the Sicels of the neighbourhood; so that, when he set out across country for Syracuse, he took with him 1000 'barbarians,' in addition to the troops already mentioned and some small contingents from Selinus and Gela—about 3000 men in all.

The speed of warships propelled by oars was so slight that even in the coastal areas of their action large spaces remained beyond eyesight in the daytime. Hence Nicias cannot fairly be blamed for letting one of Gylippus' ships from Leucas reach Syracuse at this moment with the much-needed news that twelve others were on their way, and that Gylippus, sent by Sparta to direct the defence, was not far off. A similar excuse does not exist in the case of an army coming by land. That Gylippus found Euryalus unguarded was apparently a surprise to himself, for he drew near it prepared for battle. But he made the ascent unnoticed, and once on the top of Epipolae nothing could prevent him from joining hands across the line of the Athenian circle with the Syracusans, who by pre-arrangement had come out of Achradina in full force to meet him. For a moment he thought of attacking the Athenians in their positions before they had recovered from their surprise, but, thinking better of it when he saw in what disarray the Syracusans advanced, he stood on the defensive. Nor despite his advantage in numbers did he try to relieve the city by driving off the Athenians; but, after first capturing Labdalum by a surprise attack, he set to work building a single wall from the city up Epipolae in a westerly direction. It was designed to intersect the Athenian circle to the north of the point to which this was finished and to reach the edge of the plateau at or south of Euryalus, thus adding, virtually, a new quarter to the city and excluding altogether the possibility of a circumvallation.

Nicias did not interfere prematurely. Before coming up to the high ground he completed the section to the Great Harbour; and, being dependent, as never before, on his water communications now that the Syracusan cavalry was at large; aware, too, of the necessity of keeping a closer watch on the comings and goings in the Syracusan ports now that relief was on its way by sea and the Syracusans were taking renewed interest in their fleet, he occupied Plemmyrium (the projecting headland by which the entrance into the Great Harbour was narrowed down on the south to three-quarters of a mile) with a chain of forts, and transferred his navy and his naval base thither. This took time; and in the meanwhile Gylippus had carried his counter-wall close to its point of inter-section with the Athenian circle, on the extension northward of which the Athenians were again busy. This brought matters to a head. Gylippus had more spirit for the offensive, Nicias greater need to attack. In the first battle the Syracusans found the Athenian army in a position between the walls where they could not use their cavalry, and being still inferior in infantry-fighting, they were repulsed. In the second battle Nicias, attacking in turn, found the Syracusans drawn up with their right wing, in which their cavalry and javelin-men were posted, well outside the corner of the two walls. And to this he owed his defeat. For the enemy's mobile troops routed his left, which thereupon carried his whole line with it in headlong flight within the fortifications.

That night Gylippus built his wall past the critical point; and, not content with this advantage, he employed thereafter all available man-power in completing the wall to the distant point selected. Syracuse was saved—as it proved, definitely.

It was now Nicias' turn to be besieged. Already Gylippus had posted one-third of his mounted troops at a hamlet near the

Olympieum, from which they so harassed and confined the crews of the ships at Plemmyrium that they could get water, firewood, and forage only with the greatest difficulty and danger. The soldiers, too, had henceforth to live cramped in their bleak camp by the edge of the Great Harbour and in the narrow passage-way which ran thence across the unhealthy lowlands to Syke on the wind-swept heights, nailed down to their stations in their elongated fortress by the enemy's cavalry and the ever-present menace of an attack in force from the city.

The sea was of course still open; but the twelve triremes from Corinth had made Syracuse in safety; and, combining their own vessels with these and manning them with men whom they could not use advantageously in their army, the Syracusans were busy, in full view of the Athenians, practising manœuvres with a sea fight in mind. They counted on not being inferior in numbers, and their ships were less run down and waterlogged than those of Nicias. Nor was it the smart, confident, battle-trained crews that had left the Piraeus sixteen months before with whom the Syracusans had now to measure themselves. The moment doubts as to ultimate success were justified, the morale of the Athenian seamen fell. The foreign conscripts among them took every opportunity to slip off for home, and the foreign mercenaries to desert to the enemy or to find employment elsewhere in Sicily. Since new drafts were not to be had, and the citizens, upon whom in these circumstances the fatigue duties mainly devolved—for the slaves, too, tended to run away and could no longer be trusted—were being decimated by the enemy's cavalry, the triremes generally came more and more to fall short of their full complements and the men that were left to lose their edge through sickness and excessive drudgery. Of course it was only during the chill winter months that these evils progressed sufficiently to put so many ships out of commission as to endanger the naval superiority of the Athenians, but they were already apparent to Nicias in October (414 B.C.); and since the siege could no longer be prosecuted, he at once sent a long despatch to Athens explaining his situation fully and recommending that the expedition be abandoned altogether or reinforced by another equally large. He asked too that he be relieved of the command on account of illness.

V. THE SECOND EXPEDITION

Neither he nor any other general, ancient or modern, could have taken the responsibility of abandoning outright an expedition on which his country set such store and which had come so near succeeding. Could it have entered into the calculations of the Athenians that, if they sent a second expedition, the combined force would be unable to withdraw when it pleased; that is to say, could they have been as wise to the issue as we are, they doubtless would have cut their losses and evacuated Sicily forthwith. But being a proud, plucky people, solicitous for their prestige, and not omniscient, they resolved to see the war through. They continued Nicias in the command, designating two officers then on the spot to share provisionally his burdens, and they put Eurymedon, whose knowledge of western affairs was second to none, and Demosthenes, their most energetic general, in charge of a second expedition, which, like the first, was to comprise both fleet and army—a selective draft of citizens and contingents from the allies. The task of organizing the new enterprise was entrusted to Demosthenes. Eurymedon sailed at once to Sicily with 120 talents, spreading the news of Athens' intentions (December, 414 B.C.). His arrival during the winter gave Nicias ten new ships and 2000 fresh seamen, a welcome addition for the sea fight that was due in the spring.

That strong reinforcements would come to Nicias was anticipated everywhere. It must therefore be the aim of Sparta, if it should do its part, to detain the Athenians at home; of Gylippus, to destroy the enemy's forces in Sicily, or at least complete their investment, before a new armada could arrive. Accordingly, taking up the gage which Athens, at the insistence of the Argives, had thrown down the previous summer, the Spartans re-opened the Peloponnesian War in the early spring (middle of March) of 413 B.C. by an invasion of Attica in which they and their allies, under the leadership of Agis, not only ravaged the country, but seized Decelea and proceeded systematically to fortify it. But they did more than thus point a gun at the heart of the Athenian Empire. They set to work sending soldiers on merchant ships from various points in the Peloponnese across the open sea to Sicily, masking the operation by threatening the Athenian patrol at Naupactus with a fleet of 25 triremes manned for the purpose by Corinth. Gylippus, for his part, spent the winter canvassing Sicily for allies, men, and ships. But he, too, failed to move the Siceliote Greeks very profoundly. They were interested rather to save Syracuse than to enable it to triumph. Notably they held back their warships. If the Syracusans were to get the better of the Athenians on the sea it must therefore be with the resources they already had.

They had obviously possessed a considerable fleet when the Athenians first arrived; for they now got ready for action 67 triremes in addition to the thirteen that came from Corinth. The crews, accustomed to regard the Athenians as their masters in the art of seamanship, found it difficult to estimate favourably their chances of success in naval warfare. The work of mental preparation was mainly taken in hand by Hermocrates, now as ever clear-sighted, resolute, patriotic, who developed an aggressive spirit among them by insisting that their adversaries had taken to the sea, not from instinct, but, like themselves, under pressure, and would lose their superiority if subjected unexpectedly to the same sort of bold attack with which they were wont to overwhelm others.

Plemmyrium was indicated as the first objective of Syracusan operations by two considerations: it was the key to the harbour in the same way as Euryalus was the key to Epipolae and the city; and it was the depot in which the Athenians kept their stock of food, goods, and naval stores, and the station in which their fleet was moored. Under cover of night Gylippus marched his whole army into positions where, screened by cavalry, they could wait in readiness to assail Plemmyrium from the land side at the right moment. The signal was to come from the fleet. This advanced in two squadrons, one of 45 triremes outside Ortygia from the Little Harbour, the other of 35 triremes from the naval station within the Great Harbour. But before they could join to press home the attack, the Athenians were able, notwithstanding the suddenness of the onset and the double threat, to meet the larger squadron entering the harbour's mouth with 35 ships and the other with a force likewise smaller by 10 ships than that opposed to it. The struggle was long drawn out, but eventually the Athenians had to give way in both areas; and, since at the right moment, when its defenders were gathered on the beach watching the sea fight, Gylippus assaulted the largest of the chain of forts protecting Plemmyrium, he took it by storm. The Athenians were then face to face with irreparable disaster. But, as Thucydides says, the Syracusans 'made them a present of their victory.' The squadron that had forced its way into the Great Harbour was somehow thrown into disorder, the ships falling foul of one another; so that the Athenians, alert in their desperation to seize every advantage, were able to put it to flight and then to rout the other division also.

But in the meantime Gylippus had occupied all Plemmyrium. Most of the guards escaped, those of the main fort with difficulty; but the stores, notably the sails and tackle of 40 triremes, were captured. The casualties of the sea fight were appreciably larger on the side of the Syracusans—eleven ships and their crews against three ships only;—but these losses were more than balanced by the moral effect produced on friends and foes alike by the demonstration that the Athenian fleet was no longer unbeatable.

The chief gain of the Syracusans, however—one from whose consequences the Athenians never escaped—was the occupation of Plemmyrium. For this left the Athenians no option but to shift their naval station to the only part of the Great Harbour now theirs—the strand in front of their camp, a shallow beach with muddy bottom on which the east wind rolls up a considerable surf. Thereafter, except when they won a passage by fighting, it was not they but the Syracusans who controlled the entrance of supplies of food and material, which, too, were further curtailed by a squadron of Syracusan ships sent to Italy to intercept them at their source. The pressure thus exerted on their line of communications and retreat was a great evil and a greater menace; and the constant activity required to ensure provisions and avoid surprise put a fearful strain on the endurance and vigilance of the Athenian crews, already stale from overwork. But what injured the Athenians most was that henceforth their fleet had to operate in waters so circumscribed as to destroy the possibility for the execution of the manœuvres of backing, enveloping, and breaking through on which its superiority mainly depended; so land-locked that the Syracusans could use skiffs and methods of attack that would have been quite inapplicable on the open sea.

Naturally Nicias did his utmost to exploit his naval success—the last perhaps of the eight victories gained by the Athenians when, according to Euripides, the gods were impartial—by destroying the Syracusan fleet. After its defeat this had taken refuge in the old dockyards directly across the Great Harbour from the new Athenian naval station. But all Nicias' efforts to come at the enemy's ships were frustrated by the Syracusans who put a stockade of piles in front of their positions and replaced it again as often as the Athenians removed it. Thus protected they carried through a project for remodelling their triremes. Being, as they saw, safeguarded against flank and rear attacks by the narrow field within which alone the Athenians could fight—for they dared not range widely since thus they would imperil their retreat to their narrow base between the Anapus and Lysimeleia

—the Syracusans sacrificed speed to strength of prow and produced a type of vessel that was distinctly better for head-on fighting.

Meanwhile Gylippus was busy bringing up reinforcements. Those from Selinus and Himera were denied passage through its territory by Acragas (which persisted in its neutrality to the last), and while following the alternative route through the land of the Sicels, they fell into an ambuscade laid for them, at Nicias' instigation, by the people of Centuripa and Halicyae, and of the 2300 men who started only 1500 arrived at Syracuse. Succours from Camarina and Gela, lent more freely now that Syracuse had mastered one attack and feared another, did not have a neutral or hostile barrage to encounter, and came up safely: 500 hoplites, 700 javelin-men, 500 horsemen and a squadron of five ships. Of the 1600 hoplites on their way in merchant ships across the open sea from the Peloponnese only the 300 Boeotians had been heard from as yet. Of the rest the 600 Helots and Neodamodes from Sparta, storm-driven to the coast of Africa, were to turn up at Selinus, but only in August, while the 700 from Corinth and Sicyon were late in starting. But the reinforcements actually on hand were very considerable—enough to give them numerical superiority in hoplites, cavalry, light-armed troops, and ships. Gylippus could not wait for the rest if he wanted to destroy the force of Nicias before that of Demosthenes arrived. In fact he had waited too long already.

He opened the engagement by advancing in full force both from the city and the Olympieum across the lowlands against the Athenian lines. This, however, was merely a feint and it deceived the enemy only for a moment. The real attack came from the sea. The interval separating the two lines of piles behind which the fleets lay was little more than a mile. But by quick work the Athenians got their triremes manned and free in time to deploy before the Syracusans were upon them. Nothing, therefore, came of the surprise. Nor was the fighting in any way conclusive. Numerically the fleets differed but slightly (80 Syracusan ships against 75 Athenian), and, except that they sank one or two of the enemy's triremes, the attackers derived little advantage from changing the prows of their vessels. Two days later the battle was renewed in identical circumstances, and again the struggle on land petered out and the struggle on sea was prolonged in indecisive skirmishing. Then the Syracusans, on the initiative of their best pilot, Ariston, son of Pyrrhicus, a Corinthian, staged a stratagem that was the undoing of the Athenians.

They backed away as if breaking off for the day, but it was in reality to take food, which was ready for them on the shore. Then, returning suddenly, they faced the Athenians anew, taken thus by surprise and supperless. Again the Syracusans fell to skirmishing with the evident intention of tiring the Athenians out. Perceiving this, the latter, abandoning the defensive rôle thus far assumed, brought the matter to an issue by a swift attack, and fighting began in earnest. Now it was that the remodelling of the Syracusan warships proved its value. Trireme after trireme of the Athenians had its slender prow stove in and became incapacitated. Nor was this the only particular in which the Athenians fought at a disadvantage. For Syracusan javelin-men, brought up on skiffs, which darted under the banks of oars, reached the rowers through the oar-holes and did them great damage. Tired and discouraged, the Athenians took to flight, with seven ships a total loss and many others unfit for action; and it was small compensation that the victors in their pursuit approached too near the merchantmen which Nicias had anchored the day before at intervals of 200 feet in front of his stockade, and had two of their vessels destroyed by the 'dolphins' with which these auxiliaries were equipped[1]. The Athenians were driven off the sea, and even if they could withstand the renewed attack that was imminent on land and water, they could not hold out long through lack of provisions. At this juncture Demosthenes and Eurymedon arrived.

The Spartans occupied Decelea when the Athenians could not have abandoned the second expedition even had they wished. For then, to enable Nicias to evacuate Sicily with safety, he needed from them reinforcements not orders. They were of course both inconvenienced and injured by the constant proximity of a strong garrison impregnably established on the south slope of Parnes, less than fourteen miles from the city, at a point whence it overlooked the entire plain of the Cephisus and dominated the road leading from Athens to Euboea. But so long as the sea was theirs they were in no danger. For their commitments in Sicily did not involve more than one-quarter of their field army. They were, indeed, taking chances with their maritime supremacy, but only in the contingency, which seemed excluded, that the 210 warships, implicated first and last in Sicily, would be a total loss. Their retort to the occupation of Decelea was in kind: they themselves seized a post in Laconia, opposite Cythera, whence they hoped to menace Sparta's hold on the Helots more effectively than from Pylos. This lodgement

[1] Thucydides VII, 41.

was effected by joint action between the fleet of 60 Athenian and
five Chian ships which Demosthenes was taking to Syracuse and a
home fleet of 30 ships, the crews of which, reinforced by hoplites
taken aboard at Argos, stayed on after Demosthenes' departure
to complete the fortifications.

At Zacynthus and Cephallenia and from Naupactus Demosthenes was joined by fresh hoplites. At Acarnania he was
met by Eurymedon, back from Syracuse with word that Plemmyrium had fallen; and from there they dispatched ten ships
to strengthen the patrol at Naupactus, which, even so, sustained
a moral defeat in a dubious victory which it shortly afterwards
gained over the Corinthians. Acarnania furnished light-armed
troops, both slingers and javelin-men, Corcyra hoplites and
fifteen triremes, the former requisitioned by Demosthenes, the
latter by Eurymedon. Then the two crossed to Italy. There
Tarentum and Locri remained hostile and Rhegium neutral, but
from Metapontum, Thurii, and the Messapians they received
two ships, 600 hoplites, and 750 javelin-men. It was accordingly
with a splendid armament of 73 triremes (51 Athenian), 5000
hoplites (1200 Athenian), 3000 bowmen, slingers, and javelin-
men, and an adequate commissariat and equipment—at least
15,000 men of all forces—that Demosthenes and Eurymedon
sailed into the Great Harbour in July 413 B.C. to the joy and
relief of the Athenians and the utter consternation of the Syracusans. It would have been better for Athens had Nicias and all
his men perished before they arrived.

Nicias being ill and discredited by defeat and Eurymedon a
colourless personality, the conduct of Athenian operations was at
once assumed by Demosthenes. He was clear on two points: the
necessity of acting at once while the impression of his arrival was
fresh, and the impossibility of continuing the siege without
mastering the counter-wall constructed by Gylippus longi-
tudinally across Epipolae. Accordingly, he first secured elbow-
room by driving the enemy out of the plain of the Anapus, and
then launched a resolute frontal attack on the wall in question;
but, since the Syracusans burned the engines with which he
sought to break through and repulsed at all points the assaults
made simultaneously, he had perforce to adopt the alternative—
an enveloping movement. The aim of such an operation, however,
was the possession of Euryalus, through which alone an entrance
existed into Epipolae in the rear of the Syracusan line. This weak
point was now defended by an advance fort with three fortified
camps in its rear; so that if an attempt were made to force it in

broad daylight, it had, Demosthenes thought, little chance of success. He, therefore, proposed, and his colleagues accepted, the hazardous plan of engaging his entire army in a night-attack, in the course of which Euryalus was to be overwhelmed and the Syracusans swept back on Achradina, so that Gylippus' wall could be breached and work on the circle resumed.

The first part of this programme was carried out successfully: the fort that guarded the approach was surprised and captured, and as the Athenians debouched on the heights they routed the troops specially allocated for the defence of Epipolae, and also drove before them the guards of the cross-wall, which they proceeded to dismantle. The real struggle began when the main Syracusan army came up. At the outset this too was thrust back. But first the Boeotian detachment, and then other Syracusan corps, stood their ground, or even threw back their assailants; so that the two lines became dove-tailed, so to speak, into one another, and a scene of indescribable confusion ensued. The light—for the moon was full—favoured the defenders; so did the homogeneity of their speech, battle-cries, and paeans. They were thus able to fight to better purpose and more compactly. Finally panic overtook the Athenians; and in their flight many threw themselves or were forced over the bluffs. Demosthenes' turning movement had failed, and failed disastrously, with great losses.

His design in this contingency was to depart immediately, especially since illness, due to the season and the marsh, was prostrating the soldiers. Nicias agreed with him that they could make no further headway by attacking, but he feared to accept the responsibility of withdrawing altogether without a vote of the people; and as for withdrawing to Thapsus or Catana, whence, as Demosthenes urged, they could continue the war both on land and sea much more advantageously and without the risk of being cut off completely, he argued that there was time enough to do this later when the enemy would be expecting it less, and when they themselves were quite sure that the Syracusans, who (he professed to know) were suffering greater hardships than they were and had reached the end of their financial resources, would not come to terms. Obstinate, timorous of responsibility, selfish, such Nicias showed himself at this time; but so great was the influence he still possessed, and so contagious the confidence he expressed that a revolution was imminent in Syracuse, by which his correspondents there would put the city into his hands, that he had his way even though Eurymedon was against him as well as Demosthenes.

VI. THE ATHENIAN DISASTER

So for the greater part of a month the departure was deferred. And disease raged in the camp; and the treason hoped for did not appear. Nor did the hired soldiers of Syracuse desert when their pay fell in arrears. Thus the grounds for remaining fell away; and eventually an argument for leaving came which even Nicias could not resist—the arrival in Syracuse of the Peloponnesian troops from Selinus and of further large reinforcements, which Gylippus, indefatigable as ever, had collected. The day for withdrawing was set and, in all secrecy, plans for the evacuation of the great army were matured. 'But after all was ready and when they were about to make their departure, the moon, which happened then to be at the full, was eclipsed (August 27, 413 B.C.). And most of the Athenians, taking the incident to heart, urged the generals to wait. Nicias, also, who was somewhat too much given to divination and the like, refused even to discuss further the question of their removal until they should have waited thrice nine days as the soothsayers prescribed. Such then,' says Thucydides[1], 'was the reason why the Athenians delayed and stayed on.'

After the disaster the Athenians were enraged at all their practitioners of the mantic art who by giving them assurances of success had sent them confidently to Sicily. Their anger was misplaced. The objects of their wrath had simply conformed to the traditions of their craft in harmonizing the signs from heaven with the political and military exigencies of the hour. The seers who were at fault were the soothsayers of Nicias who had not wit enough—or was it courage that was lacking?—to turn an eclipse to the account of a move so imperative as was departure on this occasion. The fact was that Nicias desired to remain. He could not believe that the gods would let him fail. Athens had already suffered because its general was too loyal a parliamentarian: it was now to have deep cause to regret that he was so complete a pattern of all the conventional virtues.

It was at once reported to the Syracusans that the Athenians had been on the point of withdrawing. Hence Gylippus did not give them a second chance to shift the scene of fighting to an arena of their own choosing. His preparations completed, he engaged the Athenian fleet again. He had only 76 ships to his opponents 86; but, favoured by the wind, he pressed the fighting, with the same elements of superiority as before, close to the Athenian base. Eurymedon, who commanded the Athenian right,

[1] VII, 50, transl. C. F. Smith, *Loeb Classics*.

tried to get freedom for manœuvring by sailing round the Syracusan flank; but, failing to swing out from the land inside Dascon,
and, hence, detached from his centre, which the enemy broke,
he was thrown back into the southern extension of the harbour
and perished together with his entire squadron. The Athenian
ships were everywhere driven towards the shore, some of them
outside the stockade to the north. Most of these the army saved,
inflicting in the process a severe defeat on the troops with which
Gylippus, coming from the city along the causeway, tried to
capture them. The Syracusans failed, too, to rid themselves of
their enemy by the use of a fire-ship.

But they were again masters of the sea; and, anticipating that
the next effort of the Athenians would be to force their way out
of the harbour at all costs, they narrowed down its mouth by a
line of boats—triremes placed sidewise, merchant ships, craft of
all kinds, anchored and chained together. They pictured themselves enshrined in the memory of the Hellenes as the destroyers
of the tyrant state that for two generations had carried terror
across the waters to all liberty-loving Greeks. The position of
the Athenians was indeed desperate. They could not remain
where they were because of lack of provisions. On the land side
the country for a great radius was all hostile, difficult to traverse,
and infested with the enemy's cavalry. Retreat in this direction
was obviously a last resort. A break-through by sea in the
opening left between Ortygia and Plemmyrium must be attempted.

To make this with a maximum of strength they shortened the
lines on land to a circuit by the shore which a garrison could hold.
With the troops thus set free and the crews that remained fit
they manned all the triremes they had, loading them down in a
way that lessened speed but converted them into floating fortresses, swarming with missile-throwers and boarding-parties, the
general idea being to seize the enemy's ships with grappling-
irons and thus fight a land battle on shipboard. Nicias left
nothing undone to increase the confidence of the fighters and
bring home to each man individually the seriousness of the
struggle both for himself and for Athens. Personally he chose
the harder part and stayed behind with the garrison, which he
spread out along the beach so as to enlarge as much as possible
the area on which the ships might fall back with safety when hard
pressed. Demosthenes shared with Menander and Euthydemus
the responsibility of leading the fleet into action, which, with its
110 ships in battle order, rowed straight for the harbour's mouth

(*c.* September 10, 413 B.C.). They found the Corinthians under Pythen ready to meet them. The rest of the Syracusan fleet, commanded by Sicanus and Agatharchus, was stationed in a semi-circle on either wing, and behind the ships the Syracusan army was distributed along the shore to intervene with help to save or destroy according as the vessels that came within its reach were friends or foes. The Syracusan ships (76 in all) were less numerous but more stoutly built and in much better repair.

The battle that ensued opened advantageously for the Athenians, who thrust the Corinthians back and reached the barrier of boats; but before they had mastered this obstacle, the Syracusans bore in upon them from all directions and forced them to fight at once on several fronts. At this point Thucydides fails even to suggest the factors that determined the outcome. Instead, he dwells on certain typical incidents in the confused fighting that followed, and then turns our attention to the spectators on the shore, and leaves us to infer the manifold vicissitudes of the protracted struggle from the agony of fear, joy, anxiety; the actual bodily swaying this way and that: the intense excitement breaking out in cries and lamentations, prayers and objurgations, with which both sets of eye-witnesses followed the action. A wail from the entire Athenian army announced the final triumph of the Syracusans.

Of the 110 Athenian ships that entered the engagement only 60 escaped in a seaworthy condition, but as the Syracusans could now launch still less—50 at most—Demosthenes and Nicias resolved to man the survivors at once and try again to force a passage out; but the sailors preferred to face the unknown perils of a retreat by land, and refused to embark. Had they set out for Catana that same night they might have escaped; but, tricked by Hermocrates into thinking that the way was blocked, they waited 36 hours to arrange their forces and pack up. Then they started westward for the Sicel country, leaving behind the sick and the wounded, the war-material and what remained of the fleet. With the men in a hollow square, Nicias in command of the front half and Demosthenes of the rear, they forced the crossing of the Anapus, and, in a swarm of attacking cavalry and light-armed troops, covered a distance of forty stadia ($3\frac{7}{10}$ miles)[1]. Next day,

---

[1] The assumption is commonly made that Thucydides here and elsewhere in his account of operations in Sicily reckons distances by the so-called itinerary stadium of about 164 yards, whereas generally in his history he uses the Attic stadium ($214\frac{1}{2}$ yards according to Dörpfeld, *Ath. Mitt.*, 1890, p. 171 and Dinsmoor, *A.J.A.*, 1925, p. 456).

twenty stadia (1⅞ miles) farther on, they reached a valley near a village (Floridia), where they stopped over-night for food and water; but, on resuming their march, they found the approach (Cava di Culatrello) to the elevated, ravine-flanked crest of Acraean Scaur, over which the advance lay, so strongly held by enemy troops, and the crest itself so effectually fortified, that resolute attacks on two successive days yielded only heavy casualties and no passage. Nor did a third attempt by a different approach bring them farther forward. There was no alternative but to alter their route. They determined to make a detour to the south and seek their destination by ascending the river Cacyparis (Cassibili). And in order to evade the enemy, whose Parthian tactics made headway almost impossible, they left numerous camp-fires burning and used the night for marching. The Syracusans failed to notice their departure; and at dawn the Athenians reached the coastal road to Helorum unmolested, Nicias in good order and a long way ahead, Demosthenes, who had been slow in starting, with the rear in much confusion. Since Nicias pushed rapidly on, while Demosthenes stopped to re-arrange his ranks, the two halves of the retreating army were fifty stadia (4⅔ miles) apart when at noon, not far beyond the Cacyparis (which the army crossed by fighting but did not ascend), the rear was overhauled by the Syracusan cavalry. Thus it happened that the two sections of the Athenian army made their fate doubly sure by meeting it separately.

Demosthenes was quickly surrounded on the 'Homestead of Polyzelus,' in a walled enclosure among olive trees, where his exhausted men were not sufficiently covered to escape the enemy's storm of missiles, to which, thus crowded together, they presented the best of targets. Though offered freedom if they would desert, the 'allied' troops from the islands of the Aegean Sea for the most part refused—a creditable proof of loyalty to their comrades if not of devotion to Athens. But the situation was utterly hopeless; and, on receiving a guarantee that they would not be put to death, the whole force surrendered. The survivors numbered 6000.

Except that it was in a river instead of an olive orchard, disaster overtook Nicias in almost identical circumstances. When he had verified for himself the fate of his colleague—it was the morning after, while he was encamped on a hill just beyond the river Erineus (Fiume di Noto, Falconara?), which now he purposed ascending,—he offered to pay the Syracusans their entire war expenses of more than 2000 talents if they would let his army go.

But the Syracusans refused. They had him hemmed in, and all day long they pelted him with missiles. Unable to stay longer through lack of food and water, and failing to slip off undetected during the darkness, he had no alternative but to fight his way aimlessly along the Helorine road. At the end of three miles, already practically in flight, the army reached the Assinarus river (Tellaro, Atiddaru?), into the bed and current of which the men rushed, forgetting discipline and danger in the agony of their thirst. A horrible butchery ensued, to which Nicias eventually put an end by surrendering himself to Gylippus; but not before a majority of the survivors had been taken prisoners privately by the Syracusans and their allies (c. September 20, 413 B.C.). Those captured officially numbered only 1000.

Two generals and 7000 men were all that now remained to enter Syracuse of the 45–50,000 soldiers and sailors whom Athens had sent against the city[1]. The rest had been spared this ignominy by death, desertion, or enslavement. Generosity to prisoners was not to be expected on the part of the victors; for they would not have experienced it themselves if they had been vanquished. Yet we cannot help regretting that they did not rise to the occasion for clemency as they had risen to the successive needs of the war—remodelling their government and their triremes, pouring out their treasure and their blood, pertinacious alike in their diplomacy and their fighting, showing no less than their adversaries how large, varied, and flexible were the resources of a free people. But at the end of it all they were exhausted and revengeful. Though Hermocrates and Gylippus would have saved Demosthenes and Nicias, the one from magnanimity the other to grace his own triumph, the Syracusans had no compunction about putting them to death and confining their perplexing mass of captives in their stone quarries—secure prisons, ready-made, but cold at night hot by day and hence unhealthy,—where they kept them crowded

---

[1] 27,000 in summer of 415 B.C.; 520 (?) plus 680 mounted troops plus 300 (?) 'Etruscans' in spring and summer of 414; 2000 in winter of 414; 15,000 in summer of 413; 1500 Sicels etc. at various times; equals 47,000. The Sicels etc. may have been more numerous. The view has been taken throughout that triremes carried 200 men each. If however 'transport' triremes carried more than 200, the totals will have to be increased—incalculably, as it seems to the present writer. Non-combatants have not been included. They must have been both numerous and persistent if Thucydides is right (VII, 75, 5) in estimating at 40,000 the 'entire throng' left in September 413 to begin the retreat. Recently these data have been examined, critically by Beloch (ii, 2, pp. 290 *sqq.*), conservatively by Ferrabino (*Riv. d. fil.*, 1925, pp. 352 *sqq.*).

together, dying of wounds, disease, and under-nourishment, without opportunity to remove their own filth or their dead, till December, when they picked out all but their most hated enemies —the Athenians and the Siceliote and Italian Greeks—and sold them. The rest dwindled away under this atrocious régime for six months longer. 'This,' says Thucydides, 'proved to be the most important event in the entire war, and, indeed, as it seems to me, in the whole history of Greece, unequalled alike in the glory it brought to the victors and the catastrophe it entailed for the vanquished; for there was no department in which the beaten were not utterly beaten, no misery from which they were spared. Their destruction was total in the fullest sense of the word. Ships, army, everything was lost. Of the many that went forth few returned home,' though this mercy was vouchsafed to stragglers and runaways who from time to time reached Catana, and (according to Plutarch, *Nicias*, 29) to some Athenians who won their liberty by teaching their Syracusan masters snatches from the choruses of Euripides.

CHAPTER XI

THE OLIGARCHICAL MOVEMENT
IN ATHENS

I. THE REVOLT OF CHIOS

WHEN the completeness of the disaster in Sicily became
known it was generally thought that Athens was done
for. The first idea men had was that the fleet which had triumphed
in the Great Harbour would appear off the Piraeus; and there
was a disposition on all sides to lend it a helping hand. Neutrals
bestirred themselves, islanders planned insurrection, the Lacedaemonians were jubilant, Persia was interested, and the Athenians depressed. But the Syracusans were neither willing nor
able to bear longer the chief burden of the war against Athens.
They had paid dearly for their victory in men, money, and ships;
and now that they need not fear Athenian intervention again,
they had their own policy in Sicily to prosecute. Hermocrates,

Note. We have two ancient continuous narratives for this period—one
formed by appending Xenophon (*Hellenica* I, i–iv) to Thucydides (VIII)
and the other in Diodorus (XIII, 33–69, 3). The eighth book of Thucydides
ends abruptly and is unfinished. The documents it quotes are imperfectly
set. Repetitions are alleged to be found in it but on insufficient evidence.
Omissions exist of course. Mistakes occur as in all histories. The historical
worth of the book as a whole is unimpaired by these blemishes. For the
point of junction with Xenophon see p. 342, n. 1. The *Hellenica* is planned
on a much smaller scale than the history of Thucydides and is inferior to it in
chronological exactitude, comprehensiveness and depth of political understanding; but it tells a plain unadorned story and is in general trustworthy.
Diodorus has no value till Thucydides fails us (XIII, 42). From that point
his source (Ephorus) contained an account that was independent of Xenophon.
It adds some valuable data, particularly regarding occurrences aside from
the main scene of action and much problematical data on the naval warfare.
The contribution of Plutarch's *Life* of Alcibiades (27–35) consists in the
comparatively few particulars where the biographer has not drawn on
Xenophon and Ephorus. In regard to the revolution in Athens Aristotle
(*Const. of Athens*, XXVIII–XXXIV) supplements Thucydides by quoting official
documents at some length. He enables us to trace in great detail the constitutional aspects of the episode; but to be valuable he must be read in conjunction with Thucydides, since read alone he conveys an altogether false
impression of the whole movement. His omissions amount to an apology for
Theramenes. The inscriptions dealing with this period are few but singularly
helpful. See the Bibliography.

however, was insistent on carrying the war into the Aegean, and since his influence had become paramount during the course of the siege, he succeeded in having a Sicilian fleet sent to help the Peloponnesians. It consisted of twenty Syracusan and two Selinuntian ships, but the summer of 412 B.C. was well advanced before it arrived. The other western states that took a hand in the eastern war, Thurii, Locri, and Tarentum, intervened still later.

Events in Greece did not await their coming. During the winter both Sparta and Athens were hard at work on new fleets— Sparta on a programme which called for the building of 100 triremes; Athens, under the direction of a new board of ten Advisers (*probouloi*), in equipping the triremes it already had and in collecting timber and money for additions. But these preparations took time, and the naval war began long before they were completed. It was precipitated by a serious revolt which broke out in the Athenian Empire. This contained a deadly menace to the war-revenues of which Athens had now such need. For the Sicilian expedition had eaten up all the reserves (with the exception of the 1000 talents held for a naval crisis); and already in 413 B.C. the city had been so short of funds that it had dismissed 1300 Thracians who had reached Athens too late to sail with Demosthenes. Strict measures of economy were therefore taken, among them the withdrawal of the garrison from Laconia (p. 303); and it was the necessity of augmenting its revenues which led Athens about this time to supplant the tribute by a 5 per cent. toll on maritime commerce—a change not unconciliatory in itself, but invidious because of the exemption undoubtedly granted to Athenians if not to Athenian metics. Upon communities agitated by this innovation fell the terrible blood-tax levied in Sicily. Hence 'the allies judged the situation under the influence of passion and were ready even beyond their power to revolt from the Athenians.'

The secession movement manifested itself spontaneously in several centres. Euboea and Lesbos communicated with Agis, now installed at Decelea almost as an independent ruler, Chios and Erythrae with Lacedaemon direct, all with the same purpose —to join Sparta the moment the Peloponnesian fleet arrived. In view of the number of ships the Chians possessed (no less than 60) there could not be much doubt as to the point at which the Spartans should intervene.

Their intervention was also solicited by Persia. King Darius II thought the moment opportune to regain the cities in Asia of

which the Athenians had had the undisputed possession since
448 B.C. His decision reached Tissaphernes, the new governor
of the maritime provinces (Lydia, Caria, Ionia), and Pharnabazus,
satrap of Dascylium (Phrygia, Bithynia), in the form of a request
for the tribute due by the 'rebels.' These officials got in touch
with Sparta, each aiming to secure assistance in his own territory.
Tissaphernes accordingly supported the petition of Chios and
Erythrae. He had a particular reason for resentment at Athens
in that Amorges, the son of the rebel Pissuthnes, from whom he
had had to wrest Lydia, found support in Attic Caria. In order
to satisfy everybody, a programme was agreed upon according to
which the Peloponnesian fleet was to go to Ionia first, thence to
Lesbos, and then to the Hellespont.

The fleet consisted of some sixty ships, thirty-nine at Lechaeum,
five in Laconia, and sixteen on their way back from Syracuse. It
would have suited Sparta to wait till the Sicilian squadron arrived;
but the Chians pressed for speedier action. The Athenians were
naturally suspicious of them, and the Chian aristocrats, who were
conducting both the government and the negotiations, were afraid
lest their dealings with Sparta should become prematurely known
either to their own people or to Athens. Accordingly 21 of the
ships at Lechaeum were carried across the Isthmus and started
for Chios (July 412 B.C.). But the Athenians, who had learned
of the enterprise, forced the squadron ashore at Peiraeus, a
deserted harbour near the border of Epidauria, and blockaded
it there; and a little later they routed the ships that were returning
from Syracuse. But one torch sufficed to set the heather on fire.
Undeterred by the misadventure of the main fleet, the Laconian
squadron continued on its way to Chios. The Athenians tried to
intercept it. But the Spartans pushed straight across the open sea
and reached their destination safely. The mainspring of this bold
action was Alcibiades, who, keen to strike Athens in its most
vulnerable point and glad to quit Sparta because of the enmity
of Agis, whose wife he had seduced, accompanied the expedition
as unofficial chief-of-staff to Chalcideus, its commander; and it
was by announcing the despatch of the Lacedaemonian fleet
while concealing its mishap that they precipitated the revolt.
Erythrae followed the lead of Chios; so did Clazomenae. The
Chians went by sea, the Erythraeans and Clazomenians by land,
and won Teos. Ephesus too seceded. And so the movement
spread. The adhesion of Miletus was especially desirable. To it
Alcibiades and Chalcideus sailed and they were admitted at once.

Tissaphernes joined them there and arranged with Chalcideus

the draft of a treaty of alliance against Athens. Its larger significance consisted in the admission by Sparta of Persia's right to
all the land and cities held by the King or his ancestors—a definition so wide as to make subsequent interpretation inevitable, yet
incontrovertibly surrendering to Darius the Greek communities
in Asia Minor. The agreement called, further, for common action
to prevent Athens from drawing money or supplies of any sort
from the places recognized as belonging to the King. It seems
to have been assumed that the resources thus denied to Athens
would be used for the maintenance of the Peloponnesian fleets;
but as Sparta had received a promise from Tissaphernes that he
would attend to this himself, the home government declined to
ratify the draft. The states thus bargained away can hardly have
known of this transaction. For their part the Chians had already
implicated themselves so deeply that they had everything to gain
—not least relative independence of Sparta and Persia—by en-
larging as quickly as possible the scope of the revolt. So they
manned another squadron which won Lebedus and Aerae; and
they sent still another to Lesbos, on the arrival of which both
Mitylene and Methymna on the island and Phocaea and Cyme
on the mainland revolted. The energy of Chios was thus richly
rewarded. Between the Iasic Gulf and the Gulf of Adramyttium
practically all that was left of the empire of Athens was Samos;
and as a centre of commerce in this area Chios bade fair to replace
Athens.

II. THE NAVAL WAR IN IONIA

But the counter-attack of the Athenians had already begun.
They did not underestimate the defection of Chios. They knew
what it meant for a fleet other than their own to be at large in the
Aegean in view of the pains they had taken to keep their subject
cities without sea-defences. Hence they concluded that the crisis
had arrived for which the special reserve of 1000 talents had been
created, and they made this sum available to speed up their naval
preparations. Squadron after squadron was sent to the scene of
action as quickly as they could be got ready. Chalcideus was
followed to Miletus and blockaded there. As their base in Asiatic
waters the Athenians chose Samos, which accordingly they felt
that they must secure against defection at any cost. They therefore aided the Samian proletariat in destroying the local aristocracy root and branch; and a new state was organized in which
the nobles who escaped massacre or exile were denied the right
of intermarriage with citizens, and the population subdivided

with a singularly un-Hellenic disregard for inherited gentile groupings. Then the Athenians restored to Samos its autonomy. Meanwhile sufficient forces had arrived to enable them to regain Teos and to send an expedition for the recovery of Lesbos. Its approach was altogether unexpected. Mitylene and Methymna fell into its hands and ten of thirteen Chian ships found there were destroyed or captured.

But Athens could not send 46 ships to Asia Minor without weakening the fleet that was blockading Peiraeus. The Peloponnesian ships there were able to force their way back to Cenchreae, and Astyochus, Spartan *nauarch* (admiral) for 412–1 B.C., escorted by four of them, came to Chios and made an effort to retrieve the position in Lesbos; but even when reinforced he was no match for the Athenians. They held the island, recovered Clazomenae, and then attacked Chios itself. After having driven the land forces of the defenders back within the walls, they plundered the rich country at pleasure. Since 21 Chian triremes had already been seized or destroyed and 25 others were shut up at Miletus, the people of Chios began to make trouble for the government which had got them into such a pass.

It was now well on toward autumn and the new vessels put on the stocks after the disaster in Sicily were coming into commission. Athens was the more forehanded on this occasion. It got off a fleet of 48 ships, including 25 transports, with an army of hoplites on board (1500 Argives, 1000 Athenians, and 1000 allies), the object being to invest and reduce Miletus. The landing-force succeeded in the first part of its mission. The Milesians, aided by Peloponnesian hoplites, and troops led by Tissaphernes, unwisely offered battle, and though they routed the Argives, killing one-fifth of their number, they were themselves defeated by the Athenians. The victors had already begun to throw a wall across the base of the peninsula on which Miletus lay when the approach of a powerful enemy fleet was reported. It proved to be the chief Lacedaemonian naval effort of the year, and was based on the 22 ships brought from Sicily by Hermocrates, to which the Peloponnesians had added 33 others. A Spartan, Therimenes, was its commander.

Had he come straight on from Leros he might have forced the Athenians to fight with a fair risk of losing their army. He went instead to Teichiussa on the north coast of the Iasic gulf and only sailed round to Miletus on the following day. By that time the Athenians had departed. They had been sorely tempted to risk a naval engagement rather than forfeit the advantage they had gained. But Phrynichus happened to be one of their generals, and he refused positively to give his consent to a battle where the consequences of defeat, in loss of forces and prestige, would be so great and the strength of the enemy was unknown, when by withdrawing to Samos they could concentrate their entire fleet for later action. The evacuation was effected during the night and Samos was reached safely; but the retreat was a costly one. The Argives went home angry because of their misfortune, and thenceforth Argos took no part in the war.

For the moment the initiative was left with the enemy, and they used it first to storm Iasus, the headquarters of Amorges, who was taken prisoner and handed over to Tissaphernes, and then to relieve Chios. This the massing of a Lacedaemonian fleet of 80 ships in Milesian waters had accomplished of itself; for it had led the Athenians to withdraw to Samos their entire forces. The way was thus open for the Chian fleet to return home and for Pedaritus, a Spartan, to come with some troops to Chios to take charge of its defence. Astyochus tried again to dislodge the Athenians from the places they had recently re-occupied in the north; but it was with the squadron concentrated at Chios that he made the effort, and when he failed to capture Clazomenae, he was prevented from going on to Lesbos by the baulking of the Chians. So he left in high dudgeon, taking his Peloponnesian ships with him, and went to Miletus to assume command of the main fleet.

The Athenian inferiority proved only momentary. In the autumn a further squadron of 35 ships reached Samos; so that the generals there felt strong enough to divide their fleet again and dispatch 30 triremes with a landing army on board to resume the investment of Chios, while masking Miletus, where the main Peloponnesian fleet lay, with 74 others. The ships going to Chios crossed those with which Astyochus was departing. They brought along only 1000 hoplites; but Chios, being a country of great landed proprietors, merchants, and industrialists, with a slave population several times greater than the free, had few heavy-armed troops; so that, despite the presence of Pedaritus with more than 500 Peloponnesians, the small Athenian army was able to occupy Delphinium, a strong place with a harbour about nine miles north of the city, and from it deny the citizens the use of their land and entice their slaves to run away *en masse*. Since the sea was closed to the Chians also and Astyochus left them to their own devices, Pedaritus soon had serious disaffection on his hands. But he crushed it with vigour. All through the winter

(412–1 B.C.) the siege continued. Their slaves were so numerous that the Chians had made it their policy to cow them by severity: now they were paid back with interest; and they suffered more discriminatingly at the hands of servants turned guides, ruffians, and bandits, than at the hands of the invaders. Finally, since no help came, Pedaritus made a bold effort to relieve the city by storming Delphinium. But he lost his life in the attempt and the Chians were beaten off with great losses. By spring famine had become unendurable. Hence Leon, appointed harmost in Pedaritus' place, after having managed to slip through the blockade with twelve ships from Miletus, sallied out with these and 24 Chian triremes and attacked the Athenian fleet, which consisted at that moment of 32 vessels. But though the besieged gave a good account of themselves in the fighting, night intervened before a decision was reached. At this point events elsewhere compelled the Athenians to give up the blockade. Delphinium, however, they held till 406 B.C.

III. THE POLICY OF TISSAPHERNES

Before Astyochus arrived at Miletus Therimenes had re-opened negotiations with Tissaphernes. With a fleet of 70 triremes on his hands and a large proportion of his crews mercenaries, his need of money was met only temporarily by the plunder of Iasus and the bounty of the Milesians. Tissaphernes, too, was now disposed to reconsider his earlier agreement. He had come to appreciate the danger of allowing the King's cities to form the habit of making contributions to Sparta. So these were forbidden in the new draft, and Tissaphernes himself undertook to shoulder the expense of the Peloponnesian fleet while it was in the King's service. But the wages allowed by him for the future were only a trifle over half ($3\frac{3}{11}$ obols per day) those paid for the month just past—a reduction which lessened alacrity among seamen to take or continue service with the Spartans. Yet, if paid regularly, the new wage, by which, after all, Athens was overbid, far outvalued the right of requisition which Therimenes covenanted away.

This financial transaction opened the way for the inauguration by Tissaphernes of a new general policy. By paying or withholding subsidies he acquired control over the size, efficiency and movements of the Spartan fleet; and he studied how to use it to serve his own ends. To help the Peloponnesians to an immediate and complete victory might very well mean to drive out Satan with Beelzebub. Not to help them further would doubtless permit the Athenians again to sweep the seas; for the fleet of Athens that now made cruises across from Samos was obviously superior in fighting strength to the one which lay inactive in Miletus. The wise course for Persia to follow was, he concluded, to preserve the naval equipoise in the Aegean, and let both parties wear themselves out in finances and man-power until the Persian fleet was strong enough to impose its will upon an exhausted Hellas.

In this conclusion was manifested the fine hand of Alcibiades, whom Sparta, suspecting treachery, had ordered Astyochus to assassinate, and the Persian Satrap, badly in need of an expert in Hellenic politics, had taken into his service (November, 412). Alcibiades' dominant impulse was to do Sparta an injury, but the most effective way of accomplishing this—instilling into Tissaphernes' mind sound motives for underrationing the Spartan fleet—was at the same time the most effective way of doing Athens a service. But his patriotism was not disinterested. He calculated by trafficking on Tissaphernes' favour ultimately to secure for himself recall from exile with so strong an asset, in his supposed or real influence over Persian policy, that political ascendancy in Athens would be assured to him. Unless Tissaphernes should become his dupe there was, of course, bound to be a parting of their ways; but not immediately. And the more ostentatiously Alcibiades identified himself with Tissaphernes' purposes—supplying for Hellenic understanding respectable arguments for Tissaphernes' illiberality and irregularity in giving money; supplying to Tissaphernes as a guiding principle the policy of preventing land-power and sea-power in Greece from falling into the hands of the same people—the more certainly he advanced towards his own goal.

Astyochus was not unduly moved by the plight of Chios. To reach it from Miletus he would have to run the gauntlet of the Athenians at Samos and this he rightly regarded as too risky. But the way to the south was open, both to him and to Sparta. It was thither accordingly that reinforcements from home were sent. A squadron of twelve ships, including those from Thurii, commanded by the international athlete Dorieus, crossed over to Cnidus, which had recently seceded to Tissaphernes; and half of them stayed there to defend the city and half cruised off the Triopian promontory intercepting the grain-ships from Egypt. This promptly brought an Athenian fleet from Samos, which captured the commerce-destroyers and almost captured the city. Then a Spartan fleet of 27 ships, equipped for the account of Pharnabazus, having clashed with an Athenian patrol off Melos while *en route* to Ionia, and apprehending danger if it kept on its course, turned south and reached Caunus (December, 412). It had on board a commission of eleven Spartans authorized to supersede the *nauarch* if it saw fit, and instructed to assume general direction of Lacedaemonian affairs in Asia. The commission ordered Astyochus to come to meet them. So he left a detachment behind to guard Miletus (from which subsequently Leon took twelve ships to Chios) and slipped away unobserved. Off Syme he came upon an Athenian squadron which, rashly assuming that his left wing, when it hove in sight on a rainy foggy morning, was the fleet from Caunus, attacked it vigorously, and, being itself surrounded, was lucky to escape to Halicarnassus with a loss of one-third of its strength. The two Lacedaemonian fleets then united at Cnidus; but they declined battle, though the Athenians, coming down from Samos, gave them the opportunity. They were superior in numbers (94 ships to 75), but in nothing else. For of late Tissaphernes had ceased to pay the crews regularly, and since Astyochus was suspected of having been bribed to acquiesce, discipline had fallen off, and ships showed slackness and empty benches.

The Lacedaemonian commissioners resolved to have a definite settlement with Persia. So Tissaphernes came to Cnidus for a conference with them. Lichas, the head of the mission, a blunt man but a trusted negotiator, spoke the mind of the Spartans not to honour agreements which, strictly construed, ceded to the King all Greece outside the Peloponnese, even if they had to do without Persian money altogether. Between this and the version of Alcibiades that the Spartans had come to Asia to liberate all the Greeks there was a wide discrepancy; but Tissaphernes, whose suspicions had been thoroughly aroused, read the one into the other, and broke off the negotiations abruptly.

So the fleet of Astyochus had to shift for itself. The Spartans, too, had now maritime allies and the rudiments of a tribute system. And at the moment they had a windfall. With the aid of its aristocrats they won Rhodes, where the lack of coast defences again proved the undoing of Athens. Thus Astyochus secured a large seafaring population from which to replenish his crews and a contribution of cash sufficient to tide him over the immediate crisis. The Athenians arrived too late to stop the revolt, but with their main base at Samos and advanced stations at Cos and Chalce they carried on war against the island. Astyochus did not use this revitalizing of his forces for a definite trial of strength with them. His primary object was to keep his fleet in being, and, as occasion offered, to make inroads into the Athenian Empire. But he could not support his fleet long with the resources of Rhodes; and except by risking a naval battle he could neither levy on his northern allies nor relieve Chios. So long before the winter was over his position became little short of desperate.

Though the Athenians still possessed the advantage on the sea, they felt that they could retain it and exploit it only if Persia continued to stand aside. They were so anxious to insure the complete separation of their two enemies that they let themselves be made the victims of a cruel hoax, and in the process (to use language replete with modern meaning) their front began to give way; and their home front *did* give way completely; but their war front, rallying splendidly, held fast and saved the whole situation.

IV. ALCIBIADES AND THE ATHENIAN REVOLUTION

Fear entered the hearts of the Athenians when they realized that in Sicily they had gambled away their safety. They naturally withdrew their favour from the men who had advised the expedition. Androcles and Peisander had to yield to others the primacy in the public meetings of citizens and went separate ways, the former to remain in touch with the urban masses whom the imminence of danger overawed, the latter to form new contacts with people, now much more numerous and aggressive, who thought the rule of a majority manifest folly. The Athenians were at this time critical not only of their leaders but also of their institutions. They concluded that the régime of irresponsible advisers, each one of whom tried to outbid the other for their favour had ceased to furnish the Council and Assembly with the choice of well-thought-out measures that the gravity of the situation demanded. They therefore proceeded to shift this important function to a responsible commission of ten elderly men (among them Sophocles, the tragic poet, and Hagnon, Theramenes' father, both associates of Pericles), selected by general vote on the ground of their special fitness for the task. Whether it was fear or the *probouloi* that had more to do with the efficiency of Athens in recreating a fleet of 150 triremes within a twelvemonth it is difficult to say. The office was probably important mainly because it facilitated a much more fundamental recasting of Athenian government.

The revolution that occurred in April–May 411 B.C. had been brewing for some time. It was first conceived as a war measure, designed to facilitate the recall of Alcibiades and with his aid to detach Tissaphernes and the King from Sparta and win them and their money for Athens. Alcibiades himself it was who suggested this idea. Unable to count on being ever restored by the 'rascality' which had outlawed him, he alleged that the King would not become a friend of Athens so long as Athens was ruled by the people. It is likely that Tissaphernes foresaw gain for Persia in having a man all-powerful in Athens who was under strong obligations to himself (thinking, no doubt, to use Alcibiades as Alcibiades thought to use him). Certainly he lent himself so far to Alcibiades' design as to give him a powerful lever for upsetting democracy in Athens; but to be effective the lever had to have a base on which to rest within the Athenian community.

This was found, at the beginning of the intrigue (December, 412), at Samos, among the men of wealth and position serving with the fleet—the trierarchs in particular. The Athenian propertied classes were terribly shortened in their incomes by the Decelean War, through the ruin of their estates in Attica; the running away of their slaves (to the number eventually of over 20,000), with the consequent closing of mines and factories; the increased risks and diminishing returns of maritime trade; and the impossibility of attending to their business whatever it was. At the same time they were staggering under the fiscal burdens put upon them by the state—the liturgies first and foremost, by the quick repetition of which even the largest fortunes were being impaired, and the almost yearly levies that were made on income. Athens was rapidly becoming poor. The silver and gold amassed by the city and its inhabitants from the tribute and the mines and the profits of trade were being dissipated, in considerable part abroad, in payment for war-services and materials; and the profiteers were as often as not beyond the reach of the Athenian fiscus. Property-owners had no monopoly of military service; for while *they* furnished the cavalry patrols which wore out the stock of Athenian horses on the stony roads of Attica and the hoplites who guarded the immense circuit of the walls night and day, the lower classes now furnished most of the marines and expeditionary forces, besides manning the triremes so far as this was not done by allies and mercenaries; and thus they bore the brunt of the fighting and of the casualties. But the former had to find much of the money with which the latter were paid; and the services for which pay was received were not military alone, but also civilian. The more decisively finance came to dominate the conduct of the war, the more the classes financially important came to demand a larger voice in its decisions than they possessed under the existing democracy. See above, pp. 29 *sq.* 105 and below, p. 327.

It was on soil thus prepared that the suggestion of Alcibiades fell. And a group of outstanding men at Samos took it up; and, after suitable persons had been sounded and a definite undertaking had been received from Alcibiades, and the rank and file of the crews—to whom the news was conveyed that they could have the support of Persia if they restored Alcibiades and ceased to be a democracy—appeared to acquiesce, the conspirators held a meeting at which it was decided to proceed with the undertaking; but not without opposition. For Phrynichus opposed it resolutely with arguments which, as reported by Thucydides, ought to have prevailed: that Alcibiades cared for an oligarchy no more than a democracy provided he returned home; that Persia was in no position to abandon Sparta and join them; that their subject-allies were deserting them not because they were democrats but because they were masters, and would desert them all the quicker if, on becoming aristocrats themselves, the Athenians, as was proposed, established aristocracies elsewhere, thus adding domestic masters to foreign; that above all else they should avoid civil dissension.

This was the position of a statesman; and had Phrynichus disassociated himself from the whole movement when the conspirators decided to send Peisander to Athens to win the enemies of democracy there for their design, he might have done Athens great service later. But he was rendered clear-sighted not by patriotism but by distrust of Alcibiades, whose vindictiveness he feared now that he had declared his opposition. And so unscrupulous was he, this herdsman turned advocate and general, this man of the people turned secretly club-man and oligarch, that when he could not get rid of Alcibiades by fair means he tried foul and betrayed to Astyochus the plan to win Persia for Athens. Astyochus betrayed him in turn to Alcibiades, and it was only by a scheme of almost unbelievable subtlety that Phrynichus escaped with his life from the difficult position into which he had got (December, 412 B.C.). As it was, he and another general were replaced at Samos by two of their colleagues, less unfriendly to Alcibiades.

This was the work of Peisander; who, masquerading as a democrat, laid before the Athenians the plan on which the committee in Samos was working, taking pains to characterize the new form of government required as a modified democracy that could be discarded when it had served its purpose. The protests were numerous and emphatic and concerned both the recall of Alcibiades and the abridgement of popular power. But they were overborne by the tactics of Peisander, who forced from each protestant the admission that he had no alternative by means of which, now that all their money was gone, they could hope to avoid defeat. The people with its usual intelligence recognized that safety was better than the constitution of its choice, and voted to send Peisander and ten others to arrange matters with Alcibiades and Tissaphernes.

Thus far the revolutionary movement was a response to the war situation; and men at home and men at the front had responded similarly. The price to be paid for Persian aid was to be paid to Athenians, with whom Athens could have an accounting later. But when Peisander and his colleagues came to deal with Tissaphernes they found that they had a price to pay to Persia also. For Tissaphernes, adhering to the policy of aiding the Greeks to destroy one another, concluded that it was still Sparta that needed assistance. So he made it clear that his Greek friend enjoyed his confidence yet avoided pledging help to Athens, by having Alcibiades speak for him in his interviews with the Athenian envoys and demand conditions for the King's friendship which they could not possibly accept: the cession of all Ionia and the adjacent islands, and (on this being agreed to) the right, abandoned by the convention of Callias, of navigating with a fleet of any size everywhere in Athenian waters (pp. 87, 471). No Athenian dared thus bargain away the results of Salamis, Mycale, and Eurymedon. So the envoys returned to Samos, incensed at Alcibiades, who, it seemed, had inveigled them into a dangerous movement either under false pretensions or to make sport of them. And the Samian conspirators decided to drop Alcibiades altogether.

V. THE FOUR HUNDRED

But it was too late to drop the conspiracy also. Clubs for mutual assistance in dealing with courts and officials had been a characteristic of upper-class life in Athens for some time. Their members were sworn to secrecy, and a good deal of doubt was permissible as to their loyalty to the Constitution and the propriety of their undertakings. So far as they made their political opinions vocal, they condemned democracy; and, appreciating its interdependence with empire, they condemned this also. They made Sparta their ideal, but they were quite un-Spartan in their mode and view of life. Unable to overthrow democracy they existed to circumvent it. But this was an exasperating business; and as the war lengthened out, their methods became more and more violent. It was upon an association of this sort, consisting of 22 young men, that responsibility for the mutilation of the Hermae had finally been saddled. The populace had been reassured on that occasion to ascertain that an individual club and not an aggregate of clubs was involved; but an aggregate had been conceivable, and before leaving for Asia Peisander had bestirred himself effectively to make it a reality and to enlist all the co-ordinated clubs for the revolutionary movement. Thereby a collection of groups of 'workers' was won for the cause, and men of different tendencies and purposes were brought into contact with it, given a semblance of union, and implicated in whatever was undertaken.

When there was so much plotting on foot Aristophanes did not miss the occasion to utilize it for comic purposes. In the *Lysistrata*, presented in February 411 B.C., he too unfolded a conspiracy—a general strike of all the women of Greece, who refused restitution of conjugal rights to their husbands until they had agreed to end the war. The burlesquing of Peisander's 'swindle' loses nothing by the more than Rabelaisian exploitation of the sexual situation to which the plot of the play invites. But the ribaldry is Dionysiac fretwork that runs riot round a central design. The poet's own suggestion, for which pleaded, he urged, ancient memories, wasted girlhood, disconsolate homes and devastated cities, was for the Athenians to make friends of the Spartans and not of the Persians; to amnesty political offenders, enfranchise alien residents, and take into partnership with themselves their far-flung colonies and subjects, so as thus to enlarge the bounds of their nationalism instead of contracting them. It was the voice of a statesmanlike jester insinuating into the ear of his master the gain of enthroning intelligence and fair-dealing as the governing forces in Athenian policy in place of suspicion, rancour, pride, and—democracy. But which conflicted more with Hellenic nature, a revolt on the part of Hellenic women, or peace without victory between Athens and Sparta and a common citizenship throughout the Athenian Empire, it would be hard to say. At the Great Dionysia next following (March, 411) Aristophanes produced the *Thesmophoriazusae*, notable for its parody of the dramatic makeshifts of Euripides. The situation had by then become too tense for politics.

The man who more than anyone else arranged the plot of the revolution was Antiphon, a sinister figure that moved in the background like an American 'boss,' fertile with helpful suggestions, shrinking from no act of ruthlessness. He had been denied the ordinary outlets for great ambition, energy, and forensic talent by his avowed contempt for democratic radicalism, and had built up for himself a large practice (in aristocratic circles naturally) as a *logographos* or speech-writer. He preferred to square his acts with legality when possible, but would stick at nothing likely to help establish in Athens a political régime in which he could himself find scope.

The first *mot d'ordre* given to the 'workers' was to put a wholesome terror into the democrats. A gang of young 'bloods' assassinated Androcles, who was hateful to Alcibiades as the prime mover of his exile and to the conspirators as the most vehement champion of popular government. Whoever raised his voice in protest against the methods or objects of the 'reformers' was quickly put out of the way; and since the reform was supported by the *probouloi* themselves, by demagogues like Peisander, moderates like Aristocrates and Theramenes, and others whose faithfulness to democracy seemed assured, as well as by generals, ex-generals, trierarchs, and men of distinction in art and letters, like Melanthius, Andron, Critias, and Aristoteles, it was easy for the forces of law and order to think that all was for the best. Since, too, there was no knowing who was in the plot and who was not, the number of the participants was thought to be much larger than it really was, determination of its magnitude was impeded by the cessation of mutual confidence and discussion, and a mood of uneasy acquiescence seized hold of the uninitiated masses.

This situation the revolutionists in Samos and Athens determined to exploit for oligarchic purposes notwithstanding that they had lost the leverage primarily instrumental in creating it. They had to count on defections from within their ranks. But in Phrynichus they made a gain of first-rate importance; for now that the movement was divorced from Alcibiades he put all his resoluteness and practical ability at its disposal. Nor did a proposal for restricting the franchise lack a war justification by any means. There was no escape from the problem of finance. Rather, it pressed all the more urgently for a radical solution precisely because it was not they, but Sparta, that had got Persian money.

For after breaking off negotiations with Peisander, Tissaphernes had effected a reconciliation with the Spartans. Astyochus was now in such straits from lack of funds that there was

danger lest he should risk his fleet in battle and lose it altogether, or take to plundering the King's country. Since either
of these contingencies would have ruined the Satrap's schemes,
both he and the Spartans were ready for a compromise. So a
definite treaty was concluded 'on the plain of the Maeander' to
which on behalf of Persia Pharnabazus affixed his signature as
well as Tissaphernes (April, 411 B.C.). No mention of the Greek
cities was made, but the King's land was acknowledged as Persian.
Tissaphernes agreed to give pay for the Lacedaemonian ships at
the stipulated rate, but only for those then in service and only
till the arrival of the King's fleet from Phoenicia. The old idea
was here unmistakeable of keeping the Spartan fleet down to a
fixed maximum and of postponing the day of definite action; and
not to make Sparta over-impatient for the mentioned (but not
pledged) Phoenician ships, the Spartan government was to pay
its own naval bills from the date of their appearance,—if not
immediately, at the end of the war. The important thing at the
moment was the receipt of regular pay for the crews at Camirus.
With this in hand Astyochus was able to restore the morale and
complements of his ships and to sail for the relief of Chios. But
the Athenians put themselves in his way, ready to fight if he
persisted; so he veered off to Miletus, while they again concentrated their main fleet at Samos. At this time (April–May, 411)
the oligarchic upheaval occurred.

Plans for a comprehensive reorganization of the Athenian
state and Empire on aristocratic lines had been matured on Samos
after the rupture with Tissaphernes. The avowed design was, by
limiting the active franchise to the class which could serve the
state at its own expense (specifically, 'all the Athenians best able
to render personal and financial service to the number of not
less—Thucydides says not more,—than 5000'), to remove from
the public pay roll the multitude of civilians whose indemnities
for service in Council, courts, offices, and religious festivals were
exhausting the domestic revenues of Athens, which, now that the
imperial revenues had fallen off and the private fortunes available
for levies on income and liturgies could stand the strain no longer,
were imperatively needed for building, equipping, and maintaining triremes and otherwise waging the war. This programme
commended itself widely to moderate men; but to put it into
effect meant to overcome a large and deeply interested opposition.
Hence, for both the inauguration and the subsequent safety and
efficiency of the régime, the presence of a small body of officers
(a Council of Four Hundred) was contemplated.

As concerned the Empire the reformers accepted the idea, which Phrynichus had already refuted, of putting the local 'oligarchs' in control of their respective cities in the belief that these malcontents, having got what they wanted from Athens, would lack a motive for plotting secession to Sparta. So five of the men in Peisander's embassy went round among the subject cities giving power to elements whose enmity to Athens, being grounded in love of liberty quite as much as in love of authority, endured, while their capacity for harm was increased. And to this mistaken policy Athens owed the secession of Thasos, where Diitrephes, sent on from Samos to act as commandant in Thrace, overturned the democracy; and of other places as well. The other envoys accompanied Peisander to Athens, stopping on the way at various cities setting up oligarchies, and recruiting hoplites from Tenos, Andros, Carystus, and Aegina for their mission in the capital.

On their arrival they found their general programme already well advertised and the population thoroughly silenced and intimidated. Thus they had no need to proceed unconstitutionally. The Assembly voted to add to the *probouloi* twenty citizens over forty years of age elected by the people, so as to form a commission of thirty (*syngrapheis*), which, after taking account of suggestions made by volunteers and scrutinizing the ancient constitution enacted by Cleisthenes, should have full authority to lay before the people on a fixed day whatever proposals it thought requisite for public safety. This was a well established method of initiating measures for the drafting of which special competence was required; and this commission differed from others only in the latitude of its powers. On the appointed day (14th of Thargelion, April–May, 411 B.C.) a meeting was called, not, as was usual, within the fortifications, but in the sanctuary of Poseidon at Colonus, one and a quarter miles outside the walls, where it would naturally be attended by the hoplites and cavalry—so far as they could be spared from duty—and not by the unorganized urban population whom fear of the Lacedaemonians would prevent from straggling so far afield. Thus made doubly sure against untoward incidents, the commission (after having had it made compulsory for the chairmen (*prytaneis*) to submit all proposals relevant to the business on hand) exhausted its mandate in requesting the abrogation of the constitutional safeguards of democracy, and the imposition of the death-penalty upon any one who should attempt to revive them. This was carried. When the way was thus cleared proposals followed realizing the essential objects of the reform: the reservation of all revenues for the needs of the war; the abolition of indemnities for all civil offices and services, an exception being made in the case of the nine archons and the *prytaneis* in charge, who were to continue on the pay roll; the limitation, for the duration of the war, of active citizenship to 'the Five Thousand,' upon whom was conferred notably the power to make treaties; the election of a committee of 100 cataloguers, ten by each tribe, to enroll the Five Thousand; and the constitution of a body of Four Hundred men who should act as a Council.

Since a 'slate' had, of course, been prepared beforehand, the cataloguers were chosen at once, the *taxeis*, or tribal regiments, present acting for the tribes. On the motion of Peisander the Four Hundred were constituted then and there by the nomination of five 'chairmen' (*proedroi*), who chose 100 of the number, each of whom in turn selected three additional members, possibly from his own tribe. By pre-arrangement (with the *proedroi* doubtless) the 100 cataloguers were included, probably as the first hundred, the oath of their special office being administered by the Four Hundred a week later. A further part of Peisander's motion, that the Four Hundred should convene the Five Thousand when they saw fit, completed his design of making the inner circle master of the situation[1]. The limitation of the franchise and the abolition of indemnities naturally wrought havoc in the ranks of office-holders. Hence the offices were all declared vacant with the exception of the Council of the Five Hundred and the archonships; and to tide over the crisis a new board of generals was at once chosen[2].

At the time these measures were taken the reformers seem to have thought it possible for the Four Hundred to rule without reigning till regularly constituted and inducted, possibly at the end of the year (14th Scirophorion), the routine domestic services being left for the remaining month to the Archons and *prytaneis*, the all-important military tasks being attended to for them by their generals. But at Samos things did not go at all according to programme. Three hundred of the democrats recently installed in the

---

[1] On the vexed question of the constitutional devices of this revolution and the counter-revolution which followed and the relations of the ancient accounts in Pseudo-Lysias, *For Polystratus*, Thucydides VIII, 47–54, 56, 63–77, 81–82, 86, 89–98 and Aristotle, *Const. of Athens*, XXVIII, 5–XXXIV, 1, see the works cited in the Bibliography.

[2] Thucydides VIII, 67, 3: Aristotle, *Const. of Athens*, XXXI, 2. This is precisely what was done with the offices at the time of the revolution that occurred in March 318 B.C. W. S. Ferguson, *Hellenistic Athens*, p. 32.

government of the island were found ready to set themselves up as a new 'aristocracy' and dispense with the services of their humbler comrades. So they formed a conspiracy, set upon and slew Hyperbolus, who had been living among them since his ostracism, and by this and other acts of violence, in which they had the aid of Charminus, one of the Athenian generals, they sought to pave the way by intimidation for a *coup d'état*. But the people prepared for resistance, and enlisted the support of Leon and Diomedon, two other of the Athenian generals, and of an energetic trierarch named Thrasybulus and a hoplite named Thrasyllus, who being all four out of sympathy with the revolutionary campaign and distressed at the lot in store for their loyal Samian friends, saw to it, the former pair that Athenian triremes should be at hand in case of violence, the latter that among their crews and the soldiers stationed in the city there should be found democratic stalwarts primed to take a hand against the oligarchs should fighting ensue. In these circumstances the Three Hundred came to grief completely. Their rising was crushed and thirty of their leaders were put to death. From this time on the Four Hundred had a sword of Damocles suspended over their head.

The crew of the despatch-boat *Paralus* had had a prominent part in defeating this despicable project, but on their arrival in Athens with news of the incident they found to their surprise and discomfiture the reformers already in power. But not in office. The first step of the Four Hundred, for whom an entirely new situation was created by the fiasco in Samos, was to assume office immediately—an open act of violence carried through with careful premeditation. On the day fixed (22nd of Thargelion, April–May) the citizens (all of whom were in military service) piled arms and fell out as usual, but instead of going home those among them who were partisans of the Four Hundred, acting on secret instructions, waited inconspicuously in the neighbourhood, ready to seize their weapons and strike if any opposition developed. The soldiers, too, that had been brought by Peisander were standing under orders; and a band of 120 young 'bloods' accompanied the Four Hundred as, each with a dagger concealed on his person, they broke into the Council Hall and bade the Councillors begone. They sugar-coated this brusque dismissal by paying the allowances for the balance of the session. Their own session they opened with the usual solemnities, and they divided themselves into prytanies and used the lot to determine their sequences and daily chairman. Thus, after having been first subjected legally to the *probouloi* and then actually to the Four

Hundred, the body was set aside completely, without a hand being raised in its defence, which, reproducing in miniature with a constantly changing personnel the entire commonwealth of Athens, was the strongest fashioner and expression of Athenian democracy. The 'best citizens' supplanted the 'fair sample' in the direction of all the administrative committees, so far as these too, like the general assembly and the popular courts of justice, were not dispensed with.

What were the powers of the new governing body? They were defined by Thucydides summarily as autocratic, and such they were in fact; but in a constitution issued as of the date Thargelion 14th and alleged to be the work of 100 men chosen at that time by the Five Thousand[1], they were described as provisional, as duly derived from the Five Thousand, as exercisable only through due process of law, and as transmissible to the Five Thousand, when the crisis was past—a matter of a couple of years at least—by the allocation of the Four Hundred to their respective *cadres* in the larger body. This constitution represents a concession made by the extremists among the reformers to the legal sense of their more moderate associates, the fair-sounding programme with which the movement was launched, and, especially, the opposition that had declared itself in Samos. The body from which it issued, on the motion of a certain Aristomachus, was perhaps the 100 cataloguers; and it may have been intended to govern the validation of the revolutionary régime due on Thargelion 22nd or at the first of the new year (June, 411). Simultaneously an elaborate organization was drawn up for the Five Thousand—for future use and present propaganda. The constitution of the Four Hundred was retrospectively justificatory—notably in the electoral norms set down and in its assumption that the assembly at Colonus constituted a legal meeting of the Five Thousand—and deceptively conciliatory. It did not give away the substance for the shadow. The Four Hundred reserved the right (subject to the new constitution) to make laws and enact decrees with full discretion; to appoint all officials and hold them to an accounting; notably, in replacement of the generals just appointed, to designate for the year 411–10 B.C., in the presence of the soldiers assembled for

---

[1] If the Five Thousand had actually gone through the form of voting at Colonus everybody must have known that all who participated belonged to the privileged group. If it had been clear to Aristotle that the constitution belonged to the proceedings at Colonus he would have expressed himself less ambiguously on the point. On the view taken in the text Thucydides' silence is more easily explicable: he did not need to record propaganda.

inspection, a board of ten men vested with unlimited executive authority in civil and military matters. Had the constitution been allowed to work itself out, its most important consequence would probably have been the transformation of an oligarchy of four hundred into an oligarchy of ten.

The organization drawn up for the Five Thousand consti-tuted the active citizens as 'councillors,' thus elevating the pri-vileged and leaving the rest, professedly, as they were. It was calculated to satisfy the large section of public opinion at home and at Samos which favoured only a moderate abatement of democracy, and this as a necessary condition to financing and winning the war. But to it the leaders of the Four Hundred did lip-service only. They had the cataloguers in their power, and if a list of the Five Thousand was ever drawn up while the oli-garchy lasted it was not divulged. The uncertainty that existed as to whether one's neighbour was or was not a councillor kept all quiet. Nor did the Four Hundred hesitate to make an ex-ample when they thought it needed. But those whom they put to death or exiled were few. Terror did the rest.

VI. THE FAILURE OF THE FOUR HUNDRED

The work of the Four Hundred was simply a catalogue of failures. It failed to win the adhesion of the sailors and soldiers at Samos; it failed to negotiate an honourable peace with Sparta; it failed to stem the defection of the subject allies; it failed in the prosecution of the war; it failed to reconcile the conflict of ideas and persons in its own body. A bad record for the *intelligentsia* of Athens! But these failures were not isolated or disconnected: they were simply consequences of the cardinal failure at Samos— developments inseparable from the fact that, as soon as the fleet discovered that it had been deceived, the Four Hundred lost control of the military weapon.

News of the situation in Athens reached Samos through un-friendly channels coloured by fear and exaggerated for political effect. The troops, driven to fury by the misrepresentation that the Four Hundred were abusing their wives and children and holding them as hostages for their good behaviour, were only prevented from stoning the adherents of the oligarchy in their midst by the proximity of the enemy's fleet and the influence of Thrasybulus and Thrasyllus, who bound them all, oligarchs and democrats, Athenians and Samians, by solemn oaths to stand to-gether, uphold democracy, fight the Peloponnesians vigorously, treat the Four Hundred as enemies, and have no traffic with them. Setting themselves up as the People of Athens[1], they deposed their generals and replaced them with others, among them Thrasybulus and Thrasyllus. They took the view that Athens had seceded; that with Samos to fall back upon they could conduct the war with virtually undiminished resources; that, if the worst came to the worst, they could settle down elsewhere than at Athens and found a new state. In the conduct of the 'sailor rabble' throughout this terrible crisis—their ready response to prudent and patriotic leadership, capacity for quick self-reorganization, determination to live up to their most heroic traditions—Athenian democracy was commended by its works. Nor was their energy confined to resolutions.

They had to count on the Spartans attacking during their trouble. This was all the more certain because on the outbreak of the revolution, in order not to lose the Hellespont, where the Spartan Dercyllidas, marching overland from Miletus, had started a revolt, they had been forced to raise the blockade of Chios, thus permitting the 35 ships bottled up there to join Astyochus. By the prompt arrival in the straits of the Athenian squadron from Chios Lampsacus was regained and the secession movement confined to Abydos; but in the meanwhile the Spartans were strong enough to threaten Samos. So the Athenians recalled their squadron from the Hellespont, and pending its arrival remained in the port on Astyochus' approach. The Spartan admiral had adopted the policy of fighting only on a certainty—a line of action that was approved at home; but not on shipboard, where it seemed like playing the game of Tissaphernes. But Astyochus was resolutely Fabian. He offered battle while the Athenians were divided and returned to his base the moment the Athenian reinforcements arrived. Thrasybulus and Thrasyllus followed him to Miletus. But he declined action though he had 112 ships to their 108. Since Tissaphernes was again at his old trick of withholding wages, Astyochus sought to reduce his mass of clamouring seamen by sending one-third of his fleet to the Hellespont to enter Pharnabazus' service and win Byzantium, from which proposals of revolt had come. Most of the ships were driven back by a storm, but eight proceeded on their way, reached Byzantium, and took from Athens this, the key to its Black Sea trade. Eighteen Athenian ships followed them up from Samos and shut them in the port.

The remissness of Tissaphernes in supporting the fleet at Miletus was notorious. The democrats at Samos were encouraged

[1] For an Athenian tetradrachm, probably struck at Samos, see Volume of Plates ii, 4, *a*.

by it to try once again to drive a wedge between the Spartans and him. With this in view, at the instigation of Thrasybulus, they recalled Alcibiades, and by electing him General they virtually gave him conduct of their affairs. It was a master-stroke both for themselves and for Athens. Alcibiades doubtless knew that Tissaphernes would not turn against the Spartans, but he thought it possible that the Spartan fleet might be goaded into attacking him. So he proclaimed in the most extravagant tones the satrap's readiness to subsidize the fleet of the Athenians if only he could be made sure of them:—how he had promised, if Alcibiades were restored to go surety for them, to raise funds for them even if he had to sell his own bed. In furtherance of this design of making Tissaphernes seem faithless Alcibiades, refusing, despite much urging, to turn his back on the Spartan fleet and sail forthwith to the Piraeus to put an end to the oligarchy, made it his first business, now that he was General and could speak for Athens with authority, to have an interview with the satrap. Had he not taught Tissaphernes so well, he might have succeeded in his difficult rôle. For the disaffection among the Spartan seamen, which rose to open mutiny among the free men serving on the Syracusan and Thurian ships, had now got beyond the power of Astyochus (whose term was approaching its close) to check it: they angrily demanded their pay; and when he tried to browbeat them and raised his stick against Dorieus, they came at him with a shout and he escaped stoning only by fleeing to an altar. The seamen, now thoroughly out of hand, also aided and abetted the Milesians in getting rid forcibly of the garrison which Tissaphernes had planted in their territory—an act of rebellion disavowed by Lichas but imitated not long after by Cnidus and Antandrus. But Tissaphernes was not to be moved to reply to this violence in kind. He thought it possible that if he starved the Spartan fleet into helplessness and let the Athenians destroy one another by civil war he could impose his will on all Greece. So he limited his response to the Milesian provocation to a diplomatic *démarche* at Sparta—in connection with which he took the opportunity to defend his conduct generally against Hermocrates of Syracuse, who went there as chief complainant on behalf of the crews (midsummer, 411). And then he made a gesture which arrested universal attention. He brought a Phoenician fleet of 147 ships up to Aspendus and went himself to that point to meet it.

And there he stayed, and the fleet came no farther; and the Spartans in Miletus went on suffering from want of funds. But the Athenians did not engage in civil war. From this calamity they were saved by Alcibiades. On his return to Samos he found emissaries of the Four Hundred there, newly arrived with the model constitutions in hand, to which they could refer for their contention that the government they represented was a government of the Five Thousand and not of the Four Hundred alone. The crews were not for hearing them at all and were not in the least appeased when they *did* hear them. It was little satisfaction to them to be told that 5000 was a larger number than attended even the most important Assemblies if they themselves were not included. Despite reassurances, they feared for their friends and relatives at home and suspected, not unjustly, that the oligarchs would betray the city to the Spartans. Their strong bent was to be off at once to the Piraeus, and had not Alcibiades been there with words of wisdom and super-eminent authority they would have gone, leaving all Ionia and the Hellespont to the enemy. Of the two domestic dangers imminent he had thus mastered one. Against the other—betrayal of Athens by the oligarchs—his only resource was a strong bid to the moderates among the Four Hundred to assert themselves; he had (he told them) no objection to the Five Thousand, but the Four Hundred must go and the Council of Five Hundred return; he strongly approved of any economies that would admit of more money being available for the fleet; above all they should not surrender to Sparta. As for himself he concluded that Aspendus was the right place for him to be in; for the fate of Greece was in Tissaphernes' hands. So he set out for Aspendus with thirteen ships and the news that civil war was not going to eliminate Athens from the struggle. The Spartans too found a way of maintaining their fleet on a war footing despite the non-payment of Tissaphernes' subsidies. So in the end the Persian fleet was sent back home as being too weak for its purpose. In a very real sense Alcibiades had arrested its advance.

Immediately after seizing power, the Four Hundred had addressed themselves to the task of making peace with the Lacedaemonians. But what they counted on chiefly for success—the sympathy of Sparta with oligarchy—was more than offset by the hope the Spartans formed of profiting by Athenian dissensions. Agis, to whom they turned first, met their overtures by assembling a League army and advancing to the walls of the city; but he found no signs of weakness or confusion. So he let diplomacy follow its course. The first envoys sent to Sparta (Laispodias, Aristophon, and Melesias) started on board a trireme manned by the crew of the *Paralus*, who took them to Argos instead, where they were detained. But either they or others reached their destination and offered peace on the basis of the *status quo*. The offer was rejected. Sparta demanded the total surrender of the Athenian Empire. Such terms even a democracy could have had, and for them the Four Hundred were at this time unready. But the message sent from Samos by Alcibiades proved to be a wedge inserted at the line of an old fissure that split the Four Hundred into two sections. The one, less compromised and more compromising, with Theramenes as its leader and Aristocrates as his first lieutenant, adopted the programme of establishing in fact the government of the Five Thousand. Theramenes' motives were mixed. We may admit that he saw the writing on the wall and manœuvred so as to safeguard a political career for himself when the restoration came. But we need not on that account deny to him credit for honestly believing that the reunion of the city and the fleet on the basis of a limited democracy was in the best interests of Athens, and that the course pursued by his colleagues—Antiphon, Phrynichus, Archeptolemus, Onomacles, Aristarchus, Peisander, Alexicles, to mention only the leading extremists— meant utter ruin. Nor did the latter give him any chance to save them along with himself.

They too saw the rising tide of opposition; but, expecting no mercy in the event of overthrow and despairing of being able unaided to retain the safety of power if they let the Empire go and bargained with Sparta simply for autonomy, they sent Antiphon, Phrynichus, and ten others to Sparta ostensibly to make one last effort to secure an honourable peace, really to arrange secretly to admit the Spartans into Athens.

VII. THE END OF THE FOUR HUNDRED

The Spartans had now a home fleet in readiness at Las in South Laconia to take a hand in the long projected revolt of Euboea. The design of depriving Athens of this, its substitute Attica, had been furthered by the capture of Oropus earlier in the year, and the oligarchic upheaval in Athens and on the island brought the plans of the secessionists to a head. The outbreak simply waited on the arrival of the Spartan squadron. The Athenian oligarchs had taken precautions, of course; among others, the appointment of Polystratus, one of their own number, eight days after they assumed office, to the command at Eretria. But their partisans in the Euboic cities played them false; and when the ground began to give way under their feet in Athens, it was themselves, and not Euboea, that they thought of first.

Their plan was to fortify Eetionea—the western lip of the Piraeus,—ostensibly against the 'rebels' in Samos, really to give them the means of starving Athens and admitting the enemy when the occasion arose. It was over the building of this fort that the storm broke. Theramenes divined the treason contemplated, and connected with the work the fleet at Las and the negotiations of Phrynichus and Antiphon in Sparta. At first his counter-measures were secret. But Phrynichus, the right arm of the government, was struck down in the open market-place, and all the investigation disclosed was that the assassin had many accomplices. When then the Spartan fleet came to Epidaurus and overran Aegina, Theramenes and Aristocrates and their supporters within and without the Four Hundred could keep quiet no longer. They openly denounced the plot. What was more important, they carried with them the soldiers in the Piraeus. These seized their general Alexicles and with the aid of the harbour population proceeded to tear down the fort they had been building, proclaiming at the same time the government of the Five Thousand. On the following day they marched to Athens. The oligarchy weakened. The Five Thousand, they agreed, should be made known and given discretion as to how Councils of 400 should be drafted in succession from their number[1]; and a day was fixed for a meeting in the Theatre of Dionysus to arrange the terms of a reconciliation.

For a time the two factions had been on the verge of war. Agesandridas, the Spartan admiral, tried not to miss the occasion for a 'knock out blow.' He brought his fleet to Megara, waiting for a signal perhaps. Then on the day fixed for the meeting he was observed off Salamis. The whole population of Athens took this as confirmation of their worst suspicions and hurried to the Piraeus to man the ships and coast defences. Agesandridas rowed past and went on to Oropus, and in hot haste the Athenians got off reinforcements for their squadron at Eretria. Their crews were untrained, they had only 36 ships to the enemy's 42, they had to fight before they were ready, and Eretria rose against them in their rear. The defeat which they sustained was complete. Twenty-two ships were lost, crews and all; and had the Spartans followed up their victory by a prompt attack on the Piraeus, the Athenian fleets abroad must have come to its defence and the whole Empire been lost. 'But on this occasion, as on many others, the Lace-

---

[1] Draco (Aristotle, *Const. of Athens*, IV = XXX, 2–6 with the Boeotian features subtracted), brought forward to checkmate Theramenes, perhaps.

daemonians proved the most convenient of all peoples for the
Athenians to have as enemies, especially in a naval war[1].' So the
opportunity passed; and a little later Agesandridas lost most of
his fleet in a storm off Athos. But Euboea, excepting only Oreus-
Histiaea, revolted, and with it Athens lost its chief near-by source
of money, grain, and supplies.

The effect on the city was catastrophic. The people gathered
once more in general assembly on the Pnyx and set aside the
Four Hundred (early in Boedromion, August–September, 411).
They had ruled for only four months. Peisander, Alexicles, and
Aristarchus escaped to Decelea and were condemned as traitors
in absentia. Antiphon and Archeptolemus stood their trial, and,
despite the brilliancy of Antiphon's defence, they were found
guilty of high treason and executed. Phrynichus was attainted
though dead and his bones cast beyond the frontier. Theramenes,
Andron, and Critias were particularly active in prosecuting their
former associates and they took pains that the charges brought
against them were on counts for which the Four Hundred
generally were not answerable.

VIII. THE GOVERNMENT OF THE FIVE THOUSAND

The moderates had now the upper hand. The government they
established was, Thucydides thought and Aristotle agreed with
him, the best Athens had ever had. It was based on the programme already issued[2]. The changes in the 'laws of Solon' there
called for, and the other adjustments necessary, were made in the
regular way by the aid of a constituent assembly (*Nomothetae*).
The whole freeborn male population remained citizens, but of
them only those capable of bearing arms—to the number it
proved of 9000—had active rights, which they exercised, on
reaching their thirtieth year, as 'councillors'—without pay. To
enable so large a body to transact business (it had to act as Council
and Assembly in one), it was divided into four Councils, each of
which, constituted of a fair sample on the old idea that this was
the best kind of representation, was to serve with plenary power
for a year at a time in an order determined by lot. This was roughly
how things were managed in the Boeotian cities, which were used
as a model. The officiating Council was too large to be asked to

---

[1] Thucydides VIII, 96, 5.

[2] See above, p. 331. On this identification of the constitution of the Five
Thousand with that sketched in Aristotle's *Constitution of Athens*, XXX, see
W. S. Ferguson, *The Constitution of Theramenes* in *C.P.* 1926, pp. 72–5.
See also V. Ehrenberg in P.-W. *s.v.* Losung.

sit daily as the Five Hundred had done: it, accordingly, met only once in five days and its members were constrained to be regular in attendance by being fined if absent without leave. In the interim it was represented by committees, still called prytanies, but constituted, not as theretofore of the members of each tribe in turn, but of fair samples of its entire membership designated by sortitions conducted by the nine archons. These quasi-prytanies were organized as usual with a tenth of the year as their term, and a succession and a chairman determined by lot, the latter anew each day. When a meeting of the Council occurred, the five chairmen thus designated since the previous session served as its presidents, of whom one was drawn, again by lot, to put the motions and announce the count of votes. The educative and equalizing features of the democratic régime were thus retained, their benefits being, of course, denied to the lower classes.

The distinction between magistrates chosen by election and those chosen by lot was upheld, but the former category, which had consisted essentially of military officials, was enlarged by the inclusion in it of the nine archons as before 487 B.C. (vol. IV, p. 156); of two committees of ten each (*hieropoioi* and *epimeletai*) who had charge of the great religious festivals; and of the chief exchequer officials, who were consolidated in two boards, one of ten men entitled Treasurers of Athena, with charge of all sacred monies and properties, and another of twenty men entitled Hellenic Treasurers to whom were entrusted the secular funds domestic and imperial alike. The difference between these important officers, who were approximately 100 in number, and the minor magistracies, who were elected by lot, was further accentuated in that they alone were chosen, by a double process of voting, from the members of the Council in office, in the work of which they all, with the inexplicable exception of the Hellenic Treasurers, participated. The net effect of these administrative changes was closer contact between the various branches of the government, more responsible organization of the civil services that handled and spent money, and an all-round strengthening of the executive. The moderate oligarchs, it should be noted, had no quarrel on principle with election by lot, rotation in office, proportional representation, or majority rule. The essence of their programme was to secure for high civil offices men of special competence, to reserve the privileges of the commonwealth to Athenians who could afford them, and deny a voice in political decisions to such as lacked an appreciable property-stake in the community.

As in the case of the minor magistracies, so in the case of the jury-courts (*dikasteria*), no change was needed. The alteration of personnel that followed the exclusion of the plebs from active citizenship sufficed. And it was some compensation for the cession of political power to the officiating Council that men from the other three Councils manned the *dikasteria*[1]; for it was to the judiciary that the governing bodies were responsible, and the jurisdiction of the courts in high political cases, already paramount, was increased through the suppression of the Assembly.

The constitution effected 'a judicious blending of the "few" (magistrates, Council) and the "many" (dicasts, councillors: *cives sine suffragio*) that raised the state from the evil plight into which it had fallen.' Such is the judgment of the Athenian historian who has analyzed so appreciatively the greatness of Periclean democracy. He did not complete the story that despite its success in making Athens once again mistress of the sea, this much praised polity lasted only eight months. There is no disguising the fact that, with all its rectifications of current abuses and its clever fusion of Boeotia and Cleisthenes with political theory masquerading as ancestral wisdom, it was but a makeshift. It was not a serious weakness that three-quarters of the active citizens normally looked on while the other quarter handled current business; for there was a provision of the constitution by which each member of the officiating Council might ask in another councillor on important occasions, and this probably ensured the participation in government of most of those who really cared about it. The Councils, too, were so constituted that one could be replaced by another without anything like the loss of continuity in policy that arises when one party succeeds another in the government of a modern country. Under this constitution a Themistocles or a Pericles or an Alcibiades could have been General only once in four years; and from the purely military point of view this was disadvantageous. But immediate re-election to the highest command was forbidden, in the interest of republicanism, in many Greek constitutions—those of Sparta and the Achaean League for example,—and in the case of Rome the interval of private life was as much as ten years. What denied permanency to the constitution of Theramenes was its disfranchisement of the element (in itself a majority of all Athenians) upon which the government organized under it was dependent for protection, prosperity, and empire. The very men who were

---

[1] [Plutarch], *Lives of the Ten Orators*, p. 833 D = *I.G.*[2] i, p. 298.

to save Athens by crushing the fleet that was strangling it to death enjoyed, to be sure, the protection of the Athenian laws and the proud status of Athenians, but otherwise they were without rights in their own country. They would acquiesce in this outrage to their every instinct so long as service abroad made the franchise of no practical value to them and the economies attendant on its loss highly remunerative; so long, too, as they had to give their entire attention to the enemy. But no longer. Besides, Alcibiades, whom the Five Thousand confirmed in his military command, had already declared for the restoration of the Council of the Five Hundred.

IX. THE STRUGGLE FOR THE HELLESPONT

Mindarus, the Spartan admiral for 411–10 B.C., shifted the scene of major naval operations from Ionia to the Hellespont. The fleet of Chios had yielded its maximum of results. The worst blow that could now be dealt Athens was to close the passage from the Black Sea. The aid paid for in advance by Pharnabazus could be withheld no longer. The farce at Aspendus and the misery at Miletus had brought complete, if tardy, illumination as to the motives of Tissaphernes. Hence, giving Samos a wide berth, Mindarus started for the Hellespont (Sept. 411), where an advance squadron of 16 ships awaited him, face to face with 18 Athenian vessels, now at Sestos. Storm-stayed for five or six days at Icaros, he found, on coming to Chios, that the Athenians were already at Lesbos, set on heading him off. An opportune revolt of Eresus drew them to the seaward side of the island, thus permitting him, by a combination of good luck, audacity, and speed, to pass through the channel of Mitylene and reach Rhoeteum. It was dead of night when he arrived. So the lights of his ships betrayed him to the Athenian squadron at Sestos, which saved itself by promptly slipping down the straits, losing four ships, however, in the run for Lemnos and Imbros. The Athenians from Eresus intervened in time, captured two ships of the pursuers, and then concentrated their forces at Elaeus. Thrasyllus and Thrasybulus were in command. Their ships numbered 76.

They must force a passage into the Propontis if they would regain or retain Athens' empire along its shores; for Cyzicus had already revolted and probably also Chalcedon and Selymbria. The attempt to do this brought on a battle at Cynossema in the Narrows—the first trial of strength of the main fleets since the naval war in the Aegean began. The details disclose only the superiority of the Athenians in speed and tactics, and the completeness of the defeat of the Lacedaemonians (September, 411). The proximity of the shore and Abydos enabled them to save their fleet, so that the losses on either side were comparable (21 ships to 15); but the moral ascendancy of the Athenians on the sea, which had been shattered by their misfortunes at Eretria and Syracuse, was restored, and the government of the Five Thousand entered on its career with an energy born of great encouragement.

The Athenians were now free to enter the Propontis. At Priapus they captured eight enemy ships from Byzantium, and since Cyzicus was unwalled it had to submit on their arrival. But though beaten, the Lacedaemonians were by no means out of the fighting. They took advantage of the absence of Thrasybulus and Thrasyllus to raid Elaeus. So the Athenians came back to the Hellespont, whither both they and their adversaries had summoned all the ships they possessed, and here, at Abydos, a second general engagement ensued (October–November, 411)[1]. Its issue was still in suspense when the arrival of Alcibiades, the only squadron-commander on either side absent at its beginning, inclined the balance in favour of the Athenians. The Lacedaemonians tried to save their fleet by running it ashore, and Pharnabazus came down into the water with foot and cavalry to aid in its defence; but, though they rescued the crews, they could not prevent the Athenians from towing off over thirty of their vessels. The latter were now numerically as well as tactically superior; but it was near the end of the season, and the possibility did not exist of provisioning the entire fleet with the money on hand or procurable at Sestos. So the force there was reduced to forty ships and the rest scattered for the winter. Twenty went with Thrasybulus to Thrace, others elsewhere. Thrasyllus returned to Athens to report on the situation and secure further ships and troops for a decisive effort in the spring. Alcibiades paid a visit to Tissaphernes who had come to the Hellespont to try to get the Spartans back into his service. And therewith his relation with the Satrap ended. Taken to Sardes, for thirty days he was held prisoner and then he owed his escape to his own exertions. Thenceforth he would have to compete for power in Athens without the advantage of being thought able to influence Persian policy—unless he could reach an understanding with Pharnabazus.

As soon as the sea was navigable Theramenes himself took the ships that were ready at Athens and sailed to Chalcis to try to

---

[1] Xenophon, *Hell.* I, 1. On the chronology of the years 410–6 see note 10

prevent the Boeotians and Euboeans from connecting their countries by filling in and bridging the Euripus; but when it proved that he could do nothing there, he went collecting money among the islands, to Paros notably, where he overthrew the oligarchy set up by the Four Hundred. Then he lent a hand to Archelaus, since 413 B.C. king of Macedon, who was having trouble with Pydna, and whose services throughout this critical time in facilitating the export to Athens of shipbuilding materials entitled him to assistance. Before the place was reduced, however, he got a message from Thrasybulus, then operating at Thasos, that they both were needed in the Hellespont, where a crisis had supervened. So he left part of his force behind and hastened on. On his arrival at Sestos the entire Athenian fleet was reunited under the command of Alcibiades and the final operation of this fierce struggle for the mastery of the Hellespont was begun. With the aid of Pharnabazus Mindarus had just recaptured Cyzicus and it was thither that Alcibiades sailed to encounter him. He had 86 ships to Mindarus' 60. So he feared the *nauarch* would decline to fight; but he masked his movements well and had a stroke of good luck. A rainstorm hid his approach. Suddenly it cleared, and he found the whole Spartan fleet practising manœuvres well away from the harbour of Cyzicus. Unable to reach port and badly outnumbered, Mindarus beached his ships and tried to defend them. But without success. While Thrasybulus, Thymochares, and Theramenes engaged the Spartans in front, Alcibiades landed the crews of twenty triremes and made a flank attack. Mindarus fell while trying to repel it. Only the Syracusans waited long enough to burn their vessels; the rest ran away, and the Athenians captured their ships. Once again Athens was undisputed mistress of the sea (April, 410 B.C.).

X. THE POLICY OF CLEOPHON

The effects of Sparta's naval collapse were at once felt at home and abroad, in Athens and Sparta, Syracuse and Susa. In Athens the citizen crews of the victorious fleet and the rest of the class to which they belonged regained their lost rights, and the Council was reduced to 500, reorganized as of old, and separated from the Assembly. The magistrates then in office seem to have been undisturbed till the end of the year. And even then some of the administrative improvements made, notably the consolidation of financial boards[1], were retained. Theramenes was abroad when the

---

[1] This entailed the permanent disappearance of the *Colacretae*.

Five Thousand gave way and he chose to remain abroad for a time. Cleophon, a lyre-manufacturer, the man who ousted him in the confidence of the majority, sympathized with the class that had been dispossessed. He represented the Cleon-Hyperbolus tradition. Finance was his forte, and for year after year he looked after this all-important branch of the administration with skill and integrity. With the restoration of the poor to citizenship, their claim to indemnities for time spent in civilian service had to be recognized—the more readily, doubtless, because of overconfidence in the speedy rehabilitation of their revenues. Cleophon's peculiar invention was the *diobelia*, a payment of two obols per day to the people, but to whom precisely and for what we are nowhere told. It is best interpreted as a dole distributed to needy citizens not otherwise on the public pay-roll; and it may have been financed by a reduction of indemnities to a two obol level all round. Under the régime of Cleophon and his associates the right of the masses to live was further recognized by the resumption of state building-operations, notably on the Erechtheum (409 B.C.). By the *diobelia* impoverished gentlefolk were primarily affected. The construction of the Erechtheum gave employment to labourers and artisans, whether they were slaves or freemen, aliens or citizens (see above, p. 5 *sq.*).

These expedients were directed to enabling Athens to continue the war; and for the decision so to do Cleophon bears (together with Alcibiades) the heavy responsibility. If the report of the battle of Cyzicus that reached Sparta was like the one the Athenians intercepted ('The ships are lost. Mindarus is dead. The men starve. We know not what to do.') the reaction of the Spartans needs no comment. They sent the head of the phil-Athenian faction, Alcibiades' friend, Endius, to Athens with an offer of peace on the basis of the *status quo*—Decelea to be given up in exchange for Pylos. This meant for Athens the loss of Euboea, Andros, Rhodes, Chios, Thasos, Abdera, Perinthus, Selymbria, Byzantium, and, with the exception of two or three places, all the towns on the Asiatic coast from Pamphylia to the Pontus. Yet there were many Athenians who, judging the struggle hopeless against such great odds, wished for peace even on these terms. And the future proved their wisdom. But the rejection of the offer was almost inevitable. Its acceptance would have stopped Athens from trying to regain its lost dependencies at the very moment when, with sea-power re-established and again self-supporting, it could turn unopposed to their recovery. Nor did acceptance give complete certainty that the war would not be renewed when Sparta had got upon its feet again. Over-confidence in themselves and inveterate lack of faith in Sparta clouded the judgment of the Athenians and incapacitated them from seeing that, even if the respite were brief, it would suffice to end the coalition of west Greeks, east Greeks and Persians which the impression of their weakness (now proved false) had brought into being, and also to disclose to their renegade allies that the choice between them and their adversaries was the choice of two masters, not, as fondly imagined, the choice of liberty or oppression.

XI. THE ATTEMPTED RESTORATION OF THE ATHENIAN EMPIRE

So the war continued. Alcibiades reoccupied Cyzicus, and spent the balance of the summer partly there and partly in re-establishing Athens' authority in Perinthus, Selymbria, and the Bosporus. He had not enough soldiers to lay siege to either Chalcedon or Byzantium. So he built a fortress at Chrysopolis just north of Chalcedon and left Theramenes there with a strong squadron to keep the exit from the Pontus open and collect a 10 per cent. toll on all cargoes passing out. In general his first care was to restore to Athens its revenues; for upon these all else depended. Nine ships now sufficed to guard the Hellespont. The rest had to be scattered for this winter as for the one preceding—a fact of which Sparta took advantage. As King Agis watched from his post at Decelea the Pontic grain-ships sailing into the Piraeus he realized as never before the importance of blocking the Bosporus. And with this in view he had a Spartan officer, Clearchus, sent with troopships to organize the defence of Chalcedon and Byzantium. Three of these the Athenian patrol destroyed in the Hellespont, but twelve reached their destination and increased enormously the military difficulties of the Athenians.

By the spring of 409 B.C. the Athenians were ready to make a strong effort to recover their lost allies. During the preceding season they had had their minds set at rest as regards Agis. The king had invited battle by leading his men from Decelea down to the city's walls, but when Thrasyllus mustered out the Athenian army and accepted the challenge, he had beaten a hasty retreat. Athens concluded that it could spare an expeditionary force and that Thrasyllus was the man to command it. After spending the winter in preparations, this popular general set out for Ionia with 1000 hoplites and a fleet of 50 ships, among the rowers of which were 5000 peltasts. He landed at Pygela south of Ephesus, where he met and defeated the Milesians; he won Colophon north of Ephesus and despoiled Lydia; but his main objective was Ephesus itself, and here he failed signally. For he encountered not merely the Ephesians, but horse and foot in large numbers which Tissaphernes (now at length compelled to do his own fighting) had assembled from all over his satrapy, and also the crews of the entire Sicilian squadron. So Thrasyllus sailed to the Hellespont where he joined forces with Alcibiades (whose summer had been singularly uneventful), and they devoted the winter to fortifying Lampsacus and to an unsuccessful attempt on Abydos.

The elimination of the Spartan fleet had brought the Persians face to face with the Athenians. Pharnabazus had stepped manfully into the breach. He had taken some of the shipless crews into his service and equipped them for the defence of his coast. Others he had assembled at Antandrus and set to work with timber from Mt. Ida rebuilding a fleet. Money he provided to the extent of his ability. Those who took most advantage of his assistance were the Sicilians, who worked to such purpose, notwithstanding that Syracuse, chagrined at the total loss of its fleet at Cyzicus, superseded and exiled their tried generals (autumn, 410 B.C.)—Hermocrates among them—that by the spring they had replaced all their ships and were thus able to join in the defence of Ionia. Thereafter they tried unsuccessfully to reach the Hellespont. It was in Sicily fighting against the Carthaginians that they next saw service (vol. VI, p. 110).

Their departure took the centre out of the new Lacedaemonian fleet, and permitted Alcibiades to concentrate his forces for the great object set for the 408 B.C. campaign—the winning of the Bosporus. Chalcedon was invested first. A determined effort on the part of Pharnabazus from without and the Spartan harmost from within failed to break the Athenian cordon. And to save the city from a worse fate than resumption of its old tributary relation to Athens Pharnabazus undertook to forward to Susa ambassadors to discuss peace with the King—an opportunity which the Athenians (supported by Argos) eagerly embraced. Could they obtain the neutrality of Persia they might yet win the war. Besides they were freed to proceed with the siege of Byzantium, round which too they threw a cordon. But their assaults proved fruitless. Clearchus, however, made the mistake of reserving the supplies for the garrison, whereupon certain citizens, solicitous for the civilian population, took advantage of his absence on a visit to Pharnabazus to betray the city. So Athens regained Byzantium and was relieved from anxiety for its food supply (autumn, 408 B.C.). Alcibiades had scored another striking success. And in the following May (Thargelion), after having collected 100 talents to fetch home as a sort of peace-offering, he returned to Athens, where he was received like a conquering hero, given back his property, relieved of the religious penalties imposed upon him in 415 B.C., and put in sole charge of the war for the following year. Since Thrasybulus regained Abdera and Thasos at this same time, and the enemy did not venture to show himself anywhere on the sea, Athens, far from regretting that it had refused to make peace with Sparta three years before, rejected the proffered hand yet again, even though in the interval only a fraction of its hopes had been realized, Corcyra had fallen after a bitter struggle into the hands of its oligarchs and reverted to its pre-war policy of neutrality, and the Spartans had regained Pylos (autumn, 409 B.C.) and the Megarians Nisaea.

But beyond Athens' vision, at the King's court at Susa, a decision had been reached which made its jubilation during the four months of Alcibiades' stay at home seem like tragic irony. The house of Hydarnes, to which Tissaphernes belonged, had been overwhelmed by disaster (vol. vi, p. 3). He had made the mistake of looking beyond victory to the settlement with Sparta that was bound to follow; and had lost victory itself. A Spartan embassy sent to Susa to complain of his duplicity had no difficulty in making out a case against him. Without waiting to hear from the Athenians and Argives, the King decided to put the financial resources of the empire squarely behind the one of the Greek contenders for power which lacked the means of maintaining a fleet without Persian assistance. And to give this idea effect and at the same time to humour his strong-minded wife, who desired, from ulterior motives, to enable Cyrus, her second son, whom she favoured, to build up for himself an independent position in the state, Darius appointed Cyrus 'to be lord (*karanos*) of all those whose mustering place is Castolus,' *i.e.*, governor-general of Asia Minor. Over and above the revenues of this area he gave him 500 talents with which to recreate the Spartan fleet. In the spring of 407 B.C. Cyrus met at Gordium the envoys for whose journey to Susa Pharnabazus had arranged. They naturally went no farther; but they were not allowed to return to spread the news that thenceforth Athens had to contend not with the uncertain, unsupported, and unrelated efforts of jealous satraps, but with the set purpose of the whole Persian Empire. The Peloponnesian War had entered upon its final phase.

CHAPTER XII

THE FALL OF THE ATHENIAN EMPIRE

I. LAW AND POLITICS IN ATHENS

THE mutilation of the Hermae (p. 286) became a topic of public jesting in Athens within five years of its occurrence, but the baying of the citizen pack while on the scent, true or false, of the mutilators echoed long in the memories of men in fashionable circles of the community. The union of political clubs effected in 411 B.C. had given way under the strain of cross-purposes, but men of popular sympathies did not soon forget how fear and death had stalked in their midst while it had lasted. The rule of the Four Hundred had cleft the aristocracy in twain, and its misdeeds hung like mill-stones on the necks even of those aristocrats who had done most to destroy it. The very existence of the Five Thousand had signified degradation for thousands of Athenians who in 410 B.C. obtained the capacity to avenge it; and they showed their resentment by depriving the soldiers who had remained in Athens under the Four Hundred of the right to speak in assembly or sit on the Council.

The disintegration of the body politic had proceeded so far that extraordinary measures were needed to check it. The state resorted to the methods of secret associations—the pledging

Note. Xenophon (*Hellenica*, I, iv to end and II) and Diodorus (XIII, 69, 4–XIV, 33) serve as narrative bases for this chapter as for chapter XI. Xenophon, with the knowledge of a participant concerning the convulsions in Athens, wrote long enough after the event to be dispassionate. Aristotle (*Const. of Athens*, XXXIV–XLI) furnishes a parallel account of the second oligarchy with divergences in the sequence and appreciation of events that are due seemingly to the partiality of his sources (Androtion, pamphlets?) for Theramenes. The orations of Andocides, Lysias and Isocrates cover, by exposition, allusion, attack and defence of persons, most of the events of the period; but they have to be construed in each case with reference to the object of the speaker. They reflect vividly the political controversies of the time. Plutarch's *Lives* of Alcibiades (35 to end) and Lysander (1–21) add little not derived from Xenophon and Diodorus' source (Ephorus). The additions (due to Theopompus' *Hellenica*, perhaps, as well as to the miscellaneous writers used in the biographical tradition, p. 254 *Note*) are by no means negligible. The inscriptions, though few in number, are of first-rate importance.

of each member individually by a solemn oath. All citizens vowed to uphold democracy, and to treat as foreign enemies any who thenceforward should serve an undemocratic government, slaying them if they got the chance, rewarding the slayers as tyrannicides were rewarded. To legislate that, in the case of political opponents, killing was no murder was thought necessary to overawe future revolutionists, but for democrats themselves fuller knowledge of the constitution which they were pledged to uphold was found desirable. In view of the recklessness with which this had been flouted and altered of late, one of the first steps taken after the restoration was to have the laws, as emended and completed, published in enforceable form. The registrars (*anagrapheis*) to whom the task was entrusted seem to have had little energy or authority. They simply inscribed on stone slabs the laws in sections as instructed by the people—Draco's ordinance on homicide in whole or part, the Cleisthenean statute concerning the Council of Five Hundred, the rules governing grants of maintenance in the prytaneum, etc. For six years they dilly-dallied at their task, unable of themselves to complete the codification and deprived, by other cares, of the sustained interest of the people.

Notwithstanding these measures the demos felt that the price of safety was unrelenting vigilance. The sole guardian of the laws was now the popular courts; and so widespread was the feeling that 'aristocrats' were at heart traitors, and so manifest the inability of the treasury to furnish jurors' allowances unless it were replenished by confiscations, that these tribunals gave ear to all kinds of charges against men of prominence and property. The legal system of Athens encouraged delation. It put the responsibility upon private individuals not only to seek legal redress for their own wrongs, but to initiate proceedings for the punishment of all who in any way seemed remiss in the performance of their public duties. Where the community was so small and privacy so limited, the consequences were, not so much collusions to foil justice, as an excess of litigiousness. Since, too, everyone was required to plead his own case, persons who made a profession of suit-bringing had a decided advantage in the courts; and this was only partially compensated by the practice of litigants to deliver speeches written for them by professional speech-writers.

In the administration of Athenian justice politicians, sycophants, and men of letters played a rôle that accords little with modern conceptions. Judges and jurists in the strict sense of these terms there were none. Magistrates with only the average citizen's knowledge of the law (which was, however, far from inconsiderable) decided the admissibility of cases and conducted proceedings in court; and the verdicts emanated from large bodies of men tolerably proficient but unspecialized in law. The law consisted of two elements—the code of 'Draco and Solon,' and the decrees of the Council and Assembly. The latter had been multiplied under the democracy. They were easier of enactment than new laws, and the authority which enacted them could amend or cancel them without ceremony. Constitutionally they could neither contradict nor duplicate laws, but they could enter in to cover cases, such as the creation of a new office or the formulation of a general rule, not dealt with by laws; and, in the absence of any public authority obligated and interested to look after the rights of the code, they tended steadily to trespass on its legitimate territory. The code consisted of a collection of statutes of varying dates and sources, couched in language that at times was shot with archaic names and phrases—statutes by the terms of which, in case acts of a specified kind were committed, penalties were imposed and the rules of procedure to be followed were indicated. The acts, whether treated individually, or grouped and sub-grouped according to their character under comprehensive statutes, were described in simple concrete language; and both they and their groupings reflected actual experience and testing. The statutes were arranged under the heads of the public authorities (first the Council—after 403 B.C. at least—then the magistrates generally and then the magistrates individually beginning with the archons) for the guidance of which they were in fact the official instructions. The recognition of wrongs, both public and private, was made with fulness of detail rather than through the application of general principles, with acuteness and clarity rather than with system; and the indications of procedure were at times casual and incomplete (set practice being taken for granted), at times minutely specific. The underlying rule was that officials should handle cases that arose out of their executive functions, but this was crossed by the allocation of types of cases to magistrates who, like the *euthyni*, *thesmothetae*, *eisagogeis*, and Thirty, had no executive duties whatsoever; and it was subordinated to the democratic requirement that, except in certain carefully defined instances (fines of 500 drachmae or less imposed by the Council, the punishment of criminals caught in the act, charges involving sums under ten drachmae, the reference of private disputes to an agreed private arbitrator), the people itself, as represented, in case of homicide by the Areopagus or one of its subsidiaries, in other cases by the jury-courts, and exceptionally by the Assembly, should render the actual judgment.

The jury courts at Athens were so empanelled (by the drawing by lot of a large group locally distributed) that the justice emanating from them was the justice that animated at the moment the Athenian people. The unlikeness in deciding like cases which is the essence of injustice must, in these circumstances, have vitiated legal decisions if a national familiarity with law had not been cultivated and sustained by the democratic judicial system. It also served to steady the action of the courts that, as a result of discussions carried on for two centuries, citizens had come to possess a valuable common stock of juridical ideas. Except for the uniqueness of their legal education, equity must have broken with strict law altogether. In the administration of justice there was little chance to bring in the past to correct the animus of the present. For, though both in public and private suits the complaint and, if there was one, the demurrer were put in writing by the magistrate who entered the case, the pleadings, including the evidence, were as yet presented orally, and the practice was still in its infancy for professional speech-writers to issue their speeches in permanent form. Neither, then, in legal records nor in the training, learning, and experience of those who held court was there much hope of previous decisions making themselves felt in determining verdicts. Indeed, the jurors were under oath to give their judgments (with due regard to laws and decrees and, these failing, to their own sense of right) purely on the merits of the actual case. Precedents had no legal standing in Attic courts. They could not be invoked authoritatively to restrain the predatory instincts of the jurors when the Athenian people, as in 410–405 B.C., had become embittered against its citizens of wealth and standing by injury, suspicion and misery.

The consequences were, accordingly, deplorable. A set of acrid politicians and sycophants, headed by Epigenes, Demophantus, and Cleigenes, encompassed the exile, disfranchisement, or judicial murder of many persons. Others they blackmailed by threats of indictment. Not only did the practice arise of buying off prosecutors, but worried holders of property or office took pettifoggers into their employ on the theory that it takes a thief to catch a thief; and Anytus, who showed himself later to be a good citizen, having detected a weakness in the organization of the jury courts, disclosed a possibility of judicial corruption by bribing in wholesale fashion the panel before which he was hauled for failure to rescue Pylos. Thus many Athenians suffered total or partial loss of civil rights. The shrinkage in the volume of trade and the loss of agricultural values affected holders of public franchises and leases as well as those engaged in private business, so that the ranks of the unfortunate who had suffered *capitis deminutio* were swollen by state-debtors and their bondsmen who were unable to make their payments when due. Novel kinds of disabilities were devised—exclusion from the agora, or from the Hellespont, or from Ionia.

This was the Athens from which Euripides and Agathon departed to enjoy the bounty and grace of the court of Archelaus of Macedon; in which Sophocles and Aristophanes remained, sure of intelligent appreciation of their matchless artistry. It was in this Athens that Plato became of age to consider the plan and purpose of his life, and of it he was probably thinking when long afterwards he wrote that there was in it 'but a very small remnant of honest followers of wisdom.' These, he thought, 'might be compared to a man who has fallen among wild beasts: he will not be one of them but he is too unaided to make head against them; and before he can do any good to society or his friends, he will be overwhelmed and perish miserably. When he considers this he will resolve to keep still, and to mind his own business; as it were standing aside under a wall in a storm of dust and hurricane of driving wind[1].' If he were of Plato's mind but not an honest follower of wisdom, he might await his chance to introduce the Spartans in order with their assistance to play the wild beast in turn.

II. THE DICTATORSHIP OF ALCIBIADES

In the autumn of 407 B.C. Alcibiades, now officially commander-in-chief of the Athenian forces, set out for the scene of operations with a fleet of 100 ships and an army of 1500 hoplites and 150 horsemen. He took with him extravagant hopes, bitter hatred, profound misgivings. His past and his personality made his place in the Athens we have described altogether dependent upon what some feared most—the success with which he should handle the military situation. His task, as the Athenians envisaged it during this summer of reunion and relaxation, was to continue the reconquest of the rebels. But the problem had changed meanwhile. Sparta was once more in possession of a naval force (70 ships) which, when concentrated at Ephesus, was strong enough to distract the main Athenian fleet from the consecutive isolation and leaguer of individual cities; and what was even more

[1] *Republic*, VI, 496 D, transl. Matthew Arnold.

important, Sparta had at length found a leader equal to the complications of combined Peloponnesian-Persian warfare.

The *nauarch* chosen for 408–7 B.C., Lysander, son of Aristocritus, realized that the factors which were now decisive in the war were, not Sparta and its continental allies, but Persia and the Greek communities won or to be won from Athens. So he set himself studiously to win the favour of Cyrus; and he was enough of the soldier to attract, enough of the courtier to please, and enough of the statesman to impress, the gallant young Persian prince. Tissaphernes pleaded with his new overlord not to make the greatest Greek land power supreme on the sea also; but Cyrus had come to Asia Minor to crush the Athenians at all costs. He gave Lysander sufficient money to increase to 90 ships the fleet he had concentrated in Ephesus, to pay to his crews all their arrears of wages, and to make service with Sparta thenceforth distinctly more lucrative than service with Athens. Thus subsidized, Lysander got in touch with suitable persons in the 'liberated' cities, through whom he enhanced his personal influence and converted his money into ships, supplies and sailors.

Confronted with this development, Alcibiades had to pass on from Andros before he had mastered the revolt which had occurred there. But on his arrival at Samos he could do nothing. And in the following spring the situation was unchanged, except that his crews were weaker through desertions and those of Lysander stronger in discipline and morale. Yet he brought his fleet to Notium, whence it controlled the passage in and out of Ephesus; while Thrasybulus proceeded with a subsidiary squadron to invest Phocaea. Chafing at his enforced inactivity, which was undermining his reputation at home, Alcibiades left Notium, taking with him his land forces alone, and associated himself with the operations of Thrasybulus, for the success of which his hoplites were probably essential. This was sound strategy. But he had left the fleet in wrong hands. His lieutenant, Antiochus, disobeyed orders; and provoking an engagement, in which his ships entered action piecemeal, he was beaten and lost 15 vessels (March 406 B.C.). Alcibiades hurried to Samos, whither the Athenian ships had withdrawn, and again offered battle. But Lysander had nothing to gain by precipitancy.

The Athenians profited by this vicarious defeat of Alcibiades to rid themselves of the shadow of tyranny which his supereminent figure was casting upon their city. From every quarter assailants rose against him. 'He had handed over,' so a spokesman from the field said, 'the duties of commander to men who won his confidence merely by drinking deep and reeling off sailors' yarns, in order that he himself might be free to cruise about collecting moneys and committing excesses of drunkenness and revelry with courtezans of Abydos and Ionia[1].' It was the eve of the annual elections for 406–5 B.C. The campaign of vituperation succeeded. Alcibiades was not among the ten chosen to be generals. On his return to Athens in the heyday of success in 407 B.C. he had feared for his life. To return now would have been suicide; but since his treatment at home undermined completely his military authority, to remain with the fleet was equally impossible. Hence he took a trireme and went quietly off to Thrace where he had acquired castles, in view of some such contingency, at Pactye and Bisanthe. The great war swept back and forth in his neighbourhood; but, feared and distrusted in Athens, Sparta, and Persia alike, the most brilliant man of action of his generation, whose judgment of public policies was as unerring as his personal aims, methods, and conduct were wrong, found outlet for his restless energy only in waging private war on the 'kingless' Thracians. Had Athens been able to trust him he might have saved her Empire and destroyed her liberty.

III. ARGINUSAE AND THE TRIAL OF THE GENERALS

The Spartan who, from now on, was to take Alcibiades' place in the centre of the stage had to leave it temporarily at about the same time as his discomfited rival (March 406 B.C.). His term as *nauarch* had ended long since and the Spartan system did not permit reappointment. The rule against iteration was devised to enable the home authorities to retain control of operations abroad, and Lysander was precisely the sort of person it envisaged; but its application to him now crossed the plans of others besides himself. It was disturbing to the partisans whom he was helping to power in the 'liberated' cities, and unintelligible to Cyrus. In his disappointment Lysander left nothing undone to embarrass his successor—a downright, old-fashioned, young Spartan named Callicratidas. Notably he returned to Cyrus the balances in his possession at the time, thus forcing Callicratidas to go at once to Sardes for money. There the new admiral was kept waiting so ignominiously in the prince's antechamber that he left without an audience, confirmed in his feelings that the quarrels among the Greeks should be ended as speedily as possible with a view to putting the Persians again in their place;

---

[1] Plutarch, *Alcibiades*, 36, transl. B. Perrin, *Loeb Classics*.

and in this spirit he went ahead with the war. Assembling fifty additional ships, which had been got ready in Rhodes (lately the scene of a concerted movement of population from the three ancient towns to a new city, which took the name and consolidated the resources of the island[1]), Chios, and elsewhere, he shifted his base to Miletus, where he was more independent of Persia. Then, having brought his fleet up to the imposing total of 170 vessels, he proceeded to Lesbos, where he attacked Methymna and took it by storm. This brought the Athenians on the scene.

To take Alcibiades' place Conon had come to Samos. He found the crews so impaired in quality and depleted in numbers that he put out of commission over one-third of the triremes and took the sea with only 70 ships. Athens was not in a position to do much to help him; for Agis had once again summoned the entire confederate army to Attica and had even tried to take the city by a night attack. Hence Conon made shift to support his fleet by plundering the enemy's territory, using the sea (Callicratidas declared) in the absence of its lord like a skulking adulterer; but he could not leave Lesbos utterly in the lurch. Thus he encountered the Spartan fleet, which, cutting him off from his base at Samos, chased him into Mitylene, capturing 30 of his triremes and driving the rest ashore (July 406 B.C.). With the aid of the townsfolk Conon beat off the enemy's assaults on the inner harbour, to which he retired when the outer proved untenable; but he was without resources against a blockade. His only hope was of getting help from Athens, to which he contrived to send news of his desperate situation; and to be of any use this must be both speedy and adequate. Callicratidas' policy of a vigorous offensive seemed thus on the point of being crowned by success. So Cyrus had a change of heart and renewed his subsidies.

Athens was at length face to face with the danger at which it had shuddered in 413 B.C.; and now it had no reserve of money to fall back upon. Yet the people never faltered. Mad the multitude may have been and ungovernable, but it was superb in the resolution with which it faced a world in arms. A maximum levy on private income was, doubtless, imposed. The silver plate in the temples was converted into currency; from their statues of Victory gold coins were minted; and the credit of the state was drawn on in the form of token money of copper[2] (July-August 406 B.C.). Triremes were not lacking; and to man them citizens and subjects, metics and slaves were impressed without regard to

[1] For a coin of the new city of Rhodes see Volume of Plates ii, 2, *i*.
[2] For this gold and copper coinage *ib.* ii, 4, *d*, *e*.

persons or status. By these revolutionary methods—for slave oarsmen were as abnormal in Athens as cavalry oarsmen or coins of gold or plated copper—within the space of thirty days, 110 ships were got under way, and after they reached Samos over 40 others joined them. It is hardly an exaggeration to say that all Athens was on these vessels.

The battle that ensued (August 406 B.C.) took place at the Arginusae Islands, between Mitylene and the mainland. The fleet of Callicratidas was smaller—he had had to leave his lieutenant Eteonicus with 50 ships to watch Conon—but better trained and faster; and it was he who forced the fighting. The weather was unsettled and the wind came up strong from the north in the course of the day. The Spartans advanced in a single line but the plan they had formed of breaking through the enemy's front and turning his flanks so as, by using their superior speed in getting about, to catch his ships sidewise, the Athenians frustrated by arranging their triremes checker-board fashion in two lines. The brunt of the fighting fell on the wings, and there too the decision was reached. The death of Callicratidas—he fell overboard as his ship rammed an enemy—demoralized his left. His right the Athenians defeated; whereupon, when over 69 ships had been lost, the survivors fled, part to Phocaea and part to Chios. In a few hours Sparta had sent to an abhorred death five times as many Hellenic sailors as it itself had citizens.

The Athenians were led on this occasion by eight of the board of generals elected in succession to Alcibiades: Aristocrates, Diomedon, Pericles, Erasinides, Protomachus, Thrasyllus, Lysias, and Aristogenes, each of whom commanded a squadron of 15 ships in the action. Had they been able to act as one man at the moment of victory, the decision they reached, to proceed themselves to Mitylene to crush Eteonicus and detail trierarchs—among them Theramenes and Thrasybulus—to rescue survivors from the hulks of triremes still afloat (there were 12 of these; thirteen had already sunk), might perhaps have been executed. As it was, the sea became so rough before they were ready to undertake either task that no one could venture far from the Islands, whither unfortunately they had rowed without first picking up their shipwrecked comrades. Thus the casualties of the Athenians were doubled; and the squadron blockading Conon escaped to Chios, so that when reunited the Spartan fleet still comprised 100 ships.

There was no discounting the exploit of the Athenian sailors in winning again for Athens the mastery of the sea; and this the people recognized by giving to the slaves engaged liberty and

'Plataean' citizenship[1] as promised to them when they had enlisted. But it was felt that the generals had bungled badly in letting so many precious citizens drown and so many ships escape. So they deposed the entire eight of them, and concentrated the command of the fleet in the hands of Conon and two new generals. Two of the generals, Protomachus and Aristogenes, saw how the wind was blowing and went into exile. The other six returned and all eight were impeached. In the official report of the battle the generals had attributed to the storm the failure to rescue the survivors. This neither was nor seemed a wholly satisfactory excuse. It was to be foreseen that the clamour for victims, natural in the circumstances, would be directed against the trierarchs if it was not fixed on the generals. Hence Theramenes and Thrasybulus threw the weight of their political influence against their superior officers. Their thought was probably first and foremost to save themselves, *i.e.*, their lives and their political future. Of the two Theramenes, in view of his past, had the more to fear.

The Council it was that inaugurated proceedings in such cases and the Assembly that passed judgment. On their first appearance before the people, though Theramenes held them to their own excuse, the violence of the storm, and denied its validity, imputing criminal negligence instead, they made a good impression, and at the end of the day the Council was instructed to bring in a motion at a later meeting specifying how they should be tried. The delay proved fatal. In the interval the Festival of Kinsmen (Apaturia) occurred (October, 406 B.C.), at which the relatives of the men who had perished appeared on this wonted occasion of family reunion and rejoicing clad in black with their heads shaven. They were prevailed upon by Theramenes to bring their mourning with them to the trial. The effect was overwhelming. The Council was stampeded into proposing that without further discussion the people decide by a single ballot the guilt or innocence of all eight defendants with death and confiscation of property as the penalty. Lashed to fury by a councillor named Callixenus, who acted throughout as the mouthpiece of the mob spirit, the Assembly forced the withdrawal of a protest of illegality that would have stayed action, rejected alternate

---

[1] The citizenship ([Demosthenes] LIX, 104–6) given the Plataeans after 427 B.C. (p. 220 n. 1) was now exercised by them in a commonwealth of their own at Scione (p. 266). With them the emancipated slaves were associated as fellow citizens (Hellanicus, frag. 80). Cf. Busolt, *Griech. Staatskunde*, ii, p. 947. They all returned to Athens in 405 B.C. (p. 362).

procedures safeguarding the right, based unfortunately on a decree
—that of a certain Cannonus—and not on a law, of the accused
to further hearings and individual trials, and bullied the *prytaneis*
(with the single exception of Socrates) into putting the iniquitous
motion, thus affirming in fact, if not, as Xenophon reports, in so
many words, that it was intolerable for the demos not to be
permitted to do what it pleased. The motion being declared carried
(the voting seems to have been close), the ballot thus authorized
was taken and the verdict reached was guilty. It did not matter
that those condemned had gained a victory that saved Athens
from destruction in the greatest naval battle theretofore fought
by Greeks against Greeks. Those who had braved the anger of the
people were executed, among them Diomedon and Thrasyllus,
than whom none had done more for the salvaging of democracy
in Samos and Athens in 411 B.C.; and Pericles, son of Pericles and
Aspasia. Their chief fault, perhaps, was to have been eight when
one alone was needed.

IV. AEGOSPOTAMI

Cleophon seems not to have had a hand in this 'act of violent
injustice and illegality,' by which the citizen ranks, closed
temporarily by the naval crisis, were again rent into factions
freshly embittered. Archedemus, the Blear-Eyed, and not he, was
now (406–5 B.C.) the dispenser of the dole (*diobelia*); and at least for
the moment he seems to have ousted Cleophon from the favour of
the people. But what was needed for leadership was not their
favour but their confidence, and the Athenians had lost confidence in all their leaders. But not in themselves. What they
remembered was not the terror of June but the triumph of
August. And in this respect Cleophon was a representative man.
The Spartans had made Callicratidas admiral with the set purpose
of freeing themselves of Athens in order to free themselves from
Persia. They had failed to win release by battle; and, though not
crushed as in 410 B.C., they could continue the war only as
dependents of Persia. Rather than accept longer this humiliation
they tried again to make peace, and again they offered Athens the
only conditions possible—for them to give up Decelea and then
for each to retain what it held. The situation on both sides was
such as to command acceptance. For Athens had already staked
its last drachma on the fleet which, though victorious at Arginusae,
could not settle down for the recovery of any one of the lost allies
because it had to keep plundering many in order to subsist;
while the crews of Sparta's ships, after having been forced to

become agricultural labourers on the estates of the Chians in
order to avoid starvation, were with difficulty prevented from
massacring and looting their hosts when this resource ended.
But the folly of the Athenians is explicable only on their own
theory that those whom the Gods would destroy they first make
mad. Cleophon mounted the bema without laying aside his armour
and persuaded them to reject the tender of peace unless the
Spartans should 'let go all the cities.' Rather than do this the
Spartans came to terms with the Persians.

What Cyrus requested was the reappointment of Lysander, and
in this he had the support of all those in the Greek cities with
whom this skilful organizer had done business in 407–6 B.C.
A conference was held at Ephesus and a formal request was
preferred for Lysander's nomination. There were many in Sparta
whom his inordinate ambition and the dubious policy that inspired his intrigues troubled; and among them was the new king,
Pausanias, who in 408 B.C. succeeded his father Pleistoanax on
the throne of the Agiadae. But the refusal of Athens left no
alternative. To avoid the constitutional difficulty, yet achieve the
desired object, Lysander was given the subordinate office of
epistoleus and to it were transferred the powers of the *nauarch*.

He again made Ephesus his headquarters, and since Cyrus not
only gave him money, but, on going to Media to attend his father
on his death-bed, turned over to him the revenues of his province, he succeeded in a few months in doubling the number of
his triremes and attracting to his service rowers in abundance,
including many deserters from the enemy's ships and territories. Miletus he punished for its independent spirit by
treacherously contriving the massacre of the adherents of the
popular party and putting the government into the hands of a
blood-stained subservient oligarchy. His plan of campaign,
concerted with Cyrus, was to avoid fighting, and reduce the
Athenians to extremities by attacking their empire at its most
vulnerable points, taking pains that if driven to port it should be
where he could get supplies. So he slipped away from Ephesus
and took by storm a place on the Ceramic Gulf. Then, after a
détour to Rhodes, he doubled back and followed the coast of
Asia Minor to the Hellespont, which had probably been his
objective from the start. He found it unguarded. Supported by
an army that had been assembled at Abydos, he attacked and
captured Lampsacus. There ensconced, he would intercept the
Pontic grain-ships for the arrival of which Athens waited im-
patiently, if he were not completely contained by the Athenian fleet.

The Athenians now had six generals, Conon, Adeimantus, Philocles, Menander, Tydeus, and Cephisodotus, of whom Conon alone, and possibly Menander, had the experience necessary for so responsible a position. Their best leaders, Theramenes and Thrasybulus, they did not trust. Alcibiades 'the city loved and hated and wished to have again: it felt that in him it had reared a lion's whelp and should humour it: it detested one whose quickness in doing his country harm contrasted with his sluggishness in helping it.' And thus distracted by conflicting impressions it left him in Thrace. What the Athenians needed, Aristophanes told them in the *Frogs* (January 405 B.C.), was to cease employing scoundrels, forgive the victims of 'Phrynichus' wiles,' and, discarding their silly airs of superiority and exclusiveness, admit to their civic family not the Arginusae slaves alone but all who were ready to fight with them in the naval war. But they estimated Aristophanes more highly as a poet than as a statesman. They were now too poor to compete with the enemy in the market of naval reserves by offers of wages. Yet they could not require all Athens to continue sitting on the rowers' benches. Hence to deter the Greeks from serving with the enemy they authorized their generals, despite the protests of Adeimantus, to amputate the right hands of captured seamen. Philocles carried this policy to its logical conclusion by putting to death the crews of two enemy triremes he had taken. And so strong was the impression that Athens was invincible on the sea that during this summer the Athenian generals brought up the total of noncitizens in their service to more than 30,000.

They were engaged in an attack on Chios when they learned of Lysander's presence in the Hellespont. Since the grain-supply of Athens was a life interest, they hurried with their entire fleet of 180 ships to safeguard it. On discovering the enemy's position and purpose they brought their fleet to Aegospotami, and drew it up on the strand nearly opposite Lampsacus about five miles away. For four successive days they crossed the strait and found the Spartans in the harbour, in battle-order but unwilling to engage. Alcibiades, who knew from experience the craft and enterprise of Lysander and the thoroughness with which he had his fleet in hand, came down from his near-by castle and counselled the generals to withdraw their ships to Sestos, where supplies would be accessible and the danger of a surprise eliminated. But he was told to be gone, that they were in command and not he. They thought they had Lysander cornered. And in their eagerness not to let him go and their solicitude to keep the

Straits open, misinterpreting his restraint as fear, they neglected the most elementary precautions. Every evening, on the withdrawal of the Athenians, Lysander had had them followed, and on the fifth day, on learning that they had disembarked as usual and had straggled inland for their food, he launched a swift attack (September, 405), and caught the entire fleet, with the exception of Conon's squadron, off its guard. Almost without a blow he captured 160 triremes and shortly afterwards he 'collected' most of their crews. As an act of bloody reprisals the 3000 Athenians among the prisoners were executed. Of the generals captured Adeimantus alone was spared. Conon made his escape with a few ships.

Thus with the suddenness and unexpectedness of a clap of thunder from a clear sky the great war was over.

The Delian confederacy was a voluntary association, the Athenian Empire a creation of force. The Empire was destroyed not by *force majeure* but by bad management. The issue of the Peloponnesian War was not predictable at the beginning. Nor was it a certainty at any time prior to Aegospotami. But after the disaster in Sicily the most that Athens could do was to stave off defeat. The failure of the demos to realize this made the contest from then on a gamble, in which *Athens* risked not only the remnants of its Empire but its very existence, *Sparta* fleets to which it contributed virtually nothing but the command. In 407 B.C. Persia became the real adversary of Athens. It was a formidable adversary not so much because of its inexhaustible supply of money—though without this it would have been negligible—nor yet because it disposed of the services of Sparta, indispensable though these were for cloaking its designs and confining the war to the sea: it was formidable because with these advantages it was able to mobilize the naval resources of the Aegean basin lost to Athens by revolt and unpopularity. By mismanagement of the war, due, as Thucydides takes pains to point out, to defects of leadership, Athens gave its allies a chance to revolt. They were predisposed to take this chance by the oppressiveness of Athenian government. Whether they would have taken it earlier if the policy of Athens in their regard had been conciliatory instead of authoritative is a matter of opinion. By failure to make peace, due fundamentally to the incapacity of the demos (and of other less censured bodies politic for that matter) to gauge the foreign situation at critical moments more wisely than the statesmen to whom it gave its confidence, Athens continued the war until defeat became total and irremediable.

Defects of leadership are not a peculiarity of any one system of government; nor is democracy the only polity which has shown itself incapable of managing an empire. The profound significance of Aegospotami is that it divorced the cultural and political headship of Hellas.

V. THE SIEGE OF ATHENS

Two tasks confronted the victor. One—the creation of something to replace the fallen empire—will be considered elsewhere (see vol. VI, chap. II). The other was to liquidate the war with Athens itself. As a first step to a siege, which he considered inevitable, Lysander gave all Athenians scattered, settled, or serving abroad, the option of returning home at once or of suffering the fate of their fellow-citizens recently captured. Having every reason to take Lysander at his word, they did not hesitate, and the sea was quickly filled with shipping engaged in the transport to Athens, not of the supplies it needed, but of a population it could neither feed nor reject. Its most considerable element consisted of the colonists from Scione, Torone, Potidaea, Histiaea, Melos, Aegina, Lesbos, Naxos—men, women, and children, to make place for whom thousands of Greeks had been killed or enslaved.

After his escape from Aegospotami Conon went to Cyprus and entered into the service of Evagoras of Salamis, but he sent to Athens the dispatch boat *Paralus* with the appalling tidings. It was dark when it arrived at the Piraeus, and long afterwards one present on the occasion described how 'a sound of wailing marked the passage of the news from man to man up between the Long Walls from the harbour to the city. At Athens that night none slept.' The fate in store for them seemed to be the one they themselves had canonized for such occasions, the slaughter of adult males and the sale of women and children into slavery. This being so, they naturally decided to resist to the utmost; and to give effect to this decision they chose new generals, among them Eucrates, Nicias' brother.

The enemy's armies appeared first. The second Spartan king, Pausanias, levied the troops of the entire coalition (excepting those of Argos) and joined Agis, who moved forward from Decelea, in investing the city closely on the land side. Lysander's fleet approached more deliberately, driving before it as into a net a school of fugitives and finally anchoring off the Piraeus, 150 ships strong. The city had no defence against the weapon employed for its reduction—starvation; yet it stood firm, hoping, like Nicias before Syracuse, for a miracle. Meanwhile it consolidated its ranks. By an act as rare as it was merited it bestowed its citizenship on the Samians *en bloc* because they alone of their allies (fearing the vengeance of their oligarchs) held out against the common enemy. It reduced the likelihood of betrayal and at the same time sought to effect an *union sacrée* by restoring full citizenstatus to all the many who had lost it for any reason other than blood-guiltiness or treason.

The miracle was not forthcoming, only the terrible reality of starvation; and negotiations had to be opened. Athens offered to join the Spartan alliance if left in possession of its walls and land—a proposal which the ephors refused even to consider, requiring instead the tearing down of 2000 yards of each 'leg' of the Long Walls. But the Athenians regarded it as intolerable to be put thus permanently at the mercy of any superior land power, and imprisoned a Councillor, Archestratus by name, who urged acceptance. Cleophon, to whom dependence on Sparta signified the end of democracy and incidentally of his own political career, threatened to slay with his own hand anyone who mooted surrender and on his motion the people voted not to consider the matter. Cooler heads saw the unwisdom of slamming the door to thus definitely, and with their support Theramenes succeeded in having himself sent as an envoy to Lysander for the alleged purpose of sounding the Spartans further. His real object was to arrange with Lysander and the Athenian exiles in his train for the installation in Athens of a new government; and to reopen negotiations for the salvation of the city as soon as Athens was ready to see reason.

For three months he stayed away—detained against his will, according to outward appearances. Thus famine had full time to operate. Deaths became appallingly frequent. The *union sacrée* too broke down completely, if indeed it had ever come into being. The citizens fell apart into two distinct groups (each with a recognizable bifurcation into a right and left wing), the point of divergence being rather the form of government which submission to Sparta portended than the terms of submission themselves. To one group the abrogation of radical democracy, desired in differing degrees by Sparta and Lysander, was also desirable; and to make ground for it the oligarchic clubs, which had again got into touch with one another, set over themselves an invisible committee of five, styled ephors, with subordinates whose special mission was to organize the knights—now, as always, the part of the military establishment most amenable to 'aristocratic' intrigue. They made such headway, with starvation as their adjutant, in detaching men of moderation and men of no character from the democratic group that they won the Council for their purposes; and on being denounced by Cleophon as a nest of traitors, this body accepted a flimsy indictment brought against him and procured his condemnation by associating itself with the jurors designated to try the case.

Thus Cleophon paid for his mistakes with his life; and a politician who gambled as recklessly as he did with his country's existence earned his fate. But those who profited by having him removed from their path had less human sympathy and less honesty and patriotism than he had; and for all their superior training, knowledge, and insight, they too, with one apparent exception, erred in their judgment of the political situation. The one exception was Theramenes, who by studying Sparta as well as Lysander, his fellows as well as his experiences, mapped out a course that harmonized his own ambitions and principles with the public welfare—and proceeded to his death. The time was one of too much violence and uncertainty even for cunning, intelligence, and moderation.

On his return from Lysander, Theramenes, with nine others, was sent to Sparta with full powers to conclude a peace. That meant virtually the acceptance of Sparta's terms whatever they should prove to be. They were in fact harsher than those previously submitted—the dismantling of the Piraeus as well as the destruction of the Long Walls, the cession of all their cities (including Lemnos, Imbros, and Scyros), the return of their exiles, and the surrender of all their triremes beyond a number to be determined by Lysander on the spot, who subsequently fixed it at twelve. These conditions were in reality not ungenerous; and when Sparta submitted them to the Congress of its allies they were opposed by the Thebans, Corinthians, and many others, who demanded the uprooting of the entire Athenian population; and it was the insistence of Sparta alone that saved Athens from this fate. It was, Sparta affirmed, intolerable that a community should be destroyed which had done so much for Greece during the Persian invasions. That she left out of consideration who should occupy Attica if not the Athenians is hardly likely. At any rate she arranged to add further strength to her league by concluding on her own account an alliance with Athens, the terms of which Theramenes and his associates also carried back with them—that Athens should accept the military leadership of Sparta and make contributions of men and money as required, being otherwise self governing as of old. The ambassadors were met on their return by an anxious multitude; and though some opposition developed, the people were too overjoyed to be relieved from their sufferings not to ratify the treaties as they stood. And so it happened that on the 16th of Munychion (April) 404 B.C. 'Lysander sailed into the Piraeus, the exiles returned, and with much enthusiasm, to the music of flute-girls, they began to demolish the walls, thinking that that day was the beginning of freedom for Greece.'

VI. THE OLIGARCHY IN ATHENS

Operations against Samos required the presence of Lysander before he had found time to arrange matters in Athens to his liking; but the men whom the peace restored both of their own volition and to please their patron joined with the clubs in the city that were confederated under ephors, and, with Theramenes and his partisans, to establish an oligarchy there. The most reckless and gifted of the exiles was Critias, the son of Callaeschrus. He had been an associate of Alcibiades, and, like him, he had been accused of complicity in the mutilation of the Hermae. Like him too he had consorted with Socrates, acquiring dexterity in argument rather than solidity of thinking. He had dabbled in literature and wrote prose and verse with equal facility—elegies and tragedies, orations and treatises on government and science. His course during the revolution of 411 B.C. fell short of treason, not because of the moderation of his views, but because of the rupture of the conspirators with Alcibiades; on the setting-up of the Five Thousand it was on his motion that Alcibiades' enemy Phrynichus was attainted and Alcibiades himself recalled. On the restoration of democracy his leader either could not or did not protect him—an omission which Critias remembered later. In these circumstances a man with his past and connections—he belonged to the royal clan of the Codridae—was 'as one who had fallen among wild beasts,' to use the colourful language of his kinsman Plato, and he was exiled at the instigation of Cleophon. We next hear of him as fomenting a servile insurrection in Thessaly—an activity irreconcilable with his Athenian career, but not with his sophistic philosophy. He returned home infuriated at the *canaille* which had exiled him and ruined Athens; and he embraced the view, so agreeable to his lust for power, that the demos should be put down and kept down by the most merciless violence. Resolute and knowing his own mind, he forced his way into the management of the clubs and quickly became the real director of their activities.

He at first figured as a lieutenant of the peace-maker Theramenes, to whom naturally the task fell of inaugurating the
'ancestral constitution' (πάτριος πολιτεία), alluded to doubtless,
but not actually prescribed, in the treaty of alliance with Sparta, as
the concomitant of autonomy. It was not easy to stamp out
democracy in Athens. Even when the multitude was perishing
from starvation, opposition on its behalf had developed to the
acceptance of the peace; and significantly enough, it had
centred in the military authorities, the generals and taxiarchs of
the siege, respectable democrats like Strombichides, Eucrates,
Dionysodorus and others. Theramenes, accordingly, judged it
unwise to proceed with his task until the walls were cast down
and the city completely isolated from the sea. The delay encouraged the friends of democracy to form a 'conspiracy' for its
preservation, and as the weeks passed the danger grew that they
would raise the people against the Council and seize control of
affairs. Hence, when the work of demolition was finished, on an
information laid by a certain Agoratus, the Council had the group
of 'seditious' democrats arrested, and at a meeting of the people
held at Munychia, they were formally impeached.

It was probably at this same meeting, held, as on the inauguration of the Four Hundred seven years before, outside the walls of
Athens, and in the presence of the foreign soldiers garrisoning
the Piraeus, that the attack on democracy was pushed home. Nor
was the seizure of the popular leaders the only act of intimidation
practised. Lysander and a fleet had been sent for from Samos
to be present on the occasion. Thus safeguarded, Dracontides
introduced a motion to create a commission of Thirty to draft anew
'the ancient constitution' and govern the state meanwhile; and
when Theramenes, making little of the clamour that ensued,
'ordered' the people to accept the proposal, the Spartan con-
queror intervened to say that, since Athens had failed to demolish
the walls within the specified time, it had broken the peace, and
could escape the consequences only by changing its government.
The Thirty (three from each tribe; ten nominated by Theramenes,
ten by the ephors, and ten by those present) were thus constituted (summer 404 B.C., perhaps at the end of the official year
405–4). They were to be the instrument in Athens, corresponding to *decarchies* elsewhere (see vol. VI, p. 28) by means of which
Lysander planned to keep in his own hands the control of the
'liberated' world. The Thirty substituted new members for those
Councillors on whom they could not depend and continued the
rest in office for the coming year. To the Council thus recast and

voting openly under their presidency they conferred jurisdiction in high political cases. They filled the magistracies with men of their own choosing, and they created a committee of Ten, with Charmides at its head, to act for them in the Piraeus, now virtually a separate city. They annulled the laws by which in 461 B.C. the power of the Areopagus was destroyed and the authority of the courts extended (p. 99); and they cancelled ambiguous provisions in Solon's code. But they did not address themselves seriously to the task of constitution-making, on the completion of which their own power was to end.

Once in the saddle they fell to and cleansed the city of low politicians and sycophants, to the satisfaction of right-minded people generally; and, to strike at the root of professionalism in public life, they forbade anyone to teach the art of speaking—an interdict which was used to suppress criticism generally, notably in the case of Socrates. They also had the democratic leaders put to death. The task of maintaining the autocratic authority they had assumed the Thirty thought too much for the corps of 300 Floggers they had organized. Hence against the judgment of Theramenes they used the good offices of Lysander to have Sparta put at their disposal a garrison of 700 Lacedaemonian troops. Its commander (harmost), Callibius, a Spartan, made the Acropolis his barracks. Even if the Thirty had not been his paymaster he was too definitely Lysander's man not to support the oligarchy through thick and thin.

The stage was now set for Critias and the majority of the Thirty, which proved to be of his way of thinking, to carry out their programme of violence. They were not purely bloodthirsty and resentful: cruel from policy also, they struck down citizens whose sole offence was that they were qualified to become leaders of opposition. This was to treat as enemies men whom Theramenes and the moderates among the oligarchs regarded as actual or potential friends. And it raised squarely the issue, on which the opponents of democracy, now as in 411 B.C., were irreconcilably divided, whether the Thirty should rule tyrannically, or as the mandatory of a majority of citizens consisting of men qualified by property really to serve the state. It also brought to a head the struggle for power between Critias and Theramenes. Ousted from leadership in the Thirty by his more violent lieutenant, Theramenes looked to outside support. But Critias now held the whip-hand. He too conceded the necessity of surrounding the Thirty by a circle of citizen supporters; but he limited it, and with it citizenship, to 3000 trustworthy persons, of whom accordingly a catalogue was prepared. The clients of Theramenes were for the most part left outside. The next step was to disarm the disfranchised; and by trickery and the aid of the garrison this was done. With the concurrence, doubtless, of the Council and the Three Thousand a fiendish law was passed enabling the Thirty to put to death on their own authority anyone not on the catalogue and to confiscate his property, the privileged being safeguarded by the right to a trial before the Council.

To passion for revenge and political calculation, fiscal necessity—the Spartan troops had to be paid—and private greed came to be added as motives for the massacre and spoliation of defenceless Athenians. Nor were the resident aliens spared. The richest among them were assigned for seizure by the Thirty personally. In general, the practice was adopted of entrusting the most odious arrests to men whom the oligarchy wished to compromise. Lysias was one of the metics singled out for death, but by bribing his captor he escaped. Socrates quietly ignored the order given him to arrest Leon of Salamis. In a few months the number of victims rose to 1500—among them individuals universally respected like the Leon just mentioned and Niceratus, Nicias' son.

Against all this Theramenes protested. He could not doubt that he was taking his life in his hands; for he must have known that he would hardly be allowed twice to wreck a tyranny. But he believed that he could count on a majority of the Council. And so it proved. For the Five Hundred, before whom he was called to answer to the accusation of plotting to overthrow the government, were much more favourably impressed by the charges of ferocious folly he launched against Critias than by those of turncoat (*cothurnus*) and traitor preferred by Critias against him. But Critias did not allow them to acquit him. He brought armed men into the chamber, and, after striking Theramenes' name off the list of the Three Thousand, he pronounced the death-sentence on him in the name of the Thirty. The Eleven executed it. The leader of the moderates died with a jest on his lips—'a health'— of hemlock—'to the gentle Critias.' At the same time that they murdered Theramenes the Thirty purged the catalogue of all who had had a hand in the overthrow of the Four Hundred. Thereafter none but the privileged felt safe. Others fled from the city as opportunity offered, and the Thirty denied re-entry within the walls to all who left. The Piraeus became a place of refuge, but thither, as well as to their estates, the victims were followed, and the stream of fugitives was strengthened which flooded Thebes, Megara, Chalcis, Oropus and Argos with Athenians of every class and description.

Among those on whom the Thirty pronounced a decree of exile were Alcibiades and Thrasybulus. Others might live in Attica in the condition of Helots: for those put under the ban there was to be no asylum anywhere. To this end Sparta was found ready to collaborate with the government Lysander had established. It issued an order requiring under heavy penalties all the states in its Empire to hand over to the Thirty the Athenian exiles in their territories. Realizing his danger, Alcibiades fled from his stronghold in Thrace and sought the hospitality of Pharnabazus. But he was too dangerous a man to be allowed to live; and, notwithstanding that he and his host had recently exchanged pledges, when Lysander asked for his life, the Persian satrap was unable to refuse (404 B.C.). The Greek cities had more courage. Argos naturally declined to deliver up its exiles; and, in notable contrast to its vindictiveness toward Athens a few months earlier, Thebes did likewise. It was accordingly possible for Thrasybulus to find safety there—and assistance.

VII. THE FALL OF THE OLIGARCHY

In the early winter (December) of 404 B.C. Thrasybulus led a force of seventy men across the Boeotian frontier into Attica and seized Phyle, an impregnable position on Mt Parnes. The Thirty put the entire Three Thousand in motion against him, and (the futility of storming the place being at once disclosed) they set about enclosing Phyle with a wall, meaning, afterwards, to let a small force and starvation do the rest. But a heavy fall of snow forced them to give up the work. The respite permitted reinforcements to reach Phyle, and Thrasybulus soon had so many men—700—that he had need to take to plundering the country. To prevent this the Thirty stationed between him and Acharnae a force consisting of the Spartan garrison and two cavalry corps, but Thrasybulus attacked them at dawn after a night march and routed them, slaying one-sixth of the Lacedaemonians in the pursuit.

The Thirty tried to corrupt Thrasybulus, but without success. They then took two steps indicating alarm. They selected Eleusis as a place of refuge in case Athens should become too hot for them. To prepare it for future occupation they moved from it its adult male population, and to bind the entire Three Thousand by complicity in atrocious crime they required them to pass sentence of death on the whole body. The act was impolitic as well as inhuman; for instead of uniting to themselves all their fellow citizens it alienated a considerable fraction of them completely. Their other step was to evacuate to the Piraeus all the non-

privileged inhabitants of the city who had not yet departed of
their own volition—a precipitate expulsion of more than 5000
persons which removed one military danger by creating another.
It furnished to Thrasybulus an objective and the raw material for
an army. During the night of the fourth day after the surprise at
Acharnae he led his force, now increased to 1000, down from
Phyle, and, entering the Piraeus, he took possession of Munychia.
Critias at once marched from Athens to eject him, but though his
soldiers were much more numerous, they were met as they
advanced up the slope leading to the citadel by such a shower of
missiles that the hoplites of Thrasybulus were able to throw them
back with heavy losses, Critias himself and Charmides being
among the fallen. The death of their leaders ended the rule of the
Thirty, eight months only after its establishment (February
403 B.C.). The Three Thousand, or rather the 'innocent' among
them, did not care to bear responsibility for others' crimes now
that an accounting seemed due. They allowed their rulers to retire
to Eleusis and chose in their place a board of Ten, including
Pheidon, one of the Thirty, and Rhinon.

But the fear of an immediate *débâcle* proved groundless. The
Ten grasped the reins of government firmly, and, secure in the
knowledge that in combating Thrasybulus they had Sparta behind
them, they succeeded in getting the Three Thousand, despite
some desertions, to form an united front for the defence of their
privileges. Notwithstanding that leaders of moderate tendencies,
notably Theramenists like Anytus, Archinus and Phormisius, had
associated themselves with Thrasybulus, some of them even from
the Phyle days, there was not only too much bad blood, but also
too serious a divergence in political ideas, between the two major
parties for an attempt at reconciliation to be successful. So all
through the spring and well into the summer of 403 B.C. the
'men of the Piraeus' and the 'men of the city' waged desultory
warfare, while simultaneously the Thirty from Eleusis struck for
their own hand.

While the struggle remained indecisive, the Spartans had
nothing to gain by interfering. Eventually, however, the men of
the Piraeus got the upper hand. On the occupation of Munychia
they had opened their ranks to aliens, many of whom joined them
on the promise of being given equality with citizens (*isoteleia*).
And after repulsing the Thirty they had time to make soldiers out
of the citizen rabble they had found in the Piraeus. The Ten were
long formidable because of their superiority in cavalry, but the men
of the Piraeus, continuously reinforced by additions from within

and without Attica, gradually mastered the open country and finally closed in on the city and attacked the walls. There was nothing left for the Ten—and the Thirty—but to apply to Sparta for assistance; and there seemed nothing for Sparta to do but grant it. Such at least was Lysander's opinion. To him, as the emissaries from Athens represented, revolt against the oligarchy was rebellion against Sparta. So he had a loan of 100 talents made to the Ten and himself designated to raise an army for the suppression of the democratic rising in Athens. He made Eleusis his base of operations, and simultaneously his brother Libys, *nauarch* for the year, blockaded the Piraeus by sea with 40 triremes. Thrasybulus would have been quickly starved into submission had not unlooked-for help arrived.

For reasons discussed elsewhere (see vol. vi, p. 31) the power of Lysander was overthrown in Sparta at this moment. The new board of ephors for 403–2 B.C., contained a majority hostile to him. King Pausanias, to his great satisfaction, was authorized to raise a confederate army and take personal charge of the situation in Attica. The one thing certain was that he would not reinstate Lysander's men. This did not satisfy Corinth and Thebes. What they now desired, in view of the might and mien of Sparta, was that Athens should escape from Spartan dictation, *i.e.*, become an adjunct to Boeotia. They therefore refused to take part in Pausanias' expedition. On his arrival in Attica the king incorporated Lysander's army with his own. Overtures from the Thirty he rejected. With the less intransigent leaders of the Three Thousand, some of whom (Rhinon, for example) had been negotiating with the Piraeus on their own account, he established unofficial relations; and he used this means of organizing (under a committee of ten perhaps) a large part of the men of the city for a policy of reconciliation.

His first dealing had been with the men of the Piraeus, whom he had ordered on his arrival to disperse to their homes. When this request was ignored, he had sought to bring them to reason by threatening demonstrations, in the course of which he got involved more deeply than he intended and had to fight a serious battle in order to regain his prestige and bring this section of the Athenians to a proper realization of their position. Then matters came quickly to a head. Pausanias suggested terms of peace to the Athenian belligerents and forwarded to Sparta envoys from the Piraeus and spokesmen for his correspondents in the city to lay the proposals before his government. The Ten tried to tempt the Spartans into making a settlement more in the sense of Lysander's programme by putting themselves unreservedly in the hands of the Lacedaemonians and demanding that their adversaries do likewise. But the Spartan authorities stuck to their course and left the decision with Pausanias and fifteen Spartans whom they sent to join him in Athens. The terms of the settlement thus arrived at could not have consulted better the interests of Athens if they had been drawn up by its most sagacious and patriotic statesmen. In general they provided for the reinstatement of everybody in home and lands, with the hard, but necessary, proviso that sales of moveable property effected during the disturbance should be valid even when it had come on the market through confiscation; a complete amnesty for all that had happened during the suspension of democratic government, except in the case of the Thirty, the Ten, the Eleven, and the Decarchy in the Piraeus, who were, however, to enjoy it too provided they gave an accounting for their acts before courts empanelled from property owners; and in the case of those in the city 'who were afraid,' liberty to move to Eleusis, without loss of property, within a specified time after announcing their intention so to do, there to live as full-fledged citizens, free from Athenian control and interference.

VIII. THE RE-ESTABLISHMENT OF DEMOCRACY

The men of the Piraeus had gained the objects for which they were fighting—repatriation and democracy; and this they signalized by marching under arms into the city to offer sacrifices to Athena on the Acropolis. But they had had to swear, with the Lacedaemonians as witnesses, to lay aside all thoughts of revenge for the terrible wrongs they had sustained. Since, for reasons best known to himself, Pausanias marched his whole army off before their triumphal entry, their honour and discipline, and the resourcefulness and authority of their leaders, were put to a severe strain on this occasion and for some time thereafter. But the right of secession to Eleusis was a wholesome regulator. It lay within the possibilities that the division between Piraeus and city should be perpetuated in a schism between Athenians and Eleusinians which would give the Peloponnesians a bridgehead in Attica and neutralize effectively the power of the country. And this may have been in the back of Pausanias' mind. But the leaders of both parties joined to avert this disaster. The Ten stood their ground and, on submitting their accounts, they were acquitted—one of them, Rhinon, being elected general thereafter. Archinus above all others was the political strategist who fashioned the block of moderates—democrats and Theramenists—that carried Athens safely through this trying time. To allay the fears for their personal safety that were inclining many of the Three Thousand to emigrate to Eleusis, he suddenly shortened the time allowed to would-be secessionists to hand in their names, thus, at one and the same time, reducing the emigration to Eleusis to less nocuous proportions and strengthening the party in Athens opposed to democratic radicalism. The thought uppermost in the mind of Thrasybulus immediately after the return was to reward the non-citizens who had fought under his command. So without waiting for a Council to be constituted he laid before the Assembly a bill drafted in the non-chauvinistic spirit of Aristophanes (see above, p. 360), bestowing the franchise upon all of them—foreigners, metics, slaves. In the enthusiasm of the moment it was carried, but Archinus, mobilizing against it two kinds of exclusiveness— that of the aristocrats against the baser sort and that of the democrats against sharing their privileges with aliens—had it quashed on the score of unconstitutionality. The time was too critical to warrant any controversial innovations in the basis of citizenship. It was, of course, well known that Sparta viewed with disfavour the scope of the Athenian franchise; and, quite apart from oligarchs on principle, there were many in Athens too who, fearing for their own property if the vote and the ballot were left with the urban proletariat now that its means of subsistence was impaired by the loss of sea-power, sympathized with the Spartan desire to see citizenship withdrawn from the elements most likely to work for the recovery of empire. But notwithstanding that Phormisius, one of the chief artificers of the return, sponsored a measure for restricting citizenship to land owners, thus disfranchising 5000 Athenians, one quarter approximately of the total number, the people rejected it. Athens was set on remaining democratic, undivided and uncontaminated. It re-enacted the Periclean law of 451 B.C., and took account of the bereavements sustained by many families during the war and its calamitous aftermath, solely by confining the requirement, that both parents of an applicant for citizenship should be Athenians, to children born after the memorable archonship of Eucleides (403–2 B.C.).

A committee of Twenty (ten from each party perhaps) arranged for the selection of new Councillors and magistrates for the balance of the year, and for the election by the Attic municipalities of 500 *nomothetae* to take in hand a revision of the laws of Draco and Solon which uncompleted codification (see above, pp. 349 *sqq.*), loss of empire, and recent events necessitated. The Council organized and assisted the *nomothetae*, and a group of expert registrars (*anagrapheis*)—among them, as in 410–04 B.C., a certain Nicomachus—attended to the work of publication, which, complicated by the continuance of the legislative process, was spread over four years. Neither the resultant code, for which, as for all public documents from then on, the Ionic alphabet was used, nor the one it replaced has reached us except in disconnected fragments, so that we cannot say what changes in financial and military organization the imperial *débâcle* entailed, apart from the disappearance of Hellenotamiae, Hellespontophylaces, Episcopi, Phrourarchs, etc.

Otherwise the alterations discernible concern the administration of justice and reform of law. Their tendency was to remedy abuses which had appeared in the last days of democracy. By leaving the panels of jurors unassigned to specified tribunals till the moment of opening court and assigning them then by lot, the bribing of dicasts was rendered much more difficult, and the same end was served by introducing dicasts (if this was not done earlier) in place of *ephetae* (vol. IV, p. 30 *sq.*), into all the criminal courts except the one in which the Areopagus tried cases of wilful murder. A way was opened for impeaching evidence on the score of perjury before the verdict was returned and the sentence executed—a reform long overdue. The amnesty was covered without invalidating titles and adjudicated rights by making the laws applicable to public offences only when they were committed after the restoration, yet recognizing all legal decisions reached in private suits under the earlier democracy. To relieve the courts of the burden of civil cases, if not altogether, at least as concerned the sifting of pleas and the amassing of evidence, a well-articulated system of public arbitration was devised, the work being divided between a board of Forty, chosen annually by lot, and individuals, also designated for specific suits by lot from among all citizens in the sixtieth year of their age. Evolution must replace revolution. So to make sure that the laws were always fresh in the memories of citizens, and to guard against the accumulation once more outside the code, in the form of decrees, of what were virtually laws, the opportunity was taken, then or later, to adapt the existing machinery for amending the laws so as to ensure their being overhauled annually with a view to revision[1] if need be, at a meeting of the Assembly held each year on the 11th day of the first month. Certain fundamental ordinances were reaffirmed with emphasis—that laws should overrule decrees of the Council or Assembly; that, except when 6000 citizens voting secretly had so

---

[1] By *nomothetae* as theretofore, chosen however from among the dicasts. See Busolt, *Griech. Staatskunde*, ii, pp. 1011 *sqq.* Athens had had enough of autocratic *syngrapheis*.

decided, no law should be enacted in regard to single individuals; that account should not be taken of ordinances (laws and decrees) not included in the code. This done, Athens set out again on the great democratic adventure with an up-to-date, flexible constitution.

For two years the new régime laboured. Eleusis, where the rump of the Thirty ruled, made war on Athens. It was not easy for the democrats to let bygones be bygones; yet to do otherwise was to play into the hands of the Eleusinians, and, perhaps, of the Spartans. The leaders of the reconciliation had to exercise great patience, watchfulness, and mutual forbearance. It cannot be denied that they acquitted themselves with credit, and that the Athenians as a whole responded intelligently and patriotically to their leadership. The loan from Sparta was assumed as a public obligation notwithstanding that it had been recognized in the conventions as an obligation of the 3000 alone. Eratosthenes, one of the Thirty who stood his audit, was acquitted. Archinus took the lead in repressing vindictiveness. The validation of legal decisions in civil suits having left a loophole for sycophancy, he had an ordinance passed requiring the officers of the law to accept the amnesty as a bar to private actions contravening it; and he gave a salutary warning to the rancorous by having the Council condemn to death summarily the first citizen who violated his oath not to bear malice—an affirmation of revolutionary power on the part of this body which, on being repeated in the unlike case of Lysimachus, led to the enactment of a law, or more properly to the re-enactment of an old law, annulling the authority of the Council to pronounce sentences of death, imprisonment, or fines exceeding 500 drachmae, without appeal to the courts.

Finally in 401–0 B.C. the chance came to close the account with the Thirty. They were drawn into a trap and put to death; whereupon the Eleusinians too were amnestied, and reunited with their fellow Athenians. Then, and then only, the Athenians voted their thanks to the men who had overthrown the oligarchy—crowns of wild olive and 1000 drachmae for a monument to the hundred odd citizens who had initiated the movement; citizenship to the metics who had accompanied them on their daring night march to the Piraeus; equality with citizens (*isoteleia*), including rights of intermarriage, to metics who joined in the fighting thereafter; and lesser privileges, nicely adjusted to individual services, to the other aliens, free and unfree, who had deserved well of the republic. Thus Archinus (for this was his work) made at least partial amends for thwarting Thrasybulus in 403 B.C. Athens was again an undivided commonwealth.

CHAPTER XIII
THE AGE OF ILLUMINATION
I. THE REACTION AGAINST THE IONIAN PHILOSOPHY

THE speculations of the Ionian philosophers, their attempts to make the world intelligible (described above in vol. IV, chap. XV), had begun early in the sixth century, and by the end of the century had produced an intellectual movement which was spreading to nearly all parts of civilized Greece. We may call the period from about 530 to 400 B.C. Greece's Age of Illumination, an age in which reason was striving to assert her rule in every sphere, and many superstitions, inherited from antiquity, were being challenged and discarded. In this process of enlightenment two phases can be distinguished, and the dividing line may be drawn roughly about 450 B.C. About that time we become aware that a certain reaction has set in against Ionian philosophy and Ionian science. Some thinkers were still working on the old lines, like Anaxagoras, and it was probably just at this time that the brilliant theory of atoms was being elaborated in the brain of Leucippus (vol. IV, p. 575 *sq.*). But in the latter part of the fifth century the men of intellectual activity most prominent in the eyes of the public were not a Leucippus or a Diogenes of Apollonia but men who were most interested in other problems and who played a different kind of rôle. It was the age of the Sophists. The results of science were coming into contact with life. Hellas had passed into an age of sophistication.

There was, as has been observed above, a certain reaction against the earlier schools of philosophical speculation, and this reaction was probably due to Zeno of Elea more than to any other man. His penetrating and lively criticism of the conceptions of space, time, and motion which are fundamental in physics led to a scepticism which distrusted both cosmology and ontology, and the influence of Zeno was very wide. He influenced the intellectual activities of Protagoras, of Gorgias, and of Socrates, and the most impatient problem of philosophy was no longer, How was the world made? but How is knowledge of the world possible? Inquiry began to turn from the macrocosm to the microcosm; and concurrently problems of social conduct began to be recognized as problems on which there is as much room for argument and as little reason for dogmatism as in physical matters. It might be put that man was becoming self-conscious. Awareness of man's importance is the note of the beautiful ode of Sophocles which begins, 'Miracles in the world are many; there is no greater miracle than man.'

In considering the Hellenic culture of the fifth century, the extent of geographical knowledge must not be overlooked. Although at this stage the ideas of the Greeks as to the size and outlines of the inhabited world were slight and deficient compared with what they would be two centuries later, they had in the last few generations made great advances. Delphi was no longer the centre of the world; Phasis and the straits of Gades were no longer its extreme limits. The Milesian geographers had learned much about western Asia, and something was known of north-western Europe through the merchants of Massilia and the information they derived from the sailors of Tartessus. Pythagoreans had announced the discovery that the earth is round. Athens may be said to have taken the place of Miletus, but she did not carry on the Milesian tradition so far as the progress of geography is concerned. Geographical knowledge almost stood still till the end of the fourth century; the Ionian maps continued to be used. This pause was part of the reaction against Ionian speculation; we can see it in Herodotus who is always bent on criticizing the geographical views of Hecataeus.

II. THE SOPHISTS

The researches of scientific men in Ionia and in Magna Graecia had enlarged the range of knowledge and the number of subjects of which any one aspiring to be a man of culture must have some knowledge, and thus a demand arose for higher education—for instruction in astronomy, geography, mathematics, physics, history. This demand was met by the Sophists who were simply itinerant professors; collectively they performed the functions of a university in Greece. They were polymaths; the Sophist engaged to give a complete training to a pupil, to impart instruction in every possible subject and prepare him for a good life, and for all the duties devolving on a citizen. As to the cost of such an education we have not much evidence. Some of the Sophists had fixed charges. Those who had a big reputation like Protagoras could charge high fees and were probably employed only by people of some wealth. The fee of Euenus of Paros was 5 minae; that of Protagoras is said to have been 100 minae. Protagoras said himself that it was his habit, in case a pupil demurred to pay what he asked for, to request him to go into a temple and declare what he considered the teaching worth, and that he then accepted the sum named. He was said to have made more money than the artist Pheidias.

With the growth of democracies in so many cities, ability to speak in public and persuade your audience, whether in a court of law or in meetings of the Assembly or the Council or of a political club, was every year becoming more necessary for the man who wished to take part in public life, and desirable as a weapon of self-defence even for those who had no such ambitions. Instruction in the art of public speaking—rhetoric—involving not only diction and elocution but also the arrangement of the topics and arguments was much sought, and the art itself was carefully elaborated by its exponents. The greatest of these was the Sicilian Gorgias, who was one of the two most eminent Sophists of the fifth century. He made prose a fine art and this is his great title to be remembered by posterity. In his hands an oration became as technical a composition as a dithyramb. But while he was first of all a stylist and his true *métier* was the teaching of rhetoric, Gorgias, like all these eminent teachers, had studied deeply the knowledge and philosophy of the day. He had imbibed the scepticism and learned the method of Zeno and he wrote a metaphysical book defending three theses which to the ordinary man were quite incomprehensible and must have sounded appalling: Being does not exist; if it did exist, it would be unknowable; if it were knowable, the knowledge of it could not be communicated by one mind to another.

The oldest and perhaps the most eminent and typical of the Sophists was Protagoras of Abdera. He has a distinct and considerable place in the history of philosophy through having propounded the doctrine which may be called, in modern jargon, the subjectivity of knowledge and which he expressed in the formula 'Man is the measure of all things; of the being of things that are and of the non-being of things that are not.' The meaning of this pronouncement has indeed been disputed, but the most probable interpretation is that what appears to you to be true, is true for you, and what appears to me to be true, is true for me; '*é così se vi pare*'; there is no objective standard to which anyone can appeal. It seems not improbable that Protagoras may have drawn the conclusion that for practical purposes what seems true to the majority of minds is true. We do not know how he worked it out. But one important corollary was deduced. On every and any matter two opposite statements can be made and maintained, which may be distinguished as the stronger and the weaker, the stronger being that which is more commonly accepted, and generally taken for granted as true. But the weaker can always be strengthened by an able exponent. One of the things which can be learned and which an expert Sophist can teach is the art of strengthening the weaker statement—an art indispensable for success in public debates and in litigation— that dangerous art which is now called sophistry and which in the hands of a virtuoso can often secure the victory of injustice. This theory of the two statements was held up to ridicule in a scene of his *Clouds* by Aristophanes, where they appear on the stage personified as the Just and the Unjust Statement.

In ethics and politics, Protagoras does not appear to have taught or promoted any revolutionary doctrines but to have been content with explaining the value of conventional morality and the generally accepted views of political virtue. It is probable that in religion too he was conventional, so far as practice was concerned, and believed in the ethics of conformity, although speculatively he was a sceptic. He wrote a book *On the Gods*, of which one sentence is preserved: 'Concerning the gods I am unable to say whether they exist or not, nor, if they do, what they are like; there are many things which hinder us from knowing; there is the obscurity of the subject and the shortness of human life.' Such a statement, taken out of its context, was sure to be interpreted by the public as a shameless declaration of atheism; and the story was that he was prosecuted and condemned; whereas it may be compatible with a quite orthodox view if Protagoras admitted, as he probably did, that where there is no possibility of knowledge, one opinion may be more probable than another.

As the Sophists professed to train aspirants to a political career, they were considered experts in political science, and it is not surprising to find that Protagoras was chosen by Pericles to draw up a constitution for the colony which was founded at Thurii under Athenian auspices (443 B.C., above, p. 169).

Athens was now becoming the intellectual capital of Greece, the place where ideas were exchanged and Hellenic public opinion created, drawing from the periphery savants and thinkers of all kinds and appreciating them. It is significant that she became the chief centre of the book trade in Greece[1]. This position of his city as a centre and example of culture was what Pericles aimed at. Most of the Sophists of the fifth century are known chiefly in connection with Athens.

It has been said by a learned modern critic that the Sophists were 'half-professors, half-journalists.' It is difficult, however,

[1] In this her chief rival seems to have been Sicily.

to see the aptitude of the comparison with journalists. It is probable that most of them were publicists; that was a useful and natural form of self-advertisement, but there is nothing to show that even the less reputable were newsmongers or political propagandists. Another Sophist who enjoyed a high reputation at Athens, though his talents were more commonplace than those of Protagoras and Gorgias, was Prodicus of the island of Ceos. He was a man of delicate health and a pessimist who maintained that the bad things in men's lives are more numerous than the good. He specialized in the study of diction and wrote a treatise on synonyms; but that he taught cosmology at Athens and some theory of the origin of the world is evident from a play of Aristophanes whose Birds, when they propound a fanciful version of the genesis of the world, urge the audience to bid Prodicus pack with his preaching (Προδίκῳ κλάειν εἴπητε τὸ λοιπόν).

All the Sophists were versatile and could teach almost any subject but perhaps the most versatile of all was the fourth of the great Sophists of pan-Hellenic fame, Hippias of Elis. It was on his versatility that he particularly prided himself, and he certainly excelled in the variety of his accomplishments. He was proud to be self-sufficing; he could make all his own clothes. He kept abreast of mathematical research, worked at the classical problems of finding geometrical constructions to trisect an angle, and to 'square the circle' and discovered a new curve, the 'quadratrix,' with the help of which they might be solved. He worked also at antiquarian studies, and compiled a chronological list of victors in the Olympic games, with the help of the inscriptions on their statues in the Altis (see above, vol. III, pp. 762 *sqq.*), and so laid the foundations for the later Greek system of dating by Olympiads which was first introduced by the historian Timaeus. Two other names among the prominent Sophists may be mentioned, Antiphon of Athens (not to be confounded with the orator and politician) and Thrasymachus of Chalcedon.

The considerable demand for the education which such teachers could give shows how enlightenment was spreading in Greece, and nowhere perhaps are the rationalistic tendencies of the time more strikingly shown than in the rise of the new medical school of Cos, inaugurated by Hippocrates, who was born probably about 460 B.C. and had been profoundly affected by the scientific speculations of the preceding generation. His treatise on 'Airs, Waters, and Places,' dealing with the effects of climate and locality on the human organism, shows a wide philosophical view reaching beyond the ordinary outlook of a medical practitioner. He and his school emancipated themselves from old superstitions, and a religious man of the stamp, say, of Nicias, would have been quite justified in calling them godless. They did not believe that particular diseases were divine visitations. Epilepsy had always been regarded as sent direct from heaven; its name in Greek was 'the sacred malady' (ἱερὰ νόσος). The following comments on this belief indicate the spirit of the new school, and are probably due to the master himself.

'With regard to the so-called "sacred disease" it appears to me to be in no respect more divine or sacred than other diseases, but to have a natural origin like other complaints. Men regard its nature and cause as divine, from ignorance and wonder because it is not like other diseases; and its divine character is maintained because men find it difficult to understand and easy to cure, since the means used for curing it are purifications and incantations. But if it is considered divine because it is wonderful, then sacred maladies will be numerous, not merely one. For I will show that there are other maladies just as wonderful and amazing which no one considers sacred. Quotidian, tertian and quartan fevers appear to be as sacred and as much sent by a god as this disease, even if they be not wonderful. They who first consecrated this disease appear to me to have been men of the same kind as the magicians and purifiers and mountebanks and impostors of the present day who pretend to be extremely religious and to have greater knowledge than others. They use the divinity as a cloak and screen to cover their own inability to benefit the patient, and to hide their ignorance, and consider this affection "sacred".'[1]

The revolution in medicine by the adoption of the principle that diseases are always due to natural causes only is one of the most impressive signs of the growth of the rationalistic temper. The same spirit manifested itself in the criticism of legendary traditions. The first drastic critic of Hellenic mythology had been Xenophanes, but a tendency to deal more or less freely with myth and not to believe all that is handed down had appeared in Stesichorus and appears in Pindar, neither of whom had heterodox inclinations. The kind of speculation which would finally be systematized by Euhemerus had already begun; a well-known example is 'the story of Heracles' by Herodorus who, living towards the end of the fifth century, attempted to produce a biography of the hero that should be humanly credible by explaining away incidents that were plainly miraculous. But this

[1] Περὶ ἱερῆς νόσου *ad init.*

sophisticated temper is most clearly and fully shown by the historians, Herodotus who rebels against accepting things that are miraculous or incredible and tentatively explains them away, and Thucydides who silently and magisterially ignores them.

III. BLASPHEMY TRIALS AT ATHENS

In such an age disturbance was naturally caused in many Hellenic cities to old beliefs and prejudices, outraged and endangered by new, subversive ideas. Of this conflict it is at Athens that we can particularly find traces. At Athens during the second third of the century, the leading statesman's personal interest in philosophical questions, his belief in expert knowledge, his freedom from prejudice must have helped sensibly towards the realization of his great aim to make this city the centre of Hellenic enlightenment, and his political opponents found it easy to excite ill-will against him on account of his eccentric intellectual proclivities. Two of his intimate friends were Anaxagoras the physicist and Damonides, the expert in music, and it was believed that both of them advised him on political matters. It can be imagined with what resentment an Aristides or a Cimon would have spoken of 'those damned professors' being consulted or allowed to interfere in politics. Both these friends of Pericles suffered. Damonides was ostracized[1].

It seems to have been early in the political career of Pericles[2] that Anaxagoras was prosecuted for irreligion, and his accusers went to some trouble in the matter. We do not know what particular offences were comprised under the name *asebeia*, 'irreligion' or 'impiety,' by the laws of Solon, but as the law stood, Anaxagoras had done nothing to expose him to the charge, for in order to make him liable to prosecution it was found necessary to pass a special decree through the Assembly, which had the effect of widening the definition of 'impiety.' This decree was introduced by one Diopeithes and it authorized the impeachment of persons who do not conform to the religious observances of the city, or who teach doctrines concerning things in the sky. The general public in Athens doubtless regarded the doctrines of Anaxagoras, who denied that the sun and the moon are divine beings, as extremely irreligious, just as to-day many people in the United States of America consider Darwinism irreligious and

[1] Aristotle, *Const. of Athens*, XXVII. It is virtually certain that he was the same as Damon, the musician.

[2] A date, not later than about 450 B.C. has been argued for by A. E. Taylor, *C.Q.* XI, pp. 81 *sqq.*; see vol. IV, p. 569 *sq.*

would like to suppress as illegal the teaching of Evolution. But Anaxagoras would probably have been suffered to live and speculate in peace if it had not been for his friendship with Pericles. It is to be noted that the charge of irreligion was reinforced by a charge that he had intrigued with Persia. The impeachment of the philosopher has always been accounted for as an attempt of political opponents to discredit that statesman. Anaxagoras was condemned to death presumably, and all Pericles could do was to aid him to escape from Athens. He withdrew to Lampsacus where he was welcomed and there spent the rest of his life. It is worthy of notice that in this enlightened age, the study of astronomy was forbidden for nearly half a century (up to the archonship of Eucleides in 403 B.C.) in the city which was the centre of Greek culture.

During the latter part of the fifth century there were some other impeachments for irreligion at Athens, and of these we know even less. There was the case of Aspasia; we are not told of what particular blasphemous acts or words she was accused, but the charge of impiety was reinforced by a charge of a totally different kind (see above, p. 175). Then there was a certain Diagoras of Melos (said to have been a dithyrambic poet), who was prosecuted apparently for making disrespectful and blasphemous observations about divinities and ceremonies which were recognized by the Athenian state[1]. He was declared an outlaw at sometime after the reduction of his native island (p. 281), but his name had somewhat earlier become associated with atheism and in the *Clouds*, performed in 423 B.C., Aristophanes can speak of Socrates as 'the Melian,' with this innuendo. The other recorded prosecution is that of Euripides[2], possibly the same time as the *Clouds*. The accuser of Euripides was no less a person than Cleon the politician. But the prosecution seems to have failed; nothing happened to interfere with the usual activities of the poet. It is quite possible that Cleon was a man of very orthodox beliefs, who hated the advanced views of Euripides and considered them dangerous to society. The extreme democrats who came of the tradesman class, like Cleon and Lysicles, Eucrates and Hyperbolus, might resort to the Sophists to learn rhetoric and political craft but were doubtless as prejudiced against freedom of speculation in matters of religion as old-fashioned conservatives like Nicias. It is however quite possible that the charge of blasphemy may have been rather a pretext than the true reason, which may have been the desire of

[1] [Lysias], VI, *Against Andocides*, 17 sqq.
[2] Satyrus, *Pap. Oxyrh.* IX, p. 153.

silencing an influential critic who had access to the ears of the public, and whose ideas of justice and humanity were outraged by some political acts of Cleon, as they assuredly must have been by his proposal to put to death the population of Mitylene (see above, p. 217 *sq.*).

Another blasphemy trial has been recorded, but the record is open to suspicion. Protagoras is said to have been indicted for irreligion, on account of his treatise *On the Gods* (see above, p. 379), by Pythodorus and to have escaped from Athens before the trial came on, and the story adds that all copies of the book that could be found were burned publicly in the market place. The occurrence was dated at the time of the oligarchic revolution of 411 B.C. and what we otherwise know of the chronology of the Sophist's life makes the whole story dubious[1].

So little information is preserved as to the details of any of these prosecutions that it is difficult to judge them, especially as we do not know the laws of Solon on the offence of *asebeia*, or precisely what that term included. But our short review of the cases recorded seems to point to the conclusion that under the early Athenian democracy there was nothing that could be called a policy of religious intolerance, and that when a prosecution for blasphemy occurred there was usually some other interest than that of religion in the background.

It is only in a highly sophisticated society that it would occur to people to ask the question whether punishment is justifiable, and on what grounds. It is still debated, and it was debated in the fifth century B.C.—probably for the first time in man's history —by Pericles and other thinkers (φροντισταί). The vindictive or retributive theory which is the primitive and natural view was considered unsatisfactory, and it is interesting to find that in the speech placed by Thucydides in the mouth of Diodotus (see above, p. 218), the speaker, discussing punishment, ignores entirely the retributive theory and tacitly assumes that the only reason for punishment is the prevention of crime[2]. This is what he says: 'no law will ever prevent people from committing offences and doing wrong to others, whatever penalties it impose.

---

[1] Diogenes Laert. IX, 54, is the chief source (see also Sextus Emp. *adv. math.* IX, 55, 56). See Burnet, *Greek Philosophy*, I, p. 111 *sq.*, for reasons for rejecting the story with which the present writer is disposed to agree. If the prosecution happened, it must have been before 411 B.C., see above, p. 279.

[2] It may be that (as Mr Cornford has suggested) it was Protagoras who propagated the deterrent theory (cp. Plato, *Protag.* 324). It would be interesting to have the criminal law of Thurii.

It is the nature of all men, individually and collectively, to do wrong. Society, in the endeavour to suffer less injury from evildoers, has exhausted the whole gamut of punishments. In ancient times punishments were lighter; as time went on, they were made severer, and now death is the penalty in most cases, but crimes are still committed. Something more fearful than death must be discovered to outweigh the motives of desire and hope which prompt evildoing.'

Another question which exercised men's minds and lent itself to sophistical discussion was the justification of law, as against nature, which is violated for instance by the restraints which law lays upon those who are stronger and abler than their fellows, thus preventing them from reaping the fruits of their superior strength and ability. The right of the superior man to exercise tyranny and commit acts of injustice could be defended by an appeal to nature, and the prevailing doctrine of *Equality* of rights in a community be discredited as a principle which had no other basis than an unnatural convention. The best presentation of the argument in favour of the superior man is that which Plato puts in the mouth of Callicles in the *Gorgias*.

Of the Athenian representatives of the Illumination, who were active during the last thirty years of the fifth century, the three names most eminent and most important for posterity are Socrates, Euripides, and Thucydides. Of these, Thucydides, the founder of critical history, was then still obscure, composing his work in exile, and we know little of him personally. The two most important things we know about him are, as will be shown in the following chapter, that he would not have the gods and would not have women at any price in history. They both represented the irrational, and this was the age of reason. Of Euripides, whose influence in literature was to be immense for centuries after his death, we know little, apart from his extant plays; these show us that he was a man unchained by conventional views, that he was not a sound polytheist, that he was sceptical about oracles and omens, that he looked with wavering complacency on the institution of slavery, that his men and women were in the habit of saying things which provoked the audience to think dangerously. Of Socrates we know a good deal, much more than we know of any other man of the time. His trial and death have always been remembered as one of the notable events in the history of civilization.

IV. THE LIFE AND DEATH OF SOCRATES

The book of Xenophon on the life and teaching of Socrates, known as the *Memorabilia*, would, if it stood alone, give us little idea of what Socrates was like, and no idea of the secret of his greatness. Xenophon belonged (probably for a very short time) to the Socratic circle, but he had no notion of what philosophy really means and but a slight first-hand knowledge of the master. He produced a portrait such as a journalist with a commonplace mind might contribute to a gallery of 'good men,' and in his endeavour to show that Socrates was a good man he succeeds in concealing the fact that he was a great man. Most of the anecdotes he tells are uninstructive or insignificant, and some, as edifying stories are apt to be, simply tedious, like the remonstrances of Socrates with his son Lamprocles who could not put up with the rough side of his mother Xanthippe's tongue. Discerning as Xenophon was in many practical things he displays conspicuous want of discernment here: and for appreciating the personality of Socrates his book is almost negligible, while for most of the bare external incidents of his life that are interesting and which a biographer ought to supply, we go to him in vain[1]. He was not present at the trial of Socrates.

It is in the *Dialogues* of his companion Plato that a figure probably resembling the real Socrates appears. There we find his *animae figura*, his mind and methods, and the features of his personality, and also many details of his life. At all events, it is very difficult to resist the impression that the Platonic Socrates is a genuine life-like portrait of the original man, however unsocratically Platonic may be the argument and ideas of which he is made the spokesman.

Socrates was born about 470 B.C., and since he served as a hoplite he must have inherited some property from his father, Sophroniscus. He is said to have possessed a house and a capital sum of 70 minae which was invested for him by his friend Crito, who belonged to the same deme (Alopece). He witnessed the development of the Athenian democracy under Pericles and lived through the Peloponnesian War, serving in some of the earlier campaigns. He was a man of strong physical constitution, and of eccentric appearance and habits. His features are well known from portrait busts which are probably faithful enough to reality. With his flat nose and prominent eyes he was com-

---

[1] This has been shown by A. E. Taylor, *Plato's Biography of Socrates*, pp. 35 *sqq*.

pared by his contemporaries to a satyr. He was subject to trances of meditation; when rapt in thought he would stand for hours, unconscious of what was going on around him. He said that from his childhood he used to hear from time to time the monition of an inner voice; its monitions were always negative, never prompting him to an action, but always restraining him from doing things.

What we know of the external events of his life is not a great deal but it is interesting. In his youth he was a pupil of Archelaus, who was a disciple of Anaxagoras, and accompanied him to Samos in 440 B.C. when the Athenians were blockading it. In 437–6 B.C. he may have served as hoplite at Amphipolis[1], and in 432 B.C. he served at Potidaea; again in 424 B.C. at Delium where he exhibited remarkable presence of mind in the retreat. On these military occasions he showed extraordinary powers of endurance in sustaining cold, hunger, and fatigue; barefooted in a severe frost he could outmarch the other soldiers who were shod.

Perhaps[2] it was not till he was an elderly man that he was called upon to perform any public duty, beyond serving in the army. In 406 B.C. he was a member of the Council of Five Hundred, being one of the fifty representatives of his tribe (Antiochis). It was the year of Arginusae, and when the unhappy Generals were tried, Socrates was the only member who stood out in refusing to agree with the illegal resolution that all should be tried together (p. 358). Under the Thirty he risked his life by refusing to carry out an order which was illegal (see below, p. 391). In all the public affairs in which he happened to be concerned he displayed moral and physical courage and respect for the laws of his city. Thus remarkable for courage and justice, Socrates was no less distinguished for his sobriety and temperance, but he was not an ascetic nor a spoilsport. He would take part in potations, but his head was strong, and he was never the worse for them.

Athenians had taken no part in the scientific speculations which had been so vigorously pursued by men of Ionia and in far western Greece. Archelaus, the instructor of Socrates, was the earliest, and not a very eminent exception. The sharp intellectual curiosity of Socrates was accompanied by a sane spirit of scepticism which was confirmed by the influence of Zeno. He cannot have been much over twenty when he came under that influence which was powerful in determining the direction of his thought.

[1] See Burnet's note on Plato's *Apology*, 28 E, p. 120.
[2] Perhaps; for it is possible that he served on the Council before 406, at some unknown date; see Burnet in his edition of Plato's *Apology*, p. 133.

Parmenides, with his young friend Zeno, may have visited Athens not long after 450 B.C. and, if so, every Athenian of inquiring mind was interested in their visit. In any case, Zeno seems to have resided at Athens for several years; he was the inventor of dialectic and Socrates learned his method.

In the course of time a small circle of friends gathered around Socrates, drawn to him by the stimulus of his conversation. Knowledge he consistently professed himself unable to impart, and these friends were associated with him not as disciples but as fellow-inquirers. Their inquiries appear to have been chiefly concerned with mathematical and physical questions, the doctrines of Anaxagoras and Archelaus and Diogenes of Apollonia and of Pythagoras. In fact during the first half of his life the studies of Socrates were devoted chiefly to physical science; it was in his later years that he turned to the logical and ethical problems with which we chiefly associate his name.

Socrates and his circle became notorious in Athens as the Thinkers (φροντισταί), and comic poets seized on them as an obvious and legitimate subject for ridicule. In 423 B.C. Ameipsias produced his *Connus*, in which the chorus consisted of Thinkers and Socrates was derided, and in the same year was acted the *Clouds* of Aristophanes in which the scene was laid in the Thinking-shop (φροντιστήριον) of Socrates and his fellow-workers.

The most devoted in this group of students was a certain Chaerephon who adored Socrates so sincerely that he went to Delphi and put to the oracle the amazing question 'Is any man wiser than Socrates?' More amazing still was the categorical answer of the oracle, without any reservations, 'No one is wiser.' Socrates said that he was greatly puzzled by this reply, being acutely conscious how little he knew. If the oracle were true, it must mean that others were not so wise as they seemed, or imagined themselves to be; and in order to test its truth, he states that he went about questioning and cross-examining persons who were eminent as proficients in their special subjects—politicians, poets, handicraftsmen. None of them stood the test; they were all convinced that they were wise, but none possessed more wisdom than Socrates himself, but he was superior in that he was fully aware of his own ignorance. In this way the oracle was justified. We do not know at what time it was given, but in the later portion of his life Socrates seems to have spent much of his time, not only in his accustomed haunts, the gymnasia of the Academy and the Lyceum, but also in the market-place and the workshops of artisans, cross-examining people and exposing their erroneous convictions that they were wise, thus fulfilling, as he put it, a duty imposed upon him by the god. Defending himself at his trial he said 'People suppose that I am wise myself in those things in which I convict another of ignorance. They are mistaken. The god alone is wise, and his oracle declares that human wisdom is worth little or nothing, using the name of Socrates as an example. That man is wisest who like Socrates knows that he is worthless so far as wisdom is concerned. The disgraceful ignorance is to think you know what you do not know.' Sceptical as Socrates was and always careful to appeal to reason, we cannot fail to see, in some parts of his defence, that there was a side of his nature which was moved by reasons that reason does not know.

In all ages of active progress, the warfare between the ideas and fashions of a young critical generation, and the old strongly entrenched opinions and customs which the innovators mock and assail, always presents amusing and humorous pictures which can furnish material for comedy. Comic poets can laugh impartially at the extravagances and the prejudices of both the combatants. If Aristophanes held up to ridicule the scientific Thinkers and the modern critics of society, he did not spare the praisers of the past, the old fogies whose ideas are out of date (ἀρχαϊκὰ φρονοῦντες) who bore you with faded memories of the veterans of Marathon, and descant on bygone virtues and modern degeneracy.

We are told nothing of personal relations between Socrates and Pericles, but it is difficult to think that they were not acquainted. Socrates, though he belonged to a different class of society, had such a high repute as a thinker and talker that he could hardly have failed to arouse the curiosity and interest of Pericles, and they had many common friends. On the other hand, we hear of an intimacy between Socrates and Aspasia[1], who, it was even supposed, gave him instruction in the art of rhetoric.

Though Socrates consistently disclaimed the possession of knowledge and therefore of the power of imparting it, he was a master of dialectic, for which he had a natural gift, and he was really teaching all the time, disguising the instruction and the ideas which he communicated under the form of question and answer. Many young men attached themselves to him and were his constant companions, and among them were the men, both Athenians and foreigners, who in the next generation were to be

---

[1] Aeschines wrote a Socratic dialogue *Aspasia*. See also the *Menexenus* which U. von Wilamowitz-Moellendorff has ingeniously defended as Platonic (*Platon*, II, pp. 126 *sqq.*).

the great thinkers of Greece, the founders of philosophical schools, each emphasizing according to his own temperament a different side of the master's teaching. Plato, son of Ariston, the greatest of them all; Antisthenes, a poor man, who founded the school of the Cynics, which was the parent of Stoicism; Aristippus of Cyrene, whose Cyrenaic school was to be the parent of Epicureanism; Eucleides of Megara; Phaedo of Eretria; Aeschines, generally called 'the Socratic,' to distinguish him from Aeschines the orator. Thus Socrates was in some sense the ancestor of all the later philosophies of Greece. Outside this circle of companions, who were virtually disciples, his society was sought by men who were not interested much in philosophical questions but who were interested in listening to him cross-examining people and perhaps hoped to learn the secret of his skill. Two of the most distinguished were the versatile man of letters, Critias, and Alcibiades, of whom the second was an ardent admirer and an intimate friend of the philosopher. It was natural that Socrates should, in the popular mind, have to bear some ill fame for associating with these enemies of the democracy and be held responsible for their mischievous conduct. Although he was always loyal to existing authorities he never concealed his unfavourable opinion of democracy, which must have seemed to him an irrational form of government; Alcibiades called it bluntly 'acknowledged folly[1].'

Throughout the Peloponnesian War Socrates had with perfect impunity pursued his unpopular mission. But under the restored democracy it seemed to some of the democratic leaders that he was a dangerous and insidious anti-democratic influence and that it was desirable to silence him. The fact that he had remained at Athens unharmed during the government of the Thirty could not be made a charge against him on account of the amnesty. As a matter of fact he had barely escaped with his life from the despotism of the Thirty. Two of these oligarchs had been his friends, Critias the leader, and Charmides the uncle of Plato, and knowing that he was no admirer of the democracy they thought they were sure of his adhesion. They did not realize the unshakable strength of his respect for law and his love of justice. But they would not tolerate free speech and Critias thought it well to warn the philosopher that his discussions with the young men who sought his society must cease, and the government then made an effort to associate him with their unjust and tyran-

[1] Thucydides VI, 89, in the speech at Sparta, probably a genuine phrase of Alcibiades.

nous acts. The tyrants ordered him and four others to go to Salamis and arrest there a certain Leon whom they had resolved to put to death. Socrates said nothing and simply went home. He would have been executed for his disobedience to the government, if it had not fallen. This notorious incident however did not convince the people in power that Socrates stood quite outside party sympathies, and cared only for justice and right. They considered him disloyal to democracy, and that his criticisms were more to be feared than the plots of an oligarchical conspirator. It was therefore deemed highly desirable to rid Athens of a citizen whose influence and fearless tongue were felt to be a danger, though he took no part in politics and was the least likely of men to do anything contrary to the law. Anytus, an honest and moderate democrat and at this moment perhaps the most important Athenian statesman next to Thrasybulus, was the prime mover in preparing a prosecution intended to silence the embarrassing philosopher. No one was more determined than Anytus to observe honestly and to interpret strictly the terms of the amnesty; so that he was concerned carefully to keep out of sight the political motive for the action. He decided that the best ground of attacking Socrates successfully would be irreligion; it was common knowledge that the philosopher was far from orthodox. Accordingly an arrangement was made with a minor poet named Meletus, who was a fanatical champion of religion[1], that he should bring against Socrates a public suit for irreligion (γραφὴ ἀσεβείας) and that Anytus should support it by acting as an advocate for the prosecution (συνήγορος). Anytus associated with himself a second advocate, a rhetorician named Lycon of whom otherwise we know nothing.

Legal actions having to do with religion came into the court of the King archon. The charge which Meletus lodged against Socrates was formulated thus: 'Socrates is guilty of not worshipping the gods whom the city worships, and of introducing religious novelties. He is guilty also of corrupting the young men.' This accusation seems to prove that neglect of the worship of the

---

[1] There is a difference of opinion on the identity of this Meletus with the man who later in the same year, 399 B.C., prosecuted Andocides for impiety and part of whose speech is preserved among the works of Lysias (*Or.* VI). That two men of this name should have brought actions for impiety— such actions were not very frequent nor was the name very common—in the same year seems unlikely. It is interesting to observe that in this trial also Anytus was concerned, not however on the side of Meletus, but as a witness for Andocides, and his evidence seems to have secured an acquittal.

gods was an indictable offence under the laws of Solon; for no one could now be indicted under the decree of Diopeithes which had been passed to meet the case of Anaxagoras, inasmuch as the effect of the settlement of 403 B.C. was that no prosecution could be based solely on one decree passed before that date (see p. 375).

Meletus, in the writ of indictment, named death as the penalty which he demanded, for irreligion was one of the offences for which there was no punishment fixed by the code; the court itself determined the penalty on each occasion. But the court was limited to a choice between two penalties, that which was demanded by the prosecutor and one which it was the right of the prisoner himself to propose in case he were found guilty. It was the prisoner's interest to name a substantial penalty milder than that named in the indictment, yet not so light that it could not be entertained by the jury. A result of this curious judicial method was that the prosecutor generally assessed a penalty greater than he expected or wished to inflict. This is emphatically a case in point. There is no reason to suppose that Anytus wished Socrates to be put to death. It was doubtless expected that if he were convicted he would, as he had a right to do, propose exile as an alternative penalty and the court would assuredly be satisfied with that. To have him out of Athens was the object.

Our knowledge of this famous trial is derived from one of the most memorable and impressive books in the literature of the world, Plato's *Apology of Socrates*. The view that it was Plato's own composition used generally to be held although it was never doubted that it was based on the facts of the trial, but some critics now believe that it is the actual speech of Socrates, edited by Plato for publication, and as near to what was said as, say, a speech of Demosthenes or Cicero in its published form to the speech the orator actually delivered. The truth probably lies between these two views. We cannot suppose that the prisoner was allowed to make an address to the court after the sentence was passed. The epilogue is an addition imagined by Plato, an artistic and moving conclusion. If this is admitted, it must also be allowed that Plato may have taken other liberties with the Defence; he may have left out parts of it and considerably expanded other parts. The most grave and perilous of the charges brought against Socrates was that of being a corrupter of youth. That would count for much with the judges because they knew that leading politicians who were enemies of the democracy had cultivated his society—Critias, Alcibiades, Charmides. But this was just the proof of the accusation which Meletus and his two advocates were prohibited from touching on. The amnesty forbade them to pronounce these names. They must however have made an attempt to show in what ways the conversation of Socrates misled and injured the young men. Of this there are no indications in the Defence according to Plato, nor can we discover from that defence how Meletus explained what were the strange religious practices which he alleged that Socrates introduced, as he assuredly must have done, producing some proof of his statements. It seems to follow that the *Apology* does not supply a full account of the trial[1].

Socrates was found guilty by a majority of 60 votes, for he mentions in his Defence that he would have been acquitted if 30 of the votes recorded against him had been for acquittal. It is probable, though not certain, that the number of Athenians in the jury appointed by the king to try the case was 501. If that was so, 225 must have voted in his favour, and it is quite likely that he would have been acquitted if he had assumed a different attitude and had really been concerned to secure a verdict of 'not guilty.' But he adopted throughout a very high tone, which was far from calculated to conciliate the court though he expressed himself with his usual urbanity and politeness. He had not condescended to make the conventional appeal to pity by bringing into court his wife and children to excite the compassion of the judges by family tears, as was almost invariably done by prisoners tried on a grave issue, and the omission of which many of the judges might consider an affront to themselves.

When the verdict of his guilt was pronounced, it was for Socrates to submit a punishment less drastic than death, and there can be no question that he could have saved his life if he had proposed banishment. But Socrates was not as other men. His tone now became higher than ever and to the ears of his judges more offensive. 'Meletus,' he said, 'assesses the penalty at death. What fair counter-assessment then shall I make, Athenians? What do I deserve to suffer, or what fine to pay,

---

[1] Cp. Bury, *Trial of Socrates*, in *Rationalist Press Annual*, 1925, where it is argued that one or two points in the speech of defence may be got from Xenophon's *Apology*, that the speech of Anytus followed the speech of Meletus and dealt with the charge of corruption of the young men, while Meletus mainly confined himself to the charges of irreligion, and it is suggested that some of the points which Anytus made may possibly be gathered from the declamation (*Apologia Socratis*) in which Libanius replied to the attack on Socrates by the sophist Polycrates.

because during my life I would not keep quiet, but neglecting the things that most people care for—making money, managing their property, public offices and political clubs—I considered myself really too good for such things, and instead of entering upon these ways of life in which I should have been no good either to you or to myself I set myself on the way of benefaction, to confer the greatest of all benefactions as I assert, by attempting to persuade each of you individually not to care for any of his own belongings before he cares for himself—for his being as good and as wise as possible, nor for any of the city's belongings before he cares for the city, and on the same principle in all other matters. What then do I deserve for this? Something good surely, Athenians, and a good that would be suitable to me personally, suitable to a poor man who is a benefactor and requires leisure. There is nothing so suitable than that such a man should have free commons in the Prytaneum, far more than for one of you who has won a victory at Olympia in a horse-race or a chariot-race; because while he makes you appear happy, I make you be happy, and he does not need public support while I do. Accordingly, if I am to propose what I deserve, I propose that my sentence be free board in the Prytaneum.' This was not calculated to conciliate the judges; it was an undisguised 'contempt of court' and was quite unnecessary; it seemed as if the prisoner was determined to make it certain that he should be condemned to death. Having by this digression done what he could to dispose the judges against him he returned to business and considered possible penalties which the court might accept. He knew quite well that banishment would probably be considered adequate. 'Perhaps,' he said, 'banishment is what you think I deserve. Yet I should be fond indeed of life, Athenians, if I were so poor a reckoner as to calculate that if you who are my fellow citizens could not put up with my lectures and discourses, and if they have become so onerous and offensive, that you are now wishing to rid yourselves of them, other people will readily tolerate them. Nay, a fine life I should have, leaving my own city at my age and moving from one city to another and continually being driven out. I know that wheresoever I came the young men would listen to my talk as they do here. If I repulse them they will persuade the older men to expel me, and if I do not, their fathers and relatives will do so for their sakes.

'But it will be said: But, Socrates, when you leave Athens, why not keep quiet and hold your tongue? This is just what is so difficult to make you understand. To do that would be to disobey the god, and therefore it is impossible to keep quiet. When I say this, you will not believe me, you will take it as irony. And again if I say that a man's greatest good is to debate every day concerning virtue and the other things you hear me discussing and cross-examining myself and others about, and that the life which is not tested and proved by such examination is not worth living—when I say this, still less do you believe me to be in earnest. If I had money I should be ready to offer all I have as a fine; paying it would do me no harm. I could pay a mina. Plato, however, and Crito and two other friends bid me name 30 minae and will stand as sureties for the payment. They are solvent. So I propose this fine.'

The majority voted for death and this majority was greater than the previous one. We can understand that the tone which Socrates had adopted caused resentment among some of those who had originally voted for acquittal. One knows the type of persons who would be reasonable and fair enough to see that the accuser had failed to prove his case and would vote accordingly, yet would feel it an outrage that any prisoner should value his life so little as to neglect all the customary and obvious methods of trying to save it and take no trouble to conciliate the judges. Such an attitude was indecent and dangerous. If prisoners were not afraid of death, what could any one do? Socrates, it almost seemed, was so impertinent as to reverse the rôles of judge and accused; he had treated them as if it was they who were on trial, and had gone too far in his insolent assumption that he was a great and good man.

A month intervened between the sentence and the execution, because it happened to be the feast of the Delian Apollo when every year Athens sent a ship to Delos, and the law was that from the time the ship set sail till it returned to the Piraeus the city should not be polluted by any death inflicted by the authority of the State. The ship had been adorned with the official garlands on the day before the trial of Socrates, and, as it turned out, a month elapsed before it returned, a month which he had to spend in the public prison in chains. He seems to have been treated there with much consideration; the overseer of the prison was a humane man and did what he could to make the confinement as little irksome as possible. His friends came daily to visit him and his last days were passed in philosophical discussion. Some of his companions, particularly Crito, urged him to escape; a plan was prepared, and there is little doubt that it could easily have been managed; even the authorities might not have been very unwilling to connive; but Socrates refused to consent. It had always been his principle to obey the laws and had he not been legally condemned? And to flee from prison and death would have been glaringly inconsistent with his own attitude at the trial and rendered it obviously absurd. If to live was such an important consideration as to prompt escape, which meant abiding in exile, he ought clearly to have proposed exile as the alternative penalty.

The last hours and death of Socrates have been described by Plato in his *Phaedo*. His friends were with him to the end, and he was killed by the painless method of a draught of hemlock poison which produced a gradual paralysis. It is the one famous execution, recorded in history, of which the circumstances are quite ideal; the end of Socrates is marred, for our memory, by no violence or shedding of blood; and modern critics have often praised the Athenians for their humane methods of punishment. But it would be an error to suppose that the ways of brutal evildoers at Athens were made so easy for them, or that robbers and assassins were treated like Socrates. It is not long ago since excavations near Phalerum revealed[1] evidence that the Athenians used to inflict punishments which in agony rivalled crucifixion and hardly fell short of Assyrian atrocity. We do not know on what principle or in what cases execution by hemlock was adopted.

Among the companions of Socrates his memory was piously cherished, while they were stirred by a deep resentment against the democracy of Athens for the crime of his death. Seen through their eyes, the trial of Socrates by a jury of average practical citizens at the prosecution of an honest politician seems as absurd an event as, to use Plato's comparison, the trial of a physician in a court of little boys at the instance of a confectioner. The great memorial of Socrates is the body of Plato's works; no other man has had a more wonderful monument. Having described the last moments of his master, Plato wrote, 'Such was the end of our friend, whom I may truly call the wisest, the justest and the best of all the men I have ever known.' In the study of his imagination the revered master grew into the ideal figure of a perfect philosopher and as such has passed into history. The tragedy changed the course of Plato's own life. He had always meant to enter political life. The behaviour of the oligarchs during their short tenure of power, in which his relatives Critias and Charmides had been conspicuous, disgusted him so deeply that he was probably inclined to support the democracy, but the crowning

[1] Compare A. D. Keramopoullos, ὁ ἀποτυμπανισμός (see Bibliography to this chapter).

injustice of the condemnation of Socrates decided him to abandon the idea of a political career. More than forty years later, in a letter addressed to 'the friends and associates' of Dion of Syracuse, he recalled his experience at this time, and his decision to embrace a life of philosophy. This is what he says[1]: 'Socrates an elderly friend of mine who, I should not be ashamed to say, was the justest man among the men of the time, was sent with others by the Thirty to arrest one of the citizens, to be executed, in order that he (Socrates) might himself share in their actions whether he wished it or not; he refused and ran the extreme risk, rather than become a participant in their wicked deeds. Seeing all these things, and other similar things which were not trifling, I was disgusted and withdrew and stood aloof from the crimes of that Government. Not long afterwards the Thirty fell and the existing constitution was changed. I felt myself again drawn though slowly towards public life. The new Government had merits, though it had also defects, but it so happened that this companion of ours, Socrates, was brought into court by certain men who were in power. They preferred against him a most wicked charge and one which was least applicable to Socrates of all men in the world. They accused him of impiety, and he was condemned and put to death, the man who had refused to take part in the wicked arrest of one of their friends who was trying to flee at the time when they were themselves unfortunate.'

He goes on to explain how this experience of the new democracy finally decided him to give up the idea of a political career.

How great Socrates was as an original thinker, whether he can be set beside Pythagoras, for instance, is a question that is open to dispute, and depends much on the view that is taken of the Platonic Dialogues (see vol. VI, chapter XI, pp. 311 *sqq.*). But there can be only one opinion as to the greatness and the unique quality of his personality, and his unrivalled power as a stimulator of thought. The Athenians, with the exception of his personal friends, were quite unconscious of his greatness. Posterity looks back at him as the most remarkable figure of the Illumination; the contemporary man in the market-place of Athens probably remembered him merely as an eccentric Sophist. One can imagine what he would have said: 'Socrates—yes, an incessant talker, who fancied himself as a good-mixer. He was really an expert bore preaching for ever about virtue and other wearisome things. He got at last what he probably had richly deserved.'

[1] Plato, *Ep.* VII, 324 E–325 C.

CHAPTER XIV

HERODOTUS AND THUCYDIDES

THERE were heroes before Agamemnon, and historians before Herodotus, albeit Cicero dubbed him *Father of History*. The beginnings of Greek historiography were not a sudden creation. Imperfection of the record here, as elsewhere, induces an illusion. Herodotus and Thucydides appear to stand, together and alone, an elder and a younger contemporary, as earth-born colossi, to guard the portal of Greek history, that is to say, of Greek prose literature. But others had been at work there before them, to whom they owed, and Herodotus in especial owed, more than appears at first sight. He was not so much the sole begetter of a new type of literature, as the last and best in a procession of prose-writers, long at home in Ionia. Neither Herodotus nor Thucydides admits a conscious debt to those their predecessors. By a remarkable coincidence each names but one such author, and that in disparaging terms, the former Hecataeus of Miletus, the latter Hellanicus the Lesbian, who can hardly be reckoned among the predecessors of our elder historian, though his work belonged to a type almost as rudimentary in comparison with the panoramic achievement of Herodotus as with the reflective depth of the Thucydidean records. Contrasted with our extant historians of the Persian and the Peloponnesian wars these early *Logographoi* may well have seemed but as hewers of wood and drawers of water to the true temple-builders. Of a truth, with Herodotus and Thucydides, History as an art was born, indeed twice-born, in romantic and in classic perfection; and to their supremacy as literary artists may be ascribed the triumphant survival of their works. The bequests of their archaic predecessors could not compete for popularity, could not compare in memorable quality, with works conceived on the scale and accomplished with the felicity displayed by those supreme artists. But, the indubitable originality of Herodotus and Thucydides is exaggerated for us by the disappearance of the *Logographoi*, and the twofold suspicion will haunt us: that historical science has suffered by the wreck of those pioneers, and that their successors owed them a larger debt than we can now verify (see vol. IV, pp. 518 *sq.*).

Historians in antiquity suffered certain limitations, which the

progress of civilization has diminished to the advantage of modern
scholars, not excepting those concerned with the rediscovery of
the ancient world. The prolegomena to history are written by the
mathematician, the astronomer, the geologist, the anthropologist.
Time and place are conditions of the historic event; some sort of
chronology, some sort of geography, of the historical record.
From the days of Homer onwards the Greeks were never wholly
at a loss for a measure of time past, or for a picture of their own
environment; and sages of Ionia from Thales to Anaxagoras made
preparation by a philosophy of nature for that proper study of
mankind, of which the works of Herodotus and Thucydides were
to be the glorious first-fruits in due season. There was yet a
further condition for the birth of history which in especial made
the harvest both difficult and late. *Only the State has a history.*
The Hegelian paradox rightly interpreted is eternally true and
suggestive. The monadic form of Greek civilization, the multi-
plicity of centres of Hellenic life, the dispersion of Greek settlements east and west and north and south, from the Phasis
to the Pillars of Heracles, from Odessa to Cyrene, the self-
sufficiency of each independent city-state, at once the strength
and the weakness of Hellenism, made a history of Greece, and
still make it, the despair of your man of letters. For purposes of
historic record antecedent civilizations, inferior to Hellas in
cultural value—the great monarchies of Egypt and Asia—were
fortunate in comparison with the petty republics of the Hellenic
world. Successions of kings, ruling over large and populous
territories, provided a chronology, almost ready-made, for the
State-archives; and the power and pride of warriors and priests,
free to immortalize themselves in tomb and temple for the
homage, or the derision, of posterity, secured a sort of perspective
from generation to generation. Again, the dynastic State, however
extensive, was still a geographical unit: the writ of Hammurabi
or Ramses ran the length and breadth of the land: an empire
furnished history with geographical data for descriptive and
memorial purposes. But within the area of Greek history and
culture, from the coming of the Achaeans to the invasion of
Xerxes, there was no political sovran that could claim a universal
or even a provincial jurisdiction. Unity of a kind was there,
a spiritual, a growing unity: religion, language, institutions,
manners, ideas, sentiments, all tending that way. Nay, more:
groupings, crystallizations, amphictyonies, synoecisms, round
one or other of the stronger or more attractive nuclei—a Delphi,
a Thebes, an Athens, centres in the Peloponnese, in Ionia, in

Magna Graecia, in Libya, even on the coasts of Pontus, or away
to the wild west; but there was still no seeing the wood by reason
of the trees, and no man conceived the possibility of a common
Hellenic history, or sat down to write it. It was, then, no accident
that the Prince of Ionian History came to write his unrivalled
account of the achievements of the Greek world as he knew it, or
knew of it, in the third quarter of the fifth century before our era:
that is to say, just after the Greeks had been schooled into something more nearly approaching a single, even if brief-lived incor-
poration, by the attacks of the massed forces of the 'Barbarian,'
upon their liberties and institutions. Nor was it an accident that
in depicting the heroic effort of the Greek complex to save itself
—and thereby to save Europe, as yet unborn—for freedom, for
science, for civilization, he found himself drawn to enrich his
ample record by such report of the non-Hellenic world, whether
civilized or savage, as his researches and his experiences enabled
him to make for the profit and the pleasure of all ages. But the
genius and the industry whereby Herodotus contrived to mould
so far-flung an argument, with such apparent ease of heart and
lightness of touch, into so large and perfect a work of literary art
as we still possess, in his *Logoi*, are wonderful, thrice wonderful,
especially when we consider the technical difficulties of such an
achievement in the fifth century before our era, and within the
normal horizons of the Greek city-state.

In some respects Thucydides hit upon a more excellent way,
or at least contrived to simplify the historian's problem. From the
first the Logographi had eased their burden by restricting their
researches in subject, as in time and place. Their works comprised
genealogies, chronicles, dynastic lists, mythologic legends, special
studies in city or family archives, geography, itineraries and
voyage-routes, some of them perhaps with a practical reference.
And, further, the short story had made its appearance in Greek
prose long before Herodotus incorporated that *genre* too in his
larger logography. Thucydides returned from the wider interests
of his immediate exemplar to specialist methods, with a difference;
and obtained a simplification of his task by a restriction of his
subject to a single war: the point of greatest difference being, that
he was contemporary with his *dramatis personae*, and was writing,
with a limited reference, the history of his own times.

Thucydides, again, might seem to score against Herodotus the
advantage of simplicity under the geographical conditions of
their respective subjects. The narrative of Thucydides hardly
quits the familiar scenes of Greek life and experience. Doubtless

maps of the Hellenic peninsula and the Mediterranean coasts and
Islands, drawn by Thucydides, would have shown distortions
and mismeasurements: but even if his accounts of marches and
voyages may not always accord with our scientific maps, the error
is rarely of much importance, while his actual or implicit topography, as of Athens and Syracuse, Sphacteria and Amphipolis,
and even larger districts, is generally verifiable and authoritative.
As much may almost be said for Herodotus, when he is working,
so to speak, merely upon the Thucydidean scale, albeit in much
more numerous and widely scattered scenes. The description of
Thessaly, the topography of Artemisium and Thermopylae, the
structure of Central Greece, Attica and Peloponnese, the coasts
of the Aegean, Hellespont and Bosporus, though not figured in
the mind of Herodotus with the precision and correctness of
modern cartography, form a verifiable theatre for his narrative,
and exhibit an immense advance in empirical knowledge upon the
resources of the Homeric age. And the explicit geography of
Herodotus expands, with the growth and development of his
historical theme, to the limits of the civilized world, as then known
to its inhabitants, and even well beyond. Travel and hear-say and
(we may safely add) the treatises of Hecataeus and other Ionian
geographers extended and enriched the *mappa mundi* as conceived, or drawn, by Herodotus; and his work undoubtedly
represents the geographical knowledge, and speculation, of the
age of Pericles in palmary form. The colonial *diaspora* of the
Greeks in the period subsequent to the Trojan epoch: the reopening of Egypt to foreigners by the twenty-sixth dynasty (vol.
III, pp. 291 *sqq.*): above all, the rise and extension of the Persian
empire under the Achaemenid kings, are, perhaps, enough to
account for the vast contrast between the Herodotean geography
and that of Homer, or even that Ionian *orbis terrarum* displayed
on the bronze plaque which the Milesian Aristagoras exhibited
at Sparta about the year 500 B.C. 'showing every sea and every
river in the world' (vol. IV, p. 219).

Herodotus himself claims to have superseded all that, and even
makes fun of the old Ionian essays in cartography, which still
treated the earth as a circular disk, with the Ocean-stream flowing
round it, and made the continents huge islands parted by the
sweet waters of Tanais and Nile. His own world-geography is,
however, based upon supposed parallelisms and symmetries, for
which there is but little justification in fact: as, for example, the
too systematic zones in Libya, on the supposed parallel between
the courses of Nile and Danube. What is of major significance

is the respect for facts, where they were, or could be, ascertained, which led Herodotus to acquiesce in a Europe and an Asia of unknown extent and boundaries, north and east: an admirable example of suspended judgment. The cadastral survey presupposed in his descriptions of the Persian empire goes far to account for the relatively high standard of Asiatic geography in the pages of Herodotus; but the defects and omissions in his map of the Western Mediterranean and its hinterlands can hardly be excused by the predominance of Carthage in these waters. The Phocaeans had been in occupation of Massilia for upwards of a century; Herodotus does not report the fact though he once casually mentions the city (v, 9); and Siceliotes and Italiotes must surely have known much more of the western world than appears in the pages of Herodotus. The total omission of Rome is less astonishing than the suppression of the Rhone, the conversion of the Alps into a river, the reduction of the Pyrenees to a problematic city of the same name! But these mistakes, which further travel or hear-say might have corrected, are less important for our estimate of the progress of geographical knowledge, as attested by Herodotus, than his critical reference to the tin islands, beyond the Pillars of Heracles, his rumour of a great river (Niger) in the west of Libya (Africa), the happy accident by which he conceived the Caspian Sea as an inland lake (a point in which his geography is superior to that of his successors, not excepting Strabo), or his remarkably scientific delimitation of Europe and Asia by a frontier running east and west—a conception in which physical fact and ethnic history combine to justify him, even against the conventions of modern geography. And though Thucydides certainly names Massilia and was acquainted with the story of its foundation, as with that of the Greek settlements in Sicily, there is not much to show that he could have bettered the general map of the inner seas, as reconstructed from the data of Herodotus.

Chronological conditions and results carry reflections somewhat similar to the foregoing. Greek chronographers, even as late as the fifth century, were at a disadvantage, compared with the palace or temple recorders of Memphis or of Babylon. Scientific prerequisites for a better chronology had indeed made considerable progress: the *enneadekateris* of Meton (still in practical use, at least for ecclesiastical purposes) was published in Athens just before the outbreak of the Peloponnesian War; and that city had enjoyed a reformed Calendar, of approximate accuracy, since the Archonship of Solon (594–3 B.C.), as Herodotus quaintly implies in his famous report of the Athenian legislator's bio-chronological calculations in the presence of Croesus (I, 32). But the political atomism of the Greek world still made a common chronometry a mere desideratum: every Greek state had its own civil reckoning: the four possible points for New Year's day were all adopted in various local systems: and the plan for an approximate standardization by reference to the periodicity of the national festivals, notably the Olympian Agōn, was not devised or applied to historiography till three-quarters of a century after the close of the Peloponnesian War. From our present point of view it were better had Thucydides carried his Atticism into his chronology, boldly and systematically dating events by Attic years, months, and days of the month. He was on the verge of that invention, when he dated the outbreak of the war, 'in the year of Pythodorus, two (or, rather, four) months before its close' (II, 2), but missed his great chance and devised instead a chronology for the war based upon its intrinsic duration and seasonal division into summers and winters. That left a great deal to be desired from a modern point of view; and though the sequence of events, and occasionally their synchronisms, are preserved by the scrupulous industry of the contemporary narrator, his rather jejune annalistic method breaks down in application to the interval between the two main wars, or divisions of the war, the ten years Archidamian War (431–21) and the ten years Deceleo-Ionian War (414–4); while for the history of the antecedents of the war it was obviously inapplicable. Indeed, the Retrospect of the events of the Pentecontaetia, that is, the interval between the retreat of the Persian from Europe (Thuc. I, 89) and the invasion of Attica by Archidamus in 431 B.C., is lamentably deficient in chronological data and precision (see p. 465); while in his *aperçus* of remoter history Thucydides had obviously nothing better than the genealogical calculations of the old *Logographoi* or *Chronographoi* to go upon. Yet the modern reconstruction of the chronology of ancient history is deeply indebted to the chronology of Thucydides, such as it is: for upon his incidental notices of certain eclipses of sun and moon, dated by his narrative to the years of the war in which they occurred, the whole framework and verification of our chronology of ancient Greek history depend. The advantage of the contemporary over the not quite contemporary authority in such matters is illustrated by the fact that we cannot ascribe an equal value to notices of eclipses preserved by Herodotus, which are, one and all, rather problems of identification, than astronomically verified pillars for the reconstruction of the true perspective of the past.

But for the rest it cannot fairly be said that the chronology of Herodotus compares unfavourably with that of Thucydides, especially if regard be had to the intrinsic character of their narratives respectively. Where he is dealing with a single war on what may be called a Thucydidean scale Herodotus holds his own with his immediate successor. The Herodotean chronology of the invasion of Xerxes (481–79) as exhibited in the last three Books of his work compares favourably with the Thucydidean chronology of the Pentecontaetia, even if it be not so full, and self-consistent as, let us say, the account of the Sicilian expedition of 415–13, as narrated by Thucydides in his sixth and seventh Books. Incidentally, too, Herodotus enables us by the sincerity of his report to appreciate chronological points of special interest, the values of which were not, or were not fully, present to his own mind: as, for example, the synchronistic fighting at Thermopylae and Artemisium, the synchronisms between the battles of Himera and Salamis, of Plataea and Mycale, the occurrence of an Olympic Festival, of an Eleusinian pilgrimage and so on.

Working backwards in his pages from the accession of Xerxes (486 B.C.) the chronology of Greek history exhibits, we must confess, more and more defects inevitable under the conditions above indicated. The clearer and more trustworthy lines are based on the succession of Persian monarchs, on the pedigrees of Spartan kings, on traditions connected with great Athenian Houses, Peisistratidae, Philaidae, Alcmaeonidae, and possibly others, back to Solon, with whom the continuous story of Athens, so far as recoverable from Herodotus, begins. The Lydian monarchy, from Croesus upwards, adds a perspective of some five reigns, or generations, back to Gyges, whom we now know to have been contemporary with Ashurbanipal and Psamatik (vol. III, pp. 501, 507 *sqq.*). It was not in Babylon or Susa that Herodotus obtained still earlier glimpses of remote peoples and cultures, but in Egypt, among the monuments of six and twenty dynasties, from the calculations of native authorities, or the reports of Greeks, who had appropriated such researches. Of the value of such traditions of the non-hellenic world something remains to be said later. For the *origines* of Greek history, so far as he treats them, Herodotus had access to stores of tradition, already committed to writing; this material, so far as chronologized, probably owed its datings to the genealogies of the aristocratic families all over Greece, which rarely carried back beyond five centuries, and broke down, or up, into the eponymous hero, or god, this side the Trojan war. Pre-homeric Greece can hardly be said to exist for Herodotus, albeit he accepts the myths and legends of the prime; a Heracles, a Theseus, a Minos are historical figures for him, as for Thucydides. The unity which he obtains for his encyclopaedia as a whole has little to say to chronological niceties, least of all in annalistic precision; but there is a thread of continuous history running through it, from the coming of Cyrus, or even from the liberation of Lydia and Egypt to the defeat of Xerxes, or, we might add, in view of references to contemporary events, almost to the death of Artaxerxes (424 B.C.); and in these references he is as much the contemporary authority as Thucydides himself.

In what may, perhaps, with a somewhat extended connotation, be called the anthropological aspect of history, the contrast between the minds of Herodotus and Thucydides reaches its maximum. Thucydides was a rationalist, and his conception of historical causation is eminently rationalistic. In his view history presents the actions and fortunes of political communities, which are to be understood in the light of political, economic, and psychological factors. Thucydides is too good a psychologist to underestimate the importance of individual character and ability in human affairs: a Themistocles, a Pericles, a Nicias, an Alcibiades, a Theramenes are all in turn dominant agents in the policy of Athens: the deaths of a Brasidas, a Cleon, are important moments in the decisions for peace. Yet Thucydides has a highly impersonal method of narrative, an objective and matter of fact point of view, congruous with his deliberately adopted annalistic scheme, which orders events (with rare exceptions) in their purely empirical sequence. Such a scheme can be combined, as in the *Annals* of Tacitus, with a result which is essentially biographical; but Thucydides would never have exchanged the annals of the War, much less the history of Athens, for the biography of an individual, however eminent.

Above all, the world of Thucydides is a world of men: gods and women are conspicuous only by their absence, or in the rare and grudging references which he allows himself to make to their existence. His account of the plague at Athens, though it contains an autobiographical note, is a palmary instance of his conscientious objectivity, even if it have not enabled modern pathologists to identify the disease. His religious agnosticism could have been no detriment to the quality of his history, had it been confined to the omission of the gods of Greece from the sphere of secondary causation: but in so far as it leads him to ignore the part played by supernaturalism in determining human action, his historical argument may have suffered. At certain

points, indeed, the 'laicism' (so to speak) of Thucydides gives
way to a recognition of the religious coefficient in politics and
morals, as in the vogue of oracles at the outbreak of the war: the
disastrous effects of the mutilation of the Hermae on the eve of
the Sicilian Expedition: the costly superstition which delayed the
Athenian retreat in 413, and sealed the fate of that ill-starred adventure. But theophanies and special providences, or any rationale
transcending the recognized gamut of human motives, or natural
causes, are out of count in the historiography of Thucydides.
In discommoning *Das Ewig-weibliche* he even curtails his own
resources within the ambit of scientific psychology. The austere
puritanism of his outlook, in strongly marked contrast not merely
to the contemporary drama but also to the romantic story-telling
of his greatest predecessor, may have been at least in part a deliberate though reticent critique of both alike. There were two
things he could not abide: the sentimentalism of a Euripides,
the pietism of an Herodotus. Thucydides has shown in his
rationalist version of the heroic age, that he had little use, in sober
prose, for gods or women: therein he but applies to the age of
Agamemnon the principles on which he writes—so far as he has
written—a history of the age of Pericles. Over and above this, we
can hardly but perceive, in his silent protest against the pietistic
and the feminist motives, as historical mechanisms, his indignation
with the scandals and tittle-tattle against Pericles current at the outbreak of the war, which are pretty fully documented in Plutarch's
Life of Pericles, and have left a smudge on the jocund pages of
Aristophanes, as in his droll parody of the Proem of Herodotus
(*Acharnians* 524 ff.). All that is simply ignored in the account
given by Thucydides of the natural antecedents of the war, which
was to him (as every war has been to its historian) the most inevitable war in human history: and within limits it may be
admitted that a motivation of human action proper enough to
despotic monarchies, or even the courts of City tyrants, might
become something of an anachronism in the freer air of Periclean
or post-Periclean Athens; and certainly not less so, in the cryptic
Senates of her opponents, the ultimately victorious oligarchies.
Finally, Thucydides is a master, if not the author, of mob-
psychology; though for the mob he has as little respect as Shake-
speare himself, and would have made short work of the intervention of the *dea ex machina* in the first Restoration of Peisistratus,
which not a little exercised the good Herodotus, in one of his rare,
and perhaps late, moments of rationalistic reflection[1].

[1] Vol. IV, p. 63, and see below, p. 408.

For indeed the general contrast between the two historians, under this heading, is immense. Taking the work of Herodotus as a whole, reading it through as we find it, the double key to history might seem to have been, in his gnomology: *cherchez la femme et n'oubliez pas le Dieu!* From his racy introduction on the Rapes of Io, Medea, and Helen, through the stories of the accession of Gyges, the fate of Cyrus, the invasion of Egypt, the Scythian expedition, the exploration of the West, and so forth, there is always a woman to account for the trouble. The same motive serves to explain many a minor episode, as in the stories of Pheretime, Demaratus, Miltiades, and others. When the main narrative shifts to homelier scenes, and the Persian monarchy becomes involved in the fortunes of the Greek states, the feminist interest, except for the prominence of his country-woman Artemisia, weakens or falls out, but leaves the first principle of the Herodotean *Weltanschauung* as the ultimate and sufficient rationale of the march of events. That principle is the conception of the God in History, as a moral power, over-ruling the march of events so as to procure results conformable to man's sense of justice and desert. Such a conception is even to-day not alien either to the sincerest religious feeling or to the profoundest philosophy of history. But, introduced into the order of secondary causes, it is apt to work unfortunately twice over: first, by offering an immediate and easy explanation for every occurrence, and so arresting inquiry into the natural nexus and causality of events; secondly, by generating the false and mischievous assumption that human suffering and misfortune imply antecedent wrongdoing and culpability. These results are to be observed *passim* in the course of the Herodotean 'exhibition of history.' And unfortunately a still more vicious twist is given to this rationale of life and experience by the morbid terms in which it is expressed. The God of Herodotus is not merely a 'just' but also a 'jealous,' an 'angry,' and a 'vindictive' God. Of the four keys in which Herodotus plays his variations on the theme of the God in history, jealousy is the most pathological; and the divine jealousy is not directed against rival deities, but poured out upon any mortal whose power, or wealth, or felicity raises him much above the general level, and especially so, should he be uplifted in mind thereby: 'for the divine being suffers none to have proud thoughts save himself.'

Doubtless, as human history is largely a record of the misfortunes of men and nations, many of them only too well deserved, a first principle of this kind is in a fair way to a rough verification, and exhibits at any rate a quasi-philosophic advance on the more capricious theurgy of the Homeric world; albeit a Xenophanes had once for all supplied the antidote for such anthropomorphism, and a Sophocles was chanting formulas for the divine law at once more sane and more poetic. Still, if in harmony with a naïve folk-lore Herodotus fills his pages with signs and wonders, theophanies and special providences, yet, in so doing, he is undoubtedly reflecting the average mind of his age and people more fully and truly than the philosophic Thucydides; and on closer inspection you may discover, not without surprise, that neither his prior fallacy of the Divine Jealousy nor his superfluity of secondary interventions of the God or Gods in History, precludes 'anthropological' conceptions of the course of human affairs. You might almost come down to Montesquieu to find a firmer grasp on the relation of Physics and Politics, a clearer reference of institutions and arts to climate, soil, flora, fauna, than are displayed by Herodotus, notably in his accounts of Egypt, Scythia, Libya, and even Hellas. 'Soft countries breed soft races' is his moral of the whole story: the sea and the mountains of Greece, the poverty of her soil, and the isolation of her valleys, made her not merely the home of liberty but the nursery of heroes. On a smaller scale, and for precise problems, Herodotus has explanations natural enough, even if given by the mouths of his *dramatis personae*. The rationale of the Greek *Tyrannis* may be recovered as clearly from stories in Herodotus as from the pages of Plato and Aristotle. The victory of the Greeks in the Persian wars is no miracle in the eyes of Herodotus: their advantages in defence, equipment, discipline, mobility, *ēthos*, leading, could not be more clearly or consciously displayed than they are in his last three Books. There is not one of his battle-pieces, which does not leave us with a bundle of unresolved problems on hand, but the general result is perfectly rationalized. At times, indeed, he betrays a breath of the sophistic scepticism of the age, which blows more coldly through the pages of Thucydides. The Magi reduced the storm of Magnesia by their incantations—if the wind did not sink of its own accord: Athene appeared in person to stay the flight of the Corinthians from Salamis; but her supposed intervention on behalf of the Athenian tyrant had been 'the most naïve of devices' (vol. IV, p. 63).

Only in Delphi has the sceptic no standing with Herodotus. The triumphant apology for Apollo's desertion of Croesus, most pious of founders and benefactors, in the first Book (c. 91), should be read in connection with the implicit refutation of the charge of medism at Delphi, in the eighth Book (*cc.* 35–39), if we would understand the extent to which Herodotus succumbed to the *genius loci*. In the former case Herodotus wins an easy victory for the Oracle: a generation that had forgiven Delphi's friendships with the native tyrant was not likely to condemn its desertion of the Lydian. In the latter case, the eclipse of Delphi in the Periclean world proves that its immunity in the Persian war had lowered the Oracle in the eyes of patriotic Greeks, and that Herodotus' vindication of Delphi fell on deaf ears, at least in Atticizing circles. To do Herodotus, and Delphi, and perhaps even Athens, full justice we should further compare the Delphic Story of Glaucus (or *The fraudulent Trustee*), in the sixth Book (*c.* 86), the austere morality of which, with its touch of almost Kantian quality, goes far to explain the prestige of the Oracle, despite its unfortunate essays in international politics. All three stories were undoubtedly posted to the address of Athens, though less explicitly than the partisan utterance just before the Peloponnesian War, preserved for us by Thucydides (1, 118): but Herodotus himself seems an unconscious victim and vehicle for these pragmatic fictions. So much easier to the anthropologist is the critique of supernaturalism than the detection of the politic subtleties of human nature!

Enough perhaps has already been here set down to suggest the conclusion that Herodotus and Thucydides, though working on very different lines, were both alike creative historians and consummate literary artists. The historical value of their works, each in itself, still more if taken together, is past any easy appraisal. It arises not merely from the continuous story of the sixth and fifth centuries, which their joint narratives supply, but also indirectly, and none the less richly, from the extent to which these authors reflect their own environment, and reveal the mind and moral of their own age. Such reflection, indeed (some one may say), is the conscious mission of Thucydides: true!—But his indirect witness, his collateral implications, his self-betrayal, are that wherein he is most convincing; his expressly memorial and didactic purposes are not his most intriguing merits. With Herodotus the contrast between now and then, past and present, is, of course, everywhere and consciously perceptible. Even his Greek histories start, so to speak, in the previous generation and carry back through the Lyric age of the Despots to the Heroic Age of Homer and the Cyclic Epos; while his non-Hellenic *Logoi* raise all the immense contrast between the Greeks and the non-Hellenic civilizations and uncivilizations of the Persian age.

A vast world-wisdom is, indeed, stored in the diverse yet equally immortal products of the Ionian and of the Attic Master, there in more varied and happy measure, here in darker, more intense and merciless character. It might seem but barely possible that one and the same nation should within the quarter of a century, or so, which separated the death of Thucydides from the death of Herodotus, exhibit two phases of historic import, so sharply and so cruelly contrasted as the united Hellas of Herodotus, transfigured and glorified by the repulse of the 'Barbarian,' and the Hellas of Thucydides, rent in twain, divided against itself, Ionian against Dorian, oligarch versus democrat, even democrat versus democrat, Sparta and Athens, Athens and Syracuse at 'truceless warfare,' the whilom traitor, Thebes, as *tertius gaudens*, destined to enjoy a brief hegemony before the utter barbarians of the North and the West should make an end for ever of the parochial politics of the Greek city-states—but not, indeed, an end of the humane and amazing art and letters of the Periclean age. And in this connection Herodotus and Thucydides are mutually indispensable and complementary: the one presenting the age still suffused with the light of the great deliverance, that concrete expression of the unity of Hellas, that proof, once for all, of the dynamic and ethical superiority of European culture: the other depicting, with relentless candour, the fundamental dualism underlying the Hellenic order, its hegemonic rivalries, centrifugal ambitions, class wars, insular atomism, treacheries, disloyalties and disintegrations. Of a truth, Herodotus and Thucydides, though contemporaries, though perhaps personally acquainted, are in spirit, and in the realm of letters, worlds apart Thucydides, displaying the tragic self-destruction of the premier City-state, his native Athens, whose recent heyday and patriotic service had made the life, the travel, the achievement of Herodotus, Dorian child of subject yet sunny Ionia, possible: Herodotus, whose unexampled work was the noblest tribute ever laid at the feet of the violet-crowned Athens. Yet strange to tell, Thucydides, who all but anticipates Aristotle's inquest on the *polis*, apparently shares that philosopher's belief in the permanent possibility of the city-state, and fails to draw from history, despite his didactic tendency, its one lesson, the relativity, the instability, the impermanence of all human institutions, which the far-wandered Herodotus had expressly alleged as his chief reason for recounting the varying fortunes, and misfortunes, not of Hellas only, but of the greater part of mankind.

The due appreciation of Herodotus and of Thucydides as

artists may have suffered sometimes from two contrary mis-
conceptions; the one, regarding Herodotus as a mere child of
Nature, creating indeed a great work, but almost in sport, unconscious of design and innocent of forethought: the other,
regarding Thucydides as a sheer incarnation of science, or at
least of the scientific spirit, and repudiating on his behalf the
charge of literary artfulness, as derogatory to his conscience and
his achievement. There is some justification for each of these
exaggerations in the superficial aspects of the respective works.
But we have already seen reason to discount the exaggerated
claim advanced for Thucydides as the founder of historical
science, and that claim cannot be rehabilitated by robbing him
of his superb and tragic powers as a literary artist. So, too,
Herodotus cannot be dismissed from the schools of history as
a merely naïve globe-trotter, with an accidental turn for happy
anecdote-mongering. The fundamental test of literary art is the
contemplation of the literary work as a whole: and this test the
works of Herodotus and Thucydides triumphantly abide, as
even the barest synopsis of each work in turn might indicate.

Nor is this triumph to be diminished or discounted by the
discovery that in neither case can the whole have been originally
conceived and projected as such fully or precisely in the form
which it finally received from the Master's hand, and in which
it has fortunately come down to us. But the architectonic retractation of the work of Thucydides was all, so to speak, *in pari
materia*, and did not demand a creative effort comparable to
that unification of national and world history accomplished in
the work of Herodotus: which accordingly presents a much
more difficult problem in regard to origin and composition.
Such problems, however, in relation to either or both of the works
under review are of too searching and disputable a character
for elucidation under the necessary limits of this chapter. Nor
is it worth while to dissect the contents with a view to exhibit
the bare skeletons of the works in question[1]. But room may
still be found here for a brief survey of the sources, on which
Herodotus and Thucydides relied for their materials, and for a
suggestion, or two, of their respective methods and tendencies,
in the exploitation of those materials.

The *Quellen-lehre*, or doctrine of the 'Sources,' is a simpler
problem in the case of Thucydides than in the case of Herodotus,

---

[1] For their contents, as for discussion of the problems of origin, the reader
may be referred to the editions and commentaries named in the Bibliography
to this chapter; and for portions of Thucydides to note 9, pp. 480 *sqq.*

partly because of the difference in their themes, partly by reason of a difference in method, to say nothing of personal idiosyncrasy. In his own proper field, the history of twenty-seven years of warfare—twenty of which he has actually recorded—Thucydides was the first pioneer to break ground. He had for this record no literary predecessors or authorities. The extent to which he could have used documentary evidences was relatively small. Copies of official documents, such as treaties, in all cases presumably and in one case demonstrably authentic, occur in his text to the special delight of the modern scholar: but such a document as the Dispatch of Nicias from Sicily in the eighteenth year of the war is probably governed by the same canon as the Speeches, which Thucydides puts into the mouths of various orators, no doubt with due regard to the probabilities of the case, but seldom quite convincingly from the strictly historical point of view. It is vastly otherwise with the narrative of military events, and with the elucidation of the political situation, as it becomes integral to the warfare. Here Thucydides is the master of all those who have written histories of their own times. He was himself a prominent if not a leading personage in the Athenian state, and was one of the ten elected magistrates, or Generals, in control of the War Office at least once, in the eighth year of the war (424–3). His banishment, assuredly in consequence of his failure on service to anticipate Brasidas the Spartan at Amphipolis in that year, gave him twenty years at least of enforced leisure, to be devoted to the further collection of evidence from a wide range of witnesses, and, as he himself avers, from the side of both belligerents, for the purpose of his great literary undertaking. The results of his method, which is to extract for his readers, to all generations, a clear and chronologized narrative, the precise sources of which are seldom even indicated, must be taken or left on his authority, and on his authority alone. In general, posterity has accepted Thucydides at his own valuation. There are supplements to his history in the Inscriptions; in the extant comedies of Aristophanes; in later writers, more especially in Plutarch's Lives of Pericles, Nicias, Alcibiades, Lysander; last not least in the Aristotelian *Constitution of Athens*, which in particular calls for some readjustments in the story of the Revolution at Athens in 411 as narrated in the unfinished Eighth Book (see above, p. 312 n.): but Thucydides will never be dethroned as the sovran authority for the history of the years 433 to 411 B.C. Even for the half-century previous to the outbreak of the war his narrative ranks hardly less high, though it leaves many more *lacunae* to be filled in by supplementary evidences, the work of Herodotus included: and we may regret that Thucydides, for his pemmicanned sketch of the Pentecontaetia, has not exploited the archives of the Athenian State more freely. Where he deals with still earlier periods (never on an extensive scale), he may safely be assumed to be using literary sources, the best work of his predecessors, so far as available, Antiochus of Syracuse for the early colonization of Sicily, perhaps the Hellanicus whom he censures, for the Thesean synoecism of Attica, though as a loyal Periclean he appears to have no use for Solon, and little prejudice against Peisistratus.

The conventional fiction, that in relation whether to the politics of his own time or to the history of the past, Thucydides affords a unique example of flawless impartiality, should no longer be necessary to the full appreciation of his work as a thing of everlasting value and reality. For an active politician and place-man, for an historian of his own times, for a Greek, Thucydides may be a miracle of impartiality; but he is not quite impartial. His ludicrous depreciation of the historic importance of the Persian wars; his transparent animosity against Cleon (undoubtedly his leading colleague among the Generals of 424–3); his determination to allow no flaw in the statecraft of Pericles; his testimonials to the authors of the Revolution in 411: all this may not amount to very much, but it amounts to something, and incidentally helps to redeem the historical artist from the fate of the bare annalist. His didactic purpose, the sin which so easily besets him, and with which as artist or as annalist he should have had nothing to do, makes us wonder at times whether it is merely in the Speeches and express reflections, that he has dropped into a paedagogic rôle: whether any parts of the narrative, the story of the siege of Plataea, for example, or the reign of terror in Corcyra, have been featured for purposes of instruction. His theory, that the years from the Archonship of Pythodorus I (432–1) to that of Pythodorus II (404–3), inclusive, were all years of one continuous war, is a reasoned conviction, but it betrays a bias to magnify his office, and has somewhat the air of a sophistic thesis. The deeper argument carries further. If the warfare from 431 to 404 was all one integral struggle, why then, the duel between Sparta and Athens began in 461, and dated from the denunciation (by Pericles) of the 'alliance against the Mede' (p. 71). On Thucydidean principles the fourteen years of peace, or less, for the Peace was declared at an end in 432 at Sparta, might easily have been given the same character as the seven years Peace 421–14; while the assertion that Athens and Sparta were at the height of their powers in 431 is demonstrably false: Athens at least had been vastly more powerful from 461 to 445 than she was after the Samian war. But the lack of contemporary records for the Pentecontaetia has given the Thucydidean conception of the course of Greek history in the last three quarters of the fifth century B.C. an authority which it is easier for moderns to accept meekly than to challenge, or to challenge than to dethrone.

The most searching criticism hardly detracts from the extraordinary impressiveness of the work of Thucydides: the elements of weakness therein are so clearly defined that the historical residuum is unassailable: we have to deal with a personal equation, and the author himself makes the discount easy for us. Vastly different is the case of Herodotus. Here almost every page, and every story—especially the traditions of the Persian war, but not those only—are saturated with afterthought, prejudice, local and party and personal feeling and interests: and memories of earlier events have been distorted or idealized 'by lapse of time and men's love of the marvellous.' But little or nothing of all this belongs to the author: he is all good nature, the incarnation of sweet reasonableness, only anxious to do justice all round and to everybody, whether Greek or barbarian, bond or free. The mischief all comes of the nature of his sources, and of his deliberate purpose to repeat whatever has been reported, and to allow his hearers, or readers, to select the true or probable, and to reject the contrary, for themselves. Where there is a variant, he will not suppress alternatives, or impose his own judgment upon posterity. Even when his own mind is made up, he will allow his informants, and his public, the benefit of the doubt. After all, he is not trying to forewarn and to forearm reactionaries, but to delight and exalt common folk with visions of the derring deeds of men.

In the end this method works out quite as well for historical purposes, especially in relation to his proper undertaking, as the contrary plan of Thucydides: indeed, one shudders on reflecting what Thucydides might have made of the Herodotean theme! But the method in view is no more quite fully and consistently applied in the composition of the *Logoi*, or 'stories,' than the Thucydidean plan in the composition of the *Syngraphe* or 'history' (*cf.* Thucydides, 1, 97). For Herodotus does sometimes expressly give one of several versions of a story, and suppress the others, as for example one of three rival accounts of the coming of Cyrus (I, 95); and he does at times definitely take sides, not merely with Greek against barbarian, but with Greek against Greek, as in his famous eulogy of Athens, the saviour of Hellas (VII, 139), or in his attitude towards Corcyra for its neutrality (VII, 168), and the neutral states in Peloponnese for their medism (VIII, 73). Moreover, the rather crude philosophy of History, which is perhaps the nearest thing to a religious creed that Herodotus professed, undoubtedly affects his preferences and determines now the turn of a particular story, now the general conception of the course of affairs, whether touching private persons, an Adrastus, a Glaucus, a Hermotimus, or kings and potentates, a Croesus, a Polycrates, a Xerxes, or states and cities, as in the contrast between the power of Persia and the poverty of Greece, exaggerated the better to point a moral.

Yet for the subjects and period in which Herodotus counts as primary authority, the Persian wars, the Achaemenid dynasty, the history of the leading Greek states, and for the general description of the contemporary world his evidence is of immense, though varying, value. We may feel pretty sure that he left no available source of information unexplored. The extent to which his materials are drawn from written and inscribed documents is a problem on which there has not been complete agreement among scholars, but we may safely say that there is a much larger amount in his work directly or indirectly drawn from such sources than is expressly specified. Even for the story of the Persian invasion he will have had some literary material, mainly poetical, besides the oracles and epitaphs preserved in his text: though, oddly enough, the leading case in which we can bring this probability into court, by comparison of the account of the battle of Salamis presented by Aeschylus in the *Persae* with the account preserved by Herodotus, proves the historian only too independent of the poet. Still, Herodotus incidentally shows a wide acquaintance with extant Greek literature, though he is not out, so to speak, to parade his erudition; and lyric, gnomic, and popular poetry is probably behind many details in his history. Certain materials from their very nature will have come to him in writing: oracles, genealogies, army and navy lists, and so forth. The information gathered at great archaeological centres, Delphi, Athens, Olympia, Samos, will not all have been merely oral. The remoter history of the Greek states had been partially reduced to writing by his predecessors: he was not ignorant of their works. There is virtually nothing to prove that he commanded any language but his own, and for his accounts of non-Hellenic history and antiquities he could not himself draw on native inscriptions: the Achaemenid records which have within living memory greatly modified our knowledge of the rise and progress of the Persian power were inaccessible to Herodotus: but his account of that Empire and its organization must go back, at second or third hand, to such documents and written records. That is all doubly clear, and generally admitted as true, of his Egyptian *Logoi*. But here, again, probability points to much of the work having been done previously by Greek writers, and accepted by Herodotus at second hand. The crude blunder by which the kings of the fourth dynasty appear in his list after those of the eighteenth and nineteenth, might have come to him ready-made, whatever its accidental or technical explanation may be[1]. The earlier Books of Herodotus, especially the second, have a much closer literary texture than the subsequent Books, notably the last three, and that albeit the second Book represents Herodotus in conversation (through an interpreter, presumably) with Egyptian 'priests'—or possibly only deacons—as on the occasion which he exploits to the disadvantage of poor Hecataeus! Herodotus may still count as an authority for the history of the Greeks and Persians in Egypt, and even to some extent for the history of Egypt under the twenty-sixth dynasty: but for the older native history modern Egyptology relies more and more exclusively upon the native monuments and records. Generally speaking we must say that the stories in the first three Books of Herodotus are now not so much materials for the true history of the non-Greek and pre-Greek world as materials from which we may reconstruct the Hellenic versions, or perversions, of non-Hellenic history, for the truer version of which the modern world is going to the native records and monuments in middle and hither Asia and in Egypt, which were undecipherable and inaccessible to the Greeks of the fifth century B.C.

A review of the historian's Sources, at least in the case of writers whose works are largely based on personal experience and oral testimony, gathered soon after the event from eye-witnesses, naturally passes into a biographical inquiry of a kind which writers of works, admittedly compilations from literary and documentary sources, do not invite. For the biographies of Herodotus and Thucydides their own works are certainly the primary sources. External evidences in the case of the elder writer are surprisingly meagre. No separate biography of Herodotus, if we except a

---

[1] See above, vol. I, p. 260.

short article in Suidas, has come down from Alexandria or Constantinople; but various writers of the Roman and Byzantine period preserve jottings on the circumstances of his life, the discussion of which must not now detain us.

Oddly enough the external tradition makes nothing of Herodotus' travels, which bulk so largely in his own work, that mine of autobiographical information about the author, for whoso cares to piece together the numerous incidental notes and self-revelations. The moderns have not been weary of reconstituting the man, his life and movements, his character and methods, from his work, without, however, reaching complete agreement or finality. Some, accepting every presumable indication of *autopsia* in the text at its face value, extend his travels over the greater part of the Persian empire, including Babylon, over Greece, Upper Egypt, the parts of Libya about Cyrene, and the unconquered and uncolonized hinterlands of the Euxine, though in the West none ventures to carry him beyond the Pillars, or even to Carthage or to Marseilles. Others will be disposed to cancel the remoter stages while verifying his visits to Memphis and the Fayum, to Tyre, to Byzantium and Olbia as no less certain than his presence at one time or another in Samos, Athens, Sparta, Thebes, Delphi, Dodona, Sybaris (Thurii), and of course on the intermediate lines implied in those voyages and journeys. Such a record of private travel is surely unique, at least before the days of the Caesars and the Roman pacification of the civilized world. And everywhere he went Herodotus carried his inexhaustible interest, his insatiable curiosity, his infinite capacity for taking notes: his flair for a good story, his power of sustaining a continuous narrative, his delight in digression, aside, and *bon mot*: his certainty of self-recovery, his sense of the whole: the lightness of his touch, the grace of his language, his glory in human virtue and achievement wherever to be found: and withal the feeling of mortality, the sense of tears, the pathos of man's fate: with ever a winged word, a witty, a wise word, as the last word: but throughout all, such a modesty, and reserve of his own merely phenomenal self, that we cannot ascertain whether he was single, or married, or the name of any of his closer friends or relatives, or any of the honours or the hardships, that must have fallen to his lot, in his life-adventure in the wide world: not even, for example, if he is drawing on his personal experience, or on that of others, when he tells us that no Egyptian, whether man or woman, would kiss a Greek on the lips!

In life and character Thucydides contrasts with Herodotus no less strongly than in style. No one has ever smiled over a line of Thucydides, and he himself never unbends in his composition: it presents him to us not merely as a serious but as a proudly tragic figure. He was, as he allows us to know, an Athenian, and suffered in the plague, a magistrate, an exile for twenty years after his command 'at Amphipolis' (which is just where he was not on the fatal day in 424!). His analysis proves him as competent to diagnose the disease in the City-state, the rottenness in Hellas, as Aristotle afterwards was, but with something less than the Stagirite's aloofness: Thucydides was before all a politician, a patriot, an Athenian. There is a Dantesque austerity in his tone. His concise and consecutive narrative of military events gives the relative trivialities of old Greek warfare an importance not merely in their results, but in themselves. In his ruthless rationale of actions and events we see him at his greatest. He seems in effect to anticipate Butler's positivism, so distressing to happy-go-lucky humanity: *Things and actions are what they are, and their consequences will be, what they will be: why then should we desire to be deceived?* He brings to history the conception of politics as a sphere for the application of reason (*Nous*) though that is not his own favourite word for it: he is content with terms of a lower range. He appears himself as an incarnation of gnomic reason on the level of technical accomplishment: he is an adept of research, dialectic, judgment. His self-confidence is unbounded. He has no misgivings. He is always right. An historical *Syngraphe*, not an autobiography is what he offers us: his own name hardly appears in his work except in relation to its composition and authorship, of which he seems, perhaps, somewhat jealous: and like Julius Caesar afterwards, in the *Commentaries*, he writes of himself throughout in the third person.

Just once Thucydides whispers his father's outlandish name, Olorus (IV, 104): for further biographical details we have to consult the *literati* of the Roman and Byzantine empires. Much which reappears in the composite Biography and Critique passing under the name of Marcellinus, might be ingenious afterthought not genuine tradition: but Marcellinus proves that a long succession of writers (Zopyrus, Didymus, Cratippus, Timaeus, Antyllus) had concerned themselves with the personal fortunes of Thucydides; items, which are not obviously enlargements of autobiographical hints in his own work, may have some real tradition or archaeological evidence behind them. A second more compressed Biography, anonymous, but from a similar quarter, adds surprising particulars concerning his forensic and financial activities, which may, perhaps, be traceable to some confusion with one or other of his namesakes.

The greater attention bestowed upon the Biography of the Attic, as compared with that of the Ionic, historian corresponds roughly with the subsequent fortunes of their respective works in antiquity. The best, if not the earliest, homage to the *Logoi* of Herodotus may be seen in the *Syngraphe* of Thucydides, who owes far more of stimulus and example to his great opposite than he openly avows. Thucydides arrays himself in deliberate opposition and contrast to Herodotus, claims expressly a far greater subject, claims expressly a far sounder method, answers the entertaining sallies and mythopoetic attractions of the great unnamed, and again and again, when he crosses the path of Herodotus, puts him right *en passant*. The omission of an express mention of Herodotus or his work is indeed, all things considered, a part of the case against Thucydides: for the Athenian public he needed, no more than Aristophanes, to name his target: from posterity he deliberately withheld the name, while he carried on the tale. Thucydides begins his review of the interval between the Persian and Peloponnesian wars exactly at the point where Herodotus dropped the baton, that, moreover, being by no means a self-evident point, whether of arrival or departure; so that his record reads continuously with that of Herodotus, only one degree less obviously than the *Hellenica* of Xenophon with the *Peloponnesiaca* of Thucydides. None has ever doubted that Xenophon knew his Thucydides, nor need we doubt that Thucydides had his copy of Herodotus. Posterity, indeed, has given the twain a closer association with each other than either might have been willing to acknowledge in life. The Museum at Naples contains a double herm, presenting the busts of Herodotus and Thucydides back to back on a single column. The scarcely idealized portraits are distinct in feature, and contrasted in type, nor are they wanting in a certain verisimilitude: the one marble may be supposed to represent counterfeits of the two historians, which had plausible originals as models. Be that as it may, the juxtaposition of the twin founders of European historiography, on the same level, with opposite outlooks, was a happy thought of the synthetic sculptor, some justification for which has, perhaps, been established in the foregoing all too brief appreciation of a noble pair of immortals:— the swan song of a Phil-Hellenist well stricken in years.

CHAPTER XV

GREEK ART AND ARCHITECTURE

I. LATE ARCHAIC SCULPTURE

IN considering the sculpture of the late archaic period, we may begin, for the sake of simplicity, with the naked male figure and the clothed female figure of the types which we have learnt to know as *kouros* and *kore*[1]; for it is not until the time of the Persian Wars that these two simple but happy creations cease to be the dominant type of substantive statue. The last stage in the development of the kouros may be illustrated by the so-called Strangford Apollo in the British Museum[2]. Body, legs and head remain frontal, and the weight is still equally distributed between the two legs: the statue differs from the kouros of Tenea not in the attitude but in the far deeper understanding of the bodily forms. It is not only that the several parts of the body have a more definite and a truer shape than before, and that portions which had been slurred, such as the neck or the area between breast and groin, are now clear and precise, but also that the artist has grasped the structure of the body as a whole, he thinks of the surface forms as determined by underlying muscle and bone, he has learnt how the head sits on the shoulders and the trunk on the pelvis, so that his kouros has a new vigour and a new elasticity. The next step will be to break with the old tradition of rigid frontality and to replace the simple bilateral symmetry of the older figures by a much more complex scheme.

The Strangford statue is said to have been found in Boeotia: but that loving study and systematic exploration of the human body to which it bears witness was not confined to one part of Greece. It is customary to give the principal credit to Peloponnesian artists, but that the movement originated in the Peloponnese we cannot be absolutely certain: all we can say is that wherever we turn in the late archaic period we find the same preoccupation, and that the idea of the young athlete, perfectly shaped and perfectly developed, becomes henceforth and for ever one of the chief elements, perhaps the chief of all, in the Greek conception of a work of art.

[1] See vol. IV, pp. 589 *sqq.*   [2] See Volume of Plates ii, 18, *a*.

For the female figure and the representation of drapery we naturally recur to that splendid series of Athenian dedications to which we have already referred; and select four statues for special remark. The big flash kore 682 belongs to about the beginning of our period. It has been held by many to be not Attic but Ionic, by others to be by an Attic sculptor imitating, and seeking to outdo, Ionian models: in any case a brilliant, pretentious and vapid work, exemplifying a passing mode, and outside the main current of Attic sculpture, though not unparalleled among the multifarious dedications on the Athenian Acropolis. We find the same scheme of drapery, but a more temperate and more monumental style, in the big kore signed by Antenor, the sculptor who made the statues of the Tyrant-slayers for the young democracy of Athens. There is a somewhat similar though a subtler contrast, a decade or more later, between 674[1], with her bower-sequestered, almost spectral charm, and the giant robustness of 684[2]. The very last stage of the kore, and the advent of a new epoch, is represented by the dedication of Euthydicus[3]: all the little gleeful prettinesses of dress, hair, lip, and eye, swept away by a young, great artist. Such works as the kore by Antenor, 684, and the kore of Euthydicus are sufficient of themselves to refute the extraordinary notion that 'grace and refinement' are the characteristics of Attic art. It is not altogether true in the fourth century: in the fifth and sixth centuries it is laughable.

For all the beauty and variety of the late archaic kouroi and korai, it is not in these that late archaic sculpture finds its most perfect expression, but in the action-figures—men not being but doing—common as before in groups, especially in decoration of buildings, and becoming common now as substantive statues. On the Acropolis of Athens the long series of pedimental decorations in limestone culminates in the marble gigantomachy which filled the Peisistratid pediment of the old Temple of Athena[4]. The Athena and the giants have that truly Attic bigness of treatment which we have already admired, at an earlier stage, in the great beast pediments or in Tricorpor, and at the dawn of Attic sculpture in the Apollo of Sunium. The Alcmaeonid pediment of the Temple of Apollo at Delphi belongs to the same period as the Gigantomachy, but is not nearly so well planned. Neither of these works bears evidence of a really systematic study of the human body and its anatomy: but this we do find, only a little later, in the finely and vigorously executed

[1] See Volume of Plates ii, 18, *b*.   [2] *Ib.* 20, *a*.   [3] *Ib.* 20, *b*.
[4] See vol. IV, p. 596, and Volume of Plates ii, 22, *b*.

metopes of the Athenian Treasury at Delphi, with their scenes
from the life of Heracles and his young compeer the Attic Theseus[1].
There is another respect in which the metopes mark a new epoch:
the modelling no longer hugs the front plane, as it did, for the
most part, in earlier high relief or pedimental action-groups: the
mass of the stone is fully utilized, the trunk is often rendered in
three-quarter view, and regularly sheers away from the spectator
towards the background. From these Attic works we may turn
for a moment to an Ionian work of the same period, the exquisite
pedimental figures from the Temple of Apollo at Eretria, Theseus
carrying off the Amazonian queen in his chariot[2], with Athena
presiding; and then to those sculptures which, over a hundred
years ago, opened modern eyes to the beauty of archaic sculpture,
and which despite the desecrations of the restorer remain unsur-
passed by any subsequent discovery, the pediments of the Temple
of Aphaia at Aegina[3].

The west pediment is distinctly less advanced in style than the
east, and it is plausibly conjectured that the west belongs to the
years just before 490, the east to the years just after. The excellence of the several figures has long been recognized, and wonder
expressed, that the Aeginetan sculptors, best known in antiquity
as bronze-casters, should have been masters of marble as well:
but not until the new excavations of 1901 was it possible to form
an accurate idea of the composition. Many-figured battle-scenes,
dense yet clear; each man eager, light of foot, and trained to the
last ounce; and all the freedom of a picture in the attitudes—
darting, dying, and even falling. The theme of the pediments is
one upon which Pindar loved to dwell in his Aeginetan odes:
how the sons of Aeacus had twice taken Troy: once with Heracles,
and again with the Atreidae. Pindar composed a hymn to Aphaia,
possibly for the opening of the temple: but it is not to Pindar
that we must turn for a counterpart to the sculpture of the pediments, but to the swift Homeric hexameter, or to the swift iambics
of Aeschylus:

πολλοὺς δέ γ᾽ εὑρήσουσιν ἐν μεσημβρίας
θάλπει βραχίον᾽ εὖ κατερρινημένους.

If a single figure had to be chosen to represent ripe archaic
sculpture, would it not be the archer Heracles[3], himself tense as
a drawn bow, from the east pediment at Aegina?

[1] See Volume of Plates ii, 22, a.   [2] Ib. 24, a, b.   [3] Ib. 24, c.

II. LATE ARCHAIC PAINTING

We have seen how in the course of the sixth century the Attic potters drove their competitors from the field[1]. About 525, a new technique came in. The old black-figure method long survived, never quite died out, and produced masterpieces down to the end of the sixth century, but it waned gradually before the new red-figure method, in which the figures are not painted in black on the clay of the vase, but left in the colour of the clay, and the background painted black: the minor details are in brown lines; a purplish-red is used very sparingly; and the colour-effect is thus very sober. That manly precision, which is one of the chief characteristics of Greek vase-painting, is now imparted not by incised lines as previously, but by the wiry unerring 'relief-line.' In its relation to nature, the drawing of the earliest red-figure vases does not differ in essentials from that of the black-figured vases signed by Execias or Amasis. The great change sets in fully about ten years after the introduction of the red-figure technique. The characteristics of the new style are first, a profound interest in the individual forms of the human body, and second, a new conception of the body in space, a conception of which the most obvious manifestation is the love of certain violent yet definite foreshortenings. The first of these characteristics we know from the sculpture of the time: in painting it may be illustrated by the Antaeus of Euphronius[2], which stands at the beginning of the movement, and is full of the enthusiasm of the pioneer: the artist delights in collecting and recording the very smallest facts. Such extreme profusion of detail is hardly found in later works: by the end of the archaic period the knowledge now being amassed is common property, and though used is not displayed. The second characteristic has no exact equivalent in sculpture in the round, but it naturally appears in low relief, and to some extent in high relief. Hitherto the figures making up a picture had moved past the beholder on a plane parallel to the plane of his eyes: either the legs had been in profile and the breast frontal, or the whole figure had been in profile. In the new style of the later sixth century the figures are apt to turn towards the spectator and front him, partly or mainly: there are figures in which one leg is in profile and the other leg and the trunk frontal; and figures in which both legs are in profile and the trunk

---

[1] See vol. IV, p. 600 *sq.*   [2] See Volume of Plates ii, 26, *a.*

three-quartered. Such figures do not merely make more variety in the representation: the foreshortenings lead the eye onwards beyond the surface of the picture, and by suggesting the third dimension give the bodies more solidity and substance. The frontal figure is not a mere vehicle of action: it invites the beholder to contemplate its mass. The Thorycion of Euthymides[1] is a good example; in which we notice further that the two halves of the body are differentiated by the frontal leg, that the head, though still in profile, no longer perches rigid on a rigid neck, but bends on to the shoulder, that one hip is higher than the other, and the trunk on the eve of turning with the bend of the head. Thus, and by the turn towards us, the figure falls into line, in some degree, with the new kind of statue which we shall find taking the place of the kouros at the beginning of the next period: an earlier manifestation of the same revolutionary idea.

Besides figures seen from the front, we have figures seen from behind: with profile legs and the back three-quartered; or with one leg in profile, and trunk and the other leg in full back-view. The head is still nearly always in profile: the full face remains rare, and three-quarter faces are not attempted till after the beginning of the fifth century, and then only occasionally and for a long time unsuccessfully. Three-quartered hands add life to the gesture; the foot may make a three-quarter turn. Finally, the artist no longer shrinks from obscuring important parts of the body: the thigh of Antaeus occludes the lower half of his leg.

Thus, by purely linear devices, the painter contrives to give his picture a certain depth in space. Towards the end of the archaic period, a device of a different kind but with a kindred tendency makes its first appearance: shading. It is used very seldom and very sparingly: a flat wash of brown to give the hollow of a hat or of folds, hatched brown brush-strokes to model the rotundity of a vessel or a shield. But it is the first step towards the abolition of the linear contour and towards the replacement of outline drawing by what the modern world calls painting.

The chief interest of the vase-painter remains action. Narrative subjects—mythical and heroic—are as popular as ever, but pictures from everyday life become commoner than before, and there is a special love of athletic scenes with their straining muscles, intense movements, and countless postures; for scenes of revelry, the 'komos,' where men rush, dance, quarrel, lust, vomit, shout, and sing; and for the counterpart of the komos in the ideal sphere

[1] See Volume of Plates ii, 26, b.

—the thiasos, Dionysus with his satyrs and maenads. For all its variety, humour and unconcern, this art is not naturalistic: apart from some very old persons, crookbacked and borne-over, from a fat belly or so, a wrinkled brow, a bald head, a bad beard, or a blobby nose; god and man, Greek and barbarian, athlete, drinker and amorist, have the same well-formed bodies and the same untainted vigour.

The number of vases is so great, and the styles so individual, that it is possible to trace the history of vase-painting with a detail and precision hardly attainable in other branches of Greek art. The earliest stage of red-figure vase-painting is best represented by the anonymous artist who painted most of the works which bear the signature of the potter Andocides—probably the same Andocides who dedicated the kore signed by Antenor. In the next stage, which is marked by the introduction of the new style of drawing with its anatomy, its foreshortenings, and its corporeity, the leading painters are Euphronius and Euthymides[1]. By this time the drinking-cup had begun to engage the particular attention of the artists, and for the rest of the archaic period cup-painters and pot-painters may be said to form two distinct classes. The chief cup-painters of this third period, the late archaic, are the Panaitius painter[2], master of careering movement, who at one time worked for Euphronius; Duris[3], who began like the Panaitius painter but soon formed a staider subtle style of his own; the Brygus painter[4], at once passionate and delicious, able to put new fire even into the Panaitian style; and Macron[5], enamoured of the warm swing of women's clothes. Of the pot-painters the Berlin painter[6], the Cleophrades painter[7], and the Pan painter[8] are the chief: the first is sober and gracious; the massive power of the second anticipates Olympia and the early classical style; the third is an exquisite.

The remains of ripe archaic painting apart from vase-painting are trifling, and cannot detain us in this brief sketch. Our literary record, moreover, is extremely scanty. The great change which came over drawing in this period did not escape the notice of ancient writers. Pliny preserves an account, probably derived from Xenocrates, of the innovations ascribed to Cimon of Cleonae, which correspond in the main to those which we know from Euphronius, Euthymides and their companions: but whether Cimon was the moving spirit, or only one of those who had a hand in the movement, there is no saying.

[1] See Volume of Plates ii, 26.   [2] Ib. 28, a.   [3] Ib. 28, b.
[4] Ib. 30, a.   [5] Ib. 30, b.   [6] Ib. 32, a.   [7] Ib. 32, b.   [8] Ib. 32, c.

III. EARLY CLASSICAL SCULPTURE

The art of the period between 480 and 450 is often termed transitional, but the term is misleading. Transitional implies inferiority to that which goes before or comes after, or to both, and the great works of this period—enough to mention the sculpture of the Temple of Zeus at Olympia—are equivalent to those of any other in quality, originality and creative force.

Let us begin with two early examples of the new art, both from the Acropolis of Athens, the Critian boy, and the fair-haired head. The Critian boy[1] is so-called because of its close stylistic resemblance to the Tyrant-slayers by Critius and Nesiotes. That famous group we possess in copies only: the boy is an original of about 480. The old kouros-type, with its simple symmetry, has now disappeared and given place to a new type of substantive statue: the weight is no longer equally distributed between the two legs, but rests principally on one, here the left; the left hip is consequently higher than the right, the shoulders are uneven, the spine curves, the axis of the whole body is thrown out, and the head turns to one side instead of looking straight in front of it. In the Critian boy the turns and twists are still slight: in later statues they will be more marked: the free leg will be farther away from the stiff leg, and the body will often sheer away from the spectator: but the age-long tradition is broken, an infinite prospect opened up, and the Critian stance will persist, developed but not essentially changed or contested, until Polyclitus introduced a still more complex and subtle idea. This great formal innovation is not a mere change of mode, it is the expression of a new view of life. The old kouros stood at the ready, with much about him of the perfect machine: his successor stands at ease, and the differentiation of the two sides of the body, with the alternation of contracted parts and relaxed, of muscle in play and at rest, gives a strong suggestion of the life, within the body, which controls the mechanism. The archaic artist was concerned with the surface and the build of the body, the interest of the early classical sculptor recedes, inwards from these, to the will.

The smile has faded from the boy's lips and his look is even sombre; and a serious, even sombre face is common in the early classical period. The kouros and the kore smiled, not because the artist knew no better, but because the gay look was part of the code of behaviour at the time. It is no longer so: the statue will still smile sometimes: not a party-smile, however, or a royal

[1] See Volume of Plates ii, 34, a.

smile (though these are not unlovely things), but in Lucian's phrase, a μειδίαμα σεμνὸν καὶ λεληθός, when deep spiritual felicity transfigures the face without perceptible change of feature.

The new simplicity and the new seriousness were observable in one of the last of the korai, the maiden dedicated by Euthydicus[1]: and a second, slightly later masterpiece by the same great artist, the fair-haired head from the Acropolis[2], is the first of that long and wonderful line of fifth-century boy victors, not elated in the hour of their triumph, but grave and even troubled, as if made conscious, for the first time, of the meaning of life. The Critian boy and the fair-haired head belong to the same five years or so, but the style is totally different: the terse forms of the one point on to Myron; the larger forms of the other to Olympia. A third original, of the same period as the Tyrant-slayers, though not of the same school, is the bronze charioteer from Delphi[3], part of one of those great chariot-groups which we read of in Pausanias.

The new depth of content appears in the statues of the gods as well as in those of men: in the archaic period god and man look much alike; but now the sculptor is able to suggest a superhuman majesty and power. Significantly enough, Apollo, young, lofty, and austere, seems to have had a special attraction for the art of this time. The chief embodiment of him, for us, is the Apollo of the west pediment of the Temple of Zeus at Olympia[4]: but other noble Apollos have been preserved to us in marble copies after bronze: chief among them the Choiseul-Gouffier[5], perhaps an Argive work, and the Cassel Apollo[6], perhaps Attic.

The smile is only one of the superficial graces or ornaments which are rejected by the new age. Just as a starker or more massive habit of body prevails in the male figure, so in the female the drapery becomes simpler and heavier. This is partly owing to a change in fashion, for the plain peplos, with its big unadorned spaces and severe verticals and horizontals, is now a favourite wear, not only in the Peloponnese, but also in Attica, where it had been replaced for nearly half a century by the gayer Ionic costume, and even in Eastern Greece itself: but the truth is that change of mode and change of treatment are due to a single cause. The kore of Euthydicus showed the new love of plainness applied to the Ionic costume itself: the next step may be illustrated by the post-Persian figure from the Propylaea, a work of the seventies[7]. The garments are no longer subordinated to the forms of the

---

[1] See Volume of Plates ii, 20, *b*.   [2] *Ib.* 34, *b, c*.   [3] *Ib.* 36, *a*.
[4] *Ib.* 36, *b*.   [5] *Ib.* 38, *a*.   [6] *Ib.* 38, *c*.   [7] *Ib.* 38, *b*.

body, but live a life of their own. The austere magnificence of
the 'peplos figure' is one of the main features of the Olympian
pediments and metopes: but splendid examples of the substantive
female statues of the period have survived to us in marble copies,
and to two at least of these we must turn our attention: the so-
called Hestia Giustiniani[1], and the statue called Amelung's from
the scholar who first placed the head on the body[2]. The Hestia
wears the peplos, and presents a complete contrast to the regular
archaic kore whose elastic unvoluminous immaterial drapery clings
to her body like a glove. The forms of the body are almost concealed: the heavy garment is like a fluted column from the waist
down; the waist is not seen; and even the outlines of shoulder,
neck, and head are masked by the thick veil. Once more, the
life withdrawn from the surface into the core of the statue, where
it burns with a strong unflickering flame. There is no reason to
suppose that the goddess is Hestia—although it was a little poem
to name her so: she stands and looks with the queenliness of the
young matron: perhaps Hera, perhaps an Aeschylean Aphrodite:

> δύναται γὰρ Διὸς ἄγχιστα σὺν Ἥρᾳ·
> τίεται δ' αἰολόμητις
> θεὸς ἔργοις ἐπὶ σεμνοῖς.

Amelung's statue belongs to the same period and the same
school, probably the Argive. The costume is here the Ionic
chiton and the himation, but it is as plain, and the envelopment as
total, as in the Hestia. The tone of the figure is subtly different:
not the matron, but the bride; and it is perhaps Europa, chosen
by Zeus to be the mother of mighty kings.

Of the early classical sculptors mentioned in our literary sources,
only two are much more than names to us. The many attempts
which have been made to associate extant works with Pythagoras
or Calamis have failed: but of Critius and of Myron we can form
a notion. The bronze Tyrant-slayers by Critius and his partner
Nesiotes are preserved to us by the marble copies in Naples[3];
other fragmentary copies—especially the newly-discovered heads
of Aristogeiton in the Vatican and of Harmodius in New York—
help to supply what is missing or spoilt in the Naples group.
The exact compositional relation of the two figures to each other
is uncertain, but we are fortunate to possess, even incompletely,
a historical monument of the first interest, an admirable example
of the severe athletic art of the stage immediately after the Aeginetans, and a chronological landmark, for the group is known to

---

[1] See Volume of Plates ii, 40, *a*.   [2] *Ib.* 40, *c*.   [3] *Ib.* 40, *b*.

have been dedicated in 476. Of the Critian boy on the Acropolis we have spoken already, and other torsoes might be added.

Myron made statues of athletes victorious in 456 and 448; and was probably active from about 480 to 440. The two famous bronzes of which we possess marble copies belong to the late part of his career: both show him as a master of movement, and an artist of great variety and originality. The discus-thrower[1] is the culmination of the single action-figure to which the late archaic sculptors had paid close attention, and which would be more fully represented among our copies if it had lent itself to translation into marble. The original of the Athena and Marsyas stood on the Acropolis of Athens[2]: the half-playful theme is a peculiar one for fifth-century sculpture, and must have been inspired by some special event at which we can only guess. Here as in the Tyrant-slayers the composition is not certain in every detail, but the main movement is clear. Athena has dropped the flute and turned to pass on; the satyr who has been listening awestruck, steals up after the discarded flute, while the goddess looks round with a warning gesture, for the flute will be his death. Both in the group and in the discus-thrower the movement is so planned that it is momentary without being trivial, and strong without violence. Strength and fineness are subtly blended in the body and head of the discus-thrower, and there is a wonderful freshness in the characterization of Athena, here a quite young girl, and of the wild man's sinewy dry body and his hidebound few-featured face.

Hestia, Amelung's, Tyrant-slayers, discus-thrower, Athena and Marsyas, are all copies. In the archaic period we were able to confine ourselves to originals, but now we must consider copies as well. Most of the ancient statues in our museums are copies, made between the first century before Christ and the second after, of earlier works, and these copies preserve to us many of the masterpieces of the fifth and fourth centuries. It is considered good taste, especially in this country, where little attention has been paid to the history of Greek sculpture, to disparage these copies as made by irresponsible workmen for indiscriminating customers—'Romans.' Quality and faithfulness obviously vary: the quality is often admirable; to determine how faithful a copy is, in the loss of the original, is naturally a most delicate matter; but not necessarily impossible because delicate.

[1] See Volume of Plates ii, 42, *a*.		[2] *Ib*. 42, *b*, *c*.

The place and more than the place, which the Aeginetan pediments occupied in the ripe archaic period, is taken in the early classical by the sculptures of the Temple of Zeus at Olympia[1]. It is only recently that their overwhelming excellence has been recognized. More than one well-known writer has characterized them as 'comparatively crude and archaic': and these are the very words which other thinkers have applied to Aeschylus. The two great artists—Aeschylus and the master of Olympia—are akin in spirit; and we may add a third, the painter Polygnotus, for although no fragment from his hand has survived, passages in ancient writers enable us to form a certain notion of one who was reckoned the earliest of the great Greek painters.

The Temple seems to have been complete by 456, and the sculptures must have been made in the decade or so previous, are contemporary therefore with the latest and greatest works of the Athenian poet. The two pediments are contrasted: the west all tumult—Apollo, and the struggle between the Lapiths and the Centaurs at the wedding of Peirithous and Hippodameia; the east quiet—Zeus, and the preparations for the fateful chariot-race between Pelops and King Oenomaus. The twelve metopes deal with the labours of Heracles.

The treatment of these subjects is characteristic of the time. It has often been noticed that Polygnotus liked to represent, not the action itself, but the scene after: not the taking of Troy, delight of the archaic artist, but the morning after the taking. And so in the metopes, side by side with action-representations of the time-honoured kind, there are others in which the labour is over: Heracles is not shooting the Stymphalian birds as in the earlier versions of the subject, but offering their dead bodies to a wavering Athena; he is not grappling with the Nemean lion—a subject which the archaic artist enjoyed extremely—but resting his foot on the corpse of the monster and his head on his hand, the heroic boy exhausted by his first labour, and darkly conscious of the life of toil before him: his friend Athena stands by, her divine brow furrowed in sympathetic concern. A third metope shows Heracles supporting the firmament, while Athena lends him a hand and a kingly, a Promethean Atlas fetches him the golden apples. The idea of Heracles is greater and richer than any version of it: Aeschylus, perhaps Sophocles, might have expressed Heracles, but as far as we know did not: the metopes of Olympia are the grandest and profoundest single embodiment of Heracles.

---

[1] See Volume of Plates ii, 36, *b*; 44; 46.

The Polygnotan Troy Taken gave the time after the action, with its revulsion, resipiscence, remorse, resignation, and despair: the east pediment at Olympia gives the time before the action, with its conflicts and contrasts of emotion, its moral tension as opposed to the physical tension of Aegina, its hopes and fears, resolutions, sorrowful forebodings and anguish of expectation. Two things are to be said: first, that what we here observe in narrative art, the recession of interest from the action itself to the mental condition previous or subsequent to action, is parallel to something already noticed in the substantive statue; and secondly, that long and conflicting suspense, a knife-flash of action and that unseen, and then strange revulsion and un-ease, is the very formula, the very soul of Aeschylean tragedy. To go closer, the Troy Taken of Polygnotus finds a real counterpart in the speech of Clytaemnestra

$$Τροίαν \ ᾿Αχαιοὶ \ τῇδ᾿ \ ἔχουσ᾿ \ ἐν \ ἡμέρᾳ·$$
$$οἶμαι \ βοὴν \ ἄμεικτον \ ἐν \ πόλει \ πρέπειν.$$

So perfect a pendant for the East pediment we shall not expect to find: but every note in that harsh symphony is struck either in the *Persians*, or in *Agamemnon*, or in the *Seven*.

Are there then no representations of action itself in this period? Of course there are, and the West pediment is one. But there is a great difference between action as treated at Olympia and as treated at Aegina. At Aegina Athena is in the middle of each pediment, but who of us remembers her? At Olympia the whole scene is dominated by the contrast between the knots of frantic strugglers and the towering figure of Apollo with the great gesture of command.

The unevenness of execution in the Olympian pediments has shocked some critics: the work is meant to tell from below and at a distance, and not every part of it will stand examination at close range. Others were repelled by a strong infusion of realism, foreign to the modern cathedral close, but characteristic of the early classical period and exactly paralleled in Aeschylean tragedy; or by a disregard of trivial propriety which seems naive—to the naive. The truth is that the pediments and the metopes are one of the highwatermarks of Greek art.

Who was the artist? Pausanias gives an answer: the East pediment was by Paeonius of Mende and the West by Alcamenes. We know something about both artists, or of the work they were doing in the thirties and twenties, and Pausanias' attributions present difficulties which cannot be discussed at length. To sum up: first, it looks as if a single artist was responsible for the designs of the two pediments and the metopes; secondly, it is hard to believe that Alcamenes worked on the Temple, unless in a completely subordinate position, even in his youth; thirdly, it is a little less hard to believe that Paeonius was the artist. But it is better to call the artist not Paeonius, but the master of Olympia.

IV. EARLY CLASSICAL PAINTING

The painters and paintings of the early classical period have left more mark in our literary records than their predecessors. Popular opinion regarded Polygnotus, an Ionian from Thasos, as the earliest of the great painters, or putting it more crudely as the inventor of painting. Pausanias has left an unusually full description of the great pictures by Polygnotus in the club-house of the Cnidians at Delphi: and with the help of this, of brief references in other writers, and of contemporary vase-paintings, we can form a certain notion, if not of Polygnotus, of the painting of his kind and time. 'Troy Taken' and the 'Nekyia'—Odysseus in Hades—were huge mural decorations each comprising a great number of lifesize or nearly lifesize figures. The composition— apart, one must suppose, from a general balance—was not synoptic but episodic; and the principle on which the figures were arranged on the wall can be determined from a comparison of the language of Pausanias with such vase-paintings as the Argonaut krater in the Louvre[1]. This vase marks, for us, an epoch, for the age-old rule that the figures must share a common standing-line is abandoned: they are now disposed at different levels in the curtly-indicated landscape setting of rocks and herbage. The vase is in the ordinary red-figure technique, and its contrast of light and dark must not be transferred to Polygnotus. In Polygnotus the background was not black, but no doubt neutral and variable; the figures must have been modelled, though still very lightly, by shading; as to the colouring we hear something from our literary records, which tell us that Polygnotus was a four-colour painter, using white, red, ochre, black, and combinations of these: that is to say, restricting himself to a low, sober scheme of colour, without bright blue, bright green, and the intermediate shades for which these are necessary. The colour-scale is in the main that of Corinthian or Attic black-figure vases, but the proportions of the colours were naturally quite different in Polygnotus. A closer analogy is furnished by the white-ground cups of the early classical

---

[1] See Volume of Plates ii, 48, a.

period: but once more, in Polygnotus the effect must have been made more complex by the use of mixed and intermediate tints. An excellent example of four-colour painting is preserved to us in the mosaic of Alexander and Darius, a careful copy of a famous picture by Philoxenus, an artist of the later part of the fourth century. The colouring of the Alexander mosaic reminds one of such modern pictures as Rubens's Battle of Ivry. Rubens, as we know, did not always confine himself to the austeri colores, but used the floridi as well: all fourth-century painting was not four-colour painting; and we need not suppose that all early classical painting was four-colour either. Philoxenus models strongly in light and dark, uses high-lights, reflected lights, and cast-shadows: Polygnotus knew none of these devices, but his colouring, though simpler than Philoxenus's, was doubtless of the same kind.

Turning to the individual groups and figures, we find that Polygnotus was regarded as the earliest master of expression: Pliny says that he was the first 'to open the mouth, show the teeth, vary the countenance from its ancient rigour.' This is a crude exaggeration, but doubtless refers to some such elaboration of facial expression as distinguishes Leonardo's Last Supper from previous Italian painting: and the great expression-figures in the Lesche—Helenus 'utterly dejected,' Thamyris 'blinded, unshorn, and altogether humbled'—make one think of the words of Leonardo (although in other respects Leonardo represents a later stage in the development of the art) when he calls 'that figure most worthy of praise, which best expresses the passion which animates it.' Polygnotus painted action-pictures: but the tone of his 'Troy Taken' or 'Odysseus after the Slaying of the Suitors' was like that of the East pediment at Olympia or the Argonaut vase: not the action itself represented, but the previous tension or the subsequent reaction; as in a tragedy where the killing is done off the stage. Finally, the ethos of Polygnotus was contrasted by critics with the lack of ethos in his successors: his figures were of heroic breed, and breathed character and will. He stood as Aeschylus, or the Sophocles of the Ajax, to Euripides, or as Michael Angelo, let us say, to Paul Veronese.

The vase-painting of the early classical period is on the whole quieter than that of the late archaic. There is less calligraphic precision about body and drapery, and more breadth. The violent movement, which reached its acme in the Brygus painter, slows down. The light and nimble drinking-cup gradually loses the importance which it had acquired in the ripe archaic period, and big, imposing, more monumental vases play a greater part than before.

The art of Micon or Polygnotus sometimes inspires the vase-painter, and sometimes leads him to attempt what is beyond his powers. The thought of dignity and majesty is often in his mind: aiming at dignity, he is apt to become official; at majesty, to become grandiose. The vase-paintings of the seventies and sixties are on the whole more vigorous and significant than those of the sixties and fifties. By the middle of the century it is clear that the vase-painter, the peer of all other artists in the archaic period, is sinking to a humbler position, and can no longer keep abreast of the great transformations which are taking place in other branches of art. Vases and vase-paintings of the rarest beauty will still be produced for many a year, but ever fewer in proportion to the output, nor always with that perfect harmony not only between shape and picture, but between expression and decoration, which is the mark of the best archaic vases.

The great vase-painters of the seventies and sixties are the Penthesilea painter, the Sotades painter, and the Pistoxenus painter. The first is mainly a painter of cups: and his masterpiece, the Penthesilea cup itself[1], is in a sense a last word in cups, an audacious attempt, this once by a miracle successful, to cram an Agincourt into an oe. The grand pathos and the huge gestures of the Penthesilea cup and the Tityus cup recall Olympia, and these, with the amazonomachy on a calyx-krater in Bologna[2], bring us closer than any other vases to the breadth and passion of battle-pieces by Micon or Polygnotus. The ordinary run of the painter's works, youths and horses, satyrs and maenads, are broadly drawn with much realism and a pungent charm. The Sotades painter is akin to him: his white-ground cups are April-fresh, and for all the tiny scale, bold beyond what would have seemed possible[3]. The Pistoxenus painter is less of a realist than the other two: his masterpiece is also on a white-ground cup, the Aphrodite on the Swan[4]: it is the earliest work of classical, as opposed to archaic or early-classical, beauty. Among the vase-painters of the sixties and fifties there are two main groups. The Niobid painter and his companions paint large and somewhat heavy-handed amazonomachies and Iliuperseis, which evidently reproduce many of the features of the great wall-pictures, but not the spirit. The art of the Villa Giulia painter and his companions, derived from the later manner of Duris, loves quiet, cool scenes, and is full of harmony.

---

[1] See Volume of Plates ii, 50, a.   [2] Ib. 48, b.
[3] Ib. 52, a, b.   [4] Ib. 50, b.

V. CLASSICAL SCULPTURE: (i) THE SECOND HALF OF THE FIFTH CENTURY

It was not possible to connect the great innovations of the early classical period with particular artists: but in the ripe classical period at least one great innovation can be ascribed to its author or perfector, the Polyclitan stance. And speaking generally, the literary sources are not only somewhat less scanty, but fit in better with the actual remains. Two sculptors stand out above the others in our record: Pheidias and Polyclitus. We know a good deal about Polyclitus, and if Pheidias still outtops knowledge, we have advanced beyond the foothills: of others, Alcamenes, Agoracritus, Cresilas, Paeonius, we catch more than a glimpse.

Polyclitus, described both as a Sicyonian and an Argive, made statues of athletes victorious in 460 and 452; and late in life, about 420, the chryselephantine image of Hera at Argos. Over half a dozen of his works have come down to us in more or less adequate copies. The chief of them is the so-called Doryphorus, a naked youth shouldering a spear[1]. The best-preserved copy is the marble in Naples which formerly decorated the beautiful Hellenistic palaestra at Pompeii: but other copies give, one the head, and two the body better. The figure expresses in new and final form that general idea of which the earlier, less elaborate, and less perfect expression was the early archaic statue of the type of the Critian boy or the Choiseul-Gouffier Apollo: the idea of giving the impression of life by means of the alternation and contrast of tense and relaxed. The two legs are much more strongly differentiated than before, for the whole weight rests on the right, while the left, drawn far back, and touching ground with the toes only, is quite free; the head turns towards the supporting leg; the right arm hangs down at the side, resembling the right leg in its straightness, unlike it in being relaxed; the left arm holding the spear across the shoulder resembles the left leg in being bent, differs in being functional. The forms of the body are firm and massive, and the whole figure weighty: but there is no clumsiness, for the artist has been at pains to give each part a harmonious contour, and to make each take its place in the grand total design. It has been said that the Naples copy 'can give us but little notion of the finish of Polyclitus' style, in which his

---

[1] See Volume of Plates ii, 54, *a*.

chief excellence lay.' The first part of the sentence is true, the second not. The principal thing is after all not the finish, but the total design, and that can be appreciated perfectly well in the Naples copy, though hardly in any photograph of it, for photographs always fail to give the recession of the free leg into depth. Pliny's tag for the Doryphoros, 'viriliter puer,' evidently translates a Greek *andropais*: and truly the statue brings to memory the astounding line of the poet:

$$\beta\lambda\acute{\alpha}\sigma\tau\eta\mu\alpha\ \kappa\alpha\lambda\lambda\acute{\iota}\pi\rho\omega\rho o\nu,\ \dot{\alpha}\nu\delta\rho\acute{o}\pi\alpha\iota\varsigma\ \dot{\alpha}\nu\acute{\eta}\rho.$$

Certain ancient critics, hardly the subtlest, complained that the statues of Polyclitus were 'very square, and all alike': and the mind of Polyclitus was no doubt guided by the thoroughly Greek conception of a single ideal representation of the human figure which must be the goal of the sculptor's efforts. In the Doryphorus he felt that he had approached as near the perfect statue as he could, and he wrote a treatise on the system of proportions which it embodied. The Hermes and the Heracles of Polyclitus go with the Doryphorus: the Diadumenus[1]—an athlete, or perhaps Apollo, binding his head with the victor's fillet—is generally allowed to belong to a later period in the sculptor's life, when his art had become freer and blither. The two boys, the Dresden and the Westmacott, alter the rhythm of the Doryphorus and the other adult figures by turning the head away from the supporting leg: the assured look of early manhood gives place to modest downcast eyes.

We would gladly know how Polyclitus treated drapery and the female figure. What little is known about his Hera does not help us: and which of the Amazons preserved in copies is his has been hotly disputed. The two candidates are the Berlin type and the Capitoline. The Berlin Amazon[2] has that perfect harmony of fold and form which the Doryphorus leads us to look for: the Capitoline[3] is the work of a realist, but its forms seem the more Polyclitan. Whoever the sculptors, both are great works: two different embodiments of athletic and heroic womanhood, not in action, but in defeat and pain playing the man.

The Polyclitan stance never ousts the simpler pre-Polyclitan, but its influence shows itself wherever we turn in the later part of the fifth century: the strong swing imparted to the figure by bent knee and tiptoe foot becomes one of the dominant elements not only in naked male figures, but in draped female. But a

second motive, just encountered for the first time, is destined to
play an equally important part—the Berlin Amazon rests her left
forearm on a pillar. This is the first step towards the leaning
figures which are characteristic of fourth-century sculpture,
figures in which the axis of the statue is not within the body but
outside it. The motive is naturally common in painting long
before it appears in sculpture; and where it occurs in fifth-century
statues it usually has a strong and special justification: the
Amazon is wounded, and Aphrodite the most indolent of the
immortals. But before the end of the century it appears in male
figures also, as in a charming statue by a follower of Polyclitus,
of which we have many copies, the best-preserved in the Louvre:
the so-called Narcissus[1], really a boy athlete leaning with his hand
on one of the little pillars of the palaestra. Artists are becoming
more and more interested in the human figure not merely at ease,
but completely at rest: when the motive power is withdrawn still
farther from the surface, and there is no thought of action at all.
The deep repose of such figures as the 'Theseus' of the Parthenon,
or the nightward Moira, is another manifestation of the same
interest.

Ancient critics thought of Polyclitus as the sculptor of men,
of Pheidias as the sculptor of gods. The masterpieces of the great
Athenian were the two colossal chryselephantine images of Zeus
at Olympia and of Athena in the Parthenon at Athens. The Athena
Parthenos was finished in 438: whether the Zeus was earlier or
later is debated: Pliny gives the 83rd Olympiad (448 B.C.) as the
artist's acme, and since this date is not that of the Parthenos, it has
been held to be the date of the Zeus. Of the Zeus we have nothing
but tiny representations on Roman coins: a fourth-century head in
Boston has been thought to reflect the majesty of the Olympian
Zeus: but if we care for reflections, we had much better go to one
or two Attic heads of the fifth century[2]. Of the Parthenos we have
reduced copies, the most complete and circumstantial the little
vulgar souvenir which is known as the Varvakeion statuette.
Something of the radiance and grandeur of the original lingers in
the Hellenistic statue from Pergamum: but the Pergamene copy
makes no pretence to fidelity. The great works of the earlier,
the Cimonian, period of Pheidias have left no certain trace. At
the other end, we have some evidence for the style of two sculptors
who were described as his pupils, Alcamenes, and the Parian
Agoracritus: and there is the Parthenon. The Procne found on

the Acropolis is in all probability an original work, though a slight one, of Alcamenes; and a herm from Pergamum is a copy, perhaps on a reduced scale, of another work of his, the Hermes which stood beside the Propylaea. Small fragments of a great marble temple-statue by Agoracritus, the Nemesis of Rhamnus, still remain; fragments of the reliefs on its base, presumably carved under his supervision, quite possibly from his design; and a copy, now in Stockholm, of part of those reliefs. The list of Alcamenean works can be increased—for instance by a Pergamene copy of one of his goddesses—but it cannot yet be said that to us he stands out from his contemporaries as Myron or Polyclitus from theirs. Nor does Agoracritus. In the general disposition of the figures, the reliefs on the base of the Nemesis follow the Birth of Pandora on the base of the Parthenos: the style of the figures, which finds parallels in a number of Attic votive reliefs, and in a statue of a boy from Rhamnus itself[1], takes us a step beyond the Parthenon in the direction of softness and sunniness, anticipating one of the tendencies of the fourth century: but we must not forget that the base is probably pupil-work. Our ancient sources would suggest that the Nemesis itself stood well within the Pheidian tradition; and we may perhaps supplement our notion of it with the help of the so-called Demeter of the Vatican Rotonda, a copy, though polished up in modern times, of a stately Attic temple-statue which seems to stand close to what we know of Agoracritus.

The sculpture of the Parthenon is our third great body of original sculpture in the fifth century, the first being Aegina and the second Olympia. Thanks to inscriptions, the dates are more precise than one could have expected: 447 to 442 for the metopes, 442 to 438 for the frieze, and 438 to 433 for the pediments. Pheidias was general superintendent of the great Periclean building operations on the Acropolis; but the question just what share he took in the sculptural decoration of the Parthenon is an extremely difficult one. The metopes vary considerably not only in quality and execution but in style, and here the individual sculptors must have had very free scope. In the frieze several hands are of course observable, but it is nevertheless so homogeneous that the sculptors must all have worked to a design and followed it closely, and that design not a mere sketch but carried out in considerable detail.

The pediments, extremely fragmentary, present the most difficult problem of all. The general sketch of both would seem

[1] See Volume of Plates ii, 58, b.

to have been the work of a single person. But there are differences
between the two which go deeper than differences of execution;
as if the general design had been carried out in models by two
different persons: and it cannot be supposed that all the figures
were executed or even finished off by one hand.

Whatever the solution we must suppose an unusual organizing
ability in some one, no doubt Pheidias: more than this, in spite
of all differences from one part to another, it is possible to speak
of a style of the Parthenon: this style can be recognized in other
works as well, but to say that it is nothing more than the Attic style
of the third quarter of the fifth century is no explanation: styles
of this grandeur do not grow up, they are created by great men:
and Pheidias has a better claim to be considered the true begetter
of the style than Alcamenes, or Agoracritus, or an unknown.

The temple was Athena's, and the adornment was all concerned
with Athena, Athens, and the mission of Athens. The shield of
the image of the goddess was decorated inside with a gigantomachy, outside with an amazonomachy, and the sandals with
Lapiths fighting Centaurs, all three symbolic of the triumph of
the higher over the lower breed. The base of the statue bore a
relief of Pandora, symbol of Athens made lovely and prosperous
by Athena and the craft-god Hephaestus. In the metopes,
gigantomachy on the east side and amazonomachy opposite the
hill of Ares on the west, the taking of Troy on the north, centauromachy on the south. On the frieze under the colonnade, the
people of Athens in festal procession, and the gods looking on. In
the east pediment the birth of Athena, in the west the contest
between Athena and Poseidon for the Attic land.

Most of the metopes preserved are from the centauromachy of
the south side: the finest of these is still on the building[1], and the
quality of the rest is unequal. It is as if the centauromachy had
found its final expression in the previous generation, at Olympia
and in the great wall-pictures of the same time, and was not
thoroughly congenial to the age now beginning. But it must also
be remembered that the frieze also is less perfect on the southern,
least frequented, side than on the others. Of the pediments only
the end-figures remain (and all these incompletely), with fragments of the others: but old drawings give the state of the pediments in the seventeenth century, when the west was still fairly
well preserved, and the east somewhat better than now.

---

[1] See Volume of Plates ii, 60, *a*.

The pediments of the Parthenon[1] are far more complex than those of the Temple of Olympia. The elements which make up the total effect are more numerous and more subtly employed. It is not only that there is much more detail in the individual figures on the Parthenon, which are worked out as if for a close-view as at Aegina and not as at Olympia, and worked out with a knowledge of the ways of the body and of drapery far more intimate and more profound than that of the Aeginetans. There is something else: whereas at Olympia the general position of the individual figures and groups is either profile or full-front and the design has something of the look of a flat drawing, in the Parthenon there is much more variety in the position with regard to the spectator, the eye is continually drawn into depth, and the lines, curves, and planes with which it is concerned are multiplied, complicated, and enriched.

In the Olympian pediments the tone of the whole composition is given by a simple and powerful contrast: in the west between the violent struggle and the calm imperious Apollo, in the east between the quiet attitudes and the beating hearts. This is not the manner of the Parthenon. In the west, one instantaneous crash of unison, the tremendous apparition of the two gods on earth in glory and power. In the east, a more solemn theophany still, the birth of the Virgin goddess on Olympus: the awestruck or dreaming divinities, and every phase of movement and repose, slowing from the centre to the wings, and vastened by the cosmic setting, the upward urge of the Sun in his chariot, and night wheeling away. The beauty of Olympia grows stern and lunar beside the Parthenon; where one pediment is a blaze of noonday splendour, and the other glows with the swelling fires of dawn.

The subject of the frieze[2] is the people of Athens; not fighting, or working, but engaged in that kind of festivity—surviving in the English word holiday, but eradicated from English life—which is at once a high religious ceremony and a delight to the participant. The special quadrennial celebration of the July feast which began the Athenian year was crowned by the Panathenaic procession. It is interesting to compare these men and boys and maidens and horses with the long lines of tribute-bearers on the reliefs of Oriental palaces, or with the rulers of Rome in the Ara Pacis Augustae. In the union of common aims and individual freedom, in an order which never breaks down although constantly looking as if it would, the frieze of the Parthenon is a

---

[1] See Volume of Plates ii, 62, *a, b*.   [2] *Ib.* 60, *b, c*.

perfect illustration of that ideal of democracy which is expressed
in the funeral speech of Pericles. There is another great work
which the Parthenon, and the frieze particularly, brings to mind
at every turn; the Aeschylean Oresteia in its closing scenes. There
also the procession of young and old, the eye of the whole Thesean
land; Athena caring for her people; the same idea of freedom—
τὸ μήτ᾽ ἄναρχον μήτε δεσποτούμενον—; and the deep note of
confidence and joy:

> χαίρετε χαίρετ᾽ ἐν αἰσιμίαισι πλούτου·
> χαίρετ᾽ ἀστικὸς λεώς
> παρθένου φίλας φίλοι.

In a brief glance at the Attic style of this period, it is almost
unnecessary to go outside the Parthenon. One or two monuments
which supplement it have been mentioned already: but a word at
least must be given to the so-called Demeter of Cherchel, copy
of an Attic original belonging to the earlier part of the period of
the Parthenon[1]. It is natural to compare her with a goddess of
the early classical period, the Hestia Giustiniani[2]: the costume is
nearly the same, and the quality of the originals must have been
equal. It is Olympia and the Parthenon over again in another
field: the austerer beauty of the Hestia with the wonderful hard
straight lines; the warmer, ampler majesty of the goddess of
Cherchel.

The catchwords grace and refinement are as appropriate to
the art of the period of the Parthenon as to the Apollo of Sunium
or Tricorpor. The bodily forms are rounder and easier than in
the early classical period, but still extremely powerful and solid.
The faces are broad and well-liking, the features are large, and
the hair glows in strong heavy undulations. There is much
sweetness not of face only but of body and attitude and gesture;
but it is the sweetness of the strong.

Most of the monuments with which we have been dealing are
earlier than the outbreak of the Peloponnesian War, which is
naturally an important date in the history of Greek art. The
Archidamian War meant less work for the sculptor not only at
Athens but elsewhere. The Peace of Nicias saw a revival of
architectural and sculptural activity; at the end of the century
the ruin of Athens had to be commemorated; and there were always
employers in outlying or foreign lands. A good deal of original
work has survived from this period, and the art of sculpture

---

[1] See Volume of Plates ii, 58, *a*.   [2] *Ib.* ii, 40, *a*

did not stand still. But broadly speaking it was living on the ideas of the Parthenon; and the great discoveries and innovations were not in sculpture, but in painting. In Attica the sculpture of the Erechtheum and the Temple of Athena Nike belongs to the last twenty years of the century; in the Peloponnese, the frieze and metopes of the Temple of Apollo at Phigalea, and the metopes of the Heraeum at Argos. The influence of Polyclitus shows itself both at Argos and at Phigalea, but only in the forms not in the spirit. At Phigalea especially, the wildness of the movements and of the wind-swept draperies, and the extraordinary unevenness of the execution, are symbolical of a hurried and distracted age[1]. In Lycia, where Greek artists had long been welcome, the Nereid monument, sepulchre of a native prince, illustrates Ionic sculpture of the late fifth century as Ionic sculpture of the late archaic period was illustrated by the Harpy Tomb. The garments, clinging insistently or abandoned to the wind, seem like an exaggeration of Attic drapery as we see it in the Fates of the Parthenon; and the fairy lightness of the male figures is ill-suited to the siege, the sortie, or the clash of battle. The same general style shows itself in the sepulchral monument from Lycian Trysa, and at a somewhat earlier and fresher stage in the Lycian sarcophagus from Sidon.

From this summerstricken art it is a pleasure to turn back, in conclusion, to the Attic tombstones[2] and their tranquil representations of women with their maids, mothers with their children, young warriors and unaged men, which preserve through the war and beyond it much of the style of the Parthenon and, for all the subdued mood, much of its spirit, and silently confute the peculiar belief that the people whose poets created an unrivalled line of noble mothers, wives, maidens, and viragos, had a low opinion of womanhood; or to the boy lately discovered at Pompeii[3], a bronze copy of a fifth-century statue; or to such boy victors as the bronze Idolino in Florence[4], probably an original, and probably by a Peloponnesian master, or the figure recently acquired by New York[5], the best of several marble copies from a famous bronze. The civilization which produced such creatures perished in the storms of the late fifth century, the long war and the so-called intellectual awakening. The men of the fourth century, sculptors or not, looked for other qualities of form and mind: these boys belong to the age of Sophocles, Pheidias, and Polyclitus:

ὄφρα μὲν ἠὼς ἦν καὶ ἀέξετο ἱερὸν ἦμαρ.

---

[1] See Volume of Plates ii, 64, a.   [2] Ib. 64, b.   [3] Ib. 66, a.
[4] Ib. 66, b.   [5] Ib. 66, c.

VI. CLASSICAL PAINTING: (i) THE SECOND HALF OF THE FIFTH CENTURY

The second half of the fifth century witnessed the rise of modern painting. The great mural decorations of the early classical period yield pride of place, as a rule, to panel-pictures with not many figures. Polygnotus reaches into the period, but the great new names are Apollodorus of Athens, Zeuxis of Heraclea (which Heraclea is uncertain, the Lucanian possible), and Parrhasius of Ephesus. Apollodorus, 'the shadow-painter,' was the pioneer. Shading was used, as we saw, in the late archaic period, though most sparingly: but Apollodorus seems to have been the first to make a systematic study of light and shade, including gradation from one to the other, and cast-shadows. Zeuxis and Parrhasius elaborated the art farther. As to the general character of their work we can gather a little from our ancient authorities: Zeuxis fond of contrast and outlandishness and surprise, his style ampler and his figures robuster, Parrhasius lighter, gayer and more subtle.

Of the great progress in painting proper as opposed to drawing, the vases tell us almost nothing: their art remains linear. Throughout the third quarter of the century the tradition of the Niobid painter is carried on by the artists who may be said to form the group of Polygnotus, for the chief painter bore the same name as the famous Thasian. But most of the finest work was done in other quarters, and is to be found among the white lekythoi or the small red-figured vases. Shortly before the middle of the century, a red-figure artist, the Achilles painter, turned his attention to the sepulchral white lekythoi, and his sober, noble style set the tone in them for many a year[1]. In the lekythoi of the Achilles painter and his immediate successors, more than in any other vases, the classical style finds its purest expression. Next to these, in the vases[2], most of them small, which deal with the life of women: the wedding and the preparations for it; the mother caressing her children; the mistress or maiden, with her friends or handmaids, working or resting, playing or dressing or making music. The Eretria painter is one of the most exquisite among the artists who painted such scenes: small, graceful figures, with their flowing garments and easeful attitudes, are redeemed from prettiness by the virility of the relief-line. The painter of the Berlin dinos brings us to a later stage, and in his large works, such as the

[1] See Volume of Plates ii, 68, *a*.   [2] *Ib.* 68, *b*

Return of Hephaestus in Bologna[1], or the maenad stamnos in Naples, he makes one think of Parrhasius, his rosefed people, his rushing movement. The style of the Meidias painter[2], at the end of the century, is of the same kind, but much more florid and ornate: it ravishes us into a rotating heaven of sweetfleshed women with golden names, and moonwhite Erotes with golden wings. The best work of the Meidias painter himself is beautiful: but his imitators are distressing, and the attempt to apply the style to solemn themes leads to the vulgarity of the Talos vase. In Southern Italy, where vase-painting now flourished, the style of the late fifth century is not so honied as at Athens, and the best vases have a weighty grandeur which is rare elsewhere, though it finds an analogy in certain late white lekythoi[3]. Italiote vase-painting never fulfilled its promise, and even in its early period its masterpieces are easily counted. Its finest products are the superb series of farcical representations on the phlyax-vases; these begin before the end of the century, and have no real parallel in Attic vase-painting: but the spirit is, locally tinged, the spirit of Aristophanes, that rarest, most delicious, and most dangerous of luxuries.

VII. DORIC ARCHITECTURE IN THE EARLY FIFTH CENTURY

The masterpieces of the Doric style were almost all built before Leuctra, and most of them were already standing when Pericles died. In the fourth century Ionic established a supremacy which it has, in truth, never since lost, for Corinthian, which challenged it in the Hellenistic age and eclipsed it under Imperial Rome, is Ionic in almost everything but its capitals. But in the first half of the fifth century Doric for a time shook off the Ionic influence which was noticeable towards the close of the sixth, and entered upon a phase of austere severity, of which the finest examples are the temple of Aphaia in Aegina and the temple of Zeus at Olympia. The architects concentrated their attention upon large problems of proportion, for the solution of which traditional Doric provided an admirable field. They aimed at reducing the heaviness of sixth-century work, without elaborating ornament for its own sake.

The decades which followed Salamis and Himera were not, however, marked by great architectural activity in Greece proper, and in the middle of the fifth century Pericles could still appeal for a general restoration of the temples burnt by the Persians. It was otherwise in the West, where the great tyrannies of Syracuse and Acragas carried on the traditions of Periander and Peisistratus. It will be convenient here, starting with temples and similar buildings, to speak first of the Doric West, next to pass by Olympia to the Doric and Ionic works of Periclean Athens, and then to give some account of what little is known of fifth-century temple architecture in Asia. Other types of building, such as theatres, assembly-halls, and private houses, will be briefly discussed at the end of the chapter.

The huge temple of Apollo ('temple G') at Selinus, begun in the sixth century, was still building in the fifth. It was long the only Doric temple comparable in size to the Ionic buildings of Ephesus or Samos, but, after Himera, Theron of Acragas rivalled it with his Olympieum†[1], the 'Temple of the Giants,' which is the strangest and most daring venture of Doric architecture and forms a striking exception to the rule of simplicity which in general characterizes this period, in the West as in old Greece. The stylobate of the Olympieum was of the same order of magnitude as its largest predecessors, in the neighbourhood, that is to say, of 120 yards by 55; a scale which remained the approximate limit in temple architecture throughout ancient history. The belief that Roman megalomania overstepped Greek standards of scale is definitely false. The temple at Acragas was, in fact, measured on the stylobate, larger than any of its successors; and it was really much larger, for its outer colonnade was engaged in a continuous wall, which enclosed a rectangle of quite unparalleled size. It was overthrown by earthquakes and its ruins were quarried for an eighteenth-century harbour mole; there is consequently much dispute about its original design and appearance. Diodorus Siculus, who saw it in the time of Augustus, states that it was never fully roofed; he assumes, perhaps wrongly, that complete roofing was originally intended. There were fourteen engaged columns on each flank and seven on each front, and these carried an entablature of normal design, but built of small blocks, and partly supported by the curtain-wall. The odd number of columns on the façade is strange: elsewhere this feature hardly occurs except in combination with a single row of inner columns. A base moulding ran all round the outer wall, and round the bottom of the columns, which thus looked as if they had moulded bases. To the half-columns on the exterior

[1] In this and the following sections † with numeral refers to plan on the sheet facing p. 464.

corresponded pilasters on the inner face of the wall, and the interior was divided by two rows of square pillars, opposite the pilasters, and themselves connected, at least at the ground-level, by a curtain-wall. But here certainty almost ends. It is known that colossal male and female figures served as additional supports at some point high in the structure, but whether on the outer wall or on the inner pillars has not been finally demonstrated. A recent theory that the temple had no pediments, but a roof sloping downwards and inwards, like that of an *atrium*, is unconvincing. It should be added that one of the peculiarities of the Olympieum was partly anticipated in sixth-century Selinus, where the pteron of temple F was engaged, to about one-third of its height, in a panelled curtain-wall.

No other fifth-century Doric temple in the West calls, in so short a sketch, for a detailed description. Two of the most interesting are the 'temple of Poseidon' at Posidonia (better known as Paestum)[1], and the temple of Segesta in north-west Sicily: the former because it is exceptionally well-preserved, and retains in position part of the upper range of its inner columns, the latter because it is unfinished, and gives much information about constructional methods. The Western architects were debarred from the exquisite accuracies of marble, but they had little to learn, in technique or in higher matters, from the greatest masters of old Greece.

Of Ionic, in this period, there is little trace in Sicily or Italy, except for a temple at Locri, founded long before, but rebuilt, with magnificent workmanship, perhaps in the early part of the fifth century. At this stage it was peripteral (seven columns by seventeen), the odd number on the façades being in this case a heritage from its earlier stages, when it had a single row of inner columns. The columns of the fifth-century temple are remarkable for necking-bands, with carved ornament, like those of the Erechtheum.

Returning to Doric, in Greece proper we may first consider the great temple of Zeus at Olympia, not forgetting its debt to such beautiful pioneers as the temple of Aphaia in Aegina, which belongs to the first twenty years of the fifth century. Like Aegina, the two chief Panhellenic sanctuaries escaped Persian destruction, but, while on the slopes of Delphi the Alcmaeonid temple already occupied the only large available site, on the plain of the Altis the lord of the sanctuary still lacked a worthy house. This anomaly

---

[1] See Volume of Plates ii, 72, *a*.

was removed about 460 B.C. by the erection of one of the first great examples of classical Doric. It was built almost throughout of rough conglomerate, faced with stucco, and was entirely normal in plan, having an outer colonnade of six columns by thirteen, a cella with pronaos and opisthodomos, each containing two columns, and two inner rows of six columns, twelve in all, on the ground level, with a second tier above. The outer colonnade was deeper at the ends than along the sides, though the temple was not, like the 'Theseum' and temple of Bassae, for instance, actually pseudodipteral at front and back. There was an exterior triglyph frieze, but sculptured decoration was confined to the pediments and to the twelve metopes which were placed at each end of the cella, inside the peripteral colonnade. Since not a column still stands, the aesthetic qualities of the architecture are difficult to appreciate, and the temple is famous chiefly for its magnificent sculpture, and for the fact that it housed Pheidias' chryselephantine Zeus; but it was clearly a masterpiece of simplicity and grandeur, and a model for the architects of the Periclean age.

At this point something must be said of a tiresome mathematical problem which vexed the masters of classical Doric, and later helped Ionic to drive its rival from the field. This problem, which chiefly affects prostyle porches and rectangular peripteral colonnades, arises from the existence of two traditional rules, which gradually became irreconcilable: the rule that one triglyph must be exactly centred over every column, and one over every intercolumniation; and the rule that there must be no gaps, for metopes or part-metopes, between the adjacent pairs of triglyphs at the four corners of the frieze. For various reasons the difficulty of reconciling these rules was little felt in the earliest surviving buildings, but it became acute towards the end of the sixth century, and remained so till the virtual extinction of monumental Doric in Hellenistic and Roman times. The chief cause was perhaps the gradual establishment of the rule that, while triglyphs must be upright oblongs, the metopes, which commonly carried sculptural decoration, must be approximately square. This development made it impossible to place the corner triglyphs at the angles of the frieze, without shifting them to a noticeable degree outside the axes of the corner columns. Theoretically the difficulty could have been met by decreasing the depth, from back to front, of the architrave, for the problem in fact turns exclusively upon the mathematical relation between the width of the triglyphs and the depth of the architrave; but structurally this was impossible, since it would have weakened the whole entablature to a dangerous degree. The architects therefore accepted the necessity of narrow and decentred angle triglyphs, but did their best to minimize the consequent irregularities in the widths of the metopes. At first they were content slightly to decentre one or more of the adjacent triglyphs, but later they began also to shift the angle columns closer together. Usually only one intercolumniation was affected, but sometimes two: the two methods are known as single and double contraction. This device may seem a strange sacrifice of the more important to the less important feature: but, in fact, not only does the eye judge differences in column-spacing less confidently than differences in metope width, but it would also rest by preference on the entablature, with its bright colours and its infinite variety of subtle decoration. It was left for the architects of the fourth and third centuries, with their passion for the mechanically regular, to declare, as Vitruvius records, that the triglyph difficulty made Doric, despite its beauty and grandeur, unfit for temple architecture.

Simple contraction on all four sides seems to occur, surprisingly, in the ancient Heraeum of Olympia: otherwise it first appears, both in Greece and the West, in the second half of the sixth century, and is often, at first, confined to the façades. In the following centuries simple contraction is usual, though double contraction is characteristic of Sicily. Some widening of both triglyphs and metopes near the corners is also common.

VIII. PARTHENON AND PROPYLAEA

Fifth-century Doric and Ionic are also marked by the development of certain 'refinements' which have occasioned much controversy. Of these the Parthenon†[2] is the classical example. It is built of marble and founded on rock, so that later displacements are easily detected, and it has been surveyed with unusual care. It is undoubtedly true that many alleged 'refinements' in other temples, and some in the Parthenon, are insufficiently attested, or plainly accidental, but the sweeping scepticism of some archaeologists is unjustifiable. Discussion of 'refinements' may conveniently follow a brief description of the Parthenon[1].

The present building is not the first on its site, though that site, which now dominates the Acropolis and Athens, was naturally, for the most part, a very inconvenient slope. It is probable

[1] See Volume of Plates ii, 72, b.

that a large temple was built here, with the help of a terrace, early in the sixth century: and it is certain that the vast limestone substructure of the existing Parthenon was built before 500 B.C. This substructure, though concealed since the present temple was erected, was apparently designed as a partly visible podium for a marble temple, not covering its whole area, which was only a few feet high when the Persians sacked the Acropolis. It was to have been a hexastyle Doric building, with sixteen columns on its flanks, and tetrastyle prostyle porches at each end of its cella. The ruins were abandoned until the surviving Parthenon was begun in 447 B.C. This new temple was entirely of marble, save for clamps, dowels, roof-timbers, door-frames, and doors. Its plan owes much to its smaller predecessor, and some of the old material was re-used. The pteron was octastyle (eight by seventeen), with a coffered marble ceiling. The cella was in two distinct sections, each entered through a shallow hexastyle prostyle porch. To the east lay a great room, one hundred Attic feet long, which contained Pheidias' chryselephantine Athena Parthenos, and was surrounded on three sides by a Doric colonnade, in two tiers, which perhaps carried a timber ceiling. The room behind the west porch was shallower, and its roof or ceiling was supported by four large columns, probably Ionic. The Parthenon had other Ionic features, especially a continuous frieze, running, in place of triglyphs and metopes, above the prostyle porches, and right round the outer wall of the cella, inside the peripteral colonnade. The incomparable proportions of this temple, still overwhelmingly impressive, despite the explosion which ruined it late in the seventeenth century, defy simple arithmetical analysis: there is perhaps more hope of explaining them on geometrical lines.

The 'refinements' of the Parthenon consist, for the most part, in the substitution of curves for straight lines, and in the tilting inwards or outwards of vertical members. The surface of the stylobate is not flat: it rather resembles the edges of a mat nailed at its four corners and raised from the floor by the wind. This rise amounts to about 4 inches on the long sides, which measure nearly 230 feet, and to about $2\frac{3}{4}$ inches on the short sides, which measure just over 100 feet. The execution here is not perfect, for the corners are not all on the same level, and the lines are not true curves. This horizontal curvature is repeated in the entablature. The columns all lean slightly inwards, those at the angles having a double inclination, which incidentally eases the problem of the angle triglyph: the entablature has the same tilt; the antae beside the porches lean forwards. The columns not only taper

upwards, as Greek columns almost always did, but do so with a
subtle curve, called the 'entasis': the angle columns are a little
stouter than the rest. Most of these refinements, with some
differences, are mentioned by Vitruvius, who drew, in the time
of Augustus, on the writings of Greek architects of the Hellenistic
age, and it is clear from his words that his authorities believed
them to be designed for the correction of optical illusions. This
explanation has been disputed, and the scientific facts are far
from clear. The various refinements may well have been invented
for different purposes, curvature of the stylobate for drainage,
tilting and thickening of the columns for strength, entasis for
beauty: and though the illusion theory may well be as old as the
fifth century, it is likely that architects at that date were in truth
chiefly influenced by an instinctive dislike of mechanical straightness. These devices are rare before the fifth century, but horizontal curvature of the stylobate can be seen even in the rock-cut
foundations of the late sixth-century temple of Corinth, and
strong entasis is found at Paestum early in the same century.
The refinements of Ionic, which are often very delicate, and
seldom include tilting of the columns, are first demonstrable in
the fifth century, and were perhaps a loan from Doric: in later
centuries most of them were the common heritage of all styles,
but they were often neglected, for they involved much additional expense and labour. The accuracy of workmanship required for the erection of an angle column, for instance, with
extra thickness, double inclination, diminution, and entasis, will
be obvious from a moment's reflection. Even the Parthenon
architects failed in fact to avoid some irregularity in the measure-
ments of the entablature which these elaborately designed
columns carried.

The architects of the Parthenon were Ictinus and Callicrates:
the Propylaea†[3] were the work of Mnesicles[1]. This marvellous
structure was begun ten years after the Parthenon, in 437 B.C.,
and both buildings were far advanced before the outbreak of the
Peloponnesian War. The Propylaea, indeed, remained and remain
a torso, for their original plan, which has been gradually recovered
by the patient skill of modern students, was curtailed in many
ways, partly, perhaps, through financial exhaustion, but partly
through conservative opposition to the obliteration of ancient
sanctuaries. Fortunately their most important side, that which
faced westwards and outwards, at the top of the winding road

[1] See Volume of Plates ii, 74, a.

leading to the Acropolis, was substantially finished, and judicious restoration has made this again one of the most impressive monuments in the world. The material was marble, except for the usual timber elements, and for a very sparing use of black Eleusinian limestone. The plan is too complicated for detailed description. In essence it is of the same ancient type which we find at Troy and Tiryns, an opening in a wall, with a roofed porch within and without: but this simple scheme is here developed with unprecedented magnificence. The wall is pierced with five openings, the middle one over twenty-four feet high and nearly thirteen feet broad: both porches are treated like the fronts of hexastyle prostyle Doric temples, and the outer one, which is more than thrice as deep as the inner, contains two inner rows of six Ionic columns, which helped to carry a coffered marble ceiling[1], still unrivalled in the time of Pausanias. The ground rises from west to east, and, while the carriage road passed between the central intercolumniations and the central doorway at a steady slope, pedestrians mounted successive flights of steps first on to the stylobate of the outer porch, and thence to the higher level of the inner one. The façades of the two porches were identical in measurement, so that the roof was stepped at the point of junction: but this rather awkward feature was not noticeable from below. On the outside the approach was flanked on the north by a rectangular hall, which ran at right angles to the main porch, and stood upon an extension of the same stylobate. In plan this hall somewhat resembled a temple, having a porch with three Doric columns, but it had no pediment, and was attached to the north wall of the west porch.

Mnesicles had clearly planned a similar hall to the south, with the difference that for its west wall was to be substituted an open Doric colonnade, to give easy access to the sanctuary of Athena Nike, which already occupied a partly natural bastion at that point: this hall was much curtailed in execution, but enough was built to balance, in a general way, the opposite wing. The plans also included two longer halls, or rather porticoes, open towards the Acropolis, to flank the inner porch to north and south, but neither of these was ever erected. The Doric work of the Propylaea closely resembles that of the Parthenon: the Ionic columns are among the simplest and grandest ever designed: the capitals[2] stand in the main line of tradition between the archaic and fourth-century work of the Ephesian Artemisium, while the bases

---

[1] See Volume of Plates ii, 74, b.　　　[2] Ib. 74, c.

furnish an early and tentative example of the Attic type (two large convex mouldings, with a hollow between), which ultimately conquered the world, though it got no footing east of the Aegean for two hundred years. The central intercolumniation of each porch of the Propylaea was exceptionally wide, to give room for the carriage road, so that two triglyphs instead of one rested on this span of the architrave. Various devices were employed to relieve the pressure on these architraves and on the lintel of the great door, including an ingenious cantilever structure in the frieze: the architraves were further reinforced with iron bars. Modern architects have calculated that these precautions were really superfluous, and the Greeks were, of course, unable to calculate strains and stresses with scientific precision. But it must not be forgotten that Greece was and is a land of earthquakes.

There is no space to describe the other Doric works of fifth-century Athens and Attica: the most important that survives is the 'Theseum,' probably a temple of Hephaestus, which is better preserved, so far as the exterior goes, than any other Greek temple. It is rather later than the Parthenon, and is a hexastyle peripteros (six by thirteen). Like the Parthenon it has some Ionic features. The larger of the two temples at Rhamnus was built about the same date: the famous temple whose columns still stand on Sunium is a little later. The temple of Apollo at Bassae in Arcadia will be described at a later point.

IX. IONIC AT ATHENS

In the Parthenon Doric ἔσχε τὴν αὐτῆς φύσιν. It was perhaps a consciousness of approaching sterility that led to the reappearance of so many Ionic elements, a symptom of reawakened desire for the elaboration of ornament. This desire led, before the close of the century, to the erection of the Erechtheum, which despite its richness of detail and the singular beauty of its individual parts is notably inferior to the Parthenon and the Propylaea in grandeur and unity of design. But before we speak of this, the chief work of fifth-century Ionic, something must be said of two simpler buildings, the temple of Athena Nike, and the lost temple on the Ilissus.

The small temple of Athena Nike (or 'Wingless Victory') stands upon a rock bastion, natural but artificially enlarged, at the south-west corner of the Acropolis, to the west of the incomplete south-west wing of the Propylaea. The architect Callicrates, Ictinus' colleague on the Parthenon, was instructed to build a temple on this site soon after 450 B.C., but it would seem that most of it was not in fact built till the Propylaea were practically complete, perhaps after the Peace of Nicias. Like most works of the Periclean age, the Nike temple is of marble. It stood till late in the seventeenth century, but was then pulled down to make a Turkish battery. Luckily little of the material was lost, though some was removed by Lord Elgin, and it was rebuilt, with many mistakes but with substantial accuracy, in 1835: what survives of the frieze is now in the British Museum, being replaced on the spot by casts, and no attempt has been made to rebuild the pediments, though parts of the cornice and sima have now been identified. The temple is tetrastyle amphiprostyle, and was entered, as usual, from the east, which is here the side of the Acropolis. As in the sixth-century treasuries of Delphi, there is a continuous frieze, but no dentils. The capitals resemble those of the inner columns of the Propylaea: but the bases show a different phase of the experimentation which produced in the Erechtheum the first orthodox examples of the Attic type. The whole building has a fairy lightness and grace.

Rather older, it would seem, was the very similar but rather heavier temple on the Ilissus, which was carefully drawn and described by early visitors, but was destroyed about the close of the eighteenth century, a fact which should give pause to Lord Elgin's critics. Some surviving slabs of its sculptured frieze have lately been identified.

The Erechtheum†4 is one of the strangest works of Greek architecture: its plan is so irregular that it has been regarded, probably without reason, as only the half of an uncompleted design. Its peculiarities seem to be due to the necessity of including a number of ancient sanctuaries on a very irregular piece of ground. It was begun, at earliest, just before the Peloponnesian War—perhaps not before the Peace of Nicias—and was finished, after a long interval, between 409 and 406: it was then damaged almost at once by fire, but was immediately restored.

The kernel of the structure is a rectangular cella running east and west. This cella has at the east end a prostyle porch of six Ionic columns in one row: the door was flanked by two windows. The south side of the cella is externally on the same level as the east porch, the level of the old Polias temple immediately to its south, but the north is about ten feet lower. The two levels are joined at the north-east corner by a broad flight of steps stretching from the temple to the Acropolis wall. At the south-west corner there is no external connection, the higher level being continued westwards as a terrace, which is in fact the substructure of the pteron of the old Polias temple. The interior was cut into two chief divisions by a cross-wall nearer the east than the west end: at this point the levels changed.

The west end[1] had no porch: the difference of ground-level, combined with the fact that the architrave, frieze, and cornice ran all round the cella, made a difficult problem, which was aesthetically complicated by the proximity of two features not yet mentioned, the large north porch on the lower level, and the small porch of the Maidens on the higher, each at the extreme west end of the cella. The architect did not try to make the western façade a replica of the eastern, but treated the angles as pilasters, and placed between them four columns or half-columns, all resting on a ledge rather higher than the eastern stylobate. The exact character of the original scheme is uncertain, for what survives is a Roman reconstruction, with half-columns engaged in a wall pierced with windows: but it seems clear that the columns or half-columns were at first connected only by a wooden grille. There is evidence that the west wall was originally designed to stand two feet further to the west, and that the change has compressed some features of the temple, especially the design of the Maiden porch.

The north porch was very like the eastern, except that its six columns were arranged in a front row of four with one more on each side between the antae and the angle columns. The columns of the north porch were more than three feet taller than those at the east, but, since its stylobate was more than ten feet lower, the peak of its pediment met the north wall of the cella just below its horizontal cornice. This porch actually overlapped the north-western angle of the cella, and would have done so by some seven feet, even had the west wall been built at the point originally planned. The open space, on the lower level, just west of the Erechtheum, was the precinct of Pandrosos, and it could be entered both from the temple, by a plain door on the ground level, below the ledge which supported the half-columns, and by a small door at the south-west corner of the northern porch. The porch of the Maidens[2] overlapped the stylobate of the old Polias temple, and contained a staircase leading down to the lower level of the western part of the interior. This porch consisted of six female figures arranged like the columns of the northern porch. They stood upon a continuous pedestal and supported on their

---

[1] See Volume of Plates ii, 76, *a*   [2] *Ib.* 76, *b.*

heads an entablature of architrave, dentils, and cornice, with no pediment.

The architect of the Propylaea and the architect of the Erechtheum were both harassed by religious difficulties, but they met them in very different ways. Mnesicles fought every inch of the ground, and proclaimed his final disappointment by deliberately emphasizing the imperfections of his accomplished work: the other bowed to the storm, and hardly even attempted to produce a harmonious whole. He was content to make the main features of his temple individually beautiful, and to elaborate the details of the decoration, which are of incomparable elegance and charm: but for all its beauty, it is depressing to look at the Erechtheum after the Parthenon and the Propylaea. About those details a few words must be said.

The columns, which rest on fully developed Attic bases, have necking-bands adorned with a complicated pattern, and the actual capitals are extremely elaborate. Their most unusual features are the addition of a convex moulding, carved with a plait-band, above the echinus, and the complication of the volute member by the addition of extra mouldings, which cross the usually plain surface of the channel between the echinus and abacus and lose themselves in the revolutions of the side spirals. Besides being painted and gilt, the capitals were adorned with inlaid glass and gilt bronze. The other mouldings of the temple were similarly carved and enriched, and the ground of the frieze was of black Eleusinian stone, to which white marble figures in relief were attached. The frame of the large north door, though in its present state partly an ancient restoration, is a work of extraordinary grandeur, and has served, directly or indirectly, as a model for countless later examples. Richly ornamented doors were no novelty in Ionic, but this is the first Attic work of its kind, for the Parthenon and the other earlier temples, including the Ionic temple on the Ilissus, had wooden door-frames, probably cased in bronze. A notable feature of the Erechtheum decoration is the appearance, perhaps for the first time, of the acanthus ornament, which was destined to win so great a place in ancient art.

It is possible to exaggerate the richness of the Erechtheum, in contrast to such buildings as the Parthenon and the Propylaea: we must not forget that these Doric works were also brightly painted with elaborate ornament and that the difference lies partly in the fact that it was the tradition of the Ionic craftsmen, due, perhaps, to their early familiarity with marble, to carve patterns which in Doric were merely painted. It is notable that, whereas the large porches lack dentils, but have a continuous frieze, the Maiden porch has dentils, but no frieze. The frieze of the east porch was carried round the cella wall.

X. BASSAE AND THE CORINTHIAN CAPITAL

The temple of Apollo in his mountain sanctuary at Bassae†[5], near Phigalea in Arcadia, is interesting in many respects, but above all because it contained the first known Corinthian column. Though from the outside it had the look of a normal peripteral Doric temple, its internal arrangements were most unusual and merit description. Pausanias says that it was built by Ictinus, the architect of the Parthenon, in 430 B.C. This date is almost certainly too early, and we can feel no confidence about Ictinus. But though some archaeologists would lower its date to the fourth century, the evidence of style strongly suggests the last decades of the fifth.

The temple, which runs north and south, because of the lie of the ground, was mainly built of limestone. It was hexastyle and of narrow proportions, its outer colonnade having six columns by fifteen, with normal porches at each end of the cella: but the cella itself[1], which was entered from the north, is quite abnormal. For about three-quarters of its length it is flanked on each side by five Ionic columns engaged to the ends of short cross-walls, projecting inwards from the main wall: eight of these cross-walls project at right angles, but the two farthest from the door are inclined towards it at an angle of 45 degrees, and between them stood a free Corinthian column. The remaining quarter of the cella forms a partially isolated room, a sort of holy of holies, which has the very rare feature of a small side-door, opening into the eastern peripteral colonnade. This room forms, in effect, a small shrine, with the proper orientation, inside the larger structure: the god doubtless stood opposite the side-door, facing east. It is certain, however, that the earlier temple, of which some fragments have been found, did not, as some have supposed, occupy the site of this portion of the later one. The inner columns of the later temple were higher than those of the pteron, and carried an architrave and a marble frieze inside the cella, carved with reliefs. It is possible that the central part of the roof was modified or omitted, in order to light the frieze. The ceilings of

---

[1] See Volume of Plates ii, 78, *a*, *b*.

the porticoes, the capitals of the inner columns, and the roof tiles were of marble.

The temple has suffered much damage since it was first excavated in 1812, and for the exact forms of the capitals of the inner columns we are largely dependent upon drawings and engravings, supplemented by recent excavation and by careful measurement on the spot. The Ionic engaged columns were of a very rare type, quite outside the main line of development. The shafts have an unusually wide spread at the bottom: below that is a torus moulding, and then a tall spreading concave member, with a low one below it. These bases appear to be a free adaptation of the old Asiatic type found in the Heraeum of Samos. We may suppose that the architect was anxious to give these tongue-walls and engaged columns an individual character, and to avoid the appearance of having simply attached normal columns to the walls. The capitals were not less unusual than the bases. Their form is an extension of that of the ordinary angle capital, which has two faces juxtaposed at right angles, the volute between being carried out an angle of 45 degrees. It is obviously possible to treat all four faces and all four angles in this way, and that was in fact often done in Hellenistic Italy and at Rome: these Bassae capitals are really such four-sided capitals engaged, but only the front face was complete, the two side ones being stopped dead half-way back. The design of the capitals was abnormal in other respects: the eyes of the volutes were unusually close together, the profiles and decoration of the parts between shaft and channel were also abnormal, and the upper line of the channel was hunched up into a continuous curve. The evidence for the nature of the abacus is conflicting.

The Corinthian capital[1] of Bassae has almost entirely vanished, but we have various sources of information about it, especially the beautiful drawings made at the time of excavation by Haller von Hallerstein, and its main features are quite certain. Though it differed in many respects from all later examples, it was indisputably Corinthian. It consisted of a basket-like bell, crowned with an abacus, shaped, in plan, as a square with its four sides concave. There was a ring of acanthus leaves round the bottom of the bell, from which sprang upwards eight small spirals which supported the abacus at its four corners. There was also on each face a pair of spirals curling inwards, with an ornament between them. These are all normal Corinthian features, but their relative

[1] See Volume of Plates ii, 78, c.

proportions here were not normal, since the leaves covered only a small part of the bell, which was unusually bare, despite the abnormal largeness of the inner spirals, and despite the fact that the ornament between them—a big palmette—was on the bell, instead of on the abacus. The spirals did not spring from fluted *cauliculi*, as they did usually, though not always, in later work. The abacus was unusually high, and the whole effect was solid and heavy. The next stages in the development of the Corinthian capital belong to the fourth century, and will be described in a later chapter (vol. VI, chap. XVII).

The origin of this type of capital is uncertain. In general scheme it seems to owe something to the Egyptian palm-capital, which we saw imitated at Delphi in the sixth century. It seems also to be indebted to the Ionic angle capital, and perhaps even to the 'Aeolic' type of Neandria, while the use of acanthus leaves was perhaps suggested by such necking bands as those of the Erechtheum. Tradition ascribes the invention of Corinthian to the sculptor and metal-worker Callimachus, who lived at about this date, and this may well be true. Its delicate and fragile forms certainly suggest metal models.

It is usual to criticize the Corinthian capital as over-ornate, and to blame the Romans for their devotion to it. But its lines are in truth more expressive of its function than those of Ionic, and the expulsion of the Ionic angle capital was pure gain. The practical verdict of posterity, in mediaeval, Renaissance, and modern times, has been overwhelmingly in favour of Corinthian.

We do not know enough of fifth-century architecture in Asia Minor for confident generalization. It is likely that at Sardes, the capital of the satrapy of Lydia, the huge temple of Artemis was rebuilt, in purely Ionic fashion, soon after the destruction of a Lydian predecessor (itself probably Greek in style) in the Ionian Revolt of 499 B.C. (vol. IV, p. 222). The surviving temple seems to date from a complete reconstruction begun in the fourth century, but the foundations of the pteron columns, and some columns and capitals, appear to date from the fifth. These capitals in several respects represent a stage between those of the earlier and later Ephesian Artemisia. They are of beautiful workmanship, and, though normal in general design, have the rare feature of carved floral ornament in the channel between echinus and abacus: one even has palmettes carved on the eggs of the echinus, an enrichment paralleled only in the archaic temple of Apollo Phanaios in Chios.

A striking Asiatic work, the Nereid Monument at Xanthos in

Lycia, a tomb in temple form, has been variously dated, but can scarcely be earlier than the close of the fifth century. Its columns have Asiatic bases, but show in their capitals such close resemblance to the Erechtheum, that it is difficult to believe in their independence, though in our deep ignorance of early Ionic, the possibility of some lost common model cannot be ignored. The building, of Parian marble, stood on a high podium, and was in the form of a tetrastyle peripteral temple (four by six); the cella had a pronaos and an opisthodomos, each fairly deep, but with no supports between the antae. There was no frieze between the architrave and the very bold dentils, but the pediment contained sculpture, and the architrave itself, as at Assos, was treated as a carved frieze. There were also two friezes of different height on the podium, which was crowned with a double egg-and-tongue resting on a bead-and-reel. There were statues between the columns.

XI. THEATRES, HALLS AND HOUSES

Hitherto nothing has been said except of temples and buildings closely resembling them, and we know far more of these than of any other type: but in the fifth century, besides private houses, many important buildings of quite different kinds were erected, some traces of which still survive. The most interesting are perhaps those designed for the accommodation of large assemblies. They fall into two main types, the political meeting-place, on more or less level ground, and the theatre scooped out of the hill-side. Neither of these was normally roofed, but they combined to produce a new type of roofed building, which became in various forms an important feature of most Hellenistic cities.

The Athenian Pnyx, which is not unique, may serve as a type of the roofless political meeting-place: a *bēma* or rostrum, and some seats, were carved from the rock of a hill, but most of the citizens stood or sat upon the ground, which was in part artificially levelled or raised. The theatre is a much more complicated matter, and raises some of the most difficult problems in Greek architectural history. The auditorium was usually based upon a natural slope, as in the theatre of Dionysus at Athens, which was backed by the south face of the Acropolis. In its oldest traceable form, which is ascribed to the sixth century, this theatre seems to have had the foundations of the auditorium cut in a series of straight lines, apparently for the reception of wooden seats, but seats were normally of stone, and cut in continuous

curves. The flanks of a hillside auditorium usually needed artificial support, especially as the Greeks liked the seats to occupy
rather more than a semicircle. Below, in the centre, lay the circular
orchestra, sometimes bounded by a stone ring, flush with the
ground. Behind the orchestra stood the rectangular *skēnē*, or
stage-building. It was an isolated structure, separated from the
auditorium by two open passages, the *parodoi*. It was usually in
two storeys, and was sometimes longer than the diameter of the
orchestra. A short wing often projected from each of its front
ends. It is unlikely that any known *skēnē* is as old as the fifth
century, but there is evidence that wooden *skēnai* preceded some
of those in stone which have survived. In front of the *skēnē*
there projected, in Hellenistic times, a one-storey structure known
as the *proskēnion*. Nothing in Greek architecture has been so
hotly debated as the construction, function, and antiquity of this
feature of the Greek theatre. Was it a stage, and did it exist in
the fifth century? The Hellenistic *proskēnion* was a row of stone
columns, or pillars with columns engaged, standing on a low
stylobate, two or three yards in front of the *skēnē*. These supports
carried a stone entablature—architrave, frieze and cornice—
which was joined by stone or wooden beams to the *skēnē* wall:
the beams were covered with a platform of wooden planks,
usually from seven to thirteen feet above the ground, level with
the upper storey of the *skēnē*, and connected with it by at least
one door. Between the pillars or columns of the *proskēnion* was
removeable panelling, for which doors were substituted in the
central opening and sometimes in two of the others.

In most theatres the whole stage-building has been repeatedly
remodelled in Hellenistic and Roman times, so that facts are
difficult to ascertain and difficult to interpret. It is practically
certain, however, that no extant stone *proskēnion* is earlier than
the close of the fourth century; nor is there good evidence for
the previous use of wooden ones. It is clear therefore that our
answer to the question whether or not the *proskēnion* was a stage
cannot at present solve the problem of the presentation of fifth-
century drama, and in detail the *proskēnion* question is hardly
relevant to the present chapter. But it is interesting to observe
that recent investigation of one of the best-preserved Greek
theatres, that of Priene, has made it likely that in that case at
least the *proskēnion* became a stage (as it was for Vitruvius) only
during the second century B.C., having apparently served, since
the foundation of the theatre at the end of the fourth century, as
a background for players on the orchestra level. On the whole,

the archaeological evidence seems unfavourable to a high stage in the fifth century, and there is no external evidence for the low stage which some critics have, quite legitimately, postulated, to satisfy the internal evidence drawn from fifth-century plays (p. 121)[1].

The few known covered halls of the fifth century are more like a roofed Pnyx than a roofed theatre, though a type more like a roofed theatre appears in the fourth century, and is common in Hellenistic times. The oldest of all seems to be the Telesterion at Eleusis; nor is this surprising, for the celebration of the Mysteries called for a combination of privacy and spaciousness which no existing type of temple or meeting-place could provide. The oldest traceable form of the Telesterion appears to date from the sixth century, and this was probably burnt by the Persians. It was approximately square, with sides a little over eighty feet long, and its roof was supported, directly or indirectly, by five rows of five columns (twenty-five in all) placed at the points of intersection of a series of equidistant lines, parallel to the side-walls: there was no specially marked central space. A prostyle porch ran along the whole length of the eastern side. The evidence for the later history of the hall is complicated. It was rebuilt in Roman times, and was then very similar in plan to its archaic predecessor, though the sides were more than doubled in length. It had forty-two columns (six rows of seven) arranged as before, and also eight tiers of seats, partly rock-cut, inside the outer walls. There were six entrances, two on every side except the western, where the building ran into the Acropolis rock. In its main lines this Roman hall almost certainly reproduced the very famous fifth-century building, ascribed by Strabo and Vitruvius to Ictinus. It appears likely, from recent excavations, that Ictinus inherited plans dating from the time of Cimon, and that he was relieved of his post when Pericles fell into disfavour, being replaced by the three architects named by Plutarch, Coroebus, Metagenes, and Xenocles. There are traces of at least two schemes for the interior supports, different in detail from those of the Roman hall, though similar in idea. From Plutarch's words it appears that in the fifth-century building the inner columns, or some of them, were joined by architraves carrying an upper row, but this does not necessarily imply a complete upper storey. A great Doric prostyle porch was added to the east side in the second half of the fourth century B.C.

One of the surprises of recent years has been the discovery

[1] A selection from the modern literature dealing with Greek theatres will be found in the Bibliography.

that the Odeum or Music Hall of Pericles, which adjoined the theatre of Dionysus, was not a circular building, as a passage of Plutarch seemed to imply, but a great rectangular hall closely resembling the Eleusinian Telesterion and nearly twice as large. It probably measured about 240 feet each way, and seems to have contained about eighty columns (perhaps nine rows of nine), arranged much as in the buildings already described. Here again what survives is a later reconstruction, for the original building, which was largely of timber, was burnt in 86 B.C., and rebuilt, on the same plan, by Ariobarzanes II of Cappadocia. The chief entrance was perhaps to the South, but this has not yet been excavated. There was a conical or pyramidal roof, copied from Xerxes' captured tent, but the details of its construction and the nature of the upper parts of the building are quite uncertain.

In all these buildings the arrangement of the inner supports, which has Egyptian and Persian precedents, must greatly have interfered with their usefulness. From the fourth century onwards, various attempts were made to remove or minimize this inconvenience, notably in the Thersilion of Megalopolis and in the Ecclesiasterion of Priene: but these fall outside the limits of this section.

Among other public buildings of unusual plan erected during the fifth century may be mentioned the Lesche of the Cnidians at Delphi. This was a rectangular room, probably entered by a door in the middle of one long side, and divided by eight wooden columns on stone bases into a central space and a surrounding passage. The inner face of the walls was adorned with frescoes by Polygnotus. There was probably a complete roof, with some sort of clerestory.

For the private houses of the fifth century the chief evidence must be extracted from casual literary allusions, though many imperfect examples survive. Town-houses seem, for the most part, to have been unpretentious, built of such materials as sun-dried bricks and timber, with flat terrace roofs. It would seem that they usually had an inner courtyard, and that in the better houses these courtyards often had colonnades on one or more sides: but complete interior peristyles do not seem to have been the rule. Two storeys were probably customary, and the upper sometimes at least served as the women's quarters. In country-houses at least it was sometimes possible to isolate the women's quarters completely by the locking of a single door. The orator Lysias (1, 9) speaks of a small town-house where the upper storey was seemingly reserved for the women; but his language is not very clear. In the *Oeconomicus* of Xenophon (ix, 5) Ischomachus explains to his bride that the chief reason for the isolation of the women's quarters in his country-house by a θύρα βαλανωτός is the separation of the male and female slaves. For two courtyards in one house there seems to be little or no evidence. Thucydides mentions expensive country-houses at the outbreak of the Peloponnesian War, and Isocrates remarks that such houses were finer and richer than those confined within town walls: but we know little about them (see above, p. 20).

The invention of formal rectangular town-planning[1] is traditionally ascribed to Hippodamus of Miletus, who is said to have designed the Piraeus at an uncertain date (p. 167), Thurii in 443 B.C., and Rhodes in 408 B.C. If all these statements are true, he cannot well have been born before 475 B.C., but there is evidence which makes it almost certain that the planning of Rhodes is wrongly ascribed to him, and that he was really born at the very beginning of the fifth century. It is a plausible conjecture that regular town-planning may have started in the colonies of the seventh and sixth centuries, where the land had to be equally divided between the settlers, but the oldest real evidence is for fifth-century Miletus. Before her destruction in 494 B.C. Miletus seems to have been as irregular as other ancient towns of gradual development, but after Mycale in 479 B.C. the new city was laid out on a grand scale and on strictly geometrical lines. It is probable that the young Hippodamus learnt his work in this practical school, and that he owes his exaggerated reputation to the fact that later in life he carried these unfamiliar ideas to Periclean Athens. He seems to have written on the theory of town-planning, and doubtless introduced some original improvements.

Before leaving fifth-century architecture we may attempt to define some of its characteristics. In its broader features the art during this period remained almost stationary. The traditional forms were lightened and refined, but, despite such innovations as the Attic base and the Corinthian capital, there was no substantial change, and little sign that architects were feeling for new lines of development. It is true that there was some increase in mechanical ingenuity, but it was used only to extend artificially the possibilities of traditional construction: there was no attempt to exploit new materials or new methods. Only in the Propylaea a new spirit appears, not indeed in construction, but in general

---

[1] On the subject of town-planning, A. von Gerkan's *Griechische Städte-anlagen* should be consulted: see the Bibliography.

design. There is a boldness in the grouping and combination of these great halls and porches that was scarcely equalled even in Roman days. But Mnesicles came before his time, and little in the following centuries breathes a similar spirit. His true heirs were the great masters of the Italian Renaissance.

NOTES ON POINTS ESPECIALLY
OF CHRONOLOGY[1]

1. THE CHRONOLOGY OF *THE PENTECONTAETIA*

In dealing with the period between the Persian and Peloponnesian Wars (478–431 B.C.), the so-called 'Pentecontaetia,' we find ourselves again and again confronted with the problem of the determination of the dates. It might have been expected that for a period, the greater part of which falls within the lifetime of Herodotus and Thucydides, at least all the more important dates would be beyond discussion or dispute. Unfortunately, the reverse of this holds good. For the decade 475–465 B.C. the most that we can determine is the relative order of the events, and even for the remainder of the period a precise chronology cannot always be established. The reasons for this are not far to seek. Our primary authority, Thucydides, although he censures his predecessor Hellanicus for his inaccurate chronology, is himself only too often vague in the dating of the incidents which he records in his sketch of the rise of the Athenian Empire; and in his narrative, towards the end of Book I, of the adventures of Pausanias and Themistocles, the indications of date are as indefinite as could well be imagined. Some of the constitutional changes which fall within this period are dated in Aristotle's *Constitution of Athens* by the Archons; but apart from this, the historian on whom we are mainly dependent for our chronology is Diodorus, a writer of the first century B.C. His scheme is annalistic, being based on the list of the eponymous Archons at Athens and the Consuls at Rome; but it can be proved in any number of instances that the mere fact that a given event is recorded by him under the name of a particular Archon is far from proving that this is its true date. It can, however, be demonstrated that Diodorus in adapting his material to an annalistic scheme availed himself of what we should call a Chronological Table, and where it can be shewn that a chronological statement is derived from this source, there is a strong presumption that it may be accepted as accurate. Among the more important events the dates of which are in dispute are the expulsion of Pausanias from Byzantium and his death; the ostracism of Themistocles and his flight to Persia; the capture of Scyros, the revolt of Naxos, and the Battle of the Eurymedon; the sailing of the great Egyptian expedition, and its destruction; the return of Cimon from exile, the conclusion of the Five Years Truce and the last expedition to Cyprus. The list is sufficient to illustrate the uncertainty of the chronology. Yet the determination of the dates is not a matter of mere antiquarian interest. The view which we take of the policy of an expedition, or of the meaning of an event, must not infrequently be affected—it may be profoundly affected—by the answer to the question when the expedition was dispatched, or when the event occurred.

[1] Notes 1–6 refer to chaps. II–IV, Notes 7–9 to chaps. VII–VIII, Note 10 to chaps. XI–XII.

A. The Thessalian expedition of Leotychidas

At the very outset of this period we are called upon to solve one of the most difficult of these chronological problems, that of the expedition of King Leotychidas to Thessaly. Our primary authority for this is Herodotus (VI, 72), who gives no indication of date. He tells us that Leotychidas was sent to Thessaly in command of a Spartan force in order to expel the medizing dynasty of the Aleuadae, and that the expedition failed in its object because the king accepted a bribe from the Thessalian princes. Herodotus asserts that he was caught redhanded, squatting down in his tent on a gauntlet full of coins, and that in consequence of this he was banished from Sparta, and died in exile at Tegea in Arcadia. If this tale is to be accepted as true in all its details, the banishment of Leotychidas must have followed immediately on his return from Thessaly; and if his reign was officially terminated by his exile, the date of the expedition can be fixed from that of the end of his reign. It has been demonstrated[1] that the true date at which the reign of Leotychidas came to an end, whether by his exile or his death, is 469 B.C., and not 476 B.C. as stated by Diodorus. As it is probable that his conviction involved his deposition, it follows that we must make our choice between two alternatives: that of putting the expedition in 469 B.C., or that of assuming that the charge was trumped up against the king, some years after the expedition, when it suited the purpose of the ephors to get rid of him, and that the picturesque details given by Herodotus formed part of the evidence produced at the trial. An expedition in 469 B.C. may be ruled out on more grounds than one, and we are therefore compelled to determine the date by some other means. The famous story of Themistocles' proposal to burn the Greek fleet[2] while it lay at Pagasae in Thessaly has been generally rejected by modern critics. The setting of the tale, however, can hardly be other than historical, and it implies 'an expedition of the Greeks' to Thessaly after the retreat of Xerxes, and a fleet which had its headquarters at Pagasae where it passed the winter months, from which the Athenian contingent was absent. This expedition can be none other than that of Leotychidas, and after 480 B.C. there were only two naval expeditions which could be described as 'an expedition of the Greeks'; that which was commanded by Leotychidas at Mycale in 479 B.C., and that which was sent to Cyprus and Byzantium the next year under Pausanias. After 478 B.C. there are no more fleets or 'expeditions of the Greeks'; the fleets are either those of the Peloponnesians, or of the Athenians. Consequently, the fleet sent to Thessaly under Leotychidas must have been that which had fought at Mycale, *minus* the Athenian contingent, and it must have anchored at Pagasae in the autumn of 479 B.C.

B. The date of Pausanias' expulsion from Byzantium

In approaching the history of the Confederacy of Delos after the work of its organization had been completed, we find ourselves once more con-

---

[1] See E. Meyer, *Forschungen* II, pp. 502–509. Clinton, *Fasti Hellenici* II, pp. 260 *sqq.*
[2] Plutarch, *Themistocles*, 20.

fronted with a chronological problem, that of the expulsion of Pausanias from Byzantium by the forces of the League under Cimon. Thucydides gives us little help towards the determination of the date. All that we can gather from his narrative (I, 131) is the relative order of the events; his return from Sparta to Byzantium, his expulsion from it by the Athenians, his residence at Colonae in the Troad, and his second recall to Sparta. Between the first event in this series and the last an interval of seven years at least must be assumed. According to the view which is most generally held, this interval is to be put between his return to Byzantium and his expulsion from it, and for this ancient authority can be cited. 'Haec namque urbs condita primo a Pausania, rege Spartanorum, et per septem annos possessa fuit[1].' To the alteration of 'condita' into 'capta' there are grave objections, but without this correction the passage is mere nonsense. The most that can be argued is that the 'per septem annos' got somehow, and from somewhere, into Justin's notes. If authority, such as it is, is in favour of so late a date as 471 B.C. for the expulsion of Pausanias from Byzantium, probability is all against it. To gain possession of Byzantium, and with it the control of the Bosporus, was a matter of first importance to the Athenians and their allies, and although Pausanias must have had at his disposal a garrison of some sort or other, he had not the moral authority of Sparta behind him. He had been superseded in his command, and in those distant waters he was a mere adventurer playing for his own hand. Why then should Athens hesitate to act? If this reasoning is sound, the capture of Byzantium by Cimon must have been his first achievement, and the place must have been captured before the end of 477 B.C.

C. The second capture of Sestos

Not a few of the more recent writers on the history of this period have assumed, on the strength of a passage in Plutarch (*Cimon*, 9) that Pausanias on his return from Sparta succeeded in getting possession of Sestos, which had subsequently to be recovered by the forces under Cimon. Unfortunately, the hypothesis of a second Athenian capture of Sestos does not solve the problem presented by the passage in Plutarch. The passage implies, not merely that Cimon was in command at the siege of Sestos, but that there were Persians of high rank in the garrison which he captured. That Sestos was captured by the Athenians from the Persians is, of course, beyond dispute; the difficulty is that when it was captured the Athenian commander was Xanthippus, not Cimon. The invention of a capture of Sestos by Pausanias, and of a second siege and second capture by the Athenians, belongs to a class of expedients which had better be left to the theologians, and to a past generation of them.

D. Chronological problems connected with the career of Cimon

The problems are two: the date of his ostracism, and the date of his return from exile.

There is no doubt as to the date of his ostracism; it can only be the spring of 461 B.C. What is in dispute is whether it preceded or followed Ephialtes'

---

[1] Justin IX, i. 3.

Reform of the Areopagus. It is very commonly assumed that Plutarch can be quoted in support of the view that Ephialtes carried his measure during Cimon's absence at Ithome. This is an entire mistake. What Plutarch says is that the Areopagus was overthrown when Cimon was absent on a naval expedition: ὡς δὲ πάλιν ἐπὶ στρατείαν ἐξέπλευσε (Cimon, 15). If Theopompus, or whoever else was Plutarch's authority, had connected the Reform of Ephialtes with Cimon's absence at Ithome, he certainly would not have used so vague a phrase as this. He inferred, quite correctly, that Cimon could not have been at Athens when the reform was carried, from the fact that there was no tradition of any debate between Cimon and Ephialtes on this question, while everyone knew of the great debate between the two on the expedition to Ithome. How then was his absence to be accounted for? To a mind such as that of Theopompus the explanation lay ready to hand; Cimon was absent on one of his numerous expeditions. That the democrats, after sustaining two such reverses as those involved in the acquittal of Cimon and the sending of a contingent to the aid of Sparta, should have ventured once more to try conclusions with the Conservatives is most improbable. No ground could have been chosen less favourable to the democratic cause than the question of the Areopagus. The success of the attack is only to be explained by the complete demoralization of Cimon's party, which had been occasioned by his ostracism and by the failure of his foreign policy.

The second problem is one of the most difficult of solution in the history of this period. Plutarch's account (Cimon, chapters 17 ad fin., 18 ad init.) is self-contradictory. He says, on the one hand, that Cimon was recalled after Tanagra, and on the other, that immediately on his return he put an end to the war between Athens and Sparta and reconciled the two states, and having done this sailed for Cyprus: εὐθὺς μὲν οὖν ὁ Κίμων κατελθὼν ἔλυσε τὸν πόλεμον καὶ διήλλαξε τὰς πόλεις· γενομένης δ' εἰρήνης ... ἐπλήρου διακοσίας τριήρεις ὡς ἐπ' Αἴγυπτον καὶ Κύπρον αὖθις ἐκστρατευσόμενος. Plutarch forgets that there was an interval of six years between Tanagra and the Five Years Truce. The usual expedient is to assume that Plutarch is confusing the latter with the truce for four months which Diodorus alleges to have been concluded between the Athenians and Spartans immediately after Tanagra (XI, 80 ad fin.). The expedient is unsatisfactory. Diodorus' statement is open to grave objections (why should the Spartans conclude a truce which left Boeotia at the mercy of Athens and secured to themselves no corresponding advantage?); but apart from this, Diodorus, our sole authority for the truce, does not connect it with the name of Cimon. Further, if Cimon was recalled in 457 B.C., why is there no trace of his presence at Athens until 451 B.C.? Why, above all, was he not sent to the rescue of the Athenian force in Egypt? The story of his recall after Tanagra certainly goes back as far as Theopompus (Frag. 88 [a] G.H., = 92 Müller F.H.G.), and it may be that it can be traced back to Stesimbrotus (see Plutarch, Pericles, 10). It is noticeable, however, that in the passage in Plutarch, Cimon's recall by the decree of Pericles is connected with a secret agreement between the latter and Elpinice, by which Cimon was given a free hand against Persia. Here again it is implied that Cimon was recalled immediately before the expedition to Cyprus in 450 B.C. One hesitates to base any argument on the passage in Andocides (*de Pace*, 3), but so far as it goes, it is evidence for his return shortly before the Five Years Truce. On the whole, the probabilities of the case may be allowed to outweigh the authority of a positive statement. One thing at least is clear. There are only two alternatives: either Cimon was recalled after Tanagra, or he was not recalled at all, but came back when the ten years of his ostracism had expired. A recall, but at some other date than after Tanagra, may be left to those to whom compromise is dear.

E. M. W.

2. THE POLITICAL SITUATION IN BOEOTIA IN 457 B.C.

It is the view of E. Meyer, Busolt, and a number of other scholars, that Thebes at the time of the Spartan intervention was a democracy, that the Federal party in Boeotia was democratic, and that the anti-Federal party was oligarchic; that Sparta consequently was in alliance with the democrats, and Athens with the oligarchs. This hypothesis is based mainly on two passages: [Xenophon] *Ath. Const.* III, 11, where Athens is said to have taken the side of the oligarchs in Boeotia; and Aristotle, *Pol.* VIII (v), 3, 1302 b 25: ἐν Θήβαις μετὰ τὴν ἐν Οἰνοφύτοις μάχην κακῶς πολιτευομένων ἡ δημοκρατία διεφθάρη. The former passage is obscure, but it is difficult to see to what period it can refer other than that between 457 and 445 B.C.; the latter passage admits of the meaning that a democracy was both set up and overthrown after Oenophyta, but it also admits of the meaning that an already existing democracy was overthrown at some date after the battle. The difficulties in the way of the hypothesis appear to the present writer to outweigh the evidence of these two passages, and those who maintain it are driven to propound theories as to what happened between Oenophyta and Coronea which are complicated and improbable, as well as contradictory of one another. We are required to assume that while Athens intervened in Boeotia in 457 B.C. in the interests of the oligarchs, she was at the very same moment the ally of the democrats in Phocis, and the enemy of the oligarchs in Locris; that the oligarchs in Boeotia were her friends at Oenophyta and her enemies at Coronea; that the anti-Federal party in Boeotia was oligarchic in 457 B.C., and democratic throughout the rest of the century after Coronea, while the Federal party was democratic at the time of Tanagra and Oenophyta, and oligarchic for the next sixty years or more; and finally, that while one object of the Spartan expedition was to co-operate with the democrats in Boeotia, its other object was to co-operate with the oligarchs in Attica. There is a point at which probability must be allowed to prevail over authority.

E. M. W.

3. THE PEACE OF CALLIAS

Little has been added by way of evidence since Grote's discussion of this question (*History of Greece*, ed. 1884, vol. v, pp. 191–197). The answer depends, not upon the discovery of further evidence, but upon the use of judgment. Grote decides in favour of the Treaty, but he is clearly a little unhappy in his decision. It is based on two arguments: one, that great as are the difficulties in the statements of the Orators, they are less than that which is implied in the hypothesis that the Peace is a pure fabrication; the other that it is extravagant to suppose that Callias should have gone to Susa, and yet have gone on some other errand than the Treaty. Most historians since Grote have accepted the Peace, but at the same time they have tended to reduce it to an understanding which bears little resemblance to the Treaty of the Orators.

Firstly, as to the embassy of Callias in Herodotus, VII, 151. The date of this follows from that of the Argive embassy. The date of the latter can be determined by two considerations. Its mission was to ascertain whether the alliance with Xerxes still held good with his successor Artaxerxes. The date therefore must be soon after the accession of Artaxerxes (464 B.C.). The embassy must also have been sent at a time when Argos was in danger of being attacked, obviously by Sparta. The date therefore must lie between 462 B.C., when the alliance was formed with Athens, and 451 B.C., when the Thirty Years Truce was concluded with Sparta. The date therefore cannot be as late as 448 B.C., when Artaxerxes had been sixteen years or more on the throne and Argos was secure against Spartan attack. The date that suits best lies somewhere between 462 B.C. and 460 B.C.

Secondly, as to the statements in Diodorus and the Orators. The terms in Diodorus (XII, 4. 5) are: (1) the autonomy of the Greek cities in Asia, (2) the Persians not to come within three days of the coast, (3) the Persian fleet to keep outside Phaselis and the Cyanean Rocks (in the Bosporus), (4) the Athenians not to attack the King's dominions. Number (4) appears only in the version of Diodorus, but it seems to be implied in any treaty or understanding between the two Powers. (1) is also stated by Lycurgus (in Leocr. 73) and by Suidas. As Persia never resigned her claim to the tribute of the Greek cities in Asia (Hdt. VI, 42, Thuc. VIII, 5. 5), she can hardly have recognized their autonomy. (1) therefore is evidently false. As to (3). The northern limit, the Cyanean Rocks, is given by Suidas, Lycurgus, Plutarch (Cimon, 13), and Demosthenes (de fals. leg. 273), as well as by Diodorus. It is clearly otiose, as Persia had no naval base on the Pontus. The southern limit appears in two contradictory forms. In Plutarch and Demosthenes, it is the Chelidonian Islands (off the southeastern point of Lycia); in Isocrates and Lycurgus, as well as in Diodorus, it is the city of Phaselis, in Pamphylia. Phaselis would be excluded from the Athenian sphere by the limit of the Chelidonian Islands. That limit therefore must be false, as Phaselis was always included in the Athenian Empire. As to (2). This appears in two rival forms; as three days' journey on foot, and as one day's ride on horseback (τριῶν ἡμερῶν ὁδός, ἵππου δρόμος). It is improbable that a term so vague as either of these could figure in a treaty, and it can be shown from passages in Thucydides that no such limit was observed by Persia (e.g. I, 115 ad fin., III, 34, V, 1). In Isocrates, our earliest authority, the limit on land is given as the Halys (Areop. 80, Panath. 59). The first explicit mention of the Treaty is in the Panegyricus of Isocrates (120), which was published in 380 B.C. It is here introduced in order to be contrasted with the Peace of Antalcidas, which had been concluded half-a-dozen years before the passage in Isocrates was written. Precisely the same contrast appears in his pupil Ephorus (Diodorus XII, 26. 2). That the Treaty should not be mentioned until after the Peace of Antalcidas, and then only in order to be contrasted with it, is, to say the least, suspicious. Finally, as to the inscription in which the terms of the Peace are alleged to have been given. There is no question that there was an inscription at Athens in the fourth century which was supposed to relate to this Peace. It was included by Craterus in his *Collection of Decrees*. It was, however, pronounced by Theopompus to be a forgery, on the ground that it was written in the New Attic Alphabet which did not come into official use until the archonship of Euclides, at the very end of the fifth century B.C. If it was genuine, what did it contain? Not a formal treaty, for the Great King, even if he could have brought himself to treat with Athens as an equal, could never have bound himself by terms so humiliating. At best then, an informal under-standing, to the effect that no Persian fleet should enter the Aegean, and that Athens should not attack the Persian dominions. Yet a difficulty still remains, for informal understandings are not things that are engraved on marble. If the inscription contained the limits by sea and land, how can we account for such discrepancies in our authorities? They had only to use their eyes, and to see what stood written on the stone. As to the author of the Treaty and the time of its conclusion, Diodorus alone gives the precise date, and only he and Demosthenes (with Suidas in one version) give Callias as its author. By Plutarch and by Suidas, in the other version, it is attributed to Cimon, and it is put by Plutarch and Lycurgus after the Eurymedon. Thucydides VIII, 56. 4 does not prove the existence of the Treaty. Treaty or no Treaty, the presence of a Persian fleet in the Aegean at this moment meant an end to the Athenian Empire. Recognized 'spheres of influence' might exist without a formal treaty. See Thucydides VI, 13: ὅροις οὐ μεμπτοῖς χρωμένους.

E. M. W.

4. DEMOCRACY IN THE EMPIRE

It has often been contended that Athens did not insist on a democratic constitution in the cities included in her Empire. The arguments seem to be that we have no evidence of democracy being imposed except where there had been a revolt, or where it was the case of an entirely new constitution (*e.g.* after the expulsion of a tyrant); and that we have instances both of a state being left free to choose its own constitution and of oligarchies being tolerated. The evidence, on the contrary, warrants two conclusions; firstly, that democracy was universal in the subject states, and secondly, that no other form of constitution was tolerated by Athens. The evidence for the first conclusion is to be found in two passages: Xenophon, *Hell.* III, iv. 7 (he is speaking of the condition of things in the Greek cities of Ionia at the time of Agesilaus' arrival at Ephesus in 396 B.C.): οὔτε δημοκρατίας ἔτι οὔσης, ὥσπερ ἐπ' Ἀθηναίων, οὔτε δεκαρχίας, ὥσπερ ἐπὶ Λυσάνδρου. It is here implied that democracy was as universal under Athenian rule as the Decarchies were in the time of Lysander. According to Thucydides (VIII, 64, 65), Peisander and his fellow conspirators in 411 B.C. (p. 328) are instructed to establish oligarchies in all the cities visited by them in their cruise in the Aegean; we are then told that they pursued their voyage, and put down the democracies in the different states. It is here implied that they would find democracies wherever they went. Even more satisfactory is the evidence for the second conclusion. Thucydides (I, 19), when contrasting the moderation of Sparta towards her allies with the conduct of Athens towards her subjects, asserts that Sparta was content with securing that the states in her alliance should be oligarchically governed. The obvious implication is that Athens not only insisted on a democratic government in the cities in her alliance, but that she still further interfered with their autonomy. Our second conclusion is also implied throughout the *Athenian Constitution* of the pseudo-Xenophon, who goes so far as to assert that, if the oligarchs were allowed to get the upper hand in the subject states, there would be an end of the Athenian Empire: εἰ δὲ ἰσχύσουσιν οἱ πλούσιοι καὶ οἱ ἰσχυροὶ ἐν ταῖς πόλεσιν, ὀλίγιστον χρόνον ἡ ἀρχὴ ἔσται τοῦ δήμου τοῦ Ἀθήνησι (I, 14). In Aristotle, *Politics*, VIII (V), 7, 1307 b 20, it is expressly stated that the Athenians *everywhere* suppressed oligarchy, just as the Spartans in the days of their empire suppressed democracy: οἱ μὲν γὰρ Ἀθηναῖοι πανταχοῦ τὰς ὀλιγαρχίας, οἱ δὲ Λάκωνες τοὺς δήμους κατέλυον. In Isocrates (*Panegyr.* 105, 106; cf. *Panath.* 54 and 68) it is claimed for Athens that she conferred on her subjects the inestimable boon of her own constitution; a passage which is all the better evidence from its very *naïveté*: τῷ μὲν πλήθει βοηθοῦντες, ταῖς δὲ δυναστείαις πολεμοῦντες, τὴν αὐτὴν πολιτείαν ἥνπερ παρ' ἡμῖν αὐτοῖς καὶ παρὰ τοῖς ἄλλοις κατεστήσαμεν. Lastly, there is a clause in the Charter of the New Athenian Confederacy of 377 B.C. (*I.G.*² II, 43 = Hicks and Hill, 101) in which the allies of Athens are guaranteed that there shall be no revival of the notorious abuses of the former Empire; they are to be free and autonomous, they are to have neither garrison or magistrate imposed on them, they are to pay no tribute, and they are to choose their own form of constitution (πολιτ[ευομέν]-ωι πολιτείαν ἣν ἂν βούληται).

It seems to the present writer hard to imagine any evidence more conclusive than the sum total of all this. Selymbria (*I.G.*² I, 116 = Hicks and Hill, 77) presents no difficulty. Athens at the time (409–8 B.C.) was ready to make any concession in order to recover what she could. The only real difficulty is in Thucydides VIII, 21. If the passage means that there was a revolution at Samos, and that down to that moment an oligarchy was in power, we can only suppose that the democracy set up by Athens in 439 B.C., after the suppression of the revolt, had proved so incompetent that Athens was compelled to restore the oligarchy. But E. Meyer (*Gesch. des Alterthums*, IV, § 688 note) may be right in denying that a revolution is implied by the words of Thucydides.

E. M. W.

5. RESTORATION OF THE ASCENDANCY OF THE AREOPAGUS

One of the most startling novelties provided by Aristotle's *Constitution of Athens* is the statement (XXIII, I. 2; XXV, I) that at the time of the Battle of Salamis the Council of the Areopagus recovered its supremacy in the state, and retained it for a period of seventeen years; *i.e.* until the Reform of Ephialtes. The cause for a reaction so remarkable is stated to have been the patriotism of the Areopagites, who supplied the funds necessary for manning the fleet that fought at Salamis, the amount subscribed being sufficient to provide eight drachmae for each member of the ships' crews. This passage explains an obscure statement in the *Politics* to the effect that the reputation won by the Areopagus in the Persian Wars rendered the character of the constitution more oligarchical (Ar. *Pol.* VIII (v), 4, 1304 a. 20: ἔδοξε συντονωτέραν ποιῆσαι τὴν πολιτείαν). Plutarch, in the *Life of Themistocles* (10), quotes Aristotle as his authority for the provision of eight drachmae, but not for its consequence, the recovery of the ascendancy. It is obvious that there are grave objections to this alleged reactionary movement in favour of the Areopagus. In the first place, it is difficult to believe that the patriotic action of the Areopagites could have secured for that council, for so long a period as seventeen years, the restoration of its former control over the state. In politics gratitude is of all forces the weakest. But there are objections of a more special nature. The theory of the recovery of authority stands or falls with the act of generosity, and on this the passage in Plutarch throws a flood of light. Plutarch contrasts two versions of the means by which the fleet was manned, that of Aristotle and that of Clitodemus, or Clidemus. The latter was apparently the earliest of the Atthidographs, *i.e.* of the composers of a new form of historical literature which is known by the name of *Atthis*, or *History of Athens*. His work may be assigned to the first quarter of the fourth century B.C., possibly *c.* 380 B.C., and it is thus about fifty years earlier than Aristotle's *Constitution*. According to him the funds for manning the fleet were procured by an ingenious artifice of Themistocles, who at the moment of the evacuation of Attica issued a proclamation that the baggage of the refugees must be examined before their embarkation at the Piraeus, in order to discover the Gorgon's head which he asserted to be missing from the statue of Athena. The Gorgon's head was not indeed discovered, but 'a bundle of money was found at the mouth of each man's sack,' and a large sum was collected by the confiscation of this hidden wealth. When we compare the sparkling wine of Clitodemus with the flat, vapid stuff presented to us by Aristotle, we need little critical insight to detect which is the original tale, to the greater glory of Themistocles, and which its refutation in the Conservative interest. According to Aristotle, 'the generals were utterly at a loss how to meet the crisis,' and had issued a *sauve qui peut*, when the Areopagus came forward and saved the state. Who can these generals be but Themistocles himself? But the anecdote in Clitodemus, although it is at once earlier and more attractive than that in Aristotle, is not less unhistorical. Both anecdotes betray the familiar conditions of fourth-century Athens, when fleets might fail to be manned because the funds were insufficient to pay the rowers. In 480 B.C. the whole citizen population was called upon to go on board the fleet. Can we think so meanly of Athenian patriotism as to suppose that the citizens, at this supreme crisis of their country's fate, would go on strike until they had their wages paid in advance? Finally, it is significant that the restoration of authority to the Areopagus is stated to have been effected without the aid of any decree (οὐδενὶ δόγματι λαβοῦσι τὴν ἡγεμονίαν). Hence we may conclude that neither law nor psephism could be adduced as evidence for the alleged reaction. It is not less significant that the terms in which the ascendancy is described (διῴκει τὴν πόλιν) are practically identical with those applied to the Areopagus in the pre-Solonian epoch. The whole story is an illustration of the Areopagitic bias which is at once so conspicuous in Aristotle's work, and so characteristic of Isocrates and his school. After all, it was natural to infer that, if Ephialtes' Reform was the turning point in the history of the Athenian democracy, the powers of which the Areopagus was deprived by that Reform must have been more than considerable.

E. M. W.

6. THE PSEPHISM OF ARISTIDES

In Plutarch's *Life of Aristides* (22) there is a statement to the effect that after the victories of Plataea and Mycale Aristides proposed a decree which rendered all Athenians eligible for election to the archonship (γράφει ψήφισμα κοινὴν εἶναι τὴν πολιτείαν καὶ τοὺς ἄρχοντας ἐξ Ἀθηναίων πάντων αἱρεῖσθαι). It is melancholy to reflect that until the recovery of Aristotle's *Constitution of Athens* this passage was universally regarded as furnishing us with one of the corner stones of Athenian constitutional history. Thanks to the *Constitution*, two facts are now certain: the archons were appointed by sortition, not by election, from 487 B.C. onwards, and the two highest classes, the Pentacosiomedimni and Knights were alone eligible for this office until the year 457 B.C., when the privilege was extended to the third class, the Zeugitae. The lowest class, the Thetes, were never eligible according to the strict letter of the law (Arist. *Const. of Athens*, XXII, 5; XXVI, 2; VII *ad fin.*). It is a further objection to the statement in Plutarch that any such reform could only be effected, at this period of Athenian history, by means of a law (νόμος), and not by a decree (ψήφισμα). The statement must have been derived by Plutarch from some late and peculiarly ignorant writer. No importance of any sort or kind is to be attached to it.

E. M. W.

7. THE CHRONOLOGY OF THE YEARS 445–431 B.C.

The ostracism of Thucydides, son of Melesias (p. 166), marks the beginning of Pericles' unchallenged ascendancy at Athens. Plutarch, *Pericles*, 16, says that after the ostracism Pericles enjoyed fifteen years of uninterrupted office. If the end of this fifteen years is set at the deposition of Pericles in 430, the date of the ostracism would be early in 444 B.C.; if it is set at the death of Pericles in 429, the ostracism would be early in 443 B.C. The latter assumption is possible in view of the fact that though Pericles was deposed in the autumn of 430 B.C., he was re-elected in the spring of 429 (Thuc. II, 65). In favour of the later date is the division of the Athenian Empire into five tribute-districts which occurred in 443 B.C. and may be connected with the controversy between Pericles and Thucydides, which was at last decided in Pericles' favour by the ostracism (see E. Meyer, *Forschungen*, II, pp. 82 *sqq.*).

The sending of Phormio to Acarnania (p. 176) cannot be dated with precision. Thucydides (II, 68) only refers to it incidentally as a past event when he is describing the operations of the year 430. We may assume that it preceded 435 B.C., as otherwise it must have directly affected the course of events in North-West Greece after that year and have been mentioned by the historian. Equally, had it happened before 439 B.C., we should expect to find it mentioned in Thucydides' account of events down to the reduction of Samos with which his excursus on the growth of Athenian power ends (1, 118). We are therefore left with the choice of a date between 439 and 435, and Busolt's suggestion of about 437 B.C. may be accepted in default of precise evidence.

For the chronology of events in the years 435 to 431 B.C. it is necessary to proceed from the inscription (*I.G.*² 1, 295 = Hicks and Hill, 53) which refers to the payments to the Attic squadrons sent to Corcyra. The restoration [ἐπὶ τῆς Αἰαν]τίδος πρυτανείας πρώτης πρυ[τανευούσης] in ll. 10–11 and [ἐπὶ τῆς] Αἰαντίδος πρυτανείας [πρώτης πρυτανευούση]ς in ll. 21–2 is epigraphically highly probable and also fits the narrative of Thucydides 1, 45–50, which implies that the battle of Sybota followed immediately upon the appearance of the Corinthian fleet in Corcyraean waters and states that the second squadron arrived on the day of the battle. The alliance between Athens and Corcyra was a defensive alliance and, according to Greek practice, the *casus foederis* would not arise until the Corinthians made an offensive movement. We may therefore place the dispatch of the first Attic squadron about the time of the setting out of the Corinthian armada. Thus the interval between the dispatch of the two Attic squadrons would be short and, if the above restoration is accepted, the first squadron sailed towards the beginning and the second towards the end of August 433 B.C., *i.e.* in the first prytany of the archonship of Apseudes (433–2 B.C.). The battle is therefore to be set in the first half of September in that year, as Corcyra is about ten days sail from Athens. The Corinthian preparations had lasted some two years since the battle of Leucimne (Thuc. 1, 31. 1), which is therefore to be set in the summer of 435 B.C.

The revolt of Potidaea falls between the sending out of Archestratus and that of Callias. The latter is to be set in the second prytany of the official year 432–1 B.C., *i.e.* Aug.–Sept. 432 (*I.G.*² 1, 296, l. 6), the former towards the end of the archon year 433–2, for the list of generals for 432–1 almost certainly did not include Archestratus (see Beloch, *Griech. Gesch.* II², 2, 219 *sq.*). Between the dispatch of Archestratus and the dispatch of Callias there is an interval of some two months, as Callias started later than Aristeus (Thuc. 1, 61. 1) and Aristeus started on receiving news of the revolt which was declared between the departure and the arrival of Archestratus in the Thracian region (*ib.* 1, 59. 1). The battle before Potidaea takes place soon after the arrival of Callias, for the Athenian generals are aware of the necessity of prompt action against Potidaea (*ib.* 1, 61. 3). It may therefore be placed in Sept.–Oct. 432 B.C. The news of the Athenian success apparently reached Corinth before the first conference at Sparta (*ib.* 1, 67. 1) which preceded the change of ephors in October (cf. *ib.* 1, 85. 3, 87. 1 with II. 2. 1). Between the dispatch of Callias and the summer of 431 B.C. Phormio was sent out with reinforcements (*ib.* 1, 64. 2), possibly in the fourth prytany (Oct.–Nov.) of 432 B.C. (see *I.G.*² 1, 296, ll. 12–3). Thucydides (1, 56–7) appears to make the disaffection at least of Potidaea follow closely upon the conclusion of the Corcyraean campaign of 433 B.C. but an interval must be allowed for the intrigues of the Corinthians to bear fruit, and Potidaea might be glad to have time for preparations, while Athens, as is suggested above (p. 185), might wait until the right moment for a Peloponnesian invasion of Attica had passed. The chronological scheme of Diodorus XII, 30 *sqq.* (beginning of Corinthian-Corcyraean War 439–8; Battle of Leucimne 438–7; Battle of Sybota 436–5 B.C.; Revolt of Potidaea 435–4) is not evidence of anything but of Diodorus' methods at their worst.

The first Peloponnesian invasion of Attica, that in 431 B.C., is about 80 days after the Theban attack on Plataea (Thuc. II, 19. 1) and that attack occurred 'in the sixth month after the battle before Potidaea,' ἅμα ἦρι ἀρχομένῳ (*ib.* II, 2. 1), τελευτῶντος τοῦ μηνός (*ib.* II, 4. 2). The choice lies between the beginning of March and the beginning of April, and the former is more probably to Thucydides the beginning of spring, and the interval of five months between Sept.–Oct. 432 and March 431 is sufficiently exact (see Beloch, *op. cit.* p. 220). On the other hand, the MSS. of Thucydides II, 2. 1 make him say that the attack on Plataea occurred when the archon Pythodorus had still two months of office to run. His archonship ended at the end of July 431 and Thucydides could not well describe an event which happened at the end of May as ἅμα ἦρι ἀρχομένῳ. The number must therefore be corrupt and 'four' or 'five' must be read in the place of 'two,' according as the attack on Plataea is set at the beginning of March or the beginning of April. If the attack on Plataea is set at the beginning of March, the invasion of Attica falls at the end of May which sufficiently well suits Thucydides' other note of time, θέρους καὶ τοῦ σίτου ἀκμάζοντος (II, 19. 1), and also his estimate of the period from the invasion of Attica to the Peace of Nicias (V, 19. 1, V, 20. 1). The Peloponnesians remained in Attica until after the Athenian fleet had sailed to attack the Peloponnese (*ib.* II, 23. 2). Three payments for this expedition are recorded (*I.G.²* 1, 296, ll. 30 *sqq.*) which may have been in the ninth prytany of 432–1, that is the month of June, and a fourth in the tenth and last prytany of the year. This reconstruction, which is generally accepted, is open to the objection that it does not exactly fit the statement of Thucydides (I, 125. 2) that the interval between the second conference at Sparta and the invasion of Attica was ἐνιαυτὸς μὲν οὐ..., ἔλασσον δέ. The historian is apparently correcting a statement that the interval was one year; we should expect the interval to be longer than that from late October to the end of May, but if Thucydides roughly equated the second conference and the battle before Potidaea it is possible that he reckoned the period as between 5 and 6 months + 80 days, and that period might be covered though rather inexactly by his phrase 'not a year, but less,' see Beloch, *loc. cit.*

It remains to determine the date of the famous Megarian decree. This decree, to exclude the Megarians from the harbours of the Athenian Empire and the markets of Attica, must have been passed before the first conference at Sparta at which the Megarians complained of it (Thuc. I, 67). If it was regarded as a breach of the Thirty Years Peace, the Megarians must have challenged it immediately upon its publication, and we may assume that it was passed immediately before the Megarian complaint. Minor grievances might wait, but this was a matter that could not be delayed. Two reasons are advanced for setting it earlier than the summer of 432 B.C. The first is that Aristophanes in the *Acharnians*, 535, says that the Megarians complained ὅτε δὴ 'πείνων βάδην, but it may be doubted whether the comedian is not putting the final results of the decree in place of the actual grievance, which was its publication, and so wrongly suggesting an interval of time between the decree and outbreak of war. In the *Peace*, 608, the decree is the spark which sets the city ablaze. The second reason is that an allusion to the decree has been found in the speech of the Corinthians at Athens (Thuc. 1,42.2): τῆς...ὑπαρχούσης πρότερον διὰ Μεγαρέας ὑποψίας. It is however plain, in the context, that the Corinthians are referring to some past action directed against themselves which Athenian complaisance in the matter of Corcyra will counterbalance: ἡ γὰρ τελευταία χάρις καιρὸν ἔχουσα, κἂν ἐλάσσων ᾖ, δύναται μεῖζον ἔγκλημα λῦσαι. Such an action was the Athenian protection of the Megarians from Corinthian attacks in *c.* 459 B.C. which caused the 'extreme hatred' of the Corinthians for Athens and led directly to war (Thuc. 1, 103). The parallel with the Athenian protection of Corcyra is exact. This suggestion renders unnecessary the hypothesis that the Megarian decree had remained in operation for more than a year before it was declared to be a breach of the Thirty Years Peace. If the Megarian decree is set, as in the text, p. 186, immediately after the departure of Aristeus for Potidaea had made war practically certain, it becomes what Thucydides seems to have seen in it, not so much a cause of war as a proof of Athenian power and a test of Athenian determination. The decree of Charinus, to put to death any Megarian found on Attic territory and to invade the Megarid twice a year, a decree which in antiquity was sometimes confused with its more famous predecessor, implies the existence of a state of war between Athens and Megara and must belong to the spring of 431 B.C. Its effect is seen in the invasion of the Megarid in the autumn of that year (p. 198).

F. E. A.

8. THE ATTACKS ON THE FRIENDS OF PERICLES

Diodorus XII, 38–39 (presumably following Ephorus), repeats under the year 431 B.C. the statement that Pericles precipitated the Peloponnesian War by refusing to repeal the Megarian decree because (1) being on the point of giving an account of his public expenditure he took the advice of Alcibiades and sought not how to give an account but how not to give one, (2) his friend Pheidias was accused by his enemies of embezzlement and Pericles himself of being his accomplice, (3) a charge of impiety was brought against Anaxagoras, the teacher of Pericles, and attacks were made on Pericles himself.

Plutarch, *Pericles*, 31–2, gives as one ancient explanation of Pericles' refusal to repeal the Megarian decree (1) the prosecution and death in prison of Pheidias, (2) the prosecution of Aspasia for impiety and for acting as procuress for Pericles, (3) the fact that one Diopeithes proposed a decree to impeach those who did not accept the gods or taught about celestial phenomena (περὶ τῶν μεταρσίων), casting suspicion on Pericles by means of Anaxagoras, (4) whereupon the people, accepting these slanders, passed a decree proposed by Dracontides that Pericles should submit his accounts of public expenditure and that the jurors should vote with ballots which had lain on the altar of Athena. Hagnon amended this last clause and proposed that the case should be tried before 1500 jurors, whether it was to be called a prosecution for embezzlement and bribery or malversation (ἀδικίου) He continues that Pericles procured the acquittal of Aspasia by shedding tears and softening the hearts of the jurors, and, fearing for Anaxagoras, he sent him away from Athens. Since the Pheidias case had brought him into collision with the people, fearing the law-court, he kindled into flame a threatening and smouldering war.

It is clear that these two accounts represent one single anti-Periclean tradition.

The decree of Dracontides must have meant the suspension or deposition of Pericles from the office of general. It must therefore be connected with the only deposition and trial of Pericles of which we have respectable evidence, viz. his deposition and trial in the autumn of 430 B.C. The amendment of the procedure by Hagnon is presumably a separate decree carried by that general on his return from Potidaea. The decree of Dracontides has therefore nothing to do with the outbreak of the war, see Beloch, *Att. Politik*, pp. 330 *sqq.*

It is possible that Aspasia was prosecuted for impiety (see p. 383) but the statement that her accuser was the comic poet Hermippus, who added to it a charge of being a procuress for Pericles, makes us suspect that we have no more than a conflation of the belief in Aspasia's free-thinking and the scurrility of comedy. The charge of being a procuress was brought also by Aristophanes in the *Acharnians* (527) in order to suit his burlesque of the Herodotean account of the causes of the Persian War (see chapter XIV, p. 406). If Aspasia was prosecuted, she was acquitted. If the story of her acquittal is true, it attests the influence of Pericles.

Prof. A. E. Taylor (*C. Q.* XI, 1917, p. 81) has made it highly probable that Anaxagoras retired from Athens to Lampsacus nearly twenty years before the outbreak of the war. The decree of Diopeithes is, doubtless, historical fact, and marks some orthodox reaction; but even if it preceded the decree of Dracontides, it may belong to the year 430 B.C. and be the outcome of the emotions evoked by the plague, the visible sign of the anger of heaven (Thuc. II, 54).

There remains the charge that Pericles brought about the war in alarm caused by the disgrace of his friend Pheidias. This charge was first brought by Aristophanes, ten years after the outbreak of the war, in the *Peace* (603 *sqq.*), if we may trust the remarks of Trygaeus and the chorus that it was entirely new to them. The accusation, clearly the invention of a comic poet who rejoices in his extravagant novelty, was removed from its context and taken seriously by those who wished to blacken the character of Pericles. The phrasing in Plutarch's *Pericles* μέλλοντα τὸν πόλεμον καὶ ὑποτυφό- μένον ἐξέκαυσεν echoes the comedian's …ἐξέφλεξε τὴν πόλιν | ἐμβαλὼν σπινθῆρα μικρὸν Μεγαρικοῦ ψηφίσματος. It is possible to argue that the prosecution of Pheidias and the outbreak of the war roughly coincided in time and that the comedian did not invent anything more than the alleged causal connection between the two events. But even the coinci- dence in time appears to the present writer improbable. The scholiast on the passage in the *Peace* adduces as refuting the poet the statement of the Athenian antiquarian and historian Philochorus. The latter points out that the Pheidias affair (τὰ περὶ Φειδίαν) occurred six years before the outbreak of the war. He gives precise dates, which, however, demand discussion. According to the MSS. he put the dedication of the Athena Parthenos ἐπὶ Πυθοδώρου and the death of Pheidias, after a period of artistic activity at Elis, ἐπὶ Σκυθοδώρου. There is no such fifth-century archon as Scythodorus. It is expressly stated that six years divided the two archonships, and Palmer's proposal, to read Theodorus (archon 438–7) for Pythodorus and Pythodorus (432–1) for Scythodorus, has received general assent. The alternative suggestion of Beloch (*Griech. Gesch.* II², 1, p. 295 n. 2) that the scholiast or his source had before him a corrupt archon-list in which the archon of 432–1 was called Scythodorus and the archon of 438–7 Pythodorus appears to the present writer an improbable explanation. In the second part of the scholion, also an abridgement of the same statement by Philochorus, the MS. reading Pythodorus is either a repetition of the preceding corruption or the correct date of Pheidias' death.

The death of Pheidias at the hands of the Eleans is connected apparently by Philochorus with the Megarian decree and so belongs to the time of the outbreak of the war, and the exile is undoubtedly supposed to precede it by six years. There is no good reason to doubt that the statue of Athena was dedicated in 438 B.C. and the fact that in 434–3 B.C. gold and ivory was sold by the commissioners for the Parthenon does not prove that the statue was not already complete at that time (see Dinsmoor, *A.J.A.* XVII, p. 70 n. 1). It appears to the present writer improbable that these materials, if they had been purchased for the statue, would have been disposed of until the use of these costly materials by the artist had been checked. It is not possible to determine on grounds of style whether Pheidias was personally concerned in the execution of the Parthenon sculptures after 438–7. The argument that Pheidias could not have worked at Olympia after he had been exiled from Athens or had fled and been condemned *in absentia*, assumes that those in charge of the temple at Olympia believed him guilty, or were anxious to please the enemies of Pericles rather than Pericles himself. The precise charges brought against Pheidias cannot be determined with certainty in the haze of fiction which surrounds them. The details about the informer Menon afford no evidence of date.

The statement in Plutarch, *Pericles*, 31, that Pheidias died of disease in prison at Athens, may be an invention designed to make possible the story which follows that some said his death was due to poison, procured by the enemies of Pericles to bring odium on Pericles, a story which is to be compared with that which made the same statesman responsible for the death of Ephialtes (*ib.* c. 10).

The view taken in the text is that Pheidias was prosecuted very soon after the dedication of the statue in 438–7 B.C. and went into exile at Elis, where he died or was killed about the time of the outbreak of the Peloponnesian War. If this view is correct, then there remains no reason for supposing, what Thucydides' account of events appears to preclude, that the personal position of Pericles was shaken in the months which precede the war.

The fragments of the Geneva Papyrus may not refer to the sculptor Pheidias at all (see Robert, *Berl. S.B.* 1914, p. 806), or if they do, they supply us with nothing but some extremely dubious support for the tradition that Pheidias was first honoured by the Eleans and then, at the time of the Peloponnesian War, incurred their hatred. The papyrus apparently contains fragments of a commentary on some speech and may, as such commentaries do, have drawn upon Philochorus. If so, it has no independent value as evidence. As has been said, Philochorus, or his source, asserts that Pheidias was put to death by the Eleans, Plutarch, or his source, that he died in prison at Athens. Frickenhaus, *J.D.A.I.* XXVIII, p. 348 *sq.*, followed by Judeich, *Hermes*, LX, p. 55, combines these statements, supposing that Pheidias died in prison at Elis, after his enemies at Athens had provoked a second accusation of him for embezzlement, this time in connection with the statue of Zeus at Olympia. Other scholars seek to combine some of the statements of Philochorus with those of Plutarch by assuming that Pheidias on the completion of the Athena in 438–7 B.C. went to Elis in peace and then *c.* 432 B.C. returned to Athens, was prosecuted and condemned, and died in prison. To embark upon such 'combinations of heterogeneous traditions' in order to retain as history the statement of Aristophanes or even the deduction from it that the prosecution of Pheidias and the beginning of the war were near together in time, appears to the present writer very hazardous.

See Busolt III, 1, p. 460 n. 2, where the earlier literature is given, Beloch, *loc. cit.*, E. Meyer III, § 531, and the works of Frickenhaus, Judeich, Pareti, Rosenberg, Schrader, cited in the Bibliography.

F. E. A.

9. THE DATES OF COMPOSITION OF PARTS OF THUCYDIDES I AND II–V, 20

The scale and scope of this work preclude the discussion of the whole intricate question of the composition of the histories of Thucydides and of Herodotus, which would otherwise have appeared in Chapter XIV from the pen of Dr R. W. Macan. What follows is a statement of the view taken by the present writer of the composition of those parts of Thucydides' history which underlie the narrative in Chapters VII and VIII[1].

The account of the increase of Athenian power (1, 89–117) appears to have been composed, possibly with the use of materials collected earlier, after the publication of the *Atthis* of Hellanicus (Thucydides, 1, 97. 2), which included events belonging to the year 407–6 B.C. (Jacoby, *F.G.H.* 171–2). The reason for this digression is apparently to justify the statement (1, 23. 6) that, whereas there were two αἰτίαι ('grievances') which led to the war, the ἀληθεστάτη πρόφασις ('truest explanation') was the increase

---

[1] A valuable review of the earlier literature and discussion of the problem will be found in Dr G. B. Grundy's *Thucydides and His Age*, London, 1911, pp. 387 *sqq.* which advances the view of a retractation in the sense here suggested. The most important recent work is that of E. Schwartz, *Das Geschichtswerk des Thukydides.* Bonn, 1919. See also Beloch, *Griech. Gesch.* II², 2, pp. 7 *sqq.*

of Athenian power which alarmed the Lacedaemonians and drove them to make war[1].

On the other hand, the account of the two 'grievances' (Corcyra and Potidaea) is elaborate and contains detailed information which must have been collected near the time, *e.g.* the names of the Corinthian and Corcyraean admirals (I, 29. 2; 46. 2; 47. 1), and it appears to the present writer probable that we have here what once seemed to the historian a sufficient account of the events which led to the war τοῦ μή τινα ζητῆσαί ποτε ἐξ ὅτου τοσοῦτος πόλεμος τοῖς Ἕλλησι κατέστη (I, 23. 5). The account of the Corcyra and Potidaea affairs and the narrative of the discussions at Sparta and of the diplomatic interchanges of 432–1, which suggest that the Lacedaemonians were, in the main, reluctant to go to war, is taken as belonging to an earlier stratum of narrative, while the historian's view that the increasing strength of Athens frightened the Spartans into war is here regarded as secondary and belonging to the period (after 407–6 B.C.) in which he wrote the excursus which supports this second view. The earlier stratum implies an active Corinth goading on an inert Sparta that had no sufficiently good cause to fear Athens, and appears to be truer to fact than the secondary view, which, on the above hypothesis, was reached during the Decelean War. The power of Athens was not as great or at least not as obvious in 432 as it was twenty years before (see p. 414), and the course of the Archidamian War is of a piece with the earlier picture of an irresolute, reluctant Sparta.

Connected with this secondary view of the cause of the war is the view that the whole period 431–404 B.C. is a unity, for it is the ambition of Athens as displayed in the Sicilian Expedition and the resolution of Sparta as personified in Lysander which best support the hypothesis of the ἀληθεστάτη πρόφασις (see Grundy, *op. cit.* pp. 411 *sqq.*). When Thucydides wrote V, 20, with its elaborate calculation of the length of the Archidamian War, we may suppose him to have thought that the war ended with the Peace of Nicias. When he wrote (IV, 48. 5) of the *stasis* in Corcyra, καὶ ἡ στάσις πολλὴ γενομένη ἐτελεύτησεν ἐς τοῦτο, ὅσα γε κατὰ τὸν πόλεμον τόνδε· οὐ γὰρ ἔτι ἦν ὑπόλοιπον τῶν ἑτέρων ὅ τι καὶ ἀξιόλογον, we may fairly assume that all except the qualification ὅσα γε κατὰ τὸν πόλεμον τόνδε was written soon after the events (425 B.C.) and that the qualification was added after the end of the Archidamian War and before Thucydides had conceived of a single twenty-seven years war, of which the Archidamian was only a part. For the *stasis* at Corcyra broke out again in 411–10 B.C. a fact which presumably caused the historian to insert the qualification. If that is so, then it was not until after this qualification was made, *i.e.* after 411–10 B.C., that Thucydides came to view the whole series of struggles as one. Once he had formed that view, we need not be surprised that references are inserted here and there which reflect it, or that the historian, seeking for a deeper cause for a longer struggle, brought into Book I material to support his ἀληθεστάτη πρόφασις, though fortunately,

---

[1] For αἰτία in the sense of 'grievance,' see Cornford, *Thucydides Mythistoricus*, p. 59. To the present writer the word 'grievance' has the meaning of *casus belli*; πρόφασις the meaning of 'explanation' as in I, 133, III, 13. 1, where the sense of pretext seems out of place.

probably because he died before the task of reconstruction was complete, he has left for us the earlier stratum.

To the earlier stratum, then, we may attribute I, 24–67 (including the speeches of the Corcyraeans and Corinthians at Athens, which appear to reflect the situation in 433 B.C. and contain no necessary anticipation of the course of the war which followed,) and the account of the negotiations at Sparta and between Sparta and Athens down to March 431. Which of the speeches contained in this account are of early composition it is hard to determine with confidence. Of those attributed to speakers at the first conference at Sparta (I, 68–86) the speech attributed to the Athenian envoys may, as Schwartz suggests, *op. cit.* pp. 102 *sqq.*, throw out the balance of the composition, the original contrast being between the Corinthian speech and that of Archidamus. In support of this view is the tone of the Athenian speech which may have been adapted to the secondary view that Athen's aggressive strength was the decisive factor, and the possible allusions to the behaviour of Sparta if she becomes an Imperial power, allusions which may reflect what happened after the Fall of Athens. But while the speech attributed to the Athenians may be a late composition by Thucydides, his statement that Athenian envoys were at Sparta need not be doubted. There is no good reason to suppose that either the speech of the Corinthians or that of Archidamus were composed long after 432 B.C. The reference in Archidamus' speech to possible help from Persia (I, 82. 1–2) does not prove lateness, in view of the Spartan embassy to the Great King in 430 B.C. (II, 67). The short speech of Sthenelaidas affords no clear indication, but may have been included to balance the Athenian speech, though there is no reason to doubt that he voiced the views of the Spartan war-party at this conference. The Corinthian speech at the second conference at Sparta is often regarded as late, because of the reference to the revolts of allies and ἐπιτειχισμός. But the former was an obvious possibility at all stages in the war and the latter plays a part in the strategy of the war long before the occupation of Decelea. The speech of Pericles (I, 140 *sqq.*) replies to that of the Corinthians, and may not reflect anything other than the situation in 432 B.C. The last chapter of the book appears to belong to the earlier stratum which makes the grievances from which the war sprang begin with the Corcyraean affair.

In the view of the present writer, therefore, the first book affords material to reconstruct Thucydides' view of the origins of the war as he conceived them in the early years of the conflict.

The narrative of the Archidamian War (II–V, 20) is based on material collected, and possibly written up, not long after the events described (I, 1. 1, Θουκυδίδης ξυνέγραψε τὸν πόλεμον...ἀρξάμενος εὐθὺς καθισταμένου), though we find, as is to be expected, short passages which betray knowledge of later events or reflect a later point of view, inserted by the writer as, from time to time, he read over and elaborated what he had written (*e.g.* II, 48. 2; 100. 2; IV, 12. 3; 74. 4; 108. 4). The historian's exile in 424 B.C. increased his access to enemy evidence, and may have enabled him to improve his earlier drafts. It is at least probable that Thucydides did not delay writing his narrative of the events of 424–1 B.C. until he had access to Athenian or Spartan official sources, for, as Kirchhoff pointed out, the texts of the armistice of 423 B.C. and of the Peace of 421 B.C. appear to have been inserted in a narrative composed without full knowledge of these state documents.

As regards the speeches in the narrative of the Archidamian War the view of E. Meyer, *Forschungen* II, p. 282, that the Funeral Speech is inserted as an *Epitaphios* on Athens after her fall is here adopted. The account of Pericles in II, 65 with its references to his successors and to the Sicilian expedition may have been inserted or expanded at the same time and for the same reasons as the Funeral Oration. The speech attributed to Hermocrates at the Conference of Gela (IV, 59–64) may have been written after the Sicilian expedition, though, to the present writer, this is not a necessary assumption. The last speech of Pericles (II, 60–4) is hardly what the situation demands, but may be intended to convey an impression of Pericles' unyielding spirit at the time. With these possible exceptions the speeches in Books II–IV show no signs of composition much later than the events with which they are connected.

The work of Thucydides is incomplete, and it appears to the present writer improbable despite the second preface in V, 26 that any part of it was finally revised and published by its author. This consideration, however, does not greatly affect the main narrative of the Archidamian War, even if, here and there though not so often as has been supposed, the well-meant efforts of his 'editor' or 'literary executor' have introduced confusions of thought or language. It appears to the present writer possible that the much-suspected Chapter III, 17 is Thucydidean, but wrongly inserted in the narrative of 428 B.C. whereas its true place appears to be in the narrative of 430 B.C. (see *Camb. Hist. Journal*, I, 1925, pp. 319 *sqq.*). For a discussion of the sources available to Thucydides see above pp. 411 *sqq.* and for the literature of the whole controversy the Bibliography to Chapter XIV.

F. E. A.

10. THE CHRONOLOGY OF THE PERIOD FROM 410 TO 406 B.C.

In the *Hellenica* Xenophon based his narrative on military seasons and thus omitted to designate the calendar years by archons, ephors and olympiads. This omission was made good for Books I and II by an ancient interpolator, who, however, did his work badly. Whether his insertions of dates are commonly made at precisely the right places in the text depends upon whether the phrases by which they are introduced, τῷ δὲ ἄλλῳ ἔτει (I, 2. 1), τοῦ δ' ἐπιόντος ἔτους (I, 3. 1), τῷ δ' ἐπιόντι ἔτει (I, 6. 1; II, 1. 10; 3. 1) belong to him or to Xenophon—a contentious point; though it argues for their being his handiwork rather than Xenophon's that elsewhere in the *Hellenica*, where interpolated dates are lacking, such phrases do not occur. Certainly he failed to observe the opening of a military season in *Hell*. I, 4. 1, though the phrase used to mark its approach (ἀρχομένου δὲ τοῦ ἔαρος) admits of no ambiguity; and this oversight threw out his dating of the two preceding seasons; for, as Busolt (III, 2, p. 698; *Hermes*, XXXIII, pp. 661 *sqq.*) has pointed out, the interpolator probably worked backwards from the obvious year of the Anarchy (404–3 B.C.), entering an archon etc. for each annual period as he delimited it in the text of Xenophon.

The question on which the long-standing controversy regarding the chronology of this period hinges is whether the events of another whole year in Xenophon are left without a date. In that case the battle of Notium, the self-exile of Alcibiades, and the naval reform of Conon (I, 5. 11–20) belong to the year 407 B.C. and the arrival in Ephesus of Callicratidas and the battle of Arginusae to 406. Otherwise all these events belong to 406, the first group of them prior to March, the second later. The latter alternative is adopted by the present writer, following Dodwell, Grote, Beloch (II², 2, pp. 241 *sqq.*) and Valeton (*Mnemosyne*, 1920, pp. 34 *sqq.*). The former construction is preferred notably by Busolt (III 2, p. 1529 n. 1) and E. Meyer (IV, pp. 616 *sqq.*, 640), who accordingly date the expedition of Thrasyllus to Ionia in 410, the Athenian operations in the Bosporus in 409, and the return to Athens of Alcibiades and the advent of Cyrus in 408.

Neither scheme is without flaws. Ours leaves Alcibiades inactive in the Hellespont between the autumn of 410 and the autumn of 409; theirs leaves both Conon and Lysander inactive between the self-exile of Alcibiades and the arrival of Callicratidas a year later. Neither escapes doing violence to some non-Xenophontine materials: ours dates the loss of Pylos sixteen years after its first occupation instead of fifteen (Diod. XIII, 64. 7); theirs dates the expedition of Thrasyllus in the archonship of Theopompus (411–10) instead of in that of Glaucippus (410–09), as Dionysius of Halicarnassus (Hypothesis to Lysias, *Or.* XXXII) reports. These difficulties, however, have all been passably met in the course of the controversy, as have the minor objections to the view we prefer, that the interval between Notium (March 406) and Arginusae (August 406) is too short for the career of Callicratidas, and that Thrasyllus who came to Athens in the autumn of 411 B.C. for reinforcements did not return with them till the spring of 409 B.C.

There is, however, a decisive objection to dating Notium in 407, seventeen months or so before Arginusae (406 B.C.). The ten generals elected after Notium (Xenophon, *Hell.* I, 5. 16; Diod. XIII, 74. 1), to serve for the calendar year next following, actually served in the archonship of Callias (406–5 B.C.); for they commanded the fleet at Arginusae and this battle was admittedly fought in Callias' year. In other words the March of Notium was the March of 406. From this conclusion there is no real escape. It is simply an evasion to affirm that the same ten men were elected generals for two consecutive years (407–6 and 406–5 B.C.)—a thing improbable in itself and quite unexampled (see Beloch, II², 2, pp. 260 *sqq.*; Krause, *Athenische Strategenliste*), and it is not even an evasion to suggest that, though generals were elected for 406–5 as usual and at the usual time, the conduct of naval operations was left with their predecessors after 407–6 had ended, since, as Valeton (*loc. cit.* pp. 38 *sqq.*) has pointed out, when the generals who commanded at Arginusae were suspended from office, vacancies occurred in the generalship which had to be filled by new elections (Xenophon, *Hell.* I, 7. 1).

Since, then, Notium and Arginusae belong to 406 B.C. the interpolator left only one year archonless, and the expedition of Thrasyllus started early in 409 and not in 410. Yet another valid reason exists for not dating this expedition in 410. The Sicilian ships were all lost at the battle of Cyzicus. This battle came at the end of a campaign which opened 'at the close of winter' in 410 B.C. (Diod. XIII, 49. 2). In view of the prior doings of Theramenes (Diod. *Ib.*; *I.G.*² 1, 105; cf. Wilhelm, *Jahreshefte*, XXI, XXII, 1924, pp. 123 *sqq.*) the battle itself cannot possibly have been fought before April. Nor can it have occurred much later than April, since it was during the archonship of Theopompus (411–10 B.C.) that the Spartan offer of peace was rejected by Athens (Philochorus, frag. 117 M) and the Council of the Five Hundred restored (*I.G.*² 1, 105, cf. *Class. Phil.* 1926, p. 75). Yet by the beginning of June, *i.e.*, seventeen days after 'the time that the grain was ripening' (Xenophon, *Hell.* 1, 2. 4 *sqq.*), of the year 410 B.C., according to the hypothesis we are combating, the Sicilians had replaced their lost fleet by new ships built at Antandros and had brought it first to Miletus and then to Ephesus, so that it was at hand there on the arrival of Thrasyllus. This seems to the present writer incredible. If at this time fleets of twenty ships could have been built by their crews, or anybody else, at isolated points in Asia Minor in two months, the whole story of the Decelean War would have been different.

W. S. F.

LIST OF ABBREVIATIONS

Abh.	Abhandlungen.
Abh. Arch.-epig.	Abhandlungen d. archäol.-epigraph. Seminars d. Univ. Wien.
A.J.A.	American Journal of Archaeology.
A.J. Ph.	American Journal of Philology.
Arch. Anz.	Archäologischer Anzeiger (in J.D.A.I.).
Arch. Phil.	Archiv für Geschichte d. Philosophie.
Ath. Mitt.	Mitteilungen des deutschen arch. Inst. Athenische Abteilung.
Bay. Abh.	Abhandlungen d. bayerischen Akad. d. Wissenschaften.
Bay. S.B.	Sitzungsberichte d. bayerischen Akad. d. Wissenschaften.
B.C.H.	Bulletin de Correspondance hellénique.
Beloch	K. J. Beloch's Griechische Geschichte. 2nd Ed.
Berl. Abh.	Abhandlungen d. preuss. Akad. d. Wissenschaften zu Berlin.
Berl. S.B.	Sitzungsberichte d. preuss. Akad. d. Wissenschaften zu Berlin.
Berl. Stud.	Berliner Studien.
B.I.C.	Bulletin de l'Institut français d'archéologie orientale au Caire.
B.P.W.	Berliner Philologische Wochenschrift.
B.S.A.	Annual of the British School at Athens.
B.S.R.	Papers of the British School at Rome.
Bull. d. I.	Bullettino dell' Istituto.
Bursian	Bursian's Jahresbericht.
Bury	J. B. Bury's History of Greece. 2nd Ed. 1922.
Busolt	G. Busolt's Griechische Geschichte.
C.A.H.	Cambridge Ancient History.
Cavaignac	E. Cavaignac's Histoire de l'antiquité.
C.J.	Classical Journal.
C.P.	Classical Philology.
C.Q.	Classical Quarterly.
C.R.	Classical Review.
C.R. Ac. Inscr.	Comptes rendus de l'Académie des Inscriptions et Belles-Lettres.
Diss.	Dissertation.
D.S.	Daremberg et Saglio, Dictionnaire des antiquités grecques et romaines.
E. Brit.	Encyclopaedia Britannica. 11th Ed.
E. Meyer	E. Meyer's Geschichte des Altertums.
Ἐφ. Ἀρχ.	Ἐφημερὶς Ἀρχαιολογική.
F.H.G.	C. Müller's Fragmenta Historicorum Graecorum.
G.G.A.	Göttingische Gelehrte Anzeigen.
Gött. Nach.	Nachrichten von der Königlichen Gesellschaft der Wissenschaften zu Göttingen. Phil.-hist. Klasse.
Harv. St.	Harvard Studies in Classical Philology.
Head H.N.[2]	Head's Historia Numorum. 2nd Ed. 1912.
Hicks and Hill	E. L. Hicks and G. F. Hill, Manual of Greek Historical Inscriptions. Oxford, 1901.
H.Z.	Historische Zeitschrift.
I.G.	Inscriptiones Graecae.
I.G.[2]	Inscriptiones Graecae. Editio minor.
Jahreshefte	Jahreshefte d. österr. archäol. Instituts in Wien.
J.D.A.I.	Jahrbuch des deutschen archäologischen Instituts.

J.H.S.	Journal of Hellenic Studies.
J.P.	Journal of Philology.
Klio	Klio (Beiträge zur alten Geschichte).
Liv. A.A.	Liverpool Annals of Archaeology.
M.B.B.A.	Monatsbericht der Berliner Akademie.
Mél. Arch.	Mélanges d'archéologie et d'histoire.
Mém. Ac. Inscr.	Mémoires de l'Académie des Inscriptions et Belles-Lettres.
Michel	Michel, Recueil d'Inscriptions Grecques, 1900.
Mon. Linc.	Monumenti antichi pubblicati per cura della R. Accademia dei Lincei.
Mon. d. I.	Monumenti Antichi dell' Instituto.
Mus. B.	Musée belge.
N.F.	Neue Folge.
N.J. Kl. Alt.	Neue Jahrbücher für das klassische Altertum.
N.J.P.	Neue Jahrbücher für Philologie.
N.S.	New Series.
Num. Chr.	Numismatic Chronicle.
Num. Z.	Numismatische Zeitschrift.
Phil.	Philologus.
Proc.	Proceedings.
P.W.	Pauly-Wissowa's Real-Encyclopädie der classischen Altertumswissenschaft.
Rend. Linc.	Rendiconti dell' Accademia dei Lincei.
Rev. Arch.	Revue Archéologique.
Rev. E.G.	Revue des études grecques.
Rev. H.	Revue historique.
Rev. N.	Revue numismatique.
Rev. Phil.	Revue de philologie, de littérature et d'histoire anciennes.
Rh. Mus.	Rheinisches Museum für Philologie.
Riv. Fil.	Rivista di Filologia.
Riv. Stor. ant.	Rivista di Storia antica.
Röm. Mitt.	Mitteilungen des deutschen arch. Inst. Römische Abteilung.
S.B.	Sitzungsberichte.
S.E.G.	Supplementum epigraphicum Graecum.
St. Fil.	Studi italiani di filologia classica.
Wien Anz.	Anzeiger d. Akad. d. Wissenschaften in Wien.
Wien S.B.	Sitzungsberichte d. Akad. d. Wissenschaften in Wien.
Wien St.	Wiener Studien.
Z.N.	Zeitschrift für Numismatik.

BIBLIOGRAPHIES

These bibliographies do not aim at completeness. They include modern and standard works and, in particular, books utilized in the writing of the chapters. Many technical monographs, especially in journals, are omitted, but the works that are registered below will put the reader on their track.

The works given in the General Bibliography for Greek History are, as a rule, not repeated in the bibliographies to the separate chapters.

The first page only of articles in learned periodicals is given.

N.B. Books in English and French are, unless otherwise specified, published at London and Paris respectively.

GENERAL BIBLIOGRAPHY FOR GREEK HISTORY

I. General Histories

Beloch, K. J. *Griechische Geschichte*. Ed. 2. Strassburg, 1912–.
Bury, J. B. *History of Greece*. Ed. 2. 1922.
Busolt, G. *Griechische Geschichte*. Ed. 2. Gotha, 1893–1904.
Cavaignac, E. *Histoire de l'Antiquité*. 1913–.
Ciccotti, E. *Griechische Geschichte*. (Hartmann's Weltgeschichte.) Gotha, 1920.
De Sanctis, G. *Atthis. Storia della Repubblica Ateniese*. Ed. 2. Turin, 1912.
Freeman, E. A. *History of Sicily*. Oxford, 1891–4.
Glotz, G. *L'Histoire Générale*. I, Histoire Ancienne. II. 1925–.
Grote, G. *A History of Greece*. New ed. 1888.
—— —— *From Solon to* 403 B.C. Condensed and edited with
     Notes and Appendices by J. M. Mitchell and M. O. B. Caspari, 1907.
Holm, A. *Geschichte Griechenlands*. Berlin, 1886–94. Engl. trans. 1894–8.
—— *Geschichte Siciliens im Altertum*. Leipzig, 1870–4.
Lehmann-Haupt, C. F. *Griechische Geschichte* in Gercke and Norden (below),
     vol. III.
Meyer, Eduard. *Geschichte des Altertums*. Stuttgart, 1893–.
—— *Forschungen zur alten Geschichte*. Halle, 1892–9.
Pöhlmann, R. v. *Griechische Geschichte und Quellenkunde*. Ed. 5. Munich, 1914.
     (In Iwan Müller's *Handbuch*, III, 4.)
Rostovtzeff, M. *A History of the Ancient World*. Trans. J. D. Duff. Vol. I. *The
     Orient and Greece*. Oxford, 1926.

II. Works on Constitutional History, etc.

Busolt, G. *Griechische Staatskunde*. (In Iwan Müller's *Handbuch*, IV, I. I.)
     Munich, 1920–6. (Very fully documentated.)
Gilbert, G. *Handbuch der Griechischen Staatsaltertümer*. Leipzig, 1881–5. Eng
     trans. of vol. I, 1895.
Greenidge, A. H. J. *A Handbook of Greek Constitutional History*. 1902.
Halliday, W. R. *The Growth of the City State*. Liverpool, 1923.
Keil, B. *Griechische Staatsaltertümer* in Gercke and Norden (below), vol. III.
Swoboda, H. *Griechische Staatsaltertümer* (Hermann's *Lehrbuch*, I, iii). Tübingen,
     1913.
Wilamowitz-Moellendorff, U. von. *Aristoteles und Athen*. 2 vols. Berlin, 1893.
—— *Staat und Gesellschaft der Griechen* (Kultur der Gegenwart, II, iv, I). Ed. 2
     Leipzig and Berlin, 1923.
Zimmern, A. E. *The Greek Commonwealth*. Ed. 4. Oxford, 1924.

III. Works of Reference, Dictionaries, etc.

Clinton, H. Fynes. *Fasti Hellenici.* 3 vols. Oxford, 1834. (F.H.)

Daremberg et Saglio. *Dictionnaire des antiquités grecques et romaines.* 1877–1919. (D.S.)

Encyclopaedia Britannica. Ed. xi. Articles on Greek History. (E. Brit.)

Gercke, A. and Norden, E. *Einleitung in die Altertumswissenschaft.* Ed. 2. Leipzig and Berlin, 1914. Ed. 3, part appeared.

Hermann, K. F. *Lehrbuch der griechischen Antiquitäten.* New ed. Tübingen, various dates. (Lehrbuch.)

Iwan Müller. *Handbuch der klassischen Altertumswissenschaft.* Munich, various dates. (Handbuch.)

Lübkers Reallexikon des klassischen Altertums. Ed. 8. Edited by J. Geffcken and E. Ziebarth. Berlin, 1914.

Pauly-Wissowa-Kroll. *Real-Encyclopädie der classischen Altertumswissenschaft.* Stuttgart, 1893– (in progress). (P.W.)

Roscher, W. *Ausführliches Lexikon der griechischen und römischen Mythologie.* Leipzig, 1884– (in progress). (Roscher.)

Whibley, L. *A Companion to Greek Studies.* Ed. 3. Cambridge, 1916.

CHAPTER I

THE ECONOMIC BACKGROUND OF THE FIFTH CENTURY

I. Original Sources

A. *Inscriptions*

All Attic inscriptions dating from before 403 B.C. are collected in *I.G.*² 1, Berlin, 1924. Later discoveries and discussions are summarized periodically in the *Supplementum Epigraphicum Graecum*, Leyden, 1923 *sqq.* Among the texts in *I.G.*² 1 the following are of special importance for the questions treated in this chapter:

Decrees relative to Phaselis (16), Brea (45), Methone (57) and Aphytis (58), to the administration of public funds (91 *sq.*), to the levy and assessment of tribute (63–6), to the payment of firstfruits to the Eleusinian sanctuary (76), to the execution of public works (24 *sq.*, 44, 54, 81, 88 *sq.*, 111) and to the lease of a sacred precinct (94). See also 140, 186, 189.

Tribute quota-lists, 191–231.

Inventories of offerings in the Parthenon, 232–92 b.

Loans from Athena Polias and Nike to the state, 293–309 a.

Inventory of the treasures of 'the other gods,' 310.

Accounts and inventories of the Eleusinian sanctuary, 311–22.

Accounts of the Public Auditors (*logistae*), 324–324 a.

Sales of confiscated property, 325–34.

Accounts of public works, 335–74, especially those of

    (*a*) the Parthenon, 339–53;

    (*b*) the chryselephantine statue of Athena, 354–62;

    (*c*) the Propylaea, 363–7;

    (*d*) the Erechtheum, 372 *sqq.*

Miscellanea, 375–90 b.

Some of the above inscriptions appear in Dittenberger's *Sylloge Inscriptionum Graecarum*, 3rd edition, Leipzig, 1915–24 (*S.I.G.*³), Michel's *Recueil d'Inscriptions Grecques*, 1900, Hicks and Hill's *Manual of Greek Historical Inscriptions*, Oxford, 1901. Of inscriptions found outside Attica the following are important:

Rescript of Darius: Hicks and Hill, 20; *S.I.G.*³ 22.

Tean Commination: Hicks and Hill, 23; *S.I.G.*³ 37 *sq.*

Sales of confiscated property at Halicarnassus and Chios: *S.I.G.*³ 46; Michel, 1383.

Relations between Cnossus and Tylissus: *S.I.G.*³ 56.

Code of Gortyn: Michel, 1333; Kohler, J. and Ziebarth, E., *Das Stadtrecht von Gortyn*, Göttingen, 1912.

Commercial Treaty between Oeanthea and Chaleum: Hicks and Hill, 44.

Contributions to Sparta for the Peloponnesian War: *S.I.G.*³ 84; *I.G.* v, 1, 1.

Athenian decree imposing the use of Attic weights and currency: *S.I.G.*³ 87.

Leases of land in Ceos and Elis: *S.I.G.*³ 964; Michel, 1358.

Manumissions: *S.I.G.*³ 1204; *I.G.* v, 1, 1228, 1231.

Deposit note: *S.I.G.*³ 1213; *I.G.* v, 2, 159.

Deed of gift: *S.I.G.*³ 1214.

B. *Literary Texts*

Herodotus, III, 89–117; IV, 81, 198 *sq.*; VI, 21, 42, 46 *sq.*; VII, 118 *sqq.*, 144, 158. [Xenophon], *Athenian Constitution.*

Thucydides, *passim*, especially I, 14, 36, 80 *sqq.*, 93, 96, 99, 121 *sq.*, 141 *sqq.*; II, 13 *sqq.*, 24, 46, 70, 97; III, 17, 19; IV, 53, 102; V, 47; VI, 8, 15 *sq.*, 22 *sqq.*, 31, 43 *sq.*, 46; VII, 13 *sq.*, 27 *sqq.*, 48; VIII, 4, 15, 29, 40, 45, 96.

Aristophanes, *Acharnians*, 159 *sqq.*; *Knights*, 255; *Clouds*, 859 and Schol.; *Wasps*, 707 *sqq.*; *Birds*, 1106 *sqq.*, 1541 and Schol.; *Frogs*, 139 *sq.*, 730 *sqq.* and Schol.; and elsewhere.

Hermippus, frag. 63 (Kock, *Comicorum Atticorum Fragmenta*), quoted by Athenaeus, I, 27 E, F.

Critias, frag. 8 (*F.H.G.* II, 70).

Hellenica Oxyrhynchia, XII, 4.

Xenophon, *Anabasis*, VII, i, 27; *Hellenica*, I, i, 35, V, 3–7, VI, 12; *Memorabilia*; *Oeconomicus*; *Vectigalia*.

Aristotle, *Politics*; *Athenian Constitution*, XXII, 7.

Philochorus, frag. 90 (*F.H.G.* I, 398).

Diodorus, XI–XIII.

Cornelius Nepos, *Aristides*, 3.

Plutarch, *Aristides*, 24 *sq.*; *Pericles*, 11 *sqq.*, 17; and elsewhere.

Aelian, *Varia Historia*, II, 43; VI, 10; XI, 9; XIII, 24.

Scattered references in the orators (*e.g.* Lysias, Andocides, Isocrates, Isaeus, Demosthenes) and the lexicographers (*e.g.* Pollux, Harpocration, Photius, Hesychius, Suidas).

The original sources for the years 478–31 B.C. are collected in Hill, G. F., *Sources for Greek History between the Persian and Peloponnesian Wars*, 2nd issue, Oxford, 1907.

II. Modern Writers

Works marked † should be added to the bibliography of chapters II–IV.

A. *General*

Andreades, A. M. Ἡ δημοσία οἰκονομία τῶν Σπαρτιατῶν in Ἐπετηρὶς τοῦ Φιλολογικοῦ Συλλόγου Παρνασσοῦ. Athens, 1915
—— Ἱστορία τῆς Ἑλληνικῆς δημοσίας οἰκονομίας. Athens, 1918.

Böckh, A. *Die Staatshaushaltung der Athener*. Ed. 3. Edited and annotated by M. Fränkel. 2 vols. Berlin, 1886.

Bolkestein, H. *Het Economisch Leven in Griekenlands Bloeitijd*. Haarlem, 1923.

Bücher, K. *Die Entstehung der Volkswirtschaft*. Ed. 3. Tübingen, 1901.

De Sanctis, G. Ἀτθίς. *Storia della repubblica ateniese*. Ed. 2. Turin, 1912. pp. 486 *sqq.*

Glotz, G. *Le travail dans la Grèce ancienne*. 1920. Translated as *Ancient Greece at Work*, 1926.

†Grundy, G. B. *Thucydides and the History of his Age*. Parts III, IV. 1911.
—— *A History of the Greek and Roman World*. 1926. pp. 170 *sqq.*

Guiraud, P. *Études économiques sur l'antiquité*. Ed. 2. 1905.

†Kahrstedt, U. *Griechisches Staatsrecht*. I. Sparta und seine Symmachie. Göttingen, 1922.

Meyer, E. *Die wirtschaftliche Entwicklung des Altertums* in Kleine Schriften, pp. 79 *sqq.* Halle, 1910.

Neurath, O. *Antike Wirtschaftsgeschichte*. Ed. 2. Leipzig, 1918.

Niese, B. *Neue Beiträge zur Geschichte und Landeskunde Lakedämons*. Gött. Nach. 1906, p. 101.

Nilsson, M. P. *Die Grundlagen des spartanischen Lebens*. Klio, XII, 1912, p. 308.

Schömann, G. F. and Lipsius, J. H. *Griechische Alterthümer*. Ed. 4. 1897–1902.

Wilamowitz-Moellendorff, U. von. *Staat und Gesellschaft der Griechen und Römer*. Leipzig, 1923.

†Zimmern, A. E. *The Greek Commonwealth*. Ed. 4. Oxford, 1924.

B. *Economic Thought*

Laistner, M. L. W. *Greek Economics*. 1923.

Pöhlmann, R. *Geschichte des antiken Kommunismus und Sozialismus*. 2 vols. Munich, 1893–1901.

—— *Die Anfänge des Sozialismus in Europa*. H.Z. LXXIX, 1897, p. 385; LXXX, 1898, p. 193.

—— *Die soziale Dichtung der Griechen*. N.J. Kl. Alt. I, 1898, p. 23.

—— *Geschichte der sozialen Frage und des Sozialismus in der antiken Welt*. Ed. 3 (by F. Oertel). Munich, 1925.

Roscher, W. H. *De doctrinae oeconomico-politicae apud Graecos primordiis*. Leipzig, 1876.

Souchon, A. *Les théories économiques dans la Grèce antique*. 1898.

Stern, E. von. *Sozialwissenschaftliche Bewegungen und Theorien in der Antike*. Halle, 1921.

Trever, A. A. *A History of Greek Economic Thought*. Chicago, 1916.

C. *Serfs, Slaves, Freedmen and Aliens*

Caillemer, E. and Foucart, P. Art. Ἀπελεύθεροι in D.S.

Calderini, A. *La manomissione e la condizione dei liberti in Grecia*. Milan, 1908.

Ciccotti, E. *Del numero degli schiavi nell' Attica*. Rendiconti dell' istituto lombardo, ser. II, vol. XXX, 1897.

—— *Il tramonto della schiavitù nel mondo antico*. Turin, 1899.

Clerc, M. *Les métèques athéniens*. 1893.

—— *De la condition des étrangers domiciliés dans les différentes cités grecques*. Revue des Universités du Midi, IV, 1898.

—— Art. *Metoikoi* in D.S.

Cloché, P. *Le décret de 401–0 en l'honneur des métèques revenus de Phylè*. Rev. E.G. XXX, 1917, p. 392.

Drachmann, A. B. *De manumissione servorum apud Graecos*. Nordisk Tidskrift for Filologi, VIII, 1887, p. 1.

Ehrenberg, V. *Spartiaten und Lakedaimonier*. Hermes, LIX, 1924, p. 23.

Foucart, G. *De libertorum conditione apud Athenienses*. 1896.

Francotte, H. *De la condition des étrangers dans les cités grecques* in Mélanges de droit public grec, p. 202. Liège, 1910.

Jacob, O. *Les esclaves publics à Athènes*. Mus. B. XXX, 1926, p. 57.

Lundberg, C. *Slafveriet i forntiden*. Stockholm, 1915.

Meyer, E. *Die Sklaverei im Altertum* in Kleine Schriften, p. 169 *sqq*. Halle, 1910.

Niese, B. *Elis und seine Periöken* in Genethliakon für C. Robert, p. 3. Berlin, 1910.

Richter, W. *Die Sklaverei im griechischen Altertume*. Breslau, 1886.

Sargent, R. L. *The Size of the Slave-Population at Athens during the Vth and IVth Centuries B.C.* University of Illinois Studies in the Social Sciences, XII, 3. Urbana, 1924.

Schenkl, H. *De metoecis Atticis*. Wien St. II, 1880, p. 161.

Silverio, O. *Untersuchungen zur Geschichte der attischen Staatssklaven*. Diss. Munich, 1900.

Strack, M. L. *Die Freigelassenen in ihrer Bedeutung für die Gesellschaft der Alten*. H.Z. CXII, 1913, p. 1.

Thalheim, T. Arts. Δοῦλοι and *Freigelassene* in P.W.

Thumser, V. *Untersuchungen über die attischen Metöken*. Wien St. VII, 1885, p. 45.

Wallon, H. *Histoire de l'esclavage dans l'antiquité.* Ed. 2. 1879.

Waszyński, S. *De servis atheniensium publicis.* Diss. Berlin, 1898.

Zimmern, A. E. *Was Greek Civilization based on Slave Labour?* Sociological Review, 1909, p. 1, p. 157.

D. *Population*

Beloch, K. J. *Die Bevölkerung der griechisch-römischen Welt.* Leipzig, 1886.

—— *Griechische Aufgebote.* Klio, v, 1905, p. 341; vi, 1906, p. 34.

Bolkestein, H. *The Exposure of Children at Athens.* C.P. xvii, 1922, p. 222.

Cavaignac, E. *Population et Capital dans le monde méditerranéen antique.* Strassburg, 1923.

—— *La population du Péloponnèse aux Ve et VIe siècles.* Klio, xii, 1912, p. 261.

Fawcus, G. E. *The Athenian Army in 431 B.C.* J.H.S. xxix, 1909, p. 23.

Ferrabino, A. *Armate greche nel V secolo a. C.* Riv. Fil. liii, 1925, p. 340, p. 494.

Glotz, G. *L'exposition des enfants* in Études sociales et juridiques sur l'antiquité grecque, p. 187. 1906.

—— Art. *Expositio* in D.S.

†Grundy, G. B. *The Population and Policy of Sparta in the Fifth Century.* J.H.S. xxviii, 1908, p. 77.

Hansen, J. H. *Die Bevölkerungsdichtigkeit Attikas und ihre politische Bedeutung.* Hamburg, 1885.

Meyer, E. *Bevölkerung des Altertums* in Conrads Handbuch der Staatswissenschaft, ii, 674 *sqq.*

—— *Wehrkraft, Bevölkerungszahl und Bodencultur Attikas* in Forschungen zur alten Geschichte, ii, 149. Halle, 1899.

Østbye, P. *Die Zahl der Bürger von Athen im 5. Jahrhundert.* Christiania, 1894.

Pöhlmann, R. *Die Übervölkerung der antiken Grossstädte.* Leipzig, 1884.

Van Hook, La Rue. *The Exposure of Infants at Athens.* Trans. Amer. Philol. Assoc. 1920, p. 134.

Wilamowitz-Moellendorff, U. von. *Aristoteles und Athen,* ii, 201 *sqq.* Berlin, 1893.

E. *Agriculture, Industry and Commerce*

Ardaillon, E. *Les mines du Laurion dans l'antiquité.* 1897.

—— Art. *Metalla* in D.S.

Bazin, H. *De la condition des artistes dans l'antiquité.* Nice, 1866.

Beloch, K. J. *Die Handelsbewegung im Altertum.* Jahrbücher für National-ökonomie und Statistik, xviii, 1899, p. 626.

Bloch, J. S. *Der Arbeiterstand bei den Palästinensern, Griechen und Römern.* Vienna, 1882.

Blümner, H. *Die gewerbliche Thätigkeit der Völker des klassischen Alterthums.* Leipzig, 1869.

—— *Technologie und Terminologie der Gewerbe und Künste bei Griechen und Römern.* 4 vols. Leipzig, 1874–87 (Ed. 2 of vol. i. Leipzig, 1912).

Bonner, R. J. *The Commercial Policy of Imperial Athens.* C.P. xviii, 1923, p. 193.

Brants, V. *Les sociétés commerciales à Athènes.* Revue de l'Instruction publique en Belgique, xxv, 1882, p. 109.

—— *De la condition du travailleur libre dans l'industrie athénienne.* Revue de l'Instruction publique en Belgique, xxvi, 1883, p. 100.

Büchsenschütz, B. *Die Hauptstätten des Gewerbfleisses im klassischen Alterthume.* Leipzig, 1869.

—— *Besitz und Erwerb im griechischen Alterthume.* Halle, 1869.

Cary, M. *The Greeks and Ancient Trade with the Atlantic.* J.H.S. xliv, 1924, p. 166.

Cauer, F. *Die Stellung der arbeitenden Klassen in Hellas und Rom.* N.J. Kl. Alt. iii, 1899, p. 686.

Drumann, W. *Arbeiter und Communisten in Griechenland und Rom.* Königsberg, 1860.

Duncker, M. *Die Hufen der Spartiaten.* Berl. S.B. 1881, p. 138.

Francotte, H. *L'industrie dans la Grèce ancienne.* 2 vols. Brussels, 1900–1.

—— Art. *Industrie und Handel* in P.W.

Frohberger, H. *De opificum apud veteres Graecos condicione.* Grimm, 1866.

Fustel de Coulanges, N. D. *Étude sur la propriété à Sparte.* C.R. Ac. Sciences morales et politiques, 1880.

—— *Nouvelles recherches sur quelques problèmes d'histoire.* I. La propriété chez les Grecs. 1891.

†Gernet, L. *L'approvisionnement d'Athènes en blé au Ve et au IVe siècle.* (Bibliothèque de la Faculté des Lettres de l'Université de Paris, xxv, p. 269.) 1909.

Gigli, G. *Delle mercedi nell' antica Grecia.* Memorie dell' Accademia dei Lincei, ser. v, vol. iv, 1896, p. 4.

Guiraud, P. *La propriété foncière en Grèce jusqu'à la conquête romaine.* 1893.

—— *La main-d'œuvre industrielle dans l'ancienne Grèce.* 1900.

Hackl, R. *Merkantile Inschriften auf attischen Vasen* in Münchener archäologische Studien dem Andenken A. Furtwänglers gewidmet, p. 1. Munich, 1909.

Heitland, W. E. *Agricola.* Cambridge, 1921.

Herfst, P. *Le travail de la femme dans la Grèce ancienne.* Utrecht, 1922.

Huvelin, P. Arts. *Mercator* and *Mercatura* in D.S.

†Jardé, A. *Les céréales dans l'antiquité grecque.* 1925.

Jevons, F. B. *Work and Wages in Athens.* J.H.S. xv, 1895, p. 239.

Kahrstedt, U. *Die spartanische Agrarwirtschaft.* Hermes, liv, 1919, p. 279.

Köster, A. *Das antike Seewesen.* Berlin, 1923.

Kornemann, E. Art. *Bauernstand* in P.W. Suppl. iv, 83 *sqq.*

Kroll, W. Arts. *Schiffahrt* and *Seeraub* in P.W.

Leaf, W. *On a History of Greek Commerce.* J.H.S. xxxv, 1915, p. 161.

—— *The Commerce of Sinope.* J.H.S. xxxvi, 1916, p. 1.

Lécrivain, C. Art. *Piratae* in D.S.

Lehmann-Hartleben, K. Art. Λιμήν in P.W.

Mauri, A. *I cittadini lavoratori dell' Attica nei secoli V^o e IV° a. C.* Milan, 1895.

—— *Il salariato libero e la concorrenza servile in Atene.* Studi e documenti di storia e diritto, xvi, 97. Rome, 1895.

Neurath, O. *Zur Anschauung der Antike über Handel, Gewerbe und Landwirtschaft.* Jahrbücher für Nationalökonomie und Statistik, xxxii, 1906, p. 577; xxxiv, 1907, p. 145.

Ormerod, H. A. *Ancient Piracy in the Eastern Mediterranean.* Liv. A.A. viii, 1921, p. 105.

†—— *Piracy in the Ancient World.* Liverpool, 1924.

Orth, A. Art. *Landwirtschaft* in P.W.

—— Art. *Bergbau* in P.W. Suppl. iv, 108 *sqq.*

Otto, W. *Kulturgeschichte des Altertums,* pp. 75 *sqq.* Munich, 1925.

†Perdrizet, P. *Scaptésylé.* Klio, x, 1910, p. 1.

Richter, G. M. A. *The Distribution of Attic Vases.* B.S.A. xi, p. 224.

Richter, W. *Handel und Verkehr der wichtigsten Völker des Mittelmeeres im Altertume.* Leipzig, 1886.

Sorlin Dorigny, A. Art. *Rustica Res* in D.S.

Speck, E. *Handelsgeschichte des Altertums.* Vol. ii. Leipzig, 1901.

Stein, P. *Ueber Piraterie im Altertume*. Cöthen, 1891.
——— *Zur Geschichte der Piraterie im Altertume*. Bernburg, 1894.
Struck, A. *Zur Landeskunde von Griechenland*. Frankfurt a. M., 1912.
†Wilamowitz-Moellendorff, U. von. *Von des attischen Reiches Herrlichkeit* in Reden und Vorträge. Ed. 3, pp. 30 *sqq*. Berlin, 1913.

F. *Coinage and Banking*

For a list of the most important public and private collections of Greek coins and of the principal works on Greek numismatics see Bibliography to vol. iv, chapter v.
Billeter, G. *Geschichte des Zinsfusses im griechisch-römischen Altertum*. Leipzig, 1898.
Breccia, E. *Storia delle banche e dei banchieri nell' età classica*. Riv. Stor. ant. vii, 1903, p. 107, p. 283.
Corolla Numismatica. Oxford, 1906.
Dodd, C. H. *The Samians at Zancle-Messana*. J.H.S. xxviii, 1908, p. 56.
†Gardner, P. *Coinage of the Athenian Empire*. J.H.S. xxxiii, 1913, p. 147.
——— *The Financial History of Ancient Chios*. J.H.S. xl, 1920, p. 160.
Hasebroek, J. *Zum griechischen Bankwesen der klassischen Zeit*. Hermes, lv, 1920, p. 113.
Laum, B. *Das Eisengeld der Spartaner*. Braunsberg, 1925.
——— Art. *Banken* in P.W. Suppl. iv, 71 *sqq*.
Lehmann-Haupt, C. F. Art. *Gewichte* in P.W. Suppl. iii, 588 *sqq*.
Reinach, T. *L'histoire par les monnaies*. 1902.
Riezler, K. *Ueber Finanzen und Monopole im alten Griechenland*. Berlin, 1907.
†Weil, R. *Das Münzmonopol Athens im ersten Attischen Seebund*. Z.N. xxv, 1906, p. 52.
†——— *Das Münzrecht der ξύμμαχοι im ersten Attischen Seebund*. Z.N. xxviii, 1910, p. 351.
Woodward, A. M. *Notes and Queries on Athenian Coinage and Finance*. J.H.S. xxxiv, 1914, p. 276.
——— *A Note on the First Issue of Gold Coins at Athens*. Num. Chr. 1911, p. 351.

G. *Domestic Economy*

Barbagallo, C. *I prezzi del bestiame da macello nell' antichità classica*. Riv. Stor. ant. xii, 1908, p. 3, p. 306.
Benndorf, O. *Das griechisches Brot* in Eranos Vindobonensis, p. 372. Vienna, 1893.
Corsetti, R. *Sul prezzo dei grani nell' antichità classica*. Studi di storia antica, ii, 1893, p. 63.
Poland, F. *Das Privatleben* in F. Poland, E. Reisinger and R. Wagner, Die antike Kultur, pp. 175 *sqq*. Leipzig, 1922.
Rankin, E. M. *The Rôle of the μάγειροι in the Life of the Ancient Greeks*. Chicago, 1907.
Rider, B. C. *The Greek House*. Cambridge, 1916.
Segré, A. *Circolazione monetaria e prezzi nel mondo antico*. Rome, 1922.

H. *Public Finance*

Bannier, W. *Zu den attischen Rechnungsurkunden des 5. Jahrhunderts*. Rh. Mus. lxi, 1906, p. 202.
Beloch, K. J. *Zur Finanzgeschichte Athens*. Rh. Mus. xxxix, 1884, p. 34, p. 239; xliii, 1888, p. 104.
——— *Das Volksvermögen von Attika*. Hermes, xx, 1885, p. 237.

Beloch, K. J. *Das attische Timema*. Hermes, xxii, 1887, p. 371.

†—— *Zur Geschichte des athenischen Staatsschatzes* in Beloch, ii², 2, p. 324.

—— *Die Veranlagung der Tribute im athenischen Reiche* in Beloch, ii², 2, p. 356.

Busolt, G. *Der Phoros der athenischen Bündner von 446/5 bis 426/5*. Phil. xli, 1882, p. 652.

†Cavaignac, E. *Études sur l'histoire financière d'Athènes au Ve siècle. Le trésor d'Athènes de 480 à 404*. 1908.

—— *Le trésor sacré d'Éleusis jusqu'en 404*. Versailles, 1908.

Christ, J. C. F. *De publicis populi Atheniensis rationibus saeculo a. Ch. quinto*. Diss. Greifswald, 1879.

Ciccotti, E. *Lineamenti dell' evoluzione tributaria del mondo antico*. Milan, 1921.

†Dahms, R. *De Atheniensium sociorum tributis quaestiones septem*. Diss. Berlin, 1904.

†Fimmen, D. *Die attischen Tributquotenlisten von 439/8 bis 432/1 v. Chr*. Ath. Mitt. xxxviii, 1913, p. 231.

Fränkel, M. *Zur Geschichte der attischen Finanzverwaltung* in Historische und philologische Aufsätze E. Curtius gewidmet. Berlin, 1884.

Francotte, H. *Les Finances des Cités Grecques*. 1909.

†—— *Le tribut des alliés d'Athènes*. Mus. B. xi, 1907, p. 173.

Keil, B. *Anonymus Argentinensis*. Strassburg, 1902.

†Kirchhoff, A. *Zur Geschichte des Athenischen Staatsschatzes im fünften Jahrhundert*. Berl. Abh. 1876, ii Abt. p. 21.

Laum, B. *Entstehung der öffentlichen Finanzwirtschaft*. Handbuch der Finanzwissenschaft, Tübingen, 1926, pp. 185 *sqq*.

Levi, M. A. *Note sul tesoro ateniese nel V secolo a. C.* Atti della R. Accademia di Torino, lvi, 113.

Meyer, E. *Griechische Finanzen* in Conrads Handwörterbuch der Staatswissenschaft, Suppl. ii, 65. 1897.

†—— *Zur Geschichte der attischen Finanzen im fünften Jahrhundert* in Forschungen zur alten Geschichte, ii, 88. Halle, 1899.

†Pedroli, U. *I tributi degli alleati d'Atene*. Studi di Storia Antica, i, 99. Rome, 1891.

†Romstedt, M. A. *Die wirtschaftliche Organisation des athenischen Reiches*. Diss. Weida i. T., 1914.

†Stevenson, G. H. *The Financial Administration of Pericles*. J.H.S. xliv, 1924, p. 1.

Swoboda, H. *Über griechische Schatzverwaltung*. Wien St. x, 1888, p. 278; xi, 1889, p. 65.

Thiel, J. H. *Zu altgriechischen Gebühren*. Klio, xx, 1925, p. 54.

Note. Further references to the literature on the Athenian quota-lists will be found in the bibliographies to chapters ii–iv and vii–viii.

CHAPTERS II–IV

THE CONFEDERACY OF DELOS; ATHENS AND THE GREEK POWERS; THE PERICLEAN DEMOCRACY

I. Original Sources for chapters II–III

A. *Inscriptions*

Decrees. *I.G.*[2] i, 5–42, 45.
Tribute quota-lists. *I.G.*[2] i, 191–9.
Accounts of public works. *I.G.*[2] i, 335–40.
Miscellanea. *I.G.*[2] i, 375.
Funeral monuments. *I.G.*[2] i, 928–40, 1085.

Add to these the following inscriptions found outside Attica.

Dittenberger, *S.I.G.*[3] nos. 31, 37–40, 47, 58–61, 67.

A selection of the above will be found in Hicks and Hill's *Manual of Greek Historical Inscriptions*, Oxford, 1901, nos. 19–41.

On the quota-lists see also the bibliography to chaps. VII–VIII.

B. *Literary Texts*

Aelian, *Varia Historia*, v, 10.
Aeschines, *de fals. leg.* 75; *in Ctes.* 183–5. Schol.: *de fals. leg.* 34, 78.
Andocides, *de pace*, 3, 4, 9.
Antiphon, *de caede Herodis*, 47.
Aristophanes, *Acharn.* 502; *Wasps*, 707. Schol.: *Birds*, 556; *Clouds*, 211, 859; *Knights*, 83, 84, 814; *Lysist.* 1137; *Plut.* 627.
Aristotle, *Const. of Athens*, XXIII–VIII; *Politics*, VIII (v), 3, p. 1303 a; VIII (v), 3, p. 1302 b; VIII (v), 7, p. 1307 a; VIII (v), 7, p. 1307 b, 20.
Athenaeus, I, 29 F; XII, 533 D.
Cicero, *de amicit.* XII, 42; *de off.* III, 11, 49; *de orator.* III, 34, 138.
Ctesias, *Persica*, 29, 32–7.
Demosthenes, *in Aristocrat.* 166; *de fals. leg.* 273; *Olynth.* III, 24; *Phil.* III, 23.
Diodorus, XI, 37–XII, 68.
Eupolis, frag. 94 (Kock).
Herodotus, III, 12, 15, 160; V, 17, 32; VI, 42, 46, 72, 83, 126–31; VII, 7, 33, 106–108, 139, 151; VIII, 3, 111 *sq.*, 121; IX, 35, 75, 105 *sq.*, 114–21.
Isocrates, *Archid.* 99; *Areop.* 80; *de pace*, 86; *Panath.* 54–9, 68; *Panegyr.* 104–106, 115–20.
Justin, *Hist.* II, 15; III, 1, 6; IX, 1.
Lycurgus, *in Leocrat.* 72 *sq.*
Lysias, *Epitaphios*, 48, 55.
Nepos, *Lives of Aristides, Cimon, Pausanias, Themistocles.*
Pausanias, I, 27, 29; III, 3, 7; 7, 11; IV, 24 *sq.*; V, 23.
Plato, *Menex.* 242 (A, B).
Plutarch, *Lives of Aristides, Cimon, Pericles, Themistocles*; *de malign. Herod.* 21; *Praec. Ger. Reip.* 5.
Polyaenus, I, 34, 41; VII, 24.
Simonides, *Epigr.* 102.
Strabo, VII, pp. 337, 362.
Suidas, *Life of Cimon.*
Theopompus, frags. 88 (Grenfell and Hunt = Müller, 92), 89 (G. and H. = M. 94), 149 a (G. and H. = M. 168), 347 (G. and H. = M. 164).

Thucydides, I, 18 *sq.*, 67, 89–end; II, 8 *sq.*, 13, 69, 75, 99; III, 10 *sq.*, 19, 34, 54, 62, 67; IV, 50, 56, 75, 102; V, 1, 14, 16, 18, 28, 89, 91, 97, 105; VI, 13, 76, 82, 85, 87; VII, 57; VIII, 5, 21, 56, 64, 65.
Tyrtaeus, *Eunomia*.
Xenophon, *Hellenica*, I, 1, 8 and 12; III, 4, 7 and 25; V, 2, 3 and 7.
[Xenophon], *Athenian Constitution*.

II. ORIGINAL SOURCES FOR CHAPTER IV

Aeschines, *in Ctes.* 252.
Andocides, *de mysteriis*, sect. 84.
Aristophanes, *Acharn.* 17–42; *Ecclesiazusae*, 102–4, 183–8, 300–10, 380, 392; *Frogs*, 677; *Knights*, 128–40, 798 *sq.*, 1303 *sq.*; *Plutus*, 171, 329–31; *Wasps*, 715. Schol.: *Wasps*, 88, 300, 684; *Eccles.* 102 *sqq.*, 171.
Aristotle, *Const. of Athens*, III, 6; IV, 4; VII, 4; IX, 1; XXII; XXIII–VIII; XXIX, 3 *sq.*; XXXIV; XXXV, 2; XLI, 3; LXII, 3; *Politics*, II, 12, p. 1274 a; VIII (v), 4, p. 1304 a.
Demosthenes, *in Timocrat.* (XXIV), 154.
Diodorus, XI, 77.
Herodotus, V, 97.
Hesychius, βουλῆς λαχεῖν.
Isocrates, *de pace*, esp. sects. 63–6.
Lycurgus, *in Leocrat.* 13, 52.
Lysias, *in Eratos.* (XII), 69.
Philochorus, frags. 90, 141 b.
Plato, *Gorgias*, 515.
Plato Comicus, frags. 133, 166 *sq.*, 170 (Kock).
Plutarch, *Aristides*, 22; *Cimon*, 9, 15 *sqq.*; *Pericles*, 9–12, 37; *Themistocles*, 10.
Polyzelus, frag. 5 (Kock).
Thucydides, II, 15; III, 36; IV, 65; VIII, 1, 67, 69.
[Xenophon], *Athenian Constitution*.

III. MODERN WRITERS: CHAPTERS II–IV

See also General Bibliography

Works recorded in the bibliography to chapter I are not, as a rule, repeated here. Works in that bibliography which are especially important for these chapters are marked †. Works marked † in this bibliography are especially important for chapters VII and VIII. For other works published up to 1897 see the bibliographies and footnotes in Busolt, *Gr. Gesch.* III, part 1.

Abbott, E. *The Early History of the Delian League.* C.R. III, 1889, p. 387.
—— *Pericles and the Golden Age of Athens.* 1898.
Agricola, E. F. M. *De Aristidis censu.* Diss. Berlin, 1900.
Babelon, E. *La politique monétaire d'Athènes au Ve siècle avant notre ère.* Rev. N. XVII, 1913, p. 457.
†Bannier, W. *Die Tributeinnahmeordnung des attischen Staates.* Rh. Mus. LIV, 1899, p. 544.
Bauer, A. *Forschungen zu Aristoteles* Ἀθηναίων Πολιτεία. Munich, 1891.
Beloch, G. (= Beloch, K. J.). *Sulla costituzione politica dell' Elide.* Riv. Fil. IV, 1876, p. 225.
—— *La battaglia di Tanagra e la pace dei cinque anni.* Riv. Fil. V, 1877, p. 453.

Beloch, K. J. *Zur Finanzgeschichte Athens*. VII. Ὁ ἐπ᾽ Ἀριστείδου φόρος. Rh. Mus. XLIII, 1888, p. 104.

—— *Hipparchos und Themistokles*. Hermes, LV, 1920, p. 311.

Bodin, L. *Phanias d'Érèse*. I. L'arrivée de Thémistocle à la cour de Perse. Rev. E.G. XXVIII, 1915, p. 251.

Botsford, G. W. *Development of the Athenian Constitution*. Cornell Studies in Classical Philology, No. 4. Boston, 1893.

Busolt, G. *Das Ende der Perserkriege*. H.Z. XII, 1882, p. 385.

—— *Ueber die Verlegung des Bundesschatzes von Delos nach Athen*. Rh. Mus. XXXVII, 1882, p. 312.

—— *Zur Dienstpflicht der athenischen Bündner*. Rh. Mus. XXXVII, 1882, p. 637.

—— *Zum perikleischen Plane einer hellenischen Nationalversammlung*. Rh. Mus. XXXVIII, 1883, p. 150.

—— *Thukydides und der themistokleische Mauerbau*. Klio, V, 1905, p. 255.

†Carcopino, J. *Damon a-t-il été ostracisé?* Rev. E.G. XVIII, 1905, p. 415.

Cary, M. (= Caspari, M. O. B.). *When was Themistocles ostracised?* C.R. XXXVI, 1922, p. 161.

—— *Athens and Hestiaea: Notes on two Attic Inscriptions*. J.H.S. XLV, 1925, p. 243.

Caspari, M. O. B. *On the Egyptian Expedition of 459–4 B.C.* C.Q. VII, 1913, p. 198.

—— *On the Long Walls of Athens*. J.H.S. XXXIV, 1914, p. 242.

Cavaignac, E. *Eschyle et Thémistocle*. Rev. Phil. XLV, 1921, p. 102.

Cloché, P. *Importance des pouvoirs de la Boulè athénienne au Ve et IVe siècles avant J.-C.* Rev. E.G. XXXIV, 1921, p. 233.

Costanzi, V. *Il movimento antilaconico nel Peloponneso dopo le guerre persiane*. Riv. Stor. ant. VII, 1903, p. 659.

—— *L' anno attico della battaglia presso l' Eurimedonte*. Riv. Fil. XXXI, 1903, p. 249.

—— *La durata della terza guerra messenica*. Riv. Fil. L, 1922, p. 289.

Curtius, E. *Der Synoikismos von Elis*. Berl. S.B. 1895, p. 793.

De Sanctis, G. *La battaglia dell' Eurimedonte in Diodoro*. Riv. Fil. XXI, 1892, p. 97.

—— *Da Clistene a Temistocle*. Riv. Fil. LII, 1924, p. 289.

Dickins, G. *The Growth of Spartan Policy*. J.H.S. XXXII, 1912, p. 1.

Domaszewski, A. v. *Die attische Politik in der Zeit der Pentekontaetie*. Heidelberg S.B. Phil.-Hist. Kl. 1924–5, 4.

Duncker, M. *Der angebliche Verrath des Themistokles*. Berl. S.B. 1882, p. 377.

—— *Der Process des Pausanias*. Berl. S.B. 1883, p. 1125.

Fabricius, E. *Das Wahlgesetz des Aristeides*. Rh. Mus. LI, 1896, p. 456.

Ferguson, W. S. *Greek Imperialism*. 1913.

Filleul, E. *Histoire du siècle de Périclès*. 1873.

Fontana, G. *Aristide nella Costituzione degli Ateniesi di Aristotele*. Verona, 1892.

Fränkel, M. *Attische Geschworenengerichte*. Berlin, 1877.

Frank, K. *Bemerkungen zur Chronologie der Pentekontaëtie*. Schönberg, 1894.

Gercke, A. *Themistokles' List*. N.J. Kl. Alt. XXXI, 1913, p. 617.

Grant, A. J. *Greece in the Age of Pericles*. 1893.

Hiller von Gaertringen, F. *Athenisches Gesetz über Hestiaia um 445 v. Chr*. Gött. Nach. 1921, p. 62.

Hohl, E. *Perikles* in E. Marcks und A. K. Müller, Meister der Politik, I, p. 1. Stuttgart-Berlin, 1922.

Holzapfel, L. *Untersuchungen über die Darstellung der griechischen Geschichte von 489 bis 413 vor Chr. bei Ephoros, Theopomp, u. a. Autoren*. Leipzig, 1879.

—— *Athen und Persien von 465 bis 412 v. Chr*. Berliner Studien für classische Philologie, VII, 19. Berlin, 1888.

Jevons, F. B. *The Development of the Athenian Democracy*. 1886.

Judeich, W. *Griechische Politik und persische Politik im V. Jahrhundert v. Chr.* Hermes, LVIII, 1923, p. 1.

Kaegi, A. *Kritische Geschichte des spartanischen Staates von 500 bis 431 v. Chr.* Jahrbücher für classische Philologie, Supplementband VI, 1873, p. 435.

Kahrstedt, U. *Sparta und Persien in der Pentekontaetie.* Hermes, LVI, 1921, p. 320.

Keil, B. *Anonymus Argentinensis.* Strassburg, 1902. (This work must be used with caution: see the articles of Laqueur and Wilcken mentioned below.)

De Keulen, B. *De Pericle pacificatore.* Mnemosyne, XLVIII, 1920, p. 239.

Kirchhoff, A. *Ueber die Tributpflichtigkeit der attischen Kleruchen.* Abh. d. Akademie zu Berlin, Phil.-Hist. Klasse, 1873, p. 1.

—— *Der Delische Bund im ersten Decennium seines Bestehens.* Hermes, XI, 1876, p. 1.

Kjellberg, L. *Zur Themistoklesfrage.* Strena Philologica Upsaliensis, p. 229. Upsala, 1922.

Klussmann, M. *Die Kämpfe am Eurymedon.* Festschrift für L. Herbst, p. 16. Hamburg, 1891.

Köhler, U. *Urkunden und Untersuchungen zur Geschichte des delisch-attischen Bundes.* Berlin, 1870.

—— *Beiträge zur Geschichte der Pentekontaetie.* Hermes, XXIV, 1889, p. 85.

Koepp, F. *Ein Problem der griechischen Geschichte.* Rh. Mus. XLVIII, 1893, p. 485.

—— *Das Gemälde der Schlacht bei Oinoë in der Stoa Poikile zu Athen.* Rh. Mus. LXIX, 1914, p. 160.

Kunst, K. *Die Richtlinien der Politik Athens im fünften Jahrhundert v. Chr.* Zeitschrift für die deutschösterreichischen Gymnasien, LXIX, 1919, p. 232.

Lanzani, C. *Ricerche intorno a Pausania reggente di Sparta.* Riv. Stor. ant. VII, 1903, p. 229.

Laqueur, R. *Die litterarische Stellung des Anonymus Argentinensis.* Hermes, XLIII, 1908, p. 220.

Lehmann (=Lehmann-Haupt), C. F. *Pausanias', des Spartaners, Todesjahr.* Klio, II, 1902, p. 345.

—— *Pausanias, Heros Ktistes von Byzanz.* Mit einer Beigabe: Der Sturz des Pausanias, des Themistokles und des Leotychidas. Klio, XVII, 1921, p. 59.

Lloyd, W. W. *The Age of Pericles.* 1875.

Mahaffy, J. P. *On the Date of the Capture of Mycenae by the Argives.* Hermathena, III, 1879, p. 60, p. 277.

Meyer, E. *Die Biographie Kimons.* Forschungen zur alten Geschichte, II, 1–87. Halle, 1899.

—— *Der Mauerbau des Themistokles.* Hermes, XL, 1905, p. 561.

Morris, C. D. *The Jurisdiction of the Athenians over their Allies.* A.J. Ph. V, 1884, p. 298.

—— *Chronology of the πεντηκονταετία.* A.J. Ph. VII, 1886, p. 325.

Mosler, I. *Chronologie der Pentekontaëtie.* Diss. Berlin, 1890.

Motte, A. *La paix de Cimon.* Ghent, 1880.

†Müller-Strübing, H. *Aristophanes und die historische Kritik.* Leipzig, 1873.

Munro, J. A. R. *The Chronology of Themistocles' Career.* C.R. VI, 1892, p. 333.

Nedwed, E. *Perikles, ein Lebensbild des grössten Ministers des athenischen Reiches.* Iglau, 1889.

Niehues, B. *De Pausania, Cleombroti filio, Lacedaemonio.* Münster, 1890.

Noack, F. *Die Mauern Athens.* Ath. Mitt. XXXII, 1907, p. 123, p. 473.

Nöthe, H. *Der delische Bund, seine Einrichtung und Verfassung.* Magdeburg, 1889.

—— *Bundesrat, Bundessteuer und Kriegsdienst der delischen Bündner.* Magdeburg, 1890.

Nordin, R. *Studien in der Themistoklesfrage.* Diss. Upsala, 1893.

Pareti, L. *Ricerche sulla potenza marittima degli Spartani e sulla cronologia dei navarchi*. Memorie della R. Accad. delle Scienze di Torino, Ser. II, Tom. LIX, p. 71.

Perrot, G. *Essai sur le droit public d'Athènes*. 1867.

Pfister, F. *Zur Gesandtschaft des Themistokles nach Sparta*. B.P.W. XXXV, 1915, p. 382.

Philarétos, G. M. *Un congrès à Athènes sous Périclès pour la liberté des mers et la paix*. L'Acropole, I, 1925, p. 104.

Philippi, A. *Der Areopag und die Epheten*. Berlin, 1874.

Probandt, K. *Beiträge zur Geschichte der Pentekontaetie*. Diss. Halle, 1908.

Reuther, H. *Pausanias, Sohn des Kleombrotos*. Diss. Bonn, 1902.

Robert, C. *Archäologische Nachlese*. IV. Die Schlacht bei Oinoa. Hermes, XXV, 1890, p. 412.

Robertson, H. G. *The Administration of Justice in the Athenian Empire*. Toronto, 1924.

Rohde, H. *De Atheniensium imperio quid quinto quartoque a. Chr. n. saeculo sit iudicatum*. Diss. Göttingen, 1913.

Rosenberg, A. *Die Parteistellung des Themistokles*. Hermes, LIII, 1918, p. 308.

Savelli, A. *Temistocle dal primo processo alla sua morte*. Florence, 1893.

Schaefer, A. *De rerum post bellum Persicum usque ad tricennale foedus in Graecia gestarum temporibus*. Leipzig, 1865.

†Schmidt, A. *Perikles und sein Zeitalter* (*Das Perikleische Zeitalter*). Jena, 1877–9.

Schulte-Vaërting, H. *Die Friedenspolitik des Perikles*. Munich, 1919.

Schulthess, O. *Das attische Volksgericht*. Bern, 1921.

Schvarcz, J. *Die Demokratie von Athen*. Leipzig, 1891.

Senfftleben, F. *Sparta und sein Bund von 479 bis 445 v. Chr.* Diss. Jena, 1872.

Smith, G. *Dicasts in the Ephetic Courts*. C.P. XIX, 1924, p. 353.

Solari, A. *Sulle relazioni diplomatiche fra la Grecia e la Persia*. Riv. Stor. ant. VII, 1903, p. 380.

—— *Ricerche Spartane*. Leghorn, 1907.

Stahl, J. M. *De sociorum Atheniensium iudiciis commentatio*. Münster, 1881.

Swoboda, H. *Arthmios von Zeleia*. Archäologisch-Epigraphische Mittheilungen aus Oesterreich-Ungarn, XVI, 1893, p. 49.

—— *Zur Geschichte der attischen Kleruchien*. Serta Harteliana, pp. 28 *sqq.* Vienna, 1896.

—— Art. *Kimon* in P.W.

Taylor, A. E. *On the Date of the Trial of Anaxagoras*. C.Q. XI, 1917, p. 81.

Ure, P. N. *When was Themistocles last in Athens?* J.H.S. XLI, 1921, p. 165.

Van Hook, La Rue. *Was Athens in the Age of Pericles Aristocratic?* C.J., XIV, 1919, p. 472.

Vinogradoff, P. *Outlines of Historical Jurisprudence*. II. The Jurisprudence of the Greek City. Oxford, 1922.

Vürtheim, J. *De heliaeis atheniensibus*. Mnemosyne, XXVIII, 1900, p. 228.

Wagner, M. *Zur Geschichte der attischen Kleruchen*. Diss. Tübingen, 1915.

Walker, E. M. *The Ἀθηναίων Πολιτεία and the Chronology of the Years* 462–445. C.R. VI, 1892, p. 95.

Welzel, P. *Kallias, ein Beitrag zur athenischen Geschichte*. Breslau, 1888.

Wilamowitz-Moellendorff, U. von. *Aristoteles und Athen*. Berlin, 1893.

Wilcken, U. *Der Anonymus Argentinensis*. Hermes, XLII, 1907, p. 374.

Witkowski, S. *De pace quae dicitur Cimonica*. Lemberg, 1900.

CHAPTER V

ATTIC DRAMA IN THE FIFTH CENTURY

I. Texts

The references in this chapter are to the following texts:

Aeschylus: N. Wecklein, Berlin, 1885–93, as revised by W. G. Headlam in the critical notes to his prose translation (see below).

Sophocles: A. C. Pearson, Oxford, 1924.

Euripides: G. Murray, Oxford, 1901–9.

Aristophanes: F. W. Hall and W. M. Geldart, Oxford, ed. 2, 1906–7.

Tragicorum Graecorum Fragmenta, A. Nauck, ed. 2, Leipzig, 1889.

Comicorum Atticorum Fragmenta, T. Kock, Leipzig, 1880.

Additional fragments will be found in:

Fragmenta Tragica Papyracea, A. S. Hunt, Oxford, 1912.

Supplementum Sophocleum, E. Diehl, Bonn, 1913.

Supplementum Euripideum, H. von Arnim, Bonn, 1913.

Supplementum Comicum, J. Demianczuk, Cracow, 1912.

See also H. W. Smyth in *A. J. P.* xli, 1920, pp. 101 *sqq*, and C. H. Oldfather, *Greek Literary Texts from Greco-Roman Egypt*, Wisconsin Studies, Madison, 1923, pp. 20 *sqq*.

II. Translations

The reader is especially referred to the following:

Aeschylus: W. G. Headlam's prose translation, completed and edited by C. E. S. H., London, 1909; this is indispensable. Greek text and English prose version by H. Weir Smyth, London, 1922. Greek Text, French prose version, introductions and brief notes by P. Mazon, Paris, 1920–5. English verse, G. M. Cookson, Oxford, 1922–4.

Sophocles: English prose, R. C. Jebb, Cambridge, 1905. Greek text and English verse by F. Storr, London, 1919. Greek text, French prose version, introductions and brief notes by P. Masqueray, Paris, 1922–4. English verse, R. Whitelaw, London, ed. 2, 1897.

Euripides: English prose, A. P. Coleridge, London, 1891. Greek text and English verse by A. S. Way, London, 1912. Greek text, French prose version, introductions and brief notes by L. Parmentier and H. Grégoire, Paris, 1923.

Aristophanes: Greek text and English verse, B. B. Rogers, London, 1924. Greek text, French prose version, introductions and brief notes by V. Coulon and H. van Daele, Paris, 1923–6. Also the following plays in English verse by J. H. Frere, London, 1871, etc.: *Acharnians, Birds, Frogs, Knights, Peace*.

Much may be learnt from the admirable German versions of U. v. Wilamowitz-Moellendorff, now reprinted, Berlin, 1922–5, in four volumes with an introductory essay, 'Die griechische Tragoedie und ihre drei Dichter,' and from Gilbert Murray's verse translations of the *Agamemnon, Choephoroe* and *Eumenides*; of Sophocles, *Oedipus Rex*; of Euripides, *Bacchae, Electra, Hippolytus, Iphigeneia in Tauris, Medea, Troades*; of the *Rhesus*; and of Aristophanes, *Frogs*.

The following verse translations of separate plays may be mentioned:

Aeschylus: E. R. Bevan, *Prometheus*, London, 1902; *Septem*, London, 1912. R. C. Trevelyan, *The Oresteia*, Liverpool, 1922.

Sophocles: R. C. Trevelyan, *Ajax*, London, 1919; *Antigone*, Liverpool, 1922; J. T Sheppard, *Oedipus Tyrannus*, Cambridge, 1922; *Electra*, Cambridge, 1927.

Euripides: F. L. Lucas, *Medea*, Oxford, 1924; J. T. Sheppard, *Helen*, Cambridge, 1926; *Hecuba*, Oxford, 1926.

III. COMMENTARIES

The most useful general commentaries are the following:

Aeschylus: F. A. Paley, ed. 4, London, 1879. H. Weil, Gissae, 1858–67. U. v. Wilamowitz-Moellendorff, vol. i, Text, vol. ii, Interpretationen, Berlin, 1914.

Sophocles: R. C. Jebb, Cambridge, various dates, 1902–8. F. W. Schneidewin and A. Nauck, many editions, the latest revised by E. Bruhn or L. Radermacher, Berlin. A. C. Pearson's edition of the *Fragments*, 3 vols., Cambridge, 1917 (indispensable).

Euripides: F. A. Paley, 3 vols., ed. 2, London, 1872–80. H. Weil, seven plays, *Medea, Hippolytus, Hecuba, Electra, I. A., Orestes, I. T.*, ed. 3, Paris, 1896–1907; *Alcestis*, Paris, 1891. N. Wecklein, editions with German notes of *Bacchae, Helen, Hippolytus, I. T., ? Medea, Electra, Orestes, Andromache*, Leipzig, various dates. A. C. Pearson, *Helen*, 1903; *Heracleidae*, 1907; *Phoenissae*, 1909, Cambridge.

Aristophanes: J. van Leeuwen, Lugd. Bat., 12 vols., 1893–1906. B. B. Rogers, 6 vols., London, various dates.

The following is a selection of the more important or accessible editions of separate plays:

Aeschylus: *Supplices*, T. G. Tucker, London, 1889; *Persae*, H. Jurenka, Leipzig, 1907; *Prometheus*, H. Weil, Paris, 1906; *Septem*, T. G. Tucker, Cambridge, 1908; *Agamemnon*, W. G. Headlam, Cambridge, 1910; *Choephoroe*, T. G. Tucker, Cambridge, 1901; *Eumenides*, K. O. Müller, Berlin, 1833 (still valuable), A. W. Verrall, London, 1908.

Sophocles: *Electra*, G. Kaibel, Berlin, 1896; *Oedipus Tyrannus*, J. T. Sheppard, Cambridge, 1920.

Euripides: *Hercules Furens*, U. v. Wilamowitz-Moellendorff, ed. 2, Berlin (important); *Bacchae*, R. Y. Tyrrell, London, 1892, J. E. Sandys, ed. 4, Cambridge, 1904; *Ion*, A. W. Verrall, Cambridge, 1890, U. v. Wilamowitz-Moellendorff, Berlin, 1925; *Orestes*, N. Wedd, Cambridge, 1895.

Aristophanes: *Birds*, W. W. Merry, Oxford, 1889—also many other plays; *Knights*, R. A. Neil, Cambridge, 1901; *Frogs*, T. G. Tucker, London, 1906, E. Radermacher, Vienna, 1921; *Clouds*, W. J. M. Starkie, London, 1911; *Wasps*, W. J. M. Starkie, London, 1907; *Peace*, H. Sharpley, London, 1905.

IV. GENERAL LITERATURE

Only a short selection, with reference particularly to the probable needs of English readers, will be here attempted from the enormous literature. Further references may be found, particularly for foreign works, in Bursian, vol. CXLVII, 1910, S. Mekler for Tragedy, 1903–7—unfortunately the latest report issued on this subject—and vols. CLXXIV, 1916, CXCV, 1924 and CCVII, 1926, E. Wuest for Comedy: also in P. Masqueray's *Bibliographie Pratique de la littérature grecque*, Paris, 1914, pp. 67–124, and better still in J. Geffcken's *Griechische Literaturgeschichte*, Heidelberg, 1926, vol. i, part 2, Anmerkungen, pp. 138–235, an excellent work, published unfortunately too late for use in the preparation of this chapter.

Cook, A. B. *Zeus*. Vol. i. Cambridge, 1914. pp. 665 *sqq.*, chapter xxi, η–κ, valuable material for the 'origins.'

Cornford, F. M. *The Origin of Attic Comedy*. 1914.

Capps, E. *The Introduction of Comedy into the City Dionysia*. Chicago Decennial Publications, vi, 1904, pp. 266 *sqq.*

   See also *A.J. Ph.* XXVIII, 1907, pp. 186 *sqq.*; *Columbia University Lectures on Greek Literature*, 1912, pp. 121 *sqq.*

Croiset, M. *Aristophanes and Political Parties at Athens*. Trans. by J. Loeb. 1909.

Decharme, P. *Euripides and the Spirit of his Drama*. Trans. by J. Loeb. 1906.

Dieterich, A. Articles on *Aischylos* and *Euripides* in P.W.

Farnell, L. R. *The Cults of the Greek States*. Vol. v, 1909, pp. 204–39, 313–24.

—— *The Dionysiac and Hero Theory of the Origin of Tragedy* in Hermathena, xvii, 1913, p. 1.

Flickinger, R. C. *The Greek Theatre and its Drama*. Ed. 2. Chicago, 1922.

Goodell, T. D. *Athenian Tragedy*. New Haven, U.S.A., 1920.

Haigh, A. E. *The Attic Theatre*. Ed. 3, revised and in part re-written by A. W. Pickard-Cambridge. Oxford, 1907.

Headlam, W. G. *The Second Chorus of the Agamemnon*. Cambridge Praelections. 1906. Also many important papers, for a full list of which see L. Haward's bibliography in *Walter Headlam, Life and Poems*, 1910.

Kaibel, G. Art. *Aristophanes* in P.W.

Kroll, W. Art. *Komoedie* in P.W.

Lucas, F. L. *Euripides*. Our Debt to Greece and Rome Series, London and Boston, 1923.

Mackail, J. W. *Essay on Sophocles* in Lectures on Greek Poetry. Ed. 2. 1926.

Matthaei, L. *Studies in Greek Tragedy*. Cambridge, 1918.

Mazon, P. *Essai sur la composition des Comédies d'Aristophane*. 1904.

Murray, G. *Aristophanes and the War Party*. 1919.

—— *Euripides and his Age*. n.d. The best appreciation.

—— *Ritual Forms Preserved in Greek Tragedy* in J. E. Harrison, Themis, Cambridge, 1923, pp. 341 *sqq*.

Navarre, O. *Les origines et la structure technique de la Comédie ancienne*. Revue des Études anciennes, xiii, 1911, p. 245.

Nestle, W. *Euripides der Dichter der griechischen Aufklärung*. Stuttgart, 1901.

—— *Die Weltanschauung des Aischylos*. N.J. Kl. Alt. xix, 1907, p. 225, p. 305.

Patin, A. *Études sur les tragiques grecs*. 1884. Many editions.

Pearson, A. C. ΕΥΡΙΠΙΔΑΡΙΣΤΟΦΑΝΙΖΩΝ.

—— Important papers on the *Ajax of Sophocles* in C.Q. xvi, 1922, p. 124 and on the *Rhesus* in C.R. xxxv, 1921, p. 52.

Ridgeway, W. *The Origin of Tragedy*. Cambridge, 1910.

—— *Drama and Dramatic Dances*. Cambridge, 1916.

Robert, C. *Oidipous*. Berlin, 1915.

Sheppard, J. T. *Greek Tragedy*. Ed. 2. Cambridge, 1920.

—— *Aeschylus and Sophocles*. (Our Debt to Greece and Rome Series.) London and Boston, 1927.

—— *The Prelude of the Agamemnon*. C.R. xxxvi, 1922, p. 5.

Symonds, J. A. *Essay on Aeschylus* in Studies of the Greek Poets. 1902.

Verrall, A. W. *Euripides the Rationalist*. Cambridge, 1895.

—— *Four Plays of Euripides*. Cambridge, 1905.

—— *The Bacchants of Euripides*. Cambridge, 1910.

Weil, H. *Études sur le drame antique*. 1908.

Wilamowitz-Moellendorff, T. v. *Die dramatische Technik des Sophokles*. Berlin, 1917.

Wilamowitz-Moellendorff, U. v. *Einleitung in die griechische Tragoedie*. Reprinted from ed. 1 of his *Euripides Herakles*, Berlin, 1921.

—— *Die Spürhunde des Sophokles*. N.J. Kl. Alt. xxix, 1912, p. 449. A plea for a return to Aristotle and to common sense about 'origins.'

Wilhelm, A. *Urkunden dramatischer Aufführungen in Athen*. Vienna, 1906.

Zielinski, T. *Die Gliederung der altattischen Komoedie*. Leipzig, 1885.

CHAPTER VI

SICILY

I. Ancient Sources

Dittenberger, *Sylloge Inscriptionum Graecarum*, ed. 3, nos. 35, 40, 70, 71.

Pindar, *Olympians*, i–vi, xi, xii; *Pythians*, i–iii, vi; *Nemeans*, i, ix; *Isthmians*, ii; frags. 105, 119, 124.

Bacchylides, iii–v.

Herodotus, vii, 170.

Xenophon, *Hiero*.

Aristotle, *Politics*, viii (v), 1303 a–b, 1312 b, 1313 b.

Timaeus, frags. 84, 86, 88, 88 A, 90, 98 B, 99. (F.H.G. i, 212 *sqq.*)

Diodorus Siculus, xi, 38–92; xii, 8–36.

Dionysius of Halicarnassus, *Ant. Rom.* xx, 7.

Strabo, vi, p. 268.

Polyaenus, i, 27.

Justin, iv, 2 *sq.*; xxi, 3.

Diogenes Laertius, viii, 2.

II. Modern Works

See also General Bibliography

See articles on separate States in P.W., *e.g.* Acragas, Selinus

Beloch, J. *Sicilisches zu Diodor.* Hermes, xxviii, 1893, p. 633.

Bury, J. B. *The Constitutional Position of Gelon and Hiero.* C.R. xiii, 1899, p. 98.

Diels, H. *Gorgias und Empedokles.* Berl. S.B. 1884, pp. 343 *sqq.*

Hill, G. F. *Coins of Ancient Sicily.* London, 1903.

Jebb, R. C. *Bacchylides.* Cambridge, 1905. pp. 465 *sqq.*

Kahrstedt, U. *Zur Geschichte Grossgriechenlands im 5. Jahrhundert.* Hermes, liii, 1918, p. 180.

Pais, E. *Ricerche Storiche e Geografiche sull' Italia antica.* Turin, 1908.

—— *Il papiro di Oxyrhynchos n. 665 relativo alla storia antica della Sicilia.* Rend. Linc. xvii, 1908, p. 329.

—— *Storia della Sicilia e della Magna Grecia.* (Storia d' Italia, Parte i.) Turin, 1894.

Pareti, L. *Studi Siciliani ed Italioti.* Florence, 1920.

Pomtow, H. *Die Statue des Tyrannen Hiero.* Klio, ix, 1909, p. 177.

De Sanctis, G. *Una nuova pagina di Storia Siciliana.* Riv. Fil. xxxiii, 1905, p. 66.

Schröder, O. *Pindarica.* Phil. lxi, 1902, pp. 356 *sqq.*

Schwartz, E. *Timaeos' Geschichtswerk.* Hermes, xxxiv, 1899, p. 485.

Wilamowitz-Moellendorff, U. von. *Hiero und Pindar.* Berl. S.B. 1901, p. 1273.

CHAPTERS VII AND VIII

THE BREAKDOWN OF THE PEACE AND THE ARCHIDAMIAN WAR

A. ANCIENT SOURCES

1. *Primary*

(*a*) Inscriptions

(*a*) *Decrees, Treaties* etc.: *I.G.*² 1, 39–80, 90 *sq.*; add texts in Thucydides, IV, 118 *sq.*; V, 18 *sq.*, 23 *sq.*

(*b*) *Quota-lists*: *I.G.*² 1, 199–230.

(*c*) *Inventories*: of the Treasurers of Athena, *I.G.*² 1, 232–43, 276–81.

(*d*) *Accounts*: of the Treasurers of Athena, *I.G.*² 1, 293–6, 299–301; of the *logistae*, *ibid.* 324, 324 a; of commissions for public works, *ibid.* 329–69.

(*e*) *Miscellaneous*: *I.G.*² 1, 375–8, 395–400, 911–5, 943–9; Ditt. *Syll.*³ 59–61, 73, 78–81.

A selection of the above with commentary is to be found in Hicks and Hill, *Historical Greek Inscriptions*, nos. 40–68; also *I.G.*² 1, ed. Hiller von Gaertringen, 1924, gives references to the literature on Attic inscriptions up to 1924, with full indices. This work is indispensable and supersedes previous collections. Of more recent publications there is to be added on the tribute-lists an important series of papers (restorations, rearrangements, etc.) by A. B. West and B. D. Meritt in *A.J.A.* XXIX, 1925, and XXX, 1926 and *C.P.* XXI, 1926, and *A Revision of Athenian Tribute lists* in Harvard Studies, XXXVII, 1926, pp. 55 *sqq.* which, together with papers in *A.J.Ph.* XLVII, 1926, p. 171 and *Trans. Amer. Philol. Assoc.* LVI, 1925, p. 252, give a revision of the lists from 454 to 440–39 B.C. which marks a new stage in the study of these documents. Add also Hondius, J. J. *Novae inscriptiones Atticae*, Leyden, 1925; Davies, P. H. *Two Attic decrees of the Fifth Century*, A.J.A. XXX, 1926, p. 177 (*I.G.*² 1, 60, 71).

(*b*) Literary

Aeschines, II, 174–5.

Andocides, III, 6–9.

Antiphon, V, 76 *sqq.*

Aristophanes, Comedies and fragments, esp. *Acharnians, Knights, Wasps* and *Peace*, with scholia.

Aristotle, *Constitution of Athens*, XXIV, XXVII–XXVIII.

Atthides: Androtion, frags. 27, 43 M; Philochorus, frags. 89–108 M.

Cratinus, frags. 40, 57 *sq.*, 71, 73, 196 *sq.*, 208, 237, 240 *sq.*, 293, 300, Kock.

Eupolis, frags. 31, 94 *sq.*, 100, 116 *sq.*, 154, 181, 191, 231, 238, 290 *sqq.*, 308, Kock.

Hermippus comicus, frags. 46, 63, Kock.

Herodotus, IV, 80; VI, 91; VII, 137, 233; IX, 73.

Isocrates, VIII, 69; XV, 111, 113.

Plato comicus, frag. 191, Kock.

Telecleides, frags. 41 *sq.*, Kock.

Theopompus, frags. 99–101, 202 M.

Thucydides, I, 23–88, 115–26, 139–46; II–V, 25; VI, 6, 2.

For the literature on Thucydides see bibliography to chapter XIV, Part II.

[Xenophon], *Constitution of Athens*: Ed. E. Kalinka 1913, with full commentary and bibliography.

Minor sources, both primary and secondary, may be found referred to in their appropriate places in Busolt and E. Meyer; see also citations in Kirchner's *Prosopographia Attica*.

2. *Secondary*

Aelian, *V. H.* ii, 29; vii, 14.
Anonymus Argentinensis, ed. B. Keil, Strassburg, 1902, but see U. Wilcken in *Hermes*, xlii, 1907, p. 374 and R. Laqueur, *ib.* xliii, 1908, p. 220.
Diodorus, xii, 9–74.
Frontinus, i, 5, 23; iii, 11, 1; iv, 7, 17.
Justin, iii, 7; iv, 3.
Lucretius, vi, 1138 *sqq.*
Nepos, *Timotheus*, 1.
Oxyrh. Pap. iv, 663 (argument of Cratinus' Dionysalexandros).
Pausanias, i, 29, 4 *sqq.*; iv, 25; 36; v, 26, 1; ix, 1, 4, 7; 6, 3.
Plato, *Euthyd.* 271 c, *Gorgias*, 455 e, *Laches* 181 b, *Menexenus, Symposium* 221 a, 221 c and other scattered references.
Plutarch, *Pericles, Nicias*, 1–10; *Alcibiades*, 1–14, 17; *Aristides*, 24; *Praec. reip. ger.* 15, *etc.*
Polyaenus, i, 36–39, 1; ii, 10, 1, 2, 4, 5; iii, 1–2, 4; vi, 19, 20.
Polybius, xii, 25.
Strabo, vi, 263 *sq.*; viii, 359.

B. Modern Works

See also General Bibliography. Add to the works listed below those marked † in the bibliography to chapters ii–iv. For public finances, population and economics in general see also the bibliography to chapter i, especially sections A, D, and H. The literature up to 1896 for the period ending 435 B.C. and up to 1903 for the Archidamian War is cited by Busolt, iii, 1 and 2. Works in this bibliography marked † should be added to the bibliography to chapters xi and xii.

1. *Topographical and Military*

Awdry, H. *A new historical aspect of the Pylos and Sphacteria incidents.* J.H.S. xx, 1900, p. 14. (See also under Compton.)
Burrows, R. M. *Pylos and Sphacteria.* J.H.S. xvi, 1896, p. 55 and further articles in *C.R.* 1897, p. 1; *J.H.S.* xviii, 1898, pp. 147, 345, xxviii, 1908, p. 148.
Chandler, L. *The North-West Frontier of Attica.* J.H.S. xlvi, 1926, p. 1.
Compton, W. C. and Awdry, H. *Two notes on Pylos and Sphacteria.* J.H.S. xxvii, 1907, p. 274.
†Custance, Sir R. N. *War at Sea, Modern Theory and Ancient Practice.* Edinburgh, 1919.
†Delbrück, H. *Geschichte der Kriegskunst.* i, Ed. 3. Berlin, 1920.
—— *Die Strategie des Pericles.* Berlin, 1890.
Ferrabino, A. *Armate greche nel V Secolo.* Riv. Fil. lxii, N.S. 3, 1925, p. 340.
Gomme, A. W. *Thucydides and Sphacteria.* C.Q. xvii, 1923, p. 36.
†Graefe, F. *Flottenmanöver im Altertum.* Hermes, liv, 1919, p. 219.
†Grundy, G. B. *Thucydides and the History of his Age.* 1911. pp. 240–383.
—— *The rate of sailing of warships in the Fifth Century.* C.R. xxiii, 1909, p. 107.
—— *An investigation of the topography of the region of Sphakteria and Pylos.* J.H.S. xvi, 1896, p. 1. And further articles in *C.R.* 1896, p. 370, 1897, pp. 155, 448 and *J.H.S.* xviii, 1898, p. 232.

†Grundy, G. B. *A suggested characteristic in Thucydides' work.* J.H.S. xviii, 1898, p. 219.

—— *The topography of the battle of Plataea.* 1894.

†Henderson, B. W. *The Great War between Athens and Sparta.* 1927. (This work appeared after chapters vii–xii had gone to press.)

†How, W. W. *Arms, tactics and strategy in the Persian War.* J.H.S. xliii, 1923, p. 117 (of value for fifth-century warfare generally).

†Köster, A. *Das Antike Seewesen.* Berlin, 1923, pp. 96 sqq.

Kromayer, J. and Veith, G. *Antike Schlachtfelder.* Bd. iv, 2. Berlin, 1926. (Contains discussion of the battles of Delium and Amphipolis and review of earlier theories.)

—— *Schlachten-Atlas zur antiken Kriegsgeschichte mit begleitendem Text.* Lief. 4 = Griech. Abt. 1. Leipzig, 1926. See Blatt 3 and Text, on Pylos (G. B. Grundy and J. Kromayer), Delium, and Amphipolis.

Lammert, E. and F. Articles *Kriegskunst* and *Schlachtordnung* in P.W.

Lehmann-Hartleben, K. *Die antiken Hafenanlagen des Mittelmeers.* Klio, Beiheft 14, Leipzig, 1923.

—— Art. Λιμήν in P.W.

MacInnes, J. *The Athenian cavalry in the Peloponnesian War and at Amphipolis.* C.R. xxv, 1911, p. 193.

Pflugk-Harttung, J. v. *Perikles als Feldherr.* Stuttgart, 1884.

Tarn, W. W. *Fleetspeeds, A Reply to Dr Grundy.* C.R. xxiii, 1909, p. 184.

Wilamowitz-Moellendorff, U. v. *Sphakteria.* Berl. S.B. xvii, 1921, p. 306.

Woodhouse, W. J. *Aetolia, its geography, topography and antiquities.* Oxford, 1897.

2. General

Bauer, W. *Epigraphisches aus dem Athener Nationalmuseum.* Klio, xv, 1917, p. 188.

†Beloch, K. J. *Die attische Politik seit Perikles.* Leipzig, 1884.

—— *Die Chronologie des peloponnesischen Krieges* in Griech. Gesch. ii², 2, p. 241. (See also General Bibliography.)

—— *Die Bevölkerung Attikas.* Ib. iii², 2, p. 386.

†Bethe, E. *Athen und der peloponnesische Krieg im Spiegel des Weltkrieges.* N.J.Kl. Alt. xxxix, 1917, p. 73.

Bonner, R. J. *The Megarian Decrees.* C.P. xvi, 1921, p. 238.

Brückner, A. *Mitteilungen aus dem Kerameikos.* Ath. Mitt. xl, 1915, p. 1.

†Bruns, I. *Das literarische Porträt der Griechen.* Berlin, 1896, pp. 1–34, 147–80.

Bürchner. Art. *Korkyra* in P.W.

Ciaceri, E. *Intorno alla obbiettività storica dei discorsi Tucididei.* Riv. Fil. xliv, 1916, p. 67.

†Croiset, M. *Aristophanes and Political Parties at Athens.* Trans. J. Loeb. 1909.

†Deonna, W. *Guerre du péloponnèse (431–404) et guerre mondiale (1914–1918).* (Useful for some modern parallels, especially if read together with Bethe above.)

Dickins, G. *The True Cause of the Peloponnesian War.* C.Q. v, 1911, p. 238.

Dinsmoor, W. B. *Attic Building Accounts.* I. A.J.A. xvii, 1913, p. 53 and V. *Supplementary Notes.* A.J.A. xxv, 1921, p. 233.

Domaszewski, A. v. *Der Staatsfriedhof der Athener.* Heid. S.B. Phil.-Hist. Kl. 1917. Abh. 7.

Ferguson, W. S. *Economic Causes of International Rivalries and Wars in Ancient Greece.* Annual Report. Amer. Hist. Assoc. 1905, p. 111.

Ferrabino, A. *Per Tere, Sparadoco e Sitalce Odrisi.* Boll. di fil. classica, xviii, 1912, p. 281.

Frickenhaus, A. *Phidias und Kolotes*. I. Die Chronologie des Phidias. J.D.A.I. xxviii, 1913, p. 342.

Gäbler, H. *Zur Münzkunde Makedoniens*, vi, *Die Prägung der Stadt Olynthos und des chalkidischen Bundes*. Z.N. xxxv, 1925, p. 193.

†Gilbert, G. *Beiträge zur innern Geschichte Athens*. Leipzig, 1877.

Grundy, G. B. *The Policy of Sparta*. J.H.S. xxxii, 1912, p. 261.

—— *The true cause of the Peloponnesian War*. C.Q. vii, 1913, p. 59.

Harrison, E. *Chalkidike*. C.Q. vi, 1912, pp. 93 *sqq.*, 165 *sqq.*

Holzapfel, L. *Über die chronol. Anordnung der Begebenheiten von der Schlacht bei Leukimme bis zum ersten Einfall der Pelop. in Attika*. Berl. Stud. vii, Heft 3.

Judeich, W. *Zum Pheidias-papyrus*. Hermes, lx, 1925, p. 50.

Kahrstedt, U. Art. *Kleon* in P.W.

Kolbe, W. *Ein chronologischer Beitrag zur Vorgeschichte des peloponnesischen Krieges*. Hermes, xxxiv, 1899, p. 380.

Körte, A. *Zum attischen Scherbengericht*. Ath. Mitt. xlvii, 1922, p. 1.

†Krause, A. *Attische Strategenliste bis 146 v. Chr.* Jena Diss. 1914.

Meritt, B. D. *Peace between Athens and Bottice*. A.J.A. xxix, 1925, p. 29.

Minns, E. H. *Scythians and Greeks*. Cambridge, 1913.

Mitchell, J. M. Art. *Peloponnesian War* in E. Brit.

†Müller-Strübing, H. *Aristophanes und die historische Kritik*. Leipzig, 1873.

†Murray, G. *Aristophanes and the War Party*. 1919.

Nicole, J. *Le procès de Phidias*. Geneva, 1910.

Nissen, H. *Der Ausbruch der peloponnesischen Krieges*. H.Z. (N.F.) xxvii, 1889, p. 406.

Pareti, L. *Il processo di Fidia ed un papiro di Ginevra*. Röm. Mitt. xxiv, 1909, p. 271.

Porzio, G. *Atene, Corinto, Pericle, e le cause della guerra peloponnesiaca*. Bologna, 1911.

Rosenberg, A. *Perikles und die Parteien in Athen*. N.J. Kl. Alt. xxxv, 1915, p. 205.

Schrader, H. *Phidias*. Frankfurt a/M. 1924. pp. 23 *sqq.*

Solari, A. *Sui dinasti dei Odrisi*. Pisa, 1912.

Stern, E. v. *Die griechische Kolonisation am Nordgestade des Schwarzen Meeres im Lichte archäologischer Forschung*. Klio, ix, 1909, p. 139.

Swoboda, H. *Über den Process des Perikles*. Hermes, xxviii, p. 536.

—— *Zur Geschichte der attischen Kleruchien*. Serta Harteliana, Vienna, 1896. pp. 28 *sqq.*

Taylor, A. E. *On the date of the trial of Anaxagoras*. C.Q. xi, 1917, p. 81.

Walker, E. M. Art. *Olynthus* in E. Brit.

West, A. B. *Athenian Generals of the year 424–3 b.c.* A.J. Ph. 1924, p. 141.

—— *Methone and the assessment of 430*. A.J.A. xxix, 1925, p. 440.

—— *Pericles' Political Heirs*. C.P. xix, 1924, pp. 124 *sqq.*, pp. 201 *sqq.*

—— *The chronology of the years 432 and 431 b.c.* C.P. x, 1915, p. 34.

—— *The History of the Chalcidic League*. Madison, 1919.

—— *Thucydidean Chronology anterior to the Peloponnesian War*. C.P. xx, 1925, p. 216.

West, A. B. and Meritt, B. D. *Cleon's Amphipolitan Campaign and the assessment list of 421*. A.J.A. xxix, 1925, p. 59.

†Whibley, L. *Political Parties in Athens*. Cambridge, 1889.

CHAPTER IX

SPARTA AND THE PELOPONNESE

I. Primary Sources

1. *Documentary*

(*a*) *Decrees*: *I.G.*² i, 25, 64, 81–96, 127–90 (in part); *I.G.*² ii, 8; *I.G.* xii, 5, 480; Wilhelm, *Wien Anz.* lxi, 1924, pp. 158 *sqq.*

(*b*) *Tribute Lists*: *I.G.*² i, 220–31 (mostly).

(*c*) *Accounts*: of the Treasurers of Athena, *I.G.*² i, 301 *sq.*; of the Superintendents of Hephaestus, *I.G.*² i, 370 *sq.*

(*d*) *Inventories*: of the Treasurers of Athena, *I.G.*² i, 244 *sqq.*, 265–70, 281–5; of the Superintendents of Eleusis, *I.G.*² i, 311 *sq.*

(*e*) *Miscellaneous*: Thucydides, v, 23 *sq.*, 47, 77, 79; *I.G.*² i, 379, 843; *I.G.*¹ ii, 1650; Ditt. *Syll.*³ 88; *I.G.* v, 1, 1 (?).

2. *Literary*

(*a*) Andocides, *Or.* iii, 8, [iv]; frag. 5.
Antiphon, *Or.* v.
Atthides: Androtion, *F.H.G.* 47, 48; Philochorus, *F.H.G.* 108, 109, 168.
Isocrates, *Or.* xvi, 32 *sqq.*
Theopompus, *F.H.G.* 103.
Thucydides, v, 20–116.

(*b*) *Minor*: (these may be found cited in their appropriate places in Busolt and E. Meyer; also, listed under the names of the Athenians concerned, in Kirchner's *Prosopographia Attica*; and, less completely, in the *Fasti Attici* published in *I.G.*² i).

II. Secondary Sources

(See also Busolt, iii, 2)

1. *Ancient*

Diodorus, xii, 38, 75–81; Nepos, *Alcibiades*; Plutarch, *Nicias*, 10 *sq.*, *Alcibiades*, 1–16.

2. *Modern*

To these should be added the works marked † in the Bibliography to chapters vii–viii. See also the General Bibliography.

Cavaignac, E. *Études sur l'histoire financière d'Athènes au Vᵉ siècle.* 1908. pp. 134–60.

Delbrück, H. *Geschichte der Kriegskunst².* I. Berlin, 1908. pp. 118 *sqq.*

Dittenberger, W. *Die Familie des Alkibiades.* Hermes, xxxvii, 1902, p. 1.

Ehrenberg, V. *Spartiaten und Lakedaimonier.* Hermes, lix, 1924, p. 33.

Fougères, G. *Mantinée et l'arcadie orientale.* 1898. pp. 39 *sqq.*, 389–404, 564–8.

Francotte, H. *Les finances des cités grecques.* Liège-Paris, 1909. pp. 186 *sqq.*

Gardner, P. *Coinage of the Athenian Empire.* J.H.S. xxxiii, 1913, p. 150.

Hiller v. Gaertringen, F. and Klaffenbach, G. *Das Münzgesetz des ersten athenischen Seebundes.* Zeit. f. Num. xxxv, 1925, p. 217.

Kahrstedt, U. *Griechisches Staatsrecht.* I. Göttingen, 1922. pp. 54 *sqq.*, 200 *sqq.*, 294 *sqq.*

Kirchhoff, A. *Thukydides und sein Urkundenmaterial.* Berlin, 1895.

Körte, A. *Zum attischen Scherbengericht.* Ath. Mitt. xlvii, 1922, p. 1.

Kromayer, J. *Antike Schlachtfelder.* Bd. IV, Berlin, 1926, pp. 207 *sqq.*

Lammert, E. and F. *Schlachtordnung.* P.W. 2te Reihe, III, 446.

Meyer, E. *Zur Geschichte der attischen Finanzen im fünften Jahrhundert.* Forsch. z. alt. Gesch. II, Halle, 1899, pp. 88–136.

—— *Die Friedenszeit und die Einheit des peloponnesischen Krieges.* Forsch. z. alt. Gesch. II, Halle, 1899, pp. 351 *sqq.*

West, A. B. *Aristidean Tribute in the Assessment of* 421 B.C. A.J.A. XXIX, 1925, p. 135.

Wilamowitz-Moellendorff, U. von. *Das Bündniss zwischen Sparta und Athen* (*Thukydides,* v). Berl. S.B. 1919, p. 934.

Woodhouse, W. J. *The Campaign and Battle of Mantinea in* 418 B.C. B.S.A. XXII, 1916–18, p. 51.

Woodward, A. M. *Notes and Queries on Athenian Coinage.* J.H.S. XXXIV, 1914, p. 285.

CHAPTER X

THE ATHENIAN EXPEDITION TO SICILY

I. Primary Sources

1. *Documentary*

(*a*) *Decrees*: *I.G.*² 1, 97–100, 127–90 (in part).
(*b*) *Accounts*: of the Treasurers of Athena, *I.G.*² 1, 297, 302 *sq.*; of the Poletae, *I.G.*²
    1, 325–34.
(*c*) *Inventories*: of the Treasurers of Athena, *I.G.*² 1, 247 *sq.*, 271 *sq.*, 286.
(*d*) *Miscellaneous*: Plutarch, *Alcibiades* 22, 3; *I.G.*² 1, 770 a.

2. *Literary*

(*a*) Andocides, *Or.* I and II.
    Aristophanes, *Birds* and *Lysistrata* 387–97, with the scholia.
    Atthides: Hellanicus, *F.H.G.* 78; Philochorus, *F.H.G.* 110–13.
    Isaeus, *Or.* VI, 14.
    Isocrates, *Or.* XVI, 37.
    [Lysias], *Or.* VI.
    Thucydides, VI and VII.
    Timaeus, *F.H.G.* 105 *sqq.*

(*b*) *Minor*: (see above under Minor Sources in the Bibliography for chapter IX).

II. Secondary Sources

(See also Busolt, III, 2)

1. *Ancient*

Aristides, *Or.* XXIX, XXX (Dindorf).
Diodorus, XII, 82 *sqq.*; XIII, 2–35.
Justin, IV, 4 *sq.*
Nepos, *Alcibiades*.
Plutarch, *Nicias* 11–30; *Alcibiades* 17–23.
Polyaenus, I, 39, 2 *sqq.*; 40, 4–7; 42, 1–43, 2.

2. *Modern*

(*a*) *General*.
Cavallari, F. S. and C. and Holm, A. *Topografia archeologica di Siracusa.* Palermo,
    1883. Also, Appendice. Torino, 1891.
Freeman, E. A. *The History of Sicily.* III. Oxford, 1892.
Holm, A. *Geschichte Siciliens im Altertum.* II. Leipzig, 1874. Cf. also, *The
    History of Greece.* II. London, 1895. pp. 466–81.
Lupus, B. *Die Stadt Syrakus im Alterthum.* Strassburg, 1887.
(*b*) *Special*.
Awdry, H. *Note on the Walls on Epipolae.* J.H.S. XXIX, 1909, p. 70.
Beloch, K. J. *Die grosse athenische Expedition nach Sicilien.* Griech. Gesch. II², 2,
    pp. 290–311.
Busolt, G. *Plutarchs Nikias und Philistos.* Hermes, XXXIV, 1899, p. 280.
Conradt, C. *Zu Thukydides.* Jahr. f. cl. Phil. CXXIX, 1884, p. 534.
Domaszewski, A. von. *Eine Urkunde bei Thukydides.* Heid. S.B. 1920, Abt. 5.
Ferrabino, A. *Armate greche nel V Secolo a. C.* Riv. Fil. LIII, 1925, p. 352.

Götz, W. *Der Hermokopidenprocess.* Jahr. f. cl. Phil. Supplb. VIII, 1876, p. 535.

Heitland, W. E. *Thucydides and the Sicilian Expedition.* J.P. XXIII, 1895, p. 45. Cf. *C.R.* VIII, 1894, p. 123.

Holm, A. *Zur Topographie des Rückzuges der Athener von Syrakus 413 v. Chr.* Verhandl. der 36. Versamml. deutschen Philologen, 1882, p. 262.

Knoke, F. *Zur Topographie von Syrakus.* N.J.P. XVI, 1913, pp. 365 *sqq.*

Kromayer-Veith. *Schlachten-Atlas zur antiken Kriegsgeschichte.* Griech. Abt. Bl. 3. Also Text, col. 19 *sqq.*

Pais, E. *The Defeat of the Athenians at the Assinarus.* Ancient Italy. Chicago, 1908. pp. 147–56. = Ricerche storiche e geografiche, pp. 189 *sqq.*

CHAPTERS XI AND XII

THE OLIGARCHICAL MOVEMENT IN ATHENS
AND THE FALL OF THE ATHENIAN EMPIRE

I. PRIMARY SOURCES

1. *Documentary*

(a) *Decrees and Laws*: *I.G.*² I, 77, 101–26, 127–90 (in part); *I.G.*² II, 1–12, 1138, 1237; Aristotle, *Ath. Pol.* 29, 2–31 (?); [Plutarch], *Vit. X Or.* 833 d; Andocides, *Or.* I, 96, 77, 83; Demosthenes, XXIV, 20–23, 33; Athen. VI, p. 234 E.

(b) *Accounts*: of the Treasurers of Athena, *I.G.*² I, 298, 304–9 a; of the Superintendents of the Erechtheum, *I.G.*² I, 372 *sqq.*, Stevens, *The Erechtheum*, p. 648.

(c) *Inventories*: of the Treasurers of Athena, *I.G.*² I, 249–55, 273 *sqq.*, 287–92 b; *I.G.*¹ II, 5, 642 b; *I.G.*¹ II, 642; of the Superintendents of Eleusis, *I.G.*² I, 313–23.

(d) *Accounts or inventories*: *I.G.*² I, 380–90 b.

(e) *Miscellaneous*: *I.G.*² I, 398, 771 *sq.*, 950 *sqq.*; *I.G.*¹ II, 652, l. 31, 959, 971 (*I.G.*¹ II, 5, 971), 972, 977; *I.G.* V, 1, p. vii; *I.G.* VII, 235; *I.G.* XII, 3, 1187; 5, 109; 8, 262 *sq.*, 277, l. 81, 402; 9, 187 A; *Tit. As. Min.* I (Kalinka), 44; *Inschr. v. Olym.* (Ditt. u. Purgold), 153; *Fouilles de Delphes*, III, I (Bourguet), 506–7 (Ditt. *Syll.*³ 115), 69; Ditt. *Syll.*³ 90, 110; Aristotle, *Const. of Athens*, 39; Plutarch, *Lysander* 14, 4; Thucydides, VIII, 18, 37, 58.

2. *Literary*

(a)

Andocides, *Or.* I, II and III.

Antiphon, *Or.* VI (?); frag. 1–6, 14 (Blass); frag. III, 1, 4 (Gernet); *Apologie* (?), ed. by Nicole. Genève, 1907.

Aristophanes, *Lysistrata, Thesmophoriazusae* and *Frogs*, with scholia.

Aristotle, *Const. of Athens*, 4, 28–41; *Pol.* VI (IV), 14, 14 (p. 1298 b); 15, 11 (p. 1299 b); *Rhet.* I, 15 (p. 1375 b); III, 18 (p. 1419 a).

Atthides: Androtion, *F.H.G.* 10, 11; *Jahr. f. cl. Phil.* CIII, 1871, p. 316; Hellanicus, *F.H.G.* 80, cf. IV, p. 636; Philochorus, *F.H.G.* 114–24, 169.

Ephorus, *F.H.G.* 125, 126.

Isocrates, *Or.* XXI, XVIII, XX, XVI.

Lysias, *Or.*, especially VII, XII, XIII, XIV, XVIII, XXI, XXV, XXVI, XXX, XXXI, XXXIV, [VI], [XX], *Oxyrhy. Pap.* XIII, 1606.

Theopompus, *F.H.G.* 21, 134.

Thucydides, VIII.

Xenophon, *Hell.* I, II, VI, 5, 35 *sq.*; *Mem.* I, 1, 18; 2, 24; II, 9; IV, 4, 2; *Symp.* IV, 30 *sq.*

(b) *Minor*: (see above under Minor Sources in the Bibliography for chapter IX).

II. SECONDARY SOURCES

(See also Busolt, III, 2)

1. *Ancient*

Diodorus, XIII, 34–42, 45–53, 64–79, 97–107; XIV, 3–6, 10–13, 32 *sq.*

Frontinus, II, 7, 6; III, 9, 6; 11, 3.

Justin, V.

Nepos, *Alcibiades, Lysander, Thrasybulus.*

Oxyrhy. Pap. XV, 1800.

Pausanias, I, 23, 9; IV, 17, 3; VI, 3, 14 *sq.*; 7, 4–7; IX, 32, 9; X, 9, 9 *sqq.*
Plutarch, *Alcibiades* 24–39; *Lysander* 1–21; [Plutarch], *Vit. X Or.*: *Andocides, Antiphon, Lysias.*
Polyaenus, I, 40, 8 *sq.*; 44–45, 5; 47, 1 *sq.*; 48, 2.
Sallust, *Catilina* 51, 28.

2. *Modern*

(*a*) *General*. To these should be added the works marked † in the Bibliography to chapters VII–VIII. See also the General Bibliography.

Beauchet, L. *Histoire du droit privé de la république athénienne.* 1897.
Blass, F. *Die attische Beredsamkeit.* I². Leipzig, 1887.
Busolt, G. *Griechische Staatskunde.* (Handbuch, IV³, 1, 1.) München, 1920–26.
Calhoun, G. M. *Athenian Clubs in Politics and Litigation.* Bull. Univ. Texas, Humanistic Series, 14. Austin, 1913.
Gardner, P. *A History of Ancient Coinage,* 700–300 B.C. Oxford, 1918.
Jebb, R. C. *The Attic Orators.* I. 1893.
Lehmann-Hartleben, K. *Die antiken Hafenanlagen des Mittelmeeres.* Klio, Beiheft 14, Leipzig, 1923.
Lipsius, J. H. *Das attische Recht und Rechtsverfahren.* Leipzig, 1905–15.
Mathieu, G. *Aristote. Constitution d'Athènes.* 1915.
Vinogradoff, P. *Outlines of Historical Jurisprudence.* II. Oxford, 1922.

(*b*) *Special.*
Beloch, K. J. *Die Chronologie des peloponnesischen Krieges.* Griech. Gesch. II², 2, 241–54.
—— *Die Bevölkerung Attikas.* Griech. Gesch. III², 2, 386–418.
Börner, A. *De rebus a Graecis inde ab anno* 410 *usque ad annum* 403 *a. Chr. n. gestis quaestiones historicae.* Gött. Diss. 1894.
Bonner, R. J. *Administration of Justice under Athenian Oligarchies.* C.P. 1926, p. 209.
Botsford, G. W. *Hellenic History.* New York, 1922, pp. 322 *sqq.*
Busolt, G. *Zur Chronologie Xenophons.* Hermes, XXXIII, 1898, p. 661.
Cloché, P. *Le conseil athénien des cinq-cents et les partis.* Rev. E.G. XXXV, 1922, p. 269.
—— *L'affaire des Arginuses.* Rev. Hist. CXXX, 1919, p. 5.
Droysen, J. *De Demophanti Patroclidis Tisameni populiscitis.* Berl. Diss. 1873.
Ferrabino, A. *Armate greche nel V Secolo a. C.* Riv. Fil. LIII, 1925, p. 494.
Gantzer, P. *Verfassungs- und Gesetzrevision in Athen vom Jahre* 411 *bis auf das Archontat des Eukleides.* Halle Diss. 1894.
Gardner, P. *The Financial History of Ancient Chios.* J.H.S. XL, 1920, p. 160.
Gülde, O. *Quaestiones de Lysiae oratione in Nicomachum.* Berl. Diss. 1882.
Glover, T. R. *From Pericles to Philip.* New York, 1917, pp. 116–35.
Hardy, W. G. *The "Hellenica Oxyrhynchia" and the Devastation of Attica.* C.P. 1926, p. 346.
Holzapfel, L. *Doppelte Relationen im 8. Buche des Thukydides.* Hermes, XXVIII, 1893, p. 435.
Judeich, W. *Kleinasiatische Studien.* Marburg, 1892. pp. 23 *sqq.*
Kahrstedt, U. *Forschungen zur Geschichte des ausgehenden fünften und des vierten Jahrhunderts.* Berlin, 1910, pp. 157 *sqq.*, 237 *sqq.*
Keil, B. *Athens Amts- und Kalenderjahre im V. Jahrhundert.* Hermes, XXIX, 1894, p. 32.
—— *Das System des kleisthenischen Staatskalenders.* Hermes, XXIX, p. 321. Cf. Beloch, Griech. Gesch. II², 2, p. 230; Wilhelm, *Wien Anz.* 1922, p. 46; Kirchner, *I.G.*² I, pp. 153–56; West, *A.J.A.* XXIX, 1925, p. 8.

Kunle, L. *Untersuchungen über das achte Buch des Thukydides.* Freiburg Diss. 1909.

Ledl, A. *Das attische Bürgerrecht und die Frauen.* Wien St. xxx, 1908, pp. 38–46. 173–87.

Müller, O. *Untersuchungen zur Geschichte des attischen Bürger- und Eherechts.* Jahr. f. cl. Phil. Supplb. xxv, 1899, pp. 786–811.

Nestle, W. *Kritias. Eine Studie.* N.J.P. xi, 1903, pp. 93–107, 178–99.

Pasquali, G. *Antifonte?* Studi Storici (Pais), i, 1908, pp. 46–57.

Perrin, B. *The Rehabilitation of Theramenes.* Amer. Hist. Rev. ix, 1904, p. 649.

—— *The Death of Alcibiades.* Trans. A. P. Assoc. xxxvii, 1906, pp. 25–37.

Preuner, E. *Zum attischen Gesetz über die Speisung im Prytaneion.* Hermes, lxi, 1926, p. 471.

Rüegg, J. A. *Theramenes.* Basel, 1910.

Schwartz, E. *Quellenuntersuchungen zur griechische Geschichte.* Rh. Mus. xliv, 1889, p. 104.

Stevens, G. P. and Paton, J. M. *The Erechtheum.* Cambridge, U.S.A., 1927, pp. 452 *sqq.*

Swoboda, H. *Zur Verfassungsgeschichte von Samos.* Festschr. f. O. Benndorf, Wien, 1898, pp. 250–5.

Valeton, M. *De praetoribus Atheniensium qui victoriam reportaverunt apud Arginusas insulas.* Mnemosyne, xlviii, 1920, p. 34.

Vischer, W. *Untersuchungen über die Verfassung von Athen in den letzten Jahren des peloponnesischen Krieges.* Kleine Schriften, i, pp. 205–38.

Wilamowitz-Moellendorff, U. von. *Thukydides VIII.* Hermes, xliii, 1908, p. 578.

—— *Aristoteles und Athen.* Berlin, 1893, i, pp. 99–108, ii, pp. 113–25, 356–67; i, pp. 126–33, 161–9, ii, pp. 212–16; i, pp. 121 *sqq.*, ii, pp. 217–30.

Wilhelm, A. *Fünf Beschlüsse der Athener.* Jahreshefte, xxi–xx, 1924, pp. 123–71.

(c) Law. (See also above under *General.*)

Bonner, R. J. *Evidence in Athenian Courts.* Chicago Diss. 1905.

—— *The Institution of Athenian Arbitrators.* C.P. xi, 1916, p. 191.

Calhoun, G. M. Διαμαρτυρία, παραγραφὴ *and the Law of Archinus.* C.P. xiii, 1918, p. 169.

—— Παραγραφὴ *and Arbitration.* C.P. xiv, 1919, p. 20.

—— *Athenian Magistrates and Special Pleas.* C.P. xiv, 1919, p. 338.

—— *Oral and Written Pleading in Athenian Courts.* Trans. A. P. Assoc. l, 1919, pp. 177–93.

Gilliard, C. *Quelques réformes de Solon.* Lausanne, 1907. pp. 37–46.

Kunst. Art. Logographos in P.W. xxv, col. 1027.

Lipsius, J. H. *Zur athenischen Nomothesie.* B.P.W. 1917, col. 902.

De Sanctis, G. *Atthis².* Torino, 1912. pp. 423–57.

Schöll, R. *Ueber attische Gesetzgebung.* Bay. S.B. 1886, pp. 83–139.

Schreiner, I. *De corpore iuris Atheniensium.* Bonn Diss. 1913.

Smith, Gertrude. *Dicasts in the Ephetic Courts.* C.P. xix, 1924, p. 353.

Sondhaus, C. *De Solonis legibus.* Jena Diss. 1909.

Weiss, Egon. *Griechisches Privatrecht,* i, 1923, pp. 92 *sqq.*

(d) The Revolution of 411 B.C. (For further literature see the works of Busolt and Lenschau cited below.)

Beloch, K. J. *Die Verfassung des Theramenes.* Griech. Gesch. ii², 2, pp. 311–24.

Busolt, G. *Griechische Staatskunde.* (Handbuch, iv³, 1, 1.) München, 1920. pp. 69–78, 630 d, 260 *sqq.* ii, bearbeitet von H. Swoboda. 1926. pp. 902 *sqq.*

Caspari, M. O. B. *The Revolution of the Four Hundred at Athens.* J.H.S. xxxiii, 1913, p. 1.

Costanzi, V. *L'Oligarchia dei Quattrocento.* Riv. Fil. xxix, 1901, p. 84.

Ehrenberg, V. *Die Urkunden von* 411. Hermes, LVII, 1922, p. 613.

Ferguson, W. S. *The Constitution of Theramenes.* C.P. XXI, 1926, p. 72.

Kahrstedt, U. *Staatsrechtliches zum Putsch von* 411. Hermes, XLIX, 1914, p. 47.

Köhler, U. *Die athenische Oligarchie des Jahres* 411. Berl. S.B. 1895, p. 451.

—— *Der thukydideische Bericht über die oligarchische Umwälzung in Athen im Jahre* 411. Berl. S.B. 1900, pp. 803–17.

Ledl, A. *Die Einsetzung des Rates der Vierhundert in Athen im Jahre* 411 *v. Chr.* Wien St. XXXII, 1910, pp. 38–55.

Lenschau, T. *Der Staatsstreich der Vierhundert.* Rh. Mus. LXVIII, 1913, p. 202.

Meyer, E. *Die Revolution der Vierhundert.* Forsch. z. alt. Gesch. II, 406–36.

Micheli, H. *La révolution oligarchique des quatre-cents à Athènes et ses causes.* Genève, 1893.

Newman, W. L. *The Politics of Aristotle.* Vol. IV. Oxford, 1902. Introduction and Notes.

Smith, Frederick D. *Athenian Political Commissions.* Chicago Diss. 1920.

Thalheim, Th. *Die aristotelischen Urkunden zur Geschichte der Vierhundert in Athen.* Hermes, LIV, 1919, p. 333.

Whibley, L. *Greek Oligarchies:* Appendix C, The Four Hundred at Athens. London, 1896, pp. 192–207.

(*e*) *The Thirty Tyrants.* (For further literature see the work by Cloché cited below.)

Armbruster, O. *Ueber die Herrschaft der Dreissig.* Freiburg Diss. 1913.

Beloch, K. J. *Die zweite Oligarchie in Athen.* Griech. Gesch. III², 2, pp. 204–11.

Blank, O. *Die Einsetzung der Dreissig zu Athen.* Freiburg Diss. 1911.

Busolt, G. *Aristoteles oder Xenophon?* Hermes, XXXIII, 1898, p. 71.

Cloché, P. *La restauration démocratique à Athènes en* 403 *avant J.-C.* Paris, 1915.

—— *Les expulsions en Attique avant la prise de Phylé.* Rev. E.G. XXIV, 1911, p. 63.

—— *Le conseil athénien des cinq cents et la peine de mort.* Rev. E.G., XXXIII, 1920, p. 1.

—— *Hypothèses sur l'une des sources de l'* Ἀθηναίων πολιτεία. Mus. B. XXIX, 1925, p. 173.

De Sanctis, G. *Atene e i suoi Liberatori.* Riv. Fil. LI, 1923, p. 287.

Foucart, P. *Les combattants de Phylé.* Mém. Ac. Inscr. XLII, 1922, pp. 323–55.

Kolbe, W. *Das Ehrendekret für die Retter der Demokratie.* Klio, XVII, 1921, p. 242.

Judeich, W. *Untersuchungen zur athenischen Verfassungsgeschichte*: 2. Die Fünf athenischen Ephoren. Rh. Mus. LXXIV, 1925, p. 254.

Mess, A. von. *Aristoteles* Ἀθηναίων Πολιτεία *und die politische Schriftstellerei Athens.* Rh. Mus. LXVI, 1911, p. 356.

Roos, A. G. *Chronologisches zur Geschichte der Dreissig.* Klio, XVII, 1921, p. 1.

CHAPTER XIII

THE AGE OF ILLUMINATION

1. ANCIENT SOURCES

Aeschines Socraticus. *Relliquiae*. Ed. Krauss, H. Leipzig, 11.

Aristophanes. Works, especially the *Clouds*.

Diels, H. *Die Fragmente der Vorsokratiker*. Vol. 1. Ed. 4. Berlin, 1922. Vols. II and III, 1912.

Diogenes Laertius. *De Vitis Philosophorum*.

Euripides. Works.

Hippocrates. Works. (1) Ed. W. H. S. Jones, Vols. 1 and 11. (2) Ed. H. Kühlewein. Vols. 1 and 11. Leipzig, 1894, 1902.

Libanius. *Apologia Socratis* in Libanii Opera. Ed. R. Foerster, v, 13 *sqq*.

Plato. *Euthyphro, Apology of Socrates* and *Crito*. Edited with notes by J. Burnet, Oxford, 1924.

Satyrus. *Vita Euripidis*. Oxyrh. Pap. 1912, IX, 124.

Xenophon, *Memorabilia, Apologia Socratis*.

2. MODERN WORKS

Burnet, J. *Greek Philosophy. Thales to Plato*. Part I. 1920.

Gomperz, Th. *Griechische Denker*. Bd. 1. Leipzig, 1896. Eng. translation. Greek Thinkers. Vol. I. By L. Magnus, 1901. Vol. II. By G. G. Berry, 1905.

Grote, G. *Plato and the other companions of Socrates*. 3 vols. 1875.

—— *History of Greece*. Vol. VIII, chaps. lxvii and lxviii.

Jackson, H. Art. *Socrates* in E. Brit. ed. 11.

Keramopoullos, A. D. Ὁ ἀποτυμπανισμός (Βιβλιοθήκη τῆς ἐν Ἀθήναις ἀρχ. ἑταιρείας). Athens, 1923.

Taylor, A. E. *Plato's Biography of Socrates*. (Proc. of Brit. Acad. vol. VIII, 1917.)

—— *On the date of the Trial of Anaxagoras*. C.Q. XI, 1917, p. 81.

Wilamowitz-Moellendorff, U. v. *Platon*. 2 vols. Berlin, 1920. (Vol. II, ed. 2.)

CHAPTER XIV

HERODOTUS AND THUCYDIDES[1]

I. HERODOTUS

A. *The Greek Text*

1. Editio princeps. Venetiis in domo Aldi mense Septembri MDII. ΗΡΟΔΟΤΟΥ ΛΟΓΟΙ ΕΝΝΕΑ ΟΙΠΕΡ ΕΠΙΚΑΛΟΥΝΤΑΙ ΜΟΥΣΑΙ.
2. Jungermann, G. folio. Frankfurt, 1608. Gk. and Lat. (Valla.) The first edition in which the Books were divided into numbered chapters.
3. Gale, T. folio. London, 1679. Gk. and Lat. The first edition published in Great Britain.
4. Foulis. 9 vols. 12mo. Glasgow, 1761. Gk. and Lat. A pocket reprint of the text of Gronovius.
5. Laing. 7 vols. 8vo. Edinburgh, 1806. With Notes based on Wesseling and on Reitz: dedicated to Porson.
6. Palm, F. 3 vols. 12mo. Leipzig, 1839. The first edition exhibiting the work in three volumes.
7. Stein, H. 2 vols. 8vo. Herodoti Historiae. Berlin, 1869.
8. —— Ed. minor. 2 vols. Sm. 8vo. Berlin, 1884.
9. Holder, A. 2 vols. 8vo. Leipzig, 1886, 1888.
10. Herwerden, H. van. 4 vols. Small 8vo. Utrecht. N.D.
11. Hude, C. 2 vols. *Herodoti Historiae.* Oxford. [1908.]

B. *The Greek Text with Notes, etc.*

1. Baehr, I. C. G. *Herodoti Musae.* Leipzig, 1830–5. Ed. 2. 4 vols. 8vo. 1856–61. Latin Notes, etc.
2. Blakesley, H. Text with Commentary. 2 vols. 8vo. 1854.
3. Stein, H. Text with explanatory Notes (German). 2 vols. 8vo. Berlin, 1852–1862: constantly improved in successive editions, 1872–1877; 1893–1895; 1901–1908. Bks I and VII have reached a 6th edition.
4. Sayce, A. H. *Herodotus,* Books I–III. 8vo. 1883.
5. Wiedemann, A. *Herodots zweites Buch* (with copious notes). 8vo. Leipzig, 1890.
6. Macan, R. W. The fourth, fifth, and sixth Books (with Introduction, Notes, etc.). 2 vols. 8vo. 1895.
7. —— The seventh, eighth, and ninth Books (with Introduction, Notes, etc.). 3 vols. 8vo. 1908.

C. *Commentaries without text*

1. Turner, D. W. *Notes on Herodotus, original and selected from the best commentators.* 1847. Ed. 2, 1852.
2. How, W. W. and Wells, J. *A Commentary on Herodotus.* 2 vols. Oxford, 1912.

D. *Translations*

Valla, L. (Latin.) First printed, Venice, 1474. Frequently reprinted, with corrections, as in the editions of Jungermann, Wesseling, P. (1763) and others.
Schweighäuser, J. (Latin.) In his annotated edition (12 vols. 8vo. Strassburg, 1816). Reprinted by Priestley. 6 vols. 1818.

---

[1] In this Bibliography the various editions, translations and modern works are arranged in chronological order so as to show the progress of study on the text and main problems connected with these two authors.

Larcher, P. H. 7 vols. 8vo. (French.) With copious notes and dissertations. Paris, 1786.

Beloe, W. 4 vols. 8vo. (With notes.) 1791. Subsequent editions: 1812, 1820.

Rawlinson, G. 4 vols. 8vo. With Introduction, copious notes, appendices, etc. 1858. Ed. 3. 1875.

Macaulay, G. C. 2 vols. Cr. 8vo. 1890. (Very accurate.)

Godley, A. D. 4 vols. London and New York, 1921–6. (Loeb Classical Library, with Greek text *en face*.)

E. *Monographs, Dissertations, Articles, Chapters, etc.*[1]

Dionysius Halicarnassensis. *Epistula ad Gn. Pompeium*: also the fragment of the *De imitatione* (ed. H. Usener, Bonn, 1889).

Plutarch. περὶ τῆς Ἡροδότου κακοηθείας (*Moralia*, 855–75) [ed. Didot, II, 1065 *sqq*.]. For a French translation see Larcher, above.

Lucian. Ἡρόδοτος ἤ Ἀετίων (831–8. Teubner, I, 391). The legend of the Olympic recitation.

Rennell, J. *Geography of Herodotus.* 4vo. 1800. 2nd ed. 2 vols. 8vo. 1830.

†Dahlmann, F. C. *Herodot. Aus seinem Buche sein Leben.* Altona, 1824. Translated by Cox, C. V. *Life of Herodotus.* 1845.

Heyse, C. W. L. *De Herodoti vita et itineribus.* Berlin, 1826.

Mure, W. *Critical History of the Language and Literature of Ancient Greece.* 5 vols. London, 1853. Bk IV, chapters vi, vii (Herodotus).

†Schöll, A. *Herodots Lebenszeit.* Phil. IX (1854).

† —— *Herodots Entwicklung.* Phil. X (1855).

† —— *Herodots Vorlesungen.* Phil. X (1855).

Müller, K. O. and Donaldson, J. W. *History of the Literature of Ancient Greece.* 3 vols. London, 1858. Chapter xix (Herodotus).

†Nitzsch, O. *De prooemio Herodoteo.* Greifswald, 1860.

† —— (1) *Spuren älterer Redaction im Herodot.* (2) *Ueber den Schluss des Herodot. Werkes.* Bielefeld, 1873.

Nitzsch, K. W. *Herodots Quellen für die Geschichte der Perserkriege.* Rh. Mus., N.F., XXVII, 1872.

Matzat, H. *Ueber die Glaubwürdigkeit der geographischen Angaben Herodots über Asien.* Hermes, VI, 1872, pp. 392–486.

†Kirchhoff, A. *Ueber die Abfassungszeit des Herodotischen Geschichtswerkes.* Berlin, 1868. (Cp. Berl. Abh. 1868.) Ed. 2, enlarged. 1878.

† —— *Ueber ein Selbstcitat Herodots.* 1885 (Berl. S.B. XIX).

Wecklein, N. *Ueber die Tradition der Perserkriege.* München, 1876.

†Bauer, A. *Die Entstehung des Herodotischen Geschichtswerkes.* Wien, 1878.

—— *Herodots Biographie.* Wien, 1878.

—— *Die Benutzung Herodots durch Ephoros bei Diodor.* Leipzig, 1879.

—— *Die Kyros-Sage und Verwandtes.* Wien, 1882.

†Rose. *Hat Herodot sein Werk selbst herausgegeben?* Giessen, 1879.

Bunbury, E. H. *History of Ancient Geography.* 2 vols. 1879. Vol. I, chapters vi, vii, viii (Geography of Herodotus).

Mahaffy, J. P. *History of Classical Greek Literature.* 2 vols. 1880. Vol. II, The Prose Writers, chapter ii (Herodotus). Ed. 3. 1890.

†Ammer, E. *Herodotus Halicarnassensis quo ordine libros suos conscripserit.* Würzburg, 1881.

---

[1] Works dealing specially with the problem of the Composition of the History are marked †.

Hildebrandt, F. R. *De itineribus Herodoti Europaeis et Africanis.* Lipsiae, 1883.

Panofsky, H. *De Historiae Herodoteae fontibus.* Berlin, 1884.

†Döhler, A. *De partibus quibusdam Historiarum Herodoti earumque compositionis genere Quaestiones.* Halis Saxonum, 1886.

Diels, H. *Herodot und Hekataios.* Hermes xxii (1887), p. 411.

Kleber, P. *Die Rhetorik bei Herodot.* 1889.

—— *De genere dicendi Herodoteo.* 1890.

Trautwein, P. *Die Memoiren des Dikaios.* Berlin, 1890. Cf. Hermes, xxv, 1890, pp. 527 *sqq.*

Croiset (Frères). *Histoire de la Littérature Grecque.* 1890. Vol. ii, chapter x (Hérodote).

Krumbholz, P. *De descriptione regni Achaemenidarum.* Eisenach, 1891.

Welzhofer, H. *Zur Geschichte der Perserkriege.* Fleckeisen's Jahrbücher (1891), p. 145; (1892), p. 145.

Wilamowitz-Moellendorff, U. von. *Aristoteles und Athen.* 2 vols. Berlin, 1893. i, 29–38; ii, 9–12, 280, 288 (Herodotos).

†Hauvette, A. *Hérodote.* Paris, 1894.

Sayce, A. *The Egypt of the Hebrews and Herodotus.* 1895.

—— *The Season and Extent of the Travels of Herodotus in Egypt.* J.P. xiv, pp. 257 *sqq.*

Myres, J. L. *An attempt to reconstruct the maps used by Herodotus.* Geogr. Journ., Dec. 1896, p. 605.

—— *Herodotus and Anthropology* in Anthropology and the Classics. Oxford, 1908. pp. 121 *sqq.*

—— *Herodotus the Tragedian* in Miscellany presented to J. M. Mackay. Liverpool, 1914. pp. 88 *sqq.*

Murray, G. *A History of Ancient Greek Literature.* 1897. Chapter vi (Herodotus).

†Meyer, E. *Forschungen zur alten Geschichte.* Halle, 1899. ii, pp. 196–268 (Herodotos).

Oeri, A. *De Herodoti fonte Delphico.* Basiliae, 1899.

Dietrich, R. *Testimonia de Herodoti vita praeter itinera.* Leipzig, 1899.

Grundy, G. B. *The Great Persian War.* 1901.

†Höch, A. *Herodot und sein Geschichtswerk.* Güterslohe, 1904.

Christ, W. von. *Geschichte der Griechischen Litteratur.* 3 vols. (Ed. 6. Munich, 1912.) Vol. i, pp. 459–75 (Herodotus).

Sourdille, C. *La durée et l'étendue du voyage d'Hérodote en Égypte.* Paris, 1910.

—— *Hérodote et la religion de l'Égypte.* Paris, 1910.

†Jacoby, F. *Herodotos* in P.-W. Suppl. ii, 1913, pp. 205 *sqq.*

Bury, J. B. *Ancient Greek Historians.* 1919. Lecture ii (Herodotus).

Aly, W. *Volksmärchen Sage und Novelle bei Herodot.* Göttingen, 1921.

Wells, J. *Studies in Herodotus.* Oxford, 1923.

Glover, T. R. *Herodotus.* Cambridge, 1924.

II. Thucydides

A. *The Greek Text*

1. Editio princeps. ΘΟΥΚΥΔΙΔΗΣ. folio. Aldus. Venetiis Mense Maio. 1502.
2. Stephanus, H. folio. Paris, 1564–88. Gk. and Lat. (Vallae) c. Scholiis.
3. Hudson, J. folio. Oxon. 1696. Gk. and Lat. (Porti) c. Scholiis. The first edition in which the Books were divided into numbered chapters.
4. Duker, C. A. folio. 2 vols. Amsterdam, 1731. Gk. and Lat.
5. Bekker, I. 4 vols. 8vo. Oxon. 1821. Gk. and Lat.
6. —— Ed. 2. Berlin (Reimer), 1868. Cf. Essen, *infra.*

7. Hude, K. 2 vols. Leipzig (Teubner), 1898–91.
8. Stahl, J. M. 2 vols. 8vo. Leipzig, 1873–4.
9. Stuart Jones, H. 2 vols. Oxford (Clarendon Press) [1898].

B. *The Greek Text with Introductions, Commentary, etc.*

1. Poppo, E. F. Leipzig, 1821–40. (Ed. 2, 1851.) The major edition in 4 parts, 11 volumes, published at intervals: the first Part (2 vols.) containing Prolegomena and Dissertations (political, geographical, chronological): the second Part (4 vols.) containing the Text, Apparatus and Scholia: the third Part (4 vols.) containing Notes (commentarii) to the several Books: the fourth Part (1 vol.) containing Supplements and Indexes.
2. —— The minor edition: 4 vols. (8 sections). 8vo. Leipzig, 1843–75. Re-edited by J. M. Stahl. 1866–82.
3. Arnold, T. K. With Notes, chiefly historical and geographical. 3 vols. 8vo. Oxford, 1830–5. Ed. 7, 1868. (With excellent Indexes by R. F. G. Tiddeman.)
4. Bloomfield, S. T. With copious notes. 2 vols. 8vo. 1842–3.
5. Krüger, K. W. Θουκυδίδου Συγγραφή. 2 vols. 8vo. Berlin, 1846–7.
6. Classen, J. 8 vols. 8vo. Berlin, 1862–78 (and new edition, ed. J. Steup).
7. Forbes, W. H. Book 1. 8vo. Oxford, 1895. [Out of print.]
8. Bétant, E. A. *Lexicon Thucydideum.* 2 vols. 8vo. Geneva, 1843–7.
9. Essen, M. H. N. von. *Index Thucydideus ex Bekkeri editione stereotypa Confectus.* 8vo. Berlin, 1887.

C. *Commentaries without text*

Linwood, W. *Remarks and emendations on some passages in Thucydides.* Ed. 2, 1860.
Sheppard, J. G. and Evans, L. *Notes on Thucydides, Books I–III.* Ed. 2, 1870.

D. *Translations*

Valla, L. Valla's Latin is printed in the Stephanus edition of the text (*v.s.*) 1564, but is also, apparently, to be met with in a separate form.
Hobbes, T. *Eight Books of the Peloponnesian Warre interpreted out of the Greek.* folio. 1628. (And frequently since: *e.g.* English Works, London, 1843, vols. VIII, IX.)
Crawley, R. 1 vol. 8vo. 1874. (2 vols. Temple Classics, 1903: Everyman's Library, 1910.)
Jowett, B. 2 vols. 8vo. Oxford, 1881. (With Introduction and Notes.) Ed. 2, 1900.
Foster Smith, C. 4 vols. 12°. 1919–23. (Loeb Classical Library, with Greek text *en face.*)
Wilkins, H. M. The Speeches with Introduction and Notes. 8vo. 1870.

E. *Monographs, Dissertations, Articles, Chapters, etc.*[1]

Dionysius Halicarnassensis. *De Thucydidis idiomatis. Ad Ammaeum epistula.* Ed. H. Usener. Bonn, 1889. (Also in the fragment *De Imitatione.* Ibid.)
†Ullrich, F. W. *Beiträge zur Erklärung des Thukydides.* Hamburg, 1846.
—— *Beiträge zur Kritik des Thukydides.* (3 parts.) Hamburg, 1850–1–2.
—— *Beiträge zur Erklärung und Kritik des Thukydides.* Hamburg, 1862.
    All in Programs of the Johanneum.

[1] Works dealing specially with the problem of the composition of the history are marked †.

Mure, W. *Critical History of the Language and Literature of Antient Greece.*
5 vols. 8vo. 1853. Book iv, chapters viii, ix, x.

Sellar, W. Y. *Characteristics of Thucydides,* in *Oxford Essays,* 1857, pp. 283 ff.

Müller, K. O. and Donaldson, J. W. *History of the Literature of Ancient Greece.*
3 vols. 8vo. 1858. Chapter xxxix.

†Breitenbach, L. *Ueber die Abfassungszeit des Thukydideischen Geschichtswerkes.*
Jahr. f. cl. Phil. cvii, 1873, p. 185.

†Ćwickliński, L. *Quaestiones de tempore quo Thucydides priorum historiae suae partem composuit.* Gnesen, 1873.

†—— *Ueber die Entstehungsweise des zweiten Theiles der Thukydideischen Geschichte.*
Hermes, xii, 1877, p. 2.

Wilamowitz-Moellendorff, U. von. *Die Thukydideslegende.* Hermes, xii, 1877,
p. 326.

†—— *Curae Thucydideae.* Göttingen, 1885.

—— *Aristoteles und Athen.* (1893.) i, pp. 99–120; ii, pp. 289–303.

Schöll, R. *Zur Thukydides-Biographie.* Hermes, xiii, 1878, p. 433.

Welzhofer, H. *Thukydides und sein Geschichtswerk.* Munich, 1878.

Gilbert, O. *Zur Thukydideslegende.* Phil. xxxviii, 1879, p. 243.

Jebb, R. C. *The Speeches of Thucydides.* Hellenica, ed. E. Abbott. 8vo. 1880.
pp. 266–321.

Mahaffy, J. P. *History of Classical Greek Literature.* 2 vols. 1880. Ed. 3, 1890.
Vol. ii, chapter v.

Müller Strübing, H. *Thukydideische Forschungen.* Wien, 1881.

†Meyer, G. *Der gegenwärtige Stand der Thukydideischen Frage.* Nordhausen, 1889
(Pr. No. 297).

Croiset (Frères). *Histoire de la Littérature Grecque.* 5 vols. 8vo. 1887–99. Vol. iv
(1895), chapter ii.

†Kirchhoff, A. *Thukydides und sein Urkundenmaterial.* Berlin, 1895.

Murray, G. *History of Ancient Greek Literature.* 1897. Chapter vii.

Lange, E. *Die Arbeiten zu Thukydides seit 1890.* Heft i. Leipzig, 1897. Heft ii.
Leipzig, 1898.

Cornford, F. M. *Thucydides Mythistoricus.* 8vo. 1907.

†Grundy, G. B. *Thucydides and the History of his Age.* 8vo. 1911.

Christ, W. von. *Geschichte der Griechischen Litteratur.* Munich, 1912. Vol. i.
pp. 476–93, Thukydides.

Meyer, E. *Thukydides und die Entstehung der wissenschaftlichen Geschichtsschreibung.*
Vienna and Leipzig. 1913.

Lamb, W. R. M. *Clio Enthroned.* Cambridge. 1914.

Hutton, M. *Thucydides and History.* Transactions R.S. Canada, x (1916), p. 225.

†Bury, J. B. *Ancient Greek Historians.* 1919. Lectures iii, iv and Appendix.

†Schwartz, E. *Das Geschichtswerk des Thukydides.* Bonn, 1919.

Laskaris, K. A. Φῶς εἰς τὸ Θουκυδίδειον ἔρεβος. Athens, 1922.

Abbott, G. F. *Thucydides, A study in Historical Reality.* 1926.

III. The two Historians

1. Creuzer, G. F. *Herodot und Thucydides. Versuch einer nähern Würdigung
einiger ihrer historischen Grundsätze mit Rücksicht auf Lucians Schrift:
Wie man Geschichte schreiben müsse.* Leipzig, 1798.

2. Salomon, E. D. *De Thucydide et Herodoto quaestionum historicarum specimen.*
Berlin, 1851.

3. Schneege, G. *De Relatione historica quae intercedat inter Thucydiden et
Herodotum.* Breslau, 1884.

CHAPTER XV

GREEK ART AND ARCHITECTURE

I. Art. (Sections i–vi)

N.B. This Bibliography is not complete in itself, but supplementary to that given in Vol. IV, pp. 654 *sqq.*, which includes (1) general and comprehensive works on Greek art, (2) works on archaic Greek art.

A. *Sculpture, especially fifth-century sculpture*

Furtwängler, A. *Aegina*. Munich, 1906.

Wolters, P. *Äginetische Beiträge*. Bay. S.B. 1912. Phil.-Hist. Kl. Abh. 5.

Treu, G. *Olympia III: die Bildwerke in Stein und Thon*. Berlin, 1897.

Studniczka, F. *Die Ostgiebelgruppe vom Zeustempel in Olympia*. Abh. der Sächs. Akademie, xxxvii (1923), no. 4.

Buschor, E. and Hamann, R. *Die Skulpturen des Zeustempels zu Olympia*. Marburg, 1924.

Smith, A. H. *The Sculptures of the Parthenon*. 1910.

Collignon, M. *Le Parthénon*. 1914. Ed. 2, revised by Fougères, 1926.

Diehl, A. *Die Reiterschöpfungen der Phidiasischen Kunst*. Berlin, 1921.

Schrader, H. *Phidias*. Frankfort, 1924.

Rumpf, A. *Die Datierung der Parthenongiebel*. J.D.A.I. xl, 1925, p. 29.

Eichler, F. *Die Skulpturen des Heraions bei Argos*. Jahreshefte, xix–xx, 1919–20, p. 15.

Conze, A. *Die attischen Grabreliefs*. Berlin, 1890–1922.

Kjellberg, E. *Studien zu den attischen Reliefs des V. Jahrhunderts*. Upsala, 1926.

Amelung, W. *Archaischer Jünglingskopf in Hannover*. J.D.A.I. xxxv, 1920, p. 49.

Rumpf, A. *Relief in Villa Borghese*. Röm. Mitt. xxxviii–ix, 1923–4, p. 446.

Amelung, W. *Studien zur Kunstgeschichte Unteritaliens und Siziliens*. Röm. Mitt. xl, 1925, p. 181.

Amelung, W. *Kolossalstatue einer Göttin aus Ariccia*. J.D.A.I. xxxvii, 1922, p. 112.

Blinkenberg, Chr. *Polykleitos*. Copenhagen, 1918.

Anti, C. *Monumenti Policletei*. Mon. Linc. xxvi (1920), pp. 501 *sqq.*

Pfuhl, E. *Artemis von Ariccia, Athena von Velletri und die Amazonen*. J.D.A.I. xli, 1926, p. 1.

Arndt, P. and Amelung, W. *Photographische Einzelaufnahmen antiker Sculpturen*. 1893–.

Furtwängler, A. *Masterpieces of Greek Sculpture*. 1895.

Lippold, G. *Kopien und Umbildungen griechischer Statuen*. Munich, 1923.

Rodenwaldt, G. *Das Relief bei den Griechen*. Berlin, 1923.

Robert, C. *Archaeologische Hermeneutik*. Berlin, 1919.

Helbig, W. *Führer durch die öffentlichen Sammlungen klassischer Altertümer in Rom*. Ed. 3. With the collaboration of Amelung, Reisch and Weege. Leipzig, 1912.

Add the modern catalogues, such as

Amelung, W. *Die Sculpturen des Vatikanischen Museums*. Berlin, 1903–8: proceeding.

Arndt, P. *La Glyptothèque Ny-Carlsberg*. Munich, 1896.

Stuart Jones, H. and members of the British School at Rome. *The Sculptures of the Museo Capitolino*. Oxford, 1912.

—— *The Sculptures in the Palazzo dei Conservatori*. Oxford, 1926.

Bieber, M. *Die antiken Skulpturen und Bronzen des K. Museum Fridericianum in Cassel.* Marburg, 1915.

Caskey, L. D. *Catalogue of Greek and Roman Sculpture in the Museum of Fine Arts, Boston.* Cambridge, Mass., 1925.

B. *Painting and vases, especially late archaic and fifth-century*

A complete bibliography, to 1922, in Pfuhl's *Malerei und Zeichnung der Griechen* (see the chapter on Early Greek Art in vol. IV).

Pfuhl, E. *Masterpieces of Greek Drawing and Painting.* 1926. A good elementary work.

Hoppin, J. C. *A Handbook of Greek black-figured Vases, with a chapter on the red-figured Southern Italian vases.* Paris, 1924.

—— *A Handbook of Attic red-figured Vases signed by or attributed to the various masters of the sixth and fifth centuries B.C.* Cambridge, Mass., 1919.
(Both works consist of illustrated lists of the signed vases. Details require checking.)

Beazley, J. D. *Attic red-figured Vases in American Museums.* Cambridge, Mass., 1918.

—— *Attische Vasenmaler des rotfigurigen Stils.* Tübingen, 1925.

—— *Greek Vases in Poland.* Oxford, 1927. (Supplements the other two books.)

Langlotz, E. *Griechische Vasenbilder.* Heidelberg, 1922. (A small work, with a good selection of pictures of red-figured vases, and a good introduction.)

Fairbanks, A. *Athenian White Lekythoi.* New York, 1907–14.

Riezler, W. *Weissgrundige attische Lekythen.* Munich, 1914.

Buschor, E. *Attische Lekythen der Parthenonzeit.* Münchener Jahrbuch der Bildenden Kunst, 1925.

Jacobsthal, P. *Ornamente griechischer Vasen.* Berlin, 1927.

Caskey, L. D. *Geometry of Greek Vases.* Boston, 1922.

Corpus Vasorum Antiquorum. Paris and elsewhere, 1922–.

Albizzati, C. *Vasi antichi dipinti del Vaticano.* 1923–.

II. ARCHITECTURE. (SECTIONS VII–XI)

1. *General*

(Theatres and houses are treated in special sections at the end.)

To the list in the bibliography to vol. IV, chapter XVI (p. 656), may be added

Dombart, T. In *P.W.* Suppl. IV, 1924, col. 270, *s.v.* Entasis.

Goodyear, W. H. *Greek Refinements.* 1912. A full collection of evidence and theories, but to be used with caution: see review in *J.H.S.* XXXIII, 1913, pp. 369 *sqq.*

To the periodicals which summarize progress should be added *Gnomon*.

2. *Doric*

Important sites in alphabetical order. Those in Sicily and South Italy are grouped together.

Aegina.
See vol. IV, p. 656.

Argos (Heraeum: second temple, of late fifth century).

Waldstein, C. and others. *The Argive Heraeum.* Vol. I. Boston and New York, 1902.

Athens and Attica.

(*a*) General.

To vol. IV, p. 657, add

Dinsmoor, W. B. In *A.J.A.*, XXVI, 1922, p. 148. (For the use of iron bars etc. in Attic construction.)

Lethaby, W. R. *Greek Buildings represented by Fragments in the British Museum.* 1918. (Important for Parthenon, Propylaea, Rhamnus temples, and 'Theseum,' in Doric, and for Erechtheum, Ilissus Temple, and Nike Temple, in Ionic: also for sites outside Attica, especially Bassae and Nereid Monument.)

Penrose, F. C. *An Investigation of the Principles of Athenian Architecture.* Ed. 2, 1888. (Important especially for the refinements of the Parthenon.)

Schede, M. *Die Burg von Athen.* 1922.

Smith, A. H. *Catalogue of Sculptures in the British Museum*, I, 1892 and II, 1900 (for Parthenon, Propylaea, 'Theseum,' Erechtheum, Nike Temple, Bassae, and Nereid Monument).

(*b*) Particular buildings and sites.

Eleusis. (Telesterion.)

Earlier work will be superseded by:

Noack, F. *Eleusis: die baugeschichtliche Entwicklung des Heiligtums.* Promised for 1927. (For this reason, no plan of the Telesterion is given in this volume of *C.A.H.*)

Odeum of Pericles.

Kastriotis, P., especially Ἐφ. Ἀρχ. 1922, pp. 25 *sqq.*

Parthenon.

Collignon, M. *Le Parthénon.* See I. A, above.

Michaelis, A. *Der Parthenon.* Leipzig. 2 vols. 1870, 1871. Still valuable.

For general proportions, etc., see Dinsmoor, W. B., in *Architecture*, XLVII, 1922, pp. 177 *sqq.* and XLVIII, 1923, pp. 241 *sqq.* (summarized in *A.J.A.* XXVII, 1923, p. 469).

For various details, see Lehmann-Hartleben, K., in *Ath. Mitt.* XLVII, 1922, pp. 124 *sqq.*; Praschniker, C., in *Jahreshefte*, XIII, 1910, p. 5; Balanos, N., *C.R. Ac. Inscr.* 1925, p. 167 (important for refinements).

For the older Parthenon see vol. IV, p. 657.

Propylaea.

Bohn, R. *Die Propyläen der Akropolis zu Athen.* Berlin and Stuttgart, 1882.

Dinsmoor, W. B. In *A.J.A.* XIV, 1910, p. 143.

Dörpfeld, W. In *Ath. Mitt.* X, 1885, pp. 38, 131.

Dinsmoor, W. B., promises a monograph on *The Propylaea and the Entrance to the Acropolis.* This should supersede all previous work: till it appears, Bohn's book, though inaccurate, is indispensable.

Rhamnus. (Temples of Themis and Nemesis.)

Orlandos, A. K. In *B.C.H.* XLVIII, 1924, p. 305.

The Unedited Antiquities of Attica. 1817. pp. 41 *sqq.*

'Theseum.'

Bates, W. N. In *A.J.A.* V, 1901, p. 37.

Sauer, B. *Das sogenannte Theseion.* Berlin and Leipzig, 1899.

Sunium.

Dörpfeld, W. In *Ath. Mitt.* IX, 1884, p. 324.

Orlandos, A. K. In Ἐφ. Ἀρχ. 1917, p. 213.

Staïs, B. In Ἐφ. Ἀρχ. 1900, p. 112; 1917, p. 168.

Bassae.

Cockerell, C. R. *The Temples...at Aegina and...Bassae.* 1860.

Gütschow, M. In *J.D.A.I.* xxxvi, 1921, p. 44. (For the Corinthian capital: important.)

Kuruniotis, K. In Ἐφ. Ἀρχ. 1910, p. 271. (For the older temple.)

Rhomaios, K. A. In Ἐφ. Ἀρχ. 1914, p. 57. (Especially for the Ionic capitals.)

See also under *Athens and Attica* (*a*) above: and for origin and development of Corinthian, see Weigand, E., *Vorgeschichte des kor. Kapitells*, Würzburg, 1920; Homolle, T., in *Rev. Arch.* 1916, 2, p. 17.

Delos.

'First Temple North' or 'Temple of the Athenians' (hexastyle amphiprostyle, with many peculiarities: late fifth century).

Courby, F. *B.C.H.* xlv, 1921, p. 179 (plan Pls. I–II).

Holleaux, M. *C.R. Ac. Inscr.* 1908, p. 178.

Delphi (Lesche of Cnidians).

Bourguet, E. In *D.S. s.v.* Lesché.

Poulsen, F. *Delphi.* Translated by Richards, G. C., 1920, pp. 239 *sqq.*

Olympia. (Especially Temple of Zeus.)

To vol. iv, p. 658, add

Gardiner, E. N. *Olympia, its History and Remains.* 1925.

Smith, J. K. *Mem. Amer. Acad. Rome*, iv, 1924, p. 153.

Sicily and S. Italy.

To general and special references in vol. iv, p. 658, add

Acragas. (Olympieum.)

Pace, B. In *Mon. Linc.* xxviii, 1922, cols. 173 *sqq.*

Caulonia.

Orsi, P. In *Mon. Linc.* xxiii, 1914, cols. 685 *sqq.*

Syracuse. (Athenaion.)

Orsi, P. In *Mon. Linc.* xxv, 1918, cols. 353 *sqq.*, especially cols. 715 *sqq.*

3. *Ionic*

Locri.

See under *Sicily and South Italy* in vol. iv, p. 658.

Athens and Attica.

To general references given above, add

Erechtheum.

De la Coste Messelière, P. In *B.C.H.* xlviii, 1924, p. 323.

Dörpfeld, W. In *Ath. Mitt.* xxviii, 1903, p. 465; xxix, 1904, p. 101; xxxvi, 1911, p. 39; *J.D.A.I.* xxxiv, 1919, p. 1.

Holland, L. B. In *A.J.A.* xxviii, 1924. (Four articles: p. 1 enumerates many important earlier papers by members of the Amer. School at Athens, chiefly in *A.J.A.*)

Weller, C. H. In *A.J.A.* xxv, 1921, p. 130.

Ilissus Temple.

Stuart, J. and Revett, N. *The Antiquities of Athens.* Vol. i, 1762, pp. 7 *sqq.*

Dörpfeld, W. In *Ath. Mitt.* xxii, 1897, p. 227.

Studniczka, F. In *J.D.A.I.* xxxi, 1916, p. 169, and *Antike Denkmäler*, iii, 3, 1914–15, p. 36.

Nike Temple.

Blümel, C. *Der Fries des Tempels der Athena Nike.* Berlin, 1923.

Dinsmoor, W. B. In *A.J.A.* xxx, 1926, p. 1. (Chiefly on the sculptured parapet, which is later than the temple.)

Orlandos, A. K. In *Ath. Mitt.* XL, 1915, p. 27.
Welter, G. In *Ath. Mitt.* XLVIII, 1923, p. 190.

Sardes. (Temple of Artemis.)
Butler, H. C. *Sardis*. Vol. II, part 1. Leyden, 1925.

Xanthos. (Nereid Monument.)
Krischen, F. In *Ath. Mitt.* XLVIII, 1923, p. 69.
Niemann, G. *Das Nereiden-Monument in Xanthos*. Vienna, 1921.
See also under *Athens and Attica* (a), p. 527 above.

4. *Theatres*

From the vast literature of this subject, the following may be selected:

Bieber, M. *Die Denkmäler zum Theaterwesen im Altertum*. Berlin and Leipzig, 1920.
Dörpfeld, W. and Reisch, E. *Das griechische Theater*. Athens, 1896.
Fiechter, E. *Die baugeschichtliche Entwicklung des antiken Theaters*. Munich, 1914.
Flickinger, R. C. *The Greek Theater and its Drama*. Chicago, 1918.
Frickenhaus, A. *Die altgriechische Bühne*. Strassburg, 1917.
Gerkan, A. v. *Das Theater im Priene*. Munich, 1922. (Criticized by Dörpfeld, W., in *Ath. Mitt.* XLIX, 1924, p. 50.)
Haigh, A. E. *The Attic Theatre*. Ed. 3, by A. W. Pickard-Cambridge, 1907.
Puchstein, O. *Die griechische Bühne*. Berlin, 1901.

For recent investigations of the theatre of Dionysus at Athens, see Welter, G., in *Arch. Anz.* 1925, cols. 311 *sqq.*

5. *Houses*

The chief sites for fifth-century houses are Aegina, Athens, Dystos in Euboea, Megara, and Piraeus. See Fiechter, E., in *P.-W. s.v.* Haus, and Rider, B. C., *The Greek House*, 1916.

The especially important Dystos houses were published by Wiegand, T. and others, in *Ath. Mitt.* XXIV, 1899, pp. 458 *sqq.*

For Aegina, see Furtwängler, A. and others, *Aegina*, 2 vols., Munich, 1906 (vol. I, pp. 107 *sqq.*).

For Hippodamus of Miletus, see v. Gerkan, A., *Griechische Städteanlagen*, Berlin and Leipzig, 1924.

GENERAL INDEX[1]

Abdera, 344, 347

Abydos, 333; Athenian naval victory at, 342; A. attack upon, 346; Spartans at, 359

Acanthus, 244, 250; Brasidas at, *see* Syn.T.

Acarnania, Acarnanians, 85, 176; in Archidamian War, 198, 204, 206 *sq.*, 208, 210 *sq.*, 227–30, Syn. T.; Peace of Nicias, 252; share in Athenian expedition to Syracuse, 304

Achaea, alliance with Athens, 83; surrendered by Athens, 90; in Archidamian War, 193, 233

Acharnae, 4, 197, 369, 370

Acharnians of Aristophanes, 227, 230

Achelous River, 211

Achradina, 152, 153, 292, 294, 297, 305

Acragas: rule of Theron, 151; temple of Zeus, 151; foreigners expelled, 154; Empedocles exiled, 158; war with Syracuse, 160; splendour, 163 *sq.*; neutral in war of Athens and Syracuse, 282, 302; Olympieum, 445 *sq.*

Acropolis of Athens: Peisistratid pediment, Old Temple of Athena, 421; Critian boy, 426 *sq.*; fair-haired head, 426 *sq.*; Athena and Marsyas, 429

Acrothoï (Acroathus), 248

Adeimantus, Athenian general, 360 *sq.*

Admetus, king of the Molossians, 63

Adrastus of Sicyon and tragedy, 115

Aegina: commerce, 17 *sq.*; rivalry with Athens, 77; blockaded, 81; made subjectally, 83, 90 *sq.*; cleruchy in, 97; grievance against Athens, 187; in Archidamian War, 198, 227, 238; Spartans in, 337; school of sculptors, 422; temple of Aphaia, 422, 444, 446; in Pindar's odes, 422

Aegospotami, defeat of Athens at, 358–62

Aerae, 315

Aeschines 'the Socratic,' 390

Aeschylus, growth of his art, 117–20; the *Oresteia*, 120–6; death, 126; parallels in sculpture, 422, 430 *sq.*, 441

Aethalia (Elba), 158

Aetna (city) founded, 147; coinage, 147 *n.*; its constitution, 153; Aetnaeans transferred to Inessa, 154 *sq.*, 159

Aetolia, Athenian expedition in, 228 *sq.*, 234, Syn.T.

Agathon, tragic poet, 137, 352

Agesandridas, Spartan admiral, 337 *sq.*

Agis, king of Sparta, 226; campaigns against Argos, 269 *sq.*, 272 *sqq.*, 275; invasions of Attica, 299, 313, 335, 345, 355, 362; and Alcibiades, 314

Agoracritus, sculptor, 435, 437 *sqq.*; the Rhamnus Nemesis, 438

Agraeans, 229, 240

Agriculture in Greece and especially in Attica, 4, 11–15

Agyrrhius, 104, *see* Vol. VI, Index

Alcamenes, 431 *sq.*, 435, 437 *sqq.*

Alcibiades, 176, 261; personality and policy, 262 *sqq.*; campaign in Peloponnese, 266–74; at Argos, 271, 275; failure of war policy, 276; renewed alliance with Argos, 277 *sq.*; at Olympia, 280; Melos, 281; urged Sicilian expedition, 284 *sq.*; charged with impiety, 286; recalled from Syracuse, 288; fled to Sparta, 289; in Ionia, 314; with Tissaphernes, 319 *sq.*; with Athenians at Samos, 322 *sq.*; removal of Androcles, 326; general at Samos, 334 *sq.*; declared for the Five Hundred, 341; at Abydos, 342; prisoner of Tissaphernes, 342; at Cyzicus, 343; operations in Hellespont, 345 *sq.*; reinstated at Athens, 347; commander-inchief, 352 *sq.*; deposition and retirement to Thrace, 353 *sq.*; advice before Aegospotami rejected, 360; death, 369; and Socrates, 390, 392; *see also* 484 (chronological note)

Alcidas, Spartan admiral, 216 *sqq.*, 221, Syn.T.

Alciphron of Argos, 270

Alcmaeonidae, influence recovered, 47 *sq.*, 63; Pericles, 72; previous record, 189, 202; pediment at Delphi, 421

Alcman, 114; *see also* Vol. IV, Index

Aleuadae, 34

Alexander I of Macedonia, 58

Alexicles, 336, 337, 338

Amasis (vase-painter), 423

Ambracia, 176, 179; in Archidamian War, 193, 207, 221, 229, Syn.T.

Ameipsias, on Socrates, 388

Amelung's statue, 428, 429

Amisus (=Piraeus), 174

Amorges, 314, 317

Amorgos, 171

Amphictyonic League, 36; *see also* Vol. VI, Index

Amphipolis founded, 57 *sq.*, 172, 184; captured by Brasidas, 244–8, Syn.T.; in terms of Peace of Nicias, 250 *sq.*, 254; negotiations over, 257, 265; Athenian attack, 279

Amyntas, son of Philip, 206

Amyrtaeus, 84, 87; *see also* Vol. VI, Index

Anactorium, 193, 207, 229, Syn. T., 255

[1] Syn.T. refers to the Synchronistic Table of the Archidamian War facing p. 252.

INDEX TO MAPS

Maps containing more than a few names have each their own index and reference is made here only to the number of the map. The alphabetical arrangement ignores the usual prefixes (lake, etc.).

† *See list of towns on map 5 note*

[1] References to Hicks and Hill's *Historical Greek Inscriptions* are given in square brackets with H.-H.